The Experience
of Parenting

Malinda Jo Muzi

Community College of Philadelphia

Prentice Hall
Upper Saddle River, New Jersey 07458

Library of Congress Cataloging-in-Publication Data

Muzi, Malinda Jo.
    The experience of parenting / Malinda Jo Muzi. — 1st ed.
      p.   cm.
    Includes bibliographical references and index.
    ISBN 0-321-01160-0 (alk. paper)
    1. Parenting—Study and Teaching.   I. Title.
HQ755.7.M89   1999
649' . 1'071—dc21   99-32340
                                                CIP

Editor-in-chief: Nancy Roberts
Executive Editor: Bill Webber
Acquisitions Editor: Jennifer Gilliland
Assistant Editor: Anita Castro
Full-service Production Manager: Patti Brecht
Buyer: Tricia Kenny
Project Coordination, Text Design, and Electronic Page Makeup:
    Pre-Press Company, Inc.
Cover Designer: Joe Sengotta
Cover Illustration: Brad Goodell, "Mother and Child's Hands," courtesy of Stock
    Illustration Source, New York.
Photo Researcher: Julie Tesser

This book was set in 10/12 Stone Serif and was printed and bound by
R.R. Donnelley & Sons, Co. The cover was printed by Phoenix Color Corp.

Printed in the United States of America

10 9 8 7 6 5 4 3 2

ISBN 0-321-01160-0

Prentice-Hall International (UK) Limited, *London*
Prentice-Hall of Australia Pty. Limited, *Sydney*
Prentice-Hall Canada Inc., *Toronto*
Prentice-Hall Hispanoamericana, S.A., *Mexico*
Prentice-Hall of India Private Limited, *New Delhi*
Prentice-Hall of Japan, Inc., *Tokyo*
Pearson Education Asia Pte. Ltd., *Singapore*
Editoria Prentice-Hall do Brasil, Ltda., *Rio de Janeiro*

In memory of Robert
    Who made me a mother but not a parent

For Jarrett
    Who compelled me to learn the parenting part

Contents

To the Instructor   xi

To the Student   xiii

Acknowledgments   xiv

Chapter 1   **The Experience of Parenting**   **1**

Learning to Parent   3

Defining Parenting   8
The Informed Parent 1.1   *Myths and Realities of Parenting*   12
The Informed Parent 1.2   *Images of Parenthood*   15

Parenting Experts Throughout the Ages   16

The Decision to Parent   18
The Informed Parent 1.3   *Am I Parent Material?*   26
The Informed Parent 1.4   *The Advantages and Disadvantages of the One-Child Family*   28

Parenting: A Historical Perspective   28
The Spirit of Parenting   *A poem by Kahlil Gibran*   39
Chapter Review   40
Student Activities   41
Helping Hands   42

Chapter 2   **The Context of Parenting**   **43**

The Informed Parent 2.1   *The Effect of World Ecomony and Politics on Parenting*   45

The World of Parents and Their Children   45

The Context of Time   51

Social Class: Windows of Opportunity   57
The Spirit of Parenting   *Advice from Erma Bombeck*   58

Parenting and Gender   61
Chapter Review   63
Student Activities   64
Helping Hands   64

Chapter 3   **Parenting Across Cultures   65**

The Assumptions of Life: Culture and Ethnicity   67
    The Informed Parent 3.1   *Culturally Diverse Family Patterns*   71

Multi-Ethnicity and Parenting   72

Acculturation Affects Parents and Children   73
    The Informed Parent 3.2   *Values of the American Macroculture*   76
    The Spirit of Parenting   *An excerpt by Anne Fadiman*   87
    Chapter Review   90
    Student Activities   91
    Helping Hands   91

Chapter 4   **Parenting Within the Family   92**

The Family Socialization Process   94
    The Spirit of Parenting   *Pat Conroy from* The Prince of Tides   103

The Well-Functioning Family   103

The Changing Family Life Cycle   109
    The Informed Parent 4.1   *The Behavior and Values of Healthy Families*   110
    Chapter Review   112
    Student Activities   113
    Helping Hands   114

Chapter 5   **Parenting in Transition   115**

The Changing American Family   116

Stepparenting: A Family Challenge   131
    The Spirit of Parenting   *An excerpt by Letty Cottin Pogrebin*   136
    The Informed Parent 5.1   *The Stepping-Ahead Program*   138

Special Parenting   139
    Chapter Review   147
    Student Activities   148
    Helping Hands   148

Chapter 6   **Special Issues of Parenting   149**

The Exceptional Child   150
    The Informed Parent 6.1   *When a Child Is Not Hearing Properly*   153
    The Informed Parent 6.2   *Coping Strategies for Families
                                    With Chronically Ill Children*   157
    The Informed Parent 6.3   *Asking Questions, Getting Answers*   162

A Death in the Family 163

Maltreatment in the Family 165

Alcohol in the Family 174
    The Informed Parent 6.4 *The Seven-Step Process to Recovery* 176
    The Spirit of Parenting *An excerpt by Caroline Knapp* 177
    Chapter Review 179
    Student Activities 180
    Helping Hands 180

Chapter 7 **Effective Parenting 182**

Patterns of Parenting 184

Belief Systems and Parenting 190
    The Spirit of Parenting *Marian Wright Edelman from* The Measure
        of Our Success 191
    The Informed Parent 7.1 *Distorted Parental Thinking* 193
    The Informed Parent 7.2 *Good and Bad Criticism of Preschoolers* 195

Parental Styles 195

Parenting-Education Programs 199
    Chapter Review 200
    Student Activities 201
    Helping Hands 201

Chapter 8 **Methods and Models of Parenting 202**

Humane Parenting 204

Child-Rearing Strategies 206
    The Informed Parent 8.1 *Communicating with Children* 210
    The Informed Parent 8.2 *Dialogue with a Teen, Eating Dinner* 212
    The Spirit of Parenting Blackberry Winter *by Margaret Mead* 216

Responsible Parents, Responsible Children 216

Modifying Behavior Through Rewards and Punishments 219
    The Informed Parent 8.3 *Family Meeting Guidelines for Resolving Conflicts* 220
    The Informed Parent 8.4 *Plain Speaking* 221

A Family-Systems Model of Parenting 231
    The Informed Parent 8.5 *When You Need Professional HELP!* 232
    Chapter Review 233
    Student Activities 234
    Helping Hands 235

Chapter 9 **Parenting the Infant 236**

The Transition to Parenting 237

From Neonate to Infant 238

Patterns and Rhythms of Life 246
 The Informed Parent 9.1   *How to Soothe a Crying Infant*   248
 The Informed Parent 9.2   *Breast Milk or the Bottle?* 253
 The Spirit of Parenting   *A poem by Miller Williams*   254

**The First Relationship:
 The Emotional Bonding of Infant and Parent 254**

The Newborn Conquers the World 263
 The Informed Parent 9.3   *Stimulating the Infant Brain*   267
 The Informed Parent 9.4   *Read to Children: Early and Often*   271
 The Informed Parent 9.5   *How to Play with a Baby* 272
 The Informed Parent 9.6   *Babyproofing the Home*   274
 Chapter Review   274
 Student Activities   276
 Helping Hands   276

Chapter 10 **Parenting the Young Child 278**

Getting Up and Going Out 280

The Health and Safety of Young Children 282
 The Informed Parent 10.1   *On-the-Move Safety Tips*   286

Organizing the World 287
 The Informed Parent 10.2   *Assessing Language Development*   292
 The Informed Parent 10.3   *Talk Tactics to Extend Conversations with Children*   294
 The Spirit of Parenting   *An excerpt by Daniel N. Stern*   295

The Self-Controlled Child 296
 The Informed Parent 10.4   *Everyday Rules of Behavior* 297

Play in Early Childhood 304
 The Informed Parent 10.5   *Fostering Creativity Through Play Materials*   307

Early Childhood Education Programs 308
 The Informed Parent 10.6   *Transition from Home to Day Care or
          Preschool*   313

 Chapter Review   313
 Student Activities   315
 Helping Hands   315

Chapter 11 **Parenting the School-Age Child   316**

A Time of Industry   317

Physical Changes of Middle Childhood   320
The Informed Parent 11.1   *Childhood Obesity: Risk Factors*   324

Cognitive Changes in Middle Childhood   324

The Competent Child   332
The Informed Parent 11.2   *A School Primer for Parents*   333
The Spirit of Parenting   *A poem by Carl Sandburg*   336
The Informed Parent 11.3   *Making School a Success*   337
The Informed Parent 11.4   *Parenting Toward Cognitive Competence*   339
The Informed Parent 11.5   *Helping with Homework*   341

The Sibling Connection   344
The Informed Parent 11.6   *Living with a Difficult School-Age Child*   345

Television and Parenting   350
Chapter Review   356
Student Activities   358
Helping Hands   358

Chapter 12 **Parenting the Adolescent and Young Adult   359**

Puberty: The Matured State   361

What Should Parents Expect?   362

The Physical Changes of Adolescence   364

Cognitive Changes in Adolescence   369

Patterns of Change Within Families   375
The Spirit of Parenting   *An excerpt by James McBride*   378
The Informed Parent 12.1   *Reducing Parent-Adolescent Conflict*   384

Educating the Adolescent   384
The Informed Parent 12.2   *Negotiating Rules*   385

The Problems of Adolescence   386
The Informed Parent 12.3   *Anorexia Nervosa*   395
The Informed Parent 12.4   *When to Seek Professional Help*   397
Chapter Review   398
Student Activities   400
Helping Hands   401

Chapter 13 **Launching Children 402**

The Changing Family Life Cycle 403

Getting Along Adult to Adult 406
The Informed Parent 13.1 *Parental Expectations for Young Adults 409*
The Informed Parent 13.2 *Parent Adult-Child Residence-Sharing Issues 410*
The Informed Parent 13.3 *Career Inventories 414*

Choosing for College 414
The Informed Parent 13.4 *The Ten Fastest-Growing
                                Jobs for College Graduates: 1992–2005 415*
The Spirit of Parenting *An excerpt by Myla and Jon Kabat-Zinn 416*

Life After Launching 417
The Informed Parent 13.5 *Grandparenting Styles 422*
The Informed Parent 13.6 *Grandparenting: Pleasures and Problems 423*

The Parenting Experience: A Summing Up 424
Chapter Review 425
Student Activities 427
Helping Hands 427

Bibliography 429
Photo Credits 457
Text Permissions 458
Index 461

To the Instructor

Teaching about parenting is one of the most valuable contributions you can make to your students' education and lives. Their understanding of the complexities of raising children will benefit society and make their own existence more fruitful.

I have made a great effort to create an authoritative, research-based text that will attract and hold the interest of your students. Students who may rely on television programs and newspaper advice columns for information about parenting will benefit from understanding that there is a *science of parenting;* that is, a body of knowledge based on study and research rather than opinion. For this reason, it is the work of scores of researchers—including Jay Belsky, Eleanor Maccoby, Diane Baumrind, Edward Zigler, Murray Straus—that makes up the core the text. I have quoted directly from the most important parenting education books on the market, including those by authors such as Thomas Gordon and David Elkind. By citing an author and his or her work, students will be prompted to go out and locate the book if they want to do more detailed reading on a subject.

It is important for students to understand that the parenting experience differs across cultures and social class. Every chapter includes material about the parenting experience as it differs—from Japan to Peru, and from the hills of Appalachia to the Naigai desert. It is my intent that through these experiences students will recognize how place and natural circumstances impact the ways in which children are raised and cared for *and* what expectations of them are based on the "man-made" aspects of their lives.

To balance research with real world applications, I have included the following features:

Biographies: I have delved into the childhood backgrounds of renowned personalities such as Eleanor Roosevelt and Colin Powell for a personalized understanding of how parenting styles and beliefs have influenced history. These vignettes help students see the practical implications of a parent's style and attitudes as well as the way in which contextual forces intertwine with the parenting experience to create a life.

The Informed Parent: Textbooks such as this one cannot be built solely upon research. The practical side of parenting that includes nutrition, safety, education, and other daily concerns is reflected in "The Informed Parent" sections in each chapter. These features offer expert suggestions on how to best handle a specific situation or task—how to guide children toward reading, how best to toilet train, how to choose a preschool, and many others.

The Spirit of Parenting: Parenting is primarily about the emotional ties of a mother or father to his or her children. In "The Spirit of Parenting," well-known writers, poets, historians, and other personalities reveal important aspects of these ties from their own parenting experiences. James McBride describes his mother's distress when her daughter Helen runs away from home, Marian Wright Edelman addresses her grown sons, Miller Williams writes a poem for his newborn daughter Emily. These pieces help make the heart of parenting real for your students.

Helping Hands: Parents need help in these difficult times, and assistance is available. At the end of each chapter I have listed organizations that offer information, advice, or support on issues such as breast feeding, adolescent pregnancy, and parent-effectiveness training. Most organizations have Web sites from which they share information and communicate by e-mail. Internet addresses were included for most of the organizations listed.

The following study aids are included to help organize students' learning.

Concepts and Understanding: This list represents the key concepts and understandings of the chapter. The "Chapter Contents" presents the topics covered in the chapter.

End-of-Chapter Activities: These assignments encourage students' critical thinking skills in contexts that are practical, interesting, and engaging. Examples of practical activities include producing a brief manual for new parents, developing a reading program for one-year-olds, and analyzing a day of children's television programming.

Summaries: These end-of-chapter sections review the important concepts and information in the chapter.

Supplements: A combined Instructor's Manual and Test Bank are available with this text.

I am grateful that you have chosen this text to help guide your students though the study of parenting. I would appreciate any advice, suggestions, or comments you might have in regard to this work at my e-mail address **MJLMuzi@aol.com** or by mail at Community College of Philadelphia.

To the Student

You are about the enter the academic world of parenting and begin an experience like no other. Parenting is an activity shared by people in every country, town, avenue, hillside, and barren wayside on the planet. However, there is little agreement about how to raise children because parenting rests on beliefs and attitudes, and these factors differ according to time, place, and circumstances.

You pick up tidbits of advice about parenting from television or newspapers, neighbors, friends, and family members. Most often, these bits of information are based on subjective opinion rather than sound psychological research. In writing *The Experience of Parenting,* my intention is to introduce you to parenting through the work of those who have conducted serious study and research in this area. Although this is an academic venture, I have tried to create a text that you will find enjoyable for its biographical vignettes, trade publication pieces, and even a little poetry. Of special interest will be each chapter's "Helping Hands" and Web site listings through which you can locate just about any information available about parenting and child care.

You are fortunate to be taking a course in a subject that will have such a long-term impact on your lives. Many of you will spend a considerable part of adulthood raising children. By understanding the concepts that underpin the experience of parenting, you can ensure a better future for yourself and your children.

Please share your opinions and responses, pose questions you might have, or make suggestions on the text to **MJLMuzi@aol.com** or write to me at Community College of Philadelphia.

Acknowledgments

Because the task of writing a book is such a solitary one, no author could remain emotionally healthy and no book would reach its fullest potential without the assistance and support of the people who share the author's, personal and professional life. I have many people to thank for seeing me through the three years it took to produce *The Experience of Parenting.*

On a professional level, I am first and foremost indebted to my editor, Becky Pascal, who had the vision to contract for this book and who gently moved me forward when I got tired and cranky from the effort of writing it. Each time she read the manuscript and requested changes she improved the text significantly. It is a far better book than it would have been without this insightful editor.

It is said that no book is written, that they are all rewritten. I am grateful for the colleagues around the country who read and reviewed the manuscript. Their efforts directed my rewriting and provoked me to make each of the books drafts tighter, clearer and better organized than the last. They include: Marsha Epstein, Community College of Philadelphia, Bob Drummond, Mid-America Nazarene College; Elizabeth A. Hill, The University of Iowa; Linda Dannison, Western Michigan University; W. Dale Brotherton, Western Carolina University; Nancy Ahlander, Ricks College; Stewart Cohen, University of Rhode Island; Deena Nardi, Indiana University Northwest; Robert Orr, University of Windsor, Canada; Susan Witt, University of Akron; Chris Rodgers Arthur; University of Iowa; Aaron Ebata, University of Illinois at Urbana-Champaign; Linda Derscheid, Northern Illinois University; Phil Osborne, Hesston College; Donald M. Stanley, North Harris College; Dave Riley, University of Wisconsin-Madison; Shelly Drazen, Cornell University; Maureen Mulroy, University of Connecticut; Phyllis L. Bengston, University of MN-St. Paul; and Marilyn Finkelstein, Miami-Dade Community College.

I also want to express a belated thanks to psychology professor and author Frank McMahon, who more than twenty years ago helped me get started on my writing career.

Special thanks is owed to a colleague and friend, Joel Esterman, who encouraged me in my writing and organized the vast bibliography for me. Deepest love and appreciation to Marcia Epstein, whose own parenting style became an inspiration and model for me.

The personal life of an author remains in disarray when deadlines loom, especially when an author works best through the night, as I do. Of all the people who helped me through the writing of *The Experience of Parenting,* I most owe appreciation—and apologies—to my son, Jarrett. From the day he got his driver's license, just after I contracted to write this book, he released me from the chores of picking up typing paper, mailing out manuscript pages, running out for milk at midnight, taking the dogs to the groomer and a score of other tasks that would have diverted me from my work. He is an intelligent, talented, kind and very funny young man that I'm proud to have raised. I hope the knowledge of how much he is loved will enable him to forgive me for the missed lacrosse games, the take-out meals, the piled-up laundry, and the messy house.

And finally, a special treat is owed to my long-time companion, Christopher, a Maltese, who spent as many hours as I in front of the computer, never wavering from his spot behind me on my chair and not once requesting a change in the manuscript.

Malinda Jo Muzi
Community College of Philadelphia

Do everything right, all the time, and the child will prosper. It's as simple as that, except for fate, luck, heredity, chance, the astrological sign under which the child was born, his order of birth, his first encounter with evil, the girl who jilts him in spite of his excellent qualities, the war that is being fought when he is a young man, the drugs he may try once or too many times, the friends he makes, how he scores on tests, how well he endures kidding about his shortcomings, how ambitious he becomes, how far he falls behind, circumstantial evidence, ironic perspective, danger when it is least expected, difficulty in triumphing over circumstances, people with hidden agendas, and animals with rabies.

Ann Beattie
Picturing Will

The Experience of Parenting

Chapter Highlights

After reading Chapter 1, students should be able to:

- Recognize the importance of parenting skills
- Understand the meaning of the term "parenting"
- Recognize the reasons people have children
- Understand the bidirectionality in the parent-child relationship
- View parenting from a historical perspective

Chapter Contents

- Learning to Parent
  Research Difficulties
- Defining Parenting
  Aspects of Parenting ▪ *The Nurturance and Socialization of Children* ▪ *Bidirectionality and the Parent-Child Relationship* ▪ *The Ever-Changing Relationship* ▪ *The Changing Responsibilities of Parents as Children Age*
- Parenting Experts Throughout the Ages
- The Decision to Parent
  Motherhood or Fatherhood: Is There a Difference? ▪ *Children as Life Changers* ▪ *The Decision Not to Parent* ▪ *The Cost of Raising Children*
- Parenting: A Historical Perspective
  The Changing Faces of American Fatherhood ▪ *The Reinvention of Fatherhood* ▪ *The Good and Bad Mother* ▪ *Mothers of the Distant Past* ▪ *Angel of the House: The Victorian Mother* ▪ *Modern Mothering* ▪ *Supermom of the Twenty-first Century*

INTRODUCTION

When World War II General Douglas MacArthur attended West Point Military Academy, his mother Pinky accompanied him to the school. She moved into a nearby hotel from where she could watch the light in her son's dormitory room and determine if he was studying enough (Manchester, 1978).

In *The Measure of Our Success,* child-welfare activist Marian Wright Edelman fondly recalled her childhood as the daughter of a Baptist minister. "I went everywhere with my parents and was under the watchful eye of members of the congregation and community who were my extended parents. They kept me when my parents went out of town, they reported on and chided me when I strayed from the straight and narrow of community expectations, and they basked in and supported my achievements when I did well" (Edelman, 1993).

In the Nayar community of southwest India, the brothers of a married woman are responsible for the care and well being of her children. The husband, and father of the woman's children, remains in his own village, where he acts as father to his own sisters' children (Haviland, 1994).

"She was just a fact of life when I was growing up," feminist writer Gloria Steinem said of her mother, Ruth. "Someone to be worried about and cared for; an invalid who lay in bed with eyes closed and lips moving in occasional response to voices only she could hear; a woman to whom I brought an endless stream of toast and coffee, bologna sandwiches and dime pies, in a child's version of what meals should be" (Steinem, 1983).

Among the Mundurucu of South America's Amazon forest, parents do not live together. Until the age of thirteen, children are cared for by their mothers, apart from men. At thirteen, boys leave their mothers' houses and take up residence with the men of the village, where they remain for the rest of their lives (Haviland, 1994).

What these examples tell us about the process known as "parenting" is that child rearing is a far more complex and varied affair than most people realize. Parenting occurs in the locales from the mountain regions of western New Guinea, where female children learn to care for pigs, to the Amazon Basin of Brazil, where Wauja Indian parents teach their children to fish and revere the rock carvings at Kamukuaka. In these and other places, adult humans are engaged in the activity of raising children, usually their own but often others that have come into their lives by way of relatives, friends, or the community. These parents and their children, along with countless others, have become the subjects of more than forty years of research by people in fields including psychology, sociology, anthropology, and medicine.

To fully understand the experience of parenting, students must appreciate the impact of culture, the role of gender, the structure of the family, personality differences, the impact of marriage, developmental models, and a myriad

Figure 1.1
The Interrelated
Forces That Influence Parenting

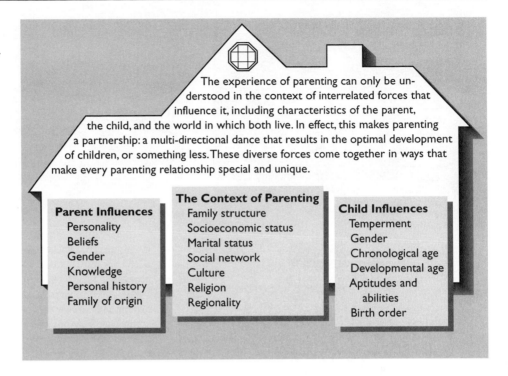

The experience of parenting can only be understood in the context of interrelated forces that influence it, including characteristics of the parent, the child, and the world in which both live. In effect, this makes parenting a partnership: a multi-directional dance that results in the optimal development of children, or something less. These diverse forces come together in ways that make every parenting relationship special and unique.

Parent Influences
Personality
Beliefs
Gender
Knowledge
Personal history
Family of origin

The Context of Parenting
Family structure
Socioeconomic status
Marital status
Social network
Culture
Religion
Regionality

Child Influences
Temperment
Gender
Chronological age
Developmental age
Aptitudes and
    abilities
Birth order

of other ingredients that comprise the parent-child mix. Figure 1.1 shows how some of these diverse forces come together.

LEARNING TO PARENT

Babies come into the world with a set of behaviors designed to ensure their survival, but the skills they eventually need to assume adult roles in society are taught and encouraged by parents, teachers, and others they come in contact with. The question is: Who teaches mothers and fathers their parenting skills? How do they learn the methods and strategies for successful child rearing? Is there such a thing as "proper" child rearing?

When people purchase an appliance such as a VCR, they are given a manual to go with it: a handbook explaining how the machine works. But when parents leave a hospital or birthing center with a color-coded (blue or pink wrapped) infant, they receive no instruction manual. For many new Moms and Dads, parenting becomes a trial and error affair—often made difficult because the world their growing children live in is radically different than the one the parents experienced.

In societies the world over, people rely on child-rearing information offered by family members and friends. This knowledge, handed down from generation to generation within a culture, is called *tradition*; and it includes

In cultures the world over, adults are involved in the process of raising children. While philosophers, clergymen, and parents themselves have long pondered the issues of child rearing, over the last fifty years the subject of parenting has become a serious discipline, an area of scientific study.

ways of thinking, feeling, and behaving toward children that are so powerful a force in family life that it functions like heredity. While this transgenerational wisdom can be exceedingly valuable (How else can an inexperienced mother or father learn the child-rearing ropes?), it can also be foolish and even harmful. A striking example of the conflict between cultural tradition and humane parenting is the 1994 case of a Nigerian woman living in Oregon. The woman requested and was granted political asylum for herself and her two daughters because her family intended to circumcise the daughters when they returned to their native country.

Today information about parenting comes from a much wider range of sources. Bookstore shelves are lined with treatises on such subjects as toilet training, sexuality, play therapy, discipline, homework, and even increasing the brain power of an infant. Scores of newspaper columnists offer parenting tips,

Parenting refers to beliefs, attitudes, and behaviors people use to help their offspring survive and prosper from birth into adulthood. Its goal is the nurturance, maintenance, guidance, and protection of children. This is accomplished in varying ways from culture to culture, family to family, and parent to parent.

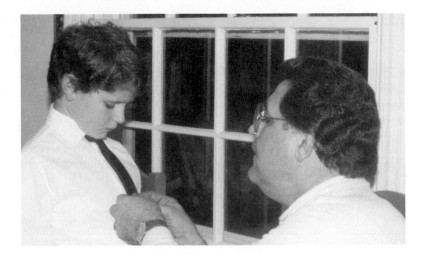

and daily television talk shows pose child-rearing problems and offer solutions. Some of the advice offered is authoritative and helpful, but much is based on subjective views and opinions that are sometimes silly and even harmful.

"It is usually assumed in our society that people have to be trained for difficult roles," write E. E. LeMasters and J. Defrain in *Parents in Contemporary America* (1983). "Most business firms would not turn a salesclerk loose on customers without some formal training; the armed forces would scarely send a raw recruit into combat without extensive and intensive training; most states now require a course in driver's education before high school students can acquire a driver's license. Even dog owners often go to school to learn how to treat their pets properly. This is not true of American parents."

The subject of parenting has become a formal discipline, an area of study open to scientific scrutiny, leading researchers to rely on natural observation and laboratory experiments to probe into every aspect of the subject. Prominent researchers in the parenting field include psychologist Mary Ainsworth, who defined the maternal role in infant attachment; Diana Baumrind, who has helped us understand the effects of parenting styles on children's behavior; child psychiatrist Stella Chess, whose work on the bidirectional influence of temperament has changed the way we view the parent-child relationship; and Alan Sroufe, whose attachment studies indicate the importance of early environmental experiences on later behavior. Other researchers are investigating issues common to a changing society like the United States—single parenting, the effects of divorce on the parent-child relationship, the stepparenting relationship, parenting in blended families, and cross-cultural parenting differences.

Adding to the information coming from scientific investigation are theories of people working in the clinical world—psychiatrists, psychologists, educators, and pediatricians. These people have daily contact with parents and their children and are thus able to offer important insights into subjects such as child care, discipline techniques, and the adolescent experience. Prominent among these theorists are T. Berry Brazelton, a well-known pediatrician who frequently writes and talks about infant behaviors, and the late Haim G. Ginott, known for his work on parent-child communication.

Parenting Research

Since the 1930s, a parenting education movement has gained great impetus in the United States because scientific research suggests to parents that much of their children's social, intellectual, and psychological development is rooted in early childhood experiences. In addition, changing social conditions in the U.S. have added great stress to family life, and with this stress has come problems with child rearing (Clark-Steward, 1978).

The primary goal of parent education programs is two-fold: to prevent, when possible, problems from developing between parents and their children, and to deal with the problems that inevitably occur in raising children (LeMasters and DeFrain, 1983). To accomplish this goal, programs offer different types of activities. Parents can join discussion groups, listen to lectures, role-play, read books, keep journals, or watch videos. Some programs assign problem-solving homework; others offer self-help therapy sessions. There are parent training programs geared to specific problems such as attention deficit disorders, stuttering, and child abuse. Parents can join support groups organized in community centers, churches, and schools across the country. Groups like La Leche League, Parents Anonymous, and Foster Grandparents provide emotional support even while addressing specific issues such as breast feeding and child mistreatment. A number of professionals—including Thomas Gordon, Michael Popkin, Adele Fabish and Elaine Mazlish—have developed parent training programs that are based on their research, clinical practices, or long-term experience with parents and their children.

Parent training models generally follow one of four major theoretical orientations, although there is considerable overlap (see Chapter 6 for a discussion of these orientations). These approaches are presented in books and on video; some offer extensive workshops with parents as participants. Some approaches focus on the parent-child relationship, particularly problem solving and conflict resolution. Others concentrate on teaching parents how to promote their children's sense of responsibility or feelings of self-worth.

Effective parenting relies on parents having broad and diverse knowledge, understanding, and skills—an understanding of themselves and the traditions they bring to parenting from their family background and culture, an awareness of their children's innate temperaments and tendencies, and the ability to use a variety of strategies that constitute humane treatment of children. Jerome Kagan (1976), one of the nation's leading child psychologists, addressed the proliferation of advice books and parenting education programs as he cautioned against focusing on *one* set way to raise children.

> Children do not require any specific actions from adults to develop optimally. There is no good evidence that children must have a certain amount

or schedule of cuddling, kissing, spanking, holding, or deprivation of privileges in order to become gratified and productive adults. The child does have some psychological needs, but there is no fixed list of parental behaviors that can be counted on to fill those requirements. The psychological needs of children vary with age and the context of their growth (Kagan, 1976).

RESEARCH DIFFICULTIES

Compiling accurate data about parenting is not without its problems. In 1989, Judith Wallerstein published her best-selling and often-quoted *Second Chances: Men, Women, and Children a Decade After Divorce,* a book based on her fifteen-year clinical investigation of the long-term effects of divorce on children. The author concluded that almost half of the children in her California study became "worried, underachieving, self-deprecating, and sometimes angry young men and women. . . ." Wallerstein's study has been criticized for its limited size, the lack of a nondivorced control group, and the fact that the subject group was overrepresented by families seeking clinical help (Cherlin and Furstenberg, 1989). With so many factors affecting the children of divorce—changing economics, the introduction of a stepparent, a continuing relationship with one or both parents—researchers are seeking additional information about the effects of marital disruption on the lives of children.

Another problem in interpreting research data has to do with estimating the influences of culture. An example of this is an attachment research conducted in northern Germany in the 1980s by Klaus and Karin Grossmann. Their research indicated that half of the children in the study tended to be avoidantly attached to their parents; that is, they were unable to form a close, loving relationship, a figure substantially higher than that in studies of American children. The researchers concluded that the high figure was due to the German children coming from a community where people tended to "distance themselves a bit from each other," (Grossmann and Grossmann, et al., 1985). After a later study of parenting in southern Germany, the Grossmanns concluded that the level of avoidant attachment was similar for Germany and America. They came to believe the avoidant attachment that they had seen among northern German children may actually have been independence, caused by the fact that those "mothers wanted to have their children self-reliant as early as possible."

Additional research showed that the northern German mothers were very sensitive to their newborn babies until about six months of age, at which time they began to discourage displays of love or need and responded less to signs of distress. The American mothers of avoidant infants were insensitive to their children from birth on. Emotional abandonment by a parent at any time during the first year of life can injure a child psychologically, but the German children showed fewer behavior problems as they aged than did the American children studied. Many parents of the avoidant northern German children were generally accepting of their children, even supporting their efforts at school and in sports activities. The mothers of avoidant American children seemed to have a more deep-seated psychological aversion to connecting with their offspring (Karen, 1994). The complexity of the Grossmanns' research shows that the same phenomenon, when studied cross-culturally, has different meanings—even when the research results are similar. While the northern Germans and some Americans raise avoidantly attached children, their motivations are different. The northern Germans raise children this way because of cultural expectations. The American parents do so for psychological reasons, against cultural norms. This does not mean that there are no similarities in outcome for the children studied. The Grossmanns found that, like their American counterparts, the German children were not able to form close friendships at the age of ten; but they also had less confidence and self-reliance and had difficulty handling stress. Whether parental rejection is due to cultural norms or psychological factors, some avoidant children suffer throughout their lives.

DEFINING PARENTING

The word "parent" can be found in any dictionary, listed as a noun. From its Latin root *pario,* parent means "life-giver" (Pai, 1952). Some standard dictionaries suggest that a parent is a mother or a father or, more scientifically, any organism that produces or generates another. Recent dictionaries have added the verb "parenting," suggesting action. The use of the word "parenting" in reference to "acting as a parent" occurred metaphorically as early as 1884, but today its literal meaning suggests there is more to raising children then feeding, sheltering, and otherwise caring for them. It is the active participation in the process of raising children; the doing something, that constitutes the experience of parenting.

It is important to understand that parenting has to do with the beliefs, attitudes, and behaviors people rely on to help their offspring survive and prosper from birth into adulthood. There are many differences in the way this is accomplished. Culture, race, social class, gender, family of origin, and environmental circumstances all influence notions about how children should be raised. China, for example, presently has a one-child policy in which male children are valued far more than female children because it is male children who will most likely care for elderly parents. This attitude is based on both tradition and economic necessity.

ASPECTS OF PARENTING

The experience of parenting is rooted first in biology and is as old as life itself. We do not know if humans carry within them an instinctual motivation for having children; nevertheless, at its essence parenting serves an evolutionary advantage. It has to do with the survival of the human species and the contribution of genes to generations that will come. Shan Guisinger and Sidney J. Blatt

(1994) pointed out that parental care results in kin selection. "If parental care benefits children," they state, "then those parents who leave more descendants as a result of their caretaking will contribute more genes to the next generation, in comparison with neglectful parents."

Ethologists like Konrad Lorenz (1971) believe that the physical characteristics of mammalian infants encourage care and protection by adults of the species. Small body size, a relatively large, rounded head, large eyes, short extremities, and clumsy movements trigger "innate releasing mechanisms" in adult mammals, including humans. Basically this means that cuddly looking mammals get cuddled. Researchers who question Lorenz's position suggest that the human response to these infantile features may be learned (Gould, 1979). The outcome, however, is the same. Whether an innate response or the result of learning, survival of a species depends on the care that young members of the group receive from adults.

Parenting is very much a sociological phenomena, in that humans evolved into a species that separates itself into social groups of quite varied living patterns. These patterns are based on climatic conditions, availability of food, economic and environmental conditions, and the beliefs and customs that come from life in this circumstance. As such, parenting is very much a learned experience, amenable to modification. It is also through social experiences that parents incorporate the values, beliefs, and attitudes about children that they will carry into the parenting experience.

There is also a strong psychological component to parenting. Children provoke emotions in their parents, ranging from incredible joy and love to the tragic anger reflected in contemporary child-abuse figures. In her landmark book, *A Natural History of Parenting,* Susan Allport (1997) relates a dream she had a year before her oldest daughter left for college. "I dreamt the other night that she had left on a trip around the world but that I had forgotten to pack her bag. In the dream it was clothes and toothpaste and shoes that I had sent her off without, but when I woke up I knew it was the less tangible things that concerned me: common sense, the ability to resist peer pressure, respect for herself and for others, focus, the courage to meet life's challenges, and the courage to love, to become attached to another human being. All the things that all mothers, and fathers, worry about. All the things that cannot possibly be packed at the last minute. Are they in the suitcase or not? How do we ever know? When do we know? Now that I was so completely attached to this child, I was having a hard time letting her go."

Given the varied faces of parenting, is there such a thing as "good" or "bad" parenting? Whether one is a Trobriand Islander in the South Pacific or a Skolt Lapp living near the Arctic Circle in Finland, are there certain things expected if one is to raise children to be fully functioning adults? Is "good" parenting essentially the same the world over—despite differences in surroundings, social class, family organization, and cultural belief systems? Is it easier to parent in some cultures than in others, because of environmental and social circumstances? Do some societies have a greater understanding of the needs and tasks of childhood than others do, and what are the long-term results of this knowledge? Most important, if it can be shown that certain parenting practices promote optimal growth and development in children, how might this information be shared with and learned by parents the world over?

THE NURTURANCE AND SOCIALIZATION OF CHILDREN

Worldwide, more than a billion babies are born each year. In the United States alone, the figure is about 4 million. These children are born into social worlds of tribes, cultures, castes, and families. It is in these worlds that children progress through infancy, childhood, and adolescence and emerge in adulthood with the expectation that they become fully functioning, competent, productive members of a society. This goal is accomplished through the nurturance and socialization of children. These are the primary tasks of parenting, responsibilities that are shared to some extent with other family members, teachers, peers, and members of the community.

To *nurture* something is to promote its development. A plant is nurtured when it is placed in the sun, given water, and has its dead leaves pruned. A musician nurtures his or her career by taking lessons and practicing. Parental nurturance refers to doing what is necessary to promote the optimal growth and development of children. This includes providing food and shelter adequate to assure basic survival, as well as offering the affection and emotional support that enable children to thrive physically and psychologically. Since children must eventually go out into the world prepared to be self-sufficient physically and economically, parents must provide experiences and offer opportunities that will help children grow intellectually and acquire competencies in areas related to their lives.

Parenting has been described as a balance between responsiveness and demandedness (Maccoby and Martin, 1983; Baumrind, 1991.) *Responsiveness* refers to the acknowledgment, acceptance, and satisfaction of a child's needs, wants, and demands. An infant demands to be fed when hungry; a three-year-old wants to pick out his own clothes in a quest for autonomy; the adolescent needs information and support if his parents decide to divorce. When parents acknowledge and assist their children appropriately, they foster individuality, self-regulation, and self-assertion. On the other hand, parents make claims upon their children. As agents of socialization, they expect their children to learn the rules—to demonstrate values and behavioral patterns accepted by the culture and society they live in. Parental expectations regarding maturity, responsibility, and specific behaviors have been labeled *demandedness*.

Individual parents have different notions concerning how willing or able they are to respond to their children, as well as the degree to which children are required to meet parental socialization demands. This is referred to as "parenting styles" (See Chapter 5). Different parenting styles lead to different eventual child-rearing outcomes. One parent may encourage a child's curiosity by supplying games and books; another believes that giving such items freely will spoil the child. An adolescent demands a degree of independence from his or her mother and she encourages a separation; another mother discourages her teenager's autonomy because she fears the child will stray from family control. Even within the same family there can be substantial differences in responsiveness-demandedness patterns based upon culture, gender differences, sibling position, and family circumstances. Responsiveness and demandedness are two sides of the parenting coin, and they determine the effectiveness of the parenting process.

In Western society, we are apt to speak of love when referring to the parent-child relationship, the intense feeling of attachment that binds people to each other. Psychoanalyst Erich Fromm (1956) described parental love as a special kind of affectionate relationship built upon four distinct but interdependent elements that are common to all forms of love: care, responsibility, knowledge, and respect. To *care* for a child is to see that it is warm and comfortable, well nourished and healthy. A parent must show the child affection and comfort it in times of stress. The optimal growth and development of the child is of primary concern. A parent who loves a child must be *responsible* for it—meaning being "able and ready to respond" to its needs, physically and psychologically. A loving parent stays with a child when it becomes frightened of an event such as a storm. A loved child can count on being given dinner every night at an appropriate hour. Caring for a child means *knowing* that child. While this may seem a simple matter for a parent, it is not. To know a child is to understand the child's temperament and idiosyncracies, to be aware of his or her secret wishes and dreams, be cognizant of the things the child likes and dislikes. A father drives a half hour back to the house because he knows his son will be miserable without the Teddy Bear he left at home. A mother remembers her daughter hates broccoli so she buys a different vegetable for the dinner table. It is Fromm's view that the more knowledge a parent has of a child, the closer the parent-child relationship will be, and the easier it will be to meet that child's needs. It is through caring, responsibility, and knowledge that parents *respect* the children they love. This respect means accepting each child's uniqueness, appreciating his or her special characteristics, and helping to make the most of the child's individuality.

BIDIRECTIONALITY AND THE PARENT-CHILD RELATIONSHIP

Before the 1950s, the parent-child relationship was seen as one in which the adult took responsibility for imparting knowledge, values, and opportunities to the child. The child was the recipient of this information, albeit an active learner—ready and able to absorb the things the adult wanted the child to know. This view reflects seventeenth century philosopher John Locke's position that the mind of a child is a *tabula rasa,* or "blank slate," on which can be written anything parents and society desire. According to this model, parenting is a unidirectional process of socialization that attributes little power to children to determine their own fates.

Since the seventeenth century, longitudinal studies of infant temperament have demonstrated that the parent-child relationship is bidirectional and built

The Informed Parent 1.1

Myths and Realities of Parenting

Most of us grow up with a romanticized view of what parenting is or will be but in truth many of the things we hear are myths.

Myth	Reality
1. Raising children is fun.	Child rearing is hard work. The fun part is created by parents and children together.
2. Children are sweet and cute.	Children are sweet and cute, as well as mean, selfish, destructive, and many other positive and negative things that challenge parents.
3. Children will turn out well if they have "good" parents.	Parents are just one influence on children's lives. Schools, the media, and peers are also powerful forces. Despite parents' best efforts at instilling appropriate values, sometimes children display problems or get into trouble.
4. Good parents can manage any child.	Some children are harder to manage than others. Temperamental differences make some children calm and others cranky, some adaptable to change and others rigid and difficult. The success of child rearing depends on how parents handle such differences.
5. One child is too few.	Only children are not necessarily lonely, nor are they generally spoiled and selfish.
6. Children appreciate parents.	Children often do not realize what their parents have done for them until they become parents themselves.
7. Love is enough in raising children.	Love is important in bringing up children but it is not enough. Parents must also have good parenting skills, energy, and patience.

upon a reciprocal influence of each on the other. In many ways, this relationship is like a dance in which the partners move rhythmically together—their steps, gestures, and turnabouts part of a unique performance. A child who is temperamentally slow moving and inactive might keep his mouth closed to force a fast-feeding parent to slow down. The nonathletic father of an active and agile child might put up a basketball hoop on the garage and even practice shots with the child after dinner. It is parents' understanding and accep-

The parent-child relationship is a perpetual give and take, one that works best when the partners are in synchrony.

tance of their child's inborn energy levels and response styles, as well as their willingness to adapt the environment to fit the child's temperamental characteristics that constitute what researchers call "goodness of fit" (Thomas and Chess, 1977).

When children have temperaments that are in synchrony with their parents, the most satisfactory relationship exists. When the partners are out of step, parents must adapt to their children's temperamental rhythms. Adaptable parents work at understanding and meeting their children's needs, whereas more rigid parents can feel guilt, anger, resentment, and even dislike toward children they don't understand.

THE EVER-CHANGING RELATIONSHIP

In *The Merchant of Venice,* Shakespeare said "It is a wise father that knows his own child." This statement implies that parents must understand the individuality and uniqueness of their children, have a knowledge of the developmental stages and tasks of childhood, and be aware of the changes that occur as children grow and develop. In Western society, the stages and tasks of childhood are more structured than in less industrialized cultures. Parental beliefs, as well as attitudes and expectations of children at specific ages, determine the style and method parents will use to regulate behaviors. The issues of independence and sexuality that concern the parents of adolescents are hardly the same as the feeding and sleep-pattern worries of parents with infants. A father who expects his two-year-old to sit quietly and unmoving at the dinner table may get upset when the child bangs his spoon against a plate. The parent who understands the need for a two-year-old to practice motor skills might offer the child a plastic spoon to play with.

Ellen Galinsky (1981) notes that as children grow and change, so does the nature of parenting. She offers a six-stage model of parenting based upon the challenges that must be faced at each stage of development, from prenatal period through adolescence.

At the *image-making stage* of parenting, parents have a picture image of what being a parent is; but a picture, or image, is a mental representation or idea of something. It is not the real thing. Parents imagine what the new baby will be like. They speculate about their parenting abilities. They prepare themselves emotionally to take on the responsibilities of raising a child. They get ready for the birth, feeling happiness and apprehension.

The *nurturing stage* begins when the baby arrives. The images parents have must be reconciled with the reality of the child. A father imagines having a daughter, but he gets a son. A mother thinks the child will have dark hair like hers, but baby is born a redhead like her paternal grandmother. An infant wakes up every two hours during the night, despite his parents' desperate need for sleep. In the nurturing stage, parents begin the task of caring for their child. They must become attached to their baby and be prepared to meet his or her needs. There are now a new set of priorities, increased time constraints, new goals for their lives. Also in this period the relationship with grandparents and other family members must be redefined.

The preschool years, as early as eighteen months, usher in the *authority stage* of parenting. This is the period in which power issues arise. Parents have expectations of their children, and they need to determine how they are going to promote their own rules and values. They can convey authority in many ways, including gentle guidance, nagging, or even physical punishment. A child's self-esteem and personal feelings of control over the environment are affected by how parents manage this stage.

The *interpretive stage* of parenting begins when children start school or are otherwise educated. At this stage parents must provide children with the tools that will help them develop the skills and competencies they need to manage in the world. Parents communicate beliefs and values to children, giving them a world view and a sense of who they are and where they are going in life.

Adolescence marks the *interdependent stage,* a time when parental authority declines and children strive for freedom. Parents are confronted with issues of their child's sexuality, limits are stretched, and plans for the child's future take center stage. Children struggle with identity issues; they worry about who they are and where they fit with their peers. Special parenting skills are needed to help children through this period.

The Informed Parent 1.2

Images of Parenthood

Stage	Time	Traits
1. Image-making stage	Pregnancy	Parent forms image of what parenting and child will be like.
2. Nurturing stage	Birth to about two	Parents becomes attached to child. Child begins to assert independence.
3. Authority stage	Two to four years	Power issues arise. Rules, regulations, and socialization emphasized.
4. Interpretative stage	Preschool to adolescence	Parents provide tools and foster competencies in their children.
5. Interdependent stage	Adolescence	Authority relationship with children reworked.
6. Departure stage	Children leave home	Evaluate experiences of parenting. Adjust to having adult children.

At the *departure stage,* children leave home and parents have as much adjusting to do as their departing offspring. Now is the time when a balance between separateness and connection is created. Parents are now faced with evaluating the job they've done as parents.

THE CHANGING RESPONSIBILITIES OF PARENTS AS CHILDREN AGE

In *Wherever You Go There You Are,* Jon Kabat-Zinn wrote, ". . . we get virtually no preparation or training for parenting, only on-the-job, moment to moment training as things unfold. At the beginning of the job there are precious few opportunities for respite. The job calls for you to be continually engaged. And the children are always pushing your limits to find out about the world and about who they are. What's more, as they grow and develop, they change. No sooner have you figured out how to relate well to one situation than they grow out of that and into something you've never seen before. You have to be continually mindful and present so that you aren't lingering with a view of things that no longer applies."

After conducting innumerable studies on the relationship between parents and their children, researcher Eleanor Maccoby (1984) concurred with this view. She defined the tasks of parents at specific times in children's lives. She states that in *infancy,* the job of a parent is mainly one of caregiving—with tasks including helping infants regulate their bodily functions. During the *preschool* years, parents help children learn to control their emotional outbursts. They monitor daily activities and provide direct feedback in response to the child's actions.

Direct contact between parents and children diminish greatly during the *school years.* Responsibilities for monitoring behavior are somewhat removed, and children become part of the family system, contributing what little they can in a modern society. Maccoby pointed out that in simpler societies, *middle-childhood* is the time during which children begin to participate in family survival enterprises that include activities such as caring for domestic animals, working in the fields, gathering wood and water, and caring for younger children. "In our own society," she says, "children's labor is not needed, and their task is to become educated."

During *adolescence* the parent-child relationship changes again as children become involved in the larger society outside the family. Parents now provide guidance and support as their children move out into the larger world sphere (Maccoby, 1984).

PARENTING EXPERTS THROUGHOUT THE AGES

There is a Greek tale of Demeter, goddess of the harvest, who turned the earth barren after her daughter Persephone was kidnapped by the god of the underworld. The story has endured for centuries because it illustrates the unrelenting love of a parent for her child. Readers are fascinated by the story of the domineering military father in Pat Conway's *The Great Santini*, and the relationship between the Chinese mothers and daughters in Amy Tan's *The Joy Luck Club*. All of these accounts allow us to model aspects of the parent-child relationship that we admire and reject aspects that we disagree with.

The written word is a powerful force in parenting. There are hundreds of texts, magazine articles, and guidebooks that point the way for struggling mothers and fathers. Some are informative and useful; others are not informative but are also harmless; and many are nonsensical and even dangerous.

Among the earliest "authorities" to dispense information on parenting was eighteenth-century philosopher Jean Jacques Rousseau, who told French parents, "Childhood has its own ways of seeing, thinking, and feeling. . . ." Rousseau insisted that if children are given the freedom to develop their own capabilities as nature intended, without interference from society, they would naturally behave well and live fully. Rousseau personally let nature run its child-rearing course when he fathered five children by an illiterate servant woman and then abandoned them all to a state foundling home.

Rousseau dispensed his parenting advice as a rebellion against John Locke's "blank slate" theory, which suggested that everything a child comes to know and be is written through learning and experience. Locke was adamant in the belief that physical punishment did more harm than good in molding a child's behavior. He believed that praise for appropriate behavior and teaching by example were the best ways to mold children in the ways parent wanted.

In the mid-nineteenth century, child-rearing books by a doctor named Daniel Schreber were so popular in Germany many went through forty printings and were translated into several languages. Among Dr. Schreber's views was a belief that a child's display of a temper might be a sign of willfulness which must be addressed "by stern words, threatening gestures, rapping on the bed . . . or if none of this helps, by appropriately mild corporal admonitions repeated persistently at brief intervals until the child quiets down or falls asleep. . . ." This child-rearing expert, whose own child was a paranoid patient in treatment with Sigmund Freud, added that in treating one's offspring this way, "you will be master of the child forever." Swiss psychiatrist Alice Miller (1990) presumed that the world catastrophe caused by Germany in the twentieth century was a direct result of the parenting practices encouraged by people like Schreber.

In the 1920s, an American behaviorist named John Watson published a popular book on child rearing. In it he warned parents about being too loving or sentimental toward their children. Watson believed that an affectionate mother was a potential danger to her child, particularly if she responded immediately to her baby's cries or demands for food. "Never hug and kiss them," Watson cautioned parents about their children, "never let them sit on your lap. If you must, kiss them once on the forehead when they say goodnight. Shake hands with them in the morning" (Watson, 1928). Watson also informed parents that their children had no inherited capacities, temperaments, or talents. In a best-selling book, he wrote, "Give me a dozen healthy infants, well-formed, and my own specified world to bring them up in and I'll guarantee to take any one at random and train him to become any type of specialist I might select—doctor, lawyer, artist, merchant chief and, yes, even beggarman and a thief, regardless of his talents, penchants, tendencies, abilities, vocations, and race of his ancestors."

Benjamin Spock, a pediatrician, also trained in psychoanalysis, wrote a child-care book in the 1950s that has sold millions of copies the world over. In it, he gave parenting advice on everything from discipline to the family bed. At one point in his book, Spock cautioned "don't be overawed by what the experts say."

Today, information about parenting comes from a far wider range of sources, including newspapers, television, ministers, and psychologists. Even presidents of the United States have been known to share their views on raising children. Harry S Truman, a doting father to his only child, Margaret, revealed the secret of his own success by saying, "I have found the best way to give advice to your children is to find out what they want and then advise them to do it."

THE DECISION TO PARENT

Men and women become parents because of choice or chance. Since the 1920s and 1930s, when contraceptive devices became effective and available, the birth of children has become less a function of fate and more the result of thought and decision making (Wells, 1988). This new-found freedom from procreation was further enhanced with the development of the birth control pill and the legalization of abortions in the United States. In the United States in 1996, the average number of children per family was slightly less than two (U.S. Bureau of the Census). This figure is a decrease from the 1960 average of 3.1 children. Today, many people are choosing to have no children at all, a change that evolved from the women's movement, concerns about overpopulation and environmental pollution, and the desire of some women to concentrate on their careers. In 1972, over one-half of white middle-class college women believed that a refusal to have children was legitimate grounds for divorcing a mate. By 1979, only one-fourth believed this (Cook, West, and Hamner, 1982). The same study showed that by 1979 almost three-fourths of the women surveyed did not believe that a happy marriage depended on their having children.

Among women who work, those in professional occupations and managerial positions are less likely to bear children then those in lower-paying jobs (White and Kim, 1987). Married couples who delay child rearing cite the need to establish careers, gain financial security, and stabilize their marriages (Soloway and Smith, 1987).

For many people, having children is viewed as an essential part of life, a source of love, and personal satisfaction. In one study, 62 percent of men questioned felt children made life richer, and 52 percent of women felt this way (see Tables 1.1 and 1.2). Others cited the lifelong benefit of giving and receiv-

TABLE 1.1 Reasons for Having Children

	Women	Men
Create new person with someone you love	60%	56%
Make life richer	52%	62%
Important part of being married	42%	42%
Someone to share things with	38%	53%
Enjoy being with children	36%	31%
Experience raising children	30%	27%
One of life's greatest accomplishments	23%	18%
Feelings about continuation of life	19%	26%
Part of being a real woman (or man)	13%	1%
Someone who loves you	9%	15%

TABLE 1.2   Reasons Not to Have Children

	Percent of All Respondents
Causes drastic change in lifestyle	68%
Financial cost is too great	65%
Children cause worry and tension	49%
Caring for children takes too much time	47%
Makes it difficult for women to work	42%
Adds to overpopulation	35%
Causes disorder in the house	26%
Endangers one's health and energy level	20%

Source: M. M. B. Asis, "The Involuntarily Childless: Is There Support for Them in American Society?" Paper presented at the meeting of the Midwest Sociological Society, Des Moines, IA, 1986.

ing love and the chance to "create a new person with someone you love" (Burnell and Norfleet, 1986).

Some parents reported their lives are more fulfilled by having children (Callan, 1987). Men, even more than women, felt that children make "life richer" (Callan and Gallois, 1983).

The wish to carry on a family name and the desire to have someone "carry on a part of oneself" are other reasons given for becoming parents (Asis, 1986). These reasons were particularly reported in regard to male children (Soloway and Smith, 1987).

The decision to have children is sometimes based on religious principles that encourage couples to "be fruitful and multiply." Married couples believe they are morally obligated to bring new members into society and the church. For them, procreation is the only acceptable intent of sexual activity, and—as a consequence—the use of contraception is immoral.

For some people, parenthood is equated with adulthood; it's the sign of being a "man" or a "woman." In one survey, 13 percent of women felt this way, but only 1 percent of men did (Burnell and Norfleet, 1986).

For some adults, having children is an opportunity to relive parts of one's own childhood and a chance to re-create some of the past. Since children by nature enjoy excitement, there are some men and women who enjoy the novelty and stimulation that comes with bringing them up. Since school activities, neighborhood gatherings, and other social events often revolve around youngsters, having children is a way to connect with one's community.

Children are often born out of the psychological needs of their parents. There are those who believe that children provide companionship and assuage loneliness. Teenage mothers desirous of love and affection often feel that a child will bring these things into their lives. Parties in an ailing marital relationship sometimes hope the birth of a child will bring them closer and distract them from the marital issues.

Women today can choose to be parents into middle age. Rosanna Della Corte, a sixty-two-year-old Italian woman gave birth to a son by caesarean section in 1994. The 7 pound 4 ounce infant, named Riccardo, was conceived by the artificial insemination of Mrs. Corte's husband's sperm and a donor's egg. In 1996, just short of her sixty-third birthday, a California woman named Arceli Keh bore a daughter, Cynthia, after five attempts at in vitro fertilization, using an anonymous donor's egg and her husband, Isagani's, sperm.

Despite the promotion of groups such as Planned Parenthood, the availability of birth control products, and the "Just Say No" campaign aimed at teens, many births are unplanned and accidental. Teen pregnancy rates rose 9 percent in the United States between 1985 and 1990. In 1990, 6 percent of all young women aged fifteen to nineteen had babies, a 13 percent increase over ten years. Reasons for this increase include poor sex education as well as a lessening of the social stigma surrounding teen parenthood. Since 1995, rates have dropped.

Reasons for having children differ across cultures. In a number of societies such as Turkey, Indonesia, the Philippines, and Thailand, children are primarily valued for their economic utility. But parents from Korea, Taiwan, and Singapore often mention stimulation and fun as their primary motives for having children (Hoffman, 1988).

MOTHERHOOD OR FATHERHOOD: IS THERE A DIFFERENCE?

The term "parenting" is generally used to describe the caregiving beliefs and behaviors of both mothers and fathers. Are the two parents viewed as interchangeable in terms of their contribution to child rearing? Do we perceive mothers and fathers as having the same roles when it comes to parenting children? Carol Gilligan (1982) pointed out that "women, universally, are largely responsible for early child care." This is true despite attempts over the past two decades to involve fathers more in the daily care of their children.

While women have more of a choice today than ever about having children, there are strong social motives that push them in this direction. The term "mothering" itself implies nurturing and care. Holding, feeding, diapering, soothing, and rocking are considered part of that care. From early childhood on, women have played at being mothers; their toys were often dolls, baby carriages, and other "mothering" paraphernalia. The television programs women watched, the games they played, the books they read—all taught the lesson that having children is an important aspect of female development. So strong is social learning in regard to mothering that a 1987 survey of 2,000 mothers found that 8 out of 10 would choose to have children again if given a second chance (Genevie and Margolies, 1987).

Fathering is not viewed the same as mothering. The traditional role of father was one of economic provider. Over the past twenty years, however, fathers have been encouraged to take an expanded role in the nurturance of their children. In Benjamin Spock's classic book *Baby and Child Care,* there is a drastic change between the 1945 edition of the book and the 1985 version.

> A man can be a warm father and a real man at the same time. . . . Of course I don't mean that the father has to give as many bottles or change just as many diapers as the mother. But it's fine for him to do these things occasionally. He might make the formula on Sunday (Spock, 1945).

> When a father does his share as a matter of course . . . it does much more than simply lighten his wife's work load and give her companionship. . . . It shows that he believes this work is crucial for the welfare of the family, that it calls for judgment and skill, and that it's his responsibility as much as it is hers. . . . This is what sons and daughters need to see in action if they are to grow up without sexist attitudes (Spock and Rothenberg, 1985).

A 1971 study found that fathers interacted with their infant children an average of 37.7 seconds per day (Rebelsky and Hanks, 1971). A number of trends over the past twenty years suggest that men in the United States are becoming more involved in child care. For example, diaper-changing tables have been placed in the men's rooms of some airports and train stations, although certainly not in the numbers as in women's rooms. In the past, mother was considered the "emotional" nurturer of her children, but now fathers are seen as providing this same kind of expressive care (Lamb, 1986). Increasingly, men are attending the births of their children and they are taking time off from work to care for them when necessary and often are enrolling in parent education classes (Lawson, 1990). A 1997 survey conducted by the Families and Work Institute showed that over the past twenty years, men are assuming more responsibility for child care and household chores. In 1977, working men put in 30 percent of the time as women on chores, including child care. In 1997, this figure rose to 75 percent. While there has been a rise in the number of two-income families in the United States, today's children under 18 are getting more attention from their working parents than did those of 20 years ago, mostly because fathers are taking more of an interest in their children. (See Figure 1.2.) In all, the survey found that working fathers spent an average of 2.3 hours during the work week caring for children, a half hour more than was reported 20 years ago. This compares to three hours each workday that mothers spend with children. It should be noted that the figures reported may be biased by the self-reporting nature of the study and the fact that some of the time spent with the children overlaps with time spent doing household chores like cooking, washing dishes, or going food shopping. Even though

Figure 1.2
Working Fathers and
Their Children

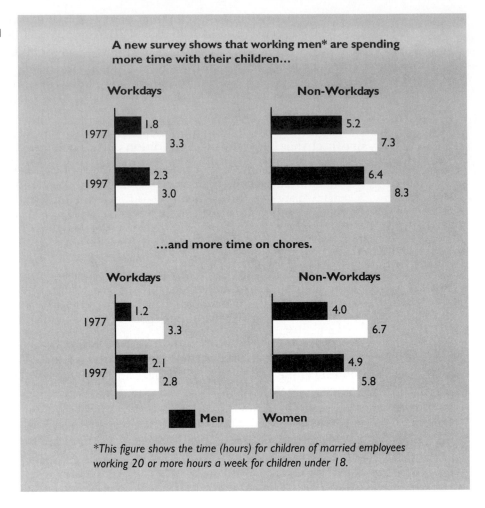

A new survey shows that working men* are spending more time with their children...

*This figure shows the time (hours) for children of married employees working 20 or more hours a week for children under 18.

parental attention is not undivided while tasks are being accomplished, parents and their children are interacting.

CHILDREN AS LIFE CHANGERS

The decision to become a parent is also a decision to change almost everything about one's life. If parents are married, the birth of a first child brings new challenges and new stresses into the marital relationship. Like it or not, a marriage is not the same once another individual becomes central to it. If a parent is unmarried and alone at the time of a child's birth, the stresses of managing the care of a baby are magnified because parenting is not being shared with a partner. Jay Belsky, chief researcher of the Penn State Child and Family Development Project (1994), looked at the issues pertaining to marriage and parenting. Belsky's work suggests that a baby's arrival tends naturally to polarize new parents, whether the marriage was happy or unhappy before a child came into it. The differences are rooted in the biological differences between men and women, socialization, personal experiences, and family background. More profoundly, Belsky discovered that few parents are realistic about what to expect after the birth of a baby.

It stands to reason that a marriage will change once a couple adds a third person into the relationship. When a baby appears, the marriage becomes a three-person system, and scarce emotional resources must be shared with the new arrival. In a study of 128 middle- and working-class couples with an average age of 29 for the husband and 27 for the wife, Belsky and his associates found that the birth of a first child led to a variety of changes. Although for at least half of the couples, there was little or no change in levels of love, conflict, and effort, for a number of them marital problems did increase. In troubled relationships, the new parents argued more, communicated less, and became uncertain about their relationship. The researchers found that a number of factors contributed to this marriage deterioration. The parents tended to be younger and less educated, with more limited financial resources available to them; one or both of the partners exhibited low self-esteem; the husbands were rated as less sensitive. The mothers who were unhappiest had infants who were somewhat difficult temperamentally (Belsky and Rovine, 1990). Interestingly, the researchers found that the couples who had more romantic relationships before the birth of their child reported more problems after the birth—because of unrealistic expectations.

While raising children is more difficult than most people believe it will be, a survey of 702 midwestern parents found that 76 percent of those interviewed were satisfied with the parenting experience, 16 percent reported being neither satisfied nor unsatisfied, and 8 percent did not like the parenting role (Meredith, Stinnet and Cacioppo, 1985). Table 1.3 lists the most satisfactory aspects of parenting.

THE DECISION NOT TO PARENT

At one time those who did not have children were referred to as "childless." (See Table 1.2.) Today, people who make a conscious decision not to have children often refer to themselves as "child-free" implying a form of liberation. The decision to forego having children often comes gradually, in stages (Houseknecht, 1987).

Couples who make the decision not to have children cite nine primary reasons for their decision:

1. Freedom from child-care responsibility.
2. A better marital relationship.
3. Monetary advantages.

TABLE 1.3   Parental Satisfaction Survey

	Percent Recording Response
Watching children grow and develop	74
Love for children	65
Pride in children's achievement	62
Sharing	54
A growth experience	45
Passing on values	44
Fun to do things with	43
General enjoyment	41
Feeling of being part of a family	40
Self-fulfillment	39
Feel needed	39
Enjoying physical contact	37
Feeling closer to spouse	36
A purpose for living	32
Enjoying the simple aspects of life	31
Companionship	27
Hope for the future	26
New appreciation for my parents	25
Adds stability to life	25
Shared marital project	24
Keeps me young	19
Pleasure for grandparents	16
More things to talk about with spouse	15

4. Career considerations.

5. General dislike of children.

6. Concern about overpopulation.

7. Doubts about parenting ability.

8. Worry about the physical aspects of childbirth.

9. Distress about world conditions.

THE COST OF RAISING CHILDREN

Historically, children—especially males—have been considered economic assets; they help financially through their personal labors, and they are expected to care for aged parents when the time comes. This view is particularly true in

Figure 1.3
Stages of Decision
Making about Not
Having Children

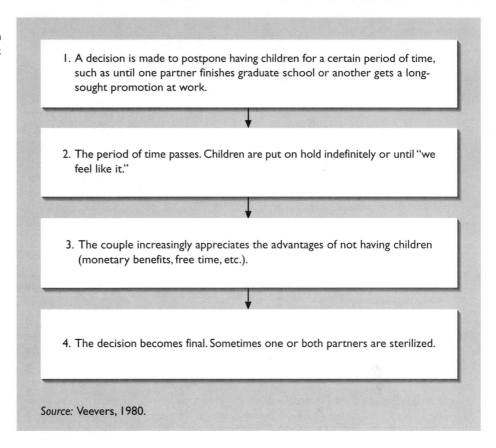

1. A decision is made to postpone having children for a certain period of time, such as until one partner finishes graduate school or another gets a long-sought promotion at work.

2. The period of time passes. Children are put on hold indefinitely or until "we feel like it."

3. The couple increasingly appreciates the advantages of not having children (monetary benefits, free time, etc.).

4. The decision becomes final. Sometimes one or both partners are sterilized.

Source: Veevers, 1980.

agrarian societies, where laborers are required to farm the land. In Western society, the shift towards manufacturing and service economies has put children more on the receiving end of financial aid.

In 1977, the estimated cost of raising a first child in a middle-class family from infancy through four years of college was $64,000. By 1990, the figure had jumped to $227,000, including four years at an in-state college or university. If one adds private schooling, the figure escalates to $310,000. In 1996, the United States Department of Agriculture surveyed 12,850 two-parent households and 3,395 single-parent households and reported the average cost of raising a child from birth to age 17, before college, at $149,820. The biggest chunk of this money, 33 percent ($49,710) is for housing. Food came next at $26,130, followed by transportation, clothing, and child care. It cost about $8,300 a year, or $694 per month, to raise one child in a two-child, two-parent, middle-income family. The figures differed depending on place of residence; for example, housing costs on the West Coast are higher than in other parts of the country. Imagine these figures in light of the 52 million middle-class households (54 percent of the population), in which 31 percent of the nation's children live and incomes range from $25,000–$100,000 per year. In

The Informed Parent 1.3

Am I Parent Material?

These questions are designed to stimulate ideas you may not have thought about. There are no right answers and no grades. Your answers are right for you and may help you decide whether *you* want to be a parent.

Does Having and Raising a Child Fit the Lifestyle I Want?

1. What do I want out of life for myself?

2. Could I handle a child and a job, or getting an education, at the same time? Would I have time and energy for both?

3. Would I be ready to give up the freedom to do what I want to do when I want to do it?

4. Would I be willing to cut back my social life and spend more time at home? Would I miss my free time and privacy?

5. Can I afford to support a child? Do I know how much money it takes to raise a child?

6. Do I want to raise a child in the neighborhood where I live now? Would I be willing and able to move?

7. How would a child affect my growth and development?

8. Am I willing to give a great part of my life, at least eighteen years, to being responsible for a child? Am I prepared to spend a large portion of my life being concerned about my child's well-being?

What's In It for Me?

1. Do I like doing things with children? Do I enjoy activities that children can do?

2. Would I try to pass my ideas and values on to my child? What if my child's ideas turn out to be different from mine?

3. Would I want my child to achieve things I didn't?

4. Would I expect my child to keep me from being lonely in my old age? Do I do that for my parents? Do my parents do that for my grandparents?

these households 70 percent are headed by married couples, 8 percent by single mothers, and 3 percent by single fathers. These are particularly astounding figures when you consider that, in 8 million American households, where 22 percent of the nation's children live, the average income is less than $15,000 (*Money*, May, 1995).

5. Do I want a boy or a girl child? What if I don't get what I want?

6. Do I expect my child to make my life happy?

Raising a Child: What's There to Know?

1. Do I like children? When I'm around children for a while, what do I think or feel about having one around all the time?

2. Is it easy for me to tell other people what I want, need, or expect of them?

3. Do I want to give a child the love he or she needs? Is loving easy for me?

4. Am I patient enough to deal with the noise, confusion, and twenty-four-hour-a-day responsibility? What kind of time and space do I need for myself?

5. What do I do when I get angry or upset? Would I take things out on a child if I lost my temper?

6. What does discipline mean to me? What does freedom, setting limits, or giving space mean? What is being too strict or not strict enough? Would I want a perfect child?

7. How do I get along with my parents? What will I do to avoid the mistakes my parents made?

8. How would I take care of my child's health and safety? How do I take care of my own?

9. What if I have a child and find out I made a wrong decision ?

Have My Partner and I Really Talked about Becoming Parents?

1. Does my partner want to have a child? Have we talked about our reasons?

2. Could we give a child a good home? Is our relationship a happy and strong one?

3. Could we share our love with a child without jealousy?

4. What would happen if we separated after having a child, or if one of us should die?

5. Do my partner and I understand each other's feelings about religion, work, family child raising, future goals? Do we feel pretty much the same way? Will children fit into these feelings, hopes, and plans?

6. Suppose one of us wants a child and the other doesn't? Who decides?

In 1998, *U.S. News & World Report* did an in-depth comparison of child-rearing costs across social class lines. They calculated into their figures the expense of wages forgone because of child-rearing duties, and also the cost of a college education. The typical middle-income family, making a 22-year investment in one child, needs just over $1.45 million dollars. This rises to $2.78 million in the top-third income bracket, and $761,871 in the bottom third.

The Informed Parent 1.4

The Advantages and Disadvantages of the One-Child Family

Advantages

Parents
Have more time to pursue own
   interests and careers
Do not have to worry about favoring
   one child over another
Less financial strain

Child
No sibling rivalry
More privacy
Enjoys closer relationship with parents
Greater financial advantage

Disadvantages

Parents
Balancing attention and indulgence
Having only one chance at parenting
Fear of being left childless in the event
   child's death

Child
Missing out on having a sibling
Feeling pressure to succeed
Having to care for aged parents alone

While these figures seem outrageous considering the median income for families with children is about $41,000 a year, the *U.S. News* report included expenses such as prenatal care, day care, medical expenses for the child, and toys (see Chapter 2).

It is not unusual today for people to have only one child. In fact, a third of American families started in 1999 will have only one child. And despite the perception that "only" children tend to be lonely and spoiled, this is not generally the case. Only children are as well-adjusted as children who have siblings; they often do better in school; and they generally have closer relationships with their parents. On the negative side, only children are sometimes subjected to greater pressure to achieve. Parents of only children usually have more financial resources available and more time to pursue their own interests and careers.

PARENTING: A HISTORICAL PERSPECTIVE

Among the "Lauues" and "Libertyes" concerning the Inhabitants of the Massachusetts, there is the Puritan belief that "if a man have a stubborn or REBELLIOUS SON, of sufficient years and understanding (viz) sixteen years of age, which will not obey the voice of his Father, or the voice of his Mother," or that of a Court, and continues to live in "sundry notorious crimes" then such a son shall be put to death. Children born into this seventeenth-century New England society, of whom a half died before the age of ten, were continually reminded that they were born into sin and were doomed to hell if they did not become obedient and compliant. To the Puritans, whose beliefs were based on the doctrine of Protestant theologian John Calvin, joyfulness and play were creations of the Devil. From the moment of their birth, children are evil beings—products of Adam's sin—and "liable to Eternal Vengeance, the Unquenchable Flames of Hell" (Heininger, et al., 1984). To ensure that their children remained passive and compliant, parents followed the dictum, "Once a day, take something from them."

The history of parenting through the ages has been called a "nightmare" by researcher Lloyd DeMause, who believes that a helping mode of parenting is a very recent force in Western society (DeMause, 1975). In tracing childhood from antiquity to the present, he encounters generation after generation of children who were brutalized and neglected by their parents. He discovered such heinous traditions as salting newborns and placing them in ice water to "harden" them, wrapping babies in swaddling bands to keep them from using their limbs, laying infants on hot ovens or hanging them on hooks to keep them out of the way; sending newborns to the countryside on wagons to be wet nursed; terrorizing children with tales of horrible figures who would spirit them away if they misbehaved; castrating male children in order to employ them in households; beating children with sticks, belts, and other household items; and leaving children by the road to die or to be carried off into slavery. Looking at the twentieth century, DeMause saw evidence of change as well as remnants of the old child care behaviors. DeMause wrote, "Children are not sent out to wet nurse at birth or to be servants at seven, but we do abandon them to hosts of nurseries, teachers, camps, and baby sitters for major portions of their young lives. Intrusive parents still find ways to restrict their baby's movements . . . and parents continue to emotionally abandon, betray, manipulate and hurt their children both overtly and covertly" (DeMause, 1975).

This notion that childhood did not exist until relatively recently is forwarded by French social historian Philip Aries (1962) who wrote a classic book, *Centuries of Childhood,* in which he illustrated how closely the parent-child relationship depends on the historical setting in which it occurs. Until the end of the Middle Ages, children were viewed as small adults. As such, they lived, worked, and played alongside their elders. According to Aries, medieval parents had many children in hopes that some would survive infancy. Families did not organize around children until the eighteenth century, when the development of schools led children to be separated from their parents.

English historian Nicholas Tucker (1993) refuted the work of DeMause and Aries by asserting that, if parenting behaviors were as awful as proposed throughout the ages, very few children would have survived. In acknowledging the work of ethologists such as Konrad Lorenz, Tucker noted that nature naturally provides infants with mechanisms that will provoke care by adults. But during unfavorable economic times and due to cultural convictions, that care may not be forthcoming. In poverty stricken societies, or in cultures where parents are forced to leave their children in order to make a living, parents tend to withdraw love from weak children or children they must abandon. For example, the Middle Ages were a particularly bad time for parents and their children. Up to 25 people lived in one home where they cooked, ate, worked, and slept in a one large chamber. People married late and died young. Life was centered around the village rather than the family unit. Many children were born into the households. Half died, and they were replaced by others. This kind of society hardly promotes the nurturance of children. Tucker cautions that worst-case scenarios of parenting do not make good psychological law. He suggests that when times are favorable, "there seems no reason to doubt that parents have always loved their babies as much as contemporary conditions made it possible for them to do so."

The effects of social class, religious beliefs, and political differences on the parenting role are illustrated in one of the volumes of *A History of Private Lives,* which describes nineteenth-century French life as relatively child oriented. The national birthrate declined, from 32.9 per thousand in 1800 to 19 per thousand in 1910. Children were seen not as individuals but as investments in the family's future. It was imperative that children carry on the family name with honor and become contributing, respected members of society. Toys for children of the middle class were manufactured on a large scale. In poor, rural families, fathers often made toys out of wood. Displays of affections were discouraged in rural areas but were tolerated by middle-class families. Children were less likely to be beaten with rods in middle-class homes than they were in aristocratic ones. Beatings were permitted in schools in order to enforce discipline. In the countryside and among the poor and petty-bourgeois segments of the urban population, "hide-tannings" or spankings were usually administered with the bare hand; sticks and whips were reserved for the masters of apprentices and guards in institutions. Physical violence was viewed in terms of masculinity and "the making of a man," although militant workers and anarchists blamed their hatred of authority on the beatings they received as children. After 1850, when children died, they were mourned as much as adults would be. At age eight, children were thought to have attained the age of reason. Girls of fifteen to eighteen were sent to boarding school to complete their moral education and prepare for a life of pleasing their husbands. Boys lived in barrack-like colleges to complete their educations.

As *Private Lives* has shown, a softening of attitudes toward children began to occur in Europe toward the end of the eighteenth century. In the United States, vast changes were occurring politically, economically, and technologically, necessitating a change in attitude toward the young. With the election of Andrew Jackson to the presidency in 1828, the country took a democratic turn. Before this time, only the wealthy had access to power. Now there were opportunities for children to rise higher in society than their parents had. To meet such responsibilities there became a need for new parenting methods, ones that focused on training children to respect authority and learn the things that would enable them to be part of the new social order. To help parents turn their children into natural resources, child rearing manuals began to appear. These manuals were especially important to the many American who had left the rural areas where they were born and raised and moved to cities where they now lived separated from the support and advice of their more experienced elders. It is in the new towns and cities of America that childhood as we know it today evolved. Toys, books, clothing, and furniture were now made specifically for young people; school attendance became compulsory; by early in the twentieth century, employing children as laborers for long hours was legally prohibited.

THE CHANGING FACES OF AMERICAN FATHERHOOD

Well into the eighteenth century, children the world over were raised by both parents, who were home together tending the farm or working side by side in a small craft shop. As a family, the father, mother, and children—along with servants, apprentices, and hired hands—planted crops, tended gardens, fed farm animals, made bread and canned food, spun clothing, made furniture and soap, and even made the family's medicines. Fathers spent a great deal of time with their children and were able to pass on their knowledge and skills during the normal day. Fathers were the dominating force in family life; wives and children generally adhered to their wishes and desires.

By the turn of the twentieth century, as fathers began to commute to factory or office jobs, their influence decreased. With the decline of the "corporate household economy," men became the primary breadwinners and women the principal nurturers of children. Fathers were now expected to increase their family's standard of living and support their children until their sons were trained in an occupation and their daughters got married. Fathers of the middle class traded time with their children for economic success. Working-class fathers lost much of their authority as they struggled to make an unpredictable and marginal living in the industrial sector. Black fathers had a particularly difficult time as they too migrated into cities from farm communities, only to find themselves excluded from all but the most menial jobs. As black fathers left the families they were unable to support, the families become overwhelmingly matriarchal. Immigrant fathers were often at odds with their children because of the gap between the culture the fathers left behind and the new culture experienced by their children. Fathers became especially alienated from their daughters as the daughters became emotionally dependent upon their mothers and female kin (Griswold, 1994).

Historian Robert L. Griswold noted that, out of concern about the declining paternal authority and family upheaval, the government took over many of the duties previously belonging to the father in the family. The state began passing laws pertaining to child abandonment, wife and child abuse, and child labor. Eventually, birth control, abortion rights, and other previously private family matters would come under government legislation. Psychologist Deborah Anna Luepnitz (1988) suggests that these new laws provided a way for men to continue to control their wives and children. Father patriarchy had been replaced by public patriarchy. The agencies of the state, as well as the male dominated media, took over control of family life.

THE REINVENTION OF FATHERHOOD

New theories of psychological development surfaced in the popular press during the 1920s as the ideas of Sigmund Freud and other researchers found their way into print. The notion of father as a necessary role model to his children brought calls for increased father involvement in the family. This father focus was coupled with concerns about the "overfeminization" of the family. What was to become of children if mother was their sole role model? Fathers were now assured by psychologists, social workers, physicians, and social reformers that self-fulfillment and meaning could come from their participation in child care. Father was now asked to be both a breadwinner and a nurturer. As Robert Griswold pointed out, the nurturer role did not include doing "unmanly" chores such as doing the children's laundry, cleaning their rooms, cooking their meals, nursing them when they become ill, or driving them places. The "new" fathers' job was to foster sex-role identification, creativity, and individualism (Griswold, 1993).

While many men were reevaluating their relationship with their children, the Great Depression of the 1930s brought despair into the lives of millions of American fathers. Unable to provide their families with financial support, men had limited power in the home. A majority of fathers still held jobs; however, those who didn't suffered a loss of self-esteem. Women were able to obtain domestic positions and other gender-based employment, which further added to family unrest. Again the government stepped in to ensure that father kept his rightful place in the family. State-funded work-relief programs favored men, in one case mandating "a woman with an employable husband is not eligible for referral, as her husband is the logical head of the family." It was suggested that any woman holding a job should give it up to a man with a family, even though the jobs were not those a family man would take.

The authority of the father in the family was reaffirmed with the coming of World War II. The nation's fathers were either in the armed services or working at high-paying jobs. Father had become the principal breadwinner again, and as such his authority in his family was reaffirmed. The social focus of America was on the re-creation of a strong, healthy family, instilled with the values that would keep America from sinking into the totalitarianism that had caused the war. Only with fathers working again and mothers staying at home to care for the children, could democracy stand. Ironically, this philosophy of life took hold while many fathers were out of the country fighting the war and the labor shortage brought mothers into the workplace in record numbers.

The war brought even more disruption to the American family; as people moved frequently because of the war effort, some marriages were made in haste, resulting in unwanted pregnancies. Some children, left on their own, drifted into delinquency. The situation was deemed so severe that in 1943 the Senate Committee on Military Affairs held hearings on a bill to exempt fathers

Hi and Lois

Reprinted with special permission of King Features Syndicate

from the draft. The bill, though popular with the public, was defeated. Newspapers, women's magazines, social workers, and psychiatrists now worried about excessive maternal influence in the family. Mothers were advised to bring father into the family through their correspondence and by reminding their children of him every day.

When the war ended, fathers returned home to children who hardly knew them and whom they hardly knew. The formerly absent serviceman-father now had to become a breadwinner, husband, and father again. Many felt their children had been "spoiled" by their mothers and by grandparents who often lived with the mother and children. Not surprisingly, conflicting views about child rearing and household management were common. As Griswold noted, "the wartime separation of children and fathers had left lasting psychological scars on both parties."

The "baby boom" of the post-war years marked a new phase in fathering. While some women continued to rise in the employment world, the majority were required to give up their jobs to returning men whether they wanted to or not, thus placing them back in the home. Younger men, eager to prove their sexual identity and be judged as responsible adults, hurried into early marriages and early fatherhood. Unmarried men were suspected of being homosexuals. Television had recently been invented and its programming closely linked manhood and fatherhood. Television also had the effect of offering dolls, toys, phones, records, dishwashers, and other items into American households, suggesting it was a father's place to provide these consumer items to his wife and children. Symbolically, the father's success at doing this proved the triumph of capitalism over the threatening sense of Communism that marked the Cold War years of the 50's. In effect, this period marks a serious separation of social classes as fathers carried their families into the middle class or stayed behind with them in the working class. Those who moved into the world of suburban housing and consumer goods did so by working long hours, often in companies that required considerable conformity and allowed little creativity. Their role as fathers consisted of being guides to right living. Their interest was in helping their children, sons in particular, develop appropriate standards of behavior. "It was middle-class men who most often treated their children in ways that promoted self-reliance, democracy, emotional stability, heterosexuality, and tolerance," wrote Griswold. Researchers of the time reported that middle-class fathers, now exposed to information on child care, moved away from strictness and the emphasis on control that marked earlier eras. Styles of parenting, expectations of children, modes of discipline, and relationships with mates differed along socioeconomic lines. Working-class fathers continued to value obedience and conformity over democracy and parental harmony, putting them at odds with a national media that promoted the values of the middle class. Attitudes about black fathers and their role in the family was particularly harsh.

A controversial 1965 report on the black family in America suggested that "the widespread family disorganization among Negros has resulted from the failure of the father to play the role in family life required by American society. . . ." (Moynihan, 1965). The report describes a long history of racism, leading to the inability of black fathers to support their families and leaving black families with a matriarchal structure that burdens them beyond their ability to survive. Historians and sociologists have countered the Moynihan Report by pointing to the strength and resilience of the black family in spite of slavery and the economic hardships that led fathers to leave home.

In 1975, 84 percent of American children under eighteen lived in two-parent families. Of these, 46 percent lived in homes where the father was the breadwinner and the mother a full-time homemaker. By 1988, the number of children living in two-parent families dropped to 78 percent, and only 29 percent lived with a full-time homemaker mother. Once again, a changing economy brought about changes in the home. Whereas a thirty-year-old man working in 1949 might experience a 63 percent increase in his income by 1959, the same age man in 1973 would see his income decline by 1983. By the mid-1960s, one-third of young white men and one-half of all young black men did not earn enough money to support a wife and family (Griswold, 1993). No longer could a middle-class father underwrite the lifestyle and consumer items desired by his wife and family. Survival of the family meant that mothers return to the workplace, a circumstance that has been the defining feature of the new fatherhood of this past decade. The role of father as breadwinner became that of father as partner in caregiving. By the 1990s, because of the change in their social status and the new expectations placed upon them at home, a large number of American men found the experience of fatherhood less and less appealing. Many delayed marriage or left the wives they had, abandoning their children financially and emotionally and leaving millions of families in impoverished circumstances. At the same time, increasing number of men became out-of-wedlock fathers. In 1960, 15 percent of teenagers who had a baby were unmarried; by the mid-1980s that number had risen to 61 percent. A number of research projects have shown that 1) many teenage fathers are interested in participating in the care of their children, and 2) if they could, they would contribute to the financial needs of their children (Robinson, 1988). Often the young men who father out-of-wedlock children do not have male role models for responsible parenting, and they are not trained or do not have enough education or training for meaningful employment.

As American society moves into the twenty-first century, the role of father continues to be redefined. It is as varied as the historical, social, and political context in which it exists. Researcher Michael Lamb (1987) emphasized the importance of a father in the home. After reviewing the scientific literature on the influence of fathers, Lamb concluded that sons become more masculine and daughters more feminine when fathers are nurturant, take their parenting role seriously, and participate actively in child care.

The changes in the American family result in divergent fatherhood paths. Some men seek to revive the old patriarchal family by subjecting their mates and children to physical abuse, sexual assault, and other forms of tyranny. Other men have accepted their new status as equal partners in the family and express a willingness to participate in child rearing. In spite of good intentions, the evolution from the patriarchical family to the egalitarian family is not yet complete. Robert L. Griswold sums up the present state of fatherhood this way:

> The ideology of male breadwinning over the course of the twentieth century has also justified men's limited commitment to child care. Despite persistent calls in this century for more fatherly commitment to offspring, men have left most of the work of rearing children to women. They have done so because of their status as providers, and their efforts as breadwinners should not be denigrated. To support a family is no small accomplishment, and men have rightfully gained a sense of self-worth and importance from doing so. But this recognition should not obscure the fact that fathers have largely left the boring, repetitious, and vexing work of child care to their wives, a division of labor that persists despite dramatic changes in the household economy. Even in homes where both parents work full-time, mothers still do the great majority of child care, a "second shift" that leaves them exhausted and resentful.

THE GOOD AND BAD MOTHER

In a 1942 book, *A Generation of Vipers,* writer Philip Wylie coined the term "momism" in warning about the smothering, over-protecting maternalism that was pervading society. In a vicious attack, Wylie blamed American mothers for everything from smashing their sons' dreams of adventure to destroying their manhood. Over the next thirty years, attacks on mothers continued as professionals in the field of child development called them "overprotective," "neglectful," "schizophrenogenic," and "self-centered." One psychiatrist, Bruno Bettelheim, suggested that the serious developmental disorder known as autism occurred because of cold mothering. Even the Moynihan Report, which lamented the abandonment of children by their fathers, suggested that there is something amiss about the matriarchal family—even while mothers struggle to economically support and emotionally care for their children. In essence, present cultural beliefs make the mother responsible for the mental health of her children, whether the father is in the home or not. This burden hasn't always been such. The role of mothers, like those of fathers, has changed according to culture, history, technology, population pressures, and society's views about women's biology.

MOTHERS OF THE DISTANT PAST

Until about A.D. 500, the world's societies revered the Great Mother. Images of her rounded, pregnant body have been found in scores of archeological sites ranging across Europe, all the way up to Siberia. She has been carved in stone and ivory, and baked in clay. The most famous of these "mother" statues is the Venus of Willendorf, discovered in Austria and dated to about 30,000 B.C. Neolithic societies linked all living things to the female, so the Great Mother became their god. Powerful images such as Earth Mother and Mother Nature come from these early beliefs. Although little is actually known about the mother-child relationship in the Stone Age or Neolithic ages, we can assume that mother and child shared an existence of food gatherers and laborers. From 3100 to 600 B.C., patriarchy became the dominant social form. With it came the descent of women's power and prestige, to the point that woman was not even acknowledged for the birth of children.

In Greek mythology, the birth mothers of the most prominent gods are male. Athena, the goddess of the battle, emerged full grown from her father Zeus's head; Aphrodite, the goddess of love and beauty, came from her father's genitals. One goddess who has a female mother is Artemis, in charge of the hunt and overseer of childbirth. But she was inadequately cared for and as a result remained childless herself. Except for Demeter, the goddess who challenged the gods on behalf of her daughter, the Greeks were an anti-female-mother society. "The mother of the child that is called here is not really its parent." wrote Aeschylus in the fifth century B.C. "She just nurses the seed that is planted with her by the child's true parent, the male. . . ." As the child's "true parent," fathers were free to decide which of their children would be raised by their mothers and which would be killed or abandoned. The children who remained, the majority of them male, were generally left in the care of wet nurses and then male slaves. Boys left their mothers' quarters as soon as they were able to join the company of men in school or the military.

In *The Myth of Motherhood*, Shari L. Thurer suggested that the notion of the "perfect mother" came into existence during the Middle Ages as Western society witnessed the appearance of Mary, the virgin mother of Jesus. This image is of a woman who has no needs of her own, is selflessly devoted to her son, and has no sexuality or life other than that of a mother. Despite the importance of this mother figure, the hard life during these times made it almost impossible to adequately nurture and care for children. Church doctrine described women as vessels of sin because of their sexuality, and it decreed that marital relations be undertaken only for the purpose of procreation and never for pleasure alone. Painful childbirth was viewed as a punishment for women's sins, leading to great misery and high death rates among medieval mothers who often had one pregnancy after another. By the end of the Middle Ages, church authorities had burned at the stake almost 200,000 "witches," many of them midwives—women who had the powerful job of overseeing childbirth. A church publication, *Witches Hammer*, blamed midwife-witches for male impotence, the birth of illegitimate children, the inability of a woman to conceive, and the death of newborns; and these women were sentenced to death. By the

Venus of Willendorf

Erich Lessing/Naturhistorisches
Museum, Vienna, Austria/
Art Resource

seventeenth century, as males took over the maternity business, childbirth continued to be a death-defying feat. The death rates for mothers rose as male pathologists alternated from corpses in morgues to birthing rooms, bringing with them the bacteria that led to puerperal (childbed) fever and horrible death. After forceps were invented to aid in difficult births, the instruments were kept secret for many years, until 1733, and their use was available only to those who could pay a high price for help in childbirth.

With the Protestant Reformation came the notion of the "good mother." It was important that the good mother rear children properly. Discipline was the key to salvation, and "sparing the rod" was believed to "spoil the child."

ANGEL OF THE HOUSE: THE VICTORIAN MOTHER

The earlier discussion of fatherhood detailed the effect of the Industrial Revolution on Western society, including that products previously made at home were now manufactured outside. As men had to become wage earners to purchase these items, the family as known was splitting apart. The woman's role in managing her household took on new importance. With the father away, parenting was left primarily to the mother; she became the emotional center of the home.

Women of the lower socioeconomic classes usually labored in domestic and other low-status occupations while trying to care for the children, many of whom were themselves full-time workers in coal mines, textile mills, canning factories, and the like before they were age fifteen. Middle-class women, attired in tight corsets and wide crinolines that restricted their movements, were expected to become socially accomplished. They played the piano, learned to speak French, read appropriate books, and supervised the household help. Even while trying to raise their own children, these women were viewed by their husbands as grown-up *kinder,* children, who had to be cared for and protected as much as the real children of the household.

MODERN MOTHERING

In the 1920s, Vassar College offered courses in motherhood. Magazines proclaimed that motherhood was a career and the only way for a women to gain true self-satisfaction. As the research of early child psychologists such as John Watson drifted into the public consciousness, child rearing became a scientific endeavor. Women, now cared for by male obstetricians rather than female midwives, began to give birth in hospitals where their newborn infants were taken away from them and placed in nurseries. Bottle-feeding came into vogue, baby food was manufactured, and feeding on demand turned into feeding on schedule. After Freudian theorists revealed children to be sexual creatures, children were expected to stay in their own beds all night.

During World War II, mothers entered the workforce. They returned home after the war (although millions worked part-time) and stayed there to raise their children during the fifties. Black women of the day were employed as domestics, working-class women were laboring in factories, and middle-class women stayed at home with their children and felt isolated from the world of adults. It is during this period that the middle-class mothers were attacked by writers and psychiatrists like Philip Wylie and Bruno Bettelheim. The stay-at-home mother was undervalued and overcriticized. She was essentially to blame for everything that went wrong with her children, physically and emotionally.

When pediatrician Benjamin Spock's *Common Sense Book of Baby and Child Care* was published in 1946, it sold millions of copies and helped turn the American family into child-oriented units. Spock advocated a more relaxed approach to parenting, encouraged autonomy for children, and recommended play and enjoyment as parts of a healthy parent-child interaction. As the primary socializer of her children, the "good mother" had to be caring, patient, understanding, empathetic, and accepting of her children—with little thought to her own needs. While American mothers tried to live up to the image of television mothers and the advice of Dr. Spock, they increasingly discovered that there might be more to life than raising children. By the 1970s, a changing economy sent mothers of all socioeconomic groups out of the house and away from their children.

Shari Thurer proposed that the notion of the "good mother" is a cultural invention, bounded by history and economics. Over the ages, mother has been worshipped, feared, rejected, and dishonored. Expectations of her are ever-changing and ambiguous.

> Motherhood—the way we perform mothering—is culturally derived. Each society has its own mythology, complete with rituals, beliefs, expectations, norms, and symbols. Our received models of motherhood are not necessar-

The Spirit of Parenting

Your children are not your children.
They are the sons and daughters of Life's longing for itself.
They come through you but not from you,
And though they are with you yet they belong not to you.
You may give them your love but not your thoughts,
For they have their own thoughts.
You may house their bodies but not their souls,
For their souls dwell in the house of tomorrow,
which you cannot visit, not even in your dreams.
You may strive to be like them, but seek not to make them like you.
For life goes not backward nor tarries with yesterday.
You are the bows from which your children as living arrows are set forth.

—Kahlil Gibran
From "On Children"

---

ily better or worse than many others. The way to mother is not writ in the stars, the primordial soup, the collective unconscious, nor in our genes. Our predecessors followed a pattern very different from our own, and our descendants may hew to one that is no less different. Our particular idea of what constitutes a good mother is only that, an idea, not an eternal verity. The good mother is reinvented as each age or society defines her anew, in its own terms, according to its own mythology (Thurer, 1994).

SUPERMOM OF THE TWENTY-FIRST CENTURY

Today the majority of households in America have no breadwinner father or homemaker mother. What has emerged is the working-homemaking mother who continues to be seen as the dominant force in the lives of children—for better or worse, with or without the father. When writer Arlie Hochschild talks about the "second shift," she is stating that mothers do double duty, even when fathers are at home (Hochschild, 1989). Research has shown that while fathers are more willing to perform child-rearing tasks such as dressing their children and driving them to birthday parties, it is mothers who shop for the clothes, buy the birthday gifts, and schedule the day (Lamb, 1987).

Diane Eyer (1996) proposed that the American culture of the nineties has turned against mothers, blaming them for raising drug addicts, rioters, and even potential terrorists. Her definitive account recounts the ways in which the medical and psychiatric community, politicians, and even parenting and women's magazines seek to make women—particularly those who work—feel guilty about their parenting skills. Eyer points out that, rather than failing their children, mothers today are carrying a disproportionate share of the responsibility for raising them. In effect, mothers are subsidizing American businesses by accepting unequal pay, inflexible hours, glass ceilings, and hostility toward absences for family obligations. This blaming of mothers, Eyer's believes, is not really about the welfare of children but rather is an attempt to restrict women's labor.

> Instead of facing the need for family-friendly business practices and public support of families by providing substantial tax cuts, paid parental leave, and regulated subsidized day care, a national blame game substitutes for a constructive family policy in this country . . . the truth is that mothers need to redirect all these fingers of blame at a society that is too cheap to care for its children, and business that is too sexist to recognize the importance of women's work. (Eyer, 1996).

Chapter Review

- Increasingly, the subject of parenting has become a discipline, an area of study open to scientific scrutiny, leading researchers to rely on natural observation as well as laboratory experiments to probe into every aspect of this process. The study of parenting encompasses over 40 years of scientific research by people working in fields including psychology, sociology, anthropology, and medicine.

- The experience of parenting must be understood in the context of the interrelated forces that influence it, including characteristics of the parent and the child and the world in which both live.

- Parenting is influenced by culture, gender, the structure of the family, personality differences, parental marriage, and available developmental models.

- Parents often learn about raising children by relying on information offered by family members and friends, this knowledge handed down from generation to generation within a culture. This knowledge is called tradition, and it refers to a way of thinking, feeling, and behaving toward children that is so powerful a force in family life that it functions much like heredity.

- Since the 1930s, the parenting-education movement in America has gained impetus as scientific research suggests that much of children's social, intellectual, and psychological development is rooted in their early childhood experiences. The primary goals of

parent-education programs are to prevent the development of problems between parents and their children when possible, and to deal with the problems that are the inevitable part of raising children.

- The experience of parenting is rooted in biology. It concerns the survival of the human species, in general, and the contribution of genes to generations that will come.

- Parenting is a learned experience, amenable to modification. It is through social experiences that parents incorporate the values, beliefs, and attitudes about children that they will carry into the parenting experience.

- There is a strong psychological component to parenting; children provoke emotions in their parents, including joy, love, anger, and other feelings.

- Parenting refers to the nurturance and socialization of children—the primary tasks of parenting: responsibilities that are shared to a lessor extent with other family members, teachers, peers, and members of the community.

- Parenting has been described as a balance between responsiveness and demandedness. Responsiveness refers to the acknowledgment, acceptance, and satisfaction of a child's needs, wants, and demands. Demandedness has to do with parental expectations regarding maturity, responsibility, and specific behaviors.

- In Western society, when referring to the parent-child relationship, we are apt to speak of love: the intense feeling of attachment that binds people to each other. Erich Fromm believes that parental love is a special kind of affectionate relationship built upon four distinct but interdependent elements common to all forms of love: care, responsibility, knowledge, and respect.

- The parent-child relationship is bidirectional, built upon the reciprocal influence of each on the other. It is parents' understanding and acceptance of their children's inborn energy levels and styles of response, combined with parents' adaption of the environment to mold with these temperamental characteristics that constitute what researchers call "goodness of fit."

- Ellen Galinsky offers a six-stage model of parenting, based on the challenges that parents must face at every stage of their child's development—from the prenatal period through adolescence. The model includes image-making, nurturing, authority, interpretive, interdependent, and departure stages.

- Over the years, there have been hundreds of texts, magazines articles, and guidebooks on the subject of parenting. Some are informative and useful, others are not informative but are also harmless, and many are nonsensical or even dangerous.

- Men and women become parents because of choice or chance. Since the 1920s and 1930s, when contraceptive devices became effective and available, the birth of children has become less a function of fate and more the result of thought and decision making. The majority of men and women view having children as an essential part of life, a source of love and personal satisfaction, and a chance to create a new person with someone you love.

- If parents are married, the birth of a first child introduces new challenges and new stresses into the marital relationship.

- There are distinct differences in the way women and men parent. But in societies throughout the world, it is mothers who have primary responsibility for raising children.

- Historically, children—especially males—have been considered economic assets. Since

Western society shifted toward manufacturing and service economies, this view is no longer realistic.

- As American society moves into the twenty-first century, the role of father is being redefined. Its definition is now as varied as the historical, social, and political context in which fathers exist. Currently, in Western society, the role of father as breadwinner has turned into that of father as a partner in caregiving.

- Motherhood is a cultural phenomenon. Each society has its own mythology of mothering, complete with rituals, beliefs, expectations, norms, and symbols.

Student Activities

1. You are the working parent of two children, ages 3 and 8. What would your ideal daily schedule be, assuming you had to put in eight hours at a workplace? How would you allocate the rest of the day's time?

2. Note the number of references to parenting in the daily newspapers, monthly magazines, and on television. Keep a notebook of the content of parenting references for one week. Do you see a pattern? What do they tell us about the parenting experience?

3. Write a letter to a present or future child. Tell him or her why you have chosen to be a parent and what expectations you have of this role.

Helping Hands

Planned Parenthood Federation of America
810 Seventh Avenue
New York, NY 10019
(212) 541-7800
http://www.plannedparenthood.org/

An organization that provides information, counseling, and medical services for people concerned with issues of reproduction, pregnancy, and sexuality.

Zero Population Growth
1400 16th St. NW, Suite 320
Washington, DC 20036
202-332-2200
http://www.zpg.org/

An organization whose goals include achieving a balance between the earth's population and environmental resources.

The Fatherhood Project
c/o James Levin
330 7th Avenue
New York, NY 10001
212-268-4846
http://www.fatherhoodproject.org/

An organization committed to working with fathers who are interested in becoming more involved in childrearing.

CHAPTER

The Context of Parenting

Chapter Highlights

After reading Chapter 2, students should be able to:

- Understand the influence of social and historical context on parenting
- Understand how both constancy and change interact in the lives of parents and their children
- Recognize the role of social class and gender in parenting

Chapter Contents

- The World of Parents and Their Children
  Urie Bronfenbrenner's Ecological Context
- The Context of Time
  Birth Cohorts ■ *Growing Up Without Childhood* ■ *Chronology: The Influence of Age*
- Social Class: Windows of Opportunity
  The Economics of Child Rearing Across Social Class ■ *Social Class and Parental Expectations*
- Parenting and Gender
  Child Rearing and Gender

INTRODUCTION

The July 1994 issue of *Money* magazine details the parenting experience of Mary and Rick Lathers, a Michigan couple who have eight girls and four boys, then ages 17 years to 11 months. According to the article, Mrs. Lathers is a homemaker and her husband works in the automobile industry. The family income is just above what the government defines as the poverty level for a family of fourteen people. Mrs. Lathers washes five loads of clothing a day in a cellar laundry and cooks for up to four hours. The house is scarcely furnished, and the cold Michigan air comes through the house's poorly insulated walls and leaky windows. Fourteen people share the one bathroom.

At first glance, it appears nearly impossible to adequately parent so many children on this family's limited resources. But parenting exists within a context, a historical and social setting that very much influence the direction parenting takes (Bronfenbrenner, 1979). At its broadest, the context of parenting takes into account cultural background, social class, nationality, neighborhood, religious orientation, and the social forces of a particular generation. More narrowly, the context of parenting includes the number of children in a family, their ages in relation to each other, the working status of parents, and the availability of each parent.

Mary Lathers is herself a child of a large family; she is the fifth of thirteen children. Both Mr. and Mrs. Lathers are devout Catholics, with an abiding belief that their children—all wanted and loved—are gifts from God. The family lives in a small rural village where housing costs are less expensive than in a city or suburb. Mr. Lathers' job provides him with health care for his entire family, as well as disability and life insurance for himself. Mrs. Lathers keeps the family food costs down by cutting coupons and cultivating a vegetable garden, and Mr. Lathers hunts deer in season, which he freezes for later use. Three of the children work outside the home to earn pocket money; all work inside the home doing unpaid chores.

While this is not the kind of parenting experience most people today desire—the average American family is 1.85 children and only one family in 3,000 (0.0003 percent) have more than five children—the example of the Lathers shows how much the context of family background, religious beliefs, economic conditions, and social circumstances impact decisions about parenting. In an unusual cultural setting, families in the ultra-religious, Orthodox Jewish community of Borough Park, a small New York neighborhood, the birthrate is double that of the city as a whole. Ten-children families are not uncommon, and some families have as many as nineteen children. These procreation rates rest on the religious belief that one must be fruitful and multiply, as well as on the desire to replenish the post-Holocaust Jewish population.

The Informed Parent 2.1

The Effect of World Economy and Politics on Parenting

In an industrialized society, it takes an average of 2.1 children per woman to maintain a specific nation's current population. Women in many developed countries are choosing, on average, to have less than this number. This change was first observed in Europe, with Italy leading the way in fertility decline, down to 1.2. Spain and Germany followed at 1.3 (Table 2.1). Ireland, a country whose fertility rate was 3.55 in 1975, has seen a drop, to 1.87 in 1995. In 1970, 19 countries had similar low birth rates. By 1995, the number had grown to 51, with Asian, Caribbean, and Eastern European countries in fertility decline. Demographers estimate that by the year 2015, 88 of the world's more than 180 countries and territories will see childbirth levels dip below 2.1 per woman.

This decline is the result a number of factors. In agrarian cultures, children are assets because they are able to work with parents on the land. As families move into urban areas, there is less need or incentive to have large families. In addition, women in some parts of the world are gaining power over their lives as a result of birth-control techniques, legal abortion, and economic independence; and these factors impact their family planning. Other reasons for the decline include higher educational levels, an eroding of the influence of religion on childbirth decisions, and concerns about global overpopulation and environmental resources.

TABLE 2.1 Fertility Rates, 1995

Fertility rates are dropping worldwide. The average number of children born per woman in all Western countries combined is now less than 2.

Country	Rate	Country	Rate
Italy	1.24 children	Japan	1.48
Spain	1.27	Cuba	1.60
Germany	1.30	Bahamas	1.95
Hong Kong	1.32	Ireland	2.01
Greece	1.38	United States	2.05

Source: New York Times

THE WORLD OF PARENTS AND THEIR CHILDREN

From the moment of their birth, children are influenced to think, feel, and behave in ways that enable them to fit into the society in which they live. The process by which this accommodation is accomplished is called *socialization*.

Although it is overwhelmingly parents who help children achieve their place in the world by instilling their own values, beliefs, and attitudes, there are others in society—including family members, teachers, clergy, and government workers—who play a part in determining how a child adjusts to his or her social group.

Developmental psychologist Urie Bronfenbrenner (1979) lamented that "we know more about children than about the environments in which they live." He defined two types of complementary conditions that must occur within a setting if development is to take place. A *primary development context* is one in which a child observes and engages in progressively more complex activities under the guidance of a person who is emotionally attached to the child and is knowledgeable about these activities. A *secondary developmental context* is one in which the child is provided with opportunities, resources, and encouragement that will enable him or her to engage in the activities learned in the primary context but now without the guidance of another person. For example, a child might watch and then help his mother cook dinner on a number of occasions. Eventually, if given a context that fosters this skill, the child will be able to cook the meal alone. Bronfenbrenner is particularly concerned with understanding the environmental supports and stressors that influence the child-rearing system. He notes that among the millions of American children who are the offspring of divorced parents, some function quite well and others exhibit problems. How a child adjusts depends upon contextual forces such as the relationship between the divorced parents, the influence of grandparents, family economics, and other factors having little to do with the actual divorce.

Urie Bronfrenbrenner emphasized the need to understand the environmental support systems and stressors that influence how people parent their children.

URIE BRONFENBRENNER'S ECOLOGICAL CONTEXT

Urie Bronfenbrenner defines human development as the phenomenon of constancy and change in a person's characteristics over a life course. He proposes that the person's characteristics at a given time in his or her life are a function of the characteristics of the person and of the environment, *jointly,* over the course of that person's life up to that time.

This definition assumes that the processes that operate in early years may or may not be the same as those in later years. It is the interaction between the changes that take place within the person and in the environment that lead to constancy and change in life. For example, a child of five might be living in a household where a grandmother takes care of him while both his parents work, and the child shares a room with his older brother. By the time the child is twelve, his grandmother might be deceased, his parents divorced, and his older sibling away at college. As he heads into adolescence, the child experiences quite a different world than the one he knew as he began elementary school. The immediate setting in which the child lives has changed, and so has the larger context in which the setting is embedded. Now that the parents are divorced, the legal system may have some impact on the lives of the child and the people close to him. His mother's friends might be different now that she is a single woman. Perhaps the mother begins to date, and a new man comes into the child's life.

Bronfenbrenner's *Ecological Systems Theory* details the importance of chronological time; that is, the experiences that occur successively over the course of a lifetime both *within the child* (first teeth, puberty, illness) and in the *external environment (*the birth of a sibling, the death of a parent, winning a lottery). One cannot understand the development of any human being without knowledge of the interaction between these forces. As Bronfenbrenner wrote:

> No characteristic of the person exists or exerts influence on development in isolation. Every human quality is inextricably embedded, and finds both its meaning and fullest expression, in particular environmental settings, of which the family is a prime example. As a result, there is always an interplay between the psychological characteristics of the person and of a specific environment; the one cannot be defined without reference to the other (Bronfenbrenner, 1989).

Bronfenbrenner proposes a four-tiered chronosystem (see Figure 2.1). The first, the *microsystem* refers to a pattern of activities, roles, and interpersonal relations experienced by a developing person in a face-to-face setting that has particular physical and material features and contains other persons with distinctive temperament, personality, and systems of belief. Home, school, peer group, and the community are settings of the microsystem. The home is where children are supposed to be adequately nurtured; the school is where they are expected to learn reading, writing, math, and other skills that will make them productive members of society. Peers provide companionship and help children gain a sense of independence; the community or neighborhood offers

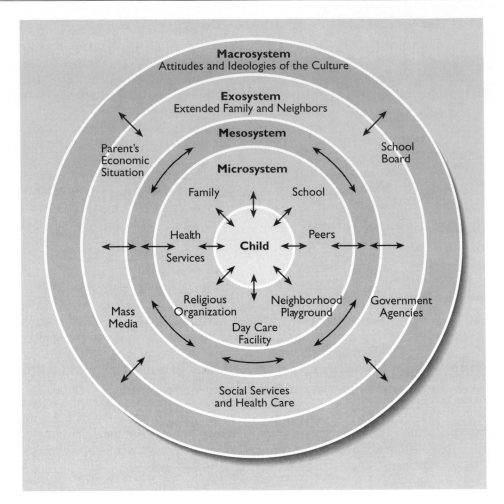

Figure 2.1
Urie Bronfenbrenner's ecological systems theory shows how complex and interrelated the socializing agents of society are and how they play out in the overall macrosystem.
Source: R. Vasta (Ed.), *Annals of Child Development* (Vol. 6). Greenwich, CT: JAI Press.

libraries, stores, food markets, and a variety of experiences unavailable to children at home.

Experiences within the microsystem vary greatly for parents and their children. In families where fathers are emotionally supportive of mothers, mothers tend to have more positive interactions with their children (Cox, et al., 1992). Parents have far more difficulty raising children in neighborhoods where drug dealers stand on corners than they do in areas where libraries are prominent. The daily experiences of urban children who can walk to friends' houses are very different from those of suburban children who need to be driven everywhere.

Child rearing is greatly affected by physical surroundings. It is far more difficult to parent in depressed or dangerous neighborhoods than in areas where children can walk down the streets safely.

The *mesosystem* refers to linkages and processes taking place between two or more settings in which the developing person is a part: a system of microsystems. The relationships between home and school, between school and the workplace, are example of mesosystems. The child who is sent off alone on the first day at school has but a single link between school and home. The more linkage between parents and the school in terms of values, experiences, and behavioral styles, the greater the chances are that a child will achieve academic success. A number of studies have shown that, when the parents and school have the same interactive style and cooperate in meeting goals, childrens' academic performance is enhanced (Epstein, 1983; Ginsburg and Bronstein, 1993). When parents invite other children over to play or encourage their youngsters to join clubs or teams, they are reinforcing mesosystem links.

The *exosystem* encompasses the linkage and processes taking place between two or more settings, at least one of which does not ordinarily contain the developing person, but in which events occur that influence processes within the immediate setting that does contain that person. For example, a child is influenced by the interaction between the home and a parent's workplace, even though the child is not part of the workplace setting. If a parent frequently works overtime, children's home lives change. They may be home alone more often and eat more take-out food, or a grandmother or babysitter might become the primary adult in the house. Similarly, a parent's friendships are part of the exosystem, in that they affect a parent's relationship with his or her children.

Parental employment or unemployment is a key determiner of child-rearing practices. Employment has been called "the long arm of the job." A parent's mood, sense of accomplishment, availability to one's children, available resources, and community status depend on what the parent does for a living (Crouter and McHale, 1993). In a study of the differences between mothers and fathers with regard to parenting and stress, it was found that mothers are as committed to their work as fathers but they feel more anxiety than do fathers over the need to balance work and parenting (Greenbergers, et al., 1989).

Paternal unemployment has negative effects on parenting behaviors. Vonnie McLoyd (1989, 1990) has shown that unemployed fathers spend more time with their children than employed fathers, however, they tend to be more negative and punitive in their dealings with the children. Unemployment affects a father's self-esteem and stresses the marital relationship, and both forces affect a father's relationship with his children (see Figure 2.2).

The *macrosystem* refers to the characteristics of a given culture, subculture, or other broader social context, with particular reference to the belief system, resources, hazards, lifestyles, opportunity structures, life course options, and patterns of social interchange that are embedded in each of the systems of the chronosystem. In other words, the macrosystem is a social blueprint consisting of belief and behavioral patterns passed down through generations and promoted by the family, school, church, government, workplace, and other cultural institutions. Social class, ethnicity, occupation, regionality, and historical cohort events are all a part of the macrosystem. A male who grew up in the

Figure 2.2
How Paternal
Economic Loss
Impacts Parenting

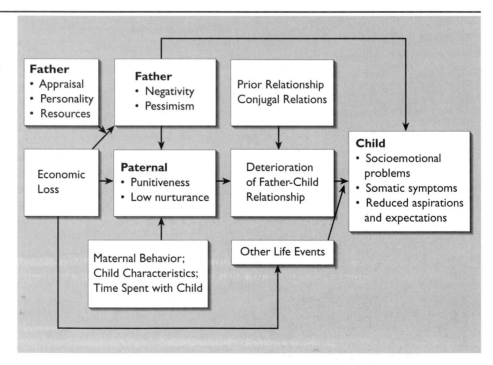

rural South—as the third child in an intact military family during the Vietnam War—experienced a much different macrosystem than a female living in Greenwich Village, New York—the only offspring of a divorced mother who worked as an attorney during the seventies and marched for women's rights.

In the United States, where there is an overall American culture as well as many different macrosystems, people perceive the world differently and therefore make judgments and behave differently. With regard to parenting, there is acceptance of spanking as a form of discipline despite innumerable studies attesting to the harm done to children. Within individual macrosystems, however, such as the Japanese, this child-rearing technique is not promoted.

THE CONTEXT OF TIME

In the United States during the 1950s children were taught to fear the Russians and their communist political philosophy. Many school classes experienced the surprise drills that sent them scurrying to the basement where blankets, pillows, and food supplies were at hand in preparation for air attacks that never came. The children of the 1990s have different fears. AIDS, guns, divorce in the family, and other social problems are just a few of the concerns that engage their attention.

Parents do not raise children in a social, political, or environmental vacuum. But issues confronting parents change from generation to generation, sometimes even year to year. This means that if a parent has more than one child, each exists in a context different from that of his or her siblings.

BIRTH COHORTS

People are born into time frames that include major historical happenings, events that influence their world view and shape the course of their lives. People born within a few years of each other are called *age cohorts* or *birth cohorts*. Obviously, parents and their children are not age cohorts; they grew up in different social, economic, and historic times. Parents who experienced the economic depression of the 1930s have different views on money and savings than do their children who were born into a time of prosperity. Parents raised in the conservative 1950s might be taken aback by the sexual openness of the 1970s. In a 1939 speech explaining the conflict between the generations born in 1890 and in 1900, social scientist Sigmund Neumann identified the time in life that most impacts birth cohorts. "Generations could be divided according to essential impressions around seventeen," said Dr. Neumann. "Modern psychology has proved that . . . impressions received in those years are deep and persistent. . . . This holds especially true of a generation of adolescents which went through experiences of weight. This gives them a unity, a common style, a new approach to life" (quoted in Gottlieb, 1987). For any generation, the most profound point in life is when children are beginning to go out into the world but are not yet settled in it (see Figure 2.3).

Figure 2.3
The Influence
of Time on
Development

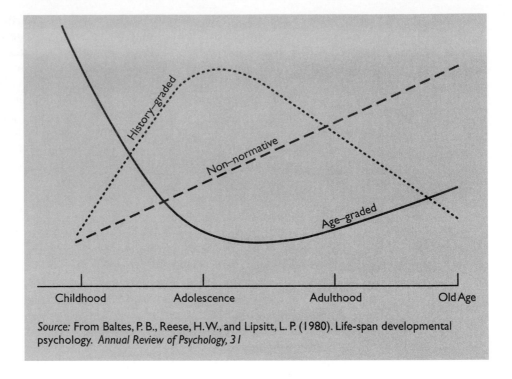

Source: From Baltes, P. B., Reese, H. W., and Lipsitt, L. P. (1980). Life-span developmental psychology. *Annual Review of Psychology, 31*

History-graded influences affect adolescents and young adults more than other age groups because these people are most involved in the nation's social life. If there is a war, or national prosperity, this age group is most affected. Age cohorts share an economic history as well as a political, social, and military one. The attitudes and world views—in fact the very style of a cohort group—reflect this shared history.

The impact of historical forces on parenting practice can be illustrated through the experience of the Vietnamese in America. For many centuries, Vietnamese child-rearing practices have been derived from Confucian principles built upon ancestor worship. Children are expected to obey their elders and promote the welfare of their kin group above personal wants or needs. Obedience and submission to the family collective are the primary social goals of child rearing (Slote, 1972). In other words, qualities of dependence rather than autonomy and individuality are most valued in Vietnamese children.

The Vietnamese migration to the United States after the Vietnam War has lead to some erosion in the parents' ability to control their children's attitudes and behaviors. A significant number of Vietnamese refugees to America have come without their parents or other, older family members who might enforce authority upon them. This has been reflected by the growth of Vietnamese American youth gangs (Vigil and Yun, 1990). Even when parents have accompanied their children, the children often forge ahead of parents in American society because they learn English faster and have more opportunities for education and job training. In addition, through television, the educational system and music, American Vietnamese youngsters are quickly exposed to the influence of American culture, a culture that values individualism. Nazli Kibria, in an exhaustive look at the Vietnamese American "family tightrope," notes that despite the problems that have come with immigration, Vietnamese youngsters continue to display strong attachment to traditional collectivist and hierarchical family values (Kibria, 1993).

In a fascinating study of the impact of historical events on the parent-child relationship, sociologist Glen Elder and his associates (Elder, 1974; Elder, 1979; Elder, Nguyen, and Casper, 1985; Elder and Hareven, 1993) studied the experiences of 167 California children born between 1920 to 1929, during the Depression. In families hardest hit by the poor economy, fathers lost their jobs along with their status at home and in the community, a loss that often led to emotional distress. Mothers gained more influence at home, particularly if they were working. Children were required to do more; girls generally had domestic chores and boys often got outside jobs. In a longitudinal analysis of the effect of this childhood experience on adult life, Elder found that effects of the Depression depended upon how old the child was when the family went through such loss and change. If these events occurred when children were preadolescents, their school work suffered, and they became less stable; in adulthood they had fewer successful work experiences and reported more emotional problems than did children whose families did not suffer through the Depression. These effects may result from parents being less attentive to their children's needs during hard economic times (Conger, et al., 1994). Children who were teenagers when their families were hit by the Depression fared better then their preteen counterparts. They did better in school and were more likely to attend college. In later life, they had happier marriages, better careers, and were even happier than children whose families were not affected by hard times. Interestingly the researchers found that adults whose families were especially deprived during the Depression fared better than those whose families were not seriously hurt by the poor economy. Elder noted that adolescents caught within their family's problems were thrust into the responsibilities of adulthood earlier then they might have been if the economy had not turned bad. He proposes that, in the long run, children who contribute to their family's well-being gain from such experiences. He laments that since World War II children remain dependent much longer on their parents, leading society to support "a large quota of nonproductive members." He suggests that a childhood that shelters the young from the hardships of life fails to develop or test adaptive capacities that are required in life crises.

Nothing illustrates the influence of historical events on the raising of children as strikingly as the effect of the AIDS epidemic on the children of Africa today. In rural areas of East Africa four of every ten children age fifteen have lost one parent (United Nations Aids Report, 1998). In 1997, the disease orphaned 1.7 million children, most of them living in Africa south of the Sahara. In Zambia alone, there are one-half million orphans, and this figure expected to double as we go into the twenty-first century. The result is that many thousands of children are living on the streets of African cities, stunted in growth because of insufficient food and victims of physical and sexual abuse.

Figure 2. 4

The Orphans of Africa

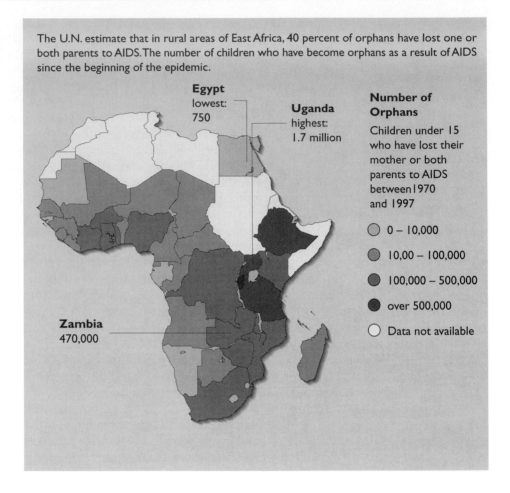

The U.N. estimate that in rural areas of East Africa, 40 percent of orphans have lost one or both parents to AIDS. The number of children who have become orphans as a result of AIDS since the beginning of the epidemic.

Egypt
lowest:
750

Uganda
highest:
1.7 million

Zambia
470,000

Number of Orphans

Children under 15 who have lost their mother or both parents to AIDS between 1970 and 1997

○ 0 – 10,000

● 10,00 – 100,000

● 100,000 – 500,000

● over 500,000

○ Data not available

GROWING UP WITHOUT CHILDHOOD

In *Children Without Childhood* (1983), Marie Winn proposed that in America today children are not being sheltered from crisis but rather they are being treated like miniature adults—the way they had been perceived in earlier eras. The rise of the two-career family, increased divorce rates, high levels of violence on the street, and television programming that brings crime, drugs, AIDS, and vivid sex into homes—all of these have made today's children more sophisticated than their cohorts of previous generations and more distrusting and less respectful of adults. In remembering what she calls the "golden age" of childhood: the fifties and sixties, when children played games on the street, read storybooks, and walked their neighborhoods freely. Winn insists that children need "the lengthy experience of being a child, of being dependent, of being totally protected and nurtured by loving parents" so they will gain the ability to be successful, protective, and nurturing parents themselves.

The roaring twenties and the "hippie" movement are reflections of the times. The birth cohorts of the nineties living in the United States have been influenced by the environmental movement, the AIDS epidemic, and the nation's banking scandals. One of the greatest challenges parents have is to understand the historical and social influences affecting their children.

Psychologist David Elkind (1988) worries about what he calls the "hurried child." He notes that in a well-defined, stable society parents are free from the stress of adapting to constant social change. This leaves them the time and energy to focus their adaptive powers on their growing and ever-changing children. Much change has come to Western society over the past thirty years—acute economic inflation that has necessitated the two-income family, computerization of every aspect of life, employment anxiety as jobs leave the country or change, concerns about the environment, gender-wage differences, absent fathers, and a myriad of other instabilities. Stressed parents have become self-absorbed, so much so that they are unable to consider the needs and interests of their children. Children have become burdened with age-inappropriate expectations and tasks. Competition for grades, trophies, and possessions are sapping their energy and optimism, to the point that suicide among teens is at an all-time high. For example, in some families, ten-year-olds are expected to handle the household cooking and cleaning, as well as the care of younger offspring. At the other extreme, toddlers are seen on ski slopes in Aspen, wearing expensive outfits that imitate those of their parents. Elkind believes that parents who pressure their children unreasonably, whether in sports or school pursuits, are dissatisfied with their own jobs and perhaps their own lives.

If child-rearing necessarily entails stress, then by hurrying children to grow up, or by treating them as adults, we hope to remove a portion of our burden of worry and anxiety and to enlist our children's aid in carrying life's load. We do not mean our children harm in acting thus—on the contrary, as a society we have come to imagine that it is good for young people to mature rapidly. Yet we do our children harm when we hurry them through childhood. (Elkind, 1988).

This does not mean that having children help with chores or participate in adult activities always results in a hurried child. The key is in not overburdening the child. It is one thing to have a child help with the family laundry; it is quite another to put the entire burden on the child. Assigning chores to children is often necessary in today's family life, but these same children must not be denied opportunities to play, dance, laugh, sing, have friendships, and do the other things that characterize childhood. David Elkind insists, "It is children's right to be children, to enjoy the pleasures, and to suffer the pains of a childhood that is infringed by hurrying. In the end, a childhood is the most basic human right of children."

CHRONOLOGY: THE INFLUENCE OF AGE

When children enter puberty, their bodies begin to change. This is a fact of life for normal young people ages eleven to fifteen. Adolescence is the period when many young American children strive for independence from parents, while seeking limits that make them feel safe and close to home. At about the time children are venturing from the family nest, parents are in their thirties, forties, and even fifties; and they are experiencing their own changes. A parent aged thirty might be moving up the career ladder when his daughter needs him to drive her to social functions; a father aged forty can be starting to feel the physical effects of middle age just as his son is starring at Little League baseball; and a fifty-year-old mother might be caring for an ailing parent and experiencing menopause while trying to keep tabs on her adolescent daughter. The normal changes in life are called "age-graded" influences; they are a function of chronological time. At specific points along the life span, normal physical, cognitive, psychological, and social changes occur in the lives of parents and their children. A son gets his first tooth; a daughter walks and then runs. Twins call out their first words within a month of each other. Sometimes the changes that parents and their children are making are compatible; other times they are not. Concerns about age-graded influences on the parent-child relationship have increased since medical advances have made it possible for older women—even post-menopausal woman—to give birth.

For parents, adjusting to the changes in their children is one of life's greatest challenges, because parents must change also if they are to meet their children's needs. Psychiatrist M. Scott Peck (1978) believes that parents gain more from their children's changes than the children do. He suggests that parents who cannot adjust will be left behind by their children and the world. "Learn-

Turn of the century immigrant families were far larger than the typical American family today. The average number of children born into American families today is less than 2, a far cry from the record held by Leontina Albina, a Chilean woman who—prior to May 1988—had given birth to 59 children, including 5 sets of triplets (*Guiness Book of World Records*). Clearly times change and, with them, attitudes about parenting.

ing from their children," he says, "is the best opportunity most people have to assure themselves a meaningful old age."

SOCIAL CLASS: WINDOWS OF OPPORTUNITY

In just about every world culture, there are differences in the degree of prestige, influence, and power that specific individuals and families have. This is called "social class." In Western society, a person's level of education, the schools attended, the job held, the money available, family name, and neighborhood lived in are all criteria that determine a person's position in society. In India, with its rigid caste (class) system, it is difficult for people to move from one level of influence to another. In the United States, there is a four-tiered system (upper class, middle class, working class, and underclass); mobility between the classes, both upward and down, occurs although generally the children's friends and adult guests in the home come from the same socioeconomic class.

THE ECONOMICS OF CHILD REARING ACROSS SOCIAL CLASS

In estimating the cost of raising one child from birth through college, a 1998 *U.S. News & World Report* calculated the differences due to social class. Food costs for a middle-class child born in 1997 will be $54,795 by the time he or she reaches age 18. In higher income families, this cost will climb to $67,805; and in lower income families the cost will be about $45,797. These figures do not hold if a second child is born, as costs decrease when housing and transportation are shared. (See Table 2.2.)

The Spirit of Parenting

In retrospect, it was only a matter of time before the Family Dinner Hour passed into history and fast foods took over. I knew its days were numbered the day our youngest propped my mouth open with a fork and yelled into it, "I want a cheeseburger and two fries and get it right this time". . . .

So, day by day I watched the family go outside of the home for meals where there were no tables to set and no clean hands required, and where green was not considered a happy color. The warm smells of Mother's kitchen gave way to the back seat of a station wagon littered with supermarket flyers, dry cleaning, schoolbooks, ropes, chains, jumper cables, and dog hairs.

The old rules for eating at home—sit up straight, chew your food, and don't laugh with cottage cheese in your mouth—didn't fit the new ambiance. A new set of rules emerged.

When ordering from the back seat of the car, do not cup your mouth over Daddy's ear and shout into it. Wait quietly until you are asked what you want. Follow this with "Thank you."

Never order more than you can balance between your knees. Remember, ice that spills between your legs dampens not only the spirit. . . .

If by chance you receive a sandwich that is not yours, do not spit on it and throw it on the floor. Simply pass it back to the driver of the car and tell him a mistake has been made. . . .

Conversation while dining in a car should be restricted to school happenings, future social events, and a polite exchange about non-controversial issues. It is quite improper to carry on a discourse as to what the secret sauce reminds you of . . . .

Remember, you are basically dining in public. This means no French fries hung from the nose . . . very few diners will find this amusing . . . each person should be responsible for his/her trash and should contain it in a bag. Two-week-old onion rings in the ashtray are not a pretty sight.

—Erma Bombeck
Family—The Ties That Bind—and Gag

An important feature of the *U.S. News* statistics is foregone income, the income a working mother gives up to raise a child. An unwed teenage mother who rears her child alone has a slightly higher average income at age 19 than a childless woman, probably due to welfare payments. However, by age 29 women who were not teenage mothers have earned about $72,191 more.

In a middle or upper class, dual-income family, the decision to stay home and raise a child may cost half the family's income. It is not surprising, then, that middle-age women with graduate degrees are three times more likely to be childless than women who drop out of high school. Similarly, dual-income married couples earning more than $75,000 a year are 70 percent more likely to be childless than people earning $10,000 to $20,000 a year.

TABLE 2.2 The Cost of Raising Children

Monthly Estimates, US Dept. of Agriculture (USDA). Monthly Costs for a Two-Parent Family. Estimated monthly expenditures* per child by husband-wife families, overall United States, 1995

Age of child	Total	Housing	Food	Transportation	Clothing	Health Care	Child Care and Education	Miscellaneous**
Gross Income: Less than $33,700 (Average = $21,000)								
0-2	$458	$175	$65	$58	$31	$31	$53	$45
3-5	468	173	73	57	30	30	59	46
6-8	478	168	93	66	34	34	35	48
9-11	481	151	112	72	38	38	21	51
12-14	547	168	118	81	63	38	15	64
15-17	538	136	127	108	56	40	25	47
Gross Income: $33,700–$56,700 (Average = $44,800)								
0-2	$634	$237	$78	$88	$37	$41	$86	$69
3-5	651	235	90	85	36	39	95	71
6-8	656	229	114	94	39	45	61	73
9-11	655	213	135	100	43	48	40	76
12-14	715	230	136	109	73	49	29	88
15-17	726	198	151	138	66	52	50	72
Gross Income: More than $56,700 (Average = $84,800)								
0-2	$943	$377	$103	$123	$48	$47	$129	$117
3-5	962	374	117	120	48	45	141	118
6-8	958	368	141	129	52	52	97	120
9-11	953	353	163	135	56	56	68	123
12-14	1023	370	172	144	93	56	52	136
15-17	1046	338	181	175	84	59	91	118
Gross Income: Less than $33,700 (Average = $14,100)								
0-2	$388	$158	$72	$55	$28	$15	$33	$28
3-5	435	178	76	48	30	23	44	36
6-8	492	190	96	56	35	26	41	48
9-11	459	183	111	40	35	33	19	38
12-14	495	183	111	46	60	35	24	37
15-17	553	193	121	73	70	35	18	43
Gross Income: $33,700 or more (Average = $51,100)								
0-2	$883	$338	$111	$167	$40	$34	$80	$113
3-5	947	360	118	160	42	46	101	121
6-8	1,009	371	141	168	48	53	94	133
9-11	976	363	170	153	48	63	55	123
12-14	1,037	364	167	158	80	68	78	122
15-17	1,073	375	176	172	92	67	63	128

*Monthly amounts calculated by dividing the yearly amounts by 12 and rounding to the nearest dollar.
**Miscellaneous expenses include personal care items, entertainment, and reading materials.
NOTE: Totals may not add due to rounding.
Source: Lino, Mark (1996). *Expenditures on Children by Families, 1995 Annual Report,* 1528–1995, USDA, p. 21.

SOCIAL CLASS AND PARENTAL EXPECTATIONS

Social class affects not only family economics but also parental expectations and attitudes, as well as opportunities available to children. Middle-class mothers tend to talk to their children, ask them questions, and praise them more than do lower income mothers. The structure and syntax of their language is more complex, leading to differences in language ability. A middle-class mother might tell her boisterous children, "Please quiet down, guys. I'm trying to talk on the phone." A working-class mother is more likely to say a simpler, "Keep quiet!" Parents from lower socioeconomic backgrounds rely more on criticism and physical punishment as techniques of control than do middle- or upper-class parents (Hoffman, 1984). Working-class and lower-income parents tend to stress obedience, whereas middle-class mothers tend to value self-control. Children of the lower socioeconomic classes are more likely to be expected to stay quiet in the company of adults; they are taught to accept the standards of these adults. Children of the middle class generally interact more with adults; they are freer to express themselves verbally. Middle-class children are more likely to be encouraged to think about and set their own goals than are the children of the lower socioeconomic classes.

Achievement expectations differ along social class lines. In upper-class families where wealth is often inherited, conformity is valued as children are responsible for carrying on the family's name, heritage, and status. Children are generally sent to private schools and prestigious colleges; they are then helped in setting up careers or businesses (Levine and Havighurst, 1992; Dodge, Pettit, and Bates, 1994). Middle-class families encourage achievement through education and hard work. They value getting along well with others as a means to social and occupational success. Lower-class families focus more on behavior than internal motivation. They expect their children to obey their elders and be helpful to them. Children from these families are more likely to do household chores, care for younger children, and run errands. Whereas middle-class parents teach their children to delay gratification in the interest of meeting long-term goals, lower socioeconomic class parents find it difficult to orient their children to the future because they themselves do not envision much change in the future.

It is easier for upper- and middle-class parents to provide their children with music lessons, dance instruction, math tutoring, camp, computers, books and other experiences that will provide advantages in their future. Teenage children from the working class participate in fewer school activities than do children from the middle class, because lower-class children often must go to after-school jobs to earn money for family and personal necessities (Lindgren and Suter, 1985). After studying the effect of economic hardship on child rearing, Vonnie McLoyd (1990) found that psychological distress often makes it difficult for lower socioeconomic class parents to nurture and consistently care for their children. For this reason, in the African American culture, where it is estimated that 40 percent of children live below the poverty line, 10 percent of children live with a grandparent (Beck and Beck, 1989). This extended family relationship brings with it important financial and emotional support. Compared to two-parent families, parents who raise children alone are more likely to have limited financial resources, as well as less time and energy for parenting; because of this, they are more apt to encourage independence and autonomy at an earlier age (Spencer and Dornbusch, 1990).

Roberta M. Berns (1997) pointed out that social class impacts the parent-child relationship in a myriad of ways.

> Social class membership begins exerting its influence before birth and continues until death. Health care and diet of the mother affect the birth of the child. The incidence of birth defects is higher in the lower classes than in the middle and upper classes. Economic pressure and lack of opportunities affect the mental health of the lower-class family, as well as determining socialization practices. For example, lack of money prevents using an allowance as a reward. Lower-class children cannot be sent to their rooms as a punishment, since there may be no room they can call their own to which they can be sent. Nor can lower-class children have privileges removed, such as going to the movies, for noncompliance since they do not have those opportunities anyway. Thus, lower-class families frequently use physical punishment as a socializing technique, whereas middle- and upper-class families have more options available.

This does not mean that working- or lower-class parents do not try to give their children advantages or encourage them in their efforts, but rather, that there are fewer resources available to parents and therefore less is available to their children.

PARENTING AND GENDER

"It's a girl!" or "It's a boy!" are two of the most powerful phrases a parent can hear. In every culture, these words carry a set of expectations about the way a female or male child should be raised. Parental interaction at almost every level differs according to gender. Communication patterns, play, and social goals are directed differently to female and male children. In Western society, the difference in treatment begins the moment of birth, when parents decide on the color of the child's room, the furnishings, and the toys the child will play with. Girls' rooms are typically pink or yellow; boys' rooms are painted blue. Girls get dolls and doll furniture; boys get sports equipment, cars, and trucks (Pomerleau, et al., 1990).

CHILD REARING AND GENDER

Parents behave differently, depending upon these gender differences. Male infants are played with more vigorously than are females; they are tossed in the air and tickled more frequently. As boys grow, they are given more opportunities to explore their environments (Fagot and Leinback, 1987; Block, 1983; Burn, Mitchell, and Obradovich, 1989). Female infants are nurtured more than males; they are responded to faster when they cry (Condry, Condry, and Pogatshynik, 1978; Huston, 1983). A number of studies have shown that after the age of three months, mothers look at their daughters more than their sons, touch them more often, and hold them closer (Belsky, 1980; Goldberg and Lewis, 1969). Mothers smile at their daughters more and display more emotional expression in their presence (Clark-Stewart, 1973). They hold and comfort their fussy female babies more than they do their fussy male babies. These different behaviors do not hold true in countries such as Greece, where a strong preference for boys leads mothers to talk more to their sons (Berko-Gleason, 1989).

Differences in treatment occur throughout childhood. One research project showed that as young as age three, daughters received a negative response when they asserted themselves (Kerig, Cowan, and Cowan, 1993). Boys were given more positive reinforcement and girls more criticism when they work on solving problems (Alessandri and Lewis, 1993).

Because parents have gender preferences, their desire for a girl or a boy determines their attitude and their parenting style of the child born. Overwhelmingly, the parents of the world want sons, reflecting a desire rooted in religious tradition and economic conditions. In past generations, before technology made everyday tasks easier, sons could participate more fully than daughters in activities that relied on physical strength. Sons could hunt, plow fields, and carry bundles; they were a source of cheap labor for the family and ensured that parents would be cared for in old age. Sons carry on the family name and provide the family with a sense of continuity over the generations. This preference for sons is revealed in the national divorce rates. An analysis of the 1980 census report indicates that couples who had an only son were less likely to split up than couples who had an only daughter, and that couples who had two sons were less likely to divorce than couples with two daughters. In China and in India, selective abortion occurs on the basis of sex because couples desire only male children. In China, where laws imposed in the late 1970s legislated only one child per family, the desire for a son is so strong that millions of girl children have died from poor nutrition, inadequate medical care, abandonment, and murder. These events have led to a serious discrepancy in population gender in the 1990s, as more than eight million single men in their thirties are unable to find Chinese wives. It is estimated that, in underdeveloped countries, girl babies die at twice the rate of boys (Kishwar, 1987).

Cultural anthropologists have noted that a number of South Pacific cultures and some Native American tribes have preferred girls because property was passed through the maternal line and women were the primary source of labor and economic productivity. In some cultures, a daughter's potential involves a bride-price, a sum of money or goods paid by a husband to the woman's parents as compensation for the loss of her future labor (Williamson, 1976).

The influence of gender preference was studied for over twenty years in a longitudinal study in Sweden. Parents visiting a clinic for prenatal care during the late 1950s were asked if they desired a boy or girl. Twenty years later, the parents whose preference had been met reported higher satisfaction with their child's gender than those who did not get the gender they desired. During the growing-up years, parents reported more conflicts and problems with the children of the nonpreferred gender, especially with girls when the parents had

From the moment of their births, parents treat children differently because of their gender. The decor of a child's bedroom, the gifts received, the activities encouraged—all make clear to children what their parents expect of them.

wanted a boy. When the children of the study became adults, they were interviewed about their relationships with their parents. Women whose parents had wanted a boy reported less positive relationships with their fathers, while men whose parents had wanted a girl reported satisfactory relationships with their parents (Klackenberg-Larsson, 1991).

Chapter Review

- Parenting exists within a context, a historical and social setting that greatly influences the direction parenting takes. At its broadest, the context of parenting takes into account cultural background, social class, nationality, neighborhood, religious orientation, and the social forces of a generation. The context of parenting also includes the number of children in a family, the ages of the children in relation to each other, the working status of parents, and the availability of each parent.

- Socialization is the process that enables people to think, feel, and behave in ways that enable them to fit into the society in which they live. Parents help children achieve a place in the world by instilling values, beliefs, and attitudes.

- Urie Bronfenbrenner defines two types of complementary conditions that must occur within a setting if development is to take place. A primary development context is one in which a child observes and engages in progressively more complex activities under the guidance of a person who is emotionally attached to the child and is knowledgeable about these activities. A secondary developmental context is one that provides a child with opportunities, resources, and encouragement that enable him or her to engage in the activities learned previously, but now without the guidance of another person.

- Bronfenbrenner's ecological systems theory details the importance of chronological time, the experiences that occur successively over the course of a lifetime, both within the child and in the external environment. Bronfenbrenner proposes a four-tier chronosystem.

- Home, school, peer group, and the community are settings of the microsystem. It is in the home that children are supposed to be adequately nurtured and at school where they are expected to learn reading, writing, and other skills that will make them productive members of society.

- The mesosystem refers to linkages and processes taking place between two or more settings in which the developing person is a part; basically it is a system of microsystems.

- The exosystem encompasses the linkage and processes taking place between two or more settings, at least one of which does not ordinarily contain the developing person, but in which events occur that influence processes within the immediate setting that does contain that person.

- The macrosystem is a social blueprint consisting of beliefs and behavioral patterns passed down through generations and promoted by the family, school, church, government, workplace, and other cultural institutions.

- People are born into time frames that incorporate major historical happenings, events that influence their world view, and shape the course of their lives. At specific points along the life span, normal physical, cognitive, psychological, and social changes occur in the lives of parents and their children. The normal changes in life are called age-graded influences.

- Parents gather information, form opinions, make judgments, and generally build up a set of beliefs or assumptions about the parent-child relationship. The variations displayed by human parents is the function of culture—the beliefs, values, ideals, and standards shared by a group of people. Social class refers to differences in the degree of prestige, influence, and power that specific individuals and families have. It determines the opportunities a family can offer its children.

- Children are parented differently depending on race and gender. Black parents have the special challenge of raising children in a society that does not value black children as much as white children. Parents act differently and have different expectations of their daughters in comparison to their sons.

Student Activities

- Investigate child rearing in a social class different from your own. What kind of activities do parents share with their children? Explore a typical day in the life of the family.

- What kind of government policies would you propose to help parents in their efforts to raise children in our society?

- Watch two television programs or movies that present different values. Describe the differences you see in child rearing.

Helping Hands

The Friendship Force
Suite 575 South Tower
One CNN Center
Atlanta, GA 30303
(404) 522-9490
http://www.friendship-force.org/

An organization designed to bring people of many countries and cultures together through international exchanges.

C H A P T E R

3

Parenting Across Cultures

Chapter Highlights

After reading Chapter 3, students should be able to:

- Recognize the role of culture and ethnicity in parenting
- Understand the effects of individualistic and collective cultures on child rearing
- Understand the role of acculturation on the parent-child relationship
- Recognize the special problems of race in the parenting process

Chapter Content

- The Assumptions of Life: Culture and Ethnicity
  Culture: The Beliefs of a People ■ *Individualism and Collectivism*
- Multi-ethnicity and Parenting
- Acculturation Affects Parents and Children
  Anglo-American Parenting ■ *Latino Parenting* ■ *Asian Parenting* ■
  Parenting and Race: A Special Challenge ■ *Native American Parenting* ■
  The Rituals of Family Life

INTRODUCTION

In 1996, African American musician James McBride published *The Color of Water,* a book in which he paid tribute to his mysterious mother, Ruth McBride Jordan. This was a woman who had lived in abject poverty during the 1940s in Brooklyn's Red Hook Housing Projects, a primarily black community, where she raised twelve children and saw every one of them go on to college.

Ruth's first husband, Andrew McBride, was a Baptist minister; after his death, she married Hunter Jordan, another deeply religious Baptist. Together the parents instilled in their children the idea that "education tempered with religion was the way to climb out of poverty in America."

Growing up, James McBride knew almost nothing about his mother; he was not sure whether she was black or white. Although James's father and step-father were African Americans, those around him—including his teachers—seemed to think Ruth was white. When he asked her why she didn't look like other mothers in the neighborhood, Ruth answered, "You ask too many questions. Educate your mind. School is important." When he persisted with his questions, Ruth answered, "It doesn't matter what color you are, as long as you're educated." His curiosity unabated, James often wondered who his mother was and where she had come from. More important, he often wondered who he himself was. "Am I black or white?" he asked his mother. Ignoring matters involving race or identity, Ruth answered. "Educate yourself or you'll be a nobody."

It was as a young man that James McBride began to unravel the mystery of Ruth. He discovered that his mother, previously called Rachel, had been born in Poland and raised in the small Virginia town of Suffolk in an extremely religious Orthodox Jewish family. Her father had been a mean and abusive man; her mother a gentle but silent woman crippled by polio. As a young girl Ruth fled her brutal childhood and settled in New York City, where she changed her name, married someone of a different race and religion, and seemingly began an entirely new life.

What Ruth did not realize is that a person cannot completely leave a past behind, even with a change in location or religious faith. It is particularly true that one cannot completely leave behind some beliefs and attitudes about parenting. Whoever Ruth McBride Jordan became in her adult life, a part of her remained rooted in the household she escaped. Like her own father, Ruth was a harsh and authoritarian parent, not beyond giving her children severe beatings when they transgressed from her ideas of what was right. In observing that his mother ruled the world, James understood that Ruth's parenting style "harked back to her own traditional Orthodox upbringing, where the home was run by one dominating figure with strict rules and regulations. Despite the orchestrated chaos of our home, we always ate meals at a certain time, always

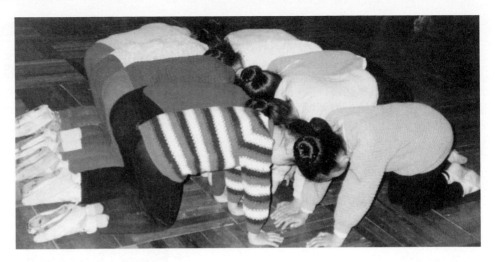

Many of the ideas that parents have about child rearing reflect the values, ideals, and standards of their culture. In Shanghai, China, young girls are taught to bow in respect. This is not a behavior expected of American youngsters.

did homework at a certain time, and always went to bed at a certain time." And like her parents, she insisted that the thing most worthy of having in the world was a good education. As James McBride noted, "It was in her sense of education, more than any others, that Mommy conveyed her Jewishness to us."

Humans are a diverse and complex species; they raise their children in various and sundry ways. Unlike animals, who prepare their offspring to go out into the world in the same basic, instinct-based manner, human parents rely primarily on *learning* to guide them through the arduous process of caring for their children. They gather information, form opinions, make judgments and generally accumulate a set of beliefs or *assumptions* about the parent-child relationship. Where does the information behind these assumptions come from? How and why do notions about parenting change over the years?

THE ASSUMPTIONS OF LIFE:
CULTURE AND ETHNICITY

The variations displayed by human parents is a function of *culture,* the beliefs, values, ideals, and standards shared by a group of people. Child-rearing differences are closely tied to cultural differences in that cultures differ in the types of competence parents encourage in their children, the age at which they expect a particular skill to be acquired, the level of accomplishment they want children to achieve, the rules for displaying emotion, and forms by which children are to express themselves (Hess, et al., 1980).

Raising children in New Guinea is a far different task from child rearing in an urban American city. In New Guinea, Kalawali parents fear their children will fall in the river and be eaten by crocodiles. They insist on crocodile initiation rites, which they believe will protect their children from harm.

In American society, where the notion of democracy is very strong, cultural differences are rarely mentioned in regard to parenting. And yet, many of the assumptions American parents make about children and the parenting role come from this determinant. Not *all* families within a culture operate exactly the same, but general parenting patterns have been observed within specific groups. As James McBride observed, even as strong a person as his mother incorporated new ideas about parenting into ones that had been instilled in her during childhood. Although her parenting attitudes came from her Jewish past, Ruth was very much influenced by the culture she lived in and adopted. "The extended black family was Mommy's hole card . . . ." he wrote. Ruth "aligned herself with any relative or friend who had any interest in any of her children and would send us off to stay with whatever relative promised to straighten us out, and many did."

CULTURE: THE BELIEFS OF A PEOPLE

In some ways, the concept of culture is a difficult one to comprehend because values, attitudes, and beliefs are abstract notions. But they are reflected in everyday behaviors and activities. In cultures that promote dependency, for example, breastfeeding may continue until a child is two or three years old, family decisions rest upon the authority of one person, children are rewarded for doing things that benefit the whole family, and signs of disobedience or independence are discouraged. In cultures that value independence, babies are left to play alone in a crib or playpen, very young children are encouraged to feed themselves, and children are organized to compete against each other for awards in school.

While individual societies have their roots in environmental conditions and responses are made to ensure survival, culture is the learned part of human community, the "person-made" aspects of the human environment.

These elements of cultural heritage or *ethnicity,* passed down from generation to generation, determine what people eat, how they work, the holidays they celebrate, the illnesses they get, the way they give birth, how they raise their children, and how they die.

To illustrate the interactive role of environment and ethnicity on child-rearing practices, anthropologist Patricia Draper (1975) compared the !Kung food foragers of Africa's Kalahari Desert to the goat-herding villagers who live nearby. Male and female !Kung children are treated alike because the experiences of their lives are very much the same. Children of both sexes spend time in the presence of both parents; tasks are assigned equally, and no burden—even that of watching younger children—falls on one gender more than the other. In the nearby village, by contrast, children are raised in a way similar to that of Western society. Men spend most of their time away from home; children spend their days with their mothers, and tasks are assigned according to gender. Girls are expected to prepare food and care for younger children, whereas boys are assigned tasks that take them away from the confines of home.

The impact of changing environmental and economic conditions on the parenting process is poignantly described by Jerre Mangione and Ben Morreale (1992) in *La Storia: Five Centuries of the Italian American Experience.* Between 1880 and 1920, more than 4 million Italians emigrated to the United States, most of them driven from seven southern, agrarian regions of Italy by economic hardship and widespread malaria. Most of those emigrants were men: the husbands, sons, brothers, and fiancés who had been the heads of households. The women left behind were traumatized by the separation from their loved ones and by the challenge of caring for themselves and their remaining children. Correspondence in *La Storia* from these years suggests, "Years ago we had family order here. . . . Children were brought up to obey their parents. Now, without close surveillance, they do as they please. . . . The number of illegitimate children is steadily increasing. And infanticide, an evil entirely unknown here a few years ago, is rapidly making itself felt." (Mangione and Morreale, 1992.)

This drastic social change led to another major consequence: the daughters left behind were now without benefit of a father or brother who would present a required dowry or financial award to a prospective husband, and they were doomed to spinsterhood. On occasion, fathers or older brothers tried to rule the Italian roost from their American homes, writing detailed instructions about how the children left behind should be raised. Once in America, parenting difficulties continued as many Italian-American parents adhered to *la via vecchia,* the old ways, while their children protested the ethnic attitudes and values as inappropriate in the new land.

Even when two cultural groups appear to hold similar values, sharp contrasts can exist in regard to child rearing. For example, Italian and Jewish cultures are both family centered. However, Italians are more likely to raise their children to stay close to home, even as grownups. An Italian saying, "Don't make your child better than you are," reflects the fear that if a child exceeds the achievements of the parents he or she will move out into the world and leave the ways of the family (Gambino, 1974; Mangione and Morreale, 1992). Italian children are often expected to put their families (parents, siblings) first, even if this obligation means abandoning their own desires.

In sharp contrast, Jewish children are their parents *nachas:* honor, fulfillment, and joy. If children in the family are successful in life, if they achieve in great measure, the parents are judged to be successful people. This means that Jewish parents must make considerable investments in their children, particularly for education and careers, even when the best opportunities carry their children far from home. Obligations in the Jewish family flow downward—from parents to children. This is reflected in the Jewish saying, "When a father helps a son, both smile. When a son helps his father, both cry." Children are expected to repay the kindness and generosity of their parents by doing the same things for their own children.

These differences in child-rearing beliefs have impact on the old age of parents. Whereas aged Italian parents almost always have their children close by to care for them, Jewish parents often find themselves living in different areas of the country than their offspring.

INDIVIDUALISM AND COLLECTIVISM

A key influence on parenting assumptions is whether a culture is built on a belief in *individualism* or *collectivism*. One researcher defines the difference this way:

> *Individualism* pertains to societies in which the ties between individuals are loose: everyone is expected to look after himself or herself and his or her immediate family. *Collectivism* as its opposite pertains to societies in which people from birth onwards are integrated into strong, cohesive ingroups, which throughout people's lifetime continue to protect them in exchange for unquestioning loyalty (Hofstede, 1991).

Most Western European cultures emphasize independence and personal responsibility. Although family life and the nurturance and support of children are important, individual identity is valued and achievement is seen as a function of one's own efforts. In cultures that promote individualism, gender roles are more egalitarian and flexible and there is more freedom to express emotions. Underlying American culture is a strong belief in individual achievement, putting the dominant society at odds with many of the ethnic groups who have emigrated to the United States since 1965.

Collective cultures are built upon group obligation. Achievement and responsibility are viewed as shared experiences. The needs of the family are paramount and come before individual desires. Researcher Patricia Greenfield (1995) pointed out that about 70 percent of the world's cultures are collective, including those from most Asian, African, and South American countries.

Because of the differences between individualist and collective cultures, it is often difficult to obtain precise information about a particular group of

The Informed Parent 3.1

Culturally Diverse Family Patterns

Cultural Beliefs	Child's Behavior
Reside in extended family household.	Shows high level of cooperation and responsibility; does not like being separated.
Family members share in all decision making.	Learns to negotiate and compromise.
Child considered an infant for two years.	Relies on contact with mother; has not learned self-help skills.
Child considered an infant until 5 years old.	May still drink from bottle.
Parent feels no pressure about developmental milestones.	
Family is strong, close-knit.	Puts family first, not self.
Child's independence is encouraged.	Has own space and toys at home.
Pride and dignity are central.	Upholds family honor; is disciplined for rude behavior and poor manners.
Family expresses feelings openly.	Cries, may have temper tantrums.
Family does not express feelings.	Does not cry or display emotion.
Discipline is harsh.	Shows obedience to authority; sometimes rebellion.

Source: Reproduced by permission. *Roots and Wings: Affirming Culture in Early Childhood Programs,* Stacey York, © 1991. Redleaf Press. St. Paul, Minnesota.

people. The U.S. Census Bureau defines a family as "two or more persons, including the householder, who are related by birth, marriage, or adoption, and who live together as one household." In collective cultures "family members" may or may not be related by birth, marriage, or adoption. In some American Indian cultures, for example, a "grandmother" may in fact be an aunt or great-aunt or even a close family friend. A "brother" may actually be a cousin or close friend. Caution must always be used in evaluating a specific culture by standards of another group

MULTI-ETHNICITY AND PARENTING

In a multi-ethnic country like the United States, enormous variation can be seen in parental customs. Even within groups, there are divisions that differ in their attitudes and values (See Figure 3.1). In addition, there is considerable intermarriage between ethnic groups in the United States. For example, Japanese Americans marry non-Japanese Americans about 65 percent of the time, a number so great that the number of children born to one Japanese parent and one non-Japanese parent exceeds the number of children born to two Japanese parents. Despite the intermingling of cultures within families, individuals carry within them a connection to a group whose commonality is transmitted over generations. How strong that connection is depends upon the length of time since migration, the group's historical experiences, whether an individual lives and works among people of the group, the language spoken by family members, the extent of intermarriage, the family's place of residence, the socioeconomic status and education of family members, the political and religious ties the family has to the ethnic group, and the degree of assimilation within the dominant American culture.

Figure 3.1
Major Ethnic Groups in the United States

The 1990 Census listed 95 ethnic and racial categories and sub-categories. The dominant groups in American society are listed here. Each places its own value system on its children and parenting in distinctive ways that reflects the needs of the culture.

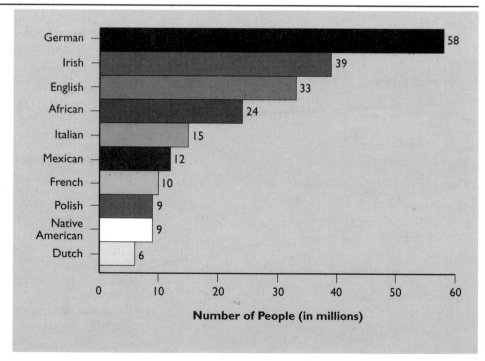

Number of People (in millions)

Sociologists Frederick Elkin and Gerald Handel (1972) pointed out that many children live in two worlds. "The child of the immigrant learns two cultures and two identities," they write in *The Child and Society,* "those of his ethnic group and those of the national society. His ethnic culture and identity are learned through hearing stories of group experiences, idealizing group heroes, observing and sympathizing with family members in their interaction with fellow ethnics and with outsiders, and generally through participating in the group's way of life. He learns the culture, not in its 'pure' form but as modified and practiced in the new country."

ACCULTURATION AFFECTS PARENTS AND CHILDREN

Parenting practices within an immigrant ethnic group may vary depending on the parents' *acculturation;* that is, the degree to which their behaviors and attitudes adhere to those of their new culture (Rogler, Cortes, and Malgady, 1991). The level of acculturation is also an index of the parents' interaction with the majority culture. The higher the degree of interaction with the majority culture, the more likely the parenting beliefs and behaviors have been influenced by the majority culture.

Acculturation can cause considerable stress if a family attempts to fit into a mainstream society and is not accepted by it. Some groups are able to do well in spite of prejudice and discrimination.

In American society, the number of child immigrants and American-born children of immigrants reached 13.7 million in 1997, up from 8 million in the 1990 U.S. Census Report. This number accounts for 1 in 5 children in the United States. In a bicoastal study tracking the children of immigrants from 1992 to 1995–96, researchers Ruben Rumbaut and Alejandro Portes (1998) found that while 9 out of 10 children of immigrants spoke a language other than English at home, 88 percent preferred to speak English by the end of high school (See Figure 3.3). In addition, the children of immigrants from some ethnic groups have higher grades in school and lower dropout rates than other American children. This is particularly true of the children of Chinese, Indian, Japanese, and Korean parents.

ANGLO-AMERICAN PARENTING

America is a nation of immigrants, with people coming from every area of the world to take up family life in the United States. The majority of the people in the United States are perceived as ethnically "white," despite the great variation displayed among the 53 categories of European Americans identified by the 1990 U.S. Census Report. The English comprised about 60 percent of the Europeans who came to the United States during Colonial times, and the dominant culture was built on their language, lifestyle, religion, values, and social institutions. One quarter of all Americans are descendants of white English colonists who arrived in the eighteenth century, bringing with them a Protestant

Figure 3.2
Composition of
Child Population
Under the Age of
18 in the United
States

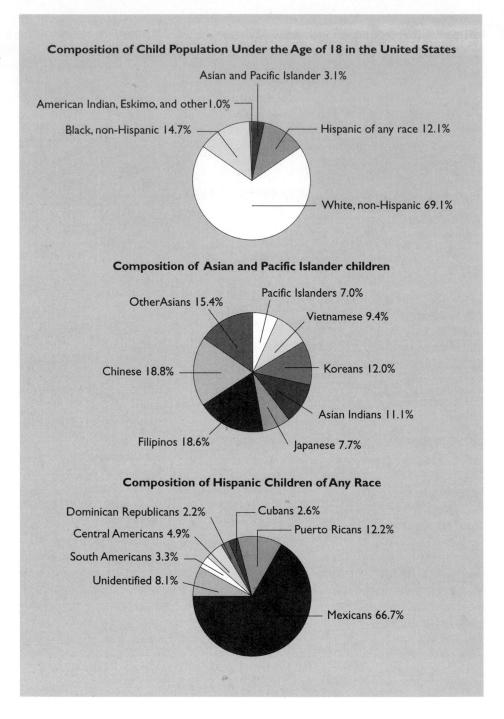

Composition of Child Population Under the Age of 18 in the United States

Asian and Pacific Islander 3.1%

American Indian, Eskimo, and other 1.0%

Black, non-Hispanic 14.7%

Hispanic of any race 12.1%

White, non-Hispanic 69.1%

Composition of Asian and Pacific Islander children

Pacific Islanders 7.0%

OtherAsians 15.4%

Vietnamese 9.4%

Koreans 12.0%

Chinese 18.8%

Asian Indians 11.1%

Filipinos 18.6%

Japanese 7.7%

Composition of Hispanic Children of Any Race

Dominican Republicans 2.2%

Cubans 2.6%

Central Americans 4.9%

Puerto Ricans 12.2%

South Americans 3.3%

Unidentified 8.1%

Mexicans 66.7%

ethic that advocates individualism, thriftiness, self-sacrifice, efficiency, and hard work as a way to reach salvation (Weber, 1930). Those new immigrants believed that upward class mobility could be obtained through hard work, thrifti-

Figure 3.3
Acculturation and
Bilingualism

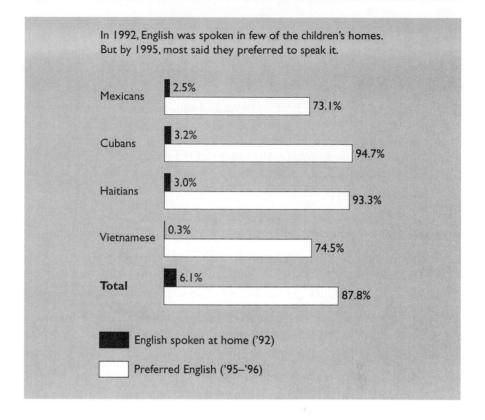

In 1992, English was spoken in few of the children's homes. But by 1995, most said they preferred to speak it.

Mexicans
2.5%
73.1%

Cubans
3.2%
94.7%

Haitians
3.0%
93.3%

Vietnamese
0.3%
74.5%

Total
6.1%
87.8%

■ English spoken at home ('92)

☐ Preferred English ('95–'96)

ness, and conformity. Wealth came by owning and working the land, and land was plentiful.

While there are regional differences among people in this group the basic emphasis on rugged individualism remains broadly espoused. Immigrant groups who followed the English sought to be assimilated into American society, and they accomplished this by adopting the ideas of the dominant Anglo culture. Also, intermarriage between ethnic group members increased the influence of Anglos in American culture.

Anglo parents raise their children to be self-contained, self-reliant and self-determining (McGoldrick, 1996.) They believe that diligence and hard work will bring success in life, and they encourage early independence and autonomy to the point that sometimes adolescent children are launched before they are emotionally and financially ready to leave home. Often the Anglo adolescent feels abandoned by the withdrawal of financial and emotional support from parents who judge that it's time for the child to be on his or her own.

Anglo-American parents are more detached from their children than most other groups; they are less emotionally involved in developmental milestones such as puberty, leaving for college, or getting married. Anglo parents also talk less to their children and, when they do, it is generally for utilitarian purposes such as discussing how to accomplish a goal. When children fail, the parents are harsh in their judgments. Clubs, sports, and hobbies are viewed as important

The Informed Parent 3.2

Values of the American Macroculture

The majority American culture is white, Anglo-Saxon, and Protestant. Its social institutions and political structure are based on a Western European tradition. Roberta M. Berns (1993) points out that, no matter what a parent or child's ethnic background is, all Americans are influenced to some degree by the values of the macroculture, including:

■ Work ethic based on individualism, independence, competitiveness, ambition, industriousness

■ Achievement valued above inheritance

■ Emphasis on mastery over passive acceptance

■ Belief in adaptation and change, rather than tradition

■ Peer relationships and equality, rather than superordinate-subordinate relationships

■ Focus on individual personality, over group identity and responsibility

■ Status based on occupation, education, and financial worth

■ New and modern considered better than old and traditional

■ Focus on future rather than present or past

■ Morality based on sense of right and wrong, not shame or dishonor

■ Communication with others direct, impersonal, objective

■ Consumer oriented, success measured by material possessions

■ Emphasis on egalitarianism: social, political, and economic equality

Source: Based on Williams, R. M. (1960). "Generic American Values." In W. Goldschmidt (Ed.), *Exploring the Ways of Mankind,* New York: Holt, Rinehart and Winston.

socialization agents, through which children learn to be both competitive and conforming.

The emphasis on rugged individualism, boundless opportunity, and prosperity poses problems for families who have not obtained or inherited land and wealth and, therefore, have been unable to meet social expectations. Children growing up in poor areas of the country, such as Appalachia often feel inferior because of their lower socioeconomic status.

LATINO PARENTING

In the United States, there are more than 20 million people of Latino origin, making this the largest U.S. subgroup and Spanish the second most commonly spoken language. This group includes Mexicans, Puerto Ricans, Cubans, Dominicans, and Brazilians (who speak Portuguese). Most follow the Catholic religion. Although these groups together are generally labeled Hispanic, each prefers to be known by its own country identity.

In Latino families, children are prized and parents are closely connected to them (Zuniga, 1992). One-third of Latino families have five or more children (U.S. Census Report, 1995). Family includes not only members of the nuclear and the extended family but also an expansive network of friends. Research by Griswold del Castillo (1984) described *compadrazgo*—the co-parenting of children by parents and godparents—to be an important feature of the Mexican-American child-rearing process. Godparents are so important in Mexican culture that they enter into special religious, social, and economic relationships with their godchildren and the parents of the children. Their presence is required for the celebration of the major religious occasions in a child's life, including baptism, first communion, and marriage. In addition, *compadres* provide discipline and emotional and financial support when needed. This system of family-network ties probably evolved as a result of economic hardship within the culture. A strong, extended family offers children care and assistance they would not receive in a closed family system (Alvarez, 1987, Vega, 1990).

While parenting practices vary among Latino groups, there is a tendency to be permissive and indulgent with young children and then change to a stricter, more authoritarian style of parenting with older children (Garcia-Apreto, 1982). Boys are socialized in keeping with the society's view of male freedom and dominance, while girls are given special protection and limits, particularly in sexual matters. Mothers and daughters are particularly close, and the lifelong interdependence among family members makes cooperation and obedience more important than independence or individual achievement.

Of all the Latino groups, Puerto Ricans occupy a unique place in American society because in 1898, after the Spanish-American War, the United States colonized Puerto Rico. While many Puerto Ricans live in the mainland United States, they have strong ties to the island and some return often to visit relatives. While there is no "traditional" Puerto Rican family and differences exist due to social class, some patterns of child rearing can be discerned.

Compared to other Latino groups in the United States, Puerto Rican families have the lowest median income, mothers are younger, and there are more children in the household. (U.S. Census Report, 1995). Adults marry young and have many children, who are seen as the poor man's wealth and symbols of their parents' fertility. Children are expected to take care of their elderly parents one day.

Some of the problems in Puerto Rican households are related to high unemployment levels, educational deficiencies, teen pregnancy, and substance abuse. Puerto Rican children living in poor, inner-city neighborhoods are more likely to suffer from asthma than children from other Latino groups. One reason for this is their exposure to tobacco smoke. Puerto Rican mothers of reproductive age smoke more than other Hispanic women, and they are less compliant with their children's necessary medical treatment than are more acculturated or bicultural mothers (Pletsch, 1994).

Puerto Rican culture values *familism,* a way of life that emphasizes the sacred bonds between relatives and obligation and duty toward kin (Rogler and Cooney, 1984). Kinship extends beyond the family as individuals not biologically related are treated like family members. Grandparents and godparents play a very important role in family decision making and financial support. In contrast to mainstream North American culture, where distinct boundaries exist between nuclear families and outsiders, Puerto Rican families will informally adopt children who are orphaned or dislocated because of family crises.

Puerto Rican parents are concerned that children be *tranquilo, obediente,* and *respetuoso* (children should be calm, obedient, and respectful), particularly in the presence of elders. They stress positive interaction with family, friends, and people they meet (Harwood, et al., 1995). In contrast to Anglo or Jewish parents, Puerto Rican parents do not often encourage their children to speak their minds freely.

Respect is valued above all attributes, as this is considered the sign of a person's worthiness. In keeping with the Spanish construct of *machismo,* males earn respect by protecting and caring for their families. Traditionally, Puerto Rican families have been patriarchal, a structure that gives men power and authority over women and children. Constructs of *marianismo* teach women that they are morally and spiritually superior to men and must therefore endure any suffering inflicted by them. *Hembrismo* denotes femaleness, with the expectation that women will be strong and persevere in meeting their duties to the workplace and home (Comas Díaz, 1989).

The power structure in Puerto Rican families changes somewhat when women go out to work. Male unemployment and marital discord has led to an increase in households headed by single females (*U.S. Census Report,* 1995).

Adolescence can be a difficult time for Puerto Rican children living in the United States, as they attempt to navigate two different cultures: one that emphasizes loyalty and family obligations and another that promotes independence and autonomy (Canino and Zayas, 1997). Parents often become very strict and overprotective with daughters who demand the freedom to date. Parents that are able to adapt to their adolescents' developmental needs are teaching their children how to live in the balance between two cultures. Parents who rigidly adhere to cultural beliefs are most likely to experience problems with their teenage children.

ASIAN PARENTING

The values of Asian families are quite different than those in Western families. Asian thought is rooted in Eastern tradition, in particular Confucianism and Buddhist principles where perseverance, self-sacrifice, and humility are high virtues. The family is primary among Asians, and children are expected to enhance the family's social status and welfare by achieving in school (Sigel, 1988). Since children are seen as products of all the generations that have come before, many family rites and ceremonies contain elements of ancestor worship. There are clearly defined roles and expectations based on age, gender, and social class. Fathers generally have the authority in the home, divorce is rare, and sons are favored over daughters.

Chinese parents are most concerned with *chiao,* the "proper development of character," in particular the internalization of beliefs that emphasize family obligations and the negation of conflict (Chaio, 1983; Ho, 1981). They view academic achievement as a way to acquire wealth and social status and as a means of overcoming discrimination in the United States (Lum and Char, 1985). Asian parents focus on training their children to bring honor to the family with connectedness the ultimate goal. Connectedness is encouraged by the close physical contact that occurs between infants and their mothers, as the babies are held much of the day. Children's needs are quickly met by a number of caregivers, including mothers, grandmothers, siblings, and other family members. Siblings are taught to look out for each other and set a good example by refraining from arguing and fighting. Relationships outside the family are not encouraged. Asian parents make most of the important decisions for their children especially as pertains to education.

In traditional Chinese culture, mothers are considered *chi* (kind) and fathers *yan (* strict). The degree of strictness depends upon the gender of the children. Chinese fathers describe themselves as stricter toward their sons because the sons inherit the family name and property and therefore must be socialized properly. Mothers value sons more and control them less than daughters because in old age mothers become dependent on their sons for support (Ho, 1987). Daughters, on the other hand, go off after marriage and join their husbands' families; however, while they live with their mothers they are expected to do household chores such as cooking and caring for younger siblings.

Variations in parenting style can be seen within Chinese culture. In a comparison of parenting in mainland China, Taiwan, and Hong Kong, researcher Thomas J. Berndt and his associates found that in Hong Kong ratings of parents' warmth is lower and strictness higher than in either Taiwan or mainland China. It is speculated that differences within the macrosystem—government policies, economic conditions, and degree of industrialization—influence parenting styles; and cosmopolitan, Westernized Hong Kong is a very different place to live in than Taiwan or mainland China (Bronfenbrenner, 1986; Kagitcibasi, 1990).

In the United States, there are more than 28 subgroups of the Asian population. Among them are the Chinese, Filipino, Japanese, Asian Indian, Korean, and Vietnamese, making Asian Americans the third largest minority group in the United States, after African Americans and Hispanics. Beliefs and rituals vary among the Asian subgroups. For example, many Chinese Americans are Buddhists, while the majority of Korean Americans are Protestant Christians. Filipinos practice Catholicism, and many Cambodians have been influenced by Hinduism. There are traditional Asian families as well as Americanized Asian families, bicultural families and interracial families.

By the year 2000, it is expected that the Asian American population will increase to nearly 10 million people (U.S. DHHS, 1996). As a group, Asian Americans' beliefs and attitudes about parenting vary according to their place

Asian cultures encourage close family and tribal ties, a respect for nature, and spirituality.

of origin, cultural traditions, language, religion, residential location, occupation, income, length of time since their immigration, and degree of acculturation.

The Chinese make up the largest Asian group in America and were the first to emigrate to the United States. Chinese Americans were victims of horrendous prejudice during the late nineteenth and early twentieth centuries; they were viewed as an unassimilated "yellow peril."

In the early years of Chinese presence in the United States, from 1850 to 1920, there was little family life as the majority of immigrants were male laborers from Guangdong province, and half of them were in America without their wives. By the 1920s, men who had managed to save some money by starting small businesses (such as laundries or restaurants) began sending for their wives and children, who not only offered companionship but were a source of free labor.

Life was particularly difficult for Chinese mothers who, in addition to working long hours in uncomfortable environments, were responsible at home for cleaning, cooking, and caring for the children. Social isolation, low status, and grief among Chinese women led to a suicide rate three times higher than that of the general population (Lin, 1986). Because children lived and worked with their parents, they were strictly supervised. To keep conflict to a minimum, discipline and cooperation were stressed, and self-expression was discouraged. Interestingly, however, as Chinese children learned to read and write English in school, there developed a reverse dependency between parents and their children. The children become the agents for their families, translating business documents, handling banking duties, negotiating with customers, and intervening with the medical and social system.

The 1960s saw a change in the structure of the Chinese family in America as the civil rights movement, new immigration laws, and greater educational and professional opportunities led to increased diversity within the culture. Thousands of new immigrants came from Hong Kong. They spoke a different language than earlier immigrants (Mandarin rather than Cantonese), most also spoke English, and they were familiar with Western ideas and ways.

Contemporary Chinese family life differs across social class lines and in degree of acculturation. Working-class Chinese tend to live in or near urban "Chinatowns," and both mothers and fathers put in long hours at work. Betty Lee Sung (1983) reported that 17 percent of Chinese high school students in New York rarely saw their mothers during the week, and 32 percent did not see their fathers. The 1960s and 1970s saw delinquency and outbreaks of gang violence among urban Chinese children, due to increased numbers of children immigrating without their parents, a breakdown of community controls, school problems, and lack of job opportunities for uneducated youngsters (Glenn, 1994).

Many affluent Chinese live in middle-class neighborhoods outside Chinatown or in the suburbs. These dual-income, professional, suburban families are more nuclear, mothers and fathers are more equal in their responsibilities and relationship, and the children are likely to have non-Chinese friends (Wong, 1985).

In comparing child-rearing practices among Chinese, immigrant Chinese and Caucasian American parents, researchers Chin-Yau Cindy Lin and Victoria Fu (1990) found that Chinese parents are more controlling of their children than are Caucasian parents. They are also less affectionate and emotionally more restrained than the Caucasian American parents. Surprisingly, the researchers found that both Chinese and immigrant Chinese parents valued and encouraged independence more than Caucasian American parents did, with the fathers of Chinese origin valuing that trait highest.

Clearly there is great variation in parenting practices within Asian cultures, and patterns of child rearing are undergoing continual change. As a consequence, Chinese parents in America are raising "bicultural" children, balancing the traditional beliefs of their ancestors and Confucian philosophy with the notions of American society at large.

PARENTING AND RACE: A SPECIAL CHALLENGE

Race is a concept that is difficult to define degree of, particularly in the United States. Many African Americans have some white ancestry and there are millions of mixed-race people in the country. The 1995 Census Report revealed that more than three million Americans are married to or living with someone of a different race and they have two million children between them. Whereas the term "race" has long had a biological application, in this text it is used to suggest the politics and culture of a group. Recently the identification "biracial" or "multiracial" is used by some children of mixed relationships, who are pressing for this category to be included in the census data.

In the centuries between 1528 and 1870, approximately fifteen million Africans were brought forcibly to the New World, most to Cuba, Brazil, America, and other areas in the Caribbean and South America (Segal, (1995). It is estimated that from 10 percent to 20 percent of these captives died during the crossing and that another 4 percent succumbed after they were sold by slavers (Black, 1993; Segal, 1995). Once in the New World, Africans were forced to give up their names and their native languages. They had to abandon their culture, religions, and customs. As slaves, they were prohibited from marrying, and extant families were often separated as they were sold to owners of different plantations. Male slaves were expected to breed new laborers, and female slaves were sexually exploited. Infant mortality rate was 200 per 1,000 births (Segal, 1995). When slavery ended in the United States, African Americans found themselves locked out of the educational and occupational opportunities Americans pride themselves on.

Prior to the mid-1980s distorted and negative images of African American families were put forth by researchers who looked at family life and parenting from a middle-class white perspective. At one point African American families were characterized as "disorganized, deprived, disadvantaged" (Moynihan, 1965). Modern researchers are more respectful of the strength, resilience, and dedication required to survive the brutality of slavery and years of discrimination and economic hardship.

African Americans comprise about 12 percent of the population of the United States, making them the largest minority group in the country (U.S. Census Bureau, 1995). It is impossible to define a "typical" African American family because of the diversity in immigration patterns. For example, people who have emigrated from Caribbean islands that were formerly British will have assimilated some of the customs and beliefs of the English. Families from Central and South America will have been influenced by the Spanish. Even African Americans who came to the United States directly from Africa are a diverse group because of geographic origins, religious background, skin color, socioeconomic status, level of acculturation, and strategies employed to cope with racism and discrimination (Hines and Boyd-Franklin, 1996). Despite these significant differences, there are some commonalities.

While the media often focuses on black families who are on public assistance or having other problems, the majority of African American families in the United States are stable, self-supporting, and well-functioning (Hopson and Hopson, 1990). A large number of these families are headed by single, female parents, about 60 percent compared to 23 percent of white families.

Motherhood is highly valued in the African American community, and black mothers are less likely than white mothers to see parenthood as a detriment to their career or social advancement (Jacobsen and Bigner, 1991). African American grandmothers have been called the "guardians of generations" (Frazier, 1939) because of their ability to raise strong families despite the economic hardship and prejudice that characterizes their life experiences.

African Americans value interpersonal relationships (Harrison, et al., 1990; Wilson, 1989). They have a very strong kinship network, which includes distant relatives, friends, and church acquaintances who are not biologically related. (Willis, 1992; Wilson, 1989). This network often results in informal adoption as relatives or family friends take over caregiving responsibility for a child on a temporary or permanent basis when natural parents are unable to (Billingsley, 1992; Boyd-Franklin, 1989). It is not unusual for an African-American child to be raised in a household that consists of a grandmother and aunts and cousins, all of whom may, at different times, take care of the child. In families where parents work, children are sometimes "parentified"; that is, an older child is given the adult responsibility for household tasks and the care of younger children—sometimes to the detriment of his or her own developmental needs. This phenomenon also occurs in other cultural groups, where parents rely on older children to care for younger children.

Religion and spirituality play an important part in African American life. The majority are Baptists, but many have joined the Jehovah's Witnesses, branches of Islam, the Catholic church, and other groups. To the African American community, church means more than simply religious services. The church offers social support, recreation, and educational programs. Family members might attend Bible study classes, sing in the choir, take part in marriage enrichment or health programs, and get together in adult or youth groups. Religious services and activities offer outlets for expressing feelings of pain, humiliation, and anger.

While disciplinary practices vary, researchers have found parenting to be more restrictive in African American families than in other cultures (Peters, 1985; Julian, et al., 1994; Baumrind, 1996). It is speculated that the emphasis African American parents place on obedience and good behavior is due to the belief that African American children are given less leeway to misbehave than children of other cultures. However, harsher parenting practices may also be the result of religious orientation.

Poverty impacts parents of all ethnic groups, as the associated stresses can reduce parents' tolerance for their children's normal behavior. The issues surrounding poverty are especially acute for African American families; 42 percent of black children in the United States (4.8 million) receive public assistance, compared to 16 percent of white children (Department of Health and Human Services, 1995).

Concerned about their children's future, African American parents encourage education as a way to improve their lives. Because there have been professional limitations due to racism, parents have encouraged their children to pursue careers that offer security rather than self-actualization (Hines and Boyd-Franklin, 1996).

One prevailing image of African American families is the absentee father (Cochran, 1997). Recent research refutes this view, suggesting that African-American fathers play an important role in their family's lives (McAdoo and McAdoo, 1994; Mirande, 1991). Rather than looking at the African American fathers who are very much a part of their children's lives, media attention and research studies have focused on the men who did not accept their parental responsibilities. (Bowman, 1993).

Another image has African American women acting as the head of household because men have not met family responsibilities (White and Parham,

1990). While there have been dramatic changes in the living arrangements of African American children over the past 20 years, these are changes that are also seen in most other cultures in America. According to 1995 census data, the number of African American children living in two-parent households has decreased from 85 percent in 1970 to 71 percent in 1993. What is rarely noted is the number of African American fathers who are raising their children alone, 2 percent in 1970 and 3 percent in 1993. Interestingly, 54 percent of these fathers have never married and 23 percent are divorced.

Researchers have noted the significant impact that economics have on men's participation in the parenting processes; this is true also for African American fathers. Even most of the fathers who are not able to provide financial support for their children and don't live with them still consider the relationship important (Wade, 1994). Employment appears to be the factor that determines whether or not an African American father marries. In one study, employed fathers living in two-income households reported that their families were strong and close. Involvement in child care was greatest among fathers who had a high level of income and education, a stable marriage, social support, a mature attitude toward family responsibility, a productive communicative style, and psychological commitment to the family (Cochran, 1997).

Contrary to public perception, most African American teenage fathers—while they may not live with their children—do help out financially if they are employed (Rivara, Sweeney, and Henderson, 1986). This is especially true if the father has a good self-image and high role expectations (Christmon, 1990). More than one-half of fathers aged 15 to 20 report that they discussed the pregnancy and child care options with the mothers of their children. While their commitment to parenting is influenced by the degree of social and emotional support they receive, many African American teenage fathers do not have the resources necessary to help raise children. As one researcher put it, "high levels of unemployment, dropout rates, and institutionalized racism, disproportionately found among African American youth, exacerbate the difficulties of early parenting" (Cochran, 1997).

Raising black children in a nation that does not value them as much as it does white children poses very special problems for black parents. Psychiatrists James P. Comer and Alvin F. Poussaint (1992), in *Raising Black Children*, suggested that black parents must deal with these special problems while also attending to all of the child-rearing issues that face every parent. One of the global tasks of parenting is to help children develop in ways that will enable them to function well as individuals, family members, and citizens. But if, by its actions and attitudes, a society denies a people a sense of belonging, as it does blacks, parents have a great deal more difficulty promoting and passing on the principles and ways of that society. In questioning what they call "mainstream or middle-class, that is, 'white ways'," the authors write, "The need to preserve our culture and community springs from a desire to maintain a real and psychological place, where we are accepted, respected, and protected. For this reason we are concerned about whether 'white psychology and child-rearing approaches' will change us, hurt us, destroy our culture."

Parents in African American families encourage strong family ties.

As Comer and Poussaint note, black parents within American society must be prepared to cope with changing attitudes and values regarding matters of family life, sex, and authority, as well as with the problems of drug use, crime and AIDS.

NATIVE AMERICAN PARENTING

The terms "Native American" and "American Indian" refer to the more than 2 million people from 500 different tribes who identify themselves this way, with the Sioux and Navajo among the largest group (Bennett, 1990). Some of these tribes are legally recognized by the United States government as sovereign nations. Despite the myth that Native Americans live on reservations, over one-half live in urban areas and many live in Alaska. There is great diversity among them, based upon language, tribal customs, religious beliefs, and economic status. For example, when a Hopi marries, the groom moves in with his wife's family; but in a Havasupai marriage, the bride moves in with her husband's family. As a group, and compared to other ethnic groups in the United States, American Indians have the highest birth rates and death rates and the shortest life expectancy. They suffer more from serious illnesses and have a high rate of suicide. In Indian society, unemployment rates are high, as are the number of children born out of wedlock (U.S. Bureau of the Census, 1995).

During the 1800s millions of American Indians died from disease and genocide as they were forced from their lands by the U.S. government. Indian children were taken away from their parents and placed in missionary boarding schools; there they were forbidden to speak their native languages or practice their religion or customs (LaDue, 1992). In the 1950s and 1960s, the uprooting continued as a relocation plan took Indians from their homes and moved them into cities. In New York alone, there are about 60,000 Indians, from more than 60 tribes. Because of dislocation, discrimination, and problems of living in an individualist American culture, American Indian rates of unemployment, suicide, and alcoholism are higher than in other ethnic groups.

Because of its multi-generational influence the boarding-school experience has most impacted the parent-child relationships in Indian culture. Children as young as five years were separated from their parents and taken far from home, where they were raised in substandard housing and neglected to the point of not even having enough food to eat. The school staff did not understand the children's languages or traditions, and they were often physically and emotionally abusive to the youngsters. The coping strategies of the generation removed from their tribes included learned helplessness, passive-aggressiveness, alcohol and drug abuse, denial and suicide (Szasz, 1977). Nadine Tafoya and Ann Del Vecchio (1996) have pointed out the effects of this treatment.

> Without positive parental role models to supply children with their culture, and without continuous exposure to nurturing, Native American adults today are forced to invent their own methods and models to negotiate both the Indian and Anglo worlds. Without positive models, Native American communities and the individuals within them have developed a set of survival skills that include numerous self-destructive behaviors, such as alcohol, drug abuse, other addictive behaviors, and suicide. Posttraumatic stress is a concomitant of the boarding-school system.

Indian tribes are collective, and the tribe and family are of primary importance. Cousins are as close as brothers and sisters, and aunts and uncles are as important as parents and grandparents. People who marry into the family do not become "in-laws"; they are new immediate-family members. In other words, the Indian family is "blended" through marriage, rather than joined. The closeness among members of a clan or tribe enables children born into this culture to experience *multiple parenting,* a system whereby children are cared for by the many adults considered kin, even those who don't actually live with the children. Names such as "The Deer Hunter" or "Dances With Wolves" are important in Indian culture, as they reflect personal identity and achievement.

Traditionally, Indians are a "giving" group, according respect to those who share their belongings with others. A family member in need is welcome to the shelter, food, clothes, and money another family member has. This is in contrast to the "acquisitiveness" of traditional American culture. This giving quality makes it difficult for families to build up the assets needed to purchase businesses, homes, and necessary goods.

Indian parents have specific expectations of their children. These include understanding their cultural heritage, which is passed to them by way of the folk tales and stories handed down through the generations; a sense of spirituality and engagement in religious practices; and learning skills that will make them capable of earning a livelihood. There is often a "generation gap" conflict between third-generation Indian children and their parents and grandparents as the family moves from reservation to urban living and the children become enculturated.

Indian children are taught to show respect for authority by displaying "good listening skills"—meaning that they are to be silent and passive in the

The Spirit of Parenting

When Lia was about three months old, her older sister Yer slammed the front door of the Lee's apartment. A few moments later, Lia's eyes rolled up, her arms jerked over her head, and she fainted. The Lees had little doubt what had happened . . . the noise of the door had been so profoundly frightening that her soul had fled her body and become lost. They recognized the resulting symptoms as *qaug dab peg,* which means "the spirit catches you and you fall down." . . . In Hmong–English dictionaries, *qaug dab peg* is generally translated as "epilepsy."

. . . seven doctors at the Merced Community Medical Center (in California) separately mentioned the case of Lia Lee to me, but each of them told me it was not worth investigation, because her parents mistrusted Americans and would almost certainly refuse to let me see Lia's medical and legal records, or to talk with me themselves . . . I often heard doctors at MCMC complain that the Hmong seemed to care less than Americans did whether their sick children got better, since they spurned the hospital's free medical care. Unbeknownst to their doctors, the Hmong actually took their children's health so seriously that they frequently budgeted large fractions of their public assistance stipends or indebted themselves to relatives in order to pay for expensive services. . . .

. . . the Lees spent $1,000 on amulets filled with sacred healing herbs from Thailand, which Lia wore constantly around her neck. They also tried a host of less costly but time-consuming therapies. Foua (Lia's mother) inserted a silver coin that said "1936 Indochine Francaise" into the yolk of a boiled egg, wrapped the egg in a cloth, and rubbed Lia's body with it; when the egg turned black, that meant the sickness had been absorbed. She massaged Lia with the bowl of a spoon. She sucked the "pressure" out of Lia's body by pressing a small cup heated with ashes against her skin, creating a temporary vacuum as the oxygen-depleted air inside the cup cooled. She pinched Lia to draw out noxious winds. She dosed Lia with tisanes infused from the gleanings of her parking-lot herb garden. Finally, she and Nao Kao (Lia's father) tried changing Lia's name to Jou, a last-ditch Hmong remedy based on the premise that if a patient is called by a new name, the *dab* (spirit) who stole her soul will be tricked into thinking she is someone else, and the soul can return.

Anne Fadiman
From *The Spirit Catches You and You Fall Down: A Hmong Child,
Her American Doctors, and the Collision of Two Cultures*

presence of adults, even dropping their heads to avoid directly looking at an elder (Yellowbird and Snipp, 1994). Much of their communication is done nonverbally, which makes it difficult for Indian children to respond and relate to others in a traditional American classroom. School and education are not primary motivators to Native American parents; tribal matters and family obligations take precedence over school attendance (Soldier, 1985; Scott, 1986).

Competition among children, expressed curiosity, and questioning are discouraged, often with the help of folk tales and legends. Children are taught to be present-oriented rather than future-oriented. Time does not mean the same thing to Indian children as it does to other ethnic and cultural groups. Indian parents view time as cyclical rather than linear. Instead of specific hours based upon clocks and calendars, Indian parents teach their children to respond to seasonal rhythms. In Anglo culture, for example, a Sunday church service has a set time to begin and end; an Indian ceremony has no set schedule: It begins when it begins, and it is over when it's over. This makes attending a traditional American school difficult for Indian children. Arriving "on time" and doing tasks in the "present" may be confusing notions.

It appears that Indian parents are permissive, to the point of ignoring inappropriate behavior or responding with a story of what the spirits will do as

In the United States, ethnic and religious diversity leads to celebrations as varied as Thanksgiving, Hanukkah, Bhai Dooj, Christmas, Kwanzaa, Loy Krathong and New Year's Day.

punishment. When there is physical and emotional abuse in an American Indian family, it can usually be linked to parental alcoholism or drug addiction.

In the recent past there has been an increased interest in Indian culture and spirituality among non-Indian Americans, and the society has shown a new respect for Indian traditions. Increased urban living and intermarriage are undoubtedly bringing changes into the home lives of today's Indian children. It remains to be seen what impact acculturation, tied to strong traditional values and beliefs, will bring to the parenting experience.

THE RITUALS OF FAMILY LIFE

Clearly there are differences in beliefs and aptitudes toward parenting that are due to culture and in a world in which people are increasingly connected, it is important to understand these variations. Children today may have friends who celebrate Christmas in December, Easter, Rosh Hashana, Ramadan, the Chinese New Year, Kwanzaa, St. Patrick's Day and a myriad of other cultural holidays. They will be exposed to foods, dances, clothing styles, and family practices their grandparents never heard of. Monica McGoldrick (1982) pointed out that ethnicity is a vital force, a major determinant of family patterns and belief systems. In regard to the United States she notes:

> The premise of equality, on which our country was founded required us to give primary allegiance to our national identity, fostering the myth of the "melting pot", the notion that group distinctions between people were unimportant. Yet, we have not "melted." There is increasing evidence that ethnic values and identification are retained for many generations after immigration and play a significant role in family life and personal development through the life cycle.

TABLE 3.1   Parenting Across Cultures

Native American Indians	Tribal and family closeness and support
	Multiple parenting
	Respect for environment
	Respect for elders and leaders
	Rich spiritual life
Asian Americans	Reverence for ancestors
	Respect for education
	Close family units
African Americans	Close family and kinship ties
	Informal adoption
	Religious values
	Emphasis on education
Anglo-Americans	Individuality
	Achievement motivation
	Emphasis on self-reliance
Latinos	Close family and kinship ties
	Informal adoption
	Emphasis on discipline and respect

Chapter Review

- Parents rely primarily on learning to guide them through the arduous process of caring for their children. They gather information, form opinions, make judgments, and generally build up a set of beliefs or assumptions about the parent-child relationship.

- The variations displayed by human parents are the function of culture: the beliefs, values, ideals and standards shared by a group of people. Cultures differ from one another in the types of competencies parents encourage in their children, the age at which they expect a particular skill to be acquired, the level of accomplishment they want children to achieve, the rules of displaying emotion, and the way children are to express themselves.

- A key influence on parenting assumptions is whether a culture is built on a belief in individualism or collectivism. Individualism pertains to societies in which the ties between individuals are loose: everyone is expected to look after himself or herself and his or her immediate family. Collectivism, as its opposite, pertains to societies in which individuals are integrated into strong, cohesive in groups, which throughout people's lifetime continue to protect them in exchange for unquestioning loyalty.

- In cultures that promote individualism, gender roles are egalitarian and flexible, and there is freedom to express emotions. Collective cultures are built upon group obligation. Achievement and responsibility are seen as shared experiences.

- In a multi-ethnic country such as the United States, there are variations in parental customs. Despite the intermingling of cultures within families, individuals carry within them a connection to a group whose commonality is transmitted over generations. How strong that connection is depends upon the length of time since migration, a group's historical experiences, whether one lives and works among people of his or her own group, the language spoken by family members, the extent of intermarriage, the family's place of residence, the socioeconomic status and education of family members, the political and religious ties a family has to the ethnic group, and the degree of assimilation within the dominant American culture.

- Parenting practices within an immigrant ethnic group vary depending on the parents' acculturation; that is, the degree to which their behaviors and attitudes match those of the new culture.

- Anglo-American parents raise their children to be self-contained, self-reliant, and self-determining. They believe that diligence and hard work will bring success in life, and they encourage early independence and autonomy.

- Many groups are called Hispanic, including Mexicans, Puerto Ricans, Cubans, Dominicans, and Brazilians. Family life often includes, not only members of the nuclear and extended family, but also an expansive network of friends. While parenting practices vary among these groups, there is a tendency to be permissive and indulgent with young children and then change to a stricter, more authoritarian style of parenting with older children. Boys are socialized according to the society's view of male dominance, whereas girls are viewed as needing special protection and limits, particularly in sexual matters.

- Among Asians, the family is primary, and children are expected to enhance the family's social status and welfare by achieving in school. Children are seen as products of all the generations that have come before, and many family rites and ceremonies contain elements of ancestor worship. There are clearly defined roles and expectations for children, based on age, gender, and social class.

- African Americans value interpersonal relationships, and they have a very strong kinship network that includes distant relatives, friends, and church acquaintances who are not biologically related. Many African American parents encourage education as a way to improve their children's lives and prospects.

- There is great diversity among Native American groups, based upon language, tribal customs, religious beliefs, and economic status. Family membership is determined by relationship rather than by blood, making the Indian family "blended" through marriage, rather than joined. Indian parents expect their children to understand their cultural heritage and learn skills that will make them capable of earning a livelihood.

- There are clear differences in beliefs and attitudes toward parenting that are due to culture, and it is important to understand these variations as people are increasingly connected.

Student Activities

1. Investigate a culture that is unfamiliar to you. Imagine you are parenting a child in that culture. What kind of things would you do or not do? What values and ideas would you try to convey?

2. Determine whether you are a member of a individualist or collective culture. Write a paper detailing a week in the life of a child who is a member of the culture different from your own. Take into consideration: meals, doing homework, bedtime, play activities, and personal interactions.

3. As the parent of a child who has friends in a number of cultures, what would you do to help your child understand his or her friends?

Helping Hands

Association on American Indian Affairs
432 Park Avenue South
New York, NY 10016
http://greatspirit.earth.com/org.html

Mexican American Cultural Center
3019 West French Place
San Antonio, TX 78228

National Black Child Development Institute
1463 Rhode Island Avenue, NW
Washington, DC 20005
(202) 387-1281
http://www.nbcdi.org

Dedicated to improving the quality of life for African American children and youth.

CHAPTER

Parenting Within the Family

Chapter Highlights

After reading Chapter 4, students should be able to:

- Recognize the importance of the family as a whole in raising children
- Understand how the family operates as a relational system
- Recognize the kind of interactions that characterize well-functioning families
- Recognize the kind of interactions that characterize problematic families

Chapter Contents

- The Family Socialization Process
  The Family as a System ▪ *Emotional Relating Within Families* ▪
  Family Maps ▪ *The Structure of the Family*
- The Well-Functioning Family
  Coping with Family Problems
- The Changing Family Life Cycle
  Family Values: The Spiritual Life of Children

INTRODUCTION

The setting was December 17, 1903, on a coastal sand dune near Kitty Hawk in North Carolina. Brothers Orville and Wilbur Wright, bicycle makers, have just made history with the world's first successful controlled flight: a twelve-second, 120-foot run, helped along by a strong wind. The triumph of the Wright brothers was due in no small part to their strange relationship. The brothers were born four years apart, with Wilbur first—the sons of clergyman Bishop Milton Wright and his wife Susan. Three years before Wilbur's birth, the death of the couple's twins, Otis and Ida, had devastated the Bishop, who continued to commemorate the twins' birthdays for over 25 years. Some historians have suggested that, despite their age difference, Wilbur and Orville began to behave like twins to make up to their father for his loss. Milton and Susan Wright had graduated college, as did their other three children. But Wilbur and Orville both dropped out of high school; neither ever married; and they never left their parents' house. Called "inseparable as twins" by their father, Wilbur wrote, "From the time we were little children, my brother Orville and myself lived together, played together, worked together, and in fact, thought together. We usually owned all of our toys in common, talked over our thoughts and aspirations so that nearly everything that was done in our lives has been the result of conversations, suggestions, and discussions between us," (McGoldrick, 1995).

Human beings are born into tribes, clans, and families; and it is within this microsystem that they first learn who they are, whether or not they are lovable, how the world works, and what possibilities the future holds. It is within families that individuals learn values, gender roles, beliefs, expectations, attitudes, and social skills. The Wright brothers came from a family in which the father encouraged dependence; Milton even boasted about the boys staying home as adults. After Wilbur's death from typhoid fever in 1912, Orville replaced him with his sister Katharine, with whom he shared a birthdate. When Katherine became engaged to be married at the age of 52, she was terrified to tell Orville. After she did, Orville never spoke to her again.

One becomes a member of such a relational group through birth, marriage, adoption, and—in rarer cases—personal choice. The word "family"—*familia*—dates back to Roman times and means property. "Kin," "clan," and "tribe" generally refer to a group of people living together in a community and claiming a common ancestor. A group of people calling themselves a family have a unique identity, and members consider this identity an important part of their being. As writer Jane Howard (1978) put it, "Families breed us, name us, succor us, embarrass us, annoy us, drive us off toward adventures as foreign to them as we can imagine, and then they lure us back. Families collapse, but families expand. They shatter, but they heal."

THE FAMILY SOCIALIZATION PROCESS

The American family has always been *in process;* that is, it is an ever changing, dynamic force affecting the lives of its members. Aside from the obvious function of caregiving and economic support, the principal role of the family is to teach children how the world works and how to live in it. From one generation to another, family members learn the social interactions that will make them responsible members of the world into which they will venture. In a multi-cultural, expansive, class-differentiated society such as the United States, this means that there are broad differences in knowledge and human interaction between people of different economic, social, and ethnic groups. Nowhere are these differences reflected in greater measure than in the parenting process.

THE FAMILY AS A SYSTEM

In the 1940s biologist Ludwig von Bertalanffy proposed that all living systems consisted of *interrelational components*. These components help interactions work as a whole rather than as a group of parts (von Bertalanffy, 1968). According to von Bertalanffy's view, the *transactional process*, the relationship taking place among the components of a system, is of greater importance than the working of any single part of the system. For example, the human respiratory system consists of six major components, or organs: the nose, pharynx, larynx, trachea, bronchi, and lungs. The pharynx or throat is a kind of hallway for the respiratory system, but it would not function if not for the trachea, which opens enough for air to reach the lungs. The respiratory system is transactional: each part works cooperatively. An imbalance in any one of the interrelated components disturbs the functioning of the whole system.

All systems work in this transactional way, from the tiniest cell to the farthest galaxies. Human behavior is governed by the same natural processes that regulate all living things. Human beings, it is theorized, exist in complex *relational systems* called *families,* and these families function in as orderly and predictible a way as the respiratory system. Family members interrelate on an emotional level so closely that a change in one person affects the behavior of all the others.

The United States is built on a belief foundation of individualism. In this orientation, children are viewed as separate beings within their families, and their behavior at any specific time is not linked to a coincidental household happening. Parenting advice manuals sometimes offer generic suggestions about behaviors such as bedwetting or temper tantrums, implying that a specific parental action will change a child's behavior. But the bedwetting or temper tantrum has different meanings depending upon a child's age, developmental level, circumstances and family interaction. In one family, bedwetting may start when parents begin to talk about divorce. In another, the child may have an undetected illness. Temper tantrums have a myriad of causes, including frustration, tiredness, hunger, or unvalidated feelings. The causes of the frustration, tiredness, and so on, also differ from family to family.

The notion that parenting must be viewed in the context of the family comes not only from Urie Bronfrenbrenner's model of development (described in Chapter 2) but also from a theoretical perspective called *family system theory,* developed by Murray Bowen. This theory is based on the view of the family as a network of interlocking relationships, a system best understood when analyzed within a multigenerational or historical framework (Goldenberg and Goldenberg, 1996).

EMOTIONAL RELATING WITHIN FAMILIES

Murray Bowen identified a number of forces that shape the emotional-relationship system of the family. The first, *differentiation of self,* refers to the individual's ability to develop as an emotionally separate person—someone able to think, feel, and act for himself or herself within the family system (See Figure 4.1). This means that life for humans is a balancing act between individuality, or *autonomy,* and togetherness, or *fusion.* The ability to function as part of a group and as an individual is a rather tricky life task. Obviously a newborn human is completely dependent on its mother for care and nurturance. In other words, infant survival depends on emotional fusion with mother, and this fusion extends to the family. This emotional partnership lasts a lifetime although the force of the connection will differ from individual to individual even within a family. It is the variance that determines how well a person will function as an adult. In a well-differentiated family, there is no

Figure 4.1

Bowen's Differentiation of Self Scale. This scale distinguishes people according to their degree of *fusion* or *differentiation* between their emotional and intellectual selves. Bowen believed that, at 0–25, people are so emotionally fused to their families that feeling completely dominates their thinking. From 25–50 some reasoning occurs, but much of goal-directed behavior is guided by the need for approval by others. At 50–75 individuals are functioning at a reasonable level of differentiation, and they are able to think things out in times of stress rather than be overwhelmed by feelings. The range of 75–100 is compromised of a small group of people who base their decisions on reason rather than emotion. A moderate-to-high level of differentiation allows people to interact with others without fear of losing their sense of self to the relationship.

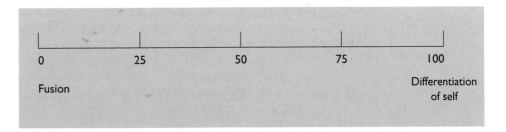

undue pressure for emotional connectedness. The child comes to view parents and siblings as distinct people with differing feelings and beliefs and learns that acceptance and approval does not depend upon "feeling" the same as everyone else in the family. In some families, however, the "togetherness force" is so strong that children are unable to separate emotionally from parents. Parental anxiety becomes a family affair; the child is pulled into the family's "emotional field" and reacts just as others do to specific situations. The rebellious adolescent is usually an *undifferentiated* child, one with a poorly developed sense of self. This child's oppositional beliefs and acting-out behaviors are a reaction to the parents' emotional immaturities.

Bowen proposed a theoretical scale for evaluating an individual's differentiation level. The scale ranges from 0, no sense of self, to 100, a strong sense of self. People at the low end of the scale are easily stressed into dysfunction; while those at the upper end function on a rational, intellectual level when confronted with stressful situations. People at the lower levels of differentiation are more likely to develop symptoms of psychological or even physical disorders.

In a stunning example, Bowen described how a 16-year-old-boy, the oldest of five children, developed cancer two years after his parents separated and divorced. The family seemed to have coped adequately until the birth of their last child, when the father began to drink heavily and had trouble keeping a job. The parent's marriage collapsed; the father moved out and stopped supporting his family. There was no help forthcoming from relatives on either side, so the mother got a job in Washington, DC, and uprooted the family from California. Shortly before the move, the mother developed serious chronic kidney problems. Although she was able to work, she increasingly relied on her oldest son,who had become a replacement for the father. Before his parents' divorce, the boy had experienced school and behavior problems; but during the two years since his parents' breakup, he had been a model son—perfectly attuned to his mother's emotional state. Within six months of the move, the youngster was diagnosed with brain cancer (Kerr and Bowen, 1988).

It is Bowen's position that the family emotional process plays an important role in the generation of problems such as autism, depression, suicide, phobias, schizophrenia, and other emotional problems that may emerge in childhood, adolescence, or early adult life. When anxiety is acted out, feelings are converted to behaviors. When anxiety is internalized and becomes an emotional symptom, feelings envelop a person's mental processes. In other words, when anxiety is externalized, the person "acts bad"; when it is internalized, the person "feels bad."

It was Bowen's goal to help parents achieve a level of differentiation of self, from each other and from their families of origin, that was high enough to allow then to learn how to parent in a way that would enable the optimal growth of children (Bowen, 1966, 1976).

While defining oneself as an individual within a family system is important for personal growth, the degree to which a person can achieve the differentiation depends on culture and even gender. Women, for example, are socialized to be concerned with and care for others to such a degree that it is sometimes difficult for them to put their own needs above those of others. In American society, differentiation and individualism are valued much more highly than in many other cultures—particularly Asian and South American.

The second force in Bowen's theory is the *triangle,* which is the basic building block in a family's emotional system (See Figure 4.2). During periods when anxiety is low and external conditions are calm, two persons may engage in a comfortable dialogue. However, the stability of the situation is threatened if one or both participants gets upset or anxious, from internal or external stress. In order to alleviate the tension, Bowen says, the twosome may "reach out" and pull in another person. The emotions may "overflow" to the third person, or that person may be emotionally "programmed" to initiate involvement. In either case, this triangle dilutes the anxiety. It is more stable and more flexible than the twosome, and it has a higher tolerance for dealing with stress. The triangle keeps any one of the relationships from "emotionally overheating." On the other hand, among parents and their children, a triangle can occur when a wife, unhappy with her husband's emotional distance, becomes increasingly involved with one of her children. Although most parents make comments from time to time—such as "Your mother is the worst driver," or "I wish your father would drink less"— complaints relayed to children about a parent set up a pattern of *triangulation.*

Bowen stresses sibling position as a clue to which child will be most emotionally attached to the parents. This is called the *family projection process.* The most attached child will have the lowest level of differentiation of self and the most difficulty separating from the family. Sometimes children are desperate to separate and employ a number of strategies. Some try geographic separation, and others rely on psychological barriers; but both are self-deceptions. Such actions make people feel "free" of their families when, in fact, they are really free only when they don't have to flee the relationship. Bowen calls this force the *emotional cutoff,* a false emancipation from unresolved emotional ties.

Figure 4.2

The Triangle. The first diagram indicates a calm relationship between persons A and B. The second diagram shows a conflict in the relationship, to the point that the more anxious person (A) draws in a third party (C). The third triangle shows that A is no longer anxious, so the conflict has shifted away from the original twosome and onto the relationship between B and C.

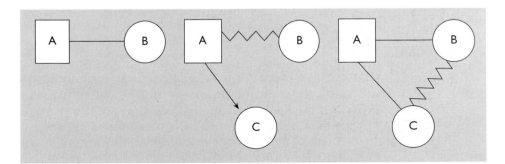

Figure 4.3a

The Genogram:
An Intergenerational
Tool

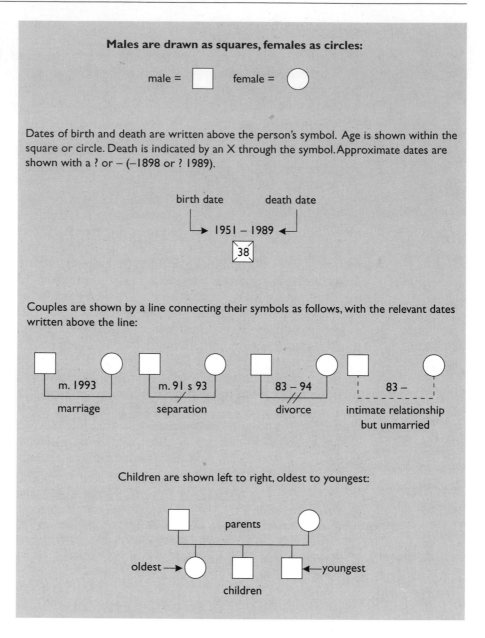

Males are drawn as squares, females as circles:

male = ☐   female = ○

Dates of birth and death are written above the person's symbol. Age is shown within the square or circle. Death is indicated by an X through the symbol. Approximate dates are shown with a ? or − (−1898 or ? 1989).

birth date   death date

1951 − 1989

38

Couples are shown by a line connecting their symbols as follows, with the relevant dates written above the line:

m. 1993   m. 91 s 93   83 − 94   83 −

marriage   separation   divorce   intimate relationship
                                                        but unmarried

Children are shown left to right, oldest to youngest:

parents

oldest →   ← youngest

children

FAMILY MAPS

One of the ways family-systems theorists learn about the intergeneration influences in parenting styles is through the construction of *genograms.* A genogram is essentially a map of one's family behavioral and social history (See Figure 4.3). Genograms were first developed by Murray Bowen in the late 1970s, as a tool for analyzing family structures. Bowen's model has been refined and standardized by Monica McGoldrick, Betty Carter, and Randy Gerson.

Figure 4.3b

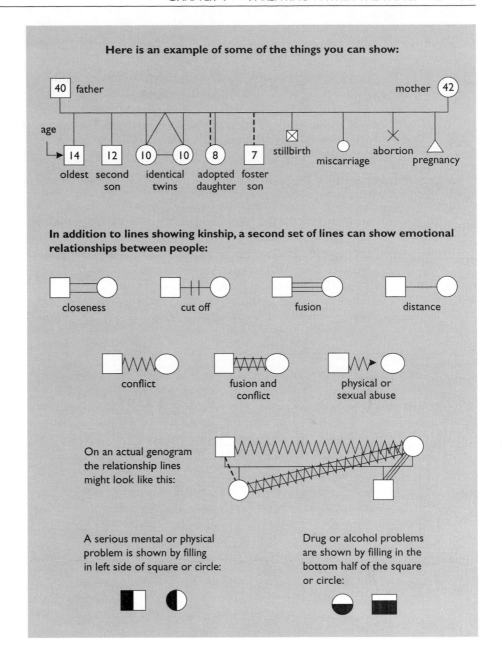

Here is an example of some of the things you can show:

In addition to lines showing kinship, a second set of lines can show emotional relationships between people:

Genograms made from a family-systems perspective are used in clinical practices when a family assessment is desired. They are composed of a series of symbols—representing factors such as gender, birth, divorce, miscarriage, and other life circumstances—developed by clinicians over a period of many years. In some ways, genograms are like family jigsaw puzzles; when the pieces are put together, it is easier to understand the complex, multigenerational patterns that characterize a particular clan. Genograms represent the story of a family's life, including the connections, secrets, and myths that impact parenting. As shown in Figure 4.3, symbols are used to denote emotional relationships such as triangles, enmeshment, and conflict.

Parental beliefs, desires, expectations, career choices, techniques, and social interactions, basically the parenting experience can be seen in the construction of this family mode.

THE STRUCTURE OF THE FAMILY

Within the parameters of ethnicity, family life flourishes throughout the world. Anthropologist Margaret Mead traveled the globe with photographer Ken Heyman. Looking into the heart of families, she wrote, "In our contemporary world, no one can think or work with a single picture of what a family is. No one can fit all human behavior, all thought and feeling, into a single pattern" (Mead and Heyman, 1965).

To truly understand how a family operates, one must look at the relationship patterns that exist between family members. Family members influence

Figure 4.4
Reading a
Genogram

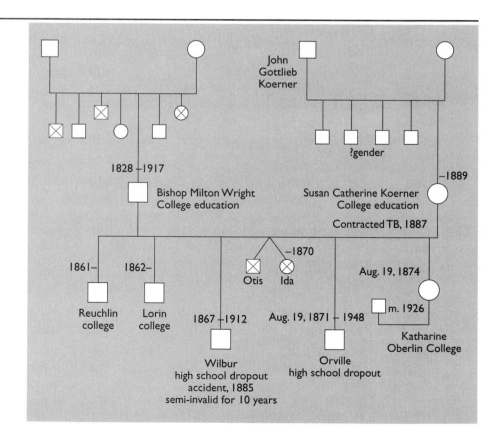

each other, and their interactions become patterns that shape the behavior of all members of the clan.

A family system is made up of coexisting subsystems, relatively stable relationships formed by generation, sex, interest, or function (Minuchin, 1974). Every member of a family belongs to several subsystems; that is, he or she has a different kind of relationship with other family members. A woman can be a wife, mother, sister, daughter, granddaughter, and grandmother all at the same time. This means playing a distinct role and interacting in each one differently. These roles sometimes conflict; for example, a child may ask his or her mother for a ride to basketball practice at the same time a husband was putting the finishing touches on a dinner for some friends. Much can be discerned about a family from noting the influence of any given subsystem. The parental subsystem largely determines the direction a family will take. And, from parental transactions, children learn about intimate relationships. If parents model kindness and consideration toward each other, children are likely to carry these behaviors into their own relationships. Inconsiderate or brutal parental relationships teach children about the harshness of interpersonal contact. Divorce or abandonment teaches a variety of lessons. In some families, the subsystems cross. For example, the oldest child is often brought into the parental subsystem when a mother tells her oldest to see that the younger ones do their homework. In families where their are marital problems, one parent may form an emotional alliance with a child, thereby creating tension between that child and the other parent.

Each subsystem has its own *boundaries* or delineations from the rest of the system, based on needs and expectations. In America, for example, one would not expect parents to double-date with their teenage son. A parent would not normally require one child to discipline another. These actions breach the borders of the parent-child and sibling subsystems. (Sometimes, however, it is necessary to mingle subsystems as in the case of grandparents who take care of their grandchildren.) Opening mail addressed to others, and listening in on phone calls not made to us, are two examples of breaching boundaries. A high school student generally will not call the principal by his or her first name unless the principal has requested this type of intimacy. Adult social interactions often depend on being able to identify boundaries. It is within the family structure that children learn the significance of interpersonal borders.

The family is a *rule-governed system* (Jackson, 1965). Each family settles on certain regulations, sometimes stated and mostly unstated but understood by all family members. For example, there may be an "unwritten rule" in the family that mother controls the money and that it's better to ask her for something after dinner when she's relaxed and in a good mood. Some families relay a silent message that sex is not to be discussed at home. In other families, speech is not regulated, even when members are screaming at each other. In some homes, it is mandated that dishes be washed immediately after use; in others, dishes can be piled in the sink until someone gets home from work and puts them in the dishwasher. In many families, specific chairs are designated for specific family members. In a well-functioning family, rules change according to needs and circumstances. Family growth can be stifled if rules become so rigid and inflexible that they do not work for the welfare of all family members.

Family life is also built upon supportive interactions and members are assigned *roles* that meet the needs and expectations of the family. These roles are based upon age, sex, and personality characteristics. Historically, roles were thought to be the function of biology. Men were seen as the stronger, more aggressive sex, and women were considered the more nurturant and dependent gender. From childhood on, families assign tasks and duties based on perceived roles. Boys may be told to take out the trash and mow the lawn, and girls expected to do the dishes and make the beds. An adult female may be counted on to make Thanksgiving dinner whether or not she is a good cook or even has any interest in to tackling this chore. An adult male might be expected to play ball with his son or fix the screen door, even if the father is not very good at or dislikes these kinds of activities. Sex-role programming teaches children how to deal with emotional feelings, what type of activities to pursue, and how to behave in relation to the other sex. Role-playing at a young age is often reflected in an adult career choice.

In societies like the United States, economic need, the feminist revolution, and rising divorce rates have led to role changes for men and women. In addition, stereotyped expectations will diminish as child rearing occupies a smaller part of many women's adult lives. Men will become increasingly involved in child care as they share more equally in the dual roles of parent and worker.

For a family to function well, it must develop clear ways of *communicating*. Family members constantly exchange information through the spoken word and through the nonverbal messages that come through gestures, facial expressions, tone of voice, and other body signs. To communicate properly,

In many families throughout the world children are considered economic assets. They are forced to work long hours in substandard conditions and are denied access to education and any degree of personal freedom.

The Spirit of Parenting

"Call me Daddy,"

"Only babies call their fathers Daddy."

"Then I'm not going to call you Daddy either," Chandler said.

"I like being called Daddy. It makes me feel adored. Girls, I want to ask you a question and I want you to answer with brutal honesty. Don't spare Daddy's feelings, just tell me what you think from the heart."

Jennifer rolled her eyes and said, "Oh, Dad, not this game again."

I said, "Who is the greatest human being you've encountered on this earth?"

"Mama," Lucy answered quickly, grinning at her father.

"Almost right," I replied. "Now let's try it again. Think of the most splendid, wonderful person you personally know. The answer should spring to your lips."

"You!" Chandler shouted.

"An angel. A pure, snow-white angel, and so smart. What do you want, Chandler? Money? Jewels? Furs? Stocks and bonds? Ask anything, darling, and your loving Daddy will get it for you."

Pat Conroy
from *The Prince of Tides*

contact must be maintained, all parties must share the same focus of attention, and they must derive the same meaning from what is being presented. When parents communicate with each other and with their children in clear and direct ways, their children develop the cognitive capacities to express their feelings and problem solve efficiently (Wynne, Jones and Al-Khayyal, 1982). If families have poor communication skills, parents often employ the silent treatment when angry, avoid eye contact when distressed, watch TV when uninterested in conversation, or leave the room when unwilling to work on a problem. Poor communication is the major complaint of families that seek professional help.

THE WELL-FUNCTIONING FAMILY

In *The Brothers Karamozov,* Russian novelist Dostoyevsky wrote, "From the house of my parents I have brought nothing but pleasant memories, for there are no memories more precious than those of one's early childhood in one's own home, and that is almost always so, if there is any love and harmony in the family at all. Indeed, precious memories may be retained even from a bad home as long as your heart is capable of finding anything precious." What Dostoyevsky knew is that while family life differs markedly from home to home, successful child rearing is marked by commonalties no matter what the context. In recent years, the terms *functional* and *dysfunctional* have been used to distinguish between families that interact in ways beneficial to all members and families who

TABLE 4.1 Family Health Scale: Relationships and Coalition Among Family Members

	Breakdown	Dysfunctional	Adequate	Optimal
PATTERN OF RELATIONSHIPS	Serious deficiencies: marked splits, scapegoating, severe triangulation, or isolation of all family members.	Serious discord or distance between members, or shifting or exclusive alignments. Children repeatedly detour parental tension or conflicts.	Satisfactory relationships but with greater closeness or distance between some family members than others.	The nature and strength of relationships between family members is constructive and appropriate to their respective ages and roles.
MARITAL RELATIONSHIP	Destructive relationship, e.g., couple fused, at war, or isolated from one another.	Overt marital difficulties, or both partners dissatisfied.	Basically satisfactory with some areas of discontent.	Mature relationship: warm, supportive, affectionate, empathic, compatible; spouses work together well.
PARENTAL RELATIONSHIP	Parents not working together at all, or extremely weak, divisive, or conflicted relationship.	Parents repeatedly disagree, act without reference to one another, or one parent repeatedly takes over or opts out.	Basic agreement on child rearing but with some deficiencies in support and/or working together.	Strong parental coalition; agreement and cooperation in child rearing; sharing of pleasure and mutual support.
PARENT-CHILD RELATIONSHIP	Both parents reject, ignore, exploit, continuously attack, or disqualify a child.	Parental attitudes and behaviors are clearly unsupportive or harmful; poor understanding of the children.	Parents support children and enjoy being with them but with minor or occasional problems in relating to the children.	Parents show care and concern; understand and pay attention to children appropriately; and are ready to participate in their activities.
CHILD-PARENT RELATIONSHIP	Children avoid, reject, continually oppose, or cling to parent(s); or show marked differentiation in their attitudes toward each parent.	One or more children show oppositional, withdrawn, overdependent, or domineering behavior toward parent(s).	Child-parent relationships are secure, but with mild difficulties in some areas or between particular dyads.	Children relate to both parents; are cooperative yet spontaneous; feel safe and show appropriate dependence.
SIBLING RELATIONSHIPS	Sibs fight continuously or ignore each other, extreme rivalry and competition for the parents' attention.	Obvious discord or distance between the sibs.	Sibs affiliate with some limited rivalry, quarreling, or lack of contact.	Sibs interact freely with shared enjoyment, affection, concern; differences can be resolved.

are unable to meet the needs of their members. Taking into consideration the variation due to ethnicity, there remains the question of what constitutes a "normal," well-functioning family, no matter what its background or heritage. Theorists Arnon Bentovim and Warren Kinston (1987) devised a series of scales that measure family functioning. These *Family Health Scales* include *optimal, adequate, dysfunctional*, and *breakdown* levels, which are based upon the relationships or coalition among family members and the degree to which parents are successful in nurturing and socializing their children. (See Tables 4.1 and 4.2).

COPING WITH FAMILY PROBLEMS

Salvador Minuchin cautioned that all families have problems. He said, "an ordinary family; that is, the couple has many problems of relating to one another, bringing up children, dealing with in-laws, and coping with the outside

TABLE 4.2   Family Health Scale: Tasks Related to Nurturing and Socializing Children

	Breakdown	Dysfunctional	Adequate	Optimal
CONFLICT RESOLUTION	Conflicts are denied or ignored, lead to continuous futile arguments, or to withdrawal and breakdown of communication.	Poorly handled conflicts disrupt completion of tasks. Members become embroiled in the conflicts of others.	Conflicts generally acknowledged and resolved, but occasional overreaction, denial, or lack of resolution.	Conflicts acknowledged and resolved by negotiation and compromise between the relevant participants.
DECISION MAKING	Decision making is severely impaired: no recognition of need for decisions; lack of acceptance of result; no action on decisions.	Making decisions is a problem for the family. The process is often disrupted or ineffective.	Decisions are generally taken and acted upon where necessary, but with occasional difficulties or dissatisfaction.	Decision processes are clear, involve members appropriately, produce satisfaction, and outcomes are accepted.
PROBLEM SOLVING	Lack of capacity for solving problems in an effective way.	Problems often not recognized, or response is delayed, inadequate, uncoordinated, or impulsive.	Problems are tackled but somewhat inflexibly, inefficiently, or simplistically.	Problems accurately perceived, tackled with flexibility and good sense; spirit of cooperation.
CHILD MANAGEMENT	Behavioral control is absent, chaotic, bizarre, or ruthless.	Overt problems managing children; unrealistic or inconsistent expectations.	Children handled fairly well, but some difficulties or inappropriate expectations.	Expectations of the children are realistic and control is flexible yet consistent.

world. Like all families, they are constantly struggling with these problems and negotiating the compromises that make a life in common possible" (Minuchin, 1974). Minuchin believes that the way a family is structured—the power hierarchy, mutual expectations, and rules—will determine the success of family life. In other words, 1) there must be a strong parental system in place so that child-rearing tasks can be successfully accomplished. 2) boundaries between subsystems must be clearly defined; and 3) the family must have the ability to adapt to the changing developmental needs of its members, as well as changes in the outside world.

Jay Haley (1980) views a family's problem-solving abilities as the primary indicator of its health. A family undergoes transitions due to changes in the ecosystem and the developmental passages of its members. The success of a transition depends on the openness and flexibility of family members and their ability to handle the problems that come from change. For example, a child's leaving home is often a major family event. The family can help the child on his or her way, or it can get so "stuck" in the crisis of change that symptoms such as substance abuse or behavioral acting-out by a family member results.

One of the best known assessments of family functioning is the Timberlawn study of healthy families (Lewis, Beavers, Gossett, and Phillips, 1976). Convinced that it is more important to understand the transactional patterns of competent families than to focus on unhealthy families, the researchers videotaped volunteer families that had at least one adolescent living at home and no family members undergoing psychiatric care. The families were given a series of tasks which were rated for competency, and then each family was categorized as "healthy," "mid-range,"or "severely dysfunctional." The study included a number of dimensions: family power structure, strength of the parental coalition, degree to which family members took individual responsibility for their actions, degree of autonomy and self-expression allowed, clarity of boundaries between family members, ability to express intimacy, degree of comfort and joy shared by family members, level of family conflict, and sensitivity of family members to each other's feelings. The volunteer families were compared to a group that was similar in structure but included an adolescent hospitalized in a private psychiatric hospital. In reviewing the Timberlawn data, Beavers (1977) proposed that the effectiveness of families can be arranged along a continuum. In highly functioning families, members are open, caring, and trusting. They value contact with each other, respect individuality, and are able to disagree or have conflict without harming the relationship. In healthy families, the power resides in the parental coalition; however, children are able to express their opinions and negotiate for their views without getting involved in a power struggle. Family members adapt realistically to loss and change. They are flexible and goal-directed. Relationships are built upon good humor, caring, warmth, and feelings of hope.

In mid-range families, parental coalitions are weak and unstable. Unresolved power issues surface, and intimidation and control mark the parent-child interactions. Attempts to communicate often lead to an invalidation of feelings. For example, the remark "I hate school" might be answered with "No, you don't. That's a silly thing to say." Relationships between family members are marked by competition, and an undercurrent of frustration and conflict is present. Beliefs may be so rigid that any change is resisted. Children in the family become "fixed" in stereotyped roles and have a limited chance of developing their individuality.

In the dysfunctional family, it is often difficult to distinguish the parents from the children. Parents do not form a coalition, individuality is discouraged, boundaries are unclear, and communication is confused. The family is unable to negotiate its differences, and interactions are hurtful and destructive. Feelings of warmth, good humor, caring, and empathy are notably lacking among family members.

Family therapist Virginia Satir (1988) proposed that unhealthy families have characteristics in common. Their self-worth is low; communication is indirect, unclear, and often dishonest; family rules are rigid, unfair, nonnegotiable, and permanent; the family has a fearful, appeasing, and often blaming relationship with the community.

Helm Stierlin (1972) proposed that, regardless of their competency level, families differ in their interaction styles. Some families are *centripetal*, which means there is a tendency for members to seek gratification predominantly from within the family. They are not comfortable going beyond family boundaries and into the outside world. At the extreme, centripetal families make it difficult for the children to leave home or develop relationships outside the family. In particular, adolescents are discouraged from separating. Centripetal families repress, suppress, or deny their negative feelings about each other, and they emphasize positive aspects of family life in order to promote togetherness. Children in centripetal families have difficulty in developing a sense of personal identity distinct from that of other family members. Beavers believes that, at the mid-range level of functioning, centripetal families produce anxious children. At a severely dysfunctional level, this type of family can produce one or more schizophrenic children.

Centrifugal families seek gratification outside the family rather than from within it. They trust relationships beyond family boundaries. At the extreme, centrifugal families oust their offspring, sometimes before they are developmentally ready to stand on their own. These families display more anger and negativism than they do affection. Their children tend to distance themselves from their families, turning to peers for needed support. Beavers believes that at the mid-range of family functioning, centrifugal families produce children who exhibit behavioral disorders. At the extreme range, they produce children who can become sociopathic and are prone to behavior that is antisocial, irresponsible, impulsive, and sometimes criminal.

The Timberlawn-Beavers study has limitations, in that its subjects were all from white, middle-class, intact families. Families were rated as "healthy" if there was an absence of emotional disturbance defined by a lack of psychiatric treatment. Furthermore, observation by videotaping most likely influences the behavior of subjects. Despite these criticisms, the Beavers work clarifies many of the characteristics that make up a well-functioning family.

In the late 1950s, researchers at McGill University in Canada began work on a family assessment technique that was refined over a period of 25 years both at McGill and Brown University in Rhode Island (Epstein, Bishop, and Baldwin, 1982). Called the *McMaster Model of Family Functioning,* the assessment focuses on three dimensions of family functioning. The *basic task area* refers to how family members handle money, food, shelter, transportation, and other necessities of life. The *developmental task area* deals with the reactions to changes that occur over time, including a birth or terminal illness in the family or a child getting ready to leave home. The *hazardous task area* refers to methods of handling serious crises that result from the loss of a job, a sudden and serious illness, or an accident. The McMaster group paid particular attention to six dimensions of family functioning and noted the healthiest responses.

1. **Problem Solving:**   How does the family solve the problems that arise? All families have problems, but, effectively functioning families resolve problems in a way that maintains optimal family functioning. Families that are able to problem solve most effectively do so in a systematic way. They clearly identify the problem, communicate with appropriate people about it, develop a set of alternative solutions, choose one of the alternatives, carry it out, and then evaluate the effectiveness of the solution.

2. **Communication:**   How is information exchanged among members of the family? In effective families, messages between members are clear and direct. People say what they mean and present their ideas to the appropriate individual—the one for whom the message is intended.

3. **Roles:**   What roles do individual family members play, and how are roles assigned? Family members use patterns of behavior to fulfill functions such as providing money and shelter, nurturing and comforting individuals, satisfying sexual needs, encouraging personal development, making decisions, and handling household tasks. In effectively functioning families, there is a clear and appropriate designation of roles. A person assigned to a task or function possesses the power and skill needed to carry out the assignment. Family members are satisfied with the distribution of the tasks; no one person is overburdened by the tasks of family life.

4. **Affective Responsiveness:**   Are family members able to respond to a specific situation with the appropriate quality and quantity of feelings? In families that function effectively, emotions such as love, joy, anger, disappointment, and sadness are experienced with reasonable intensity and duration and in a way that is not seriously disruptive to the family as a whole.

5. **Affective Involvement:**   How much interest does the family show in the activities of individual family members? Are the interests of members age-appropriate? In effectively functioning families there is active involvement and sincere interest but members do not get overly entangled in the activities of others.

6. Behavior Control: How does the family handle the behavior of members in situations that have to do with meeting biological needs, facing physical danger, and interacting socially? In effectively functioning families, behavior rules are clear, reasonable, and appropriate to the context of a situation. Parents are able to express their expectations of their children and each other. There is room for negotiation and change when the need arises.

A McGill University study carried out from 1955 to 1964 focused on the relationships between college students and their families. The study stressed that a strong, warm, supportive relationship between parents is the factor that most affects children's emotional health and happiness. Over the past thirty years there has been a rapid rise of the one-parent family, the blended family, the extended family and so on. Nonetheless, it stands to reason that the traditional family traits that were deemed important three decades ago—love, concern, encouragement, support, open communication, appropriate behavioral standards, and fair treatment—are all traits that continue to serve to foster effective family life today.

THE CHANGING FAMILY LIFE CYCLE

Only a couple of generations ago, child rearing occupied parents for almost their entire adult lives. Today, because of low birth rates and the long life span of most adults, this task takes up half that span, leaving parents with many years to contemplate and fulfill other goals. Responding to this change is difficult for parents who have defined themselves in terms of family responsibilities.

Betty Carter and Monica McGoldrick (1988) pointed out that life today is built upon transitions. So many entrances and exits, departures and returns,

Healthy families show interest in the activities of all family members—without the intense parental emotional involvement that is often seen at the sporting events of young children.

The Informed Parent 4.1

The Behavior and Values of Healthy Families

- *Display of love and acceptance.* Family members show their love and appreciation of one another. This acceptance and warmth is expressed spontaneously—physically (smile, touch, hug) or verbally ("I love you," "You're a good son/daughter"). Family members cooperate rather than compete with one another.

- *Communicativeness.* Family members are spontaneous, honest, open, and receptive to one another. They express negative as well as positive feelings. Conflicts are faced and handled, not repressed or denied into resentment.

- *Cohesiveness.* Family members enjoy spending time together. They share chores, resources, and recreational activities. They respect individual differences and encourage autonomy and independence.

- *Communication of values and standards.* Parents have definite and clear values, and they make them known to their children. These values and standards are discussed and practiced. There is also tolerance and respect for individual differences. Parents are models as well as teachers.

- *Ability to cope effectively with problems.* Stress and crisis are faced optimistically with the purpose of finding solutions. Alternatives are explored, and family members are mutually supportive.

and losses and gains are experienced in modern families that it is difficult for parents and children to negotiate this much change. As children grow and develop, parents "must shift to a less hierarchical form of relating." This shift often becomes a familiar problem because some parents encourage their adult children to be dependent and some young adults remain overly dependent or else rebel and break away in a move they believe is a strike for independence.

> The shift toward adult-to-adult status requires a mutually respectful and personal form of relating, in which young adults can appreciate parents as they are, needing neither to make them into what they are not nor to blame them for what they could not be. Neither do young adults need to comply with parental expectations and wishes at their own expense (Carter and McGoldrick,1988).

Marriage, or any other kind of union between two adults, unites two different family systems and creates a third subsystem. When children are

born into the union and the parents become caretakers to a younger generation, problems may accompany this shift. Some parents struggle with the new
responsibility, and others have an inability to behave as parents. Carter and
McGoldrick observed that "often parents find themselves unable to set limits
and exert the required authority, or they lack the patience to allow their children to express themselves as they develop." When parents make such statements as "my four-year-old is impossible to control," they are usually not accepting the generational boundary between themselves and the child. Having
children also necessitates some realignment of relationships with extended
families on both sides. Aunts, uncles, cousins, and grandparents become a part
of the new family system, albeit different from when the couple were childless.
In the face of dominant grandparents, new parents may have trouble staying
"in charge" of their children. This is particularly true when parents and
children live with grandparents, which has become increasingly common in
single-parent families.

Married couples tend to underestimate the upheaval that comes with the
birth of a first child. Working women leave their jobs as the pregnancy progresses. However, about 43 percent of new mothers returned to work within
three months, and 69 percent within twelve months. Even where there may
have been a relatively equal division of labor at home before the birth of a
child, household and child-care responsibilities become the primary job of the
mother (Ruble, et al., 1988). One study reported that the changes a baby brings
leads to a short honeymoon of one or two months, after which there is sometimes a drop in marital satisfaction (Cowan, et al., 1991). Because time becomes so limited in families where parents work and care for children, parents
have less opportunity for sleep, leisure, and sex. Researchers have reported also
that the baby's personality influences marital satisfaction. An infant who cries
a lot has a negative effect on both parents' self-perceptions. This is especially
true for fathers, although a father's dissatisfaction may have more to do with
the marital relationship than the parenting one (Belsky, et al., 1991).

Lucy Fischer has studied the effects of parenthood on the mother-
daughter and in-law relationships. The birth of a child usually decreases conflict with one's own mother, it often increases conflict with a mother-in-law
(Fischer, 1983). The reason for this change is that—while both grandmothers
give parenting advice—that offered by a woman's mother is often solicited and
therefore welcome, and that offered by a mother-in-law is often uninvited and
therefore seen as intrusive.

When children reach adolescence, the roles of parent and children take on
a different meaning. Parents must transform their view of the parenting
process enough to allow their children increased independence. At the same
time, they must maintain appropriate boundaries and structure in the family's
life. Adolescence is also a time when children begin to establish independent
relationships with extended family members, in particular grandparents. These
adjustments are especially difficult to make in today's world because there are
no built-in rituals, no markers, to guide such transitions.

Parents can no longer maintain complete authority. Adolescents can and do open the family to a whole array of new values as they bring friends and new ideals into the family arena. Families that become derailed at this stage may be rather closed to new values and threatened by them and they are frequently stuck in an earlier view of their children. They may try to control every aspect of their lives at a time when, developmentally, this is impossible to do successfully. Either the adolescent withdraws from the appropriate involvements for this developmental stage, or the parents become increasingly frustrated with what they perceive as their own impotence (Carter and McGoldrick, 1988).

What makes this phase of the parent-child saga even more difficult is the "mid-life transitions" that parents are experiencing. Sometimes mothers begin menopause just as their children begin experimenting sexually; often parents' marriage arrangements are being renegotiated, sometimes with separation or divorce the result; and parents' careers may be generating feelings of dissatisfaction or stagnation. Adolescence is also often the time when grandparents become increasingly in need of care and attention.

Of course, there is no such thing as a typical family. Ethnicity, religion, social class, and other factors determine the timing and circumstance of family transitions. It is not unusual today for children to graduate from college and return home to live with their parents. In some families, three and sometimes four generations share the same space. But whatever the home configuration, the children in families grow up; and as they do, parents must make appropriate cognitive and behavioral changes.

FAMILY VALUES: THE SPIRITUAL LIFE OF CHILDREN

One of the subjects somewhat neglected in the literature of developmental psychology is that of spirituality, especially as it relates to children. Psychiatrist Robert Coles, who spent seven years interviewing more than 1,000 children, believes that children have a powerful curiosity about where they come from and where they're going. Coles found that how children focus on aspects of religious experience depends on their religious orientations. Jewish children were interested in righteousness; Christian children were concerned with redemption and salvation; and Islamic youngsters emphasized obedience and submission. Coles believes that children are being taught neither what religion represents nor what various religious traditions have to offer. He believes schools should teach the history of the great religions; their cultural, asthetic, intellectual, moral, and spiritual aspects. He does not advocate teaching a specific religion, which is against the law in the United States, but instead teaching *about* religion and spirituality and their effects on peoples lives.

Chapter Review

- Human beings are born into tribes, clans, and families. It is within families that individuals learn values, gender roles, beliefs, expectations, attitudes, and social skills.

- In a multi-cultural, expansive, class-differentiated society such as the United States, there are broad differences in knowledge and human interaction between people of different economic, social, and ethnic groups.

Nowhere are these differences reflected in greater measure than in the parenting process.

- Human beings exist in complex relational systems called families, and these families function in as orderly and predictable a way as does the respiratory system or the solar system. Family members interrelate on an emotional level so closely that a change in one person affects the behavior of all the others.

- Family life is a balancing act between individuality, or autonomy, and togetherness, or fusion. Differentiation of self refers to the individual's ability to develop as an emotionally separate person—someone able to think, feel, and act as an individual within the family system.

- One of the ways that family-systems theorists learn about intergeneration influences on parenting styles is through the construction of a **genogram**, a map of one's family, behavioral, and social history.

- A family system is made up of coexisting subsystems, relatively stable relationships that are formed by generation, sex, interest, or function. The parental subsystem determines the direction a family will take. Each subsystem has its own boundaries: delineations between itself and the rest of the system, based on needs and expectations.

- Family life is built upon supportive interactions, and members are assigned roles that meet the needs and expectations of the family. These roles are based upon age, sex, and personality characteristics. From childhood on, families assign tasks and duties based on perceived roles.

- For a family to function well it must develop clear ways of communicating. Members of families are constantly exchanging information, not only through words but also through gestures, facial expressions, tone of voice, and other body signs.

- The primary determiner of a family's health is its problem-solving ability. The success of a transition depends on the openness and flexibility of family members and their ability to handle the problems that stem from change.

- Unhealthy families have characteristics in common. Their self-worth is low; communication is indirect, unclear, and often dishonest; family rules are rigid, unfair, nonnegotiable, and permanent; the family has a fearful, appeasing, and often blaming relationship with the community.

- Some families are centripetal, which means that members tend to seek gratification predominantly from within the family. Centrifugal families seek gratification from outside the family.

- Family life today is built upon transitions. The modern family experiences so many entrances and exits, departures and returns, and losses and gains, that it is difficult for parents and children to negotiate this much change.

Student Activities

Constructing a Genogram

To construct a genogram, you need only a piece of paper, a pencil, a key to symbols, and a family. You can get the information you need from family members, diaries, the family Bible, immigration papers, photographs, journals, scrapbooks, property records, etc. Interview your grandparents at length, asking specific questions about their backgrounds and lives.

Specifically look for repetitive symptoms, relationship or functioning patterns seen across the family and over the generations. These patterns include conflict, coalitions, triangles, and cutoffs. Note coincidences of dates such as the death of a family member falling on the date of another family event or an illness appearing at a special point in the family's history. Watch for untimely changes, such as a birth or marriage. *Do only what you are comfortable with. This is for your own enjoyment and information.*

Possible questions for each family member are:

When and where were you born?

How old were your parents at the time of your birth?

Were they married? When? Where?

Do you have siblings? How old? What is their birth order?

What kind of work do family members do?

Where did family members grow up?

How far did people in the family go in their education?

Are there adoptions, foster children, miscarriages, deaths of children in your family?

Are there separations or divorces?

What did family members die of? When? What age?

What religious and ethnic backgrounds exist in your family?

How did your parents meet? What did their respective families think of their relationship?

Is there remarriage in the family? Blended, extended families?

Note issues like custody, jealousy, favoritism, loyalty conflict, and rivalries.

Who did grandparents live with? Who inherited their estate?

How are in-laws viewed?

What kind of problems have been common in your family?

Have there been traumatic events in the family?

How are conflicts managed?

Helping Hands

National Coalition Against Domestic Violence
P.O. Box 34103
Washington, DC 20043-4103
Hotline (800) 799-7233
http://www.ncadv.org/about.htm

Dedicated to the elimination of personal and societal violence against women and their children.

CHAPTER

Parenting in Transition

Chapter Highlights

After reading Chapter 5, students should be able to:

- Identify the changing meaning of parenthood
- Understand the difficult role of the single parent
- Recognize the special nature of the stepparented family
- Understand the many and varied parenting situations that exist today

Chapter Contents

- The Changing American Family
  The Dual-Income Family ■ *Effects on Children of Dual-Income Parenting* ■
  The Single-Parent Family ■ *Single Motherhood: Myths and Realities* ■
  Stress and the Single Mother ■ *Custodial Fathers* ■ *The Dilemma*
  of the Noncustodial Father ■ *Teenage Mothers*
- Stepparenting: A Family Challenge
  Stages of the Stepparenting Family ■ *The Role of the Stepparent*
- Special Parenting
  Grandparents as Parents ■ *Gay Parenting* ■ *Adoptive Families*

INTRODUCTION

During the 1960s a Texas journalist named Liz Carpenter became press secretary to Lady Bird Johnson, the wife of Lyndon Johnson, the president of the United States. Thirty years later, when she was 71 and her children were in their forties, Mrs. Carpenter became the mother of three adolescents who were the children of her brother, who died of cancer at age 79. "A funny thing happened to me on the way to the nursing home," the late-in-life mother quipped. But in a more serious vein she also asked herself, "Could I do it? Physically? Mentally? Emotionally?" (Carpenter, 1995).

In a world that has changed the meaning of parenthood, this is the question many parents ask. Increasingly, grandparents are taking in the children of their offspring because of drug use, AIDS, mental illness, and a host of other problems that natural parents are experiencing. More and more gay couples are adopting children. Increasing numbers of single people are giving birth to and adopting children and raising them without the benefit of mates. Children are growing up in communal settings where parenting chores are shared by a number of adults. The children of divorce are dividing their lives between two parents and two homes. The number of children born to adolescents has increased substantially. Children are being raised in extended and blended families, often with a stepparent the primary caregiver. What are the implications of such dramatic social change? What is the parental role in such unusual settings? What do these changes mean to the children raised in such varying contexts? American tradition has long assumed that child rearing is most successful in a two-parent home with one parent, usually the mother, at home. This is a tradition that is being challenged by researchers who are examining the diversity of home environments and the multiplicity of parenting circumstances.

THE CHANGING AMERICAN FAMILY

Letty Cottin Pogrebin (1983) proposed that a family consists of "at least one child and one adult who live together and who make emotional claims on each other." Today there are *nuclear families* made up of a father, mother, and their children; *single-parent families,* consisting of one parent who may or may not be married, and one or more children; *blended families,* generally two divorced or widowed people marrying, with each bringing children to the new union; *homosexual families,* people of the same sexual orientation who have come together to live as a unit with or without children; and *extended families,* which include one- or two-parent arrangements, the children they have, and additional relatives such as a grandmother or friends who are considered part of the family. There are also *communal families,* groups of unrelated people who choose to live together, and *cohabiting families,* made up of unmarried couples, who live together with one or more of their children (See Table 5.1).

Today's families can consist of children from two or more marriages or relationships and a vast assortment of relatives.

TABLE 5.1   American Children and Their Parents in the 1990s

Between 1960 and 1990, changes in the economic and social environment have greatly impacted the parent-child experience.

1960		1990
5%	Children born to unmarried mothers	28%
7%	Children under 3 living with one parent	27%
90%	Children under 3 living with both parents	71%
2%	Children under 3 living with divorced parent	4%
Less than 1 %	Children under 18 experiencing parental divorce	Almost 50%
17%	Mothers returning to work within a year of a child's birth	53%
10%	Children under 18 living in one-parent family	25%
28/1000	Infant death before age 1	9/1000
27%	Children under 18 living below poverty line	21%
18.6%	Married women with children under age 6 in labor force	60%

Source: Carnegie Corporation Report; U.S. Census Bureau.

THE DUAL-INCOME FAMILY

Children who grew up in the 1950s watched "The Ozzie and Harriet Show," a nuclear-family situation comedy. The mother on the show was a homemaker, responsible for the upkeep of the house, the care of the children and the general well-being of the family, and even neighbors and friends. The father went out to make the family's living, providing food, shelter, clothes, appliances, and most of the other things his wife and children desired. Many children, particularly white and middle-class, thought this is how life would be for them. Forty years later, only 15 percent of American households have a mother at home full-time and a father who is the sole source of income (Swiss and Walker, 1993). Although many working mothers would prefer to be full-time homemakers, the economic realities of modern life have made this impossible. Thus, the advent of the two-parent both-employed family, one in which both parents work full-time, run a household, and raise children. It is estimated that 70 percent of women with children between ages 6 and 17 are in the workforce, an increase of 80 percent since 1970. The number of women coming into today's highly technical work world with a college degree is rising 1.5 times faster than the rate of well-educated men joining the work force. Professions such as law, medicine, and business are seeing an influx of women, of whom a majority will have at least one child during their working years (Swiss and Walker, 1993).

Some researchers have divided the two-parent family into categories of *dual-career* and *dual-income*. Dual-career couples are generally both professionals, working in fields such as law and medicine. These couples tend to delay childbirth until the woman's career is well established, and they then generally have one or two children. Often the women are in their thirties or even forties before giving birth. Economically well-off, dual-career parents generally have the same set of values and goals for their family, and they are both committed to parenting. Although they try to create a shared, egalitarian partnership in household and child care, in reality this is seldom accomplished (Spitze, 1991).

Life was never like Ozzie and Harriet for working-class and poor families, where working is more about survival than career development. Women often return to work soon after the birth of a baby, because it is this second income that keeps the family economically afloat. Sociologist Arlie Hochschild (1989), who has written extensively about what she calls "the second shift," found that men who were willing to share child-care duties with their wives did so because they were striving not to be like their own detached, absent, or overbearing fathers. Helpful fathers often had wives who encouraged their husbands' child-caring involvement and fostered a positive relationship between the fathers and children.

The problems of work overload and role conflict occur in dual-career and dual-income families. One survey found dual-earner couples spend an average of 16.7 hours a day working at home and on the job (Spitze, 1991). Women work approximately 15 hours longer a week than men (Hochschild, 1989). Some female physicians work as much as 70 to 80 hours a week, leaving little time for parenting or homemaking (Izraeli, 1989).

Signs of overload for working parents include fatigue, guilt over the limited time spent with the children, worry about job performance, and concern for the marital relationship. This multiple-role stress has been associated with both physical and emotional illness (Guelzow, et al., 1991).

The work world greatly impacts the parent-child relationship. Long work hours, heavy work loads, job stagnation, inflexibility in scheduling, all these put strain on a working parent. This kind of stress promotes a harsh home environment as a parent's mood affects how responsive he or she is to the children, the degree of punishment that is used, and the relationship of the parents to each other (Menaghan and Pardel, 1991). Dual-career parents promote self-reliance, independence, achievement, and psychological well-being in their children. They include their children in vacation planning, hobbies, and weekend family activities. The daughters of career mothers tend to do better academically than daughters of mothers who have not had career success. Working-class parents have different expectations of their children. They emphasize obedience, neatness, and respect for authority. Interestingly, household chores are divided along gender lines in both types of families. Daughters do 7.5 hours more chores per week at home than boys do.

EFFECTS ON CHILDREN OF DUAL-INCOME PARENTING

Regardless of the need for two-income families and the satisfaction of working parents, the concern is for the well-being of the children left at home, in day care, and in school. To date, research has not identified a universal, predictable result of child-care location, except to note that many conditions results from both parents being away from home during the day. Jay Belsky and Michael Rovin, who reviewed five studies on middle-class families, reported that more than 20 hours a week in nonmaternal care during the first year of a child's life was "associated with patterns of attachment that are commonly regarded as evidence of insecurity." Special circumstances were tied to this finding, factors such as being a boy, having a difficult temperament from birth, having a mother who is dissatisfied with her marriage, having a mother who is insensitive to the needs of others, and not having a father as an alternative caregiver. Relatively few children fit this extensive criteria. High-quality day care promotes child development in areas of language ability and socialization. Unfortunately, such care is elusive for the working class and the poor .

Arlie Hochschild is adamant that the work world will have to change in order to accommodate the needs of dual-income families. She says, "I would like to see every parent get job relief for the period of parenthood. This could be done, and it wouldn't be a loss of productivity for the company. It takes some creative thinking and coordinating of work schedules, but I think we need something that profound to really address the problems of modern parents."

THE SINGLE-PARENT FAMILY

The generic term *single-parent family* actually represents a number of different parenting arrangements, each reflecting a unique style of relating and coping in a unique social and environmental context. Single parenting can be the result of separation or divorce of parents, the death of a parent, absence of one parent due to illness or war duty, or a birth arising out of wedlock. A single-parent family may also be a grandparent raising grandchildren or an unmarried or unattached individual who has adopted a child.

Single parenting is a historical phenomena, as prior to the twentieth century the high mortality rate of mothers often left children in the care of their newly single fathers (Katz, 1979). In addition, before the late 1800s societal views and the legal system declared children to be the property of their father; in cases of divorce it was the father who claimed the children. About one-fourth of children born at the turn of the century lost a parent by the age of fifteen; some lost both parents. Children then lived with a surviving parent or were placed in foster homes and orphanages. The custody pendulum began to swing to the other extreme by the mid-1800s. The industrialization of the work world was taking fathers out of the house. Women and children were no longer seen as a man's property, the women's suffrage movement was gaining strength, and Sigmund Freud's views of the importance of early mothering were becoming popularized. For the next hundred years, judges relied on a "tender age" doctrine that stressed the mother-child bond, and they generally awarded parental custody to the mother.

In recent years, the courts have dropped the notion that one gender or another is best suited to parent a child, and while they have moved toward the problematic standard of "in the best interests of the child," in reality mothers have been favored over fathers. In 1989, approximately six and one-half million women headed households in which a child under age 18 lived. This was a 20 percent increase over a 1980 figure. By 1989, over one million single parent households were headed by men, an amazing 73 percent increase since 1980 (U.S. Bureau of the Census, 1991). This means that over those fifteen years, father-led families were the most rapidly growing form of child rearing in society. In this context, scientific debate has centered upon the relative competency levels of mothers and fathers living without each other.

More sons live in single-father households than daughters. This is because fathers are more likely to seek custody of sons than daughters, and the courts are increasingly willing to grant same-sex requests (Guttman, 1989). This preference is rooted in social learning theory and the belief that boys model and identify with their fathers and girls with their mothers, and that same-sex parents better understand the feelings and needs of a child (Gately and Schwebel, 1991). It has also been believed that the child's resemblance to a noncustodial parent may cause conflict in the relationship between the custodial parent and an opposite-sex child, or that an opposite-sex child tends to be burdened with a custodian parent's emotional needs. There is no conclusive evidence to date concerning any of these same-sex parenting speculations. There is some evidence, however, that girls in father-only households have higher educational aspirations and greater access to advanced educational tools such as computers than do girls living in mother-only homes. As a result girls in father-only families score higher on school exams. Since single fathers generally have better income levels than single mothers, the daughter-father advantage is not

Figure 5.1
Single Mothers
with Children
Under 18

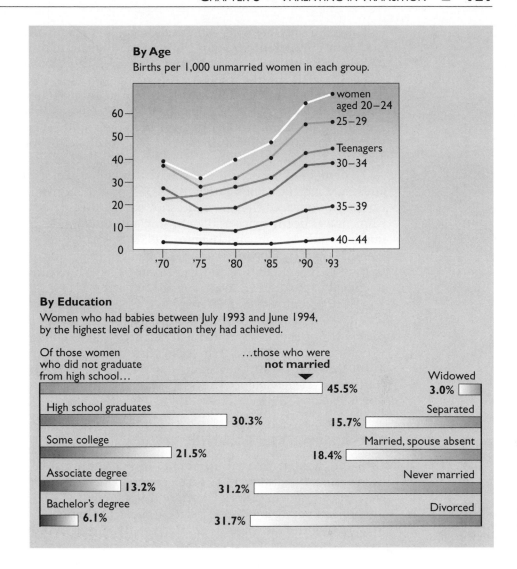

By Age
Births per 1,000 unmarried women in each group.

By Education
Women who had babies between July 1993 and June 1994,
by the highest level of education they had achieved.

due to parenting skills but rather is due more to the socioeconomic environment (Downey and Powell, 1993).

The absence of the second parent in single-parent homes decreases the time a child has with his or her custodial parent because that parent is overly burdened with the chores of work and running a household (Coleman, 1988). A study comparing the quality of family time spent by 396 adolescents from single-parent and married-parent families found that while children in single-parent families spend less time with both parents simultaneously they often spend more time with their mothers or with their mothers and siblings together than do the children from married-parent families. These children may also spend more time with extended kin such as grandparents than do children from two-parent families. During the time children from single-parent families are with their mothers, they are more likely to be doing household tasks such as shopping for food or tidying up. However, children from single-parent families who spend time with their noncustodial fathers spend more of that time in leisure activities such as eating and talking. Interestingly, adolescents in single-parent families perceive both their mothers and fathers as more friendly than do adolescents in married-parent families (Asmussen and Larson, 1991).

A number of research projects have put children at greater risk for child abuse and violence when raised in single-parent homes. A 1985 study of 802 noninstitutionalized Oregon adults showed that the frequency of abusive punishment was nearly twice as high in single-parent families than in two-parent families (Sack, Mason, and Higgins, 1985). This early project did not give the reasons for such behavior, but it has long been hypothesized that the frustrations of raising children alone leads to stress, which in turn may lead to mistreatment of children. In 1988, Richard J. Gelles surveyed 6,000 households in an attempt to understand single-parent violence toward children. He found that it wasn't the absence of another parent that led to the stress that provoked the abuse. Instead, it was noted that the stress was a result of economic deprivation and the pressures that come with poverty. What was most striking about the report was the frequency to which the poor single fathers of the study used severe violence (hitting, kicking, burning, threatening with knife or gun) when dealing with their children (Gelles, 1988).

SINGLE MOTHERHOOD: MYTHS AND REALITIES

Over the past twenty years, there has been a sharp rise in birth of children born to unmarried women. The majority of these mothers are poor or working class, with little education. Contrary to the popular belief that most unwed mothers are young and black, nearly 40 percent are non-Hispanic, white, and in their twenties (See Figure 5.2). Almost 50 percent of births to high school dropouts occur out-of-wedlock; this compares to 6 percent if a woman has finished college. While the childbirth rates for married women have declined over the past decade, seven out of ten out-of-wedlock births occur to women age 20 and older. Less than one-third of unmarried mothers are teenagers.

Often the state of unmarried motherhood is transitory. One-fourth of these women were divorced, separated or widowed before they become pregnant; 1 in 4 lives with a man who may or may not be the child's father. Of the women whose first child is born out of wedlock, four in ten marry within five years.

At the heart of the unwed-mother situation is economics and education. Today's economy makes a college education or skilled-trade education necessary if an individual expects to have a job. It is expected that a man who marries will support his family. In areas where unemployment is high among men, women are less likely to marry.

Figure 5.2
Out-of-wedlock
Births by Age and
Education

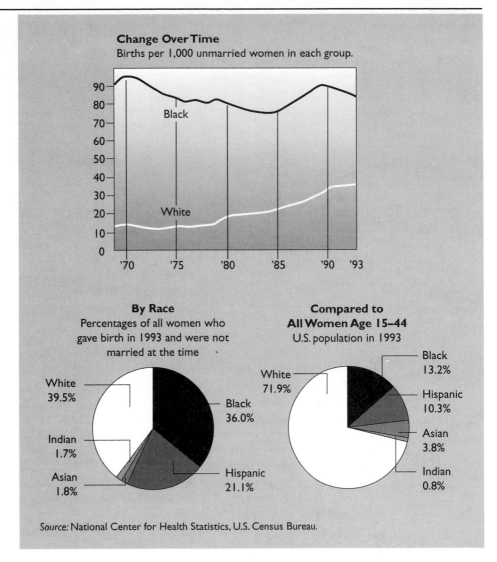

Change Over Time
Births per 1,000 unmarried women in each group.

Black

White

'70   '75   '80   '85   '90 '93

By Race
Percentages of all women who
gave birth in 1993 and were not
married at the time

White
39.5%

Indian
1.7%

Asian
1.8%

Black
36.0%

Hispanic
21.1%

**Compared to
All Women Age 15–44**
U.S. population in 1993

White
71.9%

Black
13.2%

Hispanic
10.3%

Asian
3.8%

Indian
0.8%

Source: National Center for Health Statistics, U.S. Census Bureau.

STRESS AND THE SINGLE MOTHER

The stresses of day-to-day living make single parenting a particularly challenging task. In cases of divorce, fully 38 percent of mothers change residences in the first year. This often means a new neighborhood for the children, a change in friendships, and a decline in lifestyle (McLanahan and Booth, 1991). Because single women on average earn less than men and work fewer hours, they often have difficulty making ends meet. Economics is the greatest source of stress in single-mother households. It is estimated that 66 percent of single, never-married mothers and 3 percent of divorced mothers live with their children

Figure 5. 3
Out-of-wedlock
Births for 15- to
17-year-olds in
1990

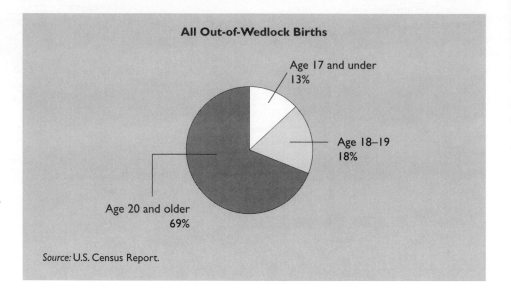

All Out-of-Wedlock Births

Age 17 and under
13%

Age 18–19
18%

Age 20 and older
69%

Source: U.S. Census Report.

below the poverty line (Holmes, 1994), compared to 10 percent for two-parent families. In 1994, the median income for two-parent households was $43,000 a year; for divorced single mothers it was $17,000, and for never-married mothers it was $9,000 (See Table 5.2). The difficult economic state of many single-mother households is often the result of an inability to collect child support and alimony payments legally due from nonresidential fathers. Only 10 percent of the income of white single mothers and 4 percent of the income of black single mothers comes from this source. It is estimated that absentee fathers owe more than $30 billion to 18 million children in the United States. Obligations are picked up by working mothers, public assistance programs, and family networks. A number of social programs provide income to single mothers.

Survivors Insurance (SI) assists single mothers who are widowed. The assistance is based on how much their husbands paid into the Social Security Fund.

TABLE 5.2   Families at Various Income Levels: 1994

Less than $10,000	7.9 percent
$10,000–$14,900	8.7
15,000–24,900	6.9
25,000–34,900	14.3
35,000–49,900	18.0
50,000–74,900	19.9
75,000–99,999	8.8
100,000 and over	8.4

Children of widows fare better than do children of unwed or divorced mothers —not only economically but personally and socially, as well. While the death of a parent deprives children of the care, economic commitment, and protection of a significant caregiver, SI benefits are higher than those given to unmarried mothers. The widowed mother and her children often receive emotional and economic support from family members on both parents' sides, and they continue to be involved with the family.

A more controversial program is the Aid to Families with Dependent Children program (AFDC), more commonly called *welfare*. This assistance is available to families who show serious economic hardship. Medicaid programs offer health insurance, and in some cases public housing is available. Some states have cut back on financial assistance to mothers who do not work, insisting instead on a "workfare" program that is intended to help them get training and jobs.

Child care is a major obstacle to working single mothers, no matter what their financial status. Sometimes extended family members care for children, and day care is available, particularly at higher income levels, but working mothers often experience anxiety because of the extended time they are away from their children. Many single mothers become exhausted and depressed from working full-time while adequately caring for children and a home (Olson and Banyard, 1993). The stresses of maintaining any kind of home are the same: cleaning, doing laundry, seeing to repairs, and doing maintenance chores, are all time-consuming activities. A study of working single mothers with preschool children showed higher stress levels associated with longer working days and a lack of control over work schedules (Campbell and Moen, 1992). Obviously, the more children a mother has, the greater the stress. Particularly problematic for working single mothers is conflict when a child or other relative needs attention and when the mother must be at work.

The ability to parent well has been directly linked to the single mother's psychological adjustment (Bank, Forgatch, Patterson, and Fetrow, 1993). Mothers who experience psychiatric symptoms, such as depression, have difficulty organizing the family's physical environment, sharing time and attention with the children, and providing age-appropriate activities for the family.

CUSTODIAL FATHERS

Today more than a 1.4 million American families are headed by single fathers, compared to 350,000 thirty years ago. Most of this change is the result of divorce. The three most frequently cited reasons for gaining custody are: the ex-wife's emotional problems, the father's superior financial status, and the children's choice to live with their father. Early studies, using small samples, portrayed custodial fathers as middle-class white, relatively well-educated, and having prestigious jobs with a high income. An extensive research project conducted in 1993 gives a clearer view of the single-father family (Meyer and Garasky, 1993). Although the incomes of father-only families are considerably higher then those of mother-only families, 18.2 percent of father-parented families live in poverty (Table 5.3). A surprising 17.5 percent of father-headed

TABLE 5.3   Single Fathers

Never married	25%
Widowed	7.5%
Living below poverty line	18%
Percentage of single-parent households	14%

families include children younger than three years old, and more than 30 percent include preschoolers.

Single fathers have many of the same stresses as single mothers: economic difficulties, child care, household management, and work schedule. Additional stress comes from disagreement with the children's mother over child-support payments and visitation rights.

A number of studies have shown that single fathers do well in raising their children, particularly when gender-role differences are less rigid. One study showed that custodial fathers are more concerned about the care and nurturance of their children than are fathers who live in dual-parent households (Tillitski, 1992).

THE DILEMMA OF THE NONCUSTODIAL FATHER

Many noncustodial fathers have little or no contact with their children, a situation that has gained national attention in recent years. Some of these fathers pay child support but most do not. It is estimated that absentee fathers owe billions of dollars in child support, and these obligations are picked up by working mothers, public-assistance programs and family networks.

A number of factors influence how involved a noncustodial father will be with his children. The circumstances of the child's birth and the father's living arrangements are significant influences (Selzer, 1991). Fathers whose children are born within a marriage are more likely to pay child support and visit with their children than are fathers with children born out of wedlock. The higher the father's economic class, the greater the likelihood he'll pay child support. And the closer he lives to his children, the more likely he is to see them.

There are serious obstacles to noncustodial fathers carrying on a positive relationship with their children. Noncustodial fathers complain that they are often denied visitation with their children, particularly if they are behind in child support payments. They frequently complain that their former mates speak negatively about them to their children, causing a loyalty split and making the children not want to be with them. Noncustodial fathers sometimes feel unimportant to the family, particularly if a stepfather lives with the children. Noncustodial fathers are often not informed when their children are ill or have school problems (Wilbur and Wilbur, 1988).

TEENAGE MOTHERS

In 1990, teenage women gave birth to approximately 500,000 babies. About 60 percent of these children were born out of wedlock, an increase from 15 percent in 1960 (Figure 5.4). The rate of teenage pregnancy in the United States is twice as high as it is in Canada, Great Britain, and France, three times as high as in Sweden, and seven times as high as in the Netherlands. In the United States, almost 40 percent of white babies and 90 percent of black babies are born into teenage single-parent families (National Commission on Children, 1991). Two percent of these births occurred to teens aged 14 and under; 36 percent to teens aged 15–17, and 62 percent to teens aged 18–19. The majority of

Figure 5.4
Birth rates for teens have been declining since 1992, with the greatest decrease among black adolescents.

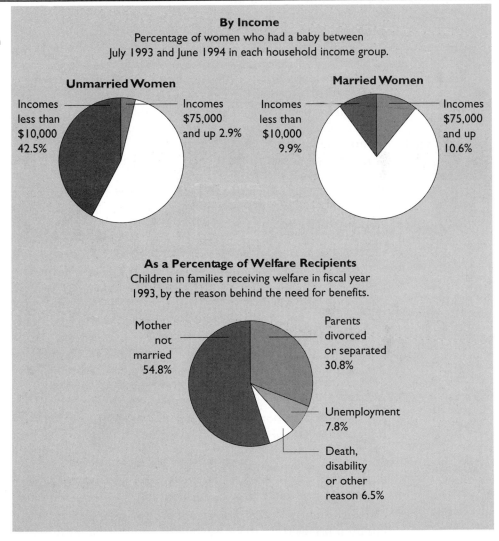

By Income
Percentage of women who had a baby between
July 1993 and June 1994 in each household income group.

Unmarried Women

Incomes less than $10,000 42.5%

Incomes $75,000 and up 2.9%

Married Women

Incomes less than $10,000 9.9%

Incomes $75,000 and up 10.6%

As a Percentage of Welfare Recipients
Children in families receiving welfare in fiscal year
1993, by the reason behind the need for benefits.

Mother not married 54.8%

Parents divorced or separated 30.8%

Unemployment 7.8%

Death, disability or other reason 6.5%

these births were unplanned and unwanted, and many were the result of sexual abuse. A 1992 study revealed that two-thirds of pregnant teens and teen mothers had been raped or sexually abused—almost always by a parent, guardian, or other relative. More than one-half of all teen mothers had been physically abused during childhood—beaten with sticks, straps, and fists; deprived of food; burned with cigarettes; or locked in a closet (Boyer and Fine, 1992). More than one-half of the babies born to teenage girls are fathered by men aged 20 and older. The younger the girl, the greater the age difference between her and her partner (Alan Guttmacher Institute, 1995). In some states, engaging in sex with an underage female is statutory rape, and increasingly these men are prosecuted when they can be identified. Adolescent white women are more likely to marry when pregnant than are black women (Cutright and Smith, 1988; Nathanson and Kim, 1989). This difference may reflect the availability of fewer employed, marriageable men in the black community, as well as a greater acceptance of nonmarital childbearing (Abrahamse, et al., 1988). While black teens have the highest birthrate—up 15 percent since 1989—the rate among Hispanic teens has risen 23 percent since that time.

The vast majority of teenage mothers (about 96 percent) choose to keep their infants, which means that parenting begins under the most difficult of circumstances (Roosa, 1991). Because they frequently do not get good prenatal care and are physically less mature, unwed teenage mothers suffer more pregnancy complications and more often have babies with physical problems than do women who are married or give birth to planned babies. Prematurity and low birth weight—which increases the likelihood of cerebral palsy, mental retardation, and epilepsy—occur most frequently in the babies of teenage mothers who do not have adequate prenatal care. The Children's Defense Fund (1988) estimates that this failure to invest in prenatal care for pregnant teens results in taxpayers' costs for intensive-care that far exceed the cost of prenatal care.

Because teenage mothers frequently do not complete their high school education, they have limited job opportunities. As a result more than 60 percent live in poverty with their children. Even when a teen parent is able to find a job, it is difficult to find adequate and affordable child care. For many adolescent mothers it is more advantageous to remain on public-assistance programs than to take a marginal job they are qualified for.

A number of research projects, have looked at the impact of early childbearing on the offspring's developmental progress. Both scholastic achievement and aptitude may be compromised in children born to very young mothers (Brooks-Gunn and Furstenberg, 1986; Hofferth, 1987). One longitudinal study of 1,242 children born into low-income, urban, black families found that children of mothers aged 17 and younger are less likely to adapt to school (Kellam, Ensminger and Turner, 1977). Subsequent research has shown that the cognitive deficits of school-age children are more likely the result of socioeconomic conditions than a consequence of maternal age (Darabi, et al., 1984).

Psychological immaturity poorly prepares many adolescent mothers to care for young children. Adolescence is a time of personal development, when children bridge the gap between childhood and adulthood by experimenting with various aspects of life, particularly career planning and social relationships. Erik Erikson calls this stage "identity," as it is during this period that teenagers discover who they are and where they want to go in life. Becoming a parent at this stage paralyzes this developmental progress.

It is during adolescence that children ideally progress from concrete to formal operational thinking, intellectual growth that allows them to think, reason and problem solve. Before this change children have difficulty differentiating between their own thoughts and the feelings of others. They create what David Elkind (1967, 1978) calls "personal fables," beliefs that their own preoccupations and concerns are shared by others. Parents who are still in this preformal stage of thinking have difficulty coming out of themselves in order to attend to the needs of their infants.

It has been proposed that some teenagers, feeling worthless and hopeless about their future, become pregnant in order to gain self-esteem, a feeling of value, and purpose in life. While teenage pregnancy is viewed as non-normative by developmental psychologists, in some cultures it is acceptable and normal. Interestingly, as many as 25 percent of teenage mothers become pregnant again within a year of their first child's birth.

Studies conducted before the 1980s showed that adolescents were often too immature to understand the long-term consequences of their behavior—that they are unable to see how limiting having a baby will be. When compared with older parents, they are less aware of and knowledgeable about developmental milestones, less sensitive to infant signals, and less likely to look at and talk to their children. In addition, they are more prone to using physical punishment to deal with behavior problems (De Lissovoy, 1975). Observers find that teen mothers often foster premature independence in their babies, pushing them to hold their own bottles, to sit up too early, and to scramble for toys before they really are able to get them. The younger the adolescent mother the less sensitive she is to the needs of her infant (McAnaarney and Hendee, 1989).

These early reports differ from recent studies, which present a more positive picture of teenage mothering, and one that sees considerable variation in the way adolescents parent (Miller and Moore, 1990). A longitudinal project involving 300 primarily urban, black, adolescents found that most of the mothers felt they were doing a good job in less than ideal circumstances (Furstenberg, Brooks-Gunn, and Morgan, 1987). As difficult as it is, many adolescent mothers do complete high school and find employment (Geronimus and Korenman, 1990). These feats are generally accomplished when a teenaged mother lives with her family of origin and receives financial and child-care support from family members. For all its benefits, the teens often complain that the price they pay for this assistance is family interference with child rearing—that they receive unsolicited advice and criticism, and that their mother's responsibilities are usurped (Richard, Barbour, and Ubenzer, 1991).

It is clear that teenage parents need substantial help for their parenthood to work out well. Health care, peer counseling, and parenting-skills education are all essential. Most importantly, teenage parents need adequate social-support systems, ones that will encourage them to continue their education.

Since at least 80 percent of adolescent and teenage parents live with their families, these families must provide the support necessary.

The reasons for the increase in teenage pregnancy and childbirth have much to do with American cultural beliefs. In countries such as the Netherlands, sex education and pregnancy prevention is considered a health issue rather than a moral one, so young people have access to contraception and abortion services. In the United States, however, adolescents get conflicting messages about sexuality. Sex is shown as exciting and desirable in the media, but teenagers are expected to abstain from engaging in it. In many areas of the country, information about sex and contraception is unavailable to adolescents because of ethnic and religious influences.

Twenty years ago, a pregnant adolescent would have left school; but that is no longer the case. Some school systems have established parenting-skills classes for pregnant teens, but in general funds for developing programs to keep teen mothers in school are scarce. This is unfortunate, because intervention programs for adolescent mothers generally have resulted in an improvement in parenting skills (Unger and Wandersman, 1985). In one study, 76 adolescent mothers were allowed to participate in a four-month program by identifying the knowledge they needed about their children's growth and development. A ten-month follow-up showed that none of the mothers who completed the program had been reported for child abuse or neglect (Fulton, A., et al., 1991).

Often left out of teenage-parent considerations is the role of the young father. Despite the social significance of the adolescent father, relatively little research has been conducted about the subject. One small study of 42 black, unwed, adolescent fathers found that young men with a positive self-image were better prepared to handle fatherhood. Also, a father's willingness to take responsibility for parenting was influenced by his role expectation (Christmon, 1990). However, many adolescent fathers were fatherless themselves and therefore had no role model to emulate in parenthood.

Family of origin support and assistance is the key factor in an adolescent's ability to parent in a positive, competent way.

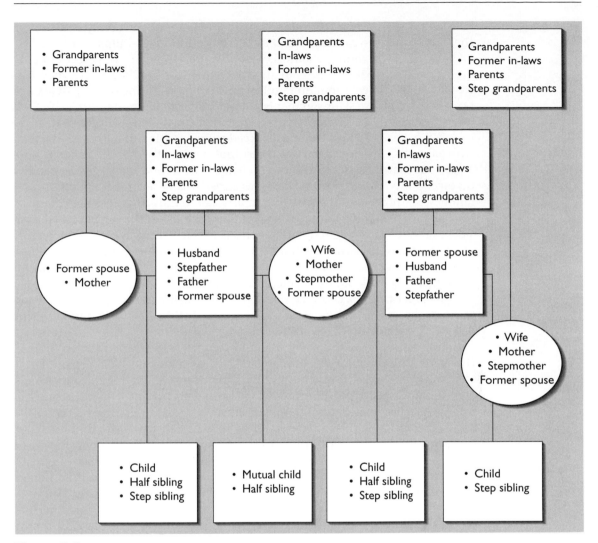

Figure 5.5
Role Demands in the Remarried Family

STEPPARENTING: A FAMILY CHALLENGE

Marriage, divorce, death, remarriage—these are standard family events in today's world. Over the past 20 years, there has been a sharp increase in the number of people who take a series of partners as their mates—often marrying, divorcing, marrying again, and divorcing again. This trend has led to *blended families, extended families,* and even the strange-sounding *reconstituted families,* as parents and children from different relationships join together. They create new family units replete with additional grandparents, aunts, uncles, and cousins and a slew of relationships within and without the family. Most often, these new units are called *stepfamilies* (Pasley and Ihinger-Tallman, 1987).

America is becoming a nation of stepfamilies, as nearly 40 percent of children born today will live in such an arrangement before they are 18 years old. In 1987, there were 11 million families in which at least one of the parents had been married before. This number is an increase from 8.9 million in 1970. Each day an estimated 1,300 new stepfamilies are formed in the United States, the majority of them formed when a divorced woman with children marries a man who either has not been married or does not have custody of the children from a previous marriage. Because about 60 percent of second marriages also end in divorce, many children in stepfamilies experience a second splitting of their families. Many second-time divorcees marry again, thus adding to the complications of the stepfamily. Most frequently "the children" in the stepfamily are considered the remarried couples' most serious problem. However, it is the quality of the relationship between stepparent and stepchildren, not that of the remarriage, that best predicts family adjustment, making it especially important for stepfamilies to work out their differences (See Figure 5.5).

Stepparenting is a complex phenomenon because so many variables determine its success or failure. What makes stepparenting especially difficult is the lack of clear guidelines concerning roles, responsibilities, financial obligations, and legal standing. What makes designing guidelines so difficult is the interactive variety that characterizes blended families. Consider some examples. A stepfamily may consist of a mother living with her biological children, plus a spouse who is not related to the children and who may or may not have children from a previous marriage or relationship. Or the family may be comprised of a father living with his children, plus a woman to whom he is not married and who may or may not bring children into the family with her. Perhaps a couple weds, uniting his children from a previous relationship and her children from two previous marriages. Practical issues such as space and household management pale next to emotional issues of power, loyalty, competition, and resentment that often emerge when families blend. Consider that while the structure of the family is changing drastically in blended family unions, the developmental needs of the children in the families are also changing. It is often difficult for members in a blended family to understand that the family members are affected to a high degree by the actions of people in households outside that of the blended family. The success or failure of stepparenting depends on many factors, such as: the prior experiences of all members of the family; the sex, ages, and developmental stages of the children in the blended family; the professional and psychological issues of the adults in the blended family; and the way differences between all family members—within and outside the blended family—are negotiated.

STAGES OF THE STEPPARENTING FAMILY

Mary F. Whiteside (1989) described the three phases of the stepparenting family. The first stage takes about two years. As new partners and their children come together, they often experience anger and a sense of loss or sadness for the life left behind. This is particularly true when a noncustodial parent has no contact with the biological children, and this is the case for half of all children whose parents divorce or separate. With an absentee, noncustodial parent, there is an extra burden for child care on a stepparent, and this adds stress to the new stepparent-stepchild relationship. Researchers have noted that behavior problems of both boys and girls increase when a stepfather is introduced into the family (Hetherington, Cox, and Cox, 1985). Sometimes an unmarried noncustodial parent feels threatened when an ex-mate brings a new partner into the child-rearing picture, fearing less time and influence with the children. A parent who has obligations to two families—a noncustodial family and a stepparented family—often has difficulty negotiating time, money, and affection among the two households (Clingempeel and Brand, 1985). Family members have hopes and expectations about the new family constellation, and some of them are unrealistic. A parent who desires to heal the biological family from the effects of divorce by bringing in a new partner may be disappointed when the healing doesn't occur. Stepparents who expect to be welcomed into the new family and loved by their stepchildren may feel hurt and resentment when the children see the stepparent as an intruder. And quite often, children maintain a fantasy that their biological parents will reunite.

The second phase of the stepparented family may last three to five years. It is a period of conflict and negotiation and the point where many marriages falter. As the stepparent begins to be part of the biological family, children may continue to resist change, and rebuff the stepparent, in loyalty to an absent biological parent. Fantasies of welcome and harmony break apart, and are replaced by feelings of anger, resentment, jealousy, confusion, and ultimately a sense of inadequacy. Biological parents may feel torn between their new adult relationships and the rejecting children. Issues arise over such things as food preferences and preparation, the organization of household chores, privacy needs, and space requirements. A number of researchers have pointed out that three to five years, longer than most families expect, are necessary for members in a blended family to learn to understand each other fully and build up positive connections (Mills, 1984; Papernow, 1984).

It is in this second stage that the family must reorganize itself—clarifying the differences between two parental households while strengthening the boundaries in the stepfamily. By now, a stepparent is less an outsider and more an individual whose ideas and beliefs are important even when they differ with those of a biological parent. It is at this stage that a biological parent must step back enough for a stepparent and stepchild to deal directly with each other. Well-functioning stepfamilies are similar to well-functioning nuclear families when it comes to making decisions that meet the individual needs of all family members. In dysfunctional stepfamilies, the parental relationship exists apart from the family; the stepparent is excluded from the biological parent-child relationship (Anderson and White, 1986).

It can take from five to seven years for a stepfamily to develop true intimacy, trust, and stability. In its third phase, the stepfamily is firmly established, and members are integrated into the blended system in keeping with their developmental needs.

Problems arise in stepparenting families when the developmental stages of the children are incompatible with a particular phase in the stepfamily's history. For example, at about three years into the new relationship, as the stepparent seeks more closeness and greater authority, an adolescent in the family might be struggling with identity, new relationships, sexuality, and plans for the future—all of which can rekindle old feelings about the divorce and remarriage (Sager, et al., 1983). The stepparenting of adolescents is a great challenge in the remarried family.

> A difficulty of conflicting developmental needs appears when the adolescent's need to become increasingly involved in the community of peers and adults outside the family competes with the stepfamily's need to build a cohesive household base. Parents become caught in the delicate balance of figuring when to insist on participation in a household event, when to insist on weekend visitation, and when to support healthy involvement outside the family. Teenagers with strong positive involvement in two households, as well as full academic and social lives, are very busy indeed. They complain about being pulled in too many directions and needing time to retreat and relax (Whiteside, 1989).

Successful stepparenting depends in part on the age of children when a stepparent enters the family and the living arrangements that are worked out between the custodial and noncustodial parents. In cases of shared custody or visitation agreements, the transition back and forth on a scheduled basis can be stressful to a young child. The child's primary attachment will be to the biological parents, and this can make a stepparent feel left out. Preschool-age children are the most likely to bond to nurturant stepparents when there is little or no contact with noncustodial parents. Children older than three years understand the family situation better, and they often feel torn between the adults in their lives. When the tie between a child and his or her custodial parent is strong, the addition of a stepparent can lead a child to feel jealous as the biological parent gives time and attention to the new relationship. This is especially true of girls who often resent the intrusion of a stepparent on their mother's time and affection. In fact, girls are more likely to drop out of school in stepparented families than in single-parent families. Although boys initially exhibit problems when a stepparent enters the picture, they often do well when a stepfather joins a mother-custody household (Hetherington, et al., 1985). Boys in stepparented families are less likely to drop out of school than boys in single-parent families.

The Role of the Stepparent

When people remarry or cohabit, they often envision the new mate as a new parent for their children. While a stepparent may provide love, support, financial assistance, and guidance to stepchildren, a stepparent is *not* a biological parent. Therein lies the problem in many families. The problem becomes particularly confusing if the children's biological parent also participates in parenting, even to a small degree. The situation is further muddled when an individual is a stepparent to some of the children in a household and a biological parent to others.

The problem in a nutshell is this: How does the stepparent role differ from that of the biological parent? Are some behaviors appropriate to biological parenting but inappropriate to stepparenting? Should a stepparent expect the same kind of consideration from stepchildren as from biological children? The complexity of the stepparent role is illustrated by variations in labeling within blended families (Dahl, Cowgill, and Asmundsson, 1987). Older children are most likely to call stepparents by their first names. Depending on the level of intimacy and the presence or absence of a biological parent, younger children use names like Mom, Dad, Mom II or Dad II, and even "my mother's husband" or "my father's wife." Children are more likely to use the term "step" than the parents themselves do. Often the children do not consider a stepparent a true part of the family.

A study by Cynthia Pill (1990) concluded that stepfamilies often come together with unrealistic expectations that are bound to lead to unhappiness. Of the families she studied, 41 percent believed that their stepparenting family would bond as closely as a biological family. The parents in these blended families expected that their noncustodial children would become close with the children of the stepfamily. In most cases neither expectation was realized. Despite parental hopes, the emotional bonds between stepparents and stepchildren are not as close as biological parent-child bonds. In situations where a noncustodial parent is out of the picture, stepparent-stepchildren relationships are more positive. In general, stepfathers have more positive relationships with stepchildren than do stepmothers. But when both parents bring children into the new family unit, stepparent-stepchildren relationships are most likely to be problematic (Coleman and Ganong, 1991).

A study of remarried families suggested that the stepparent role should not be rushed but rather requires patience and effort that only develops over a long period of time (Dahl, et al., 1987). The trust of stepchildren is earned when stepparents are consultants, coaches, friends, and mediators, rather than authority figures or intruders in the children's lives. The researchers propose that stepparents give children time to adjust to the changes that are occurring within the family, allowing space to grieve for their former lives and old relationships. They suggest that the family move to a new house if possible, or that they renovate the old house in a way that makes space for new family members to claim their own territory. Stepparents are encouraged to develop a cordial relationship with their new mate's ex-spouse, as well as with their ex-spouse's new partner if there is one. Stepparents should understand that there is a special bond between a child and his or her biological parents, a bond that must be respected. Stepparents should learn all they can about the children they are going to live with and, while stepparents and stepchildren should treat each other respectfully, it cannot be expected that they will automatically love each other. A stepparent needs to be ready to communicate openly with stepchildren, to peacefully negotiate differences, and to make compromises.

E. Mavis Hetherington of the University of Virginia (1992) warned against stepparents taking on the role of family disciplinarian. She suggests instead that a stepparent work at developing a warm, caring relationship with stepchildren. It is best that the role of disciplinarian be left to biological parents, with

The Spirit of Parenting

Spring 1954. It is an unseasonably warm afternoon. I answer the doorbell and there on the doorstep is a young woman wearing glasses and a long braid. "Hello" she says, extending her hand. "I'm Rena."

That is how I meet my father's third daughter, my other sister, who has finally come to life from the family tree in the sand. Given the drama of the moment, the twenty-seven-year-old Rena seems subdued though not at all unpleasant. Her mission is a practical one, she says, with a directness I would soon recognize as typical. She has come for "our" father's help. She wants to move out of the apartment where she has been living with her deranged mother, whose violence has escalated so alarmingly that it is not even safe for her to go back alone to pack up her things. She needs Daddy to get a court order so that she can return in the presence of a marshal or a police officer.

After a reunion with our father that can only be described as sedate, and after a dinner during which my mother seems to be trying extra hard to make her feel welcome, Rena spends the next several days with us sleeping in our attic bedroom. I rush home from school every day to spend time with her, as if she is a visiting mermaid who might disappear with the next wave. . . .

Daddy obtains the court order and helps Rena secure her belongings. She moves into an apartment of her own, but continues her regular visits, saying she wants to get to know me better. Sometimes she sleeps over for a few days at a time. Neighbors have noticed. Friends are asking questions. Mommy and Daddy tell Rena they want to acknowledge her in the community, but rather than disentangle everyone's complicated relationships at this late date, they ask if she would mind being introduced as a cousin.

To be disowned not once but twice, to be rejected after having been rediscovered, to find her father more interested in the judgments of his community than the feelings of his daughter—how that must hurt. But Rena just nods and says cousin is fine.

Letty Cottin Pogrebin
Deborah, Golda and Me

---

a stepparent only supporting that role. Hetherington believes that attempts to control stepchildren—even by warm, communicative stepparents—may be resented, especially by adolescents.

One awkward issue in the stepfamily has to do with financial obligations. Stepparents should be fully cognizant of all alimony or support orders, estate planning, debts, and other legal matters that pertain to the family (Dahl, et al., 1987). One major area of conflict in stepfamilies is resentment caused by support obligations to a child and former spouse (Lown, McFadden, and Crossman, 1989). Men are often opposed to supporting the children of their mate's previous relationship, and women often don't want to burden their new husbands with obligations for these children (Lowen, et al., 1989). Most states do not re-

TABLE 5.4.   Steps in Forming a Stepfamily

Steps	Prerequisite Attitude	Developmental Issues
1. **Entering a new relationship**	Recovery from loss of first marriage (adequate "emotional divorce")	Recommit to marriage and to forming a family, with readiness to deal with the complexity and amount of effort required
2. **Conceptualizing and planning the new marriage and family**	Accepting one's own fears and those of new spouse and children about remarriage and forming a stepfamily Accepting need for time and patience for adjustment to complexity and ambiguity of: a. Multiple new roles b. Boundaries: space, time, membership, and authority c. Affective issues: guilt, loyalty, conflicts, desire for mutuality, unresolvable past hurts	a. Work on openness in the new relationship to avoid pseudomutuality b. Plan for maintenance of cooperative co-parent relationship with ex-spouses c. Plan to help children deal with fears, loyalty conflicts, and membership in two systems d. Realign relationships with extended family to include new spouse and children e. Plan maintenance of connections for children with extended family of ex-spouse(s)
3. **Remarriage and reconstitution of the family**	Final resolution of attachment to previous spouse and ideal of "intact" family Acceptance of a different model of family, with permeable boundaries	a. Restructure family boundaries to allow for inclusion of new spouse/stepparents b. Realign relationships throughout subsystems to permit interweaving of several systems c. Make room for relationships of all children with biological (noncustodial) parents, grandparents, and other extended family d. Share memories and histories to enhance stepfamily integration

quire stepparents to support stepchildren who live with them (Fine and Fine, 1992); however there are a few areas where *in loco parentis* prevails. This position obliges a person who *acts* in place of a biological parent to financially support a child. Most states do not allow stepchildren to inherit money from an estate unless assets are noted in a will, and in wrongful death statutes, stepchildren

The Informed Parent 5.1

The Stepping-Ahead Program

Step 1: *Nurturing Your Couple Relationship*

- Plan to do something that you both enjoy doing away from your household once a week.
- Arrange to have 20 minutes of relaxed time alone with each other every day.
- Talk about the running of your household for at least 30 minutes each week.

Step 2: *Finding Personal Space and Time*

- Take time to make a "private" place for each of the adults and children in your household.
- Take two hours a week for each member to do something he or she likes to do.

Step 3: *Nourishing Family Relationships*

- Family members share with one another what they have appreciated about each other.

Step 4: *Maintaining Close Parent/Child Relationships*

- Parent and child do something fun together for 15–20 minutes once or twice a month.

Step 5: *Developing Stepparent/Stepchild Relationships*

- Stepparent and stepchild do something fun together for 15–20 minutes once or twice a month.

Step 6: *Building Family Trust*

- Schedule a family meeting once a month.

Step 7: *Strengthening Stepfamily Ties*

- Hold a family discussion every two weeks.

Step 8: *Working with the Children's Other Household*

- Give the adults in the children's other household positive feedback once a month.

are not recognized as having legal standing. At one time, stepparents had no legal rights to seek custody or visitation in cases of divorce in the blended family; however, in recent years, one-half the states have passed laws allowing third parties (stepparents, grandparents, siblings, and other significant people in the child's life) to file for such privilege. Generally, the legal community does not recognize the positive significance of stepparent-stepchildren relationships and fails to see how enduring such a connection can be.

What is most significant about the studies on stepparenting is their emphasis on how much self-searching and effort is continually required of parents in stepfamilies, not just at the beginning of this new relationship but every day thereafter. The role of the stepparent in our society is so ill defined that people often enter into a blended family situation without guidance about roles and responsibilities. As a result, noble efforts to create new families often end in confusion, conflict, stress, disappointment, and unhappiness on the part of both stepparents and stepchildren.

SPECIAL PARENTING

As society becomes more complex, variations in parenting strategies become necessary and possible. AIDS, drug problems, and divorce have left many children in vulnerable situations. Couples who previously were unable to have children are finding that they now can become parents. With these unique parenting states, come special problems.

GRANDPARENTS AS PARENTS

More than three million American children under the age of eighteen are now living in the home of a grandparent or spending a significant part of their growing up time with a grandparent. This is a 44 percent increase since 1980. In half these cases, the child's mother is also living in the grandparent's home; but in 28 percent of cases, neither parent is available. In 17 percent of cases, both parents are living with the grandparents, and in 5 percent of cases the father lives there also (Dawson, 1991; Saluter, 1992). Of all ethnic groups, black children are most likely to live with a grandparent, approximately 12 percent. This compares to 5.8 percent of Hispanics and 3.6 percent of white children (U.S. Census Report, 1991). The largest increase is for white children, from 2.4 percent in 1980 to 3.7 percent in 1991.

Custodial grandparents have legal responsibility for their grandchildren, meaning the rights and authority of a parent in making decisions for the child. *Living-with grandparents* assume all of the responsibilities for a child's care full-time, but they lack the legal authority usually because they haven't been to court to request such authority. *Day-care grandparents* offer daily care to their grandchildren for extended periods; they have no legal right to a make decisions for the child over the desires of the child's parents. Even without legal standing, living-with and day-care grandparents often make decisions about

The problems that lead to grandparent caregiving transcend race and reflect the problems of modern life: divorce in the family, teenage pregnancy, drugs and alcohol, unemployment, and mental illness.

their grandchildren by default; the children's parents are unavailable or have informally relinquished their authority.

In an attempt to understand the circumstances by which grandparents take over the parenting role, Margaret Platt Jendrek (1994) interviewed 114 white grandparents living in or near Butler County, Ohio. The sample was composed of grandparents who responded to advertisements in the media, schools, and courts. Of the group, 36 were custodial grandparents, 26 living-with grandparents, and 52 day-care grandparents.

Custodial grandparents ranged in age from 40 to 62 at the time they obtained legal rights for a grandchild. At that time the grandchildren ranged in age from newborn to fourteen and a half. Seventy-four percent of the grandparents were married, and seventy-five percent of the grandparents were related to the grandchild through their daughter.

Most of the living-in grandparents, 85 percent, had their grandchildren living in their home. These grandparents ranged in age from 40 to 64, and the grandchildren were ages newborn to nine and a half. Sixty-five percent of the grandparents were married when they began to care for their grandchildren. More then 69 percent of the living-with grandparents were related to the grandchildren through their daughter.

The day-care grandparents ranged in age from 39 to 67 at the time they began to provide care for their grandchildren. Most (81 percent) provided the care in their own homes and (71 percent) were not paid to do so. At the time the care was first provided, the grandchildren were ages newborn to three years, with the median age about one month. Again, most grandparents (89 percent) were married. About half (58 percent) were related to the grandchild through his or her mother.

Researcher Jendrek found overwhelmingly that a problem of the mother—alcohol, drugs, mental illness—was the cause of custodial grandparenting. Legal action was usually triggered by an event that attracted the attention of the police, social services, or neighbors of the child. Living-in grandparents are most motivated by wanting to help the child's parent financially or not wanting the child in day care or with a babysitter. Similarly, day-care grandparents want to help the child's parent, who often works full-time.

In many cases, grandparents take over child-rearing chores because of pressure they feel within themselves or the suggestion of a social service agency. The motivation is often fear that a grandchild will be placed in a foster home. This fear is particularly true of black grandmothers, who often downplay their own physical or health problems to take on these responsibilities (Minkler, Roe, and Price, 1992). One study of black grandparents indicated that the decision to parent grandchildren is generally made under duress, out of a fear for the child's safety if he or she is not taken in (Cherlin and Furstenberg, 1986).

More than any other ethnic group, black grandparents have traditionally taken in needy children, usually the children of family members but sometimes the children of friends or neighbors. In the past, these grandparents could rely on an extensive social network to assist them. But recent studies show that support from extended kin networks is not as forthcoming as it used to be, leaving grandparents to handle their stresses alone (Burton, 1992). The study of 60 grandmothers, grandfathers, and great-grandmothers, ages 43–82, and living in urban black communities, found 86 percent of subjects were feeling depressed and anxious most of the time; 61 percent were smoking more than they ever had in their lives; 36 percent were drinking heavily; 35 percent had heightened medical problems with diabetes and arthritis; 8 percent had had a mild stroke; and 5 percent indicated they had had a mild heart attack (Burton, 1992). In another study, many grandparent caregivers reported lifestyle changes that include problems with other family members, a decline in marital satisfaction, and a decline in contact with friends (Jendrek, 1993). Despite these hardships, most grandparents felt that they "are doing what they have to do" and found joy and satisfaction in helping their grandchildren.

GAY PARENTING

In 1995, the Virginia Supreme Court ruled that sexual orientation could be a basis for denying a parent child custody or visitation rights. In this same year, a Wisconsin court granted visitation rights to the nonbiological parent of a child from a same-sex couple who ended their relationship. The state of California has banned gay-couple adoptions, while in Illinois a lesbian couple was granted joint adoption rights to a child one of them had conceived. Also in 1995, The New York Court of Appeals, noting the "fundamental changes" that have occurred in the American family, ruled that unmarried couples, both homosexual or heterosexual, have the right to adopt children. Such is the state of gay parenting and adoption across the United States. The fact that same-sex couples are increasingly opting to raise children has led to a reinterpretation of custody laws and a redefinition of who can fulfill parental roles.

It is estimated that there are between five and six million lesbian and gay parents in the United States, a figure that may be deceptively low because many lesbian and gay parents conceal their sexual identity for fear of losing child custody or visitation rights (Lyons, 1983; Pagelow, 1980). The majority became parents while part of a heterosexual marriage, while others became parents through adoption and artificial insemination. Estimates of the number of children raised by gay parents range from six to fourteen million (Bozett, 1987).

Most of the children of gay parents are born in the context of a heterosexual relationship (Falk, 1989). If the parents divorce, one of the parents leaves the household, noncustodial parenting issues arise. If either parent gets involved in a new relationship, the new partner takes on the role of stepparent. If the partner has children, blended-family or step-sibling relationships arise.

Both single and coupled lesbians are increasingly giving birth to children through donor insemination. The donor may be a friend, relative or an unknown person. Sometimes the donor is a gay male who chooses to co-parent with a gay woman.

Psychoanalysts and social-learning theorists have generally proposed that a parent's sexual orientation has a significant impact on children's development, and this belief has always hurt gay parents when they become involved with the legal system. It has often been assumed that gay parents are not emotionally able to care for children, that the children of gay parents will themselves become gay, and that the children will suffer socially because of public attitudes about their parents. A more troubling homophobic fear has been that children living with a gay or lesbian parent are likely to be sexually mistreated by the parent or his or her acquaintances.

Research on the subject of gay and lesbian parents has been sparse. What studies have been conducted, beginning in the 1970s, focused on the children born into white, middle-class, heterosexual marriages where one of the parents later came out as gay. Generally researchers compared the children of divorced custodial lesbian mothers to the children of divorced custodial heterosexual mothers. A number of studies centered on gender identification; that is, how an individual sees himself or herself being a particular gender with its culturally determined attitudes and expectations. The studies showed that the children of lesbian and heterosexual mothers equally viewed themselves as the gender they were and had no desire to be the opposite sex (Green, 1978; Golombok, et al., 1983). Other studies found no differences between these children in toy preferences, interests, activities, or occupational choices (Kirkpatrick, 1981; Hoeffer, 1981). One researcher noted that gender choices in toys and activities are influenced more by siblings and peers than by parents (Hoeffer, 1981). In one study of the play and television preferences of about 100 children (56 children of lesbian mothers and 48 children of heterosexual mothers) it was found that the children of lesbian mothers are less likely to sex-type their activities (Green, 1986).

Closely related to sexual identity is the matter of sexual orientation, the physical attraction to one or the other sex. Twelve studies conducted over the past fifteen years, comparing 300 children of homosexual parents to the children of heterosexual parents found no differences in regard to sexual orientation, with all the children falling within normal bounds for the society at large (Patterson, 1992).

In regard to social relationships, the elementary-school-age children of homosexual and heterosexual parents choose same-sex peers as playmates; and there is no difference in the quality of these friendships (Golombok, et al., 1983). Lesbian mothers generally have more adult-male relationships—with friends and relatives—than do heterosexual mothers (Kirkpatrick, 1987). In addition, the children of lesbian mothers are more likely to have frequent contact with their fathers (at least once a week) than the children of heterosexual mothers (Golombok, 1983).

Homophobic concerns about sexual abuse in gay and lesbian families are unfounded. The majority of child-abuse cases are heterosexual in nature, with adult men abusing female children (Jones and MacFarlane, 1980).

There is of course as much variation among children within the gay community as there is within heterosexual society. One study indicated that the self-esteem among daughters of lesbian mothers with a live-in partner is higher than it is in daughters of single-parent lesbian mothers (Huggins, 1989). Self-esteem among the children of lesbian mothers was highest when other significant people in the children's lives, particularly their fathers, were either neutral or accepting of the mother's sexual orientation rather than rejecting of it (Huggins, 1989). Psychological problems related to a parent's homosexuality are found to be greatest when the children learn of it during adolescence (Schulenberg, 1985). This is a difficult period in general for young people because they are dealing with their own identity issues. In an extensive 1992 review of the data collected since the 1970s, researcher Charlotte J. Patterson has concluded the following:

> There is no evidence to suggest that psychosocial development among children of gay men or lesbians is compromised in any respect relative to that among offspring of heterosexual parents. Despite long-standing legal presumptions against gay and lesbian parents in many states, despite dire predictions about their children based on well-known theories of psychosocial development and despite the accumulation of a substantial body of research investigating these issues, not a single study has found children of gay parents to be disadvantaged in any significant respect relative to children of heterosexual parents. Indeed, the evidence to date suggests that home environments provided by gay and lesbian parents are as likely as those provided by heterosexual parents to support and enable children's psychosocial growth.

ADOPTIVE FAMILIES

Biological parents give up or lose their children for innumerable reasons: death, physical illness, unwanted pregnancy, teenage pregnancy, poverty, family

Figure 5.6
Adoptions of
Foreign Children

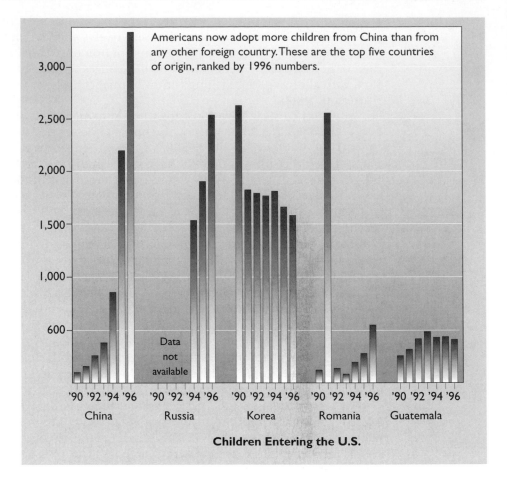

Americans now adopt more children from China than from any other foreign country. These are the top five countries of origin, ranked by 1996 numbers.

'90 '92 '94 '96   '90 '92 '94 '96   '90 '92 '94 '96   '90 '92 '94 '96   '90 '92 '94 '96
   China   Russia   Korea   Romania   Guatemala

Children Entering the U.S.

pressure, social stigma, shame, mental illness, neglect, and the legal system. Some of these children are taken in by relatives; others by strangers. Some of these children are told of their biological roots; others are raised in ignorance of their origins. Although often little is known of an adoptive child's background, particularly if the adoption is from a foreign country, sometimes the details of a child's past are well documented. All of these factors make an adoption unique to the family that makes the decision to raise a child not born directly into it.

It is estimated that about 50,000 children are legally adopted by nonrelatives each year in the United States, not including stepparents (National Committee for Adoption). This is a major drop over the last 25 years as legalized abortion, more effective contraception, and the increasing tendency for unmarried mothers to keep their infants makes fewer babies available for adoption. As a result, since the 1980s, would-be-parents have increasingly turned to adopting children from foreign countries (Gibbs, 1989). And additionally there has been an increase in the adoption of "special needs" children, who are older, and frequently nonwhite, are disabled, or have siblings that must be adopted with them.

Issues of attachment and separation naturally arise when children are adopted. Always in the background is the knowledge that the adopted child has a "real" family somewhere. An adopted child's loyalty is split between biological parents who gave the child up and adoptive parents who have invested significantly in the child's care (Boszormenyi-Nagy and Krasner, 1986). Despite the concerns, many adoptive parents become attached emotionally to their adopted children during the months that they wait for the adoption process to be completed (Butler, 1989).

One of the factors that influence the attachment process is the point in the family life cycle at which the adoptive child enters. For example, a child between the ages of 18 months and 3 years, is in a developmental period characterized by autonomy and separation/individuation. If the child enters the family at his age, he or she may not need or want as much cuddling as a new parent wants to give. The parents might feel rejected—dissatisfied and unappreciated for all their efforts on the child's behalf (Mahler, Pine, and Bergman, 1975). For reasons such as this, families need considerable information and preparation when they make the serious decision to raise a child not born to them. Since the quality of care a child has had prior to adoption is critical for his or her mental and psychological well-being, it is also particularly important for adoptive parents to know something of their child's earlier life. Obviously, the less trauma a child has suffered and the fewer the intervening placements, the less likely it is that the child will show acting out and disruptive behaviors. Psychiatrist Iris Butler (1989) has noted what can happen if a child has not been well cared for before an adoption.

> Lack of stimulation, inconsistent and non-nurturing caregivers, and physical or sexual abuse are debilitating to the child and compromise the child's and family's attachment in an adoptive process. It may be that for some children, multiple changes in environment before there is adequate language to describe what is happening may leave the children more vulnerable and mistrustful and have profound effects on the adoptive process. It may be that for some children, having to connect and disconnect repeatedly from caretakers, with a growing knowledge that they are excluded from permanent residency, may increase their anxiety and uncertainty as well as that of their adoptive families.

Butler's views are particularly significant in cases of older children adopted from foreign countries, where the children were given minimal care in state-run orphanages. Some of these children develop an *attachment disorder,* whereby they are unable to emotionally attach to their new parents and may display serious emotional and behavioral problems. Another situation that concerns potential adoptive parents is the fact that, in about 2 percent of all agency adoptions, parents either interrupt or disrupt the adoption process before it is legally final or dissolve it after the adoption is final. The disruption and dissolution rates increase with the age of the child at the time of the adoption; from 10 percent for children older than two years to 25 percent for children aged 12 to 17 (Sachs, 1990).

Children differ greatly in their vulnerability to stress, and the long-term effects of early deprivation are often unpredictable. Also families show considerable variation in their ability to nurture the children they raise. It is the strength of the adopted child's character combined with the adoptive family's ability to accept, love, and care for the child that determines the success of the adoption.

A number of controversial questions exist in regard to adoptive status. Should adoption records be open, so that a child can know who his or her biological parents are? When should a child be told of his or her adoption?

Most parents reveal their child's adoptive status gradually and continually at a young age so that the child will not be traumatized by an abrupt discovery at an older age. Problems usually arise in families where information about an adoption is ignored or kept secret. Despite reassurances, adopted children are not always convinced they are loved as much as biological children, or that an adopted parent's love will make up for their biological mother giving them up. And pronouncements to this effect can prompt adopted children to test whether parents are telling the truth. In their efforts not to alienate the adopted child, some parents behave tentatively in the face of inappropriate testing behavior. They hesitate to show firmness in their commitment as parents to this child, which is actually what the child is seeking.

A number of states have instituted "open adoptions," in which records are available to adoptees aged 18 and over. Of the adoptees who have searched for their biological mothers, about three-fourths report having positive relationships with their adoptive parents. Often, adopted children do not go in search of their birth parents, because they fear hurting their adoptive parents (Geissinger, 1984). In one study, Advid Brodzinsky found that adopted children often go through a period of emotional turmoil in adolescence when they grieve not having been wanted or raised by birth parents (in Fishman, K.D., 1992).

It takes a special adult to adopt a child, particularly if the child is older or disabled or has suffered trauma. As sociologists Mary Ann Lamanna and Agnes Riedmann point out, "any adoption entails both responsibility and risk." Prospective adoptive parents are urged to think carefully about what it means to take in a child not born to them. They are also encouraged to understand, as Iris Butler puts it,

> . . . there is an agreement that the adoptive parents will act like parents to the child, nurturing, protecting and educating him or her as if he or she were their own child. The child's side of the contract is to be parented, and to act as if he or she were a child of these parents. (Butler, 1989)

Chapter Review

- Family life has changed dramatically over the past 40 years in the United States. Today there are nuclear families, single-parent families, blended families,, homosexual families, and extended families. There are also communal families and cohabiting families.

- In the dual-income family, both parents work, run households, and raise children. Signs of overload for working parents include fatigue, guilt over the limited time spent with the children, worry about job performance, and concern for the marital relationship. This multiple-role stress has been associated with both physical and emotional illness.

- The generic term single-parent family actually represents a number of different parenting arrangements, each also reflecting a unique style of relating and coping in a unique social and environmental context. Over the past fifteen years father-led families are the most rapidly growing form of child rearing.

- A number of research projects have described children raised in single-parent homes at greater risk for child abuse and violence than when raised in two-parent homes. The main cause for this is economic deprivation and the pressures that come with poverty.

- Over the past twenty years, there has been a sharp rise in the number of children born to unmarried women. The majority of these mothers are poor or working-class women with little education. Contrary to popular belief that most are young and black, nearly 40 percent are non-Hispanic white and in their twenties.

- Today more than a 1.4 million American families are headed by single fathers, compared to 350,000 thirty years ago, most of this change being the result of divorce. The three most frequently cited reasons for a father's gaining child custody are an ex-wife's emotional problems, the father's superior financial status, and the choice of the children to live with their father.

- A number of factors influence how involved a noncustodial father will be with his chil-

dren. Fathers whose children are born within a marriage are more likely to pay child support and visit their children than fathers whose children are born out of wedlock. The higher the father's economic status, the greater the likelihood he is to pay child support. The closer in proximity he lives to his children, the more likely he is to visit them.

- Almost 40 percent of white babies and 90 percent of black babies are born into teenage single-parent families. The majority of these births are unplanned and unwanted, and many are the result of sexual abuse. Because teenage mothers frequently do not get good prenatal care and are physically less mature, they suffer more pregnancy complications and more often have babies with physical problems than do women who are married or give birth to planned babies. Prematurity and low birth weight—which increases the likelihood of cerebral palsy, mental retardation, and epilepsy—occur most frequently in the babies of teenage mothers.

- Teenage mothers need health care, peer counseling, and parenting-skills education. Most importantly, teenage parents need adequate social support systems— ones that will encourage them to stay in school and continue their education.

- Divorce is a difficult family event. Even when both parents agree to a divorce and handle the separation amicably, the family members experience stress, ambivalence, fear, doubt, and concern for the future. Reactions and effects on the children vary according to age, personality, family dynamics, religious and ethnic heritage, and socioeconomic status.

- Four factors determine the adjustment of children to a divorce in the family: the degree of conflict experienced between the parents, a continued relationship with both parents after the divorce, the kind of responsibilities given to children after the divorce, and the degree to which children accept the reasoning behind the divorce.

- Nearly 40 percent of American children born today will live in a stepparented family before they are 18 years old. What makes stepparenting difficult is the lack of clear guidelines concerning roles, responsibilities, financial obligations, and legal standing. What makes it so difficult to design guidelines is the interactive variety that characterizes blended families.

- The success or failure of stepparenting is built on factors such as prior experiences of all members of the family; the sex, ages, and developmental stages of the children in the blended family; the professional and psychological issues of the adults in the blended family; and the way the family negotiates differences between all family members— within and outside the blended family.

- More than three million American children under the age of 18 are now living in the home of a grandparent or spending a significant part of their growing-up time with a grandparent. More than any other ethnic group, black grandparents have traditionally taken in children— usually family members, but sometimes the children of friends or neighbors. Many grandparents experience great stress, leading to physical and emotional problems.

- It is estimated that there are between five and six million lesbian and gay parents in the United States. Studies show no differences between the children of homosexuals and the children of heterosexual parents in regard to sexual orientation. There is no evidence to suggest that, compared to offspring of heterosexual parents, psychosocial development among children of gay men or lesbians is compromised in any respect.

- Each year in the United States, about 50,000 children are legally adopted by nonrelatives, not including stepparents. Families also show considerable variety in their ability to nurture the children they raise. It is the adopted child's character and strength combined with the adoptive family's ability to accept, love, and care for the child that determines the success of the adoption.

Student Activities

1. Spend an entire day with a single, working parent who has two or more children. Record this parent's activities from the moment he or she arises to the moment he or she goes to bed.

2. Imagine adopting a child from a foreign country. Develop a plan that allows you as a parent to help your child keep an identity with his or her original culture while becoming a part of your family and culture.

3. Interview three children of different ages who are growing up in stepparented families. Determine what they like and dislike about the arrangement. Consider solutions to problems these children mention.

Helping Hands

The Stepfamily Foundation
333 West End Avenue
New York, New York 10023
(212) 877-3244
http://www.stepfamily.org

Stepfamily Association of America
215 Centennial Mall South, Suite 212
Lincoln, NE 68508
(402) 477-7837
http://www.stepfam.org/

Parents Without Partners
7910 Woodmont Avenue, Suite 1000
Washington, DC 20014

CHAPTER

Special Issues
of Parenting

Chapter Highlights

After reading Chapter 6, students should be able to:

- Identify the various special problems that confront parents
- Understand the challenge of raising a learning disabled child
- Understand children's reactions to a death in the family
- Recognize and understand the forces that lead to maltreatment in the family
- Understand the impact of alcoholism on the family process

Chapter Contents

- The Exceptional Child
  Physical Disabilities ▪ *Coping as a Family* ▪ *An Effective Coping Pattern* ▪ *Learning Disabilities* ▪ *Attention Deficit Disorder*
- A Death in the Family
  Children's Experience of Death ▪ *In Infancy and Toddlerhood: A Living Image* ▪ *The Preschooler's Magical Thoughts* ▪ *School-Age Children and the Silent Treatment* ▪ *Adolescence and Responsibility*
- Maltreatment in the Family
  Above All, Do No Harm ▪ *Maltreatment Myths* ▪ *The Maltreated Child* ▪ *Causes and Circumstances of Child Maltreatment* ▪ *The Hidden Victims of Family Violence*
- Alcohol in the Family
  The Roles Children Take ▪ *The Adult Children of Alcoholics*

INTRODUCTION

In August of 1996, a 10-year-old boy named Taylor Touchstone became lost in a Florida swamp. He survived for four days among poisonous snakes and alligators and violent nighttime thunderstorms before being rescued by a fisherman who found him floating in a murky river miles from where he began his ordeal. What is astounding about this rescue is that Taylor has *autism,* a developmental disorder characterized by profound aloneness, ritualistic behavior, and difficulty in relating to and communicating with others. When asked to comment on Taylor's survival against such odds, his mother said that when her son was young she decided to give him as much freedom as safely possible and to treat him like any other child. This meant letting him go swimming, visit neighbors, and roam the aisles of area stores. His self-reliance, combined with his particular disability and incredible luck, made it possible for Taylor's ordeal to end well.

Physical and cognitive disabilities are some of the special problems that confront parents as they raise their children. Others include the difficulties that arise from the dissolution of a marriage, child maltreatment, alcoholism in the family, and the death of a parent or child. These problems, once covered by secrecy, now are considered challenges to be understood and faced.

THE EXCEPTIONAL CHILD

Few events are more stressful to parents than discovering that one of their children is *exceptional;* that is, different in some way from "normal" children. "Exceptional" refers to children with special needs, including physical handicaps, emotional problems, learning disabilities, sensory impairments, difficulties in communicating, and mental retardation. Children who are especially gifted also fall under the category of exceptionality, but obviously the problems are not the same (See Table 6.1).

TABLE 6.1   Types of Exceptionality

DEFINITIONS AND PREVALENCE OF TYPES OF EXCEPTIONALITIES

Disability	Definition	Prevalence
Physical disabilities	Physical limitations that interfere with school attendance or learning to such an extent that special services, equipment, training, or facilities are required; does not include children whose primary characteristics are visual or hearing impairments.	0.05% of population

TABLE 6.1   (continued)

Disability	Definition	Prevalence
Mental retardation	Significantly subaverage general intellectual functioning (below 70–75 IQ) existing concurrently with deficits in adaptive behavior and manifested during the developmental period. May be mild, moderate, or severe.	1–3% of population; 89% mildly retarded
Learning disabilities	Substantial academic difficulties with intelligence in the normal range, creating significant discrepancy between expectations for performance and actual performance; primary cause of school-related problems; not a single condition; may be coupled with behavioral problems.	4.4% of population
Communicative disorders	Speech impairment (voice, articulation, and fluency disorders) and language impairment in the areas of form (phonology, morphology, syntax), content (semantics), and use (pragmatics).	25% of all children receiving special education services
Hearing impairments/ Deafness	Hearing impairment—Hearing is impaired but the individual can process information from sound, usually with the help of aids. Deafness—Individual has little hearing even with aids; cannot use hearing to gain information.	0.13% of population, 95% of deaf children are prelingually deaf
Visual Impairment/ Blindness	Visual impairment—Individual can read print with the use of large-print books and/or magnifying devices. Blindness— Vision is so impaired that the individual must learn to read Braille or use audiotapes and records.	0.10% of population
Emotional/ behavioral disorders	Behaviors adversely affect educational performance and are exhibited to a marked degree over a long period of time; includes schizophrenic children but not socially maladjusted unless severely emotionally disturbed; excludes children with mild forms of behavior.	3–5% of population
Developmental delay (Applies to 3–5 year-old children only; discretionary category for service eligibility)	Significant delays in one or more domains of physical, cognitive, communication, social/emotional, and adaptive development that warrant special education and related services.	
Giftedness	Evidence of high performance capability in intellectual, creative, artistic, or leadership capacity or in specific academic fields; children require services not ordinarily provided by the school to develop such capabilities fully.	3–5% of population

Source: Hallahan, D., and Kauffman, J. (1994). *Exceptional Children: Introduction to Special Education* (p. 68). Boston: Allyn and Bacon.

Parents dream of having a "perfect" child, so the knowledge that a son or daughter has a disability often comes as a shock. Normal reactions include *denial,* a repression of the knowledge so as to allow time for adjustment, *depression,* a feeling of helplessness, *anger,* questioning "why me?" and *guilt,* feeling responsible in some way for the disability. A number of researchers have noted that when parents learn of a child's disability they experience a grieving process. Depending on the severity of the child's disability, the parents have to alter or amend the expectations they had for the child. (Hinderliter, 1988). Also, the initial awareness and its accompanying feelings of panic and guilt come at a time when the mother is physically and emotionally vulnerable because of the pregnancy and childbirth.

Parents and teachers must set expectations of special-needs children that are developmentally appropriate.

The Informed Parent 6.1

When a Child Is Not Hearing Properly

It is not always easy to identify children's hearing problems. Some signs are obvious, but others are so subtle that they may go unnoticed for a long time. Here are some behaviors that a child may demonstrate:

- frequently breathes through mouth
- turns in the direction of sound
- has difficulty acquiring language; poor speech patterns
- needs things repeated
- has difficulty understanding and following directions
- mumbles or talks loudly
- does not interact with others; appears quiet and withdrawn
- responds inappropriately to requests
- voice quality is extremely high, low, hoarse, or monotonous
- rubs or pulls at ears
- uses gestures rather than words
- prefers activities that do not require hearing
- mispronounces many words

PHYSICAL DISABILITIES

Approximately 200,000 children in the United States have physical disabilities severe enough to warrant extra care and special education. Sometimes the physical disabilities are accompanied by other problems such as learning disabilities or emotional problems (Hallahan and Kauffman, 1994). Common physical disabilities include cerebral palsy, spina bifida, multiple sclerosis, polio, rheumatoid arthritis, asthma, diabetes, and hemophilia.

In the past, such physical problems were kept in the shadows. There was little practical or emotional support for the parents, and it was quite common for children like Tyler Touchstone to be placed in institutional care. In recent years, the special problems of parenting exceptional children are much more in the open. Medical advances have increased the survival rate and life expectancy of disabled children, and society has changed its perception of special children, so that they now are being accepted as valued members of families.

COPING AS A FAMILY

Today most children with special problems remain in their homes, and most families cope with this difficult and special experience. Bryan Strong and Christine DeVault (1992) have outlined the specific stresses that a family with a chronically ill or disabled member will experience. They include:

■ Strained family relationships, including resentment by the caregiver or other family members; competition for time between the ill or disabled person, the caregiver, and family members; overt or covert rejection of the ill or disabled family member; and coalitions between the ill or disabled person and the primary caregiver that leave other family members out. Overprotection may be especially prominent in families with disabled children.

■ Modifications in family activities and goals, such as reduced leisure, travel, or vacation time; change in personal or work goals (especially by the primary caregiver); and concern over having additional children if the illness or disability is genetic.

■ Increased tasks and time commitments, such as providing special diets, daily therapy, or treatments; making appointments and providing transportation to medical facilities; possible need for constant attendance.

■ Increased financial costs resulting from medication, therapy, medical consultation, and treatments, special equipment needs, and so on. Babysitting is the largest single out-of-pocket expense for families with physically disabled children.

■ Special housing requirements, including close proximity to medical facilities, optimal climate conditions, and special housing features such as wheelchair ramps.

■ Social isolation, resulting from the reactions of friends and relatives, individual or family embarrassment; limited mobility; fear of exposure to infections or conditions that might exacerbate the illness; inability to predict behavior; or lack of available time for social interactions.

■ Medical concerns, such as the individual's willingness or ability to follow prescribed treatment; obtaining competent medical care or minimizing pain and discomfort; and uncertainty of the medical prognosis.

■ Grieving over disabilities and limitations, restricted life opportunities, and, for some, anticipation of early or painful death.

In the 1980s, Jeanette Beavers and her colleagues carried out a longitudinal, cross-sectional study of families whose children were enrolled in the special education program of a Dallas (Texas) public school district. The researchers' goal was to assess each family's structure, performance, feelings, and ways of relating. The five-year project (1980–1985) focused on 157 families of preschoolers (3–5 years old at first contact) and 59 families of children at critical transition points in life (6–8 years, 12–14 years, and 18–21 years). The families represented the school population with respect to race, socioeconomic background, and family composition. The children presented a wide range of physical and cognitive disabilities.

Researchers used a structured interview, augmented by a 10-minute period of family play or picture drawing during which the interviewer withdrew. Sessions were videotaped for subsequent viewing by families, researchers, and school personnel. Assessment of the family sessions was based on the Beavers Family Assessment model of competence and style (Beavers, 1977). The competence continuum measures family structure, boundaries, power distribution, negotiating shells, ability to express feelings, conflict resolution, and general mood. Other aspects of family functioning were measured, including degree of closeness, loyalty, independence, and mutual interdependence.

"Healthy" families were shown to have clear, flexible structures and rule systems. They negotiate with each other skillfully, encourage autonomy, allow a wide range of feelings to be expressed, and are generally warm and empathic. "Mid-range" families are not as flexible in structure, and they negotiate with average difficulty. They allow only moderate individuation, are more focused on control, and repress their feelings. "Borderline" and disturbed families have either chaotic or rigidly inflexible structures. They tolerate little or no individuation and are too hostile to negotiate and resolve conflicts effectively. (Beavers and Gordon, 1983; Beavers, Hampson, Hulgus, and Beavers, 1986).

Jeanette Beavers found that families with many interests and activities coped better with the extra demands of having a special child. While babysitting arrangements were difficult to make and outings took extra work, families who managed these activities had a better sense of satisfaction. Fathers who were the most satisfied with their jobs also showed the least negative concern about their disabled children. The families rated as best adjusted to their situation were those in which members acknowledged their resentment, sadness, and fears. Siblings and disabled children were less constrained in families that encouraged this kind of flexibility in expressing their feelings. Play and humor were additional important characteristics of high-coping families.

Following is a compilation of responses the parents made when asked how the family coped with the challenge of an offspring's disability:

- Pay attention to the child. Be patient and let him know he is loved.

- Treat the child naturally and expect her to do what she can.

- As soon as you know your child has a problem, seek all the help available (information, programs, helping persons). Keep looking until you feel satisfied.

- Find things the child likes to do and work with him; the child's self-esteem grows with experience.

- It's normal to feel anger and sadness about the problem, but you need not blame yourself or feel ashamed of the child.

- Parents must help each other with feelings and responsibilities about their child.

- Don't neglect the other children; spend individual time with them, too.
- Talk about the disability naturally with the family and be open to each other's feelings about it.
- Have as many outside experiences as possible to enjoy your life.
- Find help and understanding wherever you can. Talk to other parents, join an organization, get counseling.
- Don't rush things and don't give up. It takes time, and remember you and the child are learning.

Parents of disabled children often experience ambiguity about how much help to give their child and how much independence to encourage. The National Information Center for Children and Youth with Handicaps (1990) suggests that parents examine first their own biases and expectations concerning their children. Are they being realistic about the child's capabilities? Are they being overprotective out of love and concern? Do they have a stereotypical view of the disabled child as helpless and dependent? Is this especially true of female children? The Center proposes that parents help their child to *aspire* to his or her fullest capacity. This means becoming knowledgeable and involved in educational options. This recommendation is particularly important because up to 40 percent of disabled children do not receive the medical and educational help that is available to them (Collins, 1986).

Parent using sign language.

The Informed Parent 6.2

Coping Strategies for Families with Chronically Ill Children

Strategies for coping with children who are chronically ill are the same as those for children with disabilities.

1. Maintain family integration, cooperation, and optimism about the situation.
2. Emphasize doing things as a family, thereby strengthening family relationships.
3. Maintain an overall optimistic attitude toward life, especially with the ill or disabled family member.
4. Maintain social support, self-esteem, and psychological stability by being actively involved in outside social relationships and activities.
5. Develop techniques for handling psychological tensions and strains; for example, such as taking breaks, seeking counseling, and finding additional help.
6. Develop relationships with families that have similar problems; share information and provide support for each other. Try to understand and master necessary medical information through consultations with local or available experts and by reading articles in magazines and journals.

It is difficult to calculate the amount of stress that exists in families raising a disabled child because the difficulties of caring for the child are often combined with other problems. For example almost one-fourth of the mothers are forced to give up their jobs in order to stay home with the child; 41 percent report refusing offers of paid employment. In these cases, financial burdens are added to others that come with the birth of a disabled child (Trute, 1990). Studies show that 62 percent of these caregiving mothers receive no help with household chores, and the same number never or rarely engaged babysitters so they could get a break from their routines. (Marcenko and Meyers, 1991). Mothers of disabled children spend twice as much time caring for their youngsters as do mothers of children without disabilities (Innocenti, et al., 1992).

Researchers have found, in comparing mothers and fathers in this situation, that mothers experience more stress than fathers. Mothers report more depression and feelings of incompetency, as well as increased health problems; fathers reported difficulty in attachment (Beckman, 1991).

Clearly, the parents of children with disabilities need considerable social support, particularly from each other but also from family members and

It is important for families to be open and honest about disabilities so that family, friends, and others can offer support.

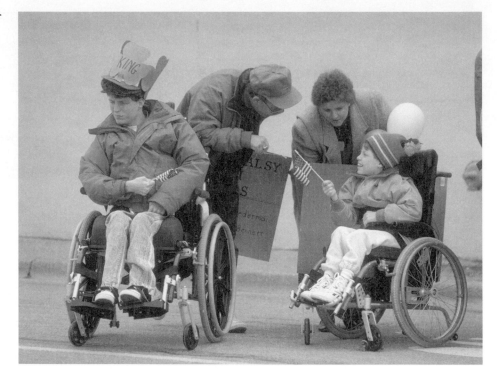

friends. Parents take a more positive approach to their situation when they have the understanding and support from the people around them (Trivette and Dunst, 1992).

AN EFFECTIVE COPING PATTERN

Jeanette Beavers cautions parents to understand that—beginning with the earliest recognition of something different about a child—the quest for a clear understanding may take several years. The need to know what is wrong, what that means, and what family members can do is a shared family task—one of varying complexity, depending on the type of handicap. She encourages open discussion about the disability within and outside the family, including how to describe it in words, what kinds of limitations to expect, and how to deal with those limitations; and she states that such discussion is essential for the family's comfort and confidence. For example, the mother of a handicapped child might say to a non-family member, "Marie has cerebral palsy and can't talk, but she likes for people to talk to her." Jeanette Beavers noted that—as with all important family tasks—being reasonably clear about a child's disability is largely a do-it-yourself process, requiring renewed efforts at different points in the life cycle and in different situations.

LEARNING DISABILITIES

It is often not until school age that parents discover their child is *learning disabled.* This catchall phrase is used to describe a variety of disabilities whose cause is a dysfunction in the brain or central nervous system. (See Table 6.2.) Children with learning disabilities generally have normal or above normal intelligence, but there is often a discrepancy between their intelligence and their performance. They may exhibit specific disorders of memory, thinking, or language use, or they may demonstrate a disorganized approach to learning (Smith and Luckasson, 1993). The National Joint Committee on Learning Disabilities (1988) defines this wide range of learning disabilities:

> Learning disabilities is a general term for a diverse group of disorders characterized by significant difficulties in the acquisition and use of listening, speaking, reading, writing, reasoning, or computing. These disorders stem from the individual and may occur across the life span. Problems in self-regulatory behaviors, social perception, and social interaction may exist with learning disabilities but do not by themselves constitute a learning disability. Learning disabilities may occur concomitantly with other handicapping conditions but are not the result of those conditions (Slavin, 1994).

Specific learning disabilities include *dyslexia,* an impairment in reading ability, *dysgraphia,* an impairment in the ability to write, and *dyscalculia,* difficulty in computing and learning math. Dyslexic children often read words

---

TABLE 6.2   Characteristics of Children with Learning Disabilities

Children who have learning disabilities may demonstrate a wide variety of problems. Some common characteristics include the following.

- Normal intelligence, and sometimes giftedness
- Discrepancy between intelligence and performance
- Attention deficit, and high level of distractibility
- Hyperactivity and impulsiveness
- Poor motor coordination and spatial-relation perception
- Problem-solving difficulties and disorganization
- Problems in perceiving numbers, letters, or words
- Difficulty with self-regulated activities
- Problems with memory, thinking, or language
- Immature social skills

Source: Adapted from Smith, D.S., and Luckasson, T. (1993), *Introduction to Special Education.* Boston: Allyn and Bacon, pp. 227–233.

backward or reverse elements, so that "good" looks like "doog." They may have slight to severe problems in reading and writing because of difficulty associating the sound of words to their written form. Dysgraphic youngsters usually take a long time with written school assignments, and their writing is difficult to read. Dyscalculic children have trouble with addition, subtraction, and other elementary computing skills.

The exact cause of these and other learning disabilities is unknown. Such difficulties often run in families, so there may be a hereditary link (Pennington and Smith, 1988). Other possible causes include prenatal exposure to a teratogen or brain injury during birth.

ATTENTION DEFICIT DISORDER

Learning disabilities are associated with problems in self-regulation, social perception, and social interaction. These problems may be a result of learning disabilities, but, they are not in themselves learning disorders. *Attention deficit disorder* (ADD) refers to the inability to focus attention and concentrate for a substantial period of time. ADD children are usually identified by second grade, because ordinary school tasks show them to be easily distracted from what they are doing and they have considerable trouble concentrating (McKinney and Speece, 1986).

Attention deficit disorder may be due to genetic endowment, exposure to teratogens such as alcohol or drugs during the prenatal period, chemical additives in the diet or vitamin deficiencies, lead poisoning, family interactions, or failure to provide adequate recreational space.

Treatment for ADD focuses on the use of proactive drugs such as Ritalin or Cylert, psychotherapy and special education, and a structuring or restructuring of the child's environment. (See Table 6.3.) Edward Hallowell and John Ratey (1994), noted for their work in this area, point out that the term *deficit* is a misnomer, because children with ADD sometimes pay attention exceptionally well, to the point of perseverating—that is, getting stuck on a task that interests them greatly. Rather than a deficiency, these children have attention *inconsistency* or *variability.*

One form of ADD, classified as *attention deficit hyperactivity disorder* (ADHD), affects about 4 percent of U.S. elementary school children—and three times as many boy as girls (Braswell and Bloomquist, 1991). Children with ADHD are unable to sit still in class, are easily distracted by stimuli in the environment, exhibit emotional outbursts, have difficulty following instructions, do not play or interact well with other children, do not stay on task, and may engage in physically dangerous activities.

Over the past twenty years there have been passed a number of federal laws that entitle learning-disabled children to special education at public expense. However, children who are enrolled in these "special education" classes are often negatively labeled and stigmatized, leading in turn to social and emotional problems and lower self-esteem (Sater and French, 1989).

TABLE 6.3   Structuring the Environment of ADD Children

Edward Hallowell and John Ratey feel children should be told the truth about their disability in words they can understand. Parents must also structure the home environment so that children can perform optimally. Here are some suggestions these researchers make to the parents of ADD children.

- Sit down with the child, or the whole family, and write down exactly what the problem areas are. It is good to define, and thereby limit, each problem instead of leaving it indefinite or vague.
- Identify specific remedies for each problem area.
- Use concrete reminders such as lists, schedules, and alarm clocks.
- Use incentive plans. Don't think of them as bribes. Children with ADD are born entrepreneurs.
- Give frequent feedback. Kids with ADD often don't see what they are doing as they are doing it. Don't wait until the house is completely torn apart before suggesting that it be put back together.
- Give responsibility whenever possible.
- Make abundant use of praise and positive feedback.
- Consider using a coach or tutor for schoolwork. Your role is that of parent, not supervisor-tutor-badgerer-teacher.
- Provide any devices the child demonstrates are helpful. Ask the child what will help, and experiment with different plans and devices.
- Always remember: Negotiate, don't struggle.

Source: Hallowell and Ratey, 1994.

Children with learning disabilities account for about 5 percent of the school population. School systems, teachers, and parents are challenged by children who have a number of other problems (Ysseldyke and Algozzine, 1990). It is important to understand that, while a child may have a particular disability, he or she could be as capable as any nondisabled child in most areas. Robert E. Slavin (1994) believes that, regardless of the age or grade level, teachers can help special-needs children fit in socially with their classmates by modeling an attitude of caring and acceptance and by helping all the children understand that people learn in many different ways. Parents and teachers must set expectations of special-needs children that are developmentally appropriate and achievement-oriented. They must provide opportunities for the children to participate fully in classroom and home routines and responsibilities and capitalize on the children's personal academic and leisure interests to bring them together with peers.

The Informed Parent 6.3

Asking Questions, Getting Answers

Parents want and need accurate information to understand children who learn differently than the majority of their peers do. Such information can be obtained from a number of organizations, including Children with Learning Disabilities (ACLD) and Children and Adults with Attention Deficit Disorders (CHADD). Following are some important questions for parents to ask of the psychologist or other professional diagnosing their child.

- What are my child's strengths?
- What are my child's weaknesses?
- How much disparity is there between the two?
- Is any further testing by medical specialists needed?
- Is a neurological examination advised?
- Will educational treatment alone be enough?
- Does my child need a special class or special school?
- Does my child need a tutor? An occupational therapist? A speech therapist?
- Does my child or my family need psychological counseling?
- Does my child need medication?
- What can the school do to help?
- What can I, as a parent, do?

Source: Adapted from *No Easy Answers: The Learning Disabled Child,* U.S. Department of Health, Education, and Welfare, 1978.

Many learning disabled children also exhibit what school authorities and parents call *social/emotional problems.* Children with learning disabilities often experience years of frustration as they struggle in school and find themselves rejected by peers and a disappointment to their parents. Interestingly, the learning disabled children often see themselves as more skilled academically and more popular with peers than do their parents (McLoughlin, Clark, Mauck, and Petrosko, 1987). Some parents, in their concern, become overly protective and overly involved in trying to correct the problem.

A parent who suspects his or her child has a learning disability should do the following:

1. Get a diagnosis from a professional in the field. Sometimes the school system will recommend or provide an expert.

2. Be clear about the skills, aptitudes, and behaviors that the expert will test.

3. Help your child understand exactly what will happen during the testing procedure. Answer the child's questions about the test honestly.

4. Request treatment recommendations from the professional. Some children need tutors, and others should be in special classes or schools.

5. Be sure to get a copy of the test results. If testing is done privately, the copy will help convince school authorities of the need for special attention.

A DEATH IN THE FAMILY

Nothing disrupts a normal family developmental process as much as a death in the family. A family death is particularly stressful in American society because our cultural forces often repress or deny this piece of the life cycle. Medical and technological advances have sometimes created the perception that death can be avoided until very old age. Consequently when families experience this kind of loss, they are often shaken to the core and are in need of much help and support to regain their equilibrium. How parents handle the grief generated by a death in the family, and how children adjust to such an event, varies greatly depending on the family's cultural and religious beliefs about death, the social and emotional supports available, the financial resources of the family after the death, and the parents' understanding of their children's capacity to understand this family event (Shapiro, 1994).

CHILDREN'S EXPERIENCE OF DEATH

Children experience the death of a parent, grandparent, sibling, friend or companion, and an animal differently as they age. As their capacities mature, children review and transform their cognitive models of the deceased and of death itself (Shapiro, 1994). When children experience grief and bereavement, they need considerable adult support; parents are often going through an emotionally difficult time themselves so they are unable to reach out to their children. At such a time, parents must be careful not to rely too much on grieving children for their own solace (See Table 6.4).

IN INFANCY AND TODDLERHOOD: A LIVING IMAGE

Infants are presumed to not have the cognitive ability to mourn until the age of 8 to 10 months, but the loss of a parent who has provided continuous, stable care can lead to childhood depression (Bowlby, 1980). In many cultures there is no caregiving interruption when a parent dies because the family has extended kinship arrangements and close social ties to the community. In isolated nuclear families, infants are more vulnerable because other attachments may be interrupted before the death. Ester Shapiro (1994) noted that if a child's caretaking

TABLE 6.4 Children's Grief Reactions

After the death of a family member or friend, children may display one or more of the following grief reactions.

- Nervousness
- Anger
- Depression
- Accident Prone
- Nightmares
- Frequent Illness
- Rebellious Behavior
- Poor Schoolwork

- Promiscuity
- Insomnia
- Overdependence
- Overeating
- Substance Abuse
- Aggressiveness
- Suicide

environment remains supportive and stable and caregivers recognize that the child has suffered a loss, the disruptive effects of death and grief can be minimized. Shapiro cautions that preverbal children who lose a parent face a difficult task as they incorporate a sense of their dead parents into their ongoing development. The image of the deceased parent continues to exist in a young child's mind through the stories, photographs, and memorabilia furnished by other family members. Often the surviving parent and relatives do not want to discuss the deceased parent because they are grief-stricken or they believe such conversations are morbid. It is important, however, for children to have a comforting relationship with a deceased parent, an internalized representation that will help in their development (Silverman, 1992).

THE PRESCHOOLER'S MAGICAL THOUGHTS

Preschool children, who are at a preoperational stage of cognitive development, believe that death is temporary or reversible. Two days after watching a pet parakeet being buried in the backyard a child at the preoperational stage might say, "When is Tweetie coming back?" When told that a loved one is "in heaven," preschool children may assume that heaven is a place one can return from. Shapiro cautions that a preschool child's exploration of death and grief requires a heroic tolerance from family members who are busy dealing with their own emotional upheaval and pain. Questions about death and dying should be openly and honestly discussed with children, as a way to help them through the healing process.

SCHOOL-AGE CHILDREN AND THE SILENT TREATMENT

Children from approximately 7 to 12 years old are able to think more logically about death, but they generally avoid discussing this event. It may therefore appear that they are unaffected by a death in the family; but this is a misunderstanding of the distress, anger, or guilt they feel but try valiantly to control. School-age children tend to repress or avoid overwhelming or painful emotional matters. Their distress is sometimes manifested in misbehavior at home or school that is misdiagnosed as attention deficit disorder (Shapiro, 1994).

ADOLESCENCE AND RESPONSIBILITY

A death in the family, particularly that of a parent, is especially difficult on adolescents who are entering the stage when they can function on an adult level, including with the deceased. Adolescents are capable of cognitively understanding the reality of death and the effects it can have on the future of the family. A death in the family can interfere with the adolescent's struggle for independence, if he or she feels responsible for the family's survival. An adolescent's adjustment after the death of a parent depends upon his or her relationship with the deceased and with the surviving parent. If a teen and a deceased parent were in conflict at the time of the death, the adolescent may feel guilt intermingled with grief. Ester Shapiro (1994), in *Grief as a Family Process,* emphasizes that, in order for adolescents to develop adequately, they need for both living and deceased parents to be present in their lives.

> Children can in fact more substantially continue their own growing up process if they are supported in sustaining a living image of the deceased parent, given the importance of both parents to the child's ongoing development . . . Young children, with limited understanding of death and its circumstances and limited knowledge of their dead parent as a multifaceted adult, need the opportunity to add new information to the evolving understanding and growing image of the dead parent. With the support of the surviving parent and other family members, the child can retain the dead parent as a developmental resource, bringing the image forward in developmental time as a living, loving, evolving presence.

MALTREATMENT IN THE FAMILY

The English drama *Ladybird, Ladybird* tells the story of Maggie Conlon, a working-class woman who has four children by four different men. Although she loves her children and tries to take care of them, Maggie lives with a man who beats her in front of the children. Maggie, who was brutalized as a child, has an uncontrollable temper. At one point, Maggie moves with the children into a welfare hotel. One day she locks the children in their flat so that she can go out drinking. The children are injured in a fire, and social services personnel place them in foster homes. Eventually Maggie meets a new man, Jorge, and they have a child. Social services comes into Maggie and Jorge's home and takes away the new baby. Maggie and Jorge have a second baby. Social services take it directly from the maternity ward. Pregnant again, Maggie is reluctant to let her baby even leave her body. "It stays where it is!" she yells while in labor.

The controversy underlying this drama centers on the question of who can have and keep children. What about people who love their children but are unable to protect them from physical or psychological damage brought on by the parents' own problems? Must parents possess certain competencies before being allowed to have children in their custody? Does an alcoholic, drug addict, or mentally ill person who loves his or her children have a right to keep them at home? Or, is it true that—as a welfare worker testifies at a hearing for Maggie Colon—"Children need more than love. They need support, and they need stability"?

ABOVE ALL, DO NO HARM

In 1874, in New York, an 8-year-old girl named Mary Ellen Wilson was discovered chained, beaten, and starved by her adoptive parents. At that time, there were no city laws to protect children, and the police refused to intervene. This case of child maltreatment was brought to trial because of the efforts of Henry Berg, the man who founded the Society for the Prevention of Cruelty to Animals (SPCA). Eventually the child was placed in an orphanage, and the adoptive mother was sent to prison for a year. Mary Ellen's plight led to the formation of the Society for the Prevention of Cruelty to Children in 1875. Subsequently it led to the establishment of agencies, orphanages, and charity homes for the protection of abandoned or abused youngsters.

For almost 100 years, the issue of child maltreatment was known primarily to the legal and social service systems in America, and there was little public awareness of this serious problem. It wasn't until the 1960s that C. Henry Kempe, a University of Colorado Medical School pediatrician, brought the plight of "the battered child" to the nation's attention (Kempe, et al., 1962). Kempe used radiological techniques that could detect old bone fractures. In essence, Dr. Kempe converted a long-standing social problem into a medical diagnosis. From there, he and his colleagues were able to make clinical observations and conduct research on this phenomenon (Newberger and Bourne, 1978). Eventually, Kempe and his associates expanded the definition of the battered child to include physical, nutritional, and emotional abuse.

Maltreatment has been defined as "the intentional, nonaccidental use of physical force or intentional, nonaccidental acts of omission, on the part of a parent or other caretaker interacting with a child in his care, aimed at hurting, injuring, or destroying that child" (Gil, 1970). In a broader definition, maltreatment includes anything that interferes with a child's optimal development. In that definition, allowing a child to miss school consistently, raising a child in a unsanitary house, or condoning delinquent behavior are all examples of maltreatment. Since the time of Mary Ellen Wilson's plight, physical, nutritional, and emotional mistreatment and neglect of children has been labeled *abuse*. In recent years, however, developmental psychologists prefer the term *maltreatment* because there are many types of mistreatment, some more serious than others. A parent can be neglectful due to a lack of knowledge about children's needs. For example, neglect may include forgetting or failing to have children inoculated for certain diseases or having *latchkey* children, who are left home alone for long periods because the parent cannot find child care for them while he or she works. These neglectful behaviors are quite different than sexual misconduct by a parent.

At the extreme, children are mistreated in a number of ways. *Physical maltreatment* of children includes assaults so severe that they suffer from bruises, welts, broken bones, burns, cuts, or other results of physical injuries. *Sexual maltreatment* includes fondling, intercourse, innuendo, photographing, making sexual comments, and otherwise engaging in any sexual exploitation of children. Children who are *physically neglected* do not receive proper nutrition, are not adequately clothed, do not get medical attention when it is needed, and often go unsupervised. *Emotional neglect* refers to the failure of parents or caregivers to show affection for a child or give emotional support. Children are *psychologically maltreated* by attacks on their self-esteem and sense of emotional and social well-being.

In serious cases of abuse or neglect it is easy to recognize the symptoms of maltreatment. One well-publicized example is parents who vacationed in Mexico while their young daughters remained home alone. It is far more difficult to identify abuse that is subtle and insidious, such as calling the child a name like "Stupid!" or hitting a child without leaving bruises. Estimates of child maltreatment range from 200,000 cases a year to 4 million, a difference being due to definition and sampling methods. For example, D. Russell (1982), who used fourteen separate questionnaires in investigating sexual abuse in San Francisco, found that 28 percent of the women responding had been victimized before they were 14 years old. Of that group, 12 percent had been victimized by a relative. A survey of 796 college students revealed that 19 percent of females and 9 percent of males had experienced sexual abuse as children (Finkelhor, 1984). Recent reports suggest that sexual maltreatment figures are much higher than the numbers reported. Whatever the true figures on child maltreatment of any form, it is clear that this phenomenon exists in epidemic proportions in the United States.

The definition of maltreatment is a controversial one in a country where physical punishment is considered an acceptable way of changing a child's behavior. Even the United States Supreme Court ruled in 1977, in the case of *Ingraham* v. *Wright,* that physical punishment in school is neither cruel nor unusual punishment. Psychologists have noted that children are the only people in America that adults are legally allowed to strike (Zigler and Hunsinger, 1977). And clearly they do so. In 1985, after surveying 3,000 parents, Murray Straus and Richard Gelles reported that 90 percent of parents of children 3 to 4 years old admitted hitting their children in the previous year. Seventy-five percent of parents of children 9 to 10 years old struck their children (Straus and Gelles, 1985).

MALTREATMENT MYTHS

Edward Zigler and Nancy Hall (1991) pointed out that a number of unfounded myths have been perpetuated in regard to child maltreatment. The most pervasive myth is a two-faceted belief that there is an intergenerational transmission of abusive behavior toward children. In this view, abused children grow up to be child abusers, and all child abusers were mistreated when they were children. Much evidence for this theory came from clinical interviews and self-reporting questionnaires completed by the parents of children who had been identified as victims of abuse (Altemeier, et al., 1982). Subsequent research has shown that the majority of parents who were themselves maltreated *do not* in turn maltreat their children (Hunter and Kilstrom, 1979; Egeland and Jacobvitz, 1984). Estimates of adult abusers who were themselves abused range from one-fifth to one-third (Kaufman and Zigler, 1987). Nonabusive parents did have common characteristics that distinguished them from abusive parents. They experienced fewer life stresses, had healthier children, and had social supports. In addition, parents who had been abused in their own childhood were less likely to be abusers if they were able to see that they had been mistreated as children.

A second false belief holds that people who mistreat their children are basically "different" than those who do not. It is more likely that parenting proceeds along a continuum, from excellent to poor. At different points in time, and depending on life circumstances, parents exhibit varying degrees of maltreatment toward their children. Almost any parent might maltreat a child during a period of trouble and feelings of isolation. There is a third view that child maltreatment is primarily a lower socioeconomic class phenomenon and associated more with nonwhites than Caucasians. Brandt G. Steele and Carl B. Pollock (1968) studied 60 families in which child maltreatment had been experienced. They found that abusive parents come from all socioeconomic classes, every educational level, and most religious and ethnic groups.

The likelihood of child maltreatment does increase with family size. Parents of two children are 50 percent more likely to abuse their children than are parents of one child. One study showed that the rate of abuse peaked at five children and declined after that number (Straus, Gelles, and Steinmetz, 1980). While it is estimated that child maltreatment rates are 75 percent higher for mothers then fathers, this figure is misleading because mothers spend considerably more time with children than fathers do. When accounting for hours spent in contact with the children, men and fathers are more likely to mistreat their children (Finkelhor, 1983).

THE MALTREATED CHILD

Some children are more "at risk" for maltreatment than others. In a number of studies, children under age 3 are overly represented in samples of maltreated children. So are premature and low-birth-weight babies and unwanted children. Other "at risk" children include those with congenital anomalies, developmental disabilities such as attention deficits or hyperactivity, and "difficult" babies. Often one child in a family is "chosen" for maltreatment because of his or her temperament, birth order, appearance, or behavior. A scapegoat child is often one who is caught in a power struggle between the parents (Blumberg, 1974). In some cultures, such as India or China, female children are at considerable risk for maltreatment. In both societies, where male children are preferred, female infanticide has been noted.

Parents, when stressed, should turn to family or friends for support, or one of the hot lines available throughout the country.

Maltreated children differ from well-treated children in a number of ways. Extending Mary Ainsworth's attachment studies, Dante Cicchetti (1987) proposed that 70 to 100 percent of abused children can be classified as insecurely attached to their caregivers. The overwhelming majority could be considered in the "disorganized" category (Main and Solomon, 1986). Ann Frodi and Michael Lamb (1980) observed that abusive mothers are more physically aroused by their infant's smiles and cries than are nonabusive mothers. However, abusive mothers are less likely to interact with their infants whether they smile or cry. Abused children's need to be cared for is coupled with fear of their caregiver. They seek connection with and avoid the caregiver at the same time. The confused, undirected behavior patterns exhibited by these children reflect disorganized attachment.

Children, particularly boys, who are physically abused tend to be aggressive. In day-care centers, physically abused toddlers are twice as likely as nonabused toddlers to assault other children (George and Main, 1979). It is likely that the parents serve as aggressive models and the children have learned to hit or kick as a way to solve problems (Parke and Slaby, 1983).

Maltreated children are more likely than nonabused to misbehave in school. They often develop learning and adjustment problems, which in turn lead to academic failure, peer problems, and sometimes substance abuse (Simons, Conger, and Whitbeck, 1988). In adolescence, these children may exhibit rebelliousness, depression, or antisocial behavior (Dean, Malik, Richards, and Stringer, 1986). Abuse and neglect as a child increases the chance of criminal behavior as an adult.

CAUSES AND CIRCUMSTANCES OF CHILD MALTREATMENT

People bring to the parent-child relationship preconceived ideas about what constitutes "good" parenting and "good" children. They have long-standing beliefs and attitudes about the nature of child-rearing tasks and about roles of the child in the relationship. These ideas originate in the parents' family of origin, the individual culture, the culture at large, and the models of parents that are portrayed in the media.

A *learning-theory* view of child maltreatment suggests that often parents are unrealistic about their children; they expect more than children are able to do or be. An insecure parent might look to a child for affection, comfort, and encouragement—the things a parent is supposed to give a child (Steele and Pollock, 1968). These parents usually lack knowledge about normal childhood growth and development, and they get little satisfaction from their role as parents. A number of studies have shown that abusive parents misread their children's cues concerning pain, hunger, and distress; and they incorrectly identify their children's emotional states. For example, a child crying because he or she is tired may be seen as being hungry. When the parent feeds the child, he or she cries more and spits out the food. The parent's frustration level grows, and the likelihood of abuse rises (Camras, et al., 1990).

A *psychiatric model* of maltreatment offers the view that child abuse is most common in families where a parent suffers from a mental or emotional disorder or addiction (Walker, Downey and Bergman, 1989). In other words, people who are immature and unable to handle stress adequately are likely to deal with their children in abusive ways (Polansky, et al., 1981). One study put the number of these immature parents at 46 percent of abusing parents (Gil, 1986) and another put the number at 10 percent (Kempe and Kempe, 1978). One researcher identified the personality traits of abusing parents as belonging in four groups. One group was characterized by chronic hostility and aggression, at war with the world in general. A second group consisted of parents who were rigid and compulsive, lacking warmth and unable to approach problems reasonably. A third group appeared depressed, unresponsive, and immature. The fourth group was experiencing extreme frustration in their personal lives (E. J. Merrill, 1962). While psychiatric or emotional problems play a part in abuse, child maltreatment is too pervasive in the general population to be attributed to psychiatric problems alone.

The *social model* proposes that societal pressure and stress on parents provoke maltreatment, particularly if the struggling families have no help or support available to them (Newberger and Newberger, 1982; Garbarino, 1983). The loss of a job, marital strife, and financial difficulties are three factors that lower parents' tolerance and lead them to strike out at their children (Dodge, Bates, and Pettit, 1990). After a study of German mothers and their newborn infants, one researcher concluded that the strongest predictors of how well or badly a child would be cared for were 1) the mother's personality traits, such as depression or composure, and 2) the condition of the parent's marriage (Engfer, 1984).

Abusing parents are often isolated from other people, even friends and relatives, because they generally mistrust others (Polansky, et al., 1985). Therefore, they have no one to turn to for help in times of stress. Spousal abuse is often a feature of the family's life. In addition, while there are laws against maltreatment of children, American culture continues to condone physical punishment as a way to discipline children, and this view is reinforced through television and films. In countries such as Sweden, where physical punishment is outlawed, child maltreatment is almost nonexistent (Zigler and Hall, 1989).

Jay Belsky (1980) integrated the work of many researchers and a number of other models in presenting an *ecological model* of child maltreatment. His model includes factors that offset maltreatment as well as factors that lead to abuse (See Table 6.5). In doing this, Belsky relied on the work of Urie Bronfenbrenner (1977, 1979) and Niko Tinbergen (1951). These two researchers believed that to comprehend a particular action one had to understand its context, as well as the historical and behavioral events leading up to the event. Belsky's model assumes four levels of interactive influence. The *ontogenetic* level focuses on the personal characteristics and background of the abuser. Does the abuser have a mental health problem? How does the abuser feel toward the maltreated child? What was the abuser's childhood like? The *microsystem* level focuses on the family environment. How many children are there in the family? Does the abuser have a mate? What is the temperament of the maltreated child? The parent's work and social worlds make up the *exosystem* level. Is the abuser employed? Does the family attend church? Are there social supports available to help the abuser? The *macrosystem* level is concerned with the cultural determinants that influence child rearing. What is society's attitude toward violence? How is corporal punishment viewed by the culture at large? Belsky's model suggests that the determinants of abuse form complexly interactive and related systems. As the systems influence each other, there are risk factors that increase the likelihood of maltreatment and compensatory factors that decrease the possibility of abuse. Other researchers have identified specific personality factors, as well as stress and household environment characteristics that contribute to abuse (See Table 6.6).

PREVENTION PROGRAMS

Two avenues to correct a national tragedy of serious proportions are preventing parental abuse and offering help to mothers and fathers who mistreat their children. High school and college courses offer parenting skills information, there are groups such as Parents Anonymous who intervene when necessary,

TABLE 6.5 Determinants of Abuse

Ontogenetic level	Microsystem level	Exosystem level	Macrosystem level
Compensatory Factors			
High IQ	Healthy children	Good social supports	Culture that promotes
Awareness of past	Supportive spouse	Few stressful events	a sense of shared re-
abuse	Economic security/	Strong, supportive	sponsibility in caring
History of a positive	savings in the bank	religious affiliation	for the community's
relationship with one		Positive school	children
parent		experiences and peer	Culture opposed to
Special talents		relations as a child	violence
Physical attractiveness		Therapeutic	Economic prosperity
Good interpersonal		interventions	
skills			
Risk Factors			
History of abuse	Marital discord	Unemployment	Cultural acceptance of
Low self esteem	Children with behavior	Isolation; poor social	corporal punishment
Low IQ	problems	supports	View of children as
Poor interpersonal	Premature or unhealthy	Poor peer relations as	possessions
skills	children	a child	Economic depression
	Single parent		
	Poverty		

and the courts often send abusive parents into family therapy or another form of counseling. The media now emphasizes the worst child-abuse cases, making what was once society's secret a feature on the evening news. When one looks at Belsky's ecological view of abuse, it appears that intervention has to come on a number of levels for abuse statistics to decline. The families of abusing parents must act to prevent the maltreatment; schools, churches, and other social agencies must offer support to parents who want to change the way they deal with their children; and cultures must reverse their view that physical violence is proper parenting behavior. Children in our society have to be viewed as valued members of the family and treated accordingly.

THE HIDDEN VICTIMS OF FAMILY VIOLENCE

Richard Gelles and Claire Cornell (1990) are among the researchers who warn that violence in the family has far-reaching and devastating effects. Violence between spouses or the parental mistreatment of children can affect the behaviors of siblings toward each other and even the relationships between adult children and their aging parents.

TABLE 6.6   Risk Characteristics of Parents and Children

A review of the research and literature pertaining to child maltreatment identifies the specific characteristics of parents, children, and households that place a given family at risk of maltreatment.

Characteristics of Parents

Mental illness
Difficulty dealing with aggressive impulses
Tendency to be rigid and domineering
Lack of social skills
Low self-esteem
Depression
Substance abuse
Poor self-understanding
History of abuse as a child
Observation of physical violence as a child
Lack of attachment to the child
Adolescent social isolation
Inadequate household and child management skills
Lack of parenting skills
Inconsistent use of discipline
Lack of knowledge regarding child development
Sole responsibility for all parenting tasks
Inability to control anger

Characteristics of Children

Behavioral problems or hyperactivity
Unwanted pregnancy
Premature birth
Physical illness
Physical or developmental disabilities
Mismatch with parent's personality
Similarity to an adult disliked by parent

Household Characteristics

Poverty or low income
Blended or reconstituted family
Single parent
Large number of children
Children less than one year apart
Chaotic family systems
Overcrowded or inadequate housing

Stress Factors

Birth of a new baby
Loss of job
Divorce or separation
Death of a close friend or family member
Sudden illness or chronic health problem
Loss of housing
Sudden financial burden

Social/Cultural Factors

Culture of poverty
Tolerance for physical punishment
Sexual stereotypes in child rearing
Community isolation
Violence in the media
Extreme notions of individual rights and
   family privacy

In studying more than 700 families with two or more children researchers found that 82 percent of the families has seen some degree of violence used against a sibling in the previous year (Straus, Gelles, and Steinmetz, 1980). The National Center on Child Abuse and Neglect estimates that almost 30 million siblings harm each other physically each year (Tiede, 1983). The highest rates occur in families with only male children, as generally boys are more violent in the home than girls. While many parents will say that conflicts between children in a family are inevitable, this does not mean that conflict has to be settled by physical force. Just as children learn to handle differences by using violence, they can also learn to solve their problems with each other in healthy and responsible ways.

Perhaps if parents realized that it is not in their best long-term interest to use violence against their children, they would cease to do so. In a statistic that shocks people, it is estimated that 2.5 million parents annually are struck by their adolescent children, including about 900,000 parents kicked, punched, bitten, or threatened with a gun or knife (Gelles and Corness, 1990). Most of these youthful attackers are between the ages of 13 and 24, with sons slightly more likely than daughters to abuse their parents. Mothers are usually the victims of this violence, probably because of their size or strength and because social norms make women less powerful and more "acceptable" targets for angry men (Gelles and Cornell, 1990).

Even more tragic are the estimates that about 500,000 elderly people—again, primarily women—are physically abused by their grown children or their grandchildren. Another 2 million are believed to be emotionally abused or neglected (Gelles and Cornell, 1990). This kind of physical and emotional mistreatment is easy to hide in cases where the elderly are confined to home, sometimes in bed or in wheelchairs, or when they suffer from mental impairments. Some elderly parents are reluctant to report maltreatment by their children for fear of being placed in an institution.

Murray Staus, Richard Gelles, and Suzanne Steinmetz in *Behind Closed Doors* (1980) made the following recommendations for societies to help families decrease their level of violence:

- Organize to stop the use of corporal punishment and encourage the use of alternative disciplinary methods.

- Provide education programs that teach parents positive strategies for dealing with family conflict.

- Establish supportive networks that include relatives, friends, and the community members who can help parents in stressful situations.

- Promote sex education and family planning so that unwanted pregnancies can be avoided.

- Discourage cultural norms that glorify violence as a way to solve problems.

ALCOHOL IN THE FAMILY

Two-thirds of Americans drink alcoholic beverages on occasion, while 5 percent of all adults are heavy drinkers—that is, they consumed at least five drinks on at least five occasions during the past month. Excessive drinking does serious harm to the families and social relationships of millions of Americans

(Steinglass, et al., 1985). The point at which a person is an *alcoholic* is debated. The label may fit when an individual drinks too much, and too often, to the point that there is a physical or psychological dependence on alcohol, or until drinking interferes with a persons job and/or home life.

Alcohol has been described as a psychoactive drug with properties that provide mood and behavior altering experiences when it is ingested into the body (Bepko and Krestan, 1985). The physiological effects of drinking include feelings of warmth, relaxation, and a loosening of inhibitions. Often the drinker experiences a more worthy sense of self and feels a greater acceptance than he or she does when not drinking. People who drink to excess—alcoholics—attempt to continually re-create the good feelings that alcohol consumption produces.

Many researchers have debated the causes underlying alcoholism. It is considered a genetic susceptibility, a learned habit, a stress reducer, or a disease (Peele, 1989). Whatever the cause, excessive drinking interferes with an individual's ability to parent effectively.

The children of alcoholics grow up in dysfunctional family environments, and they are more likely to experience sexual and physical abuse than the children of nonalcoholics (Matthew, et al., 1993; Velleman and Orford, 1993). Children of alcoholics are at an increased risk for a number of psychological problems including depression, anxiety, phobias, attention deficit disorder, and substance abuse. Additional potential problems include low self-esteem, higher than average rates of marital difficulty, and poor communication skills (Greenfield, et al., 1993).

THE ROLES CHILDREN TAKE

Claudia Bepko and Jo Ann Krestan (1985) believe that children are always affected by the alcoholism in a family because excessive drinking distorts and disrupts the functional and emotional ability of a family to evolve appropriate rules, roles, and hierarchies. Normal developmental tasks are interrupted by alcoholism, family communication becomes chaotic, parents often become neglectful or abusive, children are insufficiency nurtured, and the future become ominous. Bepko and Krestan studied at length the long-term implications of growing up in an alcoholic family:

> Children living in such an environment evolved a distinct sense that something is "wrong" with them, and that they are somehow mysteriously responsible for the disorder and unhappiness that they experience. Because they often suffer from neglect and absence of nurturing, they experience chronic feelings of sadness and depression that may continue into their adult years despite therapy or the presence of nurturing relationships in their adult environment.

Claudia Black (1982) proposed that the learned response to living in an alcoholic environment is "don't talk, don't trust, don't feel." The adult child of an alcoholic tends to have a defensive personality, one that sees the world as unfamiliar and potentially dangerous at every turn. As Black noted, the adult child of an alcoholic doesn't know how to cope with many of the emotional and functional demands of adult life.

The Informed Parent 6.4

The Seven-Step Process to Recovery

Joan K. Jackson (1954) outlined a seven-stage process to recovery after studying families of Alcoholics Anonymous members.

Stage 1: The family denies there is a problem, even after a sober adult confronts the issue. The drinker's behavior is tolerated or rationalized.

Stage 2: When the problem intensifies, the sober spouse tries to stop the drinking by threatening, bribing, or hiding the alcohol. Marital conflict increases. Both the sober spouse and the children begin to distance themselves from friends and neighbors in an attempt to hide the problem.

Stage 3: The family become disorganized as the problem can no longer be hidden from the children, friends, the drinker's employer, and others the family comes in contact with. As marital conflict increases, the children are caught between their arguing parents.

Stage 4: A first attempt is made at reorganization when the sober spouse recognizes that family life cannot go on the way it does. By now the alcoholic may be having work problems, mismanaging money, or mistreating the children. The sober spouse seeks help from a public agency or a self-help group such as Al-Anon. Sometimes the drinker promises to stop drinking. When he or she doesn't, the destructive cycle continues.

Stage 5: The family tries to escape the problem when the sober spouse seeks a separation or divorce. Sometimes the alcoholic gives up drinking for a while, but the sober spouse has already taken steps towards saving the family.

Stage 6: The family reorganizes and improves after the separation or divorce, as the sober spouse takes on the role of both parents. The drinker may attempt to reconcile with the family or to "get even" with it.

Stage 7: The family sometimes reunites after the alcoholic seeks help in therapy or a self-help group like AA and begins to control the drinking. This can be a difficult time because family roles must be reworked and feelings be reassessed.

A number of researchers have identified role responses of children in alcoholic family systems. Sharon Wegscheider (1981) believes children adopt the role of hero, scapegoat, lost child, or mascot. Each of these represents a specific way of behaving in the face of family dysfunction.

The Spirit of Parenting

My father introduced me to martinis and Spanish sherry and single-malt Scotch. More relief, a more complete protection. The summer after my senior year in high school, he took me to dinner at a Greek restaurant in downtown Boston. It was the first time we'd ever gone out to dinner alone and he ordered a martini for himself and wine for me. We sat in a red leather booth with paneled walls and when we sat down the waiter addressed my father by name. "Good evening, Dr. Knapp," he said, and my father nodded in his brusque, formal way and ordered the drinks.

I sat on my hands. I remember feeling that particularly acute brand of teenage awkwardness, unable to think of a word to say, and I remember a thick, interminable silence. I also remember an empty feeling, a wariness, something I often felt in my father's presence—looking for some nod of encouragement or approval from him, hoping for something to fill the gap between us.

But then the wine came, one glass and then a second glass. And somewhere during that second drink, the switch was flipped. The wine gave me a melting feeling, a warm light sensation in my head, and I felt like safety itself had arrived in that glass, poured out from the bottle and allowed to spill out between us. I don't remember what we talked about that night, but I do know that the discomfort was diminished, replaced by something that felt like a kind of love . . . .

What a relief it was, what release: the drink turned that weird bond of ours into something I could hold in my hand, like a treasure, instead of something that just glinted in the air between us; it allowed me to respond to my father in a new way, to align myself with him without fear, to seal our pact.

Caroline Knapp
From *Drinking: A Love Story*

- *The Hero:* Often the oldest, this child tends to be an overfunctioner who in later life will experience chronic feelings of guilt and inadequacy. This is the "parentified" child who functions as a surrogate parent and whose job is to help the nonalcoholic parent deal with the alcoholic parent.

- *The Scapegoat:* This child behaves in such an irresponsible way that the attention of the family is deflected away from the alcoholism and conflict in the marital relationship.

- *The Lost Child:* This is the "loner," the son or daughter who adapts by making no demands on the family and staying out of the way. This child receives no nurturance or support. He or she may appear independent, but in fact this facade covers feelings of worthlessness and a deep fear of depending on others.

- *The Mascot:* This child distracts the family with entertaining, childish, and immature behavior. This behavior helps the child to feel some control while living in a chaotic environment; however, this child is often limited by an inability to develop mature coping skills.

Bepko and Krestan cautioned that no child's behavior fits exactly one role. For example, the hero may be over-responsible in practical functioning, but immature on the emotional dimension. Also, roles in families may shift over time, depending on the progression of the alcoholism and changes in the family's life cycle. What is most important to remember is that normal development is interrupted when a family is troubled by alcoholism, and the legacy of addiction perpetuates itself in future generations of the family (Bepko and Krestan, 1985.)

There are a number of treatment options for parents whose drinking infers with normal family functioning. Many alcoholics seek help in individual psychotherapy, while others prefer the support they get in groups. Alcoholics Anonymous is a program based on twelve steps that function as a framework for recovery. Al-Anon is a group designed for the family and friends of alcoholics; Alateen, a part of Al-Alon, is designed specifically for the children of alcoholics.

THE ADULT CHILDREN OF ALCOHOLICS

The effects of growing up with family alcoholism linger long after children leave home to begin their adult lives. Approximately one in four children of alcoholics becomes an alcoholic, compared to one in ten in the general population. Because they came from homes in which there were no healthy adult role models, the children often repeat the dysfunctional patterns of their childhoods. The children of alcoholics often take care of their own parents. In adulthood many choose partners who also need care; they are prone to marry alcoholics or people who are troubled in some way. Because they witnessed so much unacceptable behavior, as adults the children of alcoholics tolerate high degrees of family dysfunctionality. Janet Voititz (1983) outlined a number of traits that characterize personality and behavior of the adult children of alcoholics; that is, they:

> must guess what normal behavior is.
> find it difficult to complete projects.
> often lie even when telling the truth would be easy.
> make harsh judgments of self.
> have difficulty having fun.
> have difficulty forming intimate relationships.
> need approval and affirmation from others.
> feel separate and different from others.
> act either over responsible or irresponsible.
> are extremely loyal, even when their loyalty is undeserved.
> do not consider consequences of their actions.

Chapter Review

- Exceptionality generally refers to children with special needs, including those with physical handicaps, emotional problems, learning disabilities, sensory impairments, difficulties in communicating, and mental retardation. Children who are especially gifted also fall under this category.

- Normal parental reactions to a child's exceptionality include denial, depression, anger, and guilt. A grieving process begins when parents learn of a child's disability because, depending on the degree of the disability, their expectations for the child must be amended.

- Approximately 200,000 children in the United States have physical disabilities severe enough to warrant extra care and special education. The list of physical disabilities include cerebral palsy, spina bifida, multiple sclerosis, polio, rheumatoid arthritis, asthma, diabetes, and hemophilia.

- Considerable stress characterizes families raising a disabled child. Many mothers are forced to give up their jobs; there are extra financial burdens on the family, and few social supports are available.

- Learning disability is a catchall phrase used to describe a wide variety of disabilities whose cause is thought to be in brain or central nervous system dysfunction. These disorders are characterized by significant difficulties in the acquisition and use of language—listening, speaking, reading, and writing—as well as reasoning and computing skills.

- The exact cause of specific learning disabilities is still unknown. Possibilities include heredity, prenatal factors, or brain injury.

- Attention deficit disorder (ADD) refers to the inability to focus one's attention and concentrate for long periods of time. Children so identified are easily distracted and have considerable trouble concentrating on tasks.

- Causes of attention deficit disorder include genetic endowment, exposure to teratogens, chemical additives in the diet, vitamin deficiencies, family interactions, failure to pro-

vide adequate recreational space, and lead poisoning.

- A death in the family is extremely stressful. Adjustment to grief depends upon a family's cultural and religious beliefs, the social and emotional supports available, financial resources of the family after the death, and the parental understanding of the cognitive capacities of the children in understanding this family event.

- Children experience a death in the family differently as they age. As cognitive capacities mature, children review and transform their working model—not only of the deceased but of death itself.

- Maltreatment refers to the intentional, nonaccidental use of physical force or the intentional, nonaccidental acts of omission on the part of a parent or other caretaker interacting with a child in his or her care, aimed at hurting, injuring, or destroying that child. In a broader definition, maltreatment includes anything that interferes with a child's optimal development.

- Some children are more at risk for maltreatment than others. Children under age 3 are overly represented in samples of maltreated children, as are premature and low-birthweight babies, and unwanted children. Other at-risk children include those with congenital anomalies, developmental disabilities such as attention deficits or hyperactivity, and "difficult" babies.

- A number of theories are proposed in regard to child maltreatment. A learning theory view of child maltreatment suggests that parents are unrealistic about their children and lack knowledge of normal childhood growth and development. A psychiatric model offers the view that abuse is more common in families where a parent suffers from a mental or emotional disorder or addiction. The social model proposes that societal pressure and stress on parents provoke maltreatment.

- Jay Belsky integrated the work of many researchers and a number of models in presenting an ecological model of child maltreatment that includes factors that offset maltreatment and factors leading to abuse.

- Treatment programs for abusing parents include education and support for parents who want to change, as well as cultural changes that discourage the use of physical punishment.

- Alcoholism in the family is a serious problem in many American homes. Children in these families are at increased risk for a number of psychological problems including depression, anxiety, phobias, attention deficit disorder, and substance abuse. In later life, they are likely to suffer from low self-esteem and have higher rates of marital difficulty.

- Many alcoholics seek help in individual psychotherapy, while others prefer the support they get in groups such as Alcoholics Anonymous. Al-Anon is a group geared to the family and friends of alcoholics; Alateen, a part of Al-Alon, is designed specifically for the children of alcoholics.

Student Activities

1. Spend an entire day with the parents of a physically handicapped child and describe the experience. What coping strategies are used in the course of the day?

2. Imagine that the beloved family cat died, the one that slept in your child's bed at night. Describe how you would help your child through this loss. What would you say? What, if any, rituals would you perform?

3. Develop a one-minute TV advertising program aimed at helping children understand the detriments of drinking alcohol.

Helping Hands

National Clearinghouse for Alcohol
and Drug Information
P.O. Box 2345
Rockville, MD 20852
(301) 468-2600
www.health.org/

A government-sponsored agency that provides information about drug and alcohol abuse.

Alcoholics Anonymous
475 Riverside Drive
New York, NY 10163
(212) 870-3400
www.alcoholics-anonymous/org/

An international organization devoted to helping people recover from alcoholism; local chapters exist in every state and most cities.

National Council on Alcoholism
and Drug Dependence
12 West 21st Street
New York, NY 10010
(212) 206-6770
www.ncadd.org/more.html

Works for prevention and control of alcoholism by providing information on the problem.

National Information Center for Children
and Youth with Disabilities
P.O. Box 1492
Washington, DC 20013
(703) 893-6061

Provides information to parents and educators on services for children with handicaps.

Parents Helping Parents
535 Race Street, Suite 220
San Jose, CA 95126
(408) 288-5010

Offers a wide variety of services and educational programs to help parents raise children with special needs, including birth defects.

National AIDS Information Clearinghouse
P.O. Box 6003
Rockville, MD 20849-6003
(860) 458-5231

A government-sponsored agency that provides information about AIDS and AIDS related services.

Child Help USA, Inc.
6463 Independence Avenue
Woodland Hills, CA 91370
(818) 347-7280
www.childhelpusa.org/

Promotes public awareness of child abuse through publications, media campaigns, and a speakers' bureau. Supports the National Child Abuse Hotline, (800) #-ACHILD. Callers may request information about child abuse or speak with a crisis counselor.

Parents Anonymous
520 S. Lafayette Park Place, Suite 316
Los Angeles, CA 90057
(213) 388-6685
www.parentsanon.org/

Organization dedicated to the prevention and treatment of child maltreatment. Local groups provide support and training to parents involved in or at risk of maltreatment of children.

National Center on Child Abuse and Neglect
P.O. Box 1182
Washington, DC 20013
(703) 385-7565

Helps states and communities develop programs that identify, treat, and prevent child maltreatment and neglect.

CHAPTER 7

Effective Parenting

Chapter Highlights

After reading Chapter 7, students should be able to:

- Understand different approaches to child rearing
- Recognize the impact of parents' personality on managing child-rearing tasks
- Understand how belief systems determine parental behavior
- Recognize the many styles of parenting and how they impact the behavior of children

Chapter Contents

- Patterns of Parenting
    The Person of the Parent ▪ *The Self-Aware Parent*
- Belief Systems and Parenting
    Parental Cognitions ▪ *Learning Optimism*
- Parenting Styles
    Acceptance and Expectations of Children
- Parent-Education Programs

n April of 1996, American citizens were horrified at the news of the death of 7-year-old Jessica Dubroff who, at her father's urging, attempted to fly a single-engine plane from California to Massachusetts. "Jess wants to be famous, "the father announced just before the plane she was flying crashed near the Rocky Mountains, killing Jessica, her father and a flight instructor.

From the beginning, Jessica Dubroff's life had been different. She was born in a tub of water, without benefit of doctor or midwife, so that she would experience "floating" when she came into the world. Her mother did not allow television, children's books, toys, or school. There was no set meal or bedtime. Instead of dolls and other traditional toys, Jessica was given tools to do chores with. When asked if she believed in childhood, the mother answered, "No!" When questioned about the tragic outcome of the flight, the mother said, "I'd have her do it again in a second."

This incident may seem an extreme of child rearing; however, parents throughout the world bring up children in a myriad of ways. Parents have goals for their children. Some want Olympic athletes or policemen to follow in their father's footsteps; others desire Rhodes scholars, or movie stars. For many people, the object of parenting is to raise healthy, contented, optimistic children—no matter what they become.

Is there a right or wrong way to parent? Do certain qualities of a parent lend themselves to greater competence in child rearing? Are there techniques and methods that help parents be most effective in raising their children? Undoubtedly, Jessica Dubroff's parents considered themselves competent, as do many others whose methods give us pause. "I used to think being a parent meant teaching your children things," Jessica's father said before the fatal flight. "Now I feel my job is to help them learn by exposing them to new experiences."

Is it not the role of a good parent to teach his or her children things? And is it not also important to expose one's offspring to new experiences, albeit safe ones? Children come into the world with a set of behaviors geared to ensure their survival, but the skills they need to eventually assume adult roles in society must be taught and encouraged by parents, teachers, and others they come in contact with. Parents do not rely on one particular technique when raising children. A parent's response to a child depends upon many factors including the age and personality of the child, the particular problem being addressed, the life circumstances of the parent at the time of the response, and the personality of the parent. Professionals working in the field of parent training often take an eclectic approach, using parts of differing philosophies. The problem is: Who teaches mothers and fathers how to become competent parents? How do they learn the methods and strategies that lead to successful child rearing? How do parents show children that they are loved and valued? Beyond cultural and social class influences, what forces influence the way men and women parent their children?

Masai mother and child in a warm encounter that shows parental acceptance.

PATTERNS OF PARENTING

When a Bengali mother wants to show approval and affection for her child, she might peel and seed an orange and hand it to the child. An American mother would be likely to hug or kiss her child (Rohner and Chaki-Sircar, 1988). Cultural differences in the expression of love have been studied at length by Ronald P. Rohner, who defines four principle dimensions of parental relating, using a continuum that ranges from "warm affection" to "undifferentiated rejection" (See Figure 7.1). "Parental acceptance" refers to the love that parents give their children, letting children know they are wanted, valued, and appreciated. Parental rejection denotes parents who display hostility toward their children in the form of anger, aggression, and resentment, or who show their lack of caring through neglect and indifference. According to Rohner, about 25 percent of all societies behave in ways that are consistent with the description of rejection (Rohner, 1975). However, most of these parents are behaving in ways their culture promotes as good and responsible parental behavior. Rohner points out that—even in loving families—children are likely to experience a few hurtful behaviors occasionally. He notes that a child's sense of well-being comes to a child through his or her personal relationships.

When important relationships fail or become distorted, when innermost psychological needs are unmet, subjective distress mounts. Often it erupts into disordered behavior which—over time—may lead to conduct problems, delinquency, drug abuse, psychological maladjustment, learning difficulties, problems with peers and others. To Rohner "these maladaptive behaviors seem merely to be symptoms of the underlying and unresolved hurt associated with perceived parental rejection."

> . . . individuals who have experienced so much hurt at the hands of their parents and who, as a result, often dislike themselves and are angry, insecure, and the like, come to expect little good from life. The very essence of

Figure 7.1
Parents around the world express their love (acceptance) or love-withdrawal (rejection) in four principal ways.

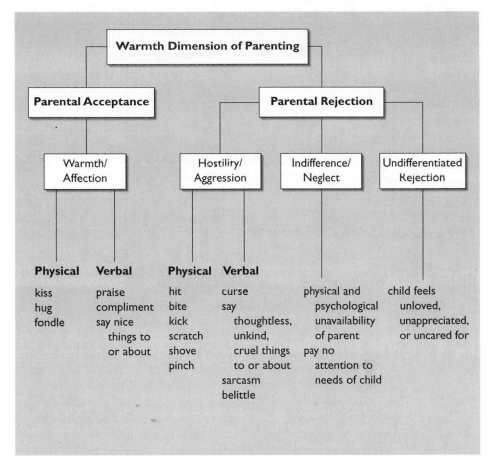

life and of existence itself for many rejected people is viewed as threatening, dangerous, and unhappy (Rohner, 1986).

The Rohner research shows how different parents are in their approach to child rearing, but it doesn't show why there are such differences. What qualities must a parent have to achieve the primary goals of parenting: to raise contented, competent children who are able to be productive, contributing members of society? British psychiatrist Donald Winnicott (1967) believes that there is a continuum of parenting, from excellent to severely pathological (See Figure 7.2). To Winnicott, children are born with a set of genetic determinants that influences their development, so their parents need only be "good enough," meaning moderately competent, in child-rearing skills. Subsequent studies by Diane Baumrind (1991) indicated that "good enough" is not really good enough, in the sense that the more effective a parent is, the happier and more competent the child becomes. In turn, the more effective parenting provides a more satisfying experience.

Eleanor Maccoby (1983) and other researchers identified three parenting constructs most likely to promote child development: *parental support, parental*

Figure 7.2
The Parenting
Continuum

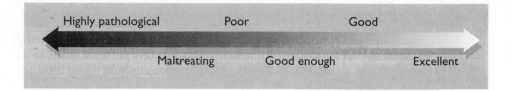

control and environmental structure. The warmth and affection of parents make children feel accepted and valued. Flexible and reasonable discipline methods foster children's self-reliance, and an organized, stimulating environment provides the consistency and order children need to feel safe and competent.

THE PERSON OF THE PARENT

Doubtless Jessica Dubroff's parents considered themselves competent to raise children, as do most parents engaged in this enterprise. But are there distinct characteristics or competencies needed to raise children effectively? What personal qualities and skills are necessary to accomplish the best child rearing?

Jay Belsky (1984) presumes that parenting is influenced by forces from within the individual parent (personality), within the individual child (characteristics of child), and from the broader social context in which the parent-child relationship is embedded (marital relations, social networks, occupational experience of parents) (See Figure 7.3). A parent's developmental history and personality actually shapes the experience of parenting *indirectly*. A troublesome marriage, for example, affects the psychological well-being of a parent, and this

Figure 7.3
Determinants
of Parenting: A
Process Model

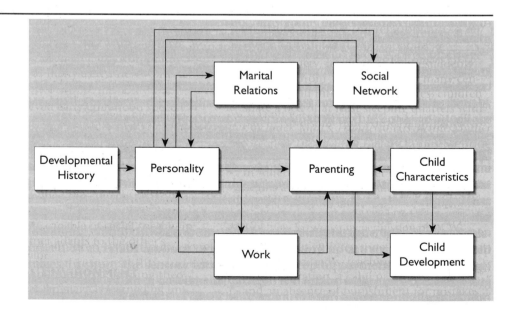

in turn impacts parenting abilities. Belsky believes that the marital relationship serves as the principal support system for parents. Fathers who feel support from their wives have a high sense of parental competence regardless of their children's temperaments. Stepping back, it is proposed that the quality of a marriage is in itself a function of parents' developmental histories and personalities. Similarly, if a parent is having employment difficulties brought on by personality problems, then that parent's life becomes more stressful, a circumstance that impacts the quality of parenting.

Since all children need parents who are *sensitively* attuned to the developmental changes that occur in growing children, it stands to reason that the psychological characteristics of a parent are a key determinant of effective parenting. Mature and mentally healthy individuals, those who score low in depression and anxiety and high in adjustment, express more positive feelings toward their children than do parents who are immature and lacking in ego strength (Cox, Owen, Lewis, and Henderson, 1989). Also, the calmness, patience, and empathy make parenting a more positive experience, whereas impatience and difficulties in handling stress make it less positive. It is Belsky's view that the healthier parents are psychologically, the better able they will be to meet the challenges of family life and withstand the stresses that come with raising children.

In some families, children are denied growth opportunities because their parents are self-absorbed, detached, and unemphathetic—in other words, narcissistic. Narcissists have an exaggerated need for reassurance and an excessive concern with external appearance over internal substance (Donaldson-Pressman and Pressman, 1994). Narcissistic parents put the parental system above the children. This is particularly true when a parent is addicted to drugs, alcohol, or gambling. Depressed mothers often create a home environment that is disruptive, hostile, and rejecting—a climate that undermines appropriate child development (Colletta, 1983).

Psychologist George Holden (1997) proposed that parental effectiveness can be gauged by looking at five areas: *attachment, social learning, social interaction, teaching,* and *environmental structure.*

Parents differ in their ability to be *involved* with their children; that is, to display a commitment to meeting their children's needs. Clearly children have basic physical and safety needs. If they are to develop optimally, they must have food, shelter, clothing, a decent home, and protection. To be effective, then, parents must commit a good part of their lives to providing for these needs and to being available when needed (Greenberger and Goldberg, 1989). Parents must also be aware of how children's needs change as they grow and develop. Problems in this area often arise when an action or behavior that was protective in childhood becomes overprotective during adolescence. Once early childhood passes, age-appropriate parent-child relationships can become such a difficulty in some families that ineffective parents disengage from their children (Hetherington and Clingempeel, 1992). In American society, involved parents watch their children play ball, attend parent-teacher conferences, and deliver and pick up children after school events.

Effective parents are *sensitive* to their children's cues. They respond appropriately to signals for food, comfort, and attention. They perceive emotional states and display a kind of "mirroring," an empathic awareness that tells children they are understood. This sensitivity is a key feature of what is called *warmth*—affection or love. Warmth is displayed in many ways, including physical affection, playfulness, generosity, expressions of approval, and caring communication.

Effective parents model appropriate behaviors and do not model undesirable behaviors. When parents cooperate with each other and with their children, they are offering a model of how to get along with others. Coping with stress, handling crises, meeting challenges, planning, and decision making are among those actions and behaviors parents must model for their children if the children are going to have these abilities as they grow up.

Effective parents encourage social interactions that are appropriate to their children's ages. They direct their children toward tasks that use skills or knowledge they already have but also present the children with new learning situations, ones that require some effort and assistance to reach a more advanced level.

Effective parents act as mentors to their children. They guide and teach their children things they have to know if they are to live successfully. According to Holden, effective parents use more positive reinforcement, questions, and feedback with young children than do less effective parents. Competent parents are more likely to converse with their children on topics that include feelings or needs of individuals, reasons for rules, and expectation of behaviors. They stimulate their children's intellects and give them a sense of responsibility (for example, teaching them to do chores appropriate to their ages).

Effective parents avoid a haphazard home setting and instead provide a consistent, predictable schedule and structure of their children's environment. By anticipating, planning, and managing activities, parents give children a chance to accomplish tasks. For example, in an observational study of mothers and their two-and-one-half-year-olds on a trip to the supermarket it was found that effective mothers were highly strategic. They anticipated behavior and directed their children to positive activities before they misbehaved. The activities ranged from engaging them in selecting grocery items to giving them something to play with or to eat (Holden, 1983). While they structure their children's environment, effective parents also monitor their children; that is, they are aware of their children's physical and emotional state as well as the status of their activities. These parents know whether homework has been completed; they know where their adolescent children are on Friday night.

Clearly, good parenting requires an enormous degree of interest, involvement, and commitment (See Table 7.1). As George Holden points out, effective parenting is influenced by culture, socioeconomic status, the environment in which children are raised, and the personality traits of children themselves. It is easier to negotiate with children, give them choices and provide a degree of freedom if they are being raised in a safe, secure environment. In dangerous neighborhoods, this kind of upbringing is essential as parental strictness and

**TABLE 7.1   Factors Affecting the Effectiveness of the
Parent-Child Relationship**

1. Cultural and social class background
2. Parental values and belief systems
3. Past experiences with children
4. Past experiences with one's own parents
5. Parental expectations
6. Personality of parent
7. Personality of child
8. Age and sex of parent
9. Age and sex of child
10. Birth order of child
11. Parental goals
12. Societal child-rearing philosophies
13. Developmental level of parent
14. Developmental level of child
15. Events of the day
16. Physical or mental health of parent
17. Pressure and influence of others in the environment
18. Stress level in family

Source: Silberman, M. *When Your Child Is Difficult,* Research Press: 1995.

insistence on obedience might keep children from harm. What is ultimately important is the outcome of parents' efforts. As Holden noted:

> What determines the effectiveness of a parent is, ultimately, how the child turns out. Some desired outcomes are universal, but others are specific to a culture or subculture. The most fundamental universal goal of parenting is to raise a child to become a physically and mentally healthy adult who is a contributing member of society. Toward that end, parents must instill in children self-esteem as well as respect for others, an ability to solve problems, and a degree of psychological health sufficient to withstand adversity. (Holden, 1983)

THE SELF-AWARE PARENT

One key attribute of maturity is *self-awareness*; indulging a realistic sense of one's strengths and weaknesses and an ability to recognize one's feelings and desires (Davidson and Moore, 1992). This means that mature adults must understand what parenting means to them and they must develop clear goals for their efforts. Self-awareness enables parents to choose how to act in any situation, and this same sense of self allows them to be flexible and change direction if they feel they have made a mistake. Sociologists J. Kenneth Davidson

Children do as their parents do; that is, they model behaviors that attract their parents' attention.

and Nelwyn Moore (1992) suggest that effective parents work at improving their competencies for parenting by accepting responsibility for self-growth, recognizing and reaffirming the significance of interpersonal relationships, and learning and using the skills of good communication. "Such accomplishments," they insist, "should be priorities for parents who wish to model principles of good mental health for their children. Beyond this base of good personal adjustment, persons must have a clear awareness of their parental role in order to succeed as a parent."

BELIEF SYSTEMS AND PARENTING

When Thurgood Marshall, the first African American to sit on the United States Supreme Court, was an adolescent, one of his uncles said, "He always was a bum, he *is* a bum, and he always will be a bum!" After attending Lincoln University, Marshall wanted to go to law school, but he had no money for tuition. His mother, who believed her son was special, said, "You're going." She pawned her engagement and wedding rings to help pay for his education.

PARENTAL COGNITIONS

Belief systems are powerful determinants of parental behavior. Psychologists use the term *cognitions* to describe the thinking, perceptions, and beliefs that cause emotional reactions, which in turn lead to behavior. In no sphere of life

The Spirit of Parenting

The Measure of Our Success

I seek your forgiveness for all the times I talked when I should have listened; got angry when I should have been patient; acted when I should have waited; feared when I should have delighted; scolded when I should have encouraged; criticized when I should have complimented; said no when I should have said yes and said yes when I should have said no. I did not know a whole lot about parenting or how to ask for help. . . . Most of all, I am sorry for all the times I did not affirm all the wonderful things you are and did that got lost in parental admonitions about things left undone or thought not well enough done. . . .

Miriam Wright Edelman
The Measure of Our Success: A Letter to My Children and Yours

do cognitions play a greater role than in the parent-child relationship. But parents differ in their beliefs about *causality* in regard to children's behaviors. For example, one parent attributes a child's crying as a signal that the child needs to be picked up and held. Another parent might believe that the child is acting "spoiled." Studies show that, as children age and develop, parents increasingly believe that misbehavior is intentional and a reflection of the child's personality. For example, a failing grade in school could be seen as willful or spiteful, rather than the result of having difficulty with a subject. Happy, social parents view their children differently than do depressed, isolated parents.

Consider a teenage girl who stays out past curfew, without calling home. This action can be interpreted in a number of ways: "She is irresponsible"; "She is doing this to spite me"; "She is having a great time and forgot to call"; and "She must have been in an accident." The emotional response to the behavior will be anger, annoyance, fear, or calm acceptance, depending on what a parent *wishes* to think. Because there is no way to know *why* the child hasn't called home until she calls or gets home, a parent's emotional state is a function of his or her own internal model. Often parent-child problems are the result of the parent's distorted, inaccurate, illogical, unrealistic, or irrational perspective.

One emotion parents exhibit frequently is anger. Anger can be in response to a child's spilling of a glass of milk, siblings fighting, or the mess in the room of a teenager. Psychiatrist David Burns (1989) believes that anger is a habitual response to actions they don't like. But anger is appropriate in only two instances: 1) when someone intentionally and unnecessarily acts in a harmful way, and 2) when the anger achieves a desired goal. Generally spilled milk is accidental, siblings quarrel because they have mutually exclusive interests, and adolescents' rooms are not health hazards. Parents often rely on anger responses because they are feeling frightened, frustrated, or hostile. For example, a parent might respond angrily to a child who runs into the street. If expressed correctly, the anger can achieve a desired goal—that of warning the child of danger. The frightened parent says, "You scared me half to death running out there. You might have gotten hit by a car!" However, if anger is expressed hostilely—"How stupid can you be? You're going to get killed the next time you do that!"—the response serves only to belittle the child.

Another powerful emotion of parents is guilt. If a child gets a poor grade in math, a parent may feel responsible for the failure. "If I had only gotten her a tutor"; "I've been working too many hours and my child is suffering"; or "My mother warned me that I'd mess up my kids." Parents who feel guilty in the face of their children's failures often judge themselves to be at fault even when there is little they could have done about them. These guilty parents are perfectionists who are convinced that if they don't do everything a certain way their children will suffer irreparable harm. They have difficulty admitting they make mistakes and are therefore unable to make necessary changes. Perfectionist parents usually raise perfectionist children who are unable to forgive themselves when things do not work out as they expect or desire. Children who are loved for what they do, rather than for who they are, often develop a "critical parent" personality. Distortions about the ability to be loved and nurtured lead parents to see their own children as unlovable.

Rudolf Dreikurs observed that making mistakes is a part of life, so parents should accept their mistakes and those of their children without dwelling on them or exaggerating their effect.

> We all make mistakes. Very few are disastrous. Many times we won't even know that a given action is a mistake until after it is done and we see the results! Sometimes we even have to make the mistake in order to find out that is a mistake. We must have the courage to be imperfect—and to allow our children also to be imperfect. Only in this way can we function, progress, and grow. Our children will maintain their courage and learn more readily if we minimize the mistakes and direct their attention toward the positive. "What is to be done now that the mistake is made" leads to progress forward and stimulates courage. Making a mistake is not nearly as important as what we do about it afterward. (Dreikurs, 1964)

LEARNING OPTIMISM

Martin Seligman of the University of Pennsylvania warns that an epidemic of depression is sweeping the psyches of today's children, with rates ten times higher than they were in the 1950s. Seligman believes that under this depression lies feelings of pessimism: a sense of hopelessness about life and a distrust of the world. This doom and gloom philosophy inevitably provokes melancholia and unhappiness. Seligman dates this wave of pessimism to the early 1960s when "feeling good" took precedence over hard work and achievement in American society. He cites consumerism, the use of recreational drugs, and grade inflation as some ways we have sought to boost our self-esteem. He

The Informed Parent 7.1
Distorted Parental Thinking

All-or-nothing thinking. A parent sees all events and situations as completely perfect or failures. A child misses some lines during a performance of a school play, so the parent rates the whole performance as "terrible."

Overgeneralization. A parent assumes an event or action in the extreme of the reality of the situation. "All the kids in the class cheated, not just my son."

Mind-reading. A parent concludes the child is thinking or doing something, without checking to see if it is true. "I know you don't want to spend time with me."

Magnification and minimization. A parent blows mistakes or events out of proportion or sees them as less than they are. "You'll never get into college with these grades." "If you got an A in the test, everybody must have."

Emotional reasoning. A parent assumes that his or her negative emotions are accurate perceptions of reality. "I feel it in my bones that your new friend is bad news, and I'm never wrong when I sense these things."

"Should and ought" statements. A parent turns a personal desire into a "right and wrong" issue. "You should call your grandmother today." "You ought to read more books."

Labeling and mislabeling. A parent assigns personal and negative labels to a child's behavior. "You are really lazy." "How dumb can you get?"

Source: Adapted from David Burns, *Feeling Good, 1980.*

believes it is the responsibility of parents to raise optimistic "ungloomy" children, who have confidence and pride in themselves, who are eager to initiate activity, and who are kind and decent to others.

Seligman is devoted to the idea of *psychological immunization;* that is, providing children with the emotional skills to ward off mental, and perhaps even physical, illness. Based on his studies of learned helplessness in dogs, Seligman suggested that optimism does not result from instilling children with positive platitudes such as "Just do it" or "Every day in every way, I'm getting better and better." Rather optimism depends on the way children think about *causation*. Seligman believes that everyone has a mode of thinking about causes—a personality trait he calls "explanatory style," which develops in childhood and often lasts a lifetime. Children consider events in their lives good or bad, depending on how they explain three dimensions of causes: *permanence, pervasiveness,* and *personalization.*

The risk of depression is higher in children who believe that the causes of bad events are permanent. To these children, the bad event will occur again because the cause is still there. Children who believe the causes of bad events are temporary will regroup after a setback. Note the effect of these two beliefs to a bad situation, such as a failing grade. One child thinks, "I'm never going to pass this course," whereas the other believes "I need to study harder so I can pass this course." When it comes to good things happening to them, optimistic children believe the cause is permanent and pessimistic children believe it is temporary.

Children who believe a causal event or situation is *specific* know that failures occurring in one realm of life will not create failures in another realm. Viewing a cause as *global* leads children to believe they will fail at everything. "I'm no good at sports" is a globalization, reflecting a different attitude than "I don't do well at basketball." Similarly, a positive event can be seen as either specific or global. Optimistic children believe that a high grade in math means they are generally smart; pessimistic children see themselves as smart only in math.

Optimism or pessimism is also a result of how a child personalizes an event or situation—whom the child blames or credits. Children who have low self-esteem habitually blame themselves for failures. Chronic self-blaming and guilt are the ingredients of depression. Optimistic children do not personalize blame in the same way. They often think the cause of a problem is outside of themselves and, when they do feel responsible, they believe they can rectify the situation.

Children learn some of their explanatory style from their parents, in particular from the way parents criticize their children. When parents communicate criticism in permanent and pervasive messages, children acquire pessimistic styles; when parents attribute bad things to temporary and specific causes, children learn optimism.

Borrowing from principles of cognitive therapy, Seligman proposed that parents have to change their own cognitions in order to help their children see things in a more positive light. He offers an ABC model of behavior change, with A standing for adversity, B for belief, and C for consequences. He teaches parents that if the *belief* about an adversity or negative event is changed, the consequence or end result also changes. For example, imagine a parent running into her teenage son at a shopping mall; he is with his friends and quickly dismisses her after she greets him. If the mother believes the boy is a disrespectful brat, the consequence will be anger. If she thinks her child is a typical teenager who doesn't want to be seen hanging around with his mother, she is likely to be amused. In other words, one activating event can lead to different reactions. Seligman's approach helps parents and children to challenge their pessimistic beliefs and to search for a more accurate understanding of the causes of life's setbacks. Once children learn to interpret the causes of problems accurately, they are able to focus on realistic problem solving.

Seligman believes that optimism is a tool that children learn in order to participate actively in the world and shape their own lives, to avoid being passive victims of whatever happens to them. When children can accurately evaluate their beliefs about the events in their lives, they are be better equipped to face adversity.

The Informed Parent 7.2

Good and Bad Criticism of Preschoolers

Permanent and Pessimistic

What's wrong with you? You are so bad.

The babysitter tells me you cried the whole day. You are a crybaby.

I asked you to pick up your toys. Why don't you ever listen to me?

Global and Pessimistic

You are a bad boy.

You're just like me, lousy in sports.

He never wants to play with other kids.

Source: Adapted from Seligman, 1996.

Changeable and Optimistic

You are misbehaving today. I don't like it.

I hear you've had a hard time being left alone today.

I asked you to pick up your toys. Why are you not doing it?

Specific and Optimistic

You are not being nice to your sister today.

You have to learn to focus on the ball.

He has a difficult time in play group.

We want our children to have lives filled with friendship and love and high deeds. We want them to be eager to learn and be willing to confront challenges. We want our children to be grateful for what they receive from us, but to be proud of their own accomplishments. We want them grow up with confidence in the future, a love of adventure, a sense of justice, and courage enough to act on that sense of justice. We want them to be resilient in the face of the setbacks and failures that growing up always brings. And when the time comes, we want them to be good parents.

PARENTING STYLES

Parental concerns change as their children pass through life stages, or transitions. During the earliest years of children's lives, parents focus on physical matters, such as sleep patterns, feeding, and illness. In middle childhood socialization and developmental competency are the emphases. The parents of the adolescent are concerned with issues of independence and sexuality. There is a common cliche that proclaims, "Little children, little problems. Big children, big problems." Parental beliefs, attitudes, and expectations of children at specific ages combine to determine the style and methods parents use to regulate behaviors. For example, if a father expects his two-year-old to sit quietly at the dinner table, he may yell at his child for banging a spoon against a plate. The parent who understands that a two-year-old needs to practice motor skills might offer the child a handful of plastic utensils with which to play.

In the past, religious texts and parenting guides recommended hitting children as an appropriate technique. Innumerable research projects have shown this method of discipline to be harmful and counterproductive.

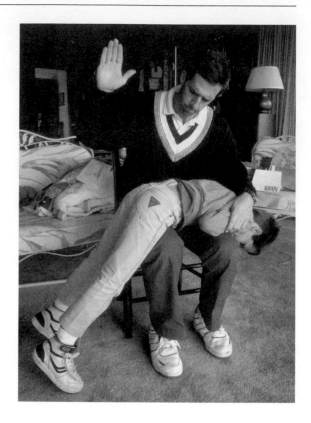

ACCEPTANCE AND EXPECTATIONS OF CHILDREN

Diane Baumrind (1971, 1989, 1991) studied the two dimensions of parenting behavior: responsiveness and demandingness. *Responsiveness* is the acknowledgment, acceptance, and satisfaction of a child's needs. *Demandingness* refers to parental expectations about their children's maturity, responsibility, and specific behaviors. As we observe the ways the two dimensions combine, we come to an understanding of how parental practices influence childhood *socialization* (See Figure 7.4).

Baumrind has proposed four primary styles of parenting. *Authoritarian* parents are very demanding of their children but they display little responsiveness to the children. Authoritarian parents are concerned with control; they demand obedience and respect for authority, and they tolerate no debate or individual differences. These parents are generally harsh and critical, and they control their children's behavior by threats, punishment, and occasional rewards. Authoritarian parents get a result quite different from what they expect. Children raised in authoritarian environments tend to become angry and rebellious. They lack self-discipline, and they are more vulnerable to stress than are children raised by other styles. They are likely to be withdrawn and fearful and are often irritable, moody, and unhappy. They have difficulty initiating activities, and they lack social skills. Baumrind noted that it is not firm control of children *per se* that leads to these problems but rather the harsh, dictatorial, and arbitrary exercise of parental power (Baumrind, 1971,1989, 1991).

Permissive-indulgent parents are responsive to their children, but they demand little in return. They do not exercise behavior control, but rather they allow excessive freedom. Limits are nonexistent and rules are not clearly communicated or not enforced. While permissive parents are somewhat warm, accepting, and encouraging, they have few expectations of their children, and they provide little structure by which their children can excel. The children of permissive parents tend to be impulsive, aimless, and lacking in self-control. They are often insecure, immature, spoiled, and disrespectful to adults.

Permissive-indifferent parents are neither responsive nor demanding. They spend little time with their children, and at the extreme they are neglectful. They rarely take an interest in their children's activities nor do they communicate much with them. Indifferent parents center their lives around their own desires and interests and show no concern for the developmental needs of their children. The children in such families are often impulsive; they are more likely to experiment with drugs, sex, and alcohol. Maccoby and Martin (1983) referred to this parenting style as *uninvolved parenting*, noting the absence of emotional attachment between these parents and their children.

Authoritative parents are warm, responsive, and demanding. They guide their children through firmness, cooperativeness, and encouragement. These parents set clear limits and standards of conduct. Rules are openly discussed and often decided upon in a democratic way. Autonomy and self-direction are

Figure 7.4
Parental Styles

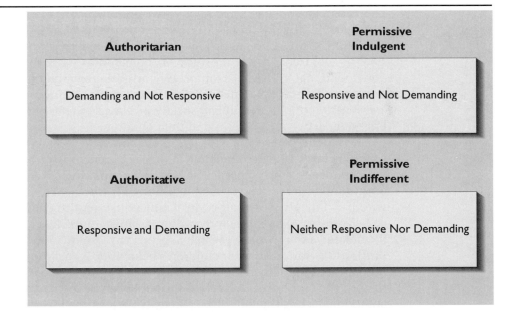

Authoritarian
Demanding and Not Responsive

Permissive Indulgent
Responsive and Not Demanding

Authoritative
Responsive and Demanding

Permissive Indifferent
Neither Responsive Nor Demanding

considered important traits for children of these parents. Authoritative families raise children who are self-disciplined and socially responsible. They are friendly toward peers, and they get along well with adults.

Baumrind has identified several other parental styles, including *directive* (obedience-oriented with moderate support), *undirective* (with no limits and moderate support), *unengaged* (providing neither control nor support), and *good enough* (providing adequate but not outstanding control and support).

Traditional views of child rearing hold that adolescence is a time for parents to extend limits and allow their children the autonomy to achieve their own sense of identity. Baumrind feels that this is true if the child's environment is secure and stable. Given the increased rates of divorce, alcohol and drug use, and the two-working-parent family, Baumrind believes that *supportive control* leads to social competence, maturity, higher scores on achievement tests, and optimism. After studying 124 white, middle-class, well-educated children born in the 1960s, the researcher proposed that authoritative parents "make it their business to know their children, how they're doing in school, and who their friends are. Their control reflects a high level of commitment to the child, and they are not afraid to confront the child" (Baumrind, 1989). Baumrind's studies have also indicated that children from authoritarian families, particularly daughters, scored lower on achievement tests than did their peers and suffered more emotional problems. The children of unengaged and nondirective parents were more likely to become involved in early sexual activity and drug use. Authoritarian and unengaged families had the highest divorce rate. Children from good-enough families did fairly well on achievement tests, and they seemed to have few serious problems. However, the daughters in good-enough families displayed very low self-esteem. One finding showed that the children of single-parent, authoritative homes were as competent and well adjusted as children from two-parent, intact families.

Baumrind's work on parenting styles points to warmth and control as interrelated, primary forces in raising caring, productive, and psychologically healthy children. One other study of the parental styles in 186 cultures also concluded that a loving but managing attitude toward child rearing was the norm in effectively parented families (Rohner and Rohner, 1981). Clearly, the socialization of children in any society is related to affectionate ties and close engagement between parents and their children.

It is a rare parent that can live up to the ideal of parenting all the time. Many factors influence the kind of parent a person is or becomes. A child's temperament inspires a particular kind of parental style. It is lot easier to be an authoritative parent to an "easy" child than it is to a "difficult" child. A child who has difficulty with self-control and adjustment to change may cause his or her parents to adopt a more authoritarian attitude. Richard Bell (1971) has formulated a *control theory*, which suggests that parents have upper and lower limits of tolerance for their children's behaviors. As a child pushes the upper limits, parents use increasingly authoritarian strategies for control. Family finances, the number of children in the family, and experience with children are additional factors that affect the parent-child relationship.

PARENT-EDUCATION PROGRAMS

Ideas about parenting are rooted in time and culture. Before the twentieth century, clergymen, philosophers, and medical doctors advised parents of their duties and goals (See Chapter 1). Eighteenth-century Methodist minister John Wesley proposed that wise parents break their children's wills; Aristotle argued that fathers were more important in children's lives than were mothers. Best-selling author/pediatrician Luther Emmett Holt (1894) told parents to keep their children on a liquid diet until their first birthday and to refrain from kissing them for fear of transmitting grave diseases.

Parent education as it exists today gained its impetus during the 1920s. At that time, social scientists began proposing that parenting was akin to having a "profession," in that study and instruction was necessary if one were to raise children to be contented, productive adults. Rather then relying on the advice of clergymen and philosophers, parents turned to the world of science for information on child rearing. Over the next fifty years, two generalizations became increasingly clear: 1) that within the limitations of culture, ethnicity, and social class, effective parenting is built upon specific beliefs and actions on the part of parents, and 2) that these actions intertwined with the genetic and psychological ingredients children bring to the mix.

Since the 1970s, the parent-education movement gave birth to a number of specific programs, including Thomas Gordon's PET (Parenting Effective Training), and the STEP program (Systematic Training for Effective Parenting). Also included were the approaches of Haim Ginott, Rudolf Dreikurs, Michael Popkin, Martin Seligman, Adele Fabish, Elaine Mazlish, and others who have based their work on research, clinical practices, and long-term experience with parents and children (See Chapter 5). These approaches are presented in books, on video, and through extensive workshops where parents are participants. Some of these approaches focus on the parent-child relationship, particularly in areas of problem solving and conflict resolution. Others concentrate on teaching parents how to encourage their children's sense of responsibility or feelings of self-worth.

Parent-training models generally follow one of four major theoretical orientations, but there is considerable overlap among them. Ginott's humanist approach focuses on understanding children's feelings; Dreikur's Adlerian model stresses the importance of learning responsibility through consequences for behavior. The behaviorist approach emphasizes the reinforcement of desired behavior. Cognitive theorists such as Seligman believe that thoughts and beliefs lie at the heart of the parent-child relationship.

When all is said and done, parenting is as much art as it is science. There is more to raising children than following a set script. An incredible number of variables go into this effort, many not under the control of parents. It is the art and spirit of parenting—in the form of openness, warmth, and awareness, and intermingled with techniques that have proven most effective—that gets parents and their children through the rough spots of this life-affirming relationship.

Parent-training programs are based on theoretical positions. Haim Ginott's humanist approach focuses on understanding children's feelings. Rudolf Dreikur's Adlerian model stresses the importance of learning responsibility through natural consequences for behavior. Cognitive theorists believe thoughts and beliefs lie at the heart of the parent-child relationship.

Chapter Review

- Parents do not rely on one particular technique when raising children. A parent's response to a child depends upon many factors including the age and personality of the child, the particular problem being addressed, the life circumstances of the parent at the time of the response, and the personality of the parent.

- Ronald P. Rohner defines four principal dimensions of parental relating, scaled on a continuum that ranges from warm affection to undifferentiated rejection.

- Eleanor Maccoby has identified three parenting constructs most likely to promote child development: parental support, parental control, and environmental structure.

- Jay Belsky presumes that parenting is influenced by forces emanating from within the individual parent, from within the individual child, and from the broader social context in which the parent-child relationship is embedded.

- George Holden has proposed that parenting effectiveness can be gauged by looking at several areas: involvement, attachment, social learning, social interaction, teaching, and environmental structure.

- Effective parents work at improving their competencies for parenting by accepting responsibility for self-growth, recognizing and reaffirming the significance of interpersonal relationships, and learning and using the skills of good communications.

- Psychologists use the term cognitions to describe the thinking, perceptions, and beliefs that cause emotional reactions, which in turn leads to behavior. Parents differ in their beliefs about causality in regard to children's behaviors.

- Martin Seligman believes that underlying children's depression are feelings of pessimism: a sense of hopelessness about life and a distrust of the world. He believes it is the responsibility of parents to raise optimistic children who have confidence in themselves and are eager to initiate new activities.

- Diane Baumrind presents two dimensions of parenting behavior: responsiveness and demandingness. Responsiveness is the acknowledgment, acceptance, and satisfaction of a child's needs. Demandingness refers to parental expectations about their child's maturity, responsibility, and specific behaviors.

- Four primary styles of parenting include *authoritarian, permissive-indulgent, permissive-neglectful,* and *authoritative.* Warmth and control are the interrelated forces that work well in raising caring, productive, and psychologically healthy children.

- The parent-education movement gained its impetus during the 1920s, when social scientists proposed that parents need information and instruction if they are to raise children to be contented, productive adults. Since the 1970s, the parenting-education movement has spawned the work of a number of researchers and clinicians.

Student Activities

1. Develop a program to help high school students become effective parents in the future. This program can consist of books, videos, lectures, or anything else you choose to include.

2. Design and produce a manual explaining the role of parents that can be given to new parents leaving a hospital after the birth of a baby.

Helping Hands

Parent Effectiveness Training
531 Stevens Avenue
Solana Beach, CA 92075
(619) 481-8121

Materials designed to help parents understand strategies and skills to be more effective. PET offers trained and certified instructors for parenting-education programs.

CHAPTER

8

Methods and Models Of Parenting

Chapter Highlights

After reading Chapter 8, students should be able to:

- Understand that parents use many methods and models of child rearing
- Recognize the methods suggested by the major parent training programs
- Understand the difference between discipline and punishment
- Understand the effects of using physical punishment to discipline children

Chapter Contents

- Humane Parenting
    Alice Miller's Poisonous Pedagogy ▪ *Parents, Children, and Haim Ginott*
- Child-Rearing Strategies
    Basic Techniques ▪ *Listening and Talking to Children* ▪ *Parent Effectiveness Training* ▪ *Self-discipline in Children*
- Responsible Parents, Responsible Children
    A Democratic, Family-Centered Approach to Parenting ▪ *The STEP Program* ▪ *The Active Parenting of Michael Popkin*
- Modifying Behavior Through Rewards and Punishments
    Do as I Do: Parents as Models ▪ *The Importance of Discipline* ▪ *Time-Out Techniques* ▪ *Discipline Does Not Mean Punishment* ▪ *The Lessons of Spanking and Hitting*
- A Family-Systems Model of Parenting

n 1927, a 23-year-old American graduate student named Margaret Mead set out for the South Pacific to begin a lifetime of study and work. Her work would eventually make her one of the most highly acclaimed anthropologists of the twentieth century. Of particular interest to Mead was the child-rearing methods of the tribes she visited. She found that the Manus of New Guinea raised their children to believe that possessions, morality, and security make people healthy, wealthy, and wise. These views were encouraged by "ghostly mentors," who punished for sexual license, for adult frivolity, and for not improving one's lot. The Arapesh of New Guinea insisted on shared parental nurturance of children, which by American standards would have both mothers and fathers considered "feminine." The Mundugumor disliked their children, sometimes to the point of tossing unwanted ones into a river. Sleeping babies were hung in rough-textured baskets in a dark place against the wall and, when a baby cried, someone would scratch gratingly on the outside of the basket. In Tchambuli families female children had more freedom than male children (Mead, 1972).

From her studies of these cultures and others, Margaret Mead picked up ideas and methods of child rearing that she would rely on years later. At age 37, while married to her third husband, renowned English anthropologist Gregory Bateson, Mead gave birth to her only child, Catherine. Rather than follow the ways of their own cultures, Margaret and Gregory picked and chose among the child-rearing methods they had observed around the world. In a tribute to her illustrious parents, Catherine Bateson wrote, "They approached the experience of parenthood with the intention of questioning forms from their two backgrounds, combining elements of the British tradition from which Gregory came and the old American tradition from which Margaret came with care and discrimination, making innovations along the way" (Bateson, 1984).

Margaret Mead had a sure advantage over most parents, in that she understood the degree to which parental attitudes and methods are bound to culture and family. She personally rejected many of the principles and practices of pregnancy, childbirth, and child rearing that were favored by American pediatricians and parents before the 1950s. "I would have to work hard," she said, "not to overprotect my child, but to ensure my child's freedom to find its own way of taking hold of life and becoming a person" (Mead, 1972).

While most parenting-advice books offer a specific approach or technique, psychologist James Windell (1991) pointed out it is necessary for parents to know and understand many different techniques, essentially "a bag full of skills" to use in raising children. Children are different and they change as they grow older, so parent methods must be adaptable to each child and each situation. Windell believes that—in addition to patience, tolerance, understanding, and flexibility—good parents know that they can never know enough about parenting.

HUMANE PARENTING

Thomas Gordon (1975), developer of the Parent Effectiveness Training program (PET), believes that parents rely almost universally on the methods of raising children and dealing with family problems that were used by their own parents, by their parents' parents, by their grandparents' parents, and so on. Most other social institutions have changed over the years but the parent-child relationship seems to have remained less changed. Gordon complains that parents are not getting the message, through no fault of their own.

> Psychology, child development, and other behavioral sciences have amassed impressive new knowledge about children, parents, interpersonal relationships, how to help another person grow, how to create a psychologically healthy climate for people. A lot is known about effective person-to-person communications, the effects of power in human relationships, constructive conflict resolution, and so on. Unfortunately, those who have uncovered new facts and developed new methods have not done a very good job of telling parents about them. We communicate to our colleagues in books and professional journals, but do not communicate as well with parents, the rightful consumers of these new methods (Gordon, 1975).

Thomas Gordon believes parents need training in order to be effective when raising children.

ALICE MILLER'S POISONOUS PEDAGOGY

Many researchers have been outspoken in the belief that parents must learn new ways of dealing with their children. Since the end of World War II, Swiss psychiatrist Alice Miller (1990) has been haunted by the Holocaust. Miller is convinced the root of such violence is in the hidden cruelty of child rearing. She believes that the practices of most parents crush the spontaneity and natural spirit in children, and may even lead their children to become criminals, drug addicts, or suicidal. The methods that do this are lying to them, laying traps to catch them in misbehavior or being untruthful, using scare tactics, withdrawing love to gain obedience, isolating children for misbehaving, humiliating them in front of others, ridiculing their ideas or character, forcing them to do things they don't want to do, and coercing them to gain obedience. Miller believes that people who insist they were not harmed by harsh treatment during their childhoods carry within them a "virus of poisonous pedagogy"—a distorted perception of what a good upbringing is, and a virus that infects the next generation. "When people who have been beaten or spanked as children attempt to play down the consequences by setting themselves up as examples, even claiming it was good for them, they are inevitably contributing to the continuation of cruelty in the world by this refusal to take their childhood tragedies seriously." Alice Miller believes we do not have to be told whether to be strict or permissive with our children, that we need only have respect for their needs, feelings, and individuality. She imagines a time that parents will regard their children not as people to be manipulated or changed, but rather "as messengers from a world we once deeply knew, but which we have long since forgotten." It is our children "who can reveal to us more about the true secrets of life, and also our own lives, than our parents were ever able to."

PARENTS, CHILDREN, AND HAIM GINOTT

One of the most renowned parenting education experts, Haim G. Ginott wrote two best-seller parenting books, *Between Parent and Child* and *Between Parent and Teenager*. In them he proposed that love is not enough when raising children. Parents are continually "confronted with concrete problems that require specific solutions" (Ginott, 1973). To Ginott, parenting is a skill, much like building a house, and it is accomplished brick by brick, window by door. In defining the goal of parenting, Ginott proposed that parents must find ways to help children become humane and strong.

> For what does it profit us if we have a neat, polite, charming youngster who could watch people suffer and not be moved to take action? What have we accomplished if we have reared a child who is brilliant—at the top of his class—but who uses his intellect to manipulate others? And do we really want children so well-adjusted that they adjust to an unjust situation? The Germans adjusted only too well to the orders of the Nazis to exterminate millions of their fellow men. Understand me: I'm not opposed to a child being polite or neat or learned. The crucial question for me is: What methods have

been used to accomplish these ends? If the methods are insults, attacks, and threats, then we can be very sure that we have also taught this child to insult, to attack, to threaten, and to comply when threatened. If, on the other hand, we use methods that are humane, then we've taught something much more important than a series of isolated virtues. We've shown the child how to be a person—a mensch, a human being who can conduct his life with strength and dignity (quoted in Faber and Mazlish, 1990).

Haim Ginott proposed that the goal of parenting must be to raise caring, humane children, capable of conducting their lives with dignity.

CHILD-REARING STRATEGIES

At the time of Catherine Bateson's birth, social changes were making it imperative for psychologists to look twice at the methods parents were using to raise their children. A number of these psychologists have shared their views and strategies in books, videos, and other materials available to parents seeking information. Each method has its own parenting philosophy, specific goal, and primary emphasis. The intent of them all is to help parents raise contented, responsible children. Of course, parents do not rely only on one particular technique when raising children. A parent's response to a child depends on many factors including the age and personality of the child, the particular problem being addressed, and the life circumstances of the parent at the time of the response. Even professionals working in the field of parent training take an eclectic approach, using parts of a number of philosophies.

Haim Ginott proposed that the goal of parenting must be to raise caring, humane children, capable of conducting their lives with dignity.

BASIC TECHNIQUES

Martin Hoffman of New York University identified three basic types of parenting techniques: power assertion, withdrawal of love, and induction. *Power-assertive* methods rely on force, in the form of commands, threats, and punishments. Physical attacks and the denial of privileges are among the tools of this technique. Generally, power assertiveness has immediate results, however, for the short run only. Since the desire to behave appropriately is not internalized by the child, compliance to parental demands generally occurs only when parents are around.

Disapproval, the silent treatment, and disregard mark the *withdrawal of love* method of parenting. The anxiety this method produces tends to change behavior temporarily but, again, the child does not internalize the parents' desires. Furthermore, feelings of being unloved may backfire as a child seeks affection and approval outside the home and acts out in attention-getting ways.

Inductive methods rely on reasoning and problem solving to instill appropriate behaviors. In particular, children are helped to understand the effects of behavior—theirs as well as that of others. Although a behavior may not change immediately, children do internalize parental expectations and the behavior usually remains in effect even when parents are absent.

It is silly to think that parents use the same techniques all the time, or that all children respond to a specific technique in the same way. A parent who is rested and relaxed on one day may take the time to reason with a child about clearing the table. On another day, after coming home from work tired or not feeling well, this same parent might revert to power assertion in order to get her child to put the dishes in the sink.

There is a cyclical aspect to parental interaction with children, based on the stresses of daily life, the behavior of children at specific times, and the emotional state of parents at the time the behavior is exhibited (Maccoby and Martin, 1993). In general, parental beliefs about the effectiveness of a particular technique influences whether or not the technique will be utilized. For example, many parents continue to rely on power-assertive methods of parenting even in the face of overwhelming research demonstrating its ineffectiveness. It takes insightful and courageous parents, or ones who are at their wit's end, to evaluate the methods they rely on and make the changes necessary to raise the kind of children they like to be around.

LISTENING AND TALKING TO CHILDREN

Haim Ginott believed emotion to be the cornerstone of the parent-child relationship. Expressing emotions—anger and fear, sadness and joy, delight and disgust—have important survival benefits in life; yet, all too often, children are educated out of knowing what they are feeling. When they hate something, they are told "it's not nice" to feel that way; when they're afraid, they are told "there's nothing to be frightened of" or "you're being silly." Sad children are told to "put on a happy face," and children in pain are expected to "be brave."

This can lead to a "mixed up" sense of one's feelings, so that later in life anger produces guilt, unhappiness is buried, and love becomes a mysterious and often misinterpreted thing. Ginott believed it is more important for children to know *what* they feel than *why they* feel it. It is the job of parents to feed back emotions that children display, in essence mirror the feeling. This technique helps children come to understand what they are really feeling, thereby making communication and problem solving easier.

Language serves as a gateway to socialization by opening up a world of communication with other people. It allows children to internalize thoughts and feelings through words; and it allows children to internalize actions so that problems can be solved without direct manipulation of physical objects in the environment. When it comes to children, parents are often not clear in the messages they give verbally, and they are often unable to pick up on what their children are telling them.

Adele Faber and Elaine Mazlish, two psychologists who studied under Haim Ginott, concentrated on helping parents reduce conflict and tensions through talking and listening to their children. In noting the direct connection between how children *feel* and how they *behave*, the two women believe that when children feel right they behave right. What makes children feel rights is having their parents accept their feelings. Following are examples of a parent *not* accepting a child's feelings:

1. *Child:* Mommy, I don't want to get up yet. I'm still tired.

   Parent: You can't be tired. You napped for two hours.

   Child: I am too tired.

   Parent: You're just a little sleepy. Here, put these clothes on and come downstairs.

2. *Child:* My hair looks terrible today. I can't go to school.

   Dad: Your hair looks fine. Finish breakfast and get on your way.

   Child: I can't be seen like this.

   Dad: You're being ridiculous. That's it, you're off to school.

3. *Child:* I hate my teacher.

   Mother: She's a nice lady.

   Child: I can't stand her. I think she's a jerk.

   Mother: Don't talk that way about your teacher.

What these communications tell children is that their feelings are not valid. Faber and Mazlish suggest acknowledging children's feelings without making judgments or giving advice. They use four techniques to do this:

1. Listen with full attention
2. Acknowledge feelings with a word, such as "Oh" . . . "I see."
3. Give the feelings a name.
4. Give children their wishes in fantasy.

Parents often only half listen when one of their children has something to say because they are generally engaged in doing something—cooking, reading the paper, watching television. It is, however, easier for children to tell their troubles to parents who take the time to fully listen. When children express themselves, often a simple acknowledgment of "Uhhh!" is enough for them to further explore their thoughts and feelings and ponder a solution to their problems. Giving feelings a name, such as "It sounds like you were embarrassed," or "You must feel very sad about losing your favorite barrette" often comforts upset children. Questioning, advising, and blaming are responses that do not solve problems. "This is the second barrette you've lost" or "How can you be so careless?" are responses that discourage children from expressing themselves again. Finally, when children want something they can't have, parents can share the fantasy instead of giving logical explanations for refusing. "It's too cold for you to go outside" might be responsively expressed as "I wish it were warmer out so you could go out and play."

Faber and Mazlish have described the common methods that are ineffectual in getting children to cooperate (see Table 8.1).

In suggesting techniques less likely to do injury to a child's self-esteem or create bad feelings, Farber and Mazlish focus on cooperation, not confrontation, between parents and their children. They suggest that parents: describe what they see, or describe the problem; give information; talk about their feelings; and sometimes write a note.

It's easier for children to solve a problem if it is clearly described to them. By saying "The refrigerator door is open," a parent describes the problem in a nonconfrontive way but still informs a child that he or she has to do something. "You always leave the refrigerator door open" blames a child for having done something in the past. Giving children information instead of insult or

TABLE 8.1   Common Ineffective Techniques in Correcting Children's Behaviors

Technique	Example
Blaming and Accusing	"You forgot to put your dishes in the sink again."
Name-Calling	"How dumb can you be, to leave the front door open?"
Threats	"Do that again and you'll be sorry."
Commands	"Take the garbage out now!"
Lecturing and Moralizing	"I can imagine what people would think of you if they knew about these grades."
Warnings	"Put your jacket on or you'll catch a cold."
Martyrdom Statements	"You kids are driving me crazy."
Comparisons	"Your sister never got a "C" in school."
Sarcasm	"If I could read Chinese I'd be able to read this homework."
Prophecy	"Keep it up and you'll never get into college."

The Informed Parent 8.1

Communicating with Children

Adele Faber and Elaine Mazlish offer suggestions for improving parents' communications with their children:

Helping Children Deal with Their Feelings

Children—even adult children—need to have their feelings accepted and respected.

1. *You can listen quietly and attentively.*
2. *You can acknowledge their feelings with a word.* "Oh . . . Mmm . . . I see . . . "
3. *You can give the feeling a name.* "That sounds frustrating."
4. *You can give the child his or her wishes in fantasy.* "I wish I could take you to Disneyworld this very afternoon." "I wish I could make that young man ask you out."

Engaging a Child's Cooperation

1. *Describe what you see, or describe the problem.* "The front door is open." "I can't find my keys."
2. *Give information.* "The cold air is coming in the door." "The milk will go bad if it's not put in the refrigerator."
3. *Say it with a word.* "The milk!" "The front door!"
4. *Describe* what you *feel.* "I don't like picking towels up off the floor."
5. *Write a note.* Please hang me on the towel rack.
6. *Problem-solve.* "How can I help you bring up your math grade?" "What can we work out so that you can borrow an item of my clothes when you need it but also so it's back in the closet and clean when I need it?"

Encouraging Autonomy

1. *Let children make choices.* "Do you want to wear your red dress or your blue one?"
2. *Show respect for a child's struggle.* "Algebra can be difficult. Maybe it would help if you got some tutoring."

blame is always more helpful in accomplishing a goal. Often, the less said, the better. "Here's your lunch!" works better than "You're forgetting your lunch again. If your head wasn't attached to you, you'd probably forget that too." Parents should express their honest feelings without attacking their children. "I get annoyed when you take my hairbrush out of my bathroom" is more effective than "You're always taking things that don't belong to you." Sometimes a written note works with children, especially if done in good spirit. A note saying, "I'd like you to tidy your room up after school today, pal. Thanks, Dad. Have a good day," encourages rather than commands. To be sure, some

3. *Don't ask too many questions.* "Did you enjoy the party?"

4. *Don't rush to answer questions.* "That's an interesting question. What do you think?"

5. *Encourage children to use sources outside the home.* "Maybe you can find the answer in the library." "Perhaps the veterinarian can answer that question."

6. *Don't take away hope.* "So you want to try out for the basketball team. That's a wonderful idea."

Praise and Self-Esteem

Instead of evaluating, describe:

1. *Describe what you see.* "I see a wonderfully made bed." "I see my keys back where they belong."

2. *Describe what you feel.* "It's delightful to come into this clean room." "I enjoyed coming to your basketball game."

3. *Sum up the child's praiseworthy behavior with a word.* "You put your dishes in the sink. That's what I call *efficient.*"

Freeing Children from Playing Roles

1. *Look for opportunities to show the child a new picture of himself or herself.* "You wore that hat when you were in elementary school."

2. *Let children overhear you say something positive about them.* "I'm thrilled that he's home for the weekend." "She handled the cavity filling like a real trooper."

3. *Model the behavior you'd like to see.* "I'm sorry for being late to your game." "I didn't get the promotion but I'm happy that a colleague in my department did."

4. *Put children in situations in which they can see themselves differently.* "Molly, would you help Daddy wash the car?" "Jed, I need you to put the icing on the cake."

5. *Be a storehouse for your child's special moments.* "Remember when you hit the homer in the last game of the season?"

6. *When the child acts according to the old label, state your feelings and/or your expectations.* "I am disappointed in you. I expect you to be polite when you're introduced to people."

of these methods will work with a particular child and others will not. However, the point of the Faber-Mazlish work is to inform parents that there are skills to be learned that will make the parent-child relationship more peaceful and rewarding.

PARENT EFFECTIVENESS TRAINING

Thomas Gordon based his parent effectiveness training (PET) program on the assumption that *parents need training, not blaming.* He advises parents to,

The Informed Parent 8.2

Dialogue with a Teen, Eating Dinner

The first version of this story leads to an argument between parent and child. The second accepts the child's feelings and allows her to use her own initiative when handling the problem.

Version A

Janetta: I hate this soup. It's too salty.

Parent: No, it's not. I hardly put any salt in it.

Janetta: You put tons of salt in it.

Parent: This isn't a restaurant. Stop complaining and eat.

Janetta: I can't eat this stuff. It's terrible.

Parent: The soup is delicious. I put healthy carrots and barley in it.

Janetta: If it's so good, you eat it.

Parent: You're rude and fresh. You'd better watch your mouth or you're going to be punished.

Janetta: I am watching my mouth. That's why I'm not eating the soup.

Parent: You're a spoiled brat. Half the people in India would love to have this soup.

Janetta: So mail it to them.

Parent: Leave the table this minute.

Version B

Janetta: I hate this soup. It's too salty.

Parent: The soup is too salty for *you*.

Janetta: Yeh, it's too salty.

Parent: It's too salty for you. It's all we have right now.

Janetta: I wish we had something better to eat in the house.

Parent: Mmmm.

Janetta: I'll eat a little of it. And I'll drink a *lot* of water.

first and foremost, accept themselves as people who have positive and negative feelings toward their children. He believes parents do not have to be consistent to be effective, and that mothers and fathers do not have to put up a common front with their children. What is essential is that parents learn to know what they are feeling. "Most people would readily agree that they feel different degrees of acceptance toward the adults they meet," Gordon notes.

"Why should it be any different in the way they feel toward children?" How accepting a parent is toward a child is partly a function of the kind of person the parent is. Because of their personalities, some parents are accepting of others, and this generalizes to their children. These parents have inner security and a high tolerance level. Other parents are generally unaccepting of others, and they are this way toward their children. These parents have a rigid sense of right and wrong and know how people "should" behave. However, parental acceptance of children and their behaviors is also dependent upon the personal characteristics and traits of the children.

Gordon's training programs emphasize effective communication between parents and their children, through conversation that does not damage a child's self-esteem. He believes most parents talk to children in ways that make them feel stupid and cause them to resist parental influence. Parents do this by sending *solution messages,* which keep children from initiating their own proper behavior. "Why don't you go out and play?" "Don't hit your brother." "Clean up that mess," are all messages that solve a problem a *parent's* way. To Gordon, the difference between ineffective and effective confrontation is the use of "you-messages" as opposed to "I-message." (See Figure 8.1).

PET training emphasizes a "no-lose" method for resolving conflicts in the family. It is a democratic system in which there is no power differential between parent and child. Parent and child encounter a conflict-of-need situation. The parent asks the child to come with a solution acceptable to both; one or both may offer possible solutions; they critically evaluate them and eventually make a decision on a final solution acceptable to both. No selling of the other is required after the solution has been selected, because both have already accepted it. No power is required to force compliance, because neither is resisting the decision (Gordon, 1975).

SELF-DISCIPLINE IN CHILDREN

Thomas Gordon has pondered the question of why parents continue to use punitive power with children when there is so little evidence it is effective. He proposes when we use the term *misbehave* in regard to children, we are judging an action to be contrary to how an adult *thinks* children should behave. He believes the "badness" of the behavior actually resides in the adult's mind, not in the child's. The child is doing what he or she chooses or needs to do to satisfy some need (Gordon, 1989). All actions of children are behaviors engaged in solely for the purpose of getting needs met; this is not much different than the motivation behind the actions of adults, who never speak of each other as "misbehaving." This does not mean that parents will always feel accepting of what their children do, but they will come to understand that the things children do to make themselves happy often conflict with an adult's own pursuit of happiness.

Studies have shown that children who rate high in self-discipline (the ability to regulate one's own behavior) had parents who did not use accusatory messages and punishment to modify their children's behavior (Baumrind, 1967). Self-discipline leads to feelings of self-esteem, which to Gordon is the foundation of positive mental health.

In helping parents deal with unwanted behaviors in nonpower ways, Gordon utilized the concept of *problem ownership*. If a child is doing something because of a need deprivation, such as getting upset because a friend has been mean, the problem "belongs" to the child, not to the parent. When the child is behaving in ways that cause problems for a parent, such as taking the car and not bringing it back when a parent needs it, the parent "owns" the problem. Gordon has presented a number of alternatives to discipline that parents can use to modify behaviors that are causing problems for either the child or the parent.

ALTERNATIVE #1   *Find Out What the Child Needs*
Is the child wet? hungry? tired? Does the child feel lonely? A problem can't be solved unless it is identified.

ALTERNATIVE #2   *Let's Make a Trade*
Try substituting an acceptable behavior for the one you find unacceptable. Give the child who is writing on the wall a piece of paper and crayons. Replace the silverware the child is banging on the table with, substituting a plastic spoon.

ALTERNATIVE #3   *Modify the Environment*
Instead of trying to change the child, change the child's environment. If you want a child to calm down before bedtime, turn off the TV and read him or her a story. If you want to keep a child from reaching things you don't want him or her to have, provide coloring books, puzzles, and other things of interest. If you want to keep children from dangerous objects, put medicines away, lock basement doors, and remove sharp objects.

ALTERNATIVE #4   *The Confrontive I-Message*
This is a nonblameful, nonevaluative message that tells children what a parent is experiencing in response to an unacceptable behavior. There is a big difference between saying to a teenager, "You're driving me crazy. Lower that stereo!" and "I can't talk to grandma on the phone when you're playing your music so loudly." You-messages bring blame, judgment, criticism and coercion with them. I-messages give the adult ownership of the problem. Children are more willing to modify their behavior if they are told in a nonblaming way that someone has a problem because of it.

ALTERNATIVE #5   *The Preventive I-Message*
A preventive I-message influences children to take a particular action in the future in order to avoid a parent's displeasure. It tells children what the parent needs or wants. "I'd like you to tell me what time you plan to be home from school so I don't worry." Preventive I-messages lead to support and cooperation in regard to parental needs.

ALTERNATIVE #6   *Shifting Gears to Reduce Resistance*
Sometimes I-messages provoke resistance, defensiveness, guilt, denial, discomfort, or hurt feelings if children come to believe that all that matters in the family is the parent's needs. This is where a shift to listening and understand-

ing comes in. "I'm upset because you didn't call to say you'd be late," might be met with "I'm sick of always having to look around for a telephone when our games go into overtime." The parent should acknowledge this inconvenience to the child and come up with a compromise that solves the problem.

ALTERNATIVE # 7   *Problem Solving*
Sometimes neither I-messages nor shifting gears modifies a child's behavior. The child wants to continue acting the way he or she does and the parent wants the behavior to change. They both now own the problem; they both will have to find a solution. Problem solving involves several steps: defining the problem by seeing what everyone's needs are, generating possible solutions, evaluating each of the solutions, finding a solution acceptable to both parent and child. Suppose a parent wants to take a nap when a teenager wants to play music. The teenager keeps putting on CDs, and the parent continues to say he or she needs to get some rest. Possible solutions might be for the teenager to listen to his music outside if weather permits, or listen in the family car, or keep the music low for a specified period of time.

ALTERNATIVE # 8   *When Angry, Find the "Primary Feeling"*
Anger is a feeling that is generated after another feeling. For parents, it can be the result of frustration at having goals blocked. A parent who yells at a child who was lost and then found in a department store is reacting with anger to an event that aroused intense fear. The yelling is a way to punish the child for terrifying the parent. When feeling anger a parent must look for the real feeling: "What's going on inside me?" "What needs of mine are being threatened?" "What feeling is really there?" "Am I hiding some other feeling?"

Figure 8.1
The Behavior
Window

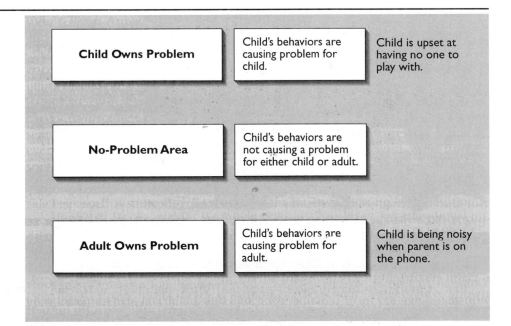

The Spirit of Parenting

Blackberry Winter

That I be not a restless ghost
Who haunts your footsteps as they pass
Beyond the point where you have left
Me standing in the newsprung grass,

You must be free to take a path
Whose end I feel no need to know,
No irking fever to be sure
You went where I would have you go.

Those who would fence the future in
Between two walls of well-laid stones
But lay a ghost walk for themselves,
A dreary walk for dusty bones.

So you can go without regret
Away from this familiar land,
Leaving your kiss upon my hair
And all the future in your hands.

Margaret Mead

RESPONSIBLE PARENTS, RESPONSIBLE CHILDREN

In the early 1900s, Viennese psychiatrist Alfred Adler, an associate of Sigmund Freud's, proposed that the goal-directed behavior of children could only be understood in the context of the social environment in which the behavior is exhibited. He believed sibling rivalry, family constellation, and parenting styles are among the variables that influence childhood and adult behavior. It was left to Rudolf Dreikurs, an associate of Adler, to bring Adler's ideas to the United States and test them in family counseling centers (Lowe, 1982). Taking his cue from family-systems theory (Chapter 4) Dreikurs believed that acceptance within the family is key to a child's well-being; therefore he recommends that parents encourage children in their abilities by word and deed. He pointed out that a parent's tone of voice, posture, and facial expression communicate feelings and attitudes. "You're too young to set the table," tells a three-year-old he is not competent. "I know you can put the napkins on the table," keeps the child away from fragile dishes but still gives him a feeling of accomplishment.

A DEMOCRATIC, FAMILY-CENTERED APPROACH TO PARENTING

Dreikurs' approach to parent training emphasizes the importance of a democratic family system—one that sets appropriate limits, shows respect for everyone in the family, and encourages collective decision making. Dreikurs did not see the democratic family as permissive or lacking in rules. Instead the entire family is involved in setting limits and goals, at regularly scheduled family meetings attended by everyone.

In characterizing children's misbehavior as "mistaken goals," in the sense that the intent is to achieve something, Dreikurs identified four purposes: the desire for attention, the pursuit of power, the need for revenge, and the attempt to display inadequacy. It is important for parents to understand the motivation behind a child's act—the feelings that provoke it—rather than focusing on the behavior alone. A teenager has a party in her family's home on a weekend her parents are out of town. Is the child looking for attention from her friends? Is she angry at her parents and getting even with them? Has the child given up on getting approval from her parents through acceptable behavior and therefore had nothing to lose by having a party? To Dreikurs, misbehavior should be met with understanding, encouragement, and love. Punishment only serves to intensify the feelings that led to the misbehavior in the first place.

THE STEP PROGRAM

The concept of the democratic family has been spread nationwide through a program known as STEP or Systematic Training for Effective Parenting, developed by Don Dinkmeyer and Gary McKay (Dinkmeyer, 1979; Dinkmeyer and Driekurs, 1996; Dinkmeyer and McKay, 1981). At its heart is the belief that the use of rewards and punishments as disciplinary techniques should be replaced with methods that rely on "natural and logical consequences" of behavior. The STEP program emphasizes the notion of *logical*, meaning reasonable and fair. Whereas punishment makes parents responsible for their children's behavior, natural and logical consequences hold children responsible for their own behavior. A mother can force a child to wear mittens to school on a cold day, but the child who refuses to do so will learn quickly enough the effect of not wearing the mittens. A teenager who misses a planned dinner hour will have to go hungry or eat a peanut butter and jelly sandwich for dinner if the family has agreed upon this option as an alternative to sharing the common meal.

The STEP program encourages parents to eliminate value-laden words such as "good," "great," and "excellent" from their praise of the children and replace them with terms that have special meaning:

Phrases that demonstrate acceptance:
"I like the way you solved that problem."
"I'm glad you enjoy playing the piano."
"Since you're unhappy about that, what do you think will please you?"

Phrases that show confidence:
"I have confidence that you can bring that grade up."
"I think you can figure out how to get there."
"You'll do it."

Phrases that focus on contributions, assets, and appreciation:
"That was thoughtful of you."
"I enjoyed being with you today."
"Thanks. I appreciate you bringing in the packages."

Phrases that recognize effort and improvement:
"It looks like you worked hard on that project."
"You've make a lot of progress on your basketball skills."
"You really gave that problem a lot of thought."

The STEP program helps parents recognize self-defeating beliefs, ideas that make it difficult for them to function as effectively as they may like. One exercise in the STEP program encourages parents to look at their parenting assumptions and amend those that interfere with optimal parenting.

Self-defeating	**Alternative**
1. It is necessary that people in the community approve of me.	I will do that which makes me freer and more self-confident and makes my children more responsible.
2. I must be competent in all aspects of parenting.	I do not get my feelings of worth from my children's behavior. I am more interested in improving my relationships than I am in perfection.
3. It is catastrophic and unacceptable when things don't turn out the way I want them to with my children.	It is annoying and unfortunate when things don't turn out the way I like. I will try to change the things I can and accept the things I don't control.
4. Disobedience is an insult to my status as a parent.	It is annoying not to be obeyed. I will try to improve the relationship so my child will want to cooperate.

The STEP program also promotes the *family meeting* as an important tool in helping children learn to respect themselves and others, to cooperate, and to develop self-esteem. At the family meeting parents and children plan the division of chores, hear concerns and complaints, express positive feelings toward each other, resolve conflicts, plan family activities, and make other decisions that affect family members. These meetings are not for griping, but rather for solving problems and discussing issues that concern individual family members. Psychologists Betty Lou Bettner and Amy Lew have noted that "when families take the time to sit down together to decide what needs to be done and how to do it, everyone may be surprised at the result. Parents who have fought with their kids over taking out the garbage may discover, when the children have input into which chores they will do, they are more likely to take on responsibility and remember to follow through. Successful meetings help family members learn to share responsibility and solve problems together" (Bettner and Lew, 1990).

THE ACTIVE PARENTING OF MICHAEL POPKIN

The ideas and methods presented by the various parent training programs overlap because many of them share a root in Alfred Adler's and Rudolf Dreikurs' work. Michael Popkin, an Adlerian, has developed his own *active parenting*, a video-based program that he supplements with reading material and small-group workshops. Like other parenting trainers, Popkin also incorporates the work of learning and cognitive theorists into his program. The concept of reinforcement, the power of consequences, and the impact of a parent's beliefs on children's behaviors are all prominent features of a learning theory orientation. Popkin's emphasis is on helping parents give children freedom with necessary limits. Here is an example of how limits and responsibilities are expanded in accordance with the child's developmental level and capabilities:

Freedom	Limit
May go outside	Stay inside the fence
Choose breakfast	Cold or hot cereal
Watch TV	"Sesame Street" or "Mr. Rogers"
Choose what to wear	From this selection for school
Select activities	If we can afford it
Select time for homework	After school, before dinner or after
Select a way to contribute to family	From a job list
Choose friends	Invite them home to meet parents
Choose bedtime	Be in your bedroom by _____; no loud music after 10:00 P.M.
Get driver's license	Take driver's education program
Borrow family car	If arranged beforehand; no drinking or drugs

Parents often lose their stance when a child says things like "I hate this house," or "I hate my life." Parents must deal with the anxiety that arises when their child says derogatory things about the parent or house. The child's anger can make parents feel unloved, often to the point of backing down. Parents have to be aware of the following things: Is there a point when you lose your ground with your child? What are your feelings then? Is your child saying something hurtful? Are you feeling attacked? Unwanted? Do you ever feel so powerless that you strike out at the child?

MODIFYING BEHAVIOR THROUGH REWARDS AND PUNISHMENTS

Parents who prize learning want their children to do well in school; a father who believes that "children should be seen and not heard" wants his children to be as quiet as possible; a religious mother expects her children to attend church services every Sunday. How do parents get the behaviors they want? What can

The Informed Parent 8.3

Family Meeting Guidelines for Resolving Conflicts

1. Agree to respect each other. Everyone can express a point of view without being attacked or ridiculed.

2. Define the problem positively. Make sure everyone agrees it is fairly stated.

3. Identify goals everyone has in common: "We all want to switch to a healthier diet."

4. Stick to the issue. Don't get sidetracked by bringing up past mistakes and behaviors, and don't allow the subject to be changed.

5. Express feelings honestly, and listen attentively to everyone else. Clarify with feedback: "It sounds as if you're saying you don't want to visit grandma every Sunday."

6. Brainstorm possible solutions. Come up with at least three alternatives. Evaluate the alternatives together. Decide which one to try.

7. Set a date for the next family meeting, when the decision will be evaluated.

Source: Adapted from Bettner and Lew, 1990.

parents do when children act in ways that are inconsistent with parental expectations? A *behavioral* model of parenting seeks to answer these questions by assuming that all of children's behavior is learned through social interaction.

The behavioral approach to parenting is based upon the work of B. F. Skinner, who described a type of learning known as *operant conditioning.* Skinner showed that when an organism operating on the environment does something, the emitted behavior is maintained and strengthened by *reinforcement* or rewards. In learning theory, reinforcement is any stimulus that increases the likelihood of a behavior being repeated. Reinforcement can be positive or negative, a very important distinction in learning theory. A positive reinforcer is a pleasant stimulus, such as a kind word or money. Praise a child for reading, and he or she will be more likely to pick up a book. A negative reinforcer *removes* an unpleasant stimulus. A child who stays alone in his bedroom to avoid his parents' arguments is being negatively reinforced for that behavior. Negative reinforcement is *not* the same thing as punishment. Punishment *decreases* the probability that a behavior will be emitted. Both positive and negative reinforcement increase the likelihood of a repeat performance.

Children act on their environments; they *do* something. How the environment responds to the behavior—positively or negatively, rewarding or not—largely determines whether or not the behavior will be repeated. Children are continually being rewarded. Sometimes the rewards are internal, as in the feeling of joy after riding a bike down the street for the first time. Parents provide external rewards. A loving hug, praise, and paying attention to a child are

The Informed Parent 8.4

Plain Speaking

It is not uncommon for parents to get into debates and arguments with children over chores, homework, privileges, and other day-to-day things. The arguments often turn unpleasant and rarely accomplish what a parent intends. Often parents are not clear and concise when they talk to their children. This leaves the door open for children to disagree, get angry, and ignore what is being said. Parents may say pointless things like "Your room looks like World War III" in an attempt to get their children to tidy a bedroom. When this is not accomplished they move to the more obvious "Your room is a mess." Sometimes they even beg. "Will you please clean up this room." Finally they threaten, "If this room is not clean by dinnertime, you can't go out with your friends this weekend."

Try a calm, direct approach, stick to the point, and don't get into debates, arguments, or discussions. Here are two scenarios concerning the room cleaning. In the first, the parent and child debate the parent's request. In the second the parent is clear and insistent, refusing to get into a discussion or argument. The parent uses a technique known as *the broken record*, a continual repeating of the request in the face of the child's delaying tactics.

Parent: Charlotte, your room is a mess. I want you to clean it.

Child: I can't today. I'm going out with Brenda.

Parent: You were supposed to clean it yesterday.

Child: I didn't have time. I'll get to it.

Parent: You said that yesterday. When will you get to it?

Child: When I come home today.

Parent: You have homework to do tonight, you won't have time.

Child: Don't worry, I'll get to it soon.

Plain Speaking

Parent: Charlotte, I want you to clean your room.

Child: I can't today. I'm going out with Brenda.

Parent: Clean your room before you go out.

Child: I don't have time. I promised Brenda I'd be at her house in 20 minutes.

Parent: Call Brenda and tell her you'll meet her after you clean your room.

Child: (angrily) I can't be late! I promised Brenda I'd be there in 20 minutes.

Parent: (calmly) The sooner you finish cleaning your room, the sooner you'll be able to meet Brenda.

Child: I hate this house. None of my friends have to do their rooms on a beautiful Sunday afternoon.

Parent: After you finish cleaning your room you can go out.

(continued)

Generally a child will comply with a parent's request after three repetitions. In cases where a child continues to try to provoke an argument, a parent can offer a clear choice.

Child: I'm doing my room later and that's it.

Parent: Charlotte, you have a choice. Clean your room now and go to Brenda's, or don't clean your room and be grounded not only tonight but the rest of the week. It's completely up to you.

social rewards; giving a child a cookie or a gold star, or buying the latest CD for a teenager is a *material* reward; taking a child to a movie or raising the bedtime hour is reward based on *privileges*.

Rewards are most effective as behavior modifiers if they are given immediately after a desired behavior is exhibited. A parent might extend the privilege of an extra half hour of television after observing that a child had cleaned her room. A gold star might go to a youngster who practices the piano.

The idea of a child's emitting a behavior and having it rewarded sounds relatively simple. The truth is that many behaviors are difficult to acquire and, once acquired, difficult to change. Children differ in the things that reinforce their behaviors. One child likes to be hugged and kissed, another finds physical contact annoying. A trip to the zoo is a pleasure to some children but a boring affair to others. Sometimes there is nothing a parent can offer that will provoke a child to do something he or she doesn't want to do. And the things that children find rewarding change as they grow and develop. Also, rewards are most effective when given immediately after a desired behavior is emitted. This is why a future reward, such as promising to take a child to Disneyworld over summer vacation if he gets good grades, is basically ineffective. It is important that rewards for a particular behavior be consistent. Given the average parent's daily activities there is often considerable inconsistency in how rewards are meted out. An unhurried, relaxed parent is more likely to remember to praise a child for putting plates in the sink. A day later, running late for work, the same parent might ignore such behavior or even punish the child by telling her to stop dawdling.

Do as I Do: Parents as Models

Behaviorists who followed B. F. Skinner agree that reinforcement plays an important role in learning; however, they propose that learning occurs in a social context. The way children perceive, analyze, and make judgments about their experiences also influences behavior. Children learn by observing the behavior of others. They expand their knowledge and develop skills by seeing and listening to the people around them. In effect, they learn vicariously how to act in the world. While considerable learning takes place from direct experience, this exceedingly important phenomenon, of *modeling*, or observational learning, enables children to learn without having to do things themselves. Through models children are taught the positive or negative consequences of actions. The most influential models for children are their parents.

Albert Bandura, a prominent social-learning theorist, believes children do not blindly respond to environmental stimuli. Rather, they pick and choose from among environmental options, basing decisions on their own insights, preferences, and past experiences. Generally, role models are family members or friends, but often they are cultural figures. For example, a high school girl dresses like Madonna although she's never met the singer; the "skinhead" look is representative of a racist subculture.

There are four processes involved in observational learning. First, the learner *observes* a model acting in a manner that catches his or her attention. Past experience and expectations shape what children will attend to in their environment, and the behavior must be acceptable and fulfill a need. Second, the information gathered from observations is filed away in *memory*. Third, the behavior is tested through *performance*. And fourth, once the modeled behavior is imitated, if it is *reinforced* by operant conditioning principles, it is repeated. A teenager feeling depressed and alone, for example, might be attracted to a religious cult that promises friendship and unconditional love. The child spends time with cult members and, if his or her feelings of aloneness are assuaged, the child will likely continue his or her relationship with the cult. Another child watches mother make cookies and find the activity appealing. After a couple of tries, the child doesn't like the messiness of cooking and she stops modeling the mother's behavior.

It is difficult to overstate the importance of models and observational learning in human development. Individuals need not be involved in direct environmental consequences to learn about the effects of specific behaviors. A child observes his older brother being punished for having a messy room. The younger child straightens his own belongings. If the older child is rewarded for earning high marks on his report card, the younger brother might attempt to improve his own grades. This is called *vicarious reinforcement.* By watching, remembering, choosing, and noting reinforcements and punishments, children learn such behaviors as how to love, display anger, and promote prejudice.

THE IMPORTANCE OF DISCIPLINE

The term *discipline* comes from *disciple*, meaning "pupil." It is also used to refer to a branch of knowledge, such as the discipline of psychology. The object of discipline, then, is to teach something. It is through learning that children are trained in the ways parents wish them to go. If parents desire certain behaviors in their children, they will have to understand the techniques and methods that make learning them possible.

There are literally scores of techniques for parents to chose from when teaching their children, each with a specific focus. In *Discipline: A Sourcebook of 50 Failsafe Techniques for Parents* (1991), James Windell categorgized the following discipline techniques:

- Discipline techniques that prevent problems
- Discipline techniques that encourage self-control
- Discipline techniques that teach lessons
- Discipline techniques that encourage and reinforce appropriate and desired behaviors
- Discipline techniques that correct behavior
- Discipline techniques that discourage inappropriate and undesired behaviors

James Windell believes rules are an important part of discipline, in that they inform children about limits for behavior. They guide children and help them change behaviors that make parents unhappy, and they give children a sense of security by ordering their day. Windell notes that for rules to be effective they must be reasonable and consistent. Many parents, however, use rules haphazardly.

Rules for young children should be few in number, simple, related to a child's age and developmental level, and stated clearly and unambiguously. A toddler can understand the straightforward "Don't hit other children," better than "Other children have rights and you should respect those rights." Parents should give reasons for rules. "Because I said so," is not as effective as "The legal curfew in this township is midnight and that's the time by which you have to be home." Parents must be aware of their reasons for insisting on a rule. What is the motivation behind, "Keep quiet," or "Children should be seen and not heard"? Parents should use consequences to enforce rules, but the consequences must be reasonable. Before deciding on the consequences, parents must consider the age and personality of a child, as well as the logic behind the consequence. For a two-year-old, a 15-minute time-out is an eternity and often will end with the child having a tantrum. And giving a time-out because the child refuses to eat or is cranky doesn't make a lot of sense. With older children time limits should be flexible. Does it really matter if a child does the dishes *before* watching a favorite TV show?

Windell cautions that children will invariably challenge rules, testing the limits of their parents' control. A teenager might come home 15 minutes after curfew; a young child might purposely make a fuss in the supermarket. Children may need a reminder of the rules and consequences from time to time. Sometimes, however, rules become inappropriate or unenforceable. For example, at some point in adolescence, it may be unnecessary or fruitless to insist on a particular bedtime. Windell insists that rules must be applied equally in families, or children will quickly recognize the hypocrisy of rules defied by some members. It is difficult for a parent to defend a rule of no smoking if the parent smokes. If children are expected to tell parents what time they'll be home, parents should do the same. A divorced parent who allows a date to "sleep over" will face an uphill battle in trying to regulate the children's sexual behavior.

By the time children are teenagers parents have to trust that their earlier rules, consistency, clarity, firmness, and fairness have produced the ultimate result: a child who knows what limits are and has learned self-discipline (Windell, 1991).

TIME-OUT TECHNIQUES

Many parents and teachers rely on a technique known as *time out,* a punishment by which a child who is behaving undesirably for a period of time is separated from his family or peers and made to stay alone in some part of the house or classroom. This technique is misused when the child is isolated for too long a time or when the technique is overemployed—used at the slightest provocation. Sometimes it is parent or teacher who needs a time out from energetic youngsters. If time out is to be used for discipline, some suggestions have been made to make this technique effective.

1. Warn the child in advance. "Please stop hitting your brother. If you don't, you are going to have to stand in the corner."

2. Give the child a few seconds to stop what she is doing. If she doesn't, take her to the corner. Remind her, "You did not stop hitting your brother. You will have to stand in the corner." Do not discuss this action with the child; ignore all crying, pleading, and begging.

3. Face the child to the wall. "You will stand here for X minutes." A few minutes is enough for children under four; from 5 to 10 minutes is enough for children ages five to eight. If the child leaves the corner, return her to it. If need be, stand nearby to make sure the child stays there.

4. State an opportunity to be released early from the punishment, and use words that reinforce appropriate behavior. "When you're willing to sit at the table without throwing food at your brother, you may return." After the child returns to the table, give some positive recognition such as, "Thank you for coming back to the table and behaving."

5. If you want the child to stay in time out for the duration stated, wait until the time is up and free the child from the corner with "Now you may go back to playing with your brother."

6. Praise the child for behaving the way you expect.

7. Recognize that time-out does not address the problem. It may cause the child to become angry.

DISCIPLINE DOES NOT MEAN PUNISHMENT

Parents can contribute to children's self-esteem by being competent disciplinarians, by giving guidance, and by being positive at the same time. If this sounds like a tall order, it is; but it can be done. What is required is discipline that is related to love and nurturing, plus a healthy respect for children and their needs at all developmental levels.

"Time outs" should be used sparingly and for good cause, or the technique will lose its effectiveness. This technique may increase misbehavior because it can increase a child's frustration when feelings that provoked misbehavior are ignored.

In an effort to shape the behavior of their children, parents try many different methods, many of them relatively ineffectual. In the name of discipline, they hit them, talk to them, take away allowances, call them names, instill guilt, sit them alone in a corner, assign chores, take away privileges, praise them, withhold food, bribe them, ground them, and ignore them. Many parents confuse discipline with punishment. Psychoanalyst Bruno Bettelheim differentiates punishment this way "Punishment teaches a child that those who have power can force others to do their will. And when a child is old enough and able, he will try to use such force himself . . . any punishment sets us against the person who inflicts it on us" (Bettelheim, 1985).

The use of punishment to shape behavior is certainly not new to the world of child rearing, but there are now questions about its effectiveness. The principle behind punishment rests on the premise that if a particular act prompts a discomfortable response, a child is less likely to repeat the act. This discomfort can come in the form of an unpleasant action, such as a slap, or the withdrawal of a pleasant action, such as removal of television privileges. As in the case of reinforcement, timing and intensity are important determinants of behavior change. In one animal experiment, for example, a rat was placed in a Skinner box wired with an electric shocker. Each time the rat pressed his food lever, it received a shock; shortly the lever-pressing activity stopped. It also stopped if the shock was administered immediately after the lever was pressed. If, however, punishment was delayed—even for as little as ten seconds—the effect of the shock was negated; that is, the rat continued to press the lever. In a similar vein, mothers who warn their children that they will be punished for misbehavior when their father gets home find little change in their youngsters' behavior.

Intensity of punishment is an important variable in modifying behavior. If punishment is mild—for example, a slight reprimand for going into the cookie jar—behavior may change only temporarily. Severe punishment, such as a hard slap or harsh scolding, may get results; however, the result may be worse than the original act. Severe punishment often leads to *suppression*, not extinction, of a behavior. The desire is still present and it merely waits for a more opportune time and place to show itself. Teenagers who are severely punished for smoking marijuana do not necessarily give up this pastime. They just try not to get caught again.

Severe punishment can lead to unfortunate emotional reactions, especially in young children. In some cases, harsh punishment leads to what Martin Seligman (1967) calls "learned helplessness." Studies of dogs have shown that when they are placed in a situation where punishment is constant and unavoidable, the dogs will give up attempts to escape and submit to punishment while showing symptoms of withdrawal, apathy, and severe depression. Depression is presently the major mental health problem in adolescents and college students, and at its root is a sense of helplessness and hopelessness. Studies of long-term life satisfaction show that powerlessness and lack of control of one's life are feelings highly instrumental in making people unhappy. In addition, a child's apprehension can provoke guilt and anxiety so strong that fears generalize. For example, young children punished for exploring their sex organs may develop sexual problems that carry into adulthood.

The most severe effects of strong punishment are the hostility and anger it provokes. Anyone who has been harshly reprimanded by a teacher or employer knows the hostility experienced. Children who are unable to express their feelings about being treated this way, for fear of greater punishment, may resort to *passive aggressiveness*, getting back at parents with behaviors such as procrastination, pouting, inattentiveness, stubbornness, or inefficiency (Coleman, Butcher, and Carson, 1984). An example of passive aggresiveness is the child who answers "I didn't hear you" after his mother calls him for dinner a half-dozen times.

Ironically, punishment can have an effect opposite from that intended. If a child views a punishment as unfair or unreasonable, the child may become so angry and resentful that he or she will ignore continued threats. In such situations, parental control is lessened. In some cases, the "bad" behavior is worth the punishment the child has to pay for it. If a child get little notice from parents for "good" behavior, he or she might write on the wall, hit a sibling, or engage in other attention-getting actions. A parent's angry response might be a satisfying experience, one that leads to a repetition of the behavior.

In short, while punishment is one way to modify behavior, it is more ineffectual than helpful. Reinforcing desired behavior has proven to be a more efficient method of promoting change. If punishment *is* to be used, there are some basic rules that make it effective. First, the punishment must reflect the "crime." To punish a failing grade on a history exam by keeping a child from a sleep over at a friend's house is meaningless, as it doesn't address the reason for the failure. Second, the timing of a punishment must be appropriate. A short "time out" *directly* after a young child has thrown food—accompanied by a loving explanation of the rules and the reason for the punishment—is more effective than denying the child the right to watch her favorite TV program an hour after dinner. Third, to be effective, an alternative to an undesired behavior must be offered. A child on time out for misbehavior during dinner should be told what is expected of her if she desires to return to the dinner table.

THE LESSONS OF SPANKING AND HITTING

In 1996, an 8-year-old boy name Korey Wax was suspended from school for misbehavior. His father, the 43-year-old superintendent of schools in a small upstate New York village, punished his son by whacking him several times across the back and chest with a three-foot rubber snake—the kind that people win in carnival booths—leaving welts on the child's skin. Someone called the state's Child Abuse Hotline and the father was arrested on charges of third-degree assault and endangering the welfare of a child. The arrest provoked a national debate about the rights of parents to discipline their children, the extent to which parents can go, and the right of government to intrude. It also points to a changing attitude about what constitutes an appropriate reaction to a child's misbehavior.

Corporal punishment can be defined as the use of physical force with the intention of causing a child to experience pain, but not injury, for the purpose of correction or control of the child's behavior. The most frequent forms of corporal punishment are spanking, slapping, grabbing or shoving roughly, and hitting with objects such as a hair brush, belt, or paddle. Corporal punishment is approved of by an overwhelming majority of Americans until it goes farther than society condones. Then, with an intent to injure and the evidence of *observable damage,* it is considered *child abuse* (Straus, 1994).

The nation's most outspoken critic of hitting and spanking children is psychologist Murray Straus, who has spent his career conducting research into the long-term effects of this parental activity. Straus believes that "the universal and chronic use of corporal punishment and its potentially harmful effects on children is the best-kept secret of American child psychology."

The notion that harsh treatment of children builds character is an ancient idea, rooted in religious tradition. The Old Testament offers this bit of advice for dealing with misbehavior. *For every one that curseth his father or his mother shall be surely put to death . . .* (Leviticus 10.9). The proverbs suggest a good dose of physical punishment in the face of a child's perceived evil. *Withhold not correction from the child: for if thou beatest him with the rod, he shall not die. Thou shalt beat him with the rod, and shalt deliver his soul from hell* (Proverbs 23:13-14). This version of the "spare the rod, spoil the child" philosophy is reflected in child-rearing attitudes in many homes. Interestingly, these views are in opposition to other biblical teachings about parenting. *Train up a child in the way he should go: and when he is old, he will not depart from it* (Proverbs 22.6). There are also suggestions in the Bible that provoking children to anger discourages them. And there is the well-known parable of the Prodigal Son, the child who is forgiven his misdeeds and welcomed back into the family.

A majority of American parents have used spanking and other forms of physical punishment in an effort to change the behavior of their children. In one study of 150 families, 148 admitted to spanking their children at least once. Boys are spanked more frequently than girls, and toddlers and preschoolers are hit more often than school-age children and adolescents (Lytton and Romney, 1991). Men are more likely to approve of using physical punishment than women, and adults who spank their children are more likely to have been spanked themselves when young (Kelder, McNamara, Carlson, and Lynn, 1991; Simons, et al., 1991).

Physical punishment by parents often leads to imitation learning in children, who see this behavior as a way to resolve conflicts with others. Behaviorist Albert Bandura (1966) conducted a famous experiment using large rubber dolls to show the effect on children of adults engaging in physical violence. Bandura had children watch a movie of an adult hitting and kicking a doll. Some children saw the film end with the adult punished for hitting the doll, others saw the adult rewarded, and a third group saw no consequences. After the viewing, the children were given the doll to play with and they acted in accordance with their film's outcome. The children who had seen the adult rewarded were exceptionally harsh on the doll; those who had viewed no consequences hit and kicked the doll less than the first group; and the children who had seen the adults punished abused the doll least. What Bandura determined from his study was that rewards *do* play a part in imitation learning—in fact to the extent that rewards create a *likelihood* of imitation performance. This is not the sole determinant of behavior, since all the children "learned" to be aggressive toward the doll; some just did not put the learning into practice.

Clearly the behavior of the punisher has as much effect on a child's behavior as the punishment itself. Parents who use punishments such as hitting and yelling tend to raise children who handle problems the same way. In one study it was reported that 100 percent of children who had been physically punished struck a sibling during the year of the study. This compares to only 20 percent of children whose parents did not use physical punishment (Straus, Gelles, and Steinmetz, 1980).

The effects of physical punishment go much further than the mere changing of a child's undesired behavior. Sometimes parents do far more harm than they intended, injuring children seriously, and even causing their death. What these parents may construe as an attempt to change a behavior is, in actuality, child abuse and subject to legal intervention. Parents generally strike children to vent their anger and reduce their frustration, not to discipline. For many, spanking is the means of communication (Larzelere, et al., 1989; Graziano and Namaste, 1990).

Children who are physically mistreated by their parents are often unpopular with their peers. They suffer from low self-esteem and possess a sense of worthlessness (Rohner, et al., 1992; Larzelere, et al., 1989). Of greatest concern is the research showing that children who are spanked by their parents often suffer from emotional instability and are more likely to exhibit delinquency in adolescence and deviant or criminal behavior in adulthood (Rohner, et al., 1991; Len, 1987; Straus, 1991).

Philip Greven (1992) believes that anxiety, anger, depression, obsessiveness and rigidity, dissociation, paranoia, sadomasochism and other emotional problems are wrought by physical punishment. But one of the most troubling and enduring consequences is the stifling of empathy and compassion for oneself and others. Greven notes that many books advocating the use of physical punishment have been written by people who have been likewise abused in childhood and that they are unable to face the reality of their mistreatment.

> . . . many advocates of corporal punishments are notably deficient in empathy for the suffering of children whose bodies bear the impact of painful assaults justified as discipline. The ability to put oneself in another's place often might seem sufficient to curb the aggressive impulses to inflict physical and emotional suffering on children, but most people hurt in childhood by their parents develop immunities to empathy that often persist for a lifetime.

Murray A. Straus (1994) is adamant that corporal punishment is the nation's major social problem, and at the heart of the pervasive violence in the culture. Domestic abuse and teenage delinquency are two long-term effects of parental use of corporal punishment. He notes that corporal punishment usually begins in infancy, it happens frequently, and it continues through the preschool years when the deepest layers of children's personalities are formed.

> Corporal punishment is deeply traumatic for young children. Most parents, psychologists, parent educators, and authors of child-rearing books apparently think that if not overdone, corporal punishment serves to correct misbehavior and has no lasting ill effect on the child. But the opposite might be true. For a child who can barely walk or talk . . . it can be truly traumatic if the most loved and trusted figure in the child's life suddenly carries out a painful attack. The consequence can be a post-traumatic stress syndrome that creates deep, lifelong psychological problems, such as depression and suicidal thinking.

What particularly concerns Straus are the high rates of depression in the United States, particularly among adolescents. While there are many reasons for this phenomenon, there is evidence that the structure and chemistry of the brain changes in response to continual stress (Holden, 1991). For children, the ever-present fear of corporal punishment causes stress that begins in early childhood and may continue through adolescence, leading to the hormonal changes that characterize depression.

Murray Straus envisions a time when corporal punishment will be outlawed in America. He notes the social benefits of this:

1. Bringing up children without hitting them will reduce the stress and trauma of being a parent and being a child. Parents will be able to bring up their children with less hassle. Young children, on the average, will be better behaved, and among older children there will be less delinquency.

2. When these children are adults and parents themselves, they will be less likely to physically abuse their spouses and children.

3. Family relationship will be more rewarding because there will be a closer bond between parents and children.

4. A society with little or no hitting of children is likely to result in fewer people who are alienated, depressed, or suicidal, and in fewer violent marriages.

5. The potential benefits for the society as a whole are equally great. These include lower crime rates, especially for violent crimes; increased economic productivity; and less money spent on controlling or treating crime and mental illness.

A FAMILY-SYSTEMS MODEL OF PARENTING

In evaluating the various child-rearing approaches, psychologist Thomas W. Roberts (1994) proposes that while gaining new skills in communicating and problem solving is always helpful, what is missing from most models of

---

TABLE 8.2   A 12-Session Parent-Education Program

Parenting education programs that emphasize a family-systems approach offer a 12-session intervention designed to help family members understand their interconnectedness.

Session 1 focuses on understanding the degree to which behavior in the family is based on reciprocal causality; that is, as a response to what is happening in the family.

Session 2 focuses on increasing knowledge of developmental issues, including physical, cognitive, and social development throughout the life cycle.

Session 3 deals with understanding moral reasoning: the ability to know right from wrong.

Session 4 emphasizes teaching parents communication skills and problem-solving strategies.

Session 5 helps parents improve the marital relationship and improve sibling relations.

Session 6 focuses on developing and maintaining triangles in the family, with emphasis on the way children are used to defuse conflict between parents.

Session 7 focuses on family boundaries and the emotional barriers that protect and identify the integrity of individual members, subsystems, and families.

Session 8 focuses on differentiation, the process by which a person controls his or her emotional reactions to other family members.

Session 9 focuses on unwritten family rules and on developing family roles.

Session 10 focuses on understanding the beneficial effects of play with children utilizing play in creating cooperative family relationships.

Session 11 focuses on storytelling as an underdeveloped and underutilized parental activity and one which directs children's behavior and gains cooperation.

Session 12 is a concluding session during which families discuss and evaluate their goals. They also discuss how the training has affected each family member.

Source: Adapted from Roberts, T.W. *A Systems Perspective of Parenting.* Brooks/Cole, 1994.

The Informed Parent 8.5

When You Need Professional HELP!

Most discipline problems can be handled by just taking the time to assess the strength of your parent-child connection, using commonsense techniques, and trying one approach after another until you find what works. Yet there are times when you need outside help. Consider two different types of counselors. Consult experienced, happy parents whose advice you value. They can offer practical tips to make living with your child easier. You may need to dig more deeply into disciplining yourself in order to discipline your child. You may require the help of a therapist. Here are some red flags that mean you are at risk for disciplining unwisely.

- **Yelling.** Do you go into frequent rages that are out of control, calling your child names ("Brat," "Damn kid") and causing your child to recoil and retreat? This means that you are letting your child punch your anger buttons too easily, that you may not have control of your anger buttons, or that there are simply too many of them.

- **Mirroring unhappiness.** Do you walk around all day reflecting to your child that you are unhappy as a person and as a parent? Kids take this personally. If they bring you no joy, they must be no good. Life is a "downer."

- **Parentifying.** Are your children taking care of you instead of vice versa? Are you crying and complaining a lot and showing immature overreactions to accidents or misbehaviors? That scares children. You're supposed to be the parent, the one in control protecting them.

- **Blame shifting.** Do you unload your mistakes on your kids or your spouse? If so, children learn that the way you deal with problems is to avoid taking personal responsibility for them, and that somehow these problems are just too big for you to manage or that you don't know how to ask for help.

- **Modeling perfection.** Are you intolerant of even trivial mistakes made by yourself or your child? The child gets the message that mistakes are horrible to make. This is particularly difficult for the "sponge child," the one who soaks up your attitudes and becomes superhard on himself.

- **Spanking more.** Are slaps and straps showing up in your corrections? Are most of your interactions with your child on a negative note?

- **A fearing family.** Is your child afraid of you? Does she cringe when you raise your voice and keep a "safe" distance from you? Is your child becoming emotionally flat, fearing the consequences of expressing her emotions?

While even the most healthy parent may experience one of these red flags occasionally, if you find they are becoming a routine way of life, for the sake of yourself and your child, get professional help.

parenting is an understanding of the way families operate (Chapter 4). Family-systems theory views children's behavior as *context dependent*, that is, a response to family dynamics. Roberts believes most models "fail to appreciate the complexity in the parent/child relationship, particularly relationships with other family members and extrafamilial relationships." A family-systems approach also takes into account the larger social network and the ecosystem of the family, including peers, work, and culture. The goal of parenting-education programs, believes Roberts, should be to improve family functioning.

> Parent education should consider the whole family and aim to improve the family's level of functioning. All members of the family should be present. The focus should be to help the family monitor itself and be able to both understand itself better and solve its own problems (Roberts, 1994).

Chapter Review

- Children change as they grow older, so parent methods must be adaptable to each child and each situation. Parents must know and understand many different techniques to use in raising children.

- Martin Hoffman has identified three basic types of parenting techniques. Power-assertive methods rely on force in the form of commands, threats, and punishment. Disapproval, the silent treatment and disregard mark the withdrawal-of-love method of parenting. Inductive methods rely on reasoning and problem solving as a way to instill appropriate behaviors.

- There is a cyclical aspect to parental interaction with children, based on the stresses of daily life, the behavior of children at specific times, and the emotional state of parents at the time behavior is exhibited.

- Haim Ginott believed emotions are the cornerstone of the parent-child relationship. Expressing emotions—anger and fear, sadness and joy, delight and disgust—have important survival benefits in life, but children are often educated out of knowing what they are feeling.

- Adele Faber and Elaine Mazlish concentrated on helping parents reduce conflict and tensions by changing the ways they talk and listen to their children. They noted the direct connection between how children feel and how they behave.

- Thomas Gordon based his parent-effectiveness training (PET) program on the assumption that parents need training, not blaming. He advises parents to first and foremost accept themselves as people who have positive as well as negative feelings toward their children. Gordon's training programs emphasize effective communication between parents and their children, conversation that does not damage a child's self-esteem.

- In helping parents deal with behaviors they don't want in nonpower ways, Gordon utilized the concept of problem ownership.

- Alfred Adler proposed that the goal-directed behavior of children can only be understood in the context of the social environment in which the behavior is exhibited. He believed sibling rivalry, family constellation, and parenting styles are among the variables that influence both childhood and adult behavior.

- Rudolf Dreikurs' approach to parent training emphasized the importance of creating a democratic family system, one that sets appropriate limits, practices respect for everyone in the family, and encourages collective decision making.

- The STEP program forwards the belief that the use of rewards and punishments as disciplinary techniques should be replaced with methods that rely on "natural and logical consequences" as determinants of behavior. The program emphasises the notion of logical, meaning that which is reasonable and sensible. The family meeting serves as an important tool in helping children learn to respect themselves and others, cooperate, and develop self-esteem.

- A behavioral model of parenting assumes that behavior on the part of children is learned through social interaction. Children act on their environments; they *do* something. How the environment responds to the behavior, positively or negatively, rewarding or not, largely determines whether or not the behavior will be repeated.

- Children learn by observing the behavior of others. They expand their knowledge and develop skills by seeing and listening to the people around them; in effect, learning vicariously how to act in the world. While considerable learning takes place from direct experience, this exceedingly important phenomenon, of modeling, or observational learning, enables children to learn without having to do things directly.

- The principle behind punishment rests on the conclusion that if a particular act produces discomfort, that act is less likely to be repeated. Intensity of punishment is an important variable in modifying behavior.

- Severe punishment leads to a number of reactions, including hostility, anger, aggression, and depression. Punishment modifies behavior, but it is more ineffectual than helpful. Reinforcing desirable behavior has proven to be a more efficient method of promoting change.

- Corporal punishment is defined as the use of physical force with the intention of causing a child to experience pain, but not injury, for the purpose of correction or control of the child's behavior.

- Physical punishment by parents often leads to imitation learning on the part of children who see this behavior as a way to resolve conflicts with others. Children who are physically mistreated are less popular with their peers. They often suffer from low self-esteem and a sense of worthlessness.

- Philip Greven believes that in addition to the anxiety, anger, depression, obsessiveness and rigidity, dissociation, paranoia, sadomasochism, and other emotional problems wrought by physical punishment, one of the most troubling and enduring consequences is the stifling of empathy and compassion for oneself and others.

- James Windell believes rules are an important part of discipline in that they regulate behavior by informing children about limits. They guide children and help them change behaviors that displease parents.

- Thomas Roberts states that what is missing from most models of parenting is an understanding of the way families operate. Family-systems theory views children's behavior as context dependent; that is, a response to family dynamics.

Student Activities

1. Ask five parents what they would do in the following situations. Select both mothers and fathers of various ages. Note differences in how they would handle these parenting problems. Whose technique or approach do they seem to be following? Are there differences due to gender or age?

   Your 17-year-old daughter says she is going to the library to meet her study group on Wednesday nights. You discover she has instead been meeting a young man you have expressed dissatisfaction with and that the pair has been going out together. How would you handle this situation when your daughter arrives home?

Your three-year-old refuses to go to day care in the morning. He cries and takes his clothes off during breakfast and says a loud "No" when asked if he wants to go to school.

Your two teenagers argue constantly about chores, TV programming, and borrowing of each other's possessions.

Helping Hands

Children's Creative Response to Conflict (CCRC)
Box 271
Nyack, NY 10960
(914) 358-4601

Trained facilitators conduct workshops for parents, children, and teachers in conflict resolution. Publisher's handbook and newsletter in English and Spanish.

CHAPTER

Parenting the Infant

Chapter Highlights

After reading Chapter 9, students should be able to:

- Understand the personal and family-life changes that mark the transition to parenthood
- Recognize how the uniqueness of every newborn affects the parenting process
- Understand the rhythm and patterns of a child's first year
- Understand the importance of emotional bonding between infants and parents
- Recognize the importance of early stimulation on the intellectual growth of children

Chapter Contents

- The Transition to Parenting
    Changes in Family Life ▪ *New-Parent Beliefs*
- From Neonate to Infant
    Reflexes: Built-in Behaviors ▪ *Temperamental Differences in Children* ▪ *Goodness of Fit*
- Patterns and Rhythms of Life
    States of Alertness ▪ *Parental Stress and Infant Crying* ▪ *Sudden Infant Death Syndrome* ▪ *The Family Bed During Infancy* ▪ *Infant Nutrition* ▪ *The Bottle or the Breast*
- The First Relationship: The Emotional Bonding of Infant and Parent
    Early Attachment ▪ *A Multi-Generational View of Attachment* ▪ *Attachment and the Microsystem* ▪ *The Blanket and the Dolly: Transitional Objects* ▪ *Attachment and Fathers*
- The Newborn Conquers the World
    The Developing Brain ▪ *Neural Competition* ▪ *Infant Communication* ▪ *Promoting Early Language Development* ▪ *Motor Development* ▪ *Gaining Control Over the Environment* ▪ *Controlling the World Manually*

In 1945, soldiers returning from World War II were about to launch a national "baby boom." That same year, a young pediatrician named Benjamin Spock wrote a book called *Baby and Child Care*. Spock's book sold millions of copies and changed the way American parents viewed their children and their own role in child rearing. In his book, Dr. Spock answered questions—about breast-feeding, nutrition, growth patterns, teething, fussy babies, and scores of other subjects of concern to mothers and fathers. To put parents at ease, Dr. Spock said "don't take too seriously all that the neighbors say" and "don't be overawed by what the experts say." He told parents to trust in their common sense and to be neither too strict nor excessively permissive.

Spock's book was not the first to offer advice to parents struggling to understand and raise the children among them. But what was different about *Baby and Child Care* was its emphasis on the uniqueness of each child and the specialness of the parent-child relationship. This book made parents look at each of their children as a distinct individuals from the moment of birth.

THE TRANSITION TO PARENTING

Parenting begins before the birth of a baby, as mothers and fathers imagine what their new child will be like. This image that parents construct in their minds will later affect their expectations of their child and themselves. A father who pictures himself playing ball with a son may find himself throwing the ball to a daughter. Parents often form *images* of what they will be like as mothers and fathers. A woman who imagines she will be a Boy Scout den mother and class-trip chaperon might find that her work schedule allows no time to accompany her school-aged child to these daytime activities. This internal picture of the child and parent is continually revised as a result of everyday experiences the parents and child share (Ferholt, 1991; Stern, 1985).

CHANGES IN FAMILY LIFE

One of the images first-time parents can hardly picture is the amount of time it takes to care for a baby. Time-consuming tasks invariably lead to changes in the parents' relationship. Regardless of educational level, employment, or any pre-birth agreement, women tend to assume the role of primary caregiver. Although more and more men are taking paternity leaves from their jobs, it is generally the woman who takes a leave from paid employment when a baby is born. In one study of physicians with children, women reported working fewer hours than did men or than did childless women physicians (Grant, et al., 1990). Unplanned pregnancies in particular often lead parents to amend their educational or employment plans.

Generally, women not only care for the baby but also carry the major responsibility for housekeeping—chores that make them tired and often resentful if their mates do not help out much. During the first two years of caring for a baby, many women comment that they have little time for the "grownup" relationships that characterized their lives before the baby was born (Bronstein, 1988; Cowan, et al., 1991). Parents of newborns report a decrease in sexual activity and in shared leisure activities, and an increase in tension between partners (Levy-Shiff, 1994).

Mothers who previously had considerable energy for work and household duties find themselves frequently fatigued from waking during the night to care for an infant. Young children average from five to nine illnesses a year, ranging from a simple cold to the flu, and sometimes more serious sickness if they go to day care. Mothers frequently pick up these infections or viruses and therefore experience more illness themselves (O'Hara, et al., 1990).

Parents usually do not predict the increased need for space. A child's "things"—diapers, clothes, furniture, toys—take up a lot of room in the home. A living room can quickly turn into a playroom, and a kitchen is likely to be filled with baby paraphernalia. Sometime parents choose to move to a bigger place or "better neighborhood" after the birth of their baby. In a survey conducted in Northern California in the 1980s, 22 percent of the respondents who were parents reported they had moved there for the "good of the children" (Fischer, 1982). Moving generally means an increase in housing costs, mortgage or rent, as well as other living expenses. Often a move to another neighborhood means a change in social relationships and outside activities. Parents' freedom is curtailed as family schedules now revolve around the new baby's needs. The partners have less time for their personal relationship and their level of intimacy changes (Belsky, et al., 1985).

NEW-PARENT BELIEFS

Men and women bring to the role of parent a set of preconceived beliefs, attitudes, and behaviors about the child-rearing process. As they become fathers and mothers, their notions do not automatically disappear and they are not suddenly imbued with child-development knowledge. In one study, mothers believed their newborns could not discriminate facial features, which they can (Miller, 1988). Other studies reveal that parents often overestimate or underestimate the capabilities of their newborns. It is exceedingly important for parents to recognize the changes that occur at every stage of their child's development so that their parental interactions and expectations will be age-appropriate and based on sound reasoning. Training programs and reading materials are widely available to help parents understand the developmental stages of children (Chapter 1), and parents who avail themselves of these resources feel more competent at parenting.

FROM NEONATE TO INFANT

The newborn is called the *neonate* for the first few weeks of life, when survival issues are paramount. The neonate comes into the world "programmed" for physical growth, emotional reactions, locomotion, speech, social interaction, and cognition—thinking and reasoning. In the first days outside the protection of the mother's womb, the neonate has to respond and adapt to dozens of physiological changes. To care for a newborn effectively, parents must understand the hard work infants do during their first year, as they change from reflexive beings into ones who can meet the world with conviction and purpose. Noted pediatrician T. Berry Brazelton (1969) stresses that—from the moment of birth, children have different levels of activity, adaptability, and responsiveness to the environment. Parents must accept and respond to these differences. Although Brazelton's advice is directed to mothers, it is sound for anyone raising children.

> I am aware that much is written for the new mother. Most of the literature, however, is aimed at giving her advice. Very little of it offers her support for her own individual reactions and intuition. . . . The different advice she receives may conflict so thoroughly that she is left in a serious quandary. When she cannot follow all this advice, she becomes even more confused and guilty. . . . In spite of this avalanche of advice, of "sure" ways to mother a child, a new mother must realize that no one of them is the only answer. She must find her own way as a mother with her own special baby. Each mother and baby is an individual. As such, each pair is stuck with its own ways of interacting. The idealized suggestions of an authority may be entirely wrong for a particular mother and her child. A young mother may be better advised to chart her own course via the markers set out by her own baby (Brazelton, 1969).

The newborn is a very capable being, "programmed" for physical growth, emotional reactions, locomotion, speech, social interaction, and thinking and reasoning.

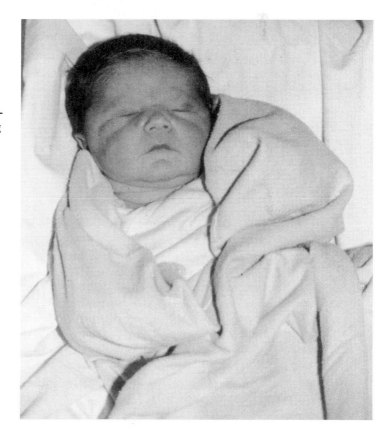

REFLEXES: BUILT-IN BEHAVIORS

Infants are born with a number of reflexes or built-in, automatic, physical responses, some of which ensure their survival after birth and others that help them adapt to their new world. Stroke an infant's cheek and he or she will turn in the direction of the touch. Offer a baby a finger and he or she will suck on it. Neonates breathe on their own before their umbilical cord is cut. If a newborn "forgets" to breathe, carbon dioxide accumulates in the blood, setting off a reaction that forces the baby to breathe. Infant reflexes help them find and take in nourishment. Infants are "prewired" to respond to temperature, touch, and noise.

Reflexive responses are such an important indicator of healthy development that a number of scales were created to gauge normal development. The most prominent of these was devised in 1973 by T. Berry Brazelton.

The *Brazelton Neonatal Behavioral Assessment Scale* measures 26 behaviors—such as rooting and sucking, irritability, and startle response—to determine the neurological status of newborns. Brazelton and his associates have categorized the scale into four groupings: motoric, state (alertness), physiological, and interaction. Motor development is evaluated by how the baby holds its head and how its legs respond when they are spread away from the body. (Do limbs remain extended or do they move back to their original position?) State or alertness refers to a baby's capacity to switch its attention and move from one state of arousal to another. (Does the infant calm down on its own when upset or must it be held by the parent? Can the infant follow an object or a sound?) To judge interaction, evaluators observe how the infant interacts socially. (Will he or she imitate mother's facial expressions?) In each category the infant is given an overall rating and profile of the areas in which the baby's responses are normal and those that indicate developmental advancement or delay (See Table 9.1).

The Brazelton Scale is not predictive of future development. Babies who show delay in the first few days or weeks of life may catch up in the first year. The scale is helpful primarily in ascertaining congenital problems, and it is used as a tool in research to compare infants living in various cultures and under differing socioeconomic conditions (Nugent, et al., 1989).

LIFE'S FIRST TEST: THE APGAR SCALE

Within a minute of birth and five minutes later infants are assessed for heart rate, respiratory effort, muscle tone, reflex irritability, and body color on a scale of 0, 1 and 2. The ratings are then totaled with a high score of 10. This assessment technique is called the *Apgar Scoring System,* named for anesthesiologist Virginia Apgar who developed it in 1953. At sixty seconds after birth 70 percent of infants score in the 8–10 range, 24 percent score 3–7, and 6 percent are at a very low point of 0–2. A score of 7–10 is considered normal, while 4–7 indicates some resuscitative measures could be needed. If a newborn scores below 3, he or she is in crisis and needs immediate resuscitation.

**TABLE 9.1   Brazelton Neonatal Behavioral Assessment
Scale Categories**

The Brazelton Scale helps parents understand that children differ in the level
of activity, adaptability, and responsiveness to the environment.

 1 Response to repeated visual stimuli
 2 Response to rattle
 3 Response to bell
 4 Response to pinprick
 5 Orienting response to inanimate visual stimuli
 6 Orienting response to inanimate auditory stimuli
 7 Orienting response to inanimate visual stimuli—examiner's face
 8 Orienting response to inanimate visual stimuli
 9 Orienting response to inanimate and auditory stimuli
10 Quality and duration of alert periods
11 General muscle tone—in resting and in response to being handled, passive, and active
12 Motor activity
13 Traction responses as he or she is pulled to sit
14 Response to being cuddled by examiner
15 Defensive movements—reaction to a cloth over his or her face
16 Consolability with intervention by examiner
17 Peak of excitement and capacity to control state
18 Rapidity of buildup to crying state
19 Irritability during examination
20 General assessment of kind and degree of activity
21 Tremulousness
22 Amount of startling
23 Change of skin color—measuring autonomic change
24 Change of states during entire examination
25 Self-quieting activity—attempts to console self and control state
26 Hand-to-mouth activity

TEMPERAMENTAL DIFFERENCES IN CHILDREN

It takes at least one child and one caregiver to creating a parenting relationship. Hence parenting is a *bidirectional* operation, and the behavior of each
party influences the nature of the alliance. This means that a parent's behavior
toward a child influences the child, and the actions of the child are equally influential in affecting the behavior of the parent. There is a *synchronicity* in the
relationship, where parent and child act in unison to create a connection.
A high-strung, intense mother who tries to rush through a feeding may be

TABLE 9.2 The Apgar Scale

Physical characteristic	0 points	1 point	2 points
A Activity (muscle tone)	Absent	Arms and legs flexed	Active
P Pulse (heart rate)	Absent	Below 100 bpm*	Above 100 bpm
G Grimace (reflex irritability)	No response	Grimace	Sneeze, cough, pulls away
A Appearance	Blue-gray, pale all over	Normal, except for extremities	Normal over entire body
R Respiration	Absent	Slow, irregular	Good, crying

*beats per minute

compelled to slow down by her dawdling, laid-back infant. If baby smiles at Dad, Dad is likely to smile at baby. If baby doesn't smile again, Dad will move closer to baby; he might even tickle the baby to get another smile response. The parent-child relationship is so bidirectional that a mother, or a father, or even a community cannot treat two children in the same way. Since each child brings its unique personality to the relationship, and each parent brings a unique temperament and set of experiences.

Temperament refers to an individual's underlying, relatively consistent, basic disposition—a pattern built into the brain's neural circuitry. Temperament determines how an individual will generally respond in life situations. Some people remain calm and cooperative in almost every circumstance, while others display a stubborn and willful posture.

Daniel G. Freedman (1974) has shown that striking differences in temperament and behavior show up from birth. In a study of Chinese and Caucasian newborns at a San Francisco hospital, Freedman found that Caucasian babies cried more easily and were harder to calm. Chinese infants adapted to almost any position they were placed in. When a cloth was pressed briefly on the babies' noses, most Caucasian babies turned their heads defensively. The Chinese babies were more likely to accept the cloths and breathe through their mouths. Subsequent studies comparing Chinese and American infants again showed Chinese infants to be significantly less active, less irritable, and less vocal then Caucasian infants (Kagan, et al., 1994).

Harvard developmental psychologist Jerome Kagan defined four temperamental types: timid, bold, upbeat, and melancholy. Timid children, called "behaviorally inhibited" by Kagan, account for 15 to 20 percent of children. Timid children become very anxious in new situations, are reluctant to try new foods, and become shy when encountering strangers. They are more reactive to stress than most other children, and they tend to talk less. Upbeat children view life as positive and enjoyable; they are able to bounce back in the face of adversity and exhibit a strong level of self-confidence. To melancholy children, life is a worry. Their world is full of obstacles, and catastrophe is only a minute away. Bold children take chances with life and welcome its challenges. They like meeting people and feel comfortable in new situations and places.

A person's temperament remains fairly stable throughout life. The shy little boy is likely to become a shy employee; and the jittery, always-moving young girl will be the TV-channel-surfing, nervous adult. This connection does not guarantee that bold children will become sky-divers or that nervous children will become adults who change jobs every six months. Upbringing, experience, and the opportunities of life ultimately define behavior. While parents have little influence on their children's temperaments, they will strengthen or weaken innate traits through the behaviors they reward or punish. Daniel Goldman emphasized the range of possibilities that exist within genetic constraints. He wrote, ". . . genes alone do not determine behavior. Our environment, especially what we experience and learn as we grow, shapes how a temperamental predisposition expresses itself as life unfolds" (Goldman, 1995).

GOODNESS OF FIT: THE SYNCHRONICITY OF PARENTING

The question of inherited temperamental traits and their influence on infant socialization has sparked the interest of attachment theorists and others who work in developmental psychology. Is a baby really born shy or sociable, adventuresome or fearful, easygoing or irritable? If so, what effect do inborn temperamental differences have on how the parents care for an infant? Child psychiatrist Alexander Thomas (1986) proposed that there must be a good match between a child's inborn temperamental characteristics and the environment he or she grows up in. Optimal development depends upon a "goodness of fit." A reciprocal relationship exists between a child's temperament and the relationship—a good fit or not—is reflected in how the parents treat the child.

In 1956, the team of Alexander Thomas, Stella Chess, and Herbert Birch (1968, 1970) began a fifteen-year study of the personality traits of 141 infants from well-educated, affluent families. The New York Longitudinal Study (NYLS), as the project was called, sought to define and classify the components of temperament (Table 9.3). The children were observed throughout their preschool years and during nursery and elementary school. At frequent intervals, parents and teachers were interviewed about the behaviors exhibited by the subjects. In addition, a number of psychological tests were administered to measure specific traits.

The researchers divided temperament into nine components and, using a three-point scale, rated the children on these basic indicators of temperament type.

Mothers and babies get caught up in an emotional dance. Under the best circumstances, they fit well together temperamentally. This mother and child are exhibiting synchrony through mutual eye contact and smiling.

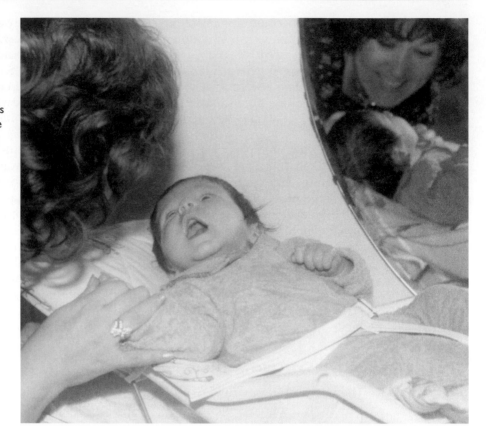

TABLE 9.3 Components of Temperament

Thomas, Birch, and Chess found that the first three components—distractibility, persistence, and sensitivity—had no relation to the child's overall temperament. These traits have been omitted from this table. The other six factors were all somewhat related to whether the child was easy, difficult, or slow-to-warm-up.

	Temperament		
Component	Easy child	Difficult child	Slow-to-warm-up child
Activity	Not related	Low	Not related
Regularity	Regular	Irregular	Not related
Responsiveness	Approaches	Withdraws	Withdraws initially
Adaptability	Flexible	Inflexible	Inflexible
Intensity of responses	Low to moderate	High	Low
Mood	Positive	Negative	Somewhat negative

Source: Chess and Thomas, 1982.

The researchers identified three fairly-well-defined personality types from the data collected. About 40 percent of the children, classified as *easy*, were regular in their habits, adaptable, and generally easy to care for. They were cheerful and positive in their mood, fitting easily into new situations and adjusting well to new people and places. About 15 percent of the children, considered *slow-to-warm-up*, exhibited a low activity level and were slow to adapt to new situations. They tended to withdraw when faced with new stimuli, they were somewhat negative in mood, and the intensity of their reactions was generally low. Another group, about 10 percent classified as *difficult*, were hard to handle from birth. They exhibited irregular bodily functions, usually showed intensity in their reactions, avoided facing new stimuli, and were generally negative in mood. The remaining 35 percent of children fit no distinct pattern.

In summarizing their results, the researchers concluded that "children do show distinct individuality in temperament in the first weeks of life, independently of their parents' handling or personality." In addition, analysis of the long-term data indicated that the original temperament indicators tend to persist in most children over the years.

Alexander Thomas cautioned parents not to attempt to change their child's temperament but rather to work with it. For example, difficult children do not respond well to parents who give them too much freedom. They tend to thrive better in structured environments.

In a study extending over eighteen months, Rudolph Schaffer and Peggy Emerson (1964) classified 36 infants into two categories—cuddlers and noncuddlers—based on their reaction to physical contact. The cuddlers snuggled against their mothers, molding their bodies to the mothers'. They tended to be more placid; they slept more; and they preferred cuddly toys (Schaffer, 1977). The noncuddlers struggled against physical closeness. They were more active and restless, and they were intolerant of such physical contact as being dressed or tucked into bed. Some mothers had to comfort their noncuddler babies by distracting them with a biscuit or bottle or by walking them around, rather than by simply holding them as the mothers would have preferred to do. Noncuddlers preferred swinging and bouncing to being held still. The differences between these two types of babies has obvious implications for the kind of paternal interventions needed to raise them. Referring to the mothers of noncuddlers, Schaffer notes that "clearly she has certain requirements of her own that she wishes to fulfill in the relationship, and a matching process must therefore take place in which the two mutually adjust to one another." A mismatch can occur if a parent tries to force physical contact on a child who cannot adjust to physical restraints, or if activity limits are placed upon a child who needs stimulation. Problems can arise from these mismatches if a parent perceives the noncuddling child as unloving or rejecting.

The effects of temperament appear to linger throughout childhood. A study of teens found that shy parents did not fare well with extroverted children, nor did anxious parents with slow-to-warm-up offspring (Nitz and Lerner, 1991). A number of research projects indicate that difficult children are most likely to be abused; in some cases these children exasperate their parents so much that they become abusive out of frustration (Korner, 1979).

Researchers Sandra Scarr and Kathleen McCartney proposed that a child's genetic makeup helps to create the environment from which they derive their experiences. In other words, rather than being passive recipients of parental desires, children evoke support and reinforcement that "fit" their genetic predispositions (Scarr and McCartney, 1983). An adventuresome children born into a quiet, reclusive family may insist on joining the Boy Scouts and attending adventure camp. A daughter who loves to be read to can force a busy parent to put work aside to make time for a story. Children often actively choose environments that complement their genetic tendencies, a correlation known as *niche-picking.* A well-coordinated child stays after school to play basketball each day; a child with a lovely singing voice joins the glee club. Niche-picking partly explains why identical twins reared apart sometimes having the same hobbies or occupations (Scarr and Weinberg, 1983).

The coordinated give-and-take, the social dance by which the behavior of children and their parents are synchronized, begins at birth; and it is an unfortunate newborn who find himself or herself out of step with a caregiver.

PATTERNS AND RHYTHMS OF LIFE

Babies come equipped with the ability to organize their daily activities, which gives them early control over aspects of their environment.

STATES OF ALERTNESS

Infants experience levels of consciousness ranging from sleeping to crying. Newborns average about sixteen hours of sleep a day, in intervals of about four hours (three asleep and one awake). As they age and their brains develop, sleep patterns change so that by three months many infants are sleeping through the night (Berg and Berg, 1979).

There are two types of sleep, quiet sleep and active or *REM* (rapid eye movement) sleep. In adults, REM sleep occupies 20 percent of total time asleep, and is the period in which dreaming occurs. For the infant, 50 percent of sleep is REM. It is believed that the REM sleep in babies represents a period of neurological self-stimulation (Berg and Berg, 1979). Preterm infants spend an even greater proportion of their time in REM sleep; this indicates that its function is related to neurological development (Roffwarg, et al., 1966). By the age of two, 25 percent of an infant's sleep is REM, about equal to that of an adult's 20–23 percent (Roffwarg, Muzio, and Dement, 1966).

In a 1966 research project, Peter Wolff observed newborns on a 24-hour basis to detect their states of arousal. Wolff devised a classification system that outlined six states, one tending to follow the other in succession, each lasting approximately twenty minutes.

■ **Regular sleep.** Represented by slow systematic breathing and little movement. Infants in this stage do not respond to mild stimulation like soft talking.

- **Irregular sleep.** Breathing rhythm is irregular. Infants squirm, twist and make interesting faces. They exhibit slight response to light stimulation.

- **Drowsiness or periodic sleep.** Infants are just falling asleep or just wakening. Breathing is regular but more rapid than in regular sleep. Eyes may intermittently be open or closed. Infants are responsive to stimulation.

- **Alert inactivity.** Breathing is irregular. Infants are responsive to environmental stimulation. Their eyes are open and their heads and bodies move. In this state infants are susceptible to learning.

- **Waking activity.** Breathing is irregular. Intense activity is brought on by a physical need such as hunger. Infants engage in vigorous activity such as kicking their legs and twisting their bodies. They begin to whimper and gradually become louder in their demands.

- **Crying.** Babies display vigorous arm and leg movements. They cry loudly and/or scream.

Peter Wolff (1969) analyzed infant crying patterns and found that there were four types of crying patterns: rhythmic cries, angry cries, cries due to pain, and cries due to hunger. Babies also cry if they are uncomfortable, bored, or ill. Crying is an adaptive response on the infant's part. An angry cry is long and loud, a cry of pain is much like a wail. Studies indicate that most mothers can identify their infants' cries and will respond most quickly to cries of pain or anger (Wolff, 1969). Most fathers are also able to make these distinctions in their infants' cries (Wiesenfeld, Malatesta, and Deloache, 1981).

As an infant's primary means of communication, crying is designed to encourage caregiving. In fact, studies show that a parent's heart rate and blood pressure can increase when they hear their baby's "cries" (Bleichfeld and Moely, 1984). Unusual crying patterns are an early sign of abnormality or illness in an infant. Brain-damaged infants often exhibit a weaker cry than normal babies, and malnourished infants have a higher-pitched cry than well-fed babies.

Although sleeping and crying are internal processes, they are also influenced by environmental factors. An agitated, crying baby can be calmed by being placed on a parent's shoulder and gently soothed. In cultures in which babies are carried by their mothers at all times, there is relatively little crying except in instances of illness (Isabell and Mckee, 1980). In 1974, a group of researchers headed by Mary Ainsworth visited the homes of newborn infants every three weeks for a year. They found that infants who were quickly soothed when distressed cried less than those infants who were made to wait before getting attention.

Parental Stress and Infant Crying

Having a baby is a stressful event in that it brings change to family life and particularly to a marriage. The baby's temperament contributes to the degree of stress experienced. Excessive crying on the infant's part can negatively affect a parent's attitudes and behaviors. A number of research projects have shown that infant irritability, crying, or colic leads to parental feelings of depression,

The Informed Parent 9.1

How to Soothe a Crying Infant

■ Lift baby to the shoulder and rock or walk.

This is the most effective soothing technique because it provides a combination of physical contact, upright posture, and motion.

■ Swaddle the baby.

Restricting movement and increasing warmth often soothes a young infant.

■ Offer a pacifier.

Sucking helps babies control their own level of arousal.

■ Talk softly or play rhythmic sounds.

Continuous, monotonous, rhythmic sounds, such as a clock ticking, a fan whirring, or peaceful music can be effective.

■ A car ride or walk in a carriage; gentle swinging in a cradle.

A gentle, rhythmic motion of any kind sometimes lulls a baby to sleep.

■ Massage the baby's body.

Stroke the baby's torso and limbs with continuous gentle motions. This can relax the baby's muscles.

■ Let the baby cry for a short period of time.

Some babies will cry for a few minutes after being laid down and before they fall asleep. If the crying goes on longer than a few minutes, try a different technique.

helplessness, anger, exhaustion, and rejection of the infant (Wilkie and Ames, 1986). In a 1979 study of mothers who responded to a magazine questionnaire, 80 percent said they felt like "bashing" their babies, and 59 percent reported this feeling was due to their infant's crying (Kirkland and Hill, 1979). A more recent study of thirty couples with 6-week-old firstborns were interviewed concerning their feelings about parenthood. Although most were not

HI AND LOIS ®

Reprinted with special permission of King Features Syndicate

Excessive infant crying stresses parental relationships. Mothers are apt to fault their infants while fathers tend to blame mothers. Less blame and more of an understanding of individual infant temperament and infant needs will help this problem.

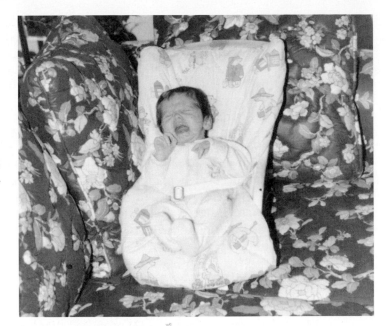

seriously stressed, the effects of infant crying were greater on fathers than on mothers. For mothers, infant crying was correlated with a lower evaluation of their baby. They perceived parenthood in more negative terms and felt they were doing as well as they could under the circumstances. For this reason they felt less inadequate than mothers of infants who cried even less. Fathers, on the other hand, did not make more negative judgments of their infants. Instead they rated themselves as less powerful as husbands but rated their wives as less powerful both as mothers and wives (Kirkland and Hill, 1979). This indicates that fathers tend to blame mothers when babies cry excessively, which may explain part of why the degree of infant crying has been linked to marital tension (Brazelton, 1962).

SUDDEN INFANT DEATH SYNDROME

Few life tragedies are as grievous as that of losing an infant to *Sudden Infant Death Syndrome* (SIDS), also known as crib death. SIDS is the abrupt death during sleep of a seemingly healthy infant. Estimates from countries reporting such statistics indicate that SIDS occurs in as many as two of every 1,000 infants born (Peterson, 1984). The vast majority of SIDS deaths occur before six months of age with most coming between two and four months. SIDS rarely occurs after age one.

SIDS infants do not appear to be much different from surviving healthy babies. Subtle weaknesses develop prenatally, however—and sometimes so seemingly insignificant as to not be apparent in the newborn. This subtle weakness, when teamed with other forces, can lead to sudden death at a particularly vulnerable time in an infant's life.

Researchers have attempted to link SIDS to a number of physical and environmental factors. SIDS has been associated with respiratory ailment, gender (higher for males), economics (lower socioeconomic class), maternal smoking, low birth weight, and drug dependence (Goyco and Beckerman, 1990). SIDS babies have higher rates of prematurity, lower birth weights, lower Apgar scores, and weaker muscle tone (Buck, et al., 1989; Shannon, et al., 1987). Clearly SIDS infants stop breathing, but the reason remains open to question. In normal children, a lack of oxygen triggers a reflexive breathing response. It has been proposed that in some children the part of the infant's brain that controls heart rate and breathing fails to respond to the drop in oxygen level that occurs when an infant stops breathing, (Hunt and Bruliette, 1987). Most SIDS deaths occur during a transitional period when respiratory functions are transferring from reflex to cortical control. At this time, breathing is gradually coming under the management of the cortex, or higher centers of the brain (Rovee-Collier and Lipsitt, 1987). The period of "disarray," when reflex activity is lessened and cognitive behaviors are not yet fully developed, is the most dangerous in terms of SIDS. It appears that a weakness in the respiratory and muscle systems prevent SIDS infants from acquiring the behaviors they need as their reflexes decline.

Lewis Lipsitt (1982) proposed that SIDS victims display a more moderate level of activity than other babies. Sucking is weaker, and interaction with the environment is less frequent. Lipsitt believes that breast-fed infants are less likely to die than bottle-fed babies because they are more skilled at breathing through their noses. Studies have also cited over-dressing infants in cold weather, a good intention that can lead to infant hypothermia.

In recent years, there has been a concerted campaign to place babies in bed on their backs rather than on their stomachs (Fleming, et al., 1990). Infants placed on their stomachs have a greater likelihood of suffocating if they get lodged among cushions or blankets, and some may not have the ability to arouse to reinitiate breathing following a long breathing pause or exposure to their own exhaled carbon dioxide.

SIDS researcher James McKenna notes that in Asian societies where infants sleep with their parents, SIDS rates are significantly lower than they are in Western societies where this sleeping arrangement is not the norm. While he does not suggest that solitary nocturnal sleep causes SIDS or that co-sleeping is right for all families, McKenna notes that infants who bed-share are breast-fed more frequently than solitary-sleeping infants and that they experience more nighttime arousals, thus spending less time in the deepest stages of sleep. McKenna points out that without small and continuous sensory-based interruptions from a co-sleeping partner, some infants may prematurely adopt adult sleep patterns without having developed the skills needed to arouse during a breathing pause (McKenna, 1996). He writes, "By sleeping alone all the time, infants may be deprived of a certain amount of practice in waking up at crucial times in sleep stages. In short, the sensory intrusions of co-sleeping partners (a sudden nudge, noise, touch, or sleep movement) provide the infant with practice in arousing within his or her natural ecology, and thus serve the infant should some internal respiratory mishap require a quick and efficient awakening."

Presently, if there is an indication of risk, parents can link their infants to monitors that will signal if there is a cessation of the child's breathing. Suggestions that will decrease the chance of SIDS include quitting smoking, placing the infant on its back or side, using less blanketing, breast-feeding, and co-sleeping. But nothing can prevent this unpredictable event from happening to some parents. Should SIDS occur, the parents will require considerable emotional support to get through this tragedy.

THE FAMILY BED DURING INFANCY

SIDS research has forced American parents to reexamine the benefits of co-sleeping, after pediatricians such as Benjamin Spock stated "it is a sensible rule not to take a child into the parents' bed for any reason" (Spock and Rothenberg, 1992). It is typically in middle- and upper-class American families that infants are separated from parents when sleeping, sometimes at birth and always after three to six months of age. This arrangement is in response to the parents' belief in the importance of independence training as well as to a desire for personal privacy. American subcultures believe differently, however. African American parents are more likely to let their children stay with them during the night. (Lozoff, et al., 1995). In the Appalachian mountains of Kentucky, infants usually remain in their parents' beds for the first two years (Abbott, 1992).

The parents in many other cultures do not take this approach to child rearing (See Figure 9.1). Japanese children sleep with their mothers throughout infancy and early childhood, and they generally have the company of a parent or someone else in the family all the way into adolescence (Takahashi, 1990). Among the Maya in rural Guatemala, infants sleep with their mothers until the next baby comes along. The older child is then moved to the father's bed or to a separate bed in the parents' room to make room for the new infant (Morelli, et al., 1992). Mayan mothers report it would trouble them to leave their babies alone at night. In cultures that emphasize co-sleeping, children are not encouraged to be independent; rather they are expected to establish an

Figure 9.1
Infant Co-sleeping
Across Cultures

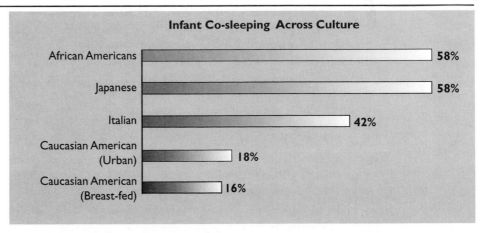

Infant Co-sleeping Across Culture

- African Americans — 58%
- Japanese — 58%
- Italian — 42%
- Caucasian American (Urban) — 18%
- Caucasian American (Breast-fed) — 16%

interdependent relationship with members of the family and larger community, thus allowing them a better chance of surviving.

The ritual of putting children in bed also differs from culture to culture. American parents have customs unheard of in other societies. In Mayan life, babies fall asleep during ongoing social activities and are carried to bed. In the United States, middle-class parents get children "ready for bed" in a series of events that may include a specific bedtime, a bath, a reading period, and—as children get older—sometimes a struggle. The American children experience nightmares and stress that are rarely seen in other societies (Kawasaki, et al., 1994). Even the need for a transitional attachment objects, such as a teddy bear, is rare in cultures where infants sleep with their caregivers (Wolf and Lozoff, 1989).

Infant Nutrition

Nutrition has been defined as "all the processes used by the adult or child to take in food and to digest, absorb, transport, utilize, and excrete food substances" (Endes and Rockwell, 1980). Proper nutrition is essential for the growth and development of the newborn. Physical size, mental ability, and psychological well-being are all dependent on receiving sufficient vitamins, minerals, proteins, fats, carbohydrates, and water. The newborn's nutritional needs are much greater than those of adults due to the rapid growth during the infant's first two years of life.

The Bottle or the Breast: An Ongoing Debate

Within two or three days after childbirth, a mother's milk production or *lactation* occurs, replacing the colostrum, a fluid previously secreted by the breasts during pregnancy. Infant suckling increases the mother's milk flow. When Benjamin Spock presented his views on breast-feeding to the mothers of the 1950s, it was designed for a generation who found this method of nourishing infants out of vogue. There were now infant formulas, dependable refrigeration, social class, and a perception of the breast as a sex object rather than a feeding tool. These changes in child rearing and lifestyle were accompanied by an increase in the number of women who had to work to help support their families. These were all factors that combined to change what had been standard means for feeding infants around the world. When Spock and others reemphasized the physical and financial benefits of breast-feeding, a resurgence of interest in breast-feeding occurred, particularly among college-educated women.

Breast milk is viewed as more advantageous to baby and mother, primarily for health reasons. Breast-feeding enables the mother's uterus to return to its nonpregnant size sooner than it would with bottle feeding. Infants digest human milk more easily than the milk of other animals. As a result, infants are less prone to diarrhea, constipation, and other intestinal problems; they are less prone to allergies and asthma; they gain weight more easily; they are protected from the diseases for which mother's milk promotes the production of antibodies in the nursing infant. Suckling a mother's breast rather than a bottle also promotes tooth and jaw development, because the nursing infant must

The Informed Parent 9.2

Breast Milk or the Bottle?

Advantages of Breast-Feeding

Milk has more iron.

Milk has more vitamins A and C.

Milk is already sterilized.

Milk supplies the newborn with antibodies
to protect it from some diseases.

Milk is easier to digest.

Babies fed breast milk have improved weight
gain.

Babies are less prone to allergies and asthma.

Milk helps prevent constipation.

Milk helps the growth of myelin.

Disadvantages of Breast-Feeding

Does not allow father's participation.

Milk may contain small amounts of alcohol,
nicotine, or medication taken by the nursing mother.

Milk may carry the HIV virus to the baby.

The mother cannot always be available to
feed her baby.

Bottled milk is more effective in promoting
muscle growth.

Source: Lozoff, 1989; Young, 1990.

make an especially energetic effort with its gums and jaw to squeeze hard
enough get nourishment.

Breast-feeding also offers emotional benefits. As nursing infants have skin
contact with their mothers and tend to be held closely when being fed, babies
enjoy the added sensory experience of touch, taste, sight, and smell as it relates
to their mothers.

Breast-feeding has its disadvantages. It does not allow a father to participate in feeding. A mother's milk may contain small amounts of alcohol, nicotine, or part of a medication she is taking. Some women find breast-feeding
physically or psychologically uncomfortable, and this feeling can affect a
woman's relationship with her infant. At times when it is impossible for a
mother to be available as her baby desires to be fed, a bottle becomes essential.
More troubling is the Centers for Disease Control's warning that the AIDS virus
may be transmitted through breast milk (1996).

The world today offers parents a number of choices for feeding. Infants are
not harmed by bottled milk, and the relationship between mothers who use
bottles with their babies is no less close than that of mothers who breast-feed
their infants. Some women try breast-feeding for a few months and then give
it up; others stay with it for a long time. There are mothers who give their infants both breast and bottled milk; they store either infant formula or breast
milk in the refrigerator for times when they go out.

By six months of age, most infants begin eating solid foods, usually cereals
and baby fruits and vegetables. Most one-year-old children can eat anything
an adult can.

The Spirit of Parenting

A Poem for Emily

Small fat and fingers and farthest one from me,
a hand's width and two generations away,
in this still present I am fifty-three.
You are not yet a full day.

When I am sixty-three, when you are ten,
and you are neither closer nor as far,
your arms will fill with what you know by then,
the arithmetic and love we do and are.

When I by blood and luck am eighty-six
and you are someplace else and thirty-three
believing in sex and god and politics
with children who look not at all like me

sometime I know you will have read them this
so they will know I love them and say so
and love their mother. Child, whatever is
is always or never was. Long ago,

a day I watched awhile beside your bed,
I wrote this down, a thing that might be kept awhile to tell you
    what I would have said
when you were who knows and I was dead
which is I stood and loved you while you slept.

Miller Williams

THE FIRST RELATIONSHIP: THE EMOTIONAL BONDING OF INFANT AND PARENT

Incredulous as it now seems, before Benjamin Spock's *Baby and Child Care*, there were doctors and psychologists who believed that the affection shown by a mother for her child was potentially dangerous. To pick up a crying baby was thought to be bad for the infant's character (Watson, 1928). World War II marks a turning point in the quest to understand mother-infant attachment. European orphanages, filled with children who had been separated from their parents, provided a huge pool of subjects for psychologists interested in studying the bonds of attachment—the sense of emotional closeness and trust that comes from being cuddled, smiled at, hugged and kissed, played with, and responded to when necessary. Since mothers are generally an infant's primary caregiver, attachment research has focused on the mother- child relationship.

Robert Karen (1994) pointed out that this research ignores other important influences on children's emotional developments, particularly the influence of fathers.

> . . . father's relationship with the child, which can have a potent effect, especially, in many families, as the child gets older and the father takes a more active role; the parents' relationship with each other, which may be warm, hostile, supportive, or undermining; sibling relationships and sibling order; general family dynamics, which may include other important figures, like grandparents who live in the home; and so on.

Karen is concerned that mothers often are made to feel that the full weight of a child's psychological well-being rests on their shoulders.

One noted researcher, British psychiatrist John Bowlby, came to believe that a child's experiences with its parents strongly influences any later capacity to form affectional bonds.

> When a baby is born he cannot tell one person from another and indeed can hardly tell person from thing. Yet, by his first birthday he is likely to have become a connoisseur of people. Not only does he come quickly to distinguish familiar from strangers but amongst his familiar he chooses one or more favorites. They are greeted with delight; they are followed when they depart; and they are sought when absent. Their loss causes anxiety and distress; their recovery, relief and a sense of security. On this foundation, it seems, the rest of his emotional life is built—without this foundation there is risk for his future happiness and health (Bowlby, 1966).

Marshall H. Klaus and John H. Kennell (1976), both pediatricians, have proposed that human mothers and babies are subjected to the same attachment mechanisms as are other animals. They believe that in the first six to twelve hours after birth, a mother's body releases hormones that enable her to form an especially close bond with her newborn. The researchers studied mothers and their newborns at one month after birth and found that mothers who had early, sustained, and close contact with their babies tended to be more affectionate, have greater eye contact, and were better able to soothe their infants than mothers who had only a limited time with their newborns after delivery. A year later, it was the infants who had extended early contact with their mothers did better on tests of physical and mental development than did those who had infrequent early contact. The researchers believe that a lack of early bonding contributes to the difficulty some women have in becoming attached to premature, malformed, and unwanted children. Klaus and Kennell have also suggested that early contact between a newborn and its father bonds the two closer, also leading to a greater attachment.

Subsequent studies have challenged the work of Klaus and Kennell. Researchers have found little long-term difference in the relationship between those who bonded early and those who did not (Macfarlane, 1977). In addition, mothers of adopted infants feel as much attachment for their babies as do biological mothers (Singer, et al., 1985). Studies on father-child attachment have been inconclusive, although it does appear that fathers who spend time alone with their babies after birth later engage in more face-to-face interaction with their children (Keller, et al., 1981). It has been speculated that a father who is present in the delivery room and spends time with his newborn also has a closer marital relationship. He is more of a "family man," which carries over into his relationship with his mate.

The Klaus and Kennell research provoked its share of debate and guilt in the childbirthing community, leading to dramatic changes in hospital policies. A mother's physical condition after a birth might interfere with early bonding; fatigue, post-partum depression, and drugs administered during the delivery can affect her ability to care for her infant immediately after birth. Some babies are born as a result of cesarean sections, others must stay in incubators for a time; there is adoption; a grandparent might have to take over the role of caregiver shortly after a birth; a stepparent might come into the family as a primary resource. Bonding between parents and their children comes in many ways and forms, on varied timetables. Attachment changes, grows, and develops just as a baby does, throughout the child's life.

EARLY ATTACHMENT

At birth, babies exhibit a generalized excitement that becomes specialized in the months afterward (See Figure 9.2). Reflexes such as rooting and sucking, grasping, and gazing into a parent's eyes are designed to keep a caregiver close and are directed indiscriminately. At about three months of age, infants focus on selected caregivers, smiling when they are near and displaying distress when they leave (Ainsworth, 1985). In American culture, infants at about nine months begin to internalize the objects of their attachment. At this point, they exhibit *stranger anxiety*, a marked distress in the presence of unfamiliar adults. A few months later they display *separation anxiety* when the object of their affection leaves them for any reason.

Alan Sroufe (1979) believes that emotional preferences are the result of cognitive changes that occur as an infant develops. At about eight months of age, as children come to anticipate the behaviors of others and understand object permanence and intentionality, they experience a wider range of emotions. Responses such as recognizing the existence of mother even when she is

Figure 9.2
Timetable of Emotional Development

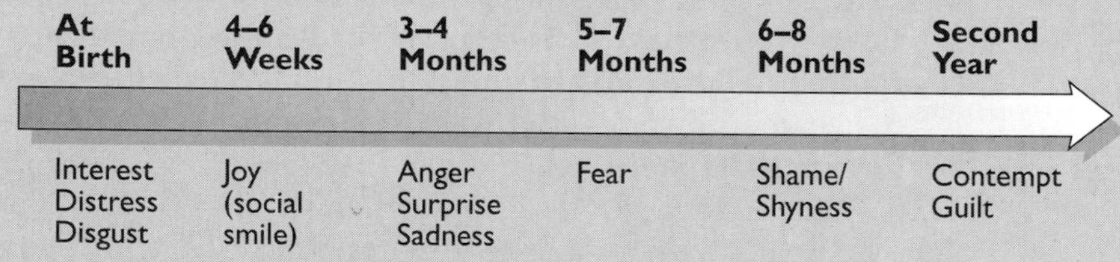

At Birth	4–6 Weeks	3–4 Months	5–7 Months	6–8 Months	Second Year
Interest Distress Disgust	Joy (social smile)	Anger Surprise Sadness	Fear	Shame/ Shyness	Contempt Guilt

Adapted from Izard, C. E. (1982) and Sroufe, L. A. (1979).

not in sight, and comparing a stranger's face to faces that are recognizable, suggest that an understanding of object permanence promotes emotional growth in young children. This lends credence to the view that cognitive development promotes emotional development.

A number of researchers have noted that an infant's reaction to strangers depends upon the behavior of the stranger and the circumstances of the interaction (Waters, Matas, and Sroufe, 1975). The expression on a stranger's face, smiling or frowning, also influences the baby's responses. When left with a caretaker, a child's separation anxiety is lessened if he or she is told that a parent is leaving. By playing "bye bye" and leaving through a frequently used door, parents can lessen the child's anxiety at being left (Littenberg, Tulkin, and Kagan, 1971, Weinraub, 1977).

After John Bowlby recognized the relational disengagement of children who had been separated from their mothers when very young, Bowlby sought to understand the dynamics of attachment. He studied how children attach emotionally to the people around them and the impact this has on their future development. His protégée was a Johns Hopkins researcher named Mary Ainsworth, who also sought to understand the attachment process. How do infants become so attached to caregivers, usually mothers, so that they internalize the values of these caregivers? And what happens if attachment and emotional development are thwarted?

From 1950 to 1954, Ainsworth and Bowlby did extensive research in the area of attachment, which Ainsworth defined as "an affectional tie that one person or animal forms between himself and another specific one—a tie that binds them together in space and endures over time" (Ainsworth, 1973). Ainsworth identified three types of attachment between infants and their mothers.

Securely attached infants have mothers who are responsive to their signals and needs. The children are fed when hungry and comforted when distressed. Care is reliable and predictable. Securely attached children see mother as a safe harbor from which they can venture into the world. These children greet mother with pleasure when she returns from being gone, and they are easily comforted by her when they are distressed (Aber and Slade, 1987).

Avoidantly attached children have mothers who are generally insensitive to their needs and are somewhat rejecting. The disappointed baby protects itself emotionally by staying uninvolved with mother; and what is often interpreted as independence and autonomy is, in actuality, a lack of trust in others and an inability to share in a close relationship.

The mothers of *ambivalently attached* infants are inconsistent in their treatment of them. Sometimes they are responsive; other times they are not. They can be warm and loving; and they can be unavailable. Ambivalently attached babies are so unsure of their mothers they want them around continually. At the same time they are angry at their mother for her unreliability, and sometimes they reject her. Ambivalently attached children are caught between a rock and a hard place, because they have learned that mother is available *sometimes*. This means that if they cry and whine enough she *might* respond. Clinginess, guilt, fussiness, and power struggles mark the relationship between them and mother.

The most striking feature of Ainsworth's research had to do with the future behavior of children who fit into the insecurely attached categories. Not surprisingly, securely attached children at ages 3 to 7 years tended to score higher on scales of social competence, self-esteem, and empathy. These children are curious and persistent in handling tasks, are popular with their peers, and possess leadership qualities (Sroufe and Cooper, 1988; Brody and Axelrad, 1978; Lieberman, 1977; Sroufe, 1983). In short, they tend to become healthy, happy, productive youngsters.

Such is not the future of insecurely attached children. Ainsworth noted that avoidant one-year-olds behave much like older children who had had long separations from their mothers when, in fact, the mothers of avoidant children had been around but rejecting or neglectful. Avoidant children are less able to engage in fantasy play; they tend to be oppositional when dealing with others, and they avoid seeking help when they need it. The avoidant child stays defended against disappointment by saying, "I don't need anybody." This kind of independence is often seen as a positive character trait when in reality the child is in deep pain. What appears to be maturity is a defensive reaction to the parent who is not able to meet the child's emotional needs. When viewed from a family-systems perspective, avoidant attachment is at the root of adult relationship problems and accompanying emotional cutoffs.

It is possible to help avoidant children. Harry Harlow discovered that his rhesus monkeys, separated from their mothers at birth, suffer the effects of maternal deprivation less if they are allowed time to play and interact with other monkeys. Similarly, sometimes an avoidant child finds a "substitute" mother—a father, an aunt, a schoolteacher, an adoptive parent—to give them the care they need and to help them overcome feelings of estrangement (Thompson, et al., 1982; Vaughn, et al., 1979; Tizard, et al., 1976). Unfortunately, it is often difficult for substitute adults to sustain a positive interest in the avoidant child because of the child's self-defeating behaviors, which are based on the belief that he or she is unlovable.

Mary Main, a one-time student of Ainsworth, added a category to Ainsworth's anxious avoidant grouping. Main found that some children are *disorganized-disoriented*. They are so unloved and uncared for that they basically are unable to function as normal children, to the point that in their mother's presence they may walk backward or stare into space.

Child psychiatrist Selma Fraiberg has been extremely concerned about the number of our children whose emotional needs are not being met. She has written in *Every Child's Birthright: In Defense of Mothering,*

> We now know that those qualities that we call "human"—the capacity for enduring love and the exercise of conscience—are not given in human biology; they are the achievement of the earliest human partnership, that between a child and his parents.
>
> And we now know that a child who is deprived of human partners in the early years of life, or who has known shifting or unstable partnerships in the formative period of personality, may suffer permanent impairment in his capacity to love, to learn, to judge, and to abide by the laws of the human community. This child, in effect, has been deprived of his humanity (Fraiberg, 1987).

A MULTI-GENERATIONAL VIEW OF ATTACHMENT

One of Mary Main's primary interests was to understand how parents come to develop their particular pattern of relating to their children. She devised the *Adult Attachment Interview,* a 60- to 90-minute interview that gauges the feelings parents have about their own childhood relationships. Main discovered that parents who talked freely and openly about their own childhoods, even if there were problems in them, were most responsive to their children's signals. These parents, called *autonomous-secure,* were able to view their childhood experiences, good and bad, in a balanced light. A second group of parents, called *dismissing,* could not recall much about their childhoods and tended to idealize their parents, although the interviews showed evidence of neglect or rejection. These parents, saw their own early attachment experiences as unimportant, so they tended to ignore their own children.

A third group of parents, *preoccupied,* showed signs of confusion when remembering the past. They were preoccupied with feelings of anger and dependency, and many were still caught up in the struggle to win their own parents' love and acceptance. This need made it difficult for them to meet the needs of their children, who tended to display ambivalent attachment patterns.

A fourth group of parents, *disorganized,* suffered from unresolved childhood trauma. Some had been severely abused and others had suffered the loss of a parent or loved one. These troubled people raised children who displayed a disorganized attachment pattern.

ATTACHMENT AND THE MICROSYSTEM

In Urie Bronfenbrenner's ecological approach to development (Chapter 2), behavior is viewed within the context of a person's physical and social world. When studying attachment, other aspects of a child's immediate world or microsystem must be considered. For example, what is a father's role in attachment? How does the condition of the parents' marriage affect how well an infant is cared for? Are there differences in families with one parent, versus those with two or even three? How do family financial problems and other life stresses influence the care a baby receives? In other words, what is the context of a particular caregiving arrangement?

A number of research projects have examined the role of temperament on the parental relationship. Parents of children with "easy" temperaments tend to view themselves more positively than do parents of "difficult" children (Sirignano and Lachman, 1985). Temperamentally difficult children create a risk in normal families. Marital dissatisfaction increases when parents feel ineffectual in their child-rearing efforts. Parents were found to be particularly distressed when an oldest daughter was difficult (Stoneman, Brody, and Burke, 1989). Unfortunately, if parents feel so inadequate to handle a difficult child that the marital relationship is strained, the changing dynamics of family life make it likely that the child will remain hard to handle or even become more difficult.

Other researchers have linked life stressors and the availability of social support to infant-parent attachment (Belsky and Isabella, 1988; Belsky, Rovine, and Taylor, 1984). In the Pennsylvania Project, it was found that the quality of parent-infant attachment was significantly influenced by changes in level of marital satisfaction after the birth of the child, as well as by the feelings of satisfaction related to social support.

Somewhat troubling is Jay Belsky's position that extensive day care, more than 20 hours a week during the first year of life, increases the risk of insecure attachment (Belsky and Rovine, 1988, Belsky and Braugart, 1991), even though a day-care provider might become an attachment figure to a child who is ignored at home (Howes, et al., 1988). About 50 percent of American mothers with children under the age of one year work outside the home, with most having gone back to work by the time the infant is 5 months old. In that context, day care is a burning issue in our society. In 1996, a large study of day care challenged the notion that affectional ties are strained when an infant is separated from mother during the day. The study suggested that day care is harmful if babies don't get enough attention at home from their mothers *in addition* to going to a poor-quality day care where the children get little attention (Weintraub, 1996). Parents who give their children a lot of nurturance and attention when they are at home can somewhat compensate for shortcomings of day care. It is more doubtful, however, that good day care can ever make up for the parents' lack of attention at home.

It is crucial to understand attachment in infancy because of the effect that early experience has on adult personality. Bowlby (1988) proposed that infants form an *internal working model* of their social world and that they carry this model through life, affecting school experiences, careers, and relationships. Because of this significance, much research is focusing on the effects of attachment beyond infancy.

It is Bowlby's view that the attachment research is important because it shows that infants are biologically prepared to signal their needs and attentive parents respond to those signals. A parent can become over involved with a child, push too hard for contact, or overstimulate in an effort to improve intellectual functioning. Parents must take their cues from the child who is exploring the world. Their role is to be available when needed. "All of us, from the cradle to the grave," writes Bowlby, "are happiest when life is organized as a series of excursions, long or short, from a secure base provided by our attachment figures" (Bowlby, 1988).

Harvard psychologist Jerome Kagan (1984) believes that both Bowlby and Ainsworth overemphasized the role of the mother figure in early experience and overlooked data on the influence of temperament. It is Kagan's position that many children deprived of love and care in childhood grow up to be healthy, productive adults. He argues that avoidant children ignore their mothers because they are constitutionally less fearful than other children and may handle stress better. He believes that many children classified as avoidant have been trained by their parents to be independent. On the other hand, children classified as securely attached according to the Ainsworth guidelines may have been raised to be dependent on their mothers, and their upset over her leaving has more to do with dependency than attachment.

THE BLANKET AND THE DOLLY: TRANSITIONAL OBJECTS

Some children form a deep attachment to an object in their environment, often a favorite blanket or doll, from which they do not like to be separated. British psychiatrist Donald Winnicott (1964, 1971) calls this special object a *transitional object* because it "represents the infant's transition from a state of being merged with the mother to a state in relation to the mother as something outside and separate." The object is a bridge to mother while existing, as the child does, outside of her.

Winnicott notes that by the age of two, children are awake most of the day, they are starting to get feedback on their behavior, and they are struggling to develop a sense of self. These combined forces may precipitate the need for a companion. The transitional object serves as a source of comfort and solace.

Dolls, teddy bears, and blankets are among the most common transitional objects, and they are held dear even when old, dirty, and tattered. Winnicott claims that the sensory stimuli from the transitional object become associated with it, becoming a vital part of the toy. The object can substitute for people who are not available to the child. Love, anger, and aggression can be acted out

The transitional object serves as a source of comfort and solace. And it gives the child something to love.

on the object. Thoughts and feelings can be projected on to it. Above all, a transitional object gives a child something to love.

ATTACHMENT AND FATHERS

Two decades ago Michael Lamb (1979) reviewed the literature concerning father-infant interaction and found that, of the time fathers spend with their children, more time is spent in playing than in caregiving. Today, however, the dual-income family and single-parent family rely on fathers for real child care, and the amount of time fathers spend caring for children is increasing. Lamb also found that fathers are more likely to pat babies while caring for them, whereas mothers are apt to talk softly to them (Yogman, et al., 1977). Fathers poke their babies and toss them in the air, while mothers play games such as pat-a-cake and peek-a-boo (Lamb, 1976). While the parent-child interactions are somewhat different, there is evidence that infants seek proximity and contact with their fathers as often as they do with their mothers (Lamb, 1977, 1981). In essence, attachment to father—like attachment to mother—depends on the quality of care given, the overall relationship between the child and parent, and other circumstances of home life.

From their appearance in delivery rooms to their increased involvement in parenting afterward, fatherhood has changed over the past twenty years. One research study called the new role *androgynous father*, referring to male and female traits (Rotundo, 1985). Surprisingly, some researchers have discovered that in dual-career families, there is greater conflict and reduced marital satisfaction

Fathers are increasingly taking part in infant child-care duties that include diapering, feeding, and other daily chores. This is a role for which many men have been ill prepared.

Doonesbury   BY GARRY TRUDEAU

when father is actively involved in child care, as well as a decrease in the father's self-esteem. This could be because, as father gets more involved in child care, he may be making career sacrifices. Also, although the father's involvement seems like a good idea, some mothers do not like their mates participating so intimately in parenting activity (Crouter, et. al., 1987, Hawkins and Belsky, 1989).

Of special interest to researchers is the impact of parenting on the marital relationship and vice versa. A father's positive marital relations have been directly associated with the easy temperament of his infant and positive feelings toward his spouse (Belsky, Youngblade, Rovine, and Volling, 1991). Interestingly, when a father's feelings of affection for his spouse decrease, he also often relates to his child more negatively. Conversely, a mother who becomes dissatisfied in her marriage often relates more positively toward her child, perhaps to compensate for her mate's withdrawal.

Today's fathers find themselves in a society whose economic structure makes it necessary that child-rearing duties be shared more equally. But there is a lack of male role models available to them when it comes to caring for their children. Mothers pick up transgenerational patterns of parenting from their grandmothers and mothers and are able to share in their parenting experiences. Fathers cannot look to the past for the information they need, and there are few resources available in the present. It may also be that, when a father participates at the level now expected of him, he will feel an unconscious "disloyalty" to the values and expectations of his father and grandfather (Cowan and Cowan, 1987).

THE NEWBORN CONQUERS THE WORLD

"Babies are smarter than anyone thinks" has become the catch phrase of the nineties for experts in the field of child development. Extraordinary data has come from research labs all over the world. Only 30 years ago, medical textbooks were reporting that newborns could not fix their eyes or respond to sounds; today researchers have inserted a hydrophone into a pregnant woman's uterus to find out just what the fetus hears before it is born.

It has been shown that each baby possesses a unique personality that influences the course of his or her life. In the first year of life, developmental changes are so dramatic that parents are often astonished. At two months, infants smile and investigate their own hands. By eight months, they are mapping their own identity and looking for hidden objects. At a year, they begin to walk and talk, and they head out into the world.

Parents can only wonder what goes on in their infant's mind as he or she experiences the world. What do infants think and feel? How can researchers tap into the hidden, subjective experience of very young children? When does a baby first sense a personal self, separate from others but related to everything in his or her environment?

The Developing Brain: A Learning Machine

Every time a parent picks up a baby, smiles at it, comforts it, or sings a song to amuse it, that parent is stimulating the infant's brain. It is during the first three years of life that parental stimulation has the most effects. Over the past ten years, startling research on infant brain activity has disproved the previously held notion that the structure of a newborn's brain is determined genetically and is pretty much set at birth. It is now known that early experiences shape the brain development of children by impacting the wiring of the neural circuits. For parents to recognize the importance of environmental stimulation they must understand how the brain works.

The adult human brain consists of more than 100 billion neurons, long, wiry cells that carry electrical messages back and forth, their stimulation coming from inside and outside the body. Each of these neurons reaches out to other neurons in a circuitry that leads to trillions of *synaptic connections* (See Figure 9.3). An infant's genes, carried from its parents' egg and sperm, provide the basic wiring for the brain, allowing the heart to beat, the kidneys to function, and the lungs to control air distribution. There is also the basic groundwork for vision, motor movement, language acquisition, and the like. But even if the ability to climb Mt. Everest or learn Spanish is programmed into the genes and made possible by brain cells, there is no guarantee that a person will later speak Spanish or display expert motor coordination. This depends on what happens to the brain before and after birth.

At birth, the infant brain consists of 100 billion neurons, which in turn form over 50 trillion connections. What is most incredible is that, in the first few months of life, the synaptic connections increase 20-fold, more connections than 1,000 trillion neural associations. But this is many more connections than the infant's brain needs. Why the abundance? And how can all these synapse connections be managed?

Neural Competition

In some ways the infant's neurons engage in a contest that will end with some connections fading out and others becoming stronger, depending on what is offered by way of stimulation. In other words, what the brain doesn't use, it loses. This is where parents come in. They are instrumental in creating the brain their children will carry through life. This does not mean that parents of

Figure 9.3
The Neural
Pruning Process

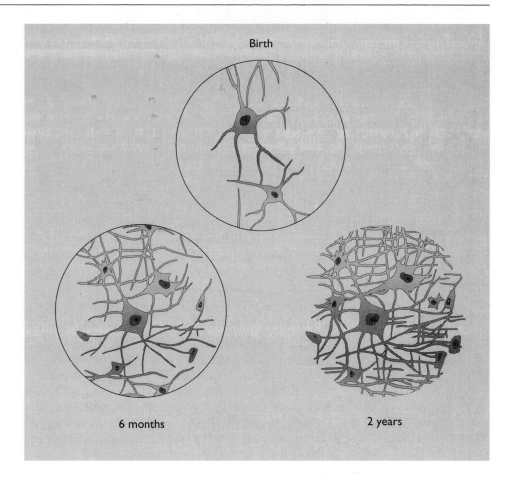

Birth

6 months

2 years

very young children should read them the names of all the presidents while holding up photos of these people; but it does mean that the environment should offer babies what they need and ask for at different stages of their development. What babies primarily need are physical contact, verbal communication, and forms of play that are age-appropriate and in tune with temperament. For example, newborns can see, but not in fine-grained detail. They cannot focus both eyes on a single object, and they lack depth perception as well as eye-hand coordination. First and foremost, parents should have their baby's eyes examined to be sure there is no weakness that can interfere with the neural connections for sight. Next, infants should be exposed to the sight of everyday things: flowers, colors, people, and such. Eye-hand coordination and other motor skills such as sitting, crawling, walking, and reaching develop when babies are allowed to explore their world as much as safety allows.

The neural circuits that control emotions are among the first constructed by the brain. At two months of age, babies experience distress or contentment; and within a few more months emotions such as joy and sadness, envy, and empathy evolve. Loving and empathetic parents provide positive emotional stimulation for the brain so that the right connections are made. If an infant is neglected, the experience of happiness or contentment can be impaired. In abused children, the areas of the brain controlling stress and anxiety may be overdeveloped. PET scans comparing the brains of normal children to those of children emotionally deprived in infancy show that the temporal lobes, the area regulating emotion, are fully functioning and active in normal brains but inactive in deprived brains. (See Table 9.4.)

Daniel Goldman (1995) has written at length about the brain's physiological reaction to emotional signals from parents. In *Emotional Intelligence* he points out that the sculpting and pruning of neural circuits, which helps us understand why emotional hardships and trauma in early childhood can affect a child all the way into adulthood. It also explains why it is so difficult to overcome early emotional mistreatment through psychotherapy.

> There are very different emotional habits instilled by parents whose attunement means an infant's emotional needs are acknowledged and met or whose discipline includes empathy, on the one hand, or self-absorbed parents who ignore a child's distress or who discipline capriciously by yelling and hitting (Goldman, 1995).

In the womb, the embryo's brain produces more neurons than are needed. A pruning process begins as some neurons are eliminated. The remaining neurons develop axons, long fibers that transmit impulses and spin out branches, which in turn reach out to targets. When electrical activity activates specific neurons, connections are reinforced. When connections are not reinforced, they fade out and are lost. After birth an explosion of new neural connections are made, particularly at two to four months, when infants really begin to notice the world around them. Sensory experiences trigger electrical activity, which in turn fine-tunes the brain's circuitry. Parents are instrumental in

---

TABLE 9.4   The Developing Brain: Eight Warning Signs

The presence of any of these signs should alert parents to neurological problems. A professional evaluation should be sought.

1. Infant "too good"; sleeps all the time.
2. Habitual poor eye contact with parents.
3. Consistent failure to respond to voices or other sounds.
4. Noticeable asymmetry of limb movements: right and left sides of the body should appear equally strong and active during the first year.
5. Noticeable delay in many or all of the commonly accepted milestones for motor development.
6. Noticeable delay in social responsiveness: doesn't participate in pat-a-cake, peek-a-boo, bye-bye.
7. Failure to develop language within appropriate time limits.
8. Abnormal over-responsiveness to physical stimuli: noises, lights, touch.

Source: Healy, J. M., *Your Child's Growing Mind*, 1994.

The Informed Parent 9.3

Stimulating the Infant Brain

Unless they are completely neglected or disabled, almost all children learn to walk and talk and engage in social interactions. But there are great variations in their ability to perceive the environment, think and reason, make associations, and manipulate the world. Neurologist William Staso (1997) notes that these variations are often due to differences in stimulation. This does not mean an infant should be bombarded with color, light, music, toys, and the like. Researcher Staso cautions that the kind of stimulation offered depends upon a child's age and temperament.

Here are some guidelines:

Month 1   Babies should be exposed to a low level of stimulation, which will increase wakefulness and alertness but reduce stress. When talking to a newborn, parents should turn off the television or radio and screen out other distracting noises.

Months 1–3   Visual areas of the brain are developed as babies are exposed to light/dark contrasts in pictures or objects. Infants should be spoken to frequently in animated tones so they can begin learning the patterns of language.

Months 3–5   Infants learn about the world primarily through vision. Parents should expose them to increasingly complex materials that represent things in the environment, such as a picture of a dog in a book or magazine. The baby's room is a good setting for the promotion of sensory skills. Mobiles, pictures, music, crib toys, textured animals, rattles, contrasting colors, and books are just a few of the things that attract babies.

Months 6–7   Infants begin to understand relationships such as cause and effect and the locations and function of objects. Parents should demonstrate how things work while explaining them. For example, "When I push this button, the television goes on."

Months 7–8   Babies make associations between sounds and environmental activity or objects. Parents can help by pointing out these associations. "Oh, the doorbell is ringing. We have a visitor." "I hear the water running. Mommy is taking a bath."

Months 9–12   Babies become increasingly interested in exploring the environment. They are able to coordinate their sensory and motor skills somewhat. While supervised, they should be encouraged to do things like turn on a light switch or push the front doorbell.

Months 12–18   An environment that offers verbal and sensory enrichment will enable infants' brains to acquire the complex associations leading to a greater understanding of the world and a better ability to live in it.

Source: Adapted from Blakeslee, S. *The New York Times,* April 17, 1997.

providing the stimulation that determines which connections will remain and which will be pruned.

Infant Communication: From Cries to Words

From the moment they are born, infants have the ability to communicate. They let others know when they are hungry, wet, cold, or in pain. Researchers believe that preverbal sounds of crying, cooing, and babbling form the foundation for learning the rules of language.

Nothing excites some parents more than hearing their baby's first word, be it "milk" or "dada." Infant language begins at approximately two months, at the point when babies have developed the muscle movements necessary for *cooing*. These utterances are strings of vowel sounds, like "ooh" and "aah." Cooing continues as the baby's only vocalizations until babbling begins, somewhere between three and six months.

Babbling consists of one-syllable consonant-vowel combinations such as "ba," "da," and "ma." Babbling appears to be self-reinforcing (Osgood, 1957), because babies repeat one sound over and over, a phenomenon called *reduplicated babbling.* Babbling strengthens infants' vocal structures, giving them practice in producing many of the sounds they will need for normal speech (Clark and Clark, 1977).

Eager parents may think their child is forming words when they babble such sounds as *da da* and *ma ma.* This gains attention from parents and may be the reason for a "conversation" between caregiver and baby. Linguistic stimulation is vital to an infant because this exposure to a parent's verbalizations has positive effects on the child's language and thought development (Masur, 1982). A study of 10-month-old babies from London, Hong Kong, Paris, and Algiers suggests that the language babies hear influences the sounds they produce, even before they speak their first word, (Boysson-Bardies, et al., 1989). This is akin to "learning the tune before the words," (Bates, et al., 1987).

Babbling is an integral part of prelanguage development. From the biological perspective, it is universal in that babies of all cultures engage in it. Babbling gradually becomes more complex as the infant's vocal structures develop and shift position. In addition, the cerebral cortex is beginning to regulate many of the baby's actions. This combination of events leads to the infant's increased ability to control and expand the vocalizations it makes (Stark, 1986).

When babies begin to babble, they also develop gestures that aid in the communication process (Bates, et al., 1987). A favorite gesture is pointing to an object or person. Accompanied by one type of sound, it is clear that the baby wants whatever he or she is pointing to. Other gestures include stretching, reaching, grabbing, and showing.

At this same time as children begin to utter their first words, they also begin to use gestures as symbols. One child pretends to take a drink, cupping his hand and raising it to his mouth. Another child flaps her arms to pretend she is a bird.

Parents sometimes find it difficult to identify exactly their child's first word. The difference between the babble *da da* and the word *dada* is that the former has no meaning or referent. The babble does not refer to an object or person, whereas the word is a deliberate attempt to identify an individual. It is not easy to ascertain when an infant's speech sounds become intentional unless the baby's first recognized words are unusual, such as "rye bread." With "rye bread" parents know for sure that intentional language has officially begun.

PROMOTING EARLY LANGUAGE DEVELOPMENT

From birth, infants have a preference for certain voices, generally that of their mother and father. Studies have shown that many parents talk to their infants in a specialized way known as *parentese* (or *motherese),* by which they speak to the infant at his or her own operational level (Reich, 1986). In essence, parentese is a "lower-level" form of speech that is characterized by the use of a high-pitched voice, very simple and abbreviated sentences, long pauses, the present tense, and often repetitive (Moskowitz, 1978). Parents speaking in parentese ask the child questions, facilitate *turn taking* when talking, and *recast* what the child has said by adding elements. For example, if a child says "Nose," mother might answer, "Yes. That's a pretty nose," or add, "Do you see Mommy's nose?" These responses give the infant cues about the correctness of language, thereby expanding and aiding speech development.

Anne Fernald observed that mothers put significant words at the conclusion of their sentences and speak these words in a louder and higher-pitched voice, as in the example of "Do you see the *doggie?"* (Fernald and Mazzie, 1991).

Presumably, the aim is to get the infant to focus on the meaningful word. Fernald also noted that at four months of age, babies focus longer on parentese than they do to normal adult speech (Fernald, 1985). This means that they probably learn more from parentese than they do from typical speech.

Laura Berk (1996) described a typical parentese conversation between a parent and an 18-month old:

MOTHER: Time to go, April.
CHILD: Go car.
MOTHER: Yes, time to go in the car. Where's your jacket?
CHILD: (Looks around, walks to the closet.) Jacket! (Points to her jacket).
MOTHER: There's that jacket! Let's put it on. (Mother helps child into the jacket.) On it goes! Let's zip it up. (Zips up the jacket.) Now, say bye-bye to Byron and Rachel.
CHILD: Bye-bye, By-on.
MOTHER: What about Rachel? Bye to Rachel?
CHILD: Bye-bye, Ta-tel.
MOTHER: Where's your doll? Don't forget your doll.
CHILD: (Looks around.)
MOTHER: Look by the sofa. See? Go get the doll. By the sofa.

The use of parentese seems to be beneficial to language development. A relationship between the mother's verbalizations and the length of the child's phrases has been shown (Furrow, et al., 1979). Those mothers who spoke parentese to their babies had children who at ages two and a half to three and a half years spoke in longer word combinations.

The social interaction approach to language development must take into account relationships besides that of infant-mother. It has been reported that 15-month old children experience more problems in communications with their fathers than they do their mothers (Tomasello, Conti-Ramsden, and Ewert, 1990). When a father doesn't understand what a child is saying, he is more likely to ignore the child, change the topic, or ask for clarification of what the child is saying. Babies often listen to and join in the conversations between others in the family (Dunn and Shatz, 1989). In families where speech is not encouraged, language deficits appear early. Children of talkative mothers know 131 more words at 20 months than children whose mothers do not talk to them. By the age of 2 years, this difference doubles, to almost 300 words.

Parentese exists in many cultures, but not all. In some societies children are rarely spoken to before the age of one year; in others, including Japan, mothers ask few questions of their babies (Toda, Fogel, and Kawai, 1990). In some families, there is a view that "children should be seen and not heard," an attitude that interferes with early language development. Certainly children can learn language without the benefit of parentese, but it seems clear that social aspects of talking enhance a child's language development. Laura Berk (1996) has observed the long-term effects of parent-infant communication.

Conversational give-and-take between parent and toddler is one of the best predictors of early language development and academic competence during the school years. It provides many examples of speech just ahead of the child's current level and a sympathetic environment in which children pick up many new cognitive skills. In fact, a major reason that twins and later-born children often acquire early language more slowly than singletons is that they have fewer opportunities to converse with parents, who must divide their time between several younger youngsters.

MOTOR DEVELOPMENT: THE WORLD EXPANDS

Next to Benjamin Spock, the man most influential in helping parents understand their newborn children was Arnold Gesell, who with Frances L. Ilg and Louise B. Ames, directed the Gesell Institute of Child Development at Yale University. Gesell and his associates published detailed profiles identifying *gradients of growth* and *maturational levels* for children. In doing so, they helped parents see that there is a sequence to development. Babies crawl, sit up, stand, and walk in a distinct order, developing according to an innate maturation blueprint. As Ames tells parents, "Give up the notion that how your child turns out is all up to you and there isn't a minute to waste. Try to appreciate the wonder of growth. Observe and relish the fact that every week and every month brings new developments" (Ames, 1971).

The Informed Parent 9.4

Read to Children: Early and Often

In addition to having conversations with children, reading to them is an activity that will most benefit them cognitively and socially as they grow and develop. Reading begins with the sound of language, and there is a strong connection between speaking fluently and learning to read. Children who are read to by an adult generally do better in school. Parents who understand how to make reading a pleasurable experience will raise children for whom reading will be a leisure-time activity. Educator Nancy Larrick (1975) points out that few activities create a warmer relationship between child and grownup than reading aloud. She notes, "it is deeply flattering to be read to and have the undivided attention of an adult. And for the adult, there is great satisfaction in sharing a child's absorption in words and pictures."

Reading material for children must be selected with background, attitude, abilities, reading skills, and interests in mind (Sutherland, 1977). Very young children like "picture books," which have little or no text. While an adult may get bored with such a book, young children like repetition and are as delighted with the picture of "doggy" at the tenth reading as they were at the first. Young children also like rhymes, songs, and lullabies, such as *Mother Goose* poems or Dr. Seuss stories.

Nancy Larrick suggests an optimal setting for reading to children:

- Choose a time when there will be no interruptions. Ignore the telephone and turn off the TV.
- Select a place away from the turmoil of the household. This can mean under a tree in the backyard or behind the closed door of a bedroom.
- Make the setting comfortable. Place a blanket on the grass, sit on soft pillows, or lay on the bed.
- Have children sit close enough to see the book and feel the warmth of a lap or comforting arm.
- Read slowly, so the words and language can be absorbed.
- Plan a regular time for reading each day so that children will look forward to that time.

Source: A Parent's Guide to Children's Reading, by Nancy Larrick, Bantam Books, 1975.

GAINING CONTROL OVER THE ENVIRONMENT

At birth, an infant's eyes roam somewhat haphazardly; but after a few days a baby can stare at objects for a brief period. This means that a patterned connection exists between the muscles that move the eyes and the nerve impulses in the brain. By four weeks of age, an infant can follow a dangling ring with his or her eyes; and at four months, a baby usually can simultaneously hold and look at a rattle. "This is a significant growth gain," wrote Gesell and

The Informed Parent 9.5

How to Play with a Baby

- Get down to the baby's level. Sit on the floor, lie on a bed, hold the baby in your lap.

- Make sure you are in a patient mood. Be sure the baby is actively interested and ready to be involved. If the infant seems passive, start a simple activity. If the baby is tired, postpone the activity until later.

- An activity must be repeated many times to firm up neural networks for proficiency. Repetition isn't boring for young children.

- Encourage children in their active exploration as they move around the environment building sensory and motor pathways. Keep playpen time and other restraints to a minimum.

- Provide low open shelves where a variety of toys, objects, and books can be accessible. Avoid boxes with jumbled toys. Toys with sound or visual input improve cognitive skills, particularly if the infant interacts with the toys. For example, banging the lids of pots together enables a baby to learn about cause and effect.

- Bring in new objects one or two at a time. While the brain responds to novelty, children are more likely to investigate new challenges when they are surrounded by familiar things.

- Call attention to specific objects or aspects of the environment: a calendar, colorful fabrics, etc. A child's visual surroundings can be varied to attract visual attention.

- Link language to sensory experience. Talk about what is happening in the child's environment.

Ilg in 1943, "It means that eyes and hands are doing teamwork, coming into more effective coordination."

The more control an infant has of voluntary motor actions—which enable reaching for things, grasping, manipulating objects, crawling, standing, and walking—the greater the infant's ability to conquer the environment. Infant motor achievements have been categorized into three areas: *postural control*, the ability to stand upright; *locomotive control*, the ability to move around; and *manual control*, the ability to manipulate objects (Keogh and Sugden, 1985). It should be cautioned that figures generally given in growth charts are based on averages, so that many children fall above and below this range. The Denver Developmental Screen Test provides *norms* under which 90 percent of children fall in motor development. (Table 9.5).

TABLE 9.5   Sequence of Motor Skills

	Age in Months			
	25%	50%	75%	90%
Lifts head up	1.3	2.2	2.6	3.2
Rolls over	2.3	2.8	3.8	4.7
Sits without support	4.8	5.5	6.5	7.8
Pulls self to stand	6.0	7.6	9.5	10.0
Walks holding on to furniture	7.3	9.2	10.2	12.7
Walks well	11.3	12.1	13.3	14.3
Walks up steps	14.0	17.0	21.0	22.0

Source: Frankenburg and Dodds, 1967

CONTROLLING THE WORLD MANUALLY

Infants like to hold on to things; this is how they learn to manipulate the world around them. At birth, there is little coordination of the chest and arms; but within four months, babies can hold themselves up while facing down, using their arms as props. Soon after, infants can sit up with support, hold on to objects, and then roll over. These activities, involving large muscle control, are said to require *gross motor skills.*

Fine motor skills refer to the more refined and delicate operations required for activities such as grasping objects with one hand and using fingers to inspect them. At birth, babies show little fine motor coordination, but within four months they can follow an object with their eyes, reach for it, and hold on to it. (Figure 9.4).

Figure 9.4
Fine Motor
Development

Source: Gallahue
and Ozman, 1995

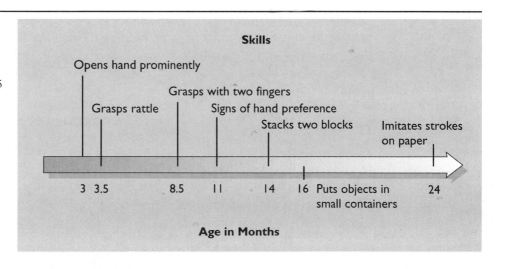

The Informed Parent 9.6

Babyproofing the Home

Babies begin to gain control over their movements at about age two and a half months, when they reach for objects. Whatever they grasp, they then put into their mouths. Parents must be keenly aware of the dangers of any objects in the environment. If in doubt about an item, don't leave it within reach of a child. Here are some additional rules for babyproofing the house.

- Never let a baby have anything small enough to swallow or choke on, or put in the nose or ears. This includes larger objects from which small parts can be detached when tugged or chewed on. The safest containers are jars with screw tops.

- Be sure painted objects given to the baby do not contain lead. Keep newsprint out of reach. Wash out empty bottles thoroughly. Do not reuse bottles that contained bleach or cleaning fluids.

- Put out of reach any items that can suffocate a baby. These include plastic bags, soft cushions, or pillows.

- Be sure all playthings are clean. Sterilize objects that have been in contact with food. Sterilize all cooking utensils before giving them to a baby. Wash other things regularly in dish washing liquid or baking soda.

Source: Adapted from Gee R., and Meredith, S., *Entertaining and Educating Babies and Toddlers*, London: Usborne Publishing, 1986.

The move from gross to fine movements is witnessed in *prehension*—the ability to pick up an object with the fingers and thumb. Prehension is a controlled act, not to be confused with the grasping reflex, which usually disappears by four months of age. Prehension is an acquired motor skill that paves the way for the development of gross and fine motor coordination.

Chapter Review

- Parenting begins even before the birth of a baby, as mothers and fathers imagine what their new child will be like. The image parents have in their minds influences their expectations of their child.

- Parenting refers to the beliefs, attitudes, and behaviors parents carry into the child-rearing process, and as such mothers and fathers form preconceived notions before their child is even born.

- It is exceedingly important for parents to recognize the changes that occur at every stage of their child's development so that interactions and expectations will be age-appropriate and based on sound reasoning.

- The newborn comes into the world preprogrammed for physical growth, emotional reactions, locomotion, speech, social interaction, and thinking and reasoning.

- Infants are born aided by a number of reflexes or built-in, automatic physical responses, some of which ensure survival after birth and others which help the newborn adapt to the world.

- A parent's behavior toward a child influences that child. The actions of the child are just as influential in affecting the behavior of the parent. There is a synchronicity to the relationship, a dance in which parent and child act in unison to create a connection.

- Temperament refers to an individual's underlying, relatively consistent, basic disposition, a pattern built into the brain's neural circuitry. It determines how an individual will generally respond in life situations. Striking differences in temperament and behavior show up from birth.

- Alexander Thomas proposes that there must be a good match between a child's inborn temperamental characteristics and the environment he or she grows up in. Optimal development depends upon a goodness of fit. A reciprocal relationship exists between the child's temperament and that of his or her parents and this is reflected in how the parents treat the child.

- A child's genetic makeup helps to create the environment from which they derive their experiences. Rather than being passive recipients of parental desires, children evoke support and reinforcement from parents that "fit" their genetic predispositions.

- Infants experience differing levels of consciousness, ranging from sleeping to crying. Peter Wolff devised a classification system outlining six states of consciousness, one tending to follow the other in succession, and each lasting approximately twenty minutes.

- Crying is an adaptive response on the infant's part. Peter Wolff analyzed infant crying patterns and found that there were four types of crying: rhythmic, angry, pain, and hunger. Babies also cry if they are uncomfortable, bored, or ill.

- SIDS is the abrupt and puzzling death of a seemingly healthy infant during sleep. SIDS has been associated with respiratory ailment, gender, economics, maternal smoking, low birth weight, and drug dependence. SIDS babies have higher rates of prematurity, lower birth weights, lower Apgar scores, and weaker muscle tone.

- It is typically a middle- and upper-class American phenomena that infants be separated from parents when sleeping, sometimes at birth and generally after three to six months of age. Parents in many other cultures favor a co-sleeping approach to child rearing.

- Proper nutrition is essential for the growth and development of the newborn. Physical size, mental ability, and psychological well-being are all dependent on receiving sufficient vitamins, minerals, proteins, fats, water, and carbohydrates.

- Breast-feeding is viewed as advantageous to baby and mother, primarily for health reasons. Infants digest human milk more easily than the milk of other animals, making them less prone to diarrhea, constipation, and other intestinal problems. Breast-fed infants are also less prone to allergies and asthma. They are protected from some diseases because mothers' milk promotes the production of antibodies.

- Marshall H. Klaus and John H. Kennell have proposed that human mothers and babies are subject to the same attachment mechanisms as other animals. They believe that in the first six to twelve hours after birth, maternal hormones are released that enable an especially close bond to form between a newborn and its mother. Subsequent studies have challenged this work. Researchers have found little long-term difference in the relationship between those who bonded early and those who did not.

- At about three months of age, infants focus on selected caregivers, smiling when they are near and displaying distress when they leave. In American culture, infants at about nine months begin to internalize the objects of their attachment. At this point, they exhibit stranger anxiety, a marked distress in the presence of unfamiliar adults. A few months later, they display separation anxiety when the object of their affection leaves them for any reason.

- Mary Ainsworth and John Bowlby did extensive research in the area of attachment, which Ainsworth defined as "an affectional tie that one person or animal forms between himself and another specific one—a tie that binds them together in space and endures over time." Ainsworth identified three types of attachment between infants and their mothers: securely attached, avoidantly attached, and ambivilantly attached.

- Jay Belsky believes that more than twenty hours a week of day care during the first year of life increases the risk of insecure attachment. However, a day-care provider might become an attachment figure to a child who is not responded to at home. Day care is harmful if babies don't get enough attention at home and go to a day care facility where they also get little attention.

- Attachment to father, like attachment to mother, depends on the quality of care given, the overall relationship between the child and father, and other circumstances of home life.

- Early experiences shape the brain development of children by impacting the wiring of the neural circuits. Parents provide the stimulation needed for optimal development.

- From the moment they are born, infants have the ability to communicate. Researchers believe that preverbal sounds of crying, cooing, and babbling form the foundation for learning the rules of language. Many parents talk to their infants in a specialized way known as parentese (which speaks to the infant at his or her own operational level).

- The more control an infant has of his or her voluntary motor actions—which enable reaching for things, grasping, manipulating objects, crawling, standing, and walking—the greater his or her ability to conquer the environment. Activities involving large muscle control, are called gross motor skills and include the ability to sit up with support, hold on to objects and then roll over. Fine motor skills refer to activities involving more refined and delicate operations, such as grasping an object with one hand and using fingers to inspect it.

Student Activities

1. Visit a local book store and investigate the materials available for children ages birth to eighteen months. Find books you would consider appropriate for each of these periods: birth to five months, six to twelve months, thirteen to eighteen months. Discuss why you would pick a certain book for a particular age level.

2. Imagine you are a parent with very limited resources. Using everyday items, create several stimulating objects for a baby to play with during its first year.

3. Plan a day's outing for a child of age one year, keeping in mind stimulation and energy levels.

Helping Hands

National Center for Clinical Infant Programs
2000 14th Street N., Suite 380
Arlington, VA 22202-2500
(703) 528-4300

Organization interested in promoting optimal development of infants and toddlers by encouraging quality intervention services.

Association for Childhood Educational International (ACEI)
11501 Georgia Avenue, Suite 312
Wheaton, MD 20902
(301) 942-2443

Organization devoted to promoting competent educational practices from infancy through adolescence.

Healthy Mothers, Healthy Babies
409 Twelfth Street, SW, Suite 309
Washington, DC 20024-2188
www.hmhb.org

A group of national and state organizations whose focus is maternal and child health. Information on nutrition, injury prevention, and infant health is shared.

La Leche League International
P.O. Box 1209
Franklin Park, IL 60131
(708) 455-7730
www.lalecheleague.org

Provides information and support to breast-feeding mothers.

National Sudden Infant Death Syndrome
Clearinghouse
8201 Greensboro Drive, Suite 600
McLean, VA 22102
(703) 821-8955

Provides SIDS information to professionals and the public.

National Sudden Infant Death Sydrome
Foundation (NSIDSF)
10500 Little Patuxent Parkway, No. 420
Columbia, MD 21004
(410) 964-8000
www.sidsnetwork.org

Provides support to parents who have lost a baby to SIDS. Helps families in caring for infants at risk due to heart and respiratory problems.

CHAPTER

Parenting the Young Child

Chapter Highlights

After reading Chapter 10, students should be able to:

- Understand how the physical changes of early childhood lead to an expansion of children's worlds
- Understand how children organize their world through the use of language
- Recognize the importance of regulation and self-control to the development of skills
- Recognize the importance of play and friendship to promote social skills during childhood
- Understand the function of preschool educational programs in cognitive and social development

Chapter Contents

- Getting Up and Going Out
  The Body Grows and Changes ▪ *Motor Activity*
- The Health and Safety of Young Children
  The Accidental Environment ▪ *Illness*
- Organizing the World
  Egocentrism ▪ *Expanding the World Through Language* ▪ *The Growth of Vocabulary* ▪ *Engaging in Conversation* ▪ *Language and the Development of the Self*
- The Self-Controlled Child
  Childhood Fears ▪ *Sleeping and Dreaming* ▪ *The Family Bed During Childhood* ▪ *Toilet Training* ▪ *Temper Tantrums* ▪ *Sexuality and Sex Roles*

■ Play in Early Childhood
    Types of Play ■ *Cognitive Development and Children's Humor* ■
    Childhood Friendships
■ Early Childhood Education Programs
    Preschool Enrichment Programs ■ *Constructive Day Care*

In 1924, an English writer named Alan Alexander Milne published a book of verse inspired by his four-year-old son, Christopher Robin. He soon expanded his work to include the story of Christopher Robin's love for a bear named Winnie the Pooh. The Pooh books have a terrific appeal for preschool children who are physically and mentally venturing out into the world and who see the little bear as a perfect companion. In his series of tales about Pooh, A. A. Milne sends Christopher Robin in and out of a forest where he meets not only his bear friend, but Piglet, Eeyore the donkey, Kanga, and Tigger.

Milne had an uncanny ability to understand the mind and actions of young children. He saw their need for make-believe, their self-centeredness, and their love of animals, toys, and adventure. Using monosyllables that appeal to children working hard to learn language, Milne delights young audiences by having Pooh get stuck in a doorway, fly in a balloon, imitate a cloud, and take a bath.

Child and dog exploring the world.

Early childhood, the period ranging from approximately eighteen months to six years, is a time of social expansion when children venture into the world seeking novel experiences and new connections. It is a time for friendship, when same-aged youngsters come together to talk, play, and share fantasies of who they are and who they hope to be. It is a special period for children because, in the midst of building new relationships, they are starting to uncover their true selves. Early childhood is a time when self-control becomes increasingly important. It is during this period that children strongly model and identify with the adults they see, meet, and know. In late infancy, children first understand themselves as separate from others, but it is still too early for them to have a realistic knowledge of who they are. By early childhood, children begin to build a self-concept based on their socialization, the gender roles they model, and their accomplishments.

Early childhood is an odd stage of development, in the sense that the need to become an individual comes up against the need to join in community with others. When children are denied opportunities to express individuality and to explore the world around them, if they are unable to seek out friends, playmates, the parents of playmates, teachers, and other adult figures, their journey through life can be lonely and difficult, particularly as it relates to discovering who one is as a person. For parents, this is an especially difficult time, because what is often labeled as "the terrible twos" is actually a time when children attempt to define themselves as separate from their parents.

GETTING UP AND GOING OUT

Like Christopher Robin and Winnie the Pooh, young children need fresh air, sunshine, nurturance, nourishment, and stimulation to blossom. Children at this stage grow in height and weight, and they change in shape and size. The brain grows, and as it does, changes in cognitive functioning occur. New worlds open up to the child who can move easily around the environment, absorbing sights and sounds, touching this and that, experiencing everything in reach. If information is power, then the years between one and six bring newfound authority and control over the world. A four-year old born among the Bushmen of the Kalahari reaches for a water-bearing root in the desert. The same age child living in New York City reaches for the remote control of a TV or VCR.

THE BODY GROWS AND CHANGES

Young children grow physically at a steady pace, but not nearly at the rate of growth during infancy. Growth in children is generally measured using a set of *norms,* or quantitative measures that are a standard by which to gauge variations. From ages two to six, the average North American child grows 12 inches and gains 20 pounds, up to an average total of 45 pounds and 43 inches (See Figure 10.1). However, the variation between children can be substantial, with one six-year-old weighing 35 pounds and another 50 pounds. Height varies also as children this age range from 40 to 50 inches tall.

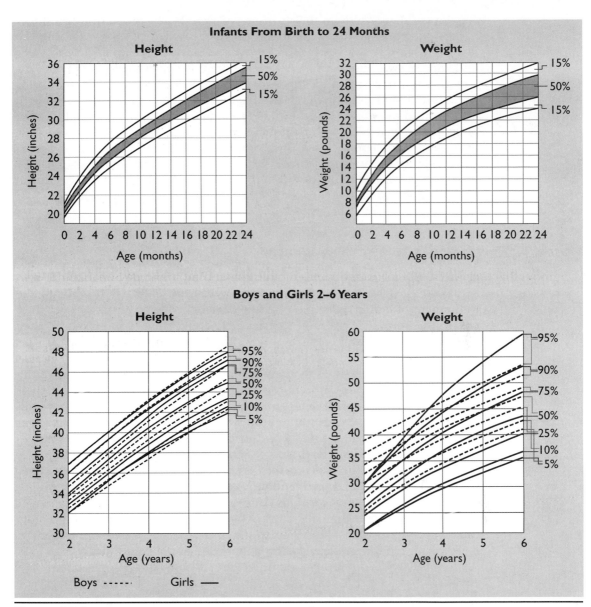

Figure 10.1
Growth Chart

As preschool children mature, they lose their baby fat. The six-year-old may have only 50 precent of the fat he or she had at one year of age. This phenomenon explains why children lose what families call their "baby faces." The remaining fat gradually redistributes away from the waist and toward the hips and shoulders. Preschool children, then not only grow in size, but they change shape, gradually looking more like adults (Sinclair, 1978). One predictive rule of thumb is that boys will ultimately grow to twice their height at 18 months and girls double the height they reach at two years (Lowry, 1978).

Boys and girls differ in their patterns of growth. The differences begin prenatally and continue until physical maturity is reached (Tanner, 1898). In the first six months of life, boys tend to grow at a faster pace than girls. But by age four, girls overtake boys in rate of development. Between age four and puberty, growth tends to even out for the sexes (Smith, 1977).

Howard Meredith (1978) reviewed over 200 studies of preschool-aged children around the world. He determined that differences in height are linked to biological as well as environmental factors. Environmental influences include nutrition, socioeconomic class, birth order, and maternal smoking during pregnancy. Children who experience severe psychological stress may also display growth problems. Malnutrition in children under five is particularly harmful to the growth process. It affects not only height, but intellectual and emotional development (Tanner, 1978).

MOTOR ACTIVITY: GOING TO MEET THE WORLD

Learning to walk has been called "a kind of second birth" that enables children to pass from helpless to active beings (Montessori, 1966). It is through the refinement of motor skills that children develop a degree of power over their environment. When children first learn to walk, they look awkward; they stumble and often walk with their feet turned outward to maintain balance. They toddle, hence the terms *toddler,* and *toddlerhood*, in honor of this period of motor activity. Changes in body size and proportion eventually give the toddler greater control and coordination. Preschoolers gain much of their weight in the form of muscle. At three years of age, gross motor skills have improved to the point where children can walk with their feet forward, hands at their sides. They run around, proud of their ability to control their movements. The four-year-old rides a three-wheeler, skips, and jumps. Children at this age walk down the stairs one foot per step. By five, children can ride a two-wheel bicycle, play jump rope, and do some gymnastics. Through play, young children practice their motor skills (Hughes, 1991).

Activities such as drawing, cutting out paper dolls, and buttoning a shirt call for fine motor skills. It appears to take until the age of five for children to have the dexterity necessary to dress themselves completely.

THE HEALTH AND SAFETY OF YOUNG CHILDREN

In his famous children's book, *Charlotte's Web* author E. B. White writes about the mystery of barns, farm tools, animals, friendship, and all the things that attract children away from home. Because of their curiosity and adventuresomeness, young children are vulnerable to accidents.

THE ACCIDENTAL ENVIRONMENT

From birth to four years of age, children's deaths from burns, drowning, poisoning, and vehicular accidents occur as much as four times more frequently than for older children and adults (National Safety Council Accident Facts 1983), accounting for more deaths than from all diseases combined. In fact, accidents are by far the leading cause of death among children of all ages, with vehicular accidents topping the list (See Figures 10.2. and 10.3).

Statistics indicate that U.S. children of all socioeconomic classes, are more likely to be injured than children in other Western countries. It seems clear that a serious parental education program on child safety is needed. Children are particularly at risk for accidents because they combine a developing mobility with a thirst for exploration, set against a backdrop of inexperience. Between 1985 and 1988, the National Safety Council gathered statistics about the danger of everyday home life. The council found that falls on stairs, ramps, and floors were responsible for almost 1.5 million injuries. Bicycles accounted for over one-half million accidents. Next were knives, followed by beds, pillows and mattresses, chairs and sofas. Outside the home, drowning occurs most frequently at age two and being hit by a car is more common at three. Given their increased motor activity it is almost impossible to keep children safe all the time. Many children have fractured a bone or required stitches by the age of ten.

The National Center for Health Statistics also reports that children of low-income families have a greatly increased chance of being injured than children of higher socioeconomic families. In poorer families, it is often difficult for adults to adequately supervise children who frequently play on inner-city streets and in neighborhoods where there are many places and ways to get hurt (Matheny, 1987). There are also gender and cultural differences in regard to childhood injuries. Because they take more risks and are more active, boys have double the rate of injury as girls by age five. African American youngsters have a higher incidence of death by accident than their Caucasian counterparts. Asian American children are injured less than children of other ethnic groups because their parents generally are more protective (Kurokawa, 1969).

Figure 10. 2
Death By Accidents for Children Ages 1–4

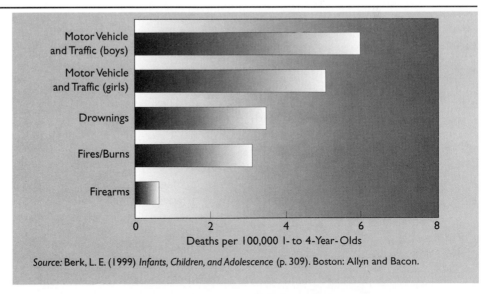

Source: Berk, L. E. (1999) *Infants, Children, and Adolescence* (p. 309). Boston: Allyn and Bacon.

Figure 10.3
Automobile
Fatalities Among
Children

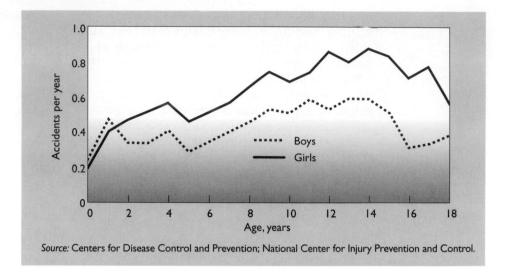

Source: Centers for Disease Control and Prevention; National Center for Injury Prevention and Control.

There is speculation that some children are accident prone, specifically children who have underdeveloped neuromuscular control for the level of activity in which they engage. They have difficulty adjusting to changing situations and are unable to prejudge the outcome of their behavior (Wright, Schaefer, and Solomon, 1979).

The risk to children can be minimized by adult supervision and the provision of a safe play environment for young children (See Table 10.1). Many states have mandated that young children be placed in car seats while in cars and yet almost half of all parents do not do so (Wilson and Baker, 1987). Townships across the country insist that swimming pool areas be fenced, but home pools are still the site of the majority of child drownings. It is relatively easy to place medicine in a place unreachable by young children and to put smoke detectors in strategic parts of a house.

ILLNESS

Communicable diseases are ones that can be transmitted from one person to another. Early childhood is a prime time for getting a number of communicable illnesses such as chicken pox, measles, or respiratory infections, because of the close contact youngsters have with others at day care centers, nursery schools, and play groups. Children do not have sufficient antibodies to defend against certain kinds of infections, and for this reason it is imperative that they be immunized throughout their growing years. The Children's Defense Fund (1991) reports an increase in infectious diseases in preschool children because a large number of youngsters in the United States are not immunized. The incidence of measles alone, up 16 percent between 1983 and 1991 to over 25,000 cases, illustrates the severity of this problem. The increase may be because low-income families in America have limited access to the health care system, compared to citizens of European countries such as Holland or Norway—where government-sponsored health care enables all children to have medical protection.

TABLE 10.1   Accidents, Remedies, and Prevention

Accidents	What to Do	How to Prevent
Drowning	Unless you are trained in water safety, extend a stick or other device. Use heart massage and mouth-to-mouth breathing when and as long as needed.	Teach children to swim as early in life as possible; supervise children's swim sessions closely; stay in shallow water.
Choking on small objects	If a child is still breathing, do not attempt to remove object; see a doctor instead. If breathing stops, firmly strike child twice on small of back. If this does not help, grab child from behind, put your fist just under his or her ribs, and pull upward sharply several times.	Do not allow children to put small objects in mouth; teach them to eat slowly, taking small bites; forbid vigorous play with objects or food in mouth.
Cuts with serious bleeding	Raise cut above level of heart; apply pressure with cloth or bandage; if necessary, apply pressure to main arteries of limbs.	Remove sharp objects from play areas; insist on shoes wherever ground or floor may contain sharp objects; supervise children's use of knives.
Fractures	Keep injured limb immobile; see doctor.	Discourage climbing and exploring in dangerous places, such as trees and construiction sites; allow bicycles only in safe areas.
Burns	Pour cold water over burned area; keep it clean; then cover with sterile bandage. See a doctor if burn is extensive.	Keep matches out of reach of children; keep children well away from fires and hot stoves.
Poisons	On skin or eye, flush with plenty of water; if in stomach, phone poison control center doctor for instructions; induce vomiting only for selected substances.	Keep dangerous substances out of reach of children; throw away poisons when no longer needed. Keep syrup of ipecac in home to induce vomiting, but use *only* if advised by doctor.
Animal bites	Clean and cover with bandage; see a doctor.	Train children when and how to approach family pets; teach them caution in approaching unfamiliar animals.
Insect bites	Remove stinger, if possible; cover with paste of bicarbonate of soda (for bees) or a few drops of vinegar (for wasps and hornets).	Encourage children to recognize and avoid insects that sting, as well as their nests; encourage children to keep calm in presence of stinging insects.
Poisonous plants (e.g., poison ivy)	Remove affected clothing; wash affected skin with strong alkali soap as soon as possible.	Teach children to recognize toxic plants; avoid areas where poisonous plants grow.

Source: Berk, L. E. (1993) *Infants, children and adolescents.* Boston: Allyn & Bacon.

The Informed Parent 10.1

On-the-Move Safety Tips

Parents must take extra safety precautions once children become mobile.
Here are some of them.

- Keep doors and gates shut and, if necessary, locked so the toddler cannot get out on his or her own.

- Be sure the toddler cannot gain access to the bathroom and to the freezer.

- Secure the tops and bottoms of stairs with safety gates.

- Place firescreens in front of fireplaces in such a way that they cannot be moved.

- Put safety plugs in electrical sockets.

- Be sure harmful substances and dangerous objects are up high enough that children cannot reach them. Be particularly careful with bleach and other cleaning fluids, medicines, alcohol, tools, knives, pins, matches, plastic bags, perfumes, and razors.

- Turn saucepan handles inward so they do not protrude over the edge of the stove. Keep coffee pots, coffee-filled mugs, and other hot beverages or food away from toddlers.

- Use a harness in high chairs and strollers.

- Always place children in car seat belts or infant seats.

- Choose toys that do not have sharp edges or corners. Be sure toy pieces are larger than the size of a plum. Beware of toxic paints and surfaces on toy products.

Illness has been linked to poverty. Poverty does not cause childhood illness per se, but impoverished environments increase the likelihood of problems such as lead poisoning, anemia, and sensory deficiencies (Egbuono and Starfield, 1982).

Lead poisoning is one of the most prevalent childhood health problems in the United States. It is estimated by the Public Health Service that one in five preschool children has blood lead levels sufficient to cause behavioral and neurological problems. Since lead accumulates in the body, low-dose exposures to lead build up over time, causing serious physical/neurological damage. Even small doses of lead can lead to lowered intelligence, hearing impairment, posture problems, and stunted growth.

Symptoms of lead poisoning include:

- Bizarre behavior
- Decreased play activity
- Listlessness
- Absence of emotion
- Small losses of newly obtained skills

- Inability to coordinate voluntary muscle movements
- Seizures
- Anorexia
- Vomiting
- Occasional stomach pains

Stress also plays a part in susceptibility to illness because emotional states are tied to immune system functioning. The direct effect of stress is a weakening of a child's resistance to disease. In families where a parent is especially stressed, less attention may be paid to a child's health needs, thereby opening up the possibility of increased illness (Beautrais, Fergusson, and Shannon, 1982).

A relationship has been found between certain stressful conditions and the occurrence of accidents. The strongest links were to hunger, exhaustion, illness, a death in the family, and the appearance of a new caregiver (Mofenson and Greensher, 1978).

ORGANIZING THE WORLD

The child's ability to think and reason and then turn his or her thoughts into language is the predominant developmental feature of early childhood. Early childhood is an age when children absorb sounds, words, and grammar from their world. By age two, they have entered the world of *symbols*, which means they are able to mentally represent objects or actions they perceive in the environment. The importance of symbols is illustrated in children's play, particularly in their make-believe play, where they pretend to do things and act as if imaginary things exist. Young children are fond of pretending to talk on the telephone, acting like one of their parents, or imitating a TV character. It is by make-believe play that children build up intellectual schemes and gain an understanding of the world around them. The use of symbols increases problem-solving skills and decreases the need for trial-and-error learning.

The use of language, the ultimate in symbolic representation, carries a child forward by leaps and bounds. A child can say the word "cookie," draw a picture of a cookie, and make a pretend cookie out of construction paper. The ability to allow a word or object to stand for something real frees the child from the constraints of the here-and-now and permits him or her to mentally travel into the past and future.

EGOCENTRISM

As children grow and increasingly interact with the social world it is important that they learn to distinguish their own perspective, or viewpoint from that of others. Young children are often not able to consider others' viewpoints. They believe everyone thinks and feels as they do. This kind of self-reference has been called *egocentrism*. Although the term implies a sense of selfishness and self-centeredness, it is not meant this way. Rather, it suggests a mental activity that changes as the child ages and experiences increased social interaction.

In a classic experiment on egocentrism, Jean Piaget and Bärbel Inhelder constructed a model of three mountains (Figure 10.4). Children aged 4 to 11 years were walked around the model so that they could see that the mountains looked dissimilar from different angles. The children were then seated on one side of the mountain model, and a doll was placed at the other side. Each child was shown a group of photos and asked to pick out the pictures that best repre-

Figure 10.4
Three Mountains
Problem

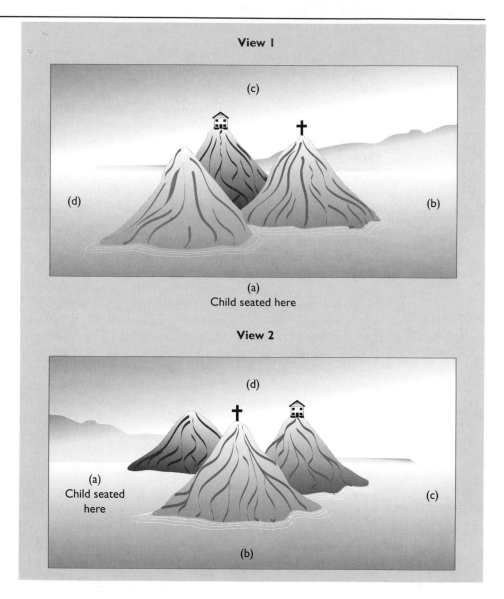

View 1

(c)

(d)

(b)

(a)
Child seated here

View 2

(d)

(a)
Child seated
here

(c)

(b)

When Christopher Robin goes to the market looking for a rabbit, he is amazed to find the market men selling mackerel and lavender when *he*, Christopher Robin wants rabbits. At Buckingham Palace's changing of the guard, the child says, "Do you think the King knows all about Me?" This is typical four-year-old egocentrism.

From "Winnie the Pooh" by A. A. Milne, illustrated by E. H. Shepard. Copyright 1926 by E. P. Dutton, renewed 1954 by A. A. Milne. Used by permission of Dutton Children's Books, a division of Penguin Books Inc.

sented what he or she saw and what the doll saw. The children from 4 to 7 years old generally chose the same photo to represent both perspectives—their own and the doll's (Piaget and Inhelder, 1948). Children this age were unable to conceptualize that the doll was would see the model from another angle.

Egocentrism is also evident in the interactions of young children, when side-by-side each child works on his or her own project, and when each child carries on a personal monologue while talking to another child. Some of the conflict between parents and their children at this stage is due to this apparent self-centered or spoiled behavior. A mother who has a headache might ask a three-year to stop making so much noise. Because the child cannot "see" the world from her position, he or she continues to make a racket.

Many researchers dispute Piaget's position on egocentrism. Some have shown that children as young as three years old can see another's point of view if the task is made simple enough. In the three mountains experiment, a measure of spatial calculation is needed to understand the various vantage points. When toys are used instead of mountains, some children can imagine another's viewpoint (Borke, 1975). It has also been observed that children as young as thirteen months old will try to comfort a crying infant by touching or hugging him, and a toddler of eighteen months will independently fetch a bandage for someone with a cut or bruise (Yarrow, 1978).

EXPANDING THE WORLD THROUGH LANGUAGE

In *The Absorbent Mind,* Italian educator Maria Montessori observed that when children learn language they also learn elements of their environment—the time and place of their growing-up years, the customs, ideas, ideals, sentiments, feelings, emotions, and religion of their culture (Montessori, 1936). Language is an agent of thought and, as their vocabulary increases, children are able to think more clearly and problem solve more effectively. Between two and six years of age, language development is rapid. Grammatical rules become more refined, and children come to understand what is expected of them by way of competent communication.

THE GROWTH OF VOCABULARY

At age two, children use about 200 words when speaking. Four years later, they have astonishing speaking vocabularies of up to 14,000 words (Carey, 1978). This means they have incorporated an average of about 10 new words a day into their speaking repertoires.

Once the first word is spoken, at roughly one year of age, the child's vocabulary mushrooms, to a repertoire of 200 words by age two. Martyn Barrett (1986) refers to this time as the *vocabulary spurt*, with children learning almost two dozen words per week. Children's first words are those referring to persons and things most relevant in their world. The first words uttered by American children are often *mama* and *dada*.

Young children have a limited speaking vocabulary, but they understand many more than they utter. A parent need only ask a child to point to his or her nose or pick up the stuffed rabbit to see that the child understands more than he or she can say. Linguists say that a child's language comprehension is greater than language production. Over the years, the gap between a child's expressive vocabulary (production) and his or her receptive vocabulary (comprehension) narrows as language develops.

Before they talk in phrases and sentences children go through an approximately 18-month to 2-year period during which they speak in two-word sentences. These brief combinations have been referred to as *telegraphic speech* because they employ a bare minimum of words to convey a thought. Dan Slobin (1970, 1972), noted that two-word sentences fall into a dozen categories—used by children in cultures as diverse as those of the South Pacific, Asia, and Europe.

Query	When eat?
Location	Ball here.
Action-object	Pet dog.
Action-direct-object	Hug me.
Action-indirect-object	Give Mommy.
Agent-action	Baby cry.
Identification	See Mommy.
Nonexistence	Doggie gone.
Negation	Not Daddy.
Recurrence	More cookie.
Possession	Mommy book.
Attribution	Blue hat.

ENGAGING IN CONVERSATION

Jean Piaget called early-childhood speech egocentric. Preschoolers engage in what Piaget called *collective monologues*. Youngsters take turns talking, but each individual proceeds along his or her own course, neither responding nor relating to another youngster's message.

Other research has questioned Piaget's idea. Some youngsters are quite capable of *social speech*, language that is strictly adapted to the speech or behavior of a partner (Garvey and Hogan, 1973). Michael Maratsos (1973) conducted an experiment in which he asked three- to five-year-olds to select a particular toy from a room that had a number of toys. When requested to choose the toy in the presence of an adult who could see what was taking place, the children pointed to the toy. However, when the adult was blindfolded, the children described the toy. Research has also shown that four-year-olds adapted their tone of voice depending on their audience. They describe items in one tone of voice when they are talking to an adult, and another tone when talking to a two-year-old (Shatz and Gelman, 1973).

Children's difficulties in communicating may be less a function of egocentrism and more a matter of information-processing skills (Menyuk, 1977). Many skills are needed to hold a conversation. A person must consider his or her own language behavior, as well as another person's perceptions, responses, and emotions. Each person must be sensitive to specific words used and sentence intonation. Jerome Bruner (1980) pointed out that children have to learn to make eye contact and to pay attention to what others say. Most adults coordinate these factors quickly and effortlessly. Young children may be able to perform all of these tasks individually, but they have difficulty spontaneously integrating them (Schmidt and Paris, 1984).

No one is sure when and how children first learn to converse. It may be that the first complete conversation comes in the form of a child responding to adult speech with actions instead of words (Dore, 1978). A parent encourages a child to say "Bye, bye," and the child waves. Children tend to repeat the words they hear spoken by adults. And usually by the age of three, children are holding a brief discourse.

The Informed Parent 10.2

Assessing Language Development

By the age of two years, children talk in two-word combinations and often in full sentences. Althought there is latitude for individual differences, certain signs should advise parents of possible problems in language development.

No speech by age two

A monotonous voice

Stuttering

Leaving out sounds, or substituting a wrong sound

Too fast or slow a rate of speech

Too soft or loud a voice

Speech that is still unintelligible by the age of three

Improper pitch

Source: L. Marotz, J. Rush, and M. Cross, 1985

The flow of a dialogue is maintained through *turnabouts*, verbalizations that prompt another person to respond. Examples include commenting on what the other person said or elaborating on a point made. Young children talk in two- or three-word sentences, making real conversation a difficult task. The number of turnabouts increases over the years from age 3 to 6 (Goelman, 1986). It is clear that adults do most of the talking in parent-child conversations. This role modeling aids in all facets of language development (Wanska and Bedrosian, 1985).

Albert Bandura (1977) and other social-learning theorists propose that language is learned by imitating parents who are role models. Reinforcement is a selective process. Sounds that fit a child's native tongue are imitated and reinforced. Unusual sounds are ignored. As a child begins to form words, parents gradually reinforce more accurate pronunciations.

Positive reinforcement also comes in the form of acceptance of what is said. Generally parents reinforce grammatically correct and incorrect sentences, choosing instead to correct only statements that are untrue, such as "I go out" when the child means "I come in" (Brown and Hanlon, 1970).

Katherine Nelson (1973) noted that children whose mothers are more critical of their speech have smaller vocabularies at age two than do children whose mothers are more tolerant. In other words, parents who consistently correct their child's utterances actually retard their language development. Another study found that mothers who are clinically depressed lack the emotional energy to tend to all the sounds their children make. Given less attention for their utterances, these children develop language at a slower pace than those with mothers who were more attentive (Breznitz and Sherman, 1987). That children require verbal attention for language development was illustrated by researchers who contrasted the language abilities of single children and twins. Because mothers of twins talk to both children together and less often to one at a time, twins develop language at a somewhat slower pace than do single children (Tomasello, Mannie, and Kruger, 1986).

By kindergarten age, there are distinct differences in the way children express themselves verbally. Some are skilled chatterers, able to speak in complex sentences, while others have such limited vocabularies that they are barely able to express ideas. A number of studies have shown girls to have more advanced language skills than boys, first-borns more advanced than later-borns, and middle-class children more advanced that lower-class children (Rebelsky, et al., 1967). Other studies have indicated that mothers talk more to their daughters than to their sons (Cherry and Lewis, 1976), parents talk more to their first-born child than those who follow (Jacobs and Moss, 1976), and middle-class parents spend more time responding to and explaining things to their children than do parents of the lower classes (Hess and Shipman, 1965). Children learn to talk if they are allowed to talk. In families or cultures that take the attitude "children should be seen and not heard," children have less well-developed language skills (Schieffelin and Eisenberg, 1984).

Jane Healy (1992) proposed that one of the best ways to stimulate a child's language development is through communication that allows the child space to think, imagine, and reflect on ideas. She notes that children learn their language—and thinking—habits in great part from their home environments. . . . Children from families that mediate situations verbally—that is, talk thoughtfully about problems or questions—are better readers, writers, communicators, and reasoners than are those from families where language is used less effectively. Healy suggests using "questions without answers" as a way of opening a child's mind. Responses like "That's interesting; tell me more," and "Why do you say that?" help children clarify their thinking. Healy describes seven "talk tactics," phrases that are helpful in extending conversations with children. She suggests opportunities for conversations with children during car rides, while doing chores, at the dinner table, and anywhere a parent has a few minutes with a child.

LANGUAGE AND THE DEVELOPMENT OF THE SELF

Daniel Stern pointed out that language serves many functions. It makes experiences more shareable, and it permits two people to create mutual experiences of meaning. Conversation permits a child to construct a narrative of his or her own life. Through the use of language, a verbal *self* emerges. The child is a person in his or her own right, single and distinct, "the agent of actions, the experiencer of feelings, the maker of intentions, the architect of plans, the transposer of experience into language, the communicator and sharer of personal knowledge" (Stern, 1985). But language ability, for all its benefits, divides experience into the part that is lived and the way it is verbally represented. The

The Informed Parent 10.3

Talk Tactics to Extend Conversations with Children

A number of techniques promote conversation between parents and children. It is a matter of listening carefully and responding in ways that extend the conversation.

Acknowledging
"That's a new idea."
"You really thought about that one."
"I see."
"Interesting."

Restating
"You're wondering if . . . ?"
"Does that mean . . . ?"
"It sounds as if you're thinking (feeling). . . ."

Clarifying
"That's interesting; tell me more."
"Can you tell me a little more about. . . ?"
"I don't quite understand what you mean. . . ."

Disagreeing
"You make an interesting point; have you considered. . . ?"
"Here's another thought. . . ."
"That's an idea I never heard before. . . ."

Challenging Thinking
"I wonder how we know . . . ?"
"Can you give me some reasons for . . . ?"

Redirecting
"Interesting idea. Let's go back to. . . ."
"Nice point, but we hadn't finished discussing. . . ."

Expanding
"I wonder what anyone else is thinking about this . . . ?"

experience of the self is subjective and interpersonal, and it is often misrepresented when transformed into the verbal word.

Meaning is a shared experience between the child and the person speaking with the child. If a mother says "Good girl," does the child experience the

The Spirit of Parenting

Joey at 20 Months

"Pumpkin": 7:05 A.M. *My room is so still. I am all alone here. I want to go where Mommy and Daddy are. There, I wrap myself in the heat that rises and falls. I bathe in the rich tide of our morning world.*

Joey gets out of bed. He stands looking about for a moment, as if thinking. He then goes quickly into his parents' bedroom and gets into their bed, slipping under the covers between them. His parents are pretty much awake by now. After a while, his father says to him, "My little pumpkin." Joey answers back, from under the covers, "Umpin." His father laughs, "That's it, you're my little pumpkin." Joey is quiet for a while. Then he comes out from the covers and announces clearly and firmly, "Me pumpkin!"

As Joey approached 18 months, he began another major maturity leap that profoundly changes his daily experience: The leap into the world of words, of symbols and self-reflection. Joey is still in the middle of this leap. In some children it starts earlier; in some, later. Like the unfolding of a flower, a uniquely human one, language blossoms overnight when the time is right . . .

So far, in respect to language, Joey has heard only its music. He hears the pure sound of the words and feels the emotions the sounds evoke in him, but he hears little of the strict meaning. But on this particular morning, Joey's father's language does not vanish into music and feeling. The word "pumpkin" stands apart, and Joey can start to explore it and play with it. His task is to master the sound and keep it, rather than just letting it wash over him.

To do this, he and his father toss the word back and forth, making it better each time. The game and the rules of alternating turns have been used by Joey and his parents for many months. They used to take turns cooing and smiling to each other when he was only three months old. The basic rules of conversation, turn taking, were long established before Joey and his parents even applied them to language. So, once again, Joey and his father follow these tried-and-true rules and send the word "pumpkin" back and forth between them.

The first time Joey tries his turn, he leaves out the exploding consonants and says, "Umpin." His father then does as most parents intuitively do in this situation: He slowly and clearly enunciates the not-yet-learned parts of the word, "Pump-kin," and leaves unstressed the already learned parts. Using this teaching technique, Joey quickly gets it right!

What happens now is truly wonderful. When a word is first unlocked, its released meaning is both a gift—in this case, a present from Joey's father—and a personal discovery and creation. Once Joey has worked on the word and let it work on him, it is his. He can now use it to refer to a new aspect of himself in the context of his relationship with his father: "Me pumpkin!"

(continued)

Joey has never heard "Me pumpkin" before. Perhaps no one has ever said it. Thus, Joey is not imitating anybody. Instead, he has created for himself a meaning, by bringing together himself ("me"), a word sound (p.u.m.p.k.i.n.) and a special experience, a way of being loved and viewed by his father ("Me pumpkin").

Diary of a Baby,
Daniel N. Stern, Basic Books (1990)

words in the same way she did when her father said them? Lev Vygotsky (1962) believes that understanding a child's language depends upon the meaning that is *negotiated* between two people sharing the process of moving from thought to word and from word to thought. Meanings are unique to the two people sharing the language. A mother's "good girl," then, is based on experiences and thoughts that are different from those that underlie a father's "good girl." As Stern notes, "Two meanings, two relations coexist." This situation presents a source of difficulty to a child who is building a personal identity and self-concept.

THE SELF-CONTROLLED CHILD

Another English writer who understood how young children think was Robert Louis Stevenson, author of *A Child's Garden of Verses,* the adventurous *Treasure Island*, and the frightening *Doctor Jekyll and Mr. Hyde.* Robert was very sickly as a young child. He spent long nights awake, wracked by painful bouts of coughing. When he did sleep, he fell into states of night terrors, imagining his bedroom walls swelling and shrinking before his eyes and creatures emerging from the clothing hanging around his room. Only his father could calm the troubled boy, and he did this by making up stories and inventing conversations to divert Robert from his night demons.

Robert Louis Stevenson's childhood trouble with sleep is not an uncommon experience for young children who are developing in leaps and bounds cognitively but having difficulty distinguishing fantasy from reality. (In Stevenson's case, a nanny compounded the boy's problems by filling his head with tales of hellfire, eternal damnation, and other horrors as punishments for bad living.) In exploring their new worlds, young children are exposed to unfamiliar people and situations. With their new exploration and imaginations running wild, children develop fears of many things. It is also at this stage in a child's life that parents' expectations increase. Parents want children to be toilet trained, eat properly at the table, play "nicely," and develop other self-regulatory behaviors that will save them in an ever-expanding social world.

The Informed Parent 10.4

Everyday Rules of Behavior

J. Heidi Gralinski and Claire Kopp have categorized the everyday rules adults make for the average child. When children are very young, parents worry most about safety issues. Gradually rules extend to areas such as table manners, self-care, and the treatment of others (Gralinski and Kopp, 1993). Rules, of course, differ from family to family (Chapter 4) and what is acceptable to one parent is not all right with another. In some families, for example, children must sit at the table until everyone is finished eating; in other families it is fine for youngsters to run off as soon as they are finished eating.

Category	Behavior
Safety	Not touching dangerous things Staying off furniture Not going into street
Protection of property	Staying away from prohibited objects Keeping away from prohibited areas Not drawing on walls or furniture
Respect for others	Not taking toys from other children Playing "nicely" with other children
Mealtime routines	Not playing with food Not spilling drinks Sitting at table until the end of the meal
Delay	Not interrupting when someone is on the phone Not interrupting others' conversations Waiting to eat
Manners	Saying "please" and "thank you"
Self-care	Dressing self Bathing and brushing teeth when told to Adhering to bedtime schedule
Family routines	Helping with chores Keeping room neat Taking care of one's posessions

CHILDHOOD FEARS

Young children fear most those things they cannot control; their strongest re-actions are to animals, the dark, snakes, falling, loud noises, and high places (Jersild, 1960; Baurer, 1976; Poznansky, 1973). Fears are physical and psycho-logical responses to real or imagined dangers, leading children to cry, tremble, withdraw, or otherwise act out their feelings. Some fears of course are reason-able. If an unfamiliar dog comes up to a young child, that child is likely to be-come anxious. Eventually the child learns that some dogs are dangerous and others are not. A fear can become irrational when it becomes generalized, as in the case of a child who compulsively fears all dogs, even those that are of no danger. This kind of maladaptive response is called a *phobia*, which, if it inter-feres with normal functioning, warrants professional help.

Parents must show patience and understanding in the face of childhood fears. An invalidation of the fear or an angry response does little to help chil-dren master their fears, but rather it makes them feel guilty about being anx-ious and injures their self-esteem (Graziano, DeGioganni, and Garcia, 1979).

SLEEPING AND DREAMING

Young children need less sleep than do infants. Preschool-age children typi-cally sleep through the night, and they may or may not take a brief afternoon nap.

About 25 percent of children aged 3 to 8 years experience either *nightmares* or *night terrors.* A nightmare is a "bad dream," which is frightening or disturb-ing to the child. Nightmares generally occur in the morning hours, near the end of the sleep cycle. Recurrent nightmares may signal a psychological prob-lem (Hartmann, 1981). Night terror is a state of severe anxiety, resulting in a sudden awakening from a deep sleep. Children who experience night terrors usually wake up screaming, but they cannot recall what they were dreaming about. When they get up in the morning, they cannot remember having been awakened during the night.

As upsetting as night disruptions are to parents, there isn't much they can do to stop such events, which appear to run in families. While children generally outgrow night terrors, medication can alleviate severe cases. During such times, it is best for parents not to focus on the dream or terror. The best approach is to soothe and comfort the child until he or she is calm and able to go back to sleep.

THE FAMILY BED DURING CHILDHOOD

Sleep is a major issue in many homes, as children and their parents often dis-agree about the "when" and "where" of bedtime. Maria Montessori suggested that "one of the greatest helps that could be given to the psychological devel-opment of a child would be to give him a bed suited to his needs and cease making him sleep longer than necessary. A child should be permitted to go to sleep when he is tired, to wake up when he is rested, and to rise when he wishes." It was Montessori's position that the beds typically used in Western society are not suited for children and that bedtime schedules fit the needs of parents more often than they do those of children.

One controversy in regard to children's sleeping problems has centered upon "the family bed." For many centuries and in many cultures children share a bed or at least sleeping quarters with parents and sometimes other family members. There appear to be strong Western taboos against this, due partly to the popularization of Freudian beliefs concerning childhood sexuality and the advice of child-care authorities such as Benjamin Spock. After World War II, middle-class America provided separate bedrooms for each family member as a sign of affluence. But more parents than generally admit it move over during the night to make room for a young child who doesn't want to sleep alone.

Anthropologist Margaret Mead considered the "family bed" one of the world's most enduring customs. She noted, "The fact that co-family sleeping occurs regularly in many human groups as it does among ours, even though the social code is opposed to this practice, is highly significant, and points to a stubborn human characteristic which is worth following up" (Thevenin, 1987). John Bowlby, in his work on separation, points to the benefits of a companion when one feels afraid, as young children often do during the night (Bowlby, 1973). There are arguments for and against the family bed, and it is best for parents to decide on a course of action that most suits a particular child and the family or its circumstance. In *The Family Bed* (1987), Tine Thevenin presents the opposing views.

Sleeping Together

- Provides a feeling of security
- Leads to a decrease in sleeping problems, such as those caused by bad dreams or nightmares
- Easier for a nursing mother
- Parents enjoy the closeness with their child
- Easier to keep an eye on an ailing child
- Soothes the child who feels lonely or afraid
- Is warmer for all in homes where there is limited heat
- Gives a feeling of family togetherness

Sleeping Apart

- Parents prefer to sleep alone
- Child is too active while sleeping
- The bed is too small
- Social customs prohibit co-sleeping
- Interferes with sexual activity of parents
- Parent fears rolling over on child
- Parent desires to make child independent
- Influenced by advice of experts or pediatrician

TOILET TRAINING

In American society, toilet training usually begins at about age 2 although, depending on the child, readiness to control elimination functions comes anywhere from 18 to 24 months of age. Any attempt to develop this habit should consider physical readiness and include teaching by instruction and observation, a calm parental attitude, and an avoidance of punishment for mistakes.

Pediatrician T. Berry Brazelton points to six readiness indicators before beginning toilet training:

1. Has the child mastered running and walking, and is he or she able to sit and play quietly for a period of time?
2. Is the child interested in being toilet trained?
3. Does the child imitate adult habits like brushing of teeth or hair brushing?
4. Does the child know when he or she has to go to the bathroom?
5. Is the child interested in being clean?
6. Is the child not fighting this attempt toward training?

Most experts view toilet training as a function of a child's natural capabilities and advise parents to encourage but not force it on children. Brazelton believes children get trained at their own pace, and he suggests allowing them to become used to a potty chair gradually. First parents can allow the child to sit on the potty while still dressed, then when undressed from the waist down. With the potty always available and parents there to remind children every so often that they may have to go to the bathroom, children should be told that they are responsible for knowing when they have to go to the potty (Brazelton, 1978).

Nathan Azrin and Richard Foxx use a system of rewards to promote toilet training. In their *Toilet Training in Less Than a Day,* they combine a number of techniques from the behaviorist and social learning perspectives, including in their program the use of dolls and reinforcements like parental praise and attention. Concerned at how often toilet training becomes a test of wills between children and their parents, Azrin and Foxx propose that children 20 months and older can be easily trained if they can pass three simple readiness tests: 1) for bladder control, 2) for physical development, and 3) for instructional readiness. In the first procedure of their technique, children learn by teaching a Doll-That-Wets to potty train herself. They suggest parents have their child guide the doll through the required motions and give approval to the doll for the correct actions, which include lowering training pants, urinating, emptying the potty, and staying dry for a few minutes at a time. The child is then encouraged to imitate the doll by preforming the same tasks. The parents motivate the child by praise like "Billy is a big boy. He is pulling his pants down," or "Here's a piece of candy for Billy for having such dry pants." These psychologists note that some children will display temper tantrums during this kind of training. They suggest parents not allow the tantrums to interrupt the training but rather wait until the child calms down and continue the program in a composed, loving way (Azrin and Foxx, 1976).

Some children, particularly boys, are toilet trained during the day, but find themselves unable to control their bladders at night, a problem seen even after age seven and into adolescence. In a small percentage of cases, bed wetting is the result of a physical problem. Other reasons include insufficient bladder capacity to last through the night and so deep a sleep pattern that children don't feel the need to go to the bathroom when they have to. Persistent bed wetting, or *enuresis*, has been linked to genetic factors as well as personality and social forces (Goldman, 1995). Children at risk for enuresis sometimes come from backgrounds where parents or siblings have the same problem. They often exhibit high levels of motor activity and aggression, have trouble adapting to new situations, are immature and overdependent, and exhibit low achievement motivation (Kaffman and Elizur, 1977).

Thomas Gordon suggests parents and children solve the problem of bed wetting together. One solution includes waking children during the night, walking them to the bathroom and putting them back in bed. Another is to have children refrain from drinking liquids before going to bed.

Behaviorists suggest using rewards such as gold stars, tokens, or praise to control bed wetting. Another technique uses a special pad that is placed under the bed sheet. When the pad becomes wet, a buzzer goes off, waking the child and reminding him or her to go to the bathroom. The buzzer has the disadvantages of waking family members other than the child and requiring that parents must get up and reset it.

The problem of bed wetting must be handled sensitively by parents, with the realization that this behavior is beyond the control of their child. The use of shame or ridicule as a technique to reverse this problem only leads to greater anxiety on the child's part and an even larger chance of having an accident.

TEMPER TANTRUMS

When children begin to explore the world that is open to them, they are bound to meet obstacles and frustrations, usually in the form of limits set by parents. The frustration may be expressed in strongly negative words like "No" or "Mine" and in crying, screaming, and stubbornness that is generally called *temper tantrums*. The challenge for parents is to avoid making childhood a battle of wills, and instead to help children gain self-control without injuring their self-esteem.

The number of temper tantrums a child has depends upon inborn temperamental differences (Chapter 9) and the parents' responses to this behavior. Haim Ginott believes that the feelings behind the tantrums should be acknowledged and accepted, and then the angry behavior redirected. Sometimes a compromise works in dealing with a child's frustration. "I know you want to play with the ball. Please take it outside and hit it against the wall" works better than simply taking the ball away from the child.

Adele Faber and Elaine Mazlish suggest that when children have temper tantrums in public, parents should leave a store, or stop the car, or otherwise take action (Faber and Mazlish, 1990). Others recommend ignoring outbursts, using a time-out technique, sending children to their rooms, and other actions aimed at calming the behavior.

Temper tantrums undoubtedly cause as much stress to parents as they do to children, but if they can be seen as a normal part of a child's attempt at independence, parents might handle them better. When parents respond to a tantrum with angry outbursts of their own, a child may become even angrier and less able to respond to the distress (Crockenberg, 1985). Managing their own distressing moods is an important part of a child's growing up (Goldman, 1995). Studies have shown that children who showed high levels of self-control at age four were more competent and better able to handle stress during middle childhood and adolescence (Toner and Smith, 1977). When parents remain firm in their guidance while helping their children calm down, they are modeling the kind of empathy and concern they want their children to develop.

SEXUALITY AND SEX ROLES

One of the most difficult notions for many parents to accept is that children are sexual beings from the day they are born. Genital play, massage, and masturbation are behaviors exhibited by a majority of toddlers and young children. Sex play between children, built upon curiosity about the body parts of others, commonly occurs between ages four and six (Gundersen, Melas, and Skar, 1981). This is the time when children ask questions about the origin of babies, play "doctor" with neighborhood friends, and begin to use words that have sexual connotations. As children develop cognitively, they are increasingly able to understand sexual matters. In 1975, Anne Bernstein and Philip Cowan studied 60 children: ten boys and ten girls at each of three age levels— 3–4, 7–8 and 11–12. The children were asked questions such as " How do people get babies?" "How did your mother get to be your mother?" "What does the word 'born' mean?" In response to a question about how a baby is made, a little girl in the age 3–7 group answered, "Well, you just make it. You put some eyes on it. . . . Put the head on, and hair, some hair, all curls. . . . You find it at a store that makes it. . . . Well, they get it and then they put it in the tummy and then it goes quickly out." A young boy in the 11–12 age group answered, "The lady has an egg and the man has a sperm, and they, sort of, he fertilized the egg, and then the egg slowly grows. . . ."

One can assume that television has caused children today to be more sophisticated about matters of sex than those of 20 years ago. At that time, Bernstein and Cowan conducted a study that showed children's beliefs about procreation follow a distinct developmental sequence and reflect their level of cognitive development (Bernstein and Cowan, 1975). On a practical level, this research tells us that—with or without adult input—children construct their own views of baby making. The research suggests that parents should answer a child's questions about sex simply and honestly, picking up cues from the child on just how much information is needed.

Parents' attitudes about sexuality are revealed overtly, by the kind of conversations they are able to have with their children, but also more subtly, in the body language, tone of voice, and attitudes conveyed in family discussions about sex. In some families, there are unwritten rules that forbid talk about sex, and in others there are open, honest discussions about the subject. Such discussions can be awkward when a single parent is raising a child of the opposite sex. Nevertheless, it is the task of parents to help their children discover and understand their own sexuality, and parents can do this by reading books such as *Where Did I Come From*, refraining from ridicule or punishment when they observe sexual behavior, and communicating openly about sexuality.

An important aspect of human sexuality is *gender identity*, a child's understanding of maleness and femaleness. Once a child is identified as "boy" or "girl" the culture he or she lives in determines what this means in terms of role behaviors. From the moment of their birth, from the names they're given to their infant clothing, children are molded into their parents' view of masculinity or femininity. Sex-role programming teaches children how to deal with emotional feelings, what type of activities to pursue, and how to behave in relation to the other sex. Until age six young children generally rely on physical cues like hair and clothing to determine male and femaleness. For example, they will insist that any long-haired person is a female (Bem, 1989). They also look to other same-sex children when establishing sex-role behaviors. From early childhood on, families assign tasks and duties based on perceived roles. A four-year old girl might help her mother make cookies while a five-year-old boy will wash the car with his father. Historically, gender roles were thought to be the function of biology. Men were seen as the stronger, more aggressive sex, and women as the more nurturant and dependent gender. In American society, some parents are taking a more androgynous approach to sex roles by giving their children unisex names, clothing, and chores.

One of the ways young children learn gender roles is through the chores assigned by parents and the modeling of what mothers and fathers do around the house.

PLAY IN EARLY CHILDHOOD

The research on attachment clearly shows that social skills are fostered when a child feels emotionally safe and secure. It is this sense of security that allows children to explore the environment to find out how things work and test their own relationship to it. No pastime is more instrumental in helping children learn about the world they live in than *play*. Catherine Garvey (1977) defines play as *an activity that is strictly pleasurable, an end unto itself (not a goal to achieving a particular goal), spontaneous, and actively participated in by the individual*. Researchers studying play note its effects on physical and cognitive development, as well as its socialization functions. Irenäus Eibl-Eibesfeldt (1967), an ethologist, calls play "an experimental dialogue with the environment" suggesting a give-and-take between exploration and an ever-changing world.

Children become social creatures by playing with others. Sharing, cooperation, conflict resolution, and intimacy are among the behaviors developed, in part, through social play. Carollee Howes (1988) believes this function of socialization is demonstrated when play helps the child learn the rules and expectations of society.

TYPES OF PLAY

The earliest form of play experienced by infants is based upon motion. Most babies love to be tickled, jiggled up and down, and even tossed in the air. They are not passive participants in this kind of play, but rather they are regulators of how active and intense the play should be. Daniel Stern (1974) notes that this kind of play is built on "pure interaction," meaning that the infant's signals of pleasure or displeasure, plus his or her reaction to stimulation, promotes or discourages continued play.

Early play progresses from peek-a-boo to make-believe. Marianne Lowe (1975) placed a number of miniature objects—a cup, a saucer, spoon, hairbrush, truck, trailer and doll—on a table and noted how differently children between the ages of 9 months and 3 years play with these items. At 9 months, a child will grasp a bright object within reach and bring it to his or her mouth. Another object will be grasped, then another. The child will bang, wave, turn, and otherwise investigate the object. At 12 months, the investigation of the object will come before banging and waving it around. At 15 months, the child understands how many of the objects are used. The child will place the cup on the saucer and sip from it. The truck will be pushed back and forth and the doll stood up. By 21 months, a child will combine objects appropriately. He or she will search for the spoon in order to stir an imaginary drink in the cup. At 24 months, the child will feed the doll, brush its hair, and lay it down for a nap. By 3 years of age, a child will make the doll pick up the cup, then wash and dry the dishes and put them away. The doll in this last scenario is acting *purposefully*, doing things with clear intent. It is over a two- to three-year span that, through play, a child progresses from learning about individual objects to transforming objects into action sequences that reflect his or her immediate world.

In a classic study, 34 children aged two to five were observed at play in a nursery school. Mildred Parten noted the various ways in which they played, and the presence or lack of interaction. From these observations, she established six categories of play behavior. Nonsocial classes of play are less mature than social types of play, and cooperative play is the most sophisticated and complex kind of play (Mildred Parten, 1932).

Unoccupied play.   Unoccupied play is not actually play. The child may stand in one place or move about: climbing on chairs, walking around the room, or sitting in one place for a period of time. Parten found that children younger than three years old spend a small amount of time in unoccupied play.

On-looker play.   Between the ages of two and three, onlooker play becomes the most common type of activity. Children engaged in onlooker play stand around watching other children play. They may talk to the children and offer advice. Although they show interest in the activity, they do not take part in it.

Solitary play.   The last category of nonsocial play is solitary play. Children play with toys that are not being used by others, occupying themselves in separate activity. In solitary play, the children make no attempt to get physically close to others, take no notice of them, and are not influenced by their behavior or play.

Parallel play.   When children participate in parallel play, they are physically close to other children, but are involved in different activities. This immature form of social play is common in children under three years of age, and it is exhibited in children up to at least five years of age. According to Parten, the child "plays with toys that are like those which the children around are using, but he plays with toys as he sees fit and does not try to influence or modify the activity of the children near him. He plays *beside* rather than *with* other children."

Associative play.   By age four, associative play becomes the most common form of play. In associative play, children may be enjoying the same activity, but each has his or her separate goal. The children do not work together toward a common end. For instance, three children may sit together, building with blocks. They will converse about their specific project, but they do not put the blocks together to build one larger structure. Instead they will each have made a separate construction.

Cooperative play.   The most socially advanced type of play is cooperative play. A common form of play for five-year-olds, cooperative play involves teamwork, designated roles, a common goal, and membership in the group. Often, one or two youngsters serve as leaders, directing the group, specifying the activity, and designating who may participate.

More recent studies of social play have broadly confirmed Parten's categories (Hartup, 1983). However, the sequence of development in social play is not rigid and straightforward. Children throughout the preschool years are involved in solitary or parallel play (Harper and Huie, 1985). The five-year-old's time in solitary play, for example, may be a means of concentrating on a specific project such as putting a puzzle together or building a model airplane (Smith, 1978). When approaching a new group, many children, regardless of age, will initially be an onlooker until becoming more comfortable with the situation. Smith found that from 34 to 41 percent of the preschooler's play remains nonsocial. There is no good or bad type of play for the preschooler. It is the quality rather than the quantity of nonsocial play that is important. Play that involves constant repetition of behavior or immature acts may signal a delay in social development.

Attachment studies have shown that securely attached children are more likely to explore their physical environment when in the presence of their mothers. These children are more sociable and are more likely to engage in cooperative games with their peers (Lieberman, 1977). Attached preschoolers function more independently at the age of two and show more curiosity by five. They are also more successful when they engage in social pretend play with other children (Howes and Rodning, 1992).

When a family is in distress, children's play is often affected. E. Mavis Hetherington and her associates (1979) compared a group of children from intact families to a group whose parents had been divorced. They found that girls from divorced families engaged in less dramatic play than did those from intact families, at two months and at one year after the divorce. The differences disappeared two years after the divorce. When boys were studied it was found that they too engaged in fewer episodes of dramatic play at all three time periods studied. Those boys who engaged in dramatic play were less imaginative and more rigid than their intact family peers. Boys of divorced parents also engaged in more immature solitary and parallel functional play activities than boys from intact families.

COGNITIVE DEVELOPMENT AND CHILDREN'S HUMOR

The ability to joke, laugh, display wit, and banter with others is an important feature of human social relationships. Parents who encourage these behaviors are enhancing their children's cognitive development while enjoying their amusing children. Very young children display a sense of humor when responding to the world around them. Psychologist Jean Piaget wrote about his two-year-old daughter's delight at playing "make-believe" with a toy telephone. This pretend game is directly related to cognitive development, as are more sophisticated forms of humor.

Paul McGhee (1979, 1988) noted that *incongruity*, or inconsistent ideas, are the basis of children's humor. As children develop cognitively, their sense of humor progresses through stages. It takes an understanding of conservation for a child to recognize a joke like: "Waiter: Should I cut your pizza into eight slices or six. Patron: Make it six. I'm on a diet." Very young children are physi-

The Informed Parent 10.5

Fostering Creativity Through Play Materials

Children's play activities are a form of experimenting with the world. Here are items parents can have available for activities that foster physical prowess, problem solving, and creativity.

Costumes for fantasy play
Bicycles and other riding toys
Push/pull toys
Sliding boards, swings, and other playground apparatus
Puzzles and books
Clay, sand, and playdough
Stuffed animals and dolls
Art equipment
Construction toys (blocks, Legos®)

cally involved with many objects, so incongruity in regard to these object becomes the focus of their humor. Placing a pair of pants on his head to make it a hat will cause a two-year-old to laugh. Once children can speak, humor involves verbal incongruities. Two-year-olds think it's funny to call objects by other names, so that a dog becomes a cat and Daddy is called Mommy. By age three, children are amused by incongruous ideas. A picture of Daddy in a dress will make them laugh. Children age seven and older have developed intellectually enough to understand inconsistencies in word use. They like jokes such as "Why did the father tiptoe past the medicine cabinet? He didn't want to wake the sleeping pills." Joking with children and laughing at their attempts at humor encourages children's creativity, helps them develop an important social skill, and relieves tension in emotional situations.

CHILDHOOD FRIENDSHIPS

Friendship is a dyadic relationship based on mutual interests, affection, intimacy, and trust. Friendship permits the loosening of the family bonds. It is the vehicle through which intimacy can be established. But intimacy, self-expression, and trust require a certain level of social, emotional, and cognitive development. Friendship to a four-year-old is therefore a different phenomenon than it is for a sixteen-year-old. Relationships change in depth and complexity, because they stem from the context of an individual's life. Preschoolers make friends with the children who live in the same neighborhood. They have similar interests and material things. Adolescents look to friends to help them become independent from their parents. The purpose of friendship is socialization different from that taught by parents and siblings. Through friendship, children learn to interact with peers and resolve or prevent conflicts (Hartup,

1989). Friends provide companionship and environmental or intellectual stimulation. They give physical support and ego reinforcement, and they serve as a basis for social comparison, models of moral behavior, and gender roles. Above all, friends offer intimacy and affection (Parker and Gottman, 1989).

In early childhood, friendship is equated with play. Relationships revolve around games and exchanges of toys. By age three, children begin to differentiate other children as individuals distinct from a nebulous group of others (Howe, 1987). In addition, their more advanced language and cognitive development allow preschoolers a wider range of interactions, and they engage in more complex play including pretend (Hartup, 1989). Preschoolers understand that a friend is someone with whom they play more and whom they like (Youniss, 1980). They demonstrate this knowledge by giving friends more compliments, praise, and cooperation than nonfriends (Hartup, 1983). Children in preschool programs have been observed to spend about 33 percent of their time with the one playmate for whom they express the most liking (Hinde, et al., 1985).

Preschoolers look for children with similar and familiar characteristics. Those who have the easiest time making friends are physically appealing, do well at cooperative play, and respond positively to others. Youngsters who have temper tantrums or difficulty managing their aggressive behavior are less popular with their age mates (Ladd, Price, and Hart, 1988). Children who have a secure attachment to their parents also tend to have good relationships with their peers. The friendships are non-domineering, congenial, sensitive, and happy (Parker and Waters, 1989). Sensitivity to others' needs and skills of conflict resolution are two other characteristics observed in children who are most able to make and keep friends (Gnepp, 1989, Yeates, and Selman, 1989).

Boys are socialized differently from girls with respect to the importance and meaning of friendships. Girls are raised to understand that relationships hold major significance in life. They are taught to express their emotions, be empathic, listen to others, and be nurturing. Their relationships are based on a sesitivity to others' needs. Boys are expected to be self-sufficient, motivated to succeed, and forceful. Such an orientation emphasizes the needs of the self over those of other people. This stereotypical pattern of socialization has its basis in the fact that our society has valued the woman who finds a mate and raises a family and on the man who has a successful career (Lips, 1993).

Preschoolers gravitate to members of the same sex in their play groups, and their best friends are generally the same sex (Maccoby, 1990). This preference for same-sex friends is the result of boys and girls preferring different activities. Competition and rough-and-tumble activity typify boys' play. This inclination tends to make girls anxious and therefore reluctant to play with boys.

EARLY CHILDHOOD EDUCATION PROGRAMS

Children ages three to six like to hear repetitive and funny books such as *The Cat in the Hat*. By drawing pictures, they define the world they live in. By building cities made of blocks, they feel a sense of accomplishment. Preschoolers' activities are as important to their cognitive skills development as the classes they will years later take in elementary, middle, and high school. In these early years, an interest in the world grabs hold. The desire to understand and manage words, objects, and people is rooted in children's early experiences and encouraged by sensitive parents and teachers. Children have an inner drive to reach their potential, and they search for tools in their environment that will help them reach their goals.

The years prior to kindergarten came to be known as "the preschool years," in the years when children younger than five or six generally stayed at home before starting school. Today, because parents and often grandparents are out of the house and in the workplace, alternate arrangements have to be made for the care of preschool children. *Day care* refers to providers in home or apartment settings, as well as to operations located in community centers, churches, and elementary schools. Home providers frequently have no formal training in child care, and the facilities are generally unlicensed. In some communities, home day care comes under social service supervision, and some help is available to the provider. The atmosphere of home day care varies considerably—from first-rate care in surroundings filled with toys, music, and educational equipment to basic neglect in environments where the TV is the only form of stimulation.

In center-based day care, personnel have some training, an activity program is usually in place, and the caregiver-child ratio is generally lower than in home settings. Today more children are cared for in center-based day care programs than in a home setting (Figure 10.5). A number of American companies

Figure 10.5
Child Care
Settings

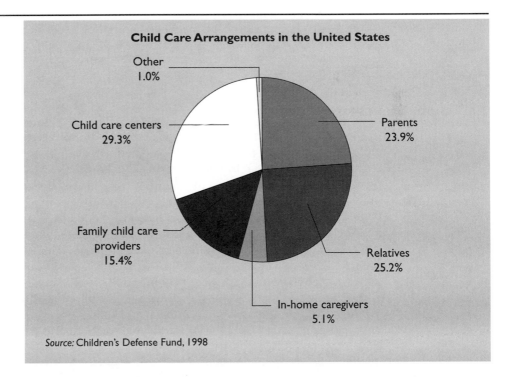

Child Care Arrangements in the United States

Other 1.0%

Child care centers 29.3%

Parents 23.9%

Family child care providers 15.4%

In-home caregivers 5.1%

Relatives 25.2%

Source: Children's Defense Fund, 1998

provide day-care centers on their premises, in an effort to relieve employees from concerns about the logistics of child care.

Nursery schools serve the same purpose as day care, and they too can be found in church basements and community centers, as well as in college classrooms and shopping malls. What they offer is formal programs designed to enhance children's cognitive and social development. They are usually licensed and staffed by trained personnel. Because costs are higher for nursery school than home or center-based day care, nursery schools generally serve the middle and upper classes.

In a study of child care effectiveness, noted researcher Alison Clarke-Stewart assessed 150 two- to four-year-olds in six different child care arrangements, including (1) care at home by a parent, (2) care at home by a sitter, (3) care in a day care home, (4) full-time care in a day care center, (5) part-time care in a day care center or nursery school, (6) and part-time care in a center plus part-time care at home with a sitter (Clarke-Stewart, 1984; Clarke-Stewart and Gruber, 1984).

> In sum, preschool children who have spent some time in center child care are, on the average, socially and intellectually advanced over their peers who have only been at home. This advanced development is likely to arise from a combination of factors, not a single critical cause. Experiences at home, including those initiated or evoked by the child, may contribute to the advanced development of children whose parents have chosen to put them in centers. Even more important, the advanced development of children in centers is likely to be the result of lessons to foster social and intellectual skills, instructions in recognizing and following rules, opportunities to practice skills and follow rules with a variety of peers and nonparental adults, and encouragement of independence and self-direction by trained and nonauthoritarian teachers. The experiences of children in centers are substantially different from those children are likely to have at home. (Clarke-Stewart, 1991)

PRESCHOOL ENRICHMENT PROGRAMS

In some preschools, children play and listen to stories. In others, they learn the alphabet and how to print one's name. There are even preschools that give instruction in computer literacy and foreign language. Many children enter preschool having been exposed to books, toys, museum trips, and travel. But many others who are raised in impoverished settings lack these advantages. Over the past few decades, programs have developed to enhance the cognitive and social development of children from disadvantaged environments.

One of the best-known enrichment programs, Head Start, was implemented in 1965. It was designed to provide four-year-old underprivileged children with a one-year enrichment program that would prepare them for kindergarten. Activities include singing, drawing, cutting, block building and puzzle solving. Children learn colors, numbers, and shapes. Readiness for reading and language arts is stressed. Head Start also provides health care for youngsters, children receive medical and dental examinations, and are immunized. Hot lunches and snacks are served, and parents are included in the educational process. Parents are offered classes in home economics, child care, and food preparation. Originally designed as an eight-week summer program, in its first year, Head Start served 20,000 children. There are now approximately 1,300 Head Start centers operating year-round, with an enrollment of about 800,000 children. Since its inception, Head Start has served millions of preschoolers across the country.

Head Start programs vary so greatly that it is difficult to study their success or failure. Some centers are well funded and staffed by professionals. Others operate marginally, in substandard facilities, with few learning materials available. Edward Zigler, one of the program's designers, believes that less than one-half of Head Start centers are adequate and that many should be closed down altogether. He also warns that too much is expected of a one-year program, if one considers the deprivation of many of the Head Start children as well as the family problems of unemployment and poor housing that remain (Zigler, 1987). For these reasons, it seems best to look at the nonacademic benefits of the program. On a practical level, Head Start offers meals and medical care to children who might otherwise not be properly fed or cared for. In addition, this program has offered parents a chance to get involved in their children's education. As a result, they develop relationships with the school system and work more effectively with teachers (Wasik, Ramey, Bryant, and Sparling, 1990). Zigler has viewed parents as the key to Head Start's long-lasting effects on children. One study indicates that mothers' gains in psychological well-being were related to their participation in the supportive activities of Head Start. Specifically these mothers reported fewer psychological problems, greater feelings of mastery, and an increased sense of life satisfaction (Parker, Piotrkowski, and Peay, 1987). A review of the program indicated that children who attend Head Start programs are less likely to become delinquent. This fact may be due to increased parental involvement in the children's lives, as a result of the program. One controversial study at the Perry Preschool in Ypsilanti, Michigan, suggests that educational intervention in the lives of disadvantaged children leads to increased incomes, more stable relationships, and a decrease in drug use or criminal behavior in adulthood. Compared to the average Head Start program, the Perry School had better educated teachers, offered smaller class sizes, and spent double the amount of money per child.

To date, research concerning the adult effect of the Head Start experience has yet to be accomplished (Zigler, 1993). Edward Zigler defends the Head Start project vigorously, concentrating on what the program offers on a daily basis.

> Head Start has focused on the whole child, not just his or her educational needs. Head Start is America's largest provider of health care services to poor children. Every child gets medical and dental screening and is referred for treatment for any health problems observed. Immunizations are brought up to date.
>
> Head Start helps families get social services and tries to find jobs for parents. Many find them with Head Start—as bus drivers, receptionists, and

classroom assistants. Some pursue further education to become Head Start teachers and directors . . .

Head Start's approach to the whole child and commitment to involving parents have defined the components of effective intervention. (Zigler, 1993)

A review of the studies on Head Start suggests that immediate effects are less dramatic than long-range results. The greatest benefits come when schools have a low teacher-child ratio, a trained special education staff, a curriculum that emphasizes cognitive skills, and a classroom environment that fosters creative play (Haskins, 1989).

CONSTRUCTIVE DAY CARE

In early studies of the effects of day care, researchers focused on the issue of potential harm resulting from the child-parent separation (Zaslow, 1991). Subsequent research has concentrated on the positive outcomes of day care. Questions asked include: How does the quality of a day care influence a child's experiences in it? How are cognitive and social skills affected by the variations in day care experience? How do the socioeconomic and psychological effects of the family fit into the day care experience?

A number of studies have looked at the structure of day care and found that children have more positive experiences when placed in small groups supervised by well-trained caregivers, and where space is well organized (Howes, 1983). A caregiver's education was also associated with the amount of time spent enhancing children's language development through interpretive and informative interactions (Berk, 1985). High turnover rates among staff were predictive of lower scores on measures of language development (Whitebook, et al., 1989). In family day care settings, increased social development was associated with the amount of time providers talked with, read to, and touched the children they cared for (Clarke-Stewart, 1987).

It is difficult to gauge the effect of a particular day care experience on later development because many children attend multiple care settings before reaching elementary school. However, quality of care is a factor in later cognitive and social development. One study found that poor-quality care during the preschool period led to greater hostility and difficulty with task orientation in kindergarten (Howes, 1987).

Family background impacts the experience of day care economically and psychologically. Children from higher socioeconomic and better-educated families experience a better quality of day care than children from less advantaged homes (Anderson, et al., 1981). Families with few resources have to rely on lower quality care for their children. These families are also burdened with more difficult lives, making family stress factors (parents living apart, long work hours, overcrowding) as much a part of the day care equation as quality of care. In other words, the effects of day care cannot be assessed without considering the context of a child's life (Poteat, et al., 1992). As previously noted (Chapter 9) day care is most harmful to children if they do not get the love and nuturance they need when they come home.

The Informed Parent 10.6

Transition From Home to Day Care or Preschool

It is important for parents and children to be prepared for the change from home to day care or preschool. Here are way to help in this transition.

- Tour the day care facility with your child.
- Talk with your child about going to preschool for several weeks before he or she actually goes.
- Request a phase-in period for your child.
- Reassure your child that you will return for him or her.
- If your child is more comfortable going to the center or school with a blanket, favorite toy, or stuffed animal, take it along.
- Try to enroll your child at the beginning of a term.
- If your child has just experienced a major illness or the family has been going through a crisis, delay your child's start of day care or preschool.
- Don't punish your child for clinging behaviors.
- Look for guidance from the day care staff or preschool teachers.

Source: Adapted from *52 Ways to Evaluate Your Day Care Options and Gain Peace of Mind,* Jan Dargatz. Nashville: Thomas Nelson Publishers, 1994.

Chapter Review

- Early childhood, ranging from approximately eighteen months to six years is a period of social expansion, a time when children venture into the world seeking novel experiences and new connections.

- Physical growth in young children continues at a steady pace, but not nearly at the rate of growth during infancy. Growth in children is generally measured using a set of norms, quantitative measures that are a standard by which to gauge growth variations.

- Boys and girls differ in their patterns of growth. The differences begin prenatally and continue until physical maturity (Tanner, 1898). In the first six months of life, boys tend to grow at a faster pace than girls. By age four girls overtake boys; then between age four and puberty, growth tends to even out for the sexes.

- Changes in body size and proportion eventually enable greater physical control and coordination. Preschoolers gain much of their weight in the form of muscle. At three years of age, gross motor skills have improved to the point where children can walk with their feet forward and hands at their sides. They run about, proud of their ability to control their movements.

- From birth to four years of age, deaths from burns, drowning, poisoning and vehicular accidents occur as much as four times more frequently than for older children and adults, accounting for more deaths than all diseases combined. Accidents are the leading cause of death among children of all ages.

- Early childhood is a prime time for contracting a number of communicable illnesses, such as chicken pox, measles, or respiratory infections. The close contact youngsters have with others at day care centers, nursery schools, and play groups accounts for these illnesses.

- Poverty does not cause childhood illness, but impoverished environments increase the likelihood of problems such as lead poisoning, anemia, and sensory deficiencies. Stress also plays a part in susceptibility to illness because emotional states are tied to immune-system functioning.

- The child's ability to think and reason and then turn thoughts into language is the predominant feature of development in early childhood. Children absorb sounds, words, and grammar from the world they live in. By age two they have entered the world of symbols, which means they are able to mentally represent objects or actions they perceive in the environment.

- Young children are often not able to consider the viewpoints of others. They believe everyone thinks and feels as they do. This form of self-reference has been called egocentrism, relating to mental activity that changes as the child ages and experiences increased social interaction.

- At age two, children speak about 200 words. Four years later, they have astonishing vocabularies of up to 14,000 words—which means they have been able to incorporate, on the average, as many as ten new words a day into their repertoire.

- Jean Piaget believed early childhood speech is egocentric. Preschoolers engage in what Piaget called collective monologues. Youngsters take turns talking, but each proceeds along his or her own course, neither responding or relating to the other's message. Other research has questioned the concept that all young children's speech is egocentric. Some children are quite capable of social speech, in which each partner adapts to the other's speech or behavior.

- Albert Bandura and the social learning theorists propose that language is learned by imitating parents who serve as role models. Reinforcement is viewed as a selective process. Sounds that fit a child's native tongue are imitated and reinforced; unusual sounds are ignored. As a child begins to form words, parents gradually reinforce accurate pronunciations.

- Jane Healy proposes that one of the best ways to stimulate a child's language development is through communication that allows the space to think, imagine, and reflect on ideas.

- Lev Vygotsky believes that understanding a child's language depends on the meaning that is negotiated between two people sharing the back-and-forth process of moving from thought to word and from word to thought. This means that meanings are unique to the two people sharing language.

- In exploring their new world, young children are exposed to unfamiliar people and situations. Along with their new exploration, imaginations run wild and children develop fears of lot of things. At this stage in life, expectations of children increase. Parents want their children to become toilet trained, eat properly at the table, play "nicely," and develop other self-regulatory behaviors that will carry them into an ever-expanding social world.

- Sleeping difficulties often arise in early childhood. Night terrors are states of severe anxiety, resulting in being suddenly awakened from a deep sleep. For many centuries and in innumerable cultures, children share a bed or at least sleeping quarters with parents and sometimes other family members. There are strong Western taboos against co-sleeping arrangements.

- In American society, toilet training usually begins at about age two, although, depending on the child, readiness to control elimination functions comes anywhere from 18 to 24 months of age. Any attempt to develop this habit in children must take into account physical readiness, teaching by instruction and observation, a calm parental attitude, and an absence of punishment for mistakes.

- As children reach a point that the world is open to them, they come up against obstacles and frustrations, usually in the form of limits set by parents. The result can be a strong negativism, expressed in the words "No," and "Mine," and in the crying, screaming, and stubbornness generally called temper tantrums.

- Genital play, massage, and masturbation are sexual behaviors exhibited by a majority of toddlers and young children. Parental attitudes about sexuality are most significant in teaching children about human sexuality, not only in an overt way by the kind of conversations they are able to have with their children, but more subtly also, in the body language, tone of voice, and attitudes conveyed in the family about sex.

- An important aspect of human sexuality is gender identity, a child's understanding of maleness and femaleness. Once a child is identified as "boy" or "girl," the family's culture determines what this means in terms of role behaviors.

- Children become social creatures by playing with others. Sharing, cooperation, conflict resolution, and intimacy are among the behaviors developed in part through social play. This function of socialization is demonstrated when play helps the child learn the society's rules and expectations.

- In early childhood, friendship is equated with play. Relationships revolve around games and exchanges of toys. By age three, children begin to differentiate other children as individuals rather than as a nebulous group of others. More advanced language and cognitive development allow preschoolers a wider range of interactions and more complex play activity.

- Because of social changes that take parents out of the house and into the workplace, alternate arrangements have to be made for the care of preschool children. Nursery-school, day care, babysitter, and Head Start programs are some child care options.

Student Activities

1. Plan a party for ten children ages three and four. Include in the plan the food you will serve, the decorations you will use, and the activities in which you would involve the children during the festivities.

2. Visit a day care center and rate it on an evaluation scale you have developed.

3. Write a story that you think would appeal to three-year-olds and enhance their verbal skills.

Helping Hands

National Head Start Association
201 N. Union Street, Suite 320
Alexandria, VA 22314
(703) 739-0875
www.nhsa.org

Association of Head Start director, parents and staff, and others working to upgrade Head Start services.

National Association for Family Day Care
725 15th Street, NW, Suite 505
Washington, DC 20005
(202) 347-3356
www.nafcc.org/about.html

Association of caregivers, parents and others interested in promoting high-quality family day care.

Child Care Information Exchange
Box 2890
Redmond, WA 98052
(206) 883-9394
www.ccie.com/

A publication written for day care directors. Articles cover practical issues of running a day care facility, including health and safety issues.

U.S. Consumer Product Safety Commission
5401 Westbard Avenue
Bethesda, MD 20207
(800) 638-2772

Establishes and enforces product safety standards. Operates a hotline with information about consumer products.

CHAPTER

Parenting the School-Age Child

Chapter Highlights

After reading Chapter 11, students should be able to:

- Recognize the importance of helping school-age children gain mastery over their environments
- Understand the physical, cognitive, and social changes of middle childhood
- Recognize the forces that develop a positive self-esteem
- Recognize the influence of sibling relationships on self-concept
- Understand the influence of television on school-age children

Chapter Contents

- A Time of Industry
  The Work of School
- Physical Changes of Middle Childhood
  Growth Patterns and Changes ▪ *Variations in Height* ▪ *Motor Skills in Middle Childhood* ▪ *Growth and Health* ▪ *Physical Fitness*
- Cognitive Changes in Middle Childhood
  Preoperational Stage ▪ *Concrete Operational Stage* ▪ *Truth and Deception* ▪ *Parental Perceptions of the Importance of Thinking* ▪ *Multiple Intelligences* ▪ *Triarchic Theory of Intelligence* ▪ *Moral Behavior*
- The Competent Child
  The Development of Self-Esteem ▪ *Peer Relations and Friendship* ▪ *The Allowance Balance*
- The Sibling Connection
  Birth Order ▪ *Siblings and Gender* ▪ *Physical Appearance* ▪ *Idiosyncratic Experiences* ▪ *Sibling Sameness* ▪ *Sibling Rivalry*
- Television and Parenting
  Family Viewing Patterns ▪ *Television and Cognitive Development* ▪ *Television and Violence* ▪ *Prosocial Behavior and Television* ▪ *Children and Commercialism* ▪ *Television Guidelines*

n April 12, 1945, Harry S Truman, a Missouri farmer's son, became president of the United States. Handicapped by poor eyesight as a child, Harry liked to stay close to home and in the company of his mother, Mattie. A pleasant, easy-going boy, he learned early the importance of having people like him. "When I was growing up, it occurred to me to watch the people around me to find out what they thought and what pleased them most. . . . I used to watch my father and mother closely to learn what I could do to please them, just as I did with my schoolteachers and playmates."

Intent on giving her adored son a good education, Mattie Truman convinced her husband John to leave the family farm and move to Independence, where Harry could go to a good school. Harry's first-grade teacher remembered that "he just smiled his way along" in school. His second-grade report card shows consistent high grades for spelling, reading, and deportment. He skipped the third grade and went directly into the fourth. By this time, he was reading "everything I could get my hands on—histories and encyclopedias and everything else." For his tenth birthday, his mother gave him an illustrated series of books, *Great Men and Famous Women*, a gift he considered a turning point in his life. He was particularly enthralled with the biography of Andrew Jackson, who was his mother's idol and a farmer who had become a president.

Middle childhood is in many ways a mirror into adult life, as the intellectual and social competencies of infancy and early childhood stabilize during the childhood years from six to ten. The school-aged Harry Truman—optimistic, intellectual, social, and pleasant—foretold the adult Harry Truman: the piano-playing president devoted to his family and friends and to the job he inherited when Franklin Roosevelt died suddenly. Luckily for Harry, at his most important stage of development, he had parents who not only encouraged him to develop his skills but gave him a sense of himself as a loved and valued human being.

A TIME OF INDUSTRY

In cultures throughout the world, the middle childhood period marks the time when children are expected to begin functioning as useful members of their society. In some societies, this is accomplished informally; elders teach children to make spears and other tools, to hunt and fish, to gather and prepare food, and to join in the rituals of the culture. Moral teaching is done through the oral tradition, storytelling and singing.

Much of the world relies on a formal tradition of educating its children through schooling. From ages six through approximately twelve years, most youngsters spend a large part of their day in organized schools, being taught by professional teachers. During these years, children change dramatically in terms of physical and cognitive development. The intention of the elementary school experience is to expose children to the world outside the home. Increased intellectual options and a greater range of social experiences help children develop the competencies they will need to eventually enter the worlds of adolescence and adulthood. Middle childhood is a bridge to those worlds. Whether children cross that bridge feeling worthwhile and competent, or inferior and incompetent, depends upon parents, teachers, and what the environment has to offer. Parents' tasks at this juncture are to help their children interpret the world outside the home, to assist them in meeting the demands of school, and to teach them how to manage the stresses and disappointments they inevitably encounter.

THE WORK OF SCHOOL

Now the child, aged from six or seven to approximately eleven years begins, in Erik Erikson's words, "to comprehend the tool worlds of his culture." In this stage, children receive some type of systematic instruction or schooling. The child now becomes a worker, winning recognition by producing things. In Western society, the educational system offers a culture of its own, with its specific goals, limits, achievements, and disappointments. Success at this stage depends on home and school environments.

The school-age-stage conflict is one of the periods Erik Erikson refers to as "industry." The key to its success is a sense of *competence*. Referring to this stage as one of *industry versus inferiority,* Erikson warns that, "many a child's development is disrupted when family life has failed to prepare him for school life, or when school life fails to sustain the promises of earlier stages." Feelings of inadequacy and inferiority result when a child is unable to learn those things his or her culture expects.

Cultures are distinct by the tools they use to live and work by. Middle childhood is a crucial time for children to learn to use these tools—be they fishing poles, plows, or computers.

During this stage of development, children establish work habits that will carry them through life. They develop a view of themselves that will influence their future choices and relationships. It is here that parental attitudes toward children make them feel "good" or "bad" about themselves. Children who are loved and accepted by their parents and seen as smart and capable, develop a positive self-concept—one that will motivate them to continue working hard toward their goals. These children show higher academic achievement during their school years than children who are not viewed positively by their parents (Chapman, Lambourne, and Silva, 1990). When parents are judgmental and unaccepting of their children's abilities, the children feel inadequate and they become dependent. Often this sense of worthlessness leads to hostility and aggression (Rahner, 1980).

At this point in their development, children begin to venture away from the family and their parents, and peer group activities become important. This is the time to join the Cub Scouts, play sports, take music lessons, join church groups, and so on. Problems arise when parents deny their children opportunities to be with others who share the children's interests, or force their children to do an activity they don't want to do on their after-school time.

Nurturing a child at this stage means providing an orderly and quiet space to do homework, making books and other reading materials available, and making children's friends welcome in the home. Clearly the challenge for parents during this stage is to accept that the child is pulling away from the relationship as it was. "Letting go" is a parent's most difficult task. Some of the feelings of loss can be assuaged by changing the parent-child relationship. The

A typical child in the United States today has books, maps, television, and even a computer at his or her disposal.

family can make time for shared cultural activities, such as visits to an art museum or a vacation that consists of everyone enjoying mutually-agreed-upon activities.

PHYSICAL CHANGES OF MIDDLE CHILDHOOD

Middle childhood is about competence: mastery of the environment, not just exploration of it. It is a time of increased physical skill and the ability to engage in more organized, group activities. New-found strengths in these physical-growth areas are directly related to the cognitive and social changes that are going on.

GROWTH PATTERNS AND CHANGES

Between the ages of six and twelve, children's faces take on a more mature look; the face becomes larger, the forehead flattens, the nose enlarges, and the jaw widens. In preadolescence, at about eleven and twelve years, girls are slightly taller and heavier than boys. Girls tend to accumulate more body fat than boys, which gives them a more curved shape. Boys develop more muscle, thus gaining an edge in strength and speed (Waley and Wong, 1988). This disparity grows during adolescence, as boys eventually surpass girls in height. By the end of elementary school, the child's brain is almost 100 percent of its mature size and weight. Neural connections continue to develop and, as the brain cells form increasingly intricate and extensive connections, children develop more complex and sophisticated cognitive abilities.

VARIATIONS IN HEIGHT

Physical growth is steady and moderate during middle childhood, except for a few spurt periods. Average height at six years of age is 3½ feet and average weight is 45 pounds; boys are a little taller and heavier than girls.

Weight gain during middle childhood ranges from 4½ to 8 pounds a year, and children grow two to three inches a year (Lowry, 1978). By age eleven, on average boys stand 4 feet 9½ inches and girls 4 feet 10 inches, a half inch taller. From ages five to eleven, the average child doubles his or her weight and grows one foot taller. A group of Scottish researchers found that between the ages of three and ten, children exhibit small spurts in growth: girls at ages four and a half, six and a half, eight and a half, and ten; boys a little later at four and a half, seven, nine, and ten and a half years (Butler, McKie, and Ratcliffe, 1990). A researcher noted for his studies of physical change, James Tanner (1973) cautioned that averages or norms do not represent the wide variation in height and weight of school-age children (Figure 11.1). He notes that the range is so wide "that if a child who was exactly average height at his seventh birthday grew not at all for two years, he would still be just within the normal limits of height attained at nine."

Figure 11.1
Growth Charts

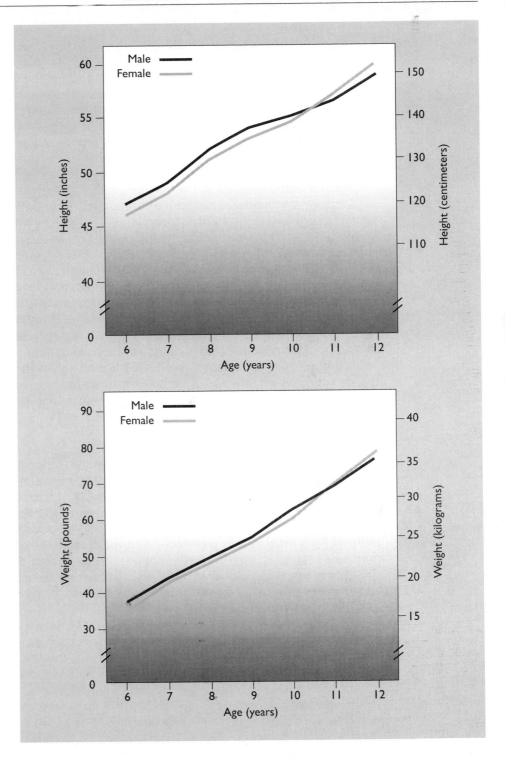

Variations in growth rate are the result of genetics, nutrition, and physical and emotional health. These differences are striking when observed cross-culturally. Howard Meredith (1973) plotted the average heights of eight-year-old boys from dozens of cultures around the world and he has found significant ethnic and cultural differences. The shortest children were found in South America, Asia, and the Pacific Islands; the tallest were in northern and central Europe, Australia, and the United States. The average eight-year-old Northern or Eastern European girl is about six inches taller than the average Indian girl. This difference may be a result of the preference for boys in India, which leads to inferior nutritional and medical care for girls (Poffenberger, 1981).

Studies of the changes in the pattern of physical growth in this century have shown that school-aged children in America are about four inches taller on average than were school-aged children of 40 years ago (Roche, 1979). Meredith suggests that, beginning at about the turn of the century, American children between the ages of six and fifteen grew about one inch taller every decade. In addition, they reached their adult height sooner, by about age fifteen (Meredith, 1976).

Children's bones grow longer and broaden in middle childhood, sometimes causing children discomfort, particularly at night. Children who grow rapidly might complain of pain when they are as young as four years. Parents should be cautioned that overly rigorous physical training can injure a child because the bones and ligaments are not fully mature at this age. Injuries to the shoulder, elbow, wrist, knee, and ankle are common among children participating in Little League programs and other demanding sports.

Motor Skills in Middle Childhood

Middle childhood is the time in which children develop mastery and control over their muscles (Lansdown and Walker, 1991). Most six-year-olds can tie their shoes, eight-year-olds can write in cursive, and ten-year-olds can play musical instruments. School-age children can build models, sew, make cookies, and groom themselves. Most studies show that boys are superior at activities involving gross motor movement, and they tend to be stronger and more muscular than girls. Girls are better coordinated, are more flexible, and have superior balance (Lansdown and Walker, 1991). Boys are generally better in activities like throwing, catching, and hitting balls, and girls do better in activities like gymnastics and rope jumping.

Physical differences alone do not account for female or male superiority in many sports activities. Boys generally have more experience in outdoor play that relies on gross motor activities (Harper and Sanders, 1979), and boys are more competitive than girls (Stoneman, Brody and MacKinnon, 1984). In a study of twelve-year-olds playing dodge ball, youngsters were divided into four groups: boys of low and high skills and girls of low and high skills. The high-skill girls were clearly bigger and better at dodge ball than the low-skill boys. Yet when these girls competed with the low-skill boys, they invariably lost the game. The results were the same whether the children were African American from a large urban environment or Hopi children from a reservation in Arizona. When the research team scrutinized the films of the games, they noticed that the girls pitted against the boys were easily distracted, did not give their full attention to the game, and played below their level. Some girls even stood around eating snacks. When the same girls were pitted against other girls they were sharp, alert, and competitive (Weisfield, Weisfield, and Callaghan, 1982). Expectations account for differences in performance by the girls. When boys and girls participated in the same physical education program with the same expectations, girls did as well as boys in activities such as situps, 50-yard dash, and broad jump. Both sexes improved with age and, after three years of the same training, girls on average surpassed the boys (Hall and Lee, 1984).

GROWTH AND HEALTH

While the common cold and other minor illnesses still occur in middle childhood, this stage is generally a healthy time for children. The number of ear infections and illnesses common to early childhood decrease as children's physical immunities build. The start of school is a good time for parents to check their children's eyesight and hearing, as there is a sharp increase in the diagnosis of nearsightedness, or myopia, at this time, and the inability to do well in school is sometimes due to difficulty in hearing the teacher.

Accidents are the leading cause of middle-childhood injuries and death, primarily because more coordinated children engage in more dangerous pastimes, such as roller blading and skateboarding. Team sports such as baseball and football involve potentially harmful bodily contact and injury from projectiles like pucks and baseballs. In a specific example, there has been a great increase in the number of injuries to children when in-line skating. In 1993, the number of children ages five to fourteen who were injured in this sport was 49.91 per 100,000. By 1995, the figure jumped almost 200 percent, to 146.19 per 100,000.

In 1987, the overall dath rate from acidental injuries was 15.56 per 100,000 children aged fourteen and under. By 1995, the number had decreased 26.4 percent to 11.45 per 100,000 children (National Center for Health Statistics, 1996). The specific reason for this decline is an increased use of seat belts and bike helmets, as well as an increased use of fire detectors and other safety items.

PHYSICAL FITNESS

Children are less active today than they were 30 years ago. Air conditioning, television, extension phones, and other conveniences—as well as family lifestyles—keep children in the house and excessively inactive. As a result, activities that promote the optimal functioning of the heart, lungs, muscles, and blood vessels are not as available to children as they once were. For this reason, one-fourth of school-age children are overweight; and many weigh at least 20 percent above their ideal weight, therefore being considered obese (Gortmaker, Dietz, Sobol, and Wehler, 1987).

The Informed Parent 11.1

Childhood Obesity: Risk Factors

A number of factors predispose a child to serious weight problems. Parents should try hard to teach good nutrition habits from an early age.

- Heredity plays a part in obesity. Obese children generally have one parent who is obese.
- Obesity is more common in low-income families than in middle-income families.
- Family eating habits contribute to childhood obesity. Children who are fed or rewarded with high-calorie treats are more likely to be obese than children who are fed healthy snacks.
- Obese children eat when provoked by external cues, such as the sight, taste, and smell of food, rather then by the cues of hunger.
- The more television children watch, the more likely they are to be obese.
- Obese children engage in fewer physical activities than do normal-weight children.
- Emotional trauma, such as that caused by a death in the family, abuse, or parental divorce can lead to obesity.

Source: Stunkard, et al., 1986; Kolata, 1986; Dietz and Gortmaker, 1995.

Obesity leads to physical and social problems. A majority of overweight children will be overweight adults predisposed to high blood pressure, heart disease, diabetes, and other medical problems (Epstein and Wing, 1987). Overweight children are sometimes rejected by their schoolmates, which leads to a lack of self-esteem and feelings of inadequacy. Parents must be very sensitive to children who have weight problems, as ridicule or other kinds of harsh treatment make children feel even worse about themselves.

Parents of school-age children should foster good nutrition habits, although although this is extremely difficult. Two-thirds of elementary school children eat lunches prepared at school, and most of these are too high in fat and salt content (Parcel, et al., 1987). In addition, children are exposed to television ads that promote snacks that are high in sugar, fat, and salt, and low in nutritional value. Also, working parents often rely on "fast foods" for dinner; and this generally means pizza, hamburgers and fries, and other high-calorie meals.

COGNITIVE CHANGES IN MIDDLE CHILDHOOD

During the school-age years, children become more sophisticated in their thinking, and they increasingly rely on logic and reasoning to understand the world. As they build up a pool of knowledge, they are less bound by intuitions based only on what they see, smell, and hear: Rather their thoughts become more flexible and organized, to the point where they understand the operations used to solve problems. Jean Piaget divided middle childhood into two stages of intellectual development. The first, the *preoperational* period, spans the years from about four to seven. Then a shift in thinking moves children forward in their abilities to problem solve (Cowan, 1978). Stage two is called the *concrete operational* stage, because, at about age seven, children organize their thoughts based on the properties of what they see.

PREOPERATIONAL STAGE: THE WORLD IN SYMBOLS (AGES TWO TO SEVEN)

Preschool children rapidly develop language skills and become more adept at motor skills. In the preoperational stage, they increase their use of symbols and verbal communication to manipulate the world. At this stage, their thinking is still rather rigid. Transformation or changes in the environment are not readily comprehended, although these children have some intuitive problem-solving abilities, as in enlarging a hole in a box in order to get to its contents. Most striking about this stage is the *egocentrism*, the inability to understand that others see, think, and feel differently than the child does. Preoperational children see the world only from their limited perspective. The moon follows them, and monsters come into their rooms at night. Here are some typical answers children in preoperational thought might give to questions about their environment:

Why does it get dark out?	So I can go to sleep.
Why does the sun shine?	To keep me warm.
Why is grass green?	Because green is my favorite color.

CONCRETE OPERATIONAL STAGE (AGES SEVEN TO ELEVEN)

The concrete operational stage lasts from about age seven to eleven or twelve. Although school-age children perform operations, they can only do so with concrete, tangible objects or concepts. A typical seven-year-old would have difficulty imagining what the world might be like in 100 years because no such model exists. At adolescence, this would not be a difficult task.

The concrete operational stage marks the time of logical thinking. The child now understands concepts and ideas that exist solely in the mind. He or she can think about things and figure out discrepancies and relationships. One of the most important operations of this period is called *conservation* of objects, the ability to see an object as the same even though its length, width, or shape changes. At this point, a child can understand that a tall, thin glass can hold the same amount of orange juice as a short, fat glass. If a ball of clay is strengthened into a skinny rope of clay, the quantity of clay remains the same. Piaget found that later in this stage children also begin to classify objects.

In spite of their increased cognitive capability, children in the concrete operational stage must rely on symbols and solutions based in the real world. They do not fully understand such concepts as freedom and justice. Nor can they imagine what the world would be like if men could bear children.

Children will experience a family vacation differently because of age, gender, and temperament differences. One child will love camping out in the woods; another will spend the day worrying about insects and bears. The first might write a school paper about the trip and join the Boy Scouts; the other might never mention the experience again.

The ability to reason and problem solve is not enough to ensure sucess in school. To adequately process information, children must be able to pay attention to environmental stimuli and store information in memory. Preschool children have short attention spans and are easily distracted (Kaplan, 1990). By school age, attention levels improve significantly and children have the ability to tune out distracting stimuli such as street noises or television when working on a task. Memory also improves through the school-age years, as children are able to process and recall information at adult levels (Stern, 1985).

TRUTH AND DECEPTION

Young children can have difficulty distinguishing fantasy from reality. As they grow cognitively and morally, they are better able to recognize what is true and what is deception. By that age of six or seven years, children are about to understand the difference between telling the truth and lying. Whether they do one or the other depends upon their age, their intentions, and what they have learned in the home. School-age children lie in different ways. Young children often present *fantastic lies*, those based on fantasy and most obvious to others.

"There was a green monster in my room last night," is a fantastic lie. Parents sometimes borrow from children's imaginations when they say, "If you don't go to sleep, the bogeyman will get you."

Children sometimes model their parents' exaggerations. They offer *imitative lies* when they say things like "I love you more than life itself." When parents enhance their stories to the point that they have the "worst" boss on the planet, or "the company would fall apart" if they ever left their job, children learn to make up the same kind of stories they've been hearing.

Social lies, or white lies, are used to save others from feeling badly. Children hear their parents say, "Tell Aunt Edna I'm not home," when they mean, "I don't want to talk on the phone right now." In turn they learn to be tactful in their own relationships. "My Mom won't let me" represents "I don't want to come over your house today."

Children who feel the need to escape from blame and possible punishment tell *defensive lies,* such as "The lamp was broken when I came home. The cat must have knocked it over." Parents who punish children for telling the truth about an incident, even if things have gone badly, actually reinforce the tendency to lie. If telling the truth is going to get a child into trouble, why would a child do this more than once? By accepting the truth, whatever it is, and praising a child for being honest, parents can help children accept responsibility for whatever they do.

The need for praise or acceptance leads to *compensatory lies*, as in "You're the best teacher I've ever had." Parents sometimes lie to get the attention they want, and children overhear them. "I only buy my flowers here. You have the best selection in town." When children see a parent receive a smile or special response to such a statement, they are likely to model this behavior.

Finally, there are lies built on the desire to get even with another person for a perceived grievance. A *vengeful lie* is meant to be hurtful, as in "Everyone in class thinks you're a jerk." Children learn to tell hurtful lies from the shows they watch on television and from parents who lie in this way.

Children have to be taught that credibility is important in human relationships. What people say must be true; otherwise their deceitfulness can lead to the loss of friends and other relationships. Children must know that once a person is seen as untrustworthy, it is difficult for them ever to be taken seriously—even when they do tell the truth.

Parents best accomplish modeling truthfulness by first being honest themselves and second by praising their children for telling the truth, while allowing them to accept the consequences of their behavior. "Thank you for telling me you broke the lamp. Please get the dustpan out and clean up the mess" is a more appropriate response to such an accident than punishing the act and forcing children to lie in the future when something goes wrong.

PARENTAL PERCEPTIONS OF THE IMPORTANCE OF THINKING

Psychologists define intelligence as the *capacity for learning, reasoning, and understanding*. It has always been noted that some children appear to have a better capacity than others, and therefore they are likely to perform better in school tasks. Interestingly, non-Western parents do not define intelligence the way Western psychologists do. In many non-Western cultures, intelligence is seen in the light of socially beneficial behaviors and motivations. Japanese college students, for example, include in their definition of intelligence such traits as being sympathetic and modest, and seeing another's persons point of view (Azuma and Kashiwagi, 1987); in rural African communities, intelligence is linked to social cooperativeness (Serpell, 1984).

In a large-scale study of parental beliefs and children's school performance, Lynn Okagaki and Robert Sternberg (1993) questioned parents of six cultures—Cambodian, Filipino, Vietnamese, Anglo-American, Mexican, and Mexican American. All parents thought it more important to teach first and second graders socially conforming behaviors (such as following directions and obeying school rules) than the more autonomous behaviors (such as making friends and making decisions). American-born parents saw teaching children how to ask questions and how to be creative as more important than teaching them to print and write neatly. In contrast, all of the immigrants parents thought that doing neat and orderly work was as important as learning basic information, developing their creativity, and learning to problem solve. The attitudes Okagaki and Sternberg noted take on special meaning in an increasingly competitive society built on a technological economy.

> . . . we found that parents differ in the relative importance they place on characteristics of an intelligent first-grade child. For minority parents, noncognitive attributes received ratings that were as high or higher than ratings for cognitive skills. Only Anglo-American parents generally gave higher importance ratings to cognitive abilities than to noncognitive abilities. (Okagaki and Sternberg, 1993)

The Theory of Multiple Intelligences

In referring to intelligence as "frames of mind," Howard Gardner (1993) theorizes the existence of multiple intelligences. Gardner proposes that there are at least eight kinds of cognitive competencies that make up the abilities, talents, and skills known generally as intelligence. These multiple intelligences are independent of each other, although they combine for certain kinds of thinking or skills. Gardner's eight competencies are:

1. **Linguistic Intelligence**   The ability to communicate through the use of words and phrases

2. **Musical Intelligence**   A sensitivity to and understanding of musical structures and symbols

3. **Logical–Mathematical Intelligence**   Ability to understand long chains of reasoning; the recognition of significant problems and the ability to solve them; scientific ability

4. **Spatial Intelligence**   Capacity to perceive the visual world accurately and re-create aspects of visual experience

5. **Bodily–Kinesthetic Intelligence**   Control of one's bodily motions and the capacity to handle objects skillfully

6. **Naturalist Intelligence**   Ability to relate to the environment and to adapt to the demands of the environment

7. **Interpersonal Intelligence**   Ability to notice and make distinctions among other people; a sense of other people's moods, temperaments, motivations, and intentions

8. **Intrapersonal Intelligence**   Access to one's own feelings; an understanding of one's own feelings and emotions

The eight intelligences are common to everyone, to different degrees. Sigmund Freud, for example, was extremely competent in both language ability and interpersonal intelligence, but he disliked music and had no skill at all in this area. In Western society today, linguistic and logical-mathematical intelligence are most valued; in the Inuit society of Alaska, spatial intelligence is most admired; and in the Germanic society of Mozart and Haydn, musical intelligence was most revered.

Although these intelligences are relatively independent of one another, Gardner believes they can be fashioned and combined in adaptive ways by individuals and cultures. A child can have a high level of logical-mathematical intelligence, good interpersonal skills, and deft athletic abilities. Gardner believes that there is considerable plasticity and flexibility in human growth, particularly during the early years. This plasticity operates within the confines of genetics, which predisposes individuals to carry out specific intellectual operations. Within each culture, the system of education—be it through mentoring, apprenticeships, or schools—must build upon a knowledge of these tendencies.

TRIARCHIC THEORY OF INTELLIGENCE

Robert Sternberg defines intelligence as "a kind of mental self-management—the mental management of one's life in a constructive, purposeful way." It involves the ability to shape, adapt to, and select one's environment. Sternberg describes three different ways in which intelligence is used to manage the environment.

Environmental adaptation refers to the understanding of one's life setting and the adaptation to it. An inner-city child, for example, has to be more alert to streets and cars than a child living in a rural community. When an environment proves disagreeable or maladaptive, a capacity for *environmental selection* comes into play. Knowing when to quit—because of differences in values, incompatibility, or lack of interest—is an important part of adequate functioning. At times when adaptation is impossible and selection of a new environment is too difficult to accomplish, *environmental shaping* becomes an option. A child who feels unwanted at home may turn to a teacher or relative for love and appreciation.

Sternberg identifies three types of intelligence, each able to utilize adaptation, selection, or shaping to direct one's life. *Componential intelligence* refers to acquiring information, evaluating it, and using this knowledge to problem solve. When a child is assigned a school paper, he first decides on a topic. Information is gathered on the subject, the paper is drafted and then edited and proofread for clarity, spelling, and grammar. The finished product is evaluated using criteria set by the teachers, and if anything is lacking the student reworks the paper.

Children like to take things apart and put them back together again. Often the only way to really learn something is by "hands-on experience." Building a canoe or learning to operate a computer are among the tasks that require *experiential intelligence,* a type of thinking that aids in the understanding of novel or unfamiliar tasks. Children who can see connections between past learnings and new experiences are displaying this type of creative intelligence.

Contextual intelligence colloquially known as "street smarts," is reflected in how well individuals adapt to their external environment. Contextual skills include sensitivity to what others want and need, and an understanding of environmental obstacles and how best to maneuver around them.

Eskimo children develop high levels of spatial intelligence because of the harshness of their environment. They must notice the smallest breaks in the ice, judge weather conditions accurately, and find their way back in the tundra.

MORAL BEHAVIOR: HOW CHARACTER TAKES SHAPE

Moral behavior is generally thought to include obeying rules and regulations—those laid down by parents, a school system, or the government, as well as the religious teachings and other customs in the environment that influence children's thoughts, attitudes, and values. But in actuality, moral behavior is far more. It has to do with goodness and decency, the way one individual treats another, the sympathy and empathy one person can show for another, respect for others, and basic kindness.

Children are not born "good" or "bad"; rather they acquire their moral beliefs from the people around them. Mowing the lawn for an elderly neighbor, giving up the family dog because he sheds too much, speaking politely to relatives, remembering birthdays, ignoring appointments, lying to people on the phone—are common adult behaviors that children take note of. From these interactions, children learn appropriate and inappropiate ways of dealing with others.

Social-learning researchers have proposed that moral behavior is the result of reinforcement, punishment, and imitation. If children are rewarded for following specific rules, they are more likely to repeat the behavior that won them praise. If they are punished for behaving in ways adults in their environment find unacceptable, the possibility of repeating this behavior will decrease. While noted child psychiatrist Robert Coles (1997) agrees that rewards, punishments, reprimands, reminders, sermons, lectures, and readings from books have an impact on children's behavior, he believes that the most persuasive moral teaching comes from parents and other adults who, on a daily basis and over extended time, model actions for behavior toward others. In his landmark book *The Moral Intelligence of Children,* Coles pointed out that during the elementary-school years children become intensely moral creatures. During this time they are trying to figure things out, understand the people around them, discover how to best make it in the world outside the home. While school offers them formal lessons in morality through the books, videos, songs, poems, and photos they promote, children also get "character-in-action" lessons: what their parents say, why they say it, what they do, how they speak of what they do, if they speak at all. A father who plays golf on Saturdays and Sundays, his only days off from work, sends his children a silent message about the role of family in his life. Parents who do the dishes together and chat amicably about the day's events send a different message. Coles believes that ultimately it is parents who give shape to the "goodness" or "badness" their children display.

> We grow morally as a consequence of learning how to be with others, how to behave in this world, a learning prompted by taking to heart what we have seen and heard. The child is a witness; the child is an ever-attentive witness of grown-up morality—or lack thereof; the child looks and looks for cues as to how one ought to behave, and finds them galore as we parents and teachers go about our lives, making choices, addressing people, showing in action our rock-bottom assumptions, desires, and values, and thereby telling those young observers much more than we may realize (Coles, 1997).

A majority of American households have companion animals. Children must be taught to respect animals as members of the family, entitled to good care and kindness. Under no circumstances, should children be allowed to be cruel to animals.

The Competent Child

The school-age years are truly "the wonder years" as children learn to think, study, and get along with others. As early as five years old, children learn how to count, recognize words, and write their own names. They pick up information from storybooks and television, if the information relates to their own life experiences. This is also the time they first play in groups, learn to negotiate and cooperate, tease and joke with schoolmates. By age six, children are comparing themselves to others. Socially, they become quite rule-minded. There is a freedom and easiness about children's learning as they enter school, a sense of wonder that often dissipates by the end of elementary school. In American society, parents and school officials put extreme pressure on children to achieve at levels beyond their age. Kindergarten children, who should be learning to enjoy school, are sometimes expected to do homework; first graders just learning to read are given exams in some school settings. Some states require six-year olds to pass a standardized test before entering first grade. Psychologist David Elkind worries that during this critical period in development "the child's budding sense of competence is frequently under attack, not only from inappropriate instructional practices . . . but also from the hundred and one feelings of hurt, frustration and rejection that mark a child's entrance into the world of schooling, competition and peer-group involvement" (Elkind, 1981).

The Informed Parent 11.2

A School Primer for Parents

When visiting a school, trust your eyes. What you see is what your child is going to get.

- Teachers should talk to small groups of children or individual youngsters; they shouldn't just lecture.

- Children should be working on projects, active experiments, and play; they shouldn't be at their desks all day filling in workbooks.

- Children should be dictating and writing their own stories or reading real books.

- The classroom layout should have reading and art areas and space for children to work in groups.

- Children should create freehand artwork, not just color or paste together adult drawings.

- Most importantly, watch the children's faces. Are they intellectually engaged, eager, and happy? If they look bored or scared, they probably are.

For many children, school learning is a passive experience, a part of what is called the *traditional classroom*, where children sit at desks and teachers do most of the talking. Rules, decision-making, and curriculum are the responsibility of the teacher alone. Children are expected to complete teacher-assigned tasks and respond in class when called on. Schoolwork is judged on the basis of standardized assessments. In the *open classroom,* children participate in the educational experience. Rules are more flexible; children share in decision making; and learning occurs at its own pace. Children judge themselves on the basis of their past efforts. The teacher generally moves from area to area, guiding children when they need help (Minuchin and Shapiro, 1983).

While studies show that children in traditional classrooms do slightly better academically, those in open settings enjoy school more, have more respect for classmates, and tend to be more independent (Walberg, 1986).

It is difficult to look at the education of children in general terms because there are such great differences between schools—for example, an inner-city school populated with children from low-income families, and a suburban school populated with middle- and upper-class youngsters. Jonathon Kozol (1991) has written at length about the impact of poverty on the educational system. He has described schools that are filthy and overcrowded, and some even housed in abandoned factories. Science classes are without microscopes, and reading classes are taught in bathrooms. In one elementary school, one counselor served 3,600 students. Even with the most attentive and concerned parent at home, it is hard to imagine that schooling under such circumstances can be productive for children.

Parental attitudes greatly affect the way children view school and learning. A parent who had an unsatisfying experience in school may project a negative attitude about education, and this view can influence a child's expectations and performance. Parents who value education and support the school's objectives are more likely to raise children who view school positively (Hetherington and Parke, 1993).

THE DEVELOPMENT OF SELF-ESTEEM

Eleanor Roosevelt was first lady of the United States when her husband Franklin was president. In contrast to Harry Tuman, Eleanor lived a sad and lonely existence as a child. When she was born, her mother, Anna, was disappointed that the baby wasn't a boy and she wrote that her new daughter was "a more wrinkled and less attractive baby than the average." A beautiful and vain woman, Anna took a great disliking to her plain-looking child, whom she nicknamed "Granny." Eleanor later described her childhood as a time of anxiety and fear. She was afraid of the dark, of dogs, of horses, of snakes, of other children, of being scolded, and of being disliked. Eleanor later wrote ". . . I was a solemn child, without beauty and painfully shy and I seemed like a little old woman entirely lacking in the spontaneous joy and mirth of youth" (Lash, 199).

Children begin to perceive themselves as separate and distinct human beings while they are still in infancy. This perception, called *self-concept*, is the basis of identity. A child's sense of self comes from experience with and evaluation by parents and other significant people. *Self-esteem* is a reflection of what a child thinks about his or her self. It refers to a sense of worth—the positive form of which comes down to thinking "I'm OK", "I'm a good person," "I have a lot to offer this world." While the child Eleanor Roosevelt thought herself ugly and dull because of her mother's disappointment, she did believe she had something to offer the world because her father loved her and thought she was a special person.

School-age children rate themselves on three self-esteem scales: cognitive competence, physical ability, and social worth (Harter, 1982). They combine the experiences from each of these settings into an overall sense of self-esteem. During the first years of elementary school, self-esteem often drops as children adjust their self-perceptions to fit the opinions of others and their school performance (Stipek and MacIver, 1989). From about fourth grade on, self-esteem rises, dropping again when children enter middle school (Nottelmann, 1987).

A powerful determinant of how children view their academic performance is parental expectations and standards. As early as third grade, some children underestimate their academic competence; they rely more on their parents' perceptions than they do on more objective evidence of competence, such as grades and test scores (Phillips, 1984, 1987). When very young children do not understand their own adequacies, they tend to overestimate their abilities (Phillips and Zimmerman, 1990). High-achieving children, if they believe themselves to be incompetent, often avoid challenging tasks and lack persistence in their efforts (Harter, 1983, 1985). Children who see themselves as incompetent are also placed at risk for symptoms of depression (Haley, et al., 1985).

A number of studies have linked parental warmth to the child's sense of self-worth (Baumrind, 1967, 1971; Coopersmith, 1967). Children's perceived academic competence is particularly related to father warmth, in tasks that lead to both success and failure (Wagner and Phillips, 1992).

The literature on self-esteem reveals four factors identified as significant to the development of a sense of self-worth. They include 1) the degree to which parents show respect and acceptance of their children; 2) the children's history of success and the recognition they get for their efforts; 3) the goals children have and the value placed on those goals; and 4) children's ability to defend themselves when their self-esteem is attacked (Coopersmith, 1967). Researchers point out that children must have clearly defined and enforced limits, but within those limits there is latitude for individual actions. This is basically the parenting style known as authoritative or democratic (Chapter 7). When children are raised in an environment of disrespect for who they are, and if they feel rejected, isolated, unloved, and—worse—unlovable, they come to believe that their actions have no meaning and that they have limited control over their own lives. Overprotective parents, those that want to save their children from experiencing failure, keep their children from becoming self-reliant. Children whose parents encourage them to problem solve on their own develop stronger feelings of competence in the face of school work than children whose parents solved problems for them.

It is not clear what influences school success—child-rearing practices or the messages parents give children regarding their academic efforts. What often separates children is the explanation they give for the cause of their successes and failures. High achievers attribute their successes to mastery. When they succeed, they assume the cause is their own ability. When they fail they also look to themselves, but believe that with more effort or some other change the failure can be reversed. Children with a negative sense of self often credit luck and other outside forces for their successes but look to their own abilities for their failures. They do not believe effort on their part affects performance, and therefore working harder does not seem to be a reasonable option (Chapman and Skinner, 1989; Dweck and Leggett, 1988). In a study of children who were not doing well in math, researchers found that the parents of these children felt their offspring were less capable than others and needed to work harder to do well (Parsons, Adler, and Kaczala, 1982). When things go wrong, low self-esteem children tend to give up. The result is frustration, anger, and a feeling of impotence, which can turn into vengeful behavior toward others (Schaefer and Millman, 1981).

More often than boys, girls get messages from parents and teachers that they have less ability when they don't do well. Therefore, more often than boys, girls blame their own abilities when they do poorly (Dweck and Elliott, 1983).

The Spirit of Parenting

The People, Yes

"I love you,"
    said a great mother.
"I love you for what you are,
knowing so well what you are.
And I love you more yet, child,
deeper yet than ever, child,
for what you are going to be,
knowing so well you are going far,
knowing your great works are ahead,
ahead and beyond,
yonder and far over yet."

Carl Sandburg

Sometimes parents and teachers do not realize the subtle messages they give children. In a renowned study called *Pygmalion in the Classroom,* researchers Robert Rosenthal and Lenore Jacobson (1974) identified a group of elementary-school children as "intellectual bloomers," those who were most likely to show great academic gains during the next school year. Teachers were told the names of the students who were poised to spurt ahead. Eight months later, when given IQ tests, those children identified as "intellectual bloomers" scored much higher than they had on previous tests. What is significant about this study is that Rosenthal and Jacobson deceived the teachers. The "intellectual bloomers" were in reality no different than others in their group. They had been chosen at random. What then caused these children to make the gains they showed? The researchers propose that teacher expectations provoked the advances. Once teachers thought certain children were "intellectual bloomers" they gave them extra encouragement in subtle ways—a little extra attention, a smile or nod, a word of praise. These children got the message from teachers that they were bright and talented, so they behaved like bright and talented youngsters (Rosenthal and Jacobson, 1974).

Parents have the same effect on children, and parents convey their expectations blatantly and subtly. A look at the bedrooms of children show marked differences, beginning long before children are able to express their own preferences. Boys' rooms are often loaded with sports equipment, pennants, cars, and trucks. The primary color is blue. Girls' rooms are filled with dolls, children's furniture, and kitchen goods. Pink and yellow are the colors most used in girls' rooms (Pomerleau, et al., 1990). Boy toys promote spatial skills, which boys later excel at; girl toys encourage nurturance and the caring for others.

The Informed Parent 11.3

Making School a Success

There are many steps that parents can take to help their children be successful in school. Some have to do with establishing routines for the child, some with actions parents themselves can take. If you are raising a school-age child, review this list to see how many of the steps you can incorporate into the family routine.

At Home

1. Set a daily routine for your child. Have a set time for meals, storytelling, bath, and sleep.
2. Be sure your child eats a nutritious breakfast. If your family life is too hectic in the morning, see if your school has a breakfast program.
3. Be sure the child is dressed appropriately, in clothing meant for easy movement. Be sure clothes are clean and mended.
4. Give the child enough time to get dressed in the morning. Let him or her choose the clothes, within reason, and do as much buttoning and zipping as possible.
5. Read to your child every day. Get him or her a library card and go together to the library often. Review television shows for content, and limit viewing.
6. Provide educational experiences. Take your child to the library, museums, movies, grocery stores, parks, playgrounds, concerts, and plays.
7. Give children responsibility at home. Have them take care of their own sleeping area, take out trash, feed pets, etc.

At School

1. If possible, have the child meet the teacher and see the classroom before school starts.
2. Make sure your child gets to school on time every day. Habits like good attendance begin early.
3. Send any money requested to school in an envelope labeled with your child's name, the home room, and how the money is to be used.
4. Print your child's name on all clothing, book bags, lunch boxes, etc., to prevent mixups.
5. Wait to see what supplies are asked for before buying anything.
6. Respond to teachers' notes or calls promptly.
7. Inform the school and teacher of any changes in the child's home life that may affect school experience, such as moving, a death or divorce in the family, or a new baby.
8. Attend all parent-teacher conferences. Before going, make a list of questions and concerns you have. Share information about the child with the teacher. Find out how you can help at home.

While stereotyped expectations are not as rigid as they have been in previous generations, it is very difficult for parents to give their children messages that are at odds with what has long been assumed is the proper gender role for boys and girls. Studies show that both mothers and fathers use more emotional words when talking to their daughters, and they are more likely to talk about sad events and feelings. With their sons, parents are more likely to encourage physical activity and aggression. Fathers tend to compliment their daughters on their appearance, protect them more than they do their sons, and show them more affection. They roughhouse more with sons, encourage sports participation, and punish them more harshly than they do their daughters (Siegal, 1987).

Success in school is related to parental expectations. In a study asking adults to picture an intelligent child, 57 percent of women and 71 percent of men visualize a boy. As early as first grade, parents think math and science are male domains. When girls bring home poor grades in these subjects, parents believe girls are just not as smart at boys when it comes to math and science. When boys bring home poor grades in the same subjects, they are encouraged to work harder (Snellman, 1992). When parents give girls help in math and science when they need it and encourage them to do well in difficult subjects girls succeed at the same level as boys (Houser, 1985).

Myra and David Sadker (1994) have taped hundreds of hours of class sessions in schools throughout the country and have written at length about the differences in the academic expectations for boys and girls. They propose that "sitting in the same classroom, reading the same textbooks, listening to the same teacher, boys and girls receive very different educations." In *Failing at Fairness: How America's Schools Cheat Girls*, they note that in the early grades, girls generally outperform boys on achievement tests. By the time they graduate high school, girls are behind. In the intervening years, they have been taught to speak quietly, defer to boys, and avoid math and science. Their emphasis changes; instead of academic success, girls are taught to concentrate on neatness and on their appearance. Girls also become increasingly critical of their own schoolwork and more complimentary of others' work.

While in elementary school 31 percent of white girls reported that they liked the way they looked. By middle school, their satisfaction level decreased to 11 percent, a 20-point decline. For Hispanic girls, the change was from 47 percent to 21 percent, a 26-point decline. Boys have a distinct advantage in school. They get more attention from teachers, win the majority of scholarships, and eventually end up in higher-paying jobs than girls. But the Sadkers believe boys pay a high price for these advantages. When boys—who are raised to be active, aggressive, and independent—enter schools, they are expected to be quiet, passive, and conforming. In an uneasy compromise, many walk a tightrope between compliance and rebellion. To keep the balance, schools go the extra mile for males and give them more resources and attention. Nevertheless, with expectations of boys so high, many can not make the grade. Boys at the bottom, as problems in need of special control or assistance, are more likely to fail courses, miss a promotion, or drop out of school (Sadker and Sadker, 1994).

The Informed Parent 11.4

Parenting Toward Cognitive Competence

Robert Sternberg and Wendy Williams (1995) propose that parents can foster cognitive competence in their children by mastering a number of strategies. They have suggested seven lessons on what not to do, what to do, and how to do it.

Lesson 1

- **Do not** tell children they don't have the ability to do certain kinds of things, or the personality to do other kinds of things, or the motivation to complete something they might start.
- **Do** tell children they have the ability to meet just about any challenge life offers.
- **Do** tell them they must decide how hard they are willing to work to meet these challenges.
- **Do** teach children that the main limitation on what they can do is what they tell themselves they can't do.

Lesson 2

- **Do not** encourage children to view you or their teacher as the one who should ask questions, and the student as the one to answer them.
- **Do not** perpetuate the belief that the roles of parent and of teacher are ones of teaching children the "facts."
- **Do** realize—and make sure children realize—that what matters most is not the answers to questions but rather the child's ability *to ask* the right questions.
- **Do** help children learn not only how to answer questions but also how to ask them and how to formulate the right questions.

Lesson 3

- **Do not** work with children to find things their parents had always hoped they would love to do.
- **Do** help children find what really excites them, remembering that it may not be what really excites their parents or what parents wish would really excite their children.

Lesson 4

- **Do not** always encourage children to play it safe—with courses, with teachers, with intellectual challenges.
- **Do** teach children to sometimes take intellectual risks and to develop a sense of when to take risks and when not to.

(continued)

Lesson 5

- **Do not** always look for—or allow children to look for—the outside enemy who is responsible for the child's failures (teachers, other students, illnesses, etc.).
- **Do not** always push children because you think they can't do it for themselves.
- **Do** teach children to take responsibility for themselves.
- **Do** help them develop their own internal push, so you don't have to push them: Enable them to do it for themselves.

Lesson 6

- **Do not** always reward children immediately.
- **Do not** allow children to expect immediate rewards, to get what they want right away.
- **Do not** emphasize the here-and-now at the expense of the long term.
- **Do** teach children to wait for rewards.
- **Do** teach them that the greater rewards are often those that come down the line. Show them examples in your own life and describe how these examples may apply to them.
- **Do** emphasize the long term, not just the here-and-now.

Lesson 7

- **Do not** teach children to form a point of view but not to try to understand the points of views of others.
- **Do** teach children the importance of understanding, respecting, and responding to the points of view of others.

In recent years, girls have been encouraged to take more math and science courses; books like the Sadkers', as well as teacher-training programs, have promoted gender awareness in teaching. Some parents, aware of gender differences in the schools, have opted for single-sex schooling at this point in their children's development.

School can be as difficult a place for minority children as it is for some boys. Until recently, schools did not acknowledge the cultural traditions and experiential differences of the various children in their settings. African American children are exposed to more noise, activity, and people in their lives than most white children. At school they are expected to remain still and quiet, listen to one speaker at a time, and work alone rather than with other children (Hale-Benson, 1986). Often language and speech patterns of African American children differ from those of their teachers, making communication between them difficult.

The Informed Parent 11.5

Helping with Homework

Supervising schoolwork at home puts parents on a tightrope over two fearsome chasms. On one side lies the danger of making a child overly dependent, negative, or downright defiant; on the other—school failure. What a choice! While perfect solutions are, as always, only dreams, here are some suggestions that have helped other parents.

Rule No. 1: *Wait to be asked.*
If neither your child nor his teachers ask for your help, it probably is not needed. Trying to force a child to work with you may short-circuit any desire to come to you in the future. If you sense trouble, make an appointment with the school for advice. Remember that school-work is the territory of the child, who needs to feel responsible and in control.

Rule No. 2: *Be available and supportive when help is requested.*
Your attitude toward the importance of homework will shape your child's. If a TV program is more important to you than a need to practice multiplication tables, don't be surprised if the youngster agrees.

Rule No. 3: *Focus on process, not product.*
Often the ultimate product (the answer, the perfect paragraph, one day's assignment) is secondary to the process of learning. Think about the learning you are encouraging:
a. "If I whine enough, I can get someone else to do my work for me."
b. "Every time I ask for help, we wind up in a fight because the whole thing isn't perfect enough."
c. "It was sort of fun figuring out the answers, even though neither Dad nor I really understood the questions at first."

Rule No. 4: *The final product must represent the pupil's work.*
Don't deprive your child of valuable learning because you're afraid of a bad grade. You won't get invited to go along to college or to a job.

Rule No. 5: *Children are often hardier than they would like us to believe.*
If assignments seem unreasonably long, check the following: Can she organize time effectively? Are study times at school used productively? Are telephone conversations interfering? If the child is truly overloaded, a conference at school should be scheduled so that you, your child, and the teacher can discuss the problem.

Rule No. 6: *Let him fight his own buttles whenever possible.*
Your moral support is essential, but it is the student's job to learn to get along with people in the world—including teachers!

(continued)

Rule No. 7: *Provide the tools necessary for success.*
Your child needs a quiet, well-lit place to study, a regular routine, and a moratorium on weeknight TV and video games until homework is satisfactorily completed. Be tough; this is important. Older students also may need a tape recorder, word processor with a spell checker, a good dictionary and thesaurus, and transportation to library if they give you advance notice.

Rule No. 8: *You don't have to know everything.*
Parents feel uncomfortable when they don't know everything, but admitting your confusion and working problems through with your child may be the best teaching you can do.

The American school system reflects the overall values of American society, making competition and achievement the highest motivations. Some minority cultures, like the Japanese and Chinese, stress hard work and the drive to achieve, and children from these cultures generally excel academically in school.

Peer Relations and Friendship

Self-esteem and peer relationships go hand in hand. Children who perceive themselves positively are better able to build relationships within same-age social groups known as *peers*. During middle childhood, children spend about 40 percent of their time with peers. On average, they have five close friends.

An awareness of other people and an ability to imagine what they are thinking and feeling is part of social success. In middle childhood, children build skills in *perspective-taking*. Those children best at perspective-taking are also better at problem solving in social situations (Eisenberg, et al., 1987). The ability to put oneself in another's place and also to know that others can do the same is an advantage when dealing with people. Perspective-taking children are the most popular among their peers because they are sensitive and cooperative in their relationships.

Children have a preference for other children who are physically attractive, extroverted, and supportive. Children who have poor social skills and are deficient in perspective-taking often treat others badly, and therefore they are less popular with peers. These rejected children are aggressive and immature, and given to conflictual relationships with peers (Coie and Koeppl, 1990). Often they come from homes in which anger, hostility, and punishment is the norm (Patterson, 1982). Studies show that neglected children, those whose parents do not give them adequate physical or emotional care, are often shy in social relationships and less likely to interact with their peers. However, they are often as skilled socially as average children, and they are not particularly disliked by their peers (Asher and Wheeler, 1985; Coie and Kupersmidt, 1983).

Because rejected children go through their school years feeling alienated and unhappy (French and Waas, 1985), they are at risk to drop out of school and to move into adolescent delinquency and then adult criminality (Parker and Asher, 1987).

Parents are best able to teach children the social problem-solving skills they need as they move into the world of peers, teachers, and even strangers. Now that children are cognitively able to view the world logically, parents must provide opportunities and help in problem solving. At this point, parents begin to relinquish some of the control they have had over their children. Now parent and child are engaged in *coregulation,* a transitional form of supervision in which parents exercise general oversight, while permitting children to be in charge of moment-by-moment decision making (Berk, 1993). Eleanor Maccoby describes the coregulation relationship this way:

> The parental tasks . . . are threefold: First, they must monitor, guide and support their children at a distance—that is, when their children are out of their presence; second, they must effectively use the times when direct contact does occur; and third, they must strengthen in their children the abilities that will allow them to monitor their own behavior, to adopt acceptable standards of good (conduct), to avoid undue risks, and to know when they need parental support and guidance. Children must be willing to inform parents of their whereabouts, activities, and problems so that parents can mediate and guide them when necessary (Maccoby, 1984).

THE ALLOWANCE BALANCE

In the early part of the century, American children left their farm and factory lives and headed for the schoolyard. This left them basically without money at their disposal, and thus the notion of an *allowance,* regular financial aid from parents, was born. Although middle-class parents were first to adopt this habit, eventually parents from all social classes began to think that giving children a regular allowance would help them learn to manage money wisely (Mortimer, et al., 1994). Although there is general agreement among child psychologists that children need an allowance, there is considerable debate over what this allowance should be used for. Some parents link allowance to the performance of household chores; other believe this link undermines the notion that everyone in a family should freely contribute to household maintenance. There are parents who make an allowance contingent on "good" behavior, but others believe this undermines the genuine motivation to behave well. Most experts feel children should not be paid for routine household chores, but payment for special tasks that might require hiring outside help (such as snow shoveling, washing the car, lawn mowing, or babysitting) is acceptable (Henderson, 1988). Even though many parents believe that giving children an allowance will help them learn effective money management, research has shown that this is not the case. One study found that children who received a "no-strings-attached" allowance had a better understanding of money than those whose allowance was conditional on chores or those who did not get an allowance at all (Abramovitch, Freedman, and Pliner, 1991).

In a study of class differences in England, researchers found that middle-class parents were more likely than working-class parents to give children an allowance, and at an earlier age. This of course may be due to the parents' greater financial resources. A more recent study found that children from single-parent homes are given more spending money and greater responsibility to buy their own clothes and other necessities—resulting most likely from a need to relieve parental burdens (Stipp, 1988).

In 1994, Jeyland T. Mortimer studied 1,000 Minnesota Public School ninth graders, three-fourths of whom received an average of $8.86 per week of allowance. Children who got an allowance had been receiving one for an average of five years, beginning when they were 8.8 years old. About 80 percent of the students reported that they did household work for their allowance. A majority of the students earned additional money by performing "extra" jobs for pay; their total average allowance went up to about $15 per week. Not surprisingly, more than one-half felt they didn't have enough money to buy the things they wanted. The researchers found that parents of higher socioeconomic levels were more likely to give an allowance than parents of lower socioeconomic status. And two-parent families were less likely to give children an allowance than were parents in other family types. While both boys and girls were equally likely to receive an allowance, boys more often than girls had to do chores for their money.

> The fact that boys' allowance was more likely to be contingent upon the performance of household chores may reflect parental expectations regarding the familial and economic roles of adult men and women. Females are traditionally socialized to contribute to family tasks out of love, nurturance, or a sense of obligation, while males are socialized to earn money in exchange for their work. (Mortimer, et al.,1994).

A major concern of the researchers was their finding that ninth-grade students who received a regular allowance were less likely than other students to view work generally as a source of intrinsic satisfaction. In other words, an allowance may divert attention from the rewards that work has to offer.

THE SIBLING CONNECTION

In the book *Having Our Say: The Delany Sisters' First 100 Years,* Bessie said of the 103-year-old sister she'd lived with her entire life, "If Sadie is molasses, then I am vinegar: Sadie is sugar and I'm the spice. . . . We were best friends from Day One."

The sibling relationship, which can go on for an amazing number of years, offers a special closeness. Brothers and sisters provide companionship for each other, as well as help with tasks and comfort in times of stress (Furman, et al., 1989). If mother and father are working long hours, older siblings often become surrogate parents. They cook meals, change diapers, and help younger children with their homework, taking on a role that has lifelong implications, because the caregiver sibling often takes on this role in other relationships.

The Informed Parent 11.6

Living with a Difficult School-Age Child

Here are some general strategies and solutions to help you live with a difficult youngster:

1. Establish a neutral or objective emotional climate in which to deal with your child. Try not to respond in an emotional and instinctive manner, which is unproductive.

2. Don't take your child's behavior personally. Temperament is innate, and your child is not purposely trying to be difficult or irritating. Don't blame him or her, or yourself.

3. Try to prioritize the issues and problems surrounding your child. Some are more important and deserve greater attention. Others are not as relevant and can be either ignored or put "way down the list."

4. Focus on the issues of the moment. Do not project into the future.

5. Consider your own temperament and behavior, and how they might also be difficult. Think how you might need to adjust yourself a bit to encourage a better fit with your child.

6. Anticipate impending high-risk situations, and try to avoid or minimize them. Accept the possibility that this may be a difficult day or circumstance, and be prepared to make the best of it.

7. Review your expectations of your child. Are they realistic and appropriate? When your youngster does something right, praise him or her and reinforce the specific behaviors that you like.

Psychologists view sibling behaviors in terms of a *shared environment* and a *nonshared environment.* Shared environments include those things in an environment that are the same for all the children in the family. These would include things like the basic personality of parents, the family house, the neighborhood, religious affiliation, the amount of books in the house, and the family dog. Nonshared environments refers to those things that are not the same for all the children. These include friends, relationships with relatives or other adults, and the individual way parents relate to each child in the family.

Robert Plomin and Denise Daniels (1987) reviewed studies of twins, adopted children, and other siblings in an effort to distinguish the influences of genetics from environmental experiences. They concluded that siblings are no more alike than children who happen to live across the street from one another. They believe that the small similarities noted between siblings are the result of genetics, but the terrific differences between sisters and brothers are due to their unshared environment, the distinct worlds that exist for children within the family structure. To Plomin and Daniels, factors often thought to be important in shaping personality, particularly birth order, are not nearly as influential as children's perceptions about parental treatment of the children

While siblings appear to have the same environment, each actually experiences the world in a different way. Friends, school experiences, and parental treatment all produce an *unshared environment* for siblings, leading them to develop into unique individuals. The relationship between siblings is based on competition, comparison, and cooperation.

in the family. Factors like parental love, favoritism, attention, and control affect children differently, as do popularity with peers and sibling rivalry.

Despite their claims to the contrary, parents do not treat their children alike. Innumerable studies have shown how the temperament of a child influences parent-child interactions (Chapter 9). They smile, compliment, touch, punish, and encourage children in varying degrees.

Lois Hoffman (1991) points out that children are perpetually comparing themselves to others, particularly others who are their brothers and sisters. What they often see is what social psychologists call *relative deprivation;* that is, what they are not getting, as compared to what they think their siblings are getting. Even in a loving family, a child may think himself unloved if he believes a sibling is favored. Hoffman notes that there are five primary sources of sibling differences, all influencing the parent-child relationship. These are ordinal position or birth order, the age of the child when an event in the family occurs, gender of the child, the child's physical appearance, and any idiosyncratic experiences.

BIRTH ORDER

Studies indicate that fathers talk to and touch first-born male infants more than subsequent children (Parke and Sawin, 1975). Dinner-table conversation is directed to the first-born more than to other children; first-borns are given more responsibilities than later-borns, but their activities are interfered with more (Hilton, 1967; Rothbart, 1971). Higher professional status and higher IQ scores have been linked to ordinal position, with first-borns coming out on top. But they also tend to be more anxious, and they are less popular with their peers than later-born children (Schacter, 1963; Zajonc, 1983; Lahey, et al., 1980; Miller and Maruyama, 1976).

First-borns are more likely to be Rhodes Scholars and Nobel prize winners, and they are represented disproportionately as National Merit Scholar candidates. The notion that birth order affects personality, career success, mental health, and other aspects of life has long had an appealing ring to it; but in actuality, few definitive outcomes can be linked to ordinal position because so many other variables intercede. Sigmund Freud, for example, was his mother's first-born but not his father's. Franklin Roosevelt was his mother's only child but he did have an older half-brother. Harry Truman was a first-born; John F. Kennedy was not.

In 1952, Anne Roe interviewed 64 renowned first-born scientists and described them this way: "He was the first-born child of a middle-class family, the son of a professional man. He is likely to have been a sick child or to have lost a parent at an early age. He has a very high IQ, and in boyhood began to do a great deal of reading. He tended to feel lonely and 'different' and to be shy and aloof from his classmates."

According to psychologists Brian Sutton-Smith and Ben Rosenberg, what has been lumped under the heading of birth-order research is actually research into parental age, social class, family size, and possibly even the birth order of the researchers. Sutton-Smith and Rosenberg point out that the fewer the children in a family, the greater the chance of them obtaining the higher educational levels needed for success. Middle- and upper-class families generally have fewer children and are therefore able to provide them with more educational resources. Anne Roe's eminent scientists, for example, all came from families of middle- or upper-social strata. Parents in these families valued learning and provided intellectual, aesthetic, and cultural stimulation. Why, then, aren't all the children in these families equally intelligent? Robert Zajonc (1986) has proposed that ordinal position determines the intellectual stimulation a child receives. First-borns are stimulated by social interactions with adults; later-borns interact more with siblings than they do mothers and fathers. This view explains why Roe found that successful later-borns had either lost an older sibling during early development or were separated from older siblings by a significant number of years.

For all its social, intellectual, and economic benefits, the position of first-borns has its problems. After a period of time in which the first child is the most prized and powerful member of the family, the birth of a sibling can be a real psychological shock. While first-borns have undivided parental attention for a period of time, they come into a family of inexperienced parents—mothers and fathers who often have inappropriate developmental expectations for their first child. During adolescence, for example, parents who are confronted with the clothing, music, dating, and curfew styles of the teenage culture often experience great conflict with a first-born. By the time later-born children hit their teen years, parents have a better understanding of this stage of development and the peer culture.

How the new role of big sister or brother is handled within a family affects a first-born's adjustment to the birth, but the relationship between the siblings depends upon gender and age spacing. In studying "the sibling bond," Michael Kahn and Stephen Bank (1982) noted that in three-children families, two of the children are often close and one is left as somewhat of an outsider.

SIBLINGS AND GENDER

Sons and daughters are treated differently within a family. Girls are given help more quickly when performing tasks, and they are reinforced more for dependent behaviors such as clinging to mother's skirt or seeking body contact. The same behavior is discouraged in boys (Fagot, 1978, 1985.) Parents are more likely to argue with each other in front a male child (Hetherington and Camara, 1984). Female babies are generally perceived and handled as if they were more fragile than male babies; but in fact female babies are more mature at birth. Male babies are more vulnerable to disease and infant mortality (Minton, Kagan, and Levine, 1971; Moss, 1967). Parents allow male children to cross the street by themselves at a younger age than female children; but in actuality girls are ready earlier because of differences in the maturity and impulsivity levels (Hoffman, 1975, 1977). Interestingly, the sibling who experiences more closeness to the father, whether a son or a daughter, is generally the one who expects to achieve more occupationally.

PHYSICAL APPEARANCE

Sibling differences in physical appearance influence the treatment they receive from parents. Children who are the most attractive are responded to more positively by parents, as well as by teachers, other adults, and peers (Lerner and Lerner, 1987). In a study of 150 families in which infants' attractiveness was assessed by an independent panel of judges, it was found that the most attractive babies were kissed, cooed at, smiled at, and cuddled more by their mothers, particularly if they were girls (Langlois, 1966; Langlois and Casey, 1984). This same pattern held for fathers (Parke and Sawin, 1975). In one study it was shown that fathers were more punitive and less supportive of unattractive daughters during times of economic hardship and unemployment (Elder, et al., 1986; Elder, et al., 1985). In some cases, attractive daughters in these same conditions were given increased supportivenss and lessened punitiveness.

Physical appearance affects the parent-child relationship in other ways. A child's strong resemblance to one parent causes different responses and may lead a child to identify more with the look-alike parent. A child's size also has an impact, as parents of children who are tall for their age often place higher developmental expectations on their larger offspring.

IDIOSYNCRATIC EXPERIENCES

Random differences in experiences, such as illness or witnessing a parental interaction unseen by siblings, can have a striking impact on development. Siblings inevitably have different experiences outside the family, as they meet people and develop friendships based on their personal likes and needs.

A child's age in the family has a critical effect on his or her reactions to a particular event. For example, a divorce will impact a ten-year-old far differently than a two-year-old. A classic study of children growing up during the Great Depression of the 1930s best illustrates the difference in reactions. When families entered hard times, adolescent sons who had lived in the family during times of prosperity were often required to get jobs to help support the family. Generally these sons achieved occupational success and stability in adulthood. Younger sons experienced economic deprivation during their childhoods and were not part of helping the family cope. As adults, they did not do as well occupationally as their age cohorts whose families did not go through hard times (Elder, 1974).

SIBLING SAMENESS

Lois Hoffman points out that while siblings may be different when it comes to personality traits, on values, morals, coping styles, political attitudes, work orientation, social competencies, interests, and even their own parenting styles, the siblings are similar because of a shared family environment. Factors related to parenting styles are basically the same for all children in the family. Parents who are democratic with one child are not likely to be power-oriented with another. Parents who are disinterested in religion are not likely to have children who become very involved. This tendency is particularly true if both parents hold similar values and beliefs (Grotevant, 1979).

SIBLING RIVALRY

Sibling rivalry refers to the competition between siblings for the love, attention, and recognition of one or both parents. While this is a normal phenomenon, the way parents respond to the rivalry can lead to healthy competition or to psychological problems that can last a lifetime. Sibling rivalry is most common in first-born children who don't want to share the once-undivided attention of parents. It is also more common between same-sex siblings, particularly girls; and it is most severe for rejected children who feel hurt and therefore antagonize a favored sibling (Leung and Robson, 1991). Parents' comparisons between children are often the source of resentment. A younger child might see an older sibling as favored when the older sibling is allowed to stay up later. One child in a family might be more talented, attractive, or academically superior to another. Comparisons based on differences are usually harmful.

Young children may display anger, physically and verbally, when they feel jealous and resentful. An older or bigger child may act aggressively toward a resented younger or smaller sibling—hitting, pushing, or biting. Sometimes a first-born regresses to thumb sucking or bed wetting when a new baby comes into the family. At the extreme, if the childhood feelings remain unresolved, an angry sibling might grow into a selfish, aggressive, destructive, insecure adult in need of psychiatric treatment.

Judy Dunn and Robert Plomin (1990) emphasize that parents must try hard to minimize the differences in their relationships with their children and be especially sensitive to the keenness with which children monitor the various relationships within the family.

Educators Adele Faber and Elaine Mazlish offer a number of suggestions for decreasing sibling rivalry.

- Instead of dismissing children's negative feelings about a sibling, acknowledge their feelings.
- Help children channel their hostile feelings into symbolic or creative outlets.
- Stop hurtful behavior. Show how angry feelings can be discharged safely. Refrain from attacking the attacker.
- Avoid unfavorable comparisons.
- Avoid favorable comparisons.
- Instead of worrying about giving equal amounts, focus on each child's individual needs.
- Instead of claiming equal love, show children how they are loved uniquely.
- Don't give your attention to the aggressor; give it to the injured party.
- Help the bullying child see that he or she is capable of being civil and kind.
- Help the victim see his or her strength and ability.
- Establish limits and separate children if fighting is headed toward hurting.
- Teach children how to resolve their differences peacefully.

Television and Parenting

Television has become an ingrained and extremely influential part of the childhood experience. Parents must recognize that, as an educational medium, television affects children in a number of significant areas. Researchers have focused attention on specific areas such as: cognitive function, aggressive behavior, prosocial behavior, gender roles, and consumer attitudes.

In 1950, one out of twenty American homes had a television set. Today 98 percent of homes have televisions, and many have three or four. America's 28 million children ages two to eleven watch an average of 21 hours and 38 minutes of television a week, down more than five hours since the mid-1980s when computers and videotapes took their place in the home (Nielsen Media Research, 1996). The nation's youngsters tend to spend more time watching television than conversing with family members (Singer and Singer, 1983). Many will spend more time in front of a television than they will in a classroom. Children from the most impoverished backgrounds have the highest rates of television watching (Huston, et al., 1990). Television viewing increases markedly in the preschool years, peaks in elementary school, and then declines slightly in adolescence (Liebert and Sprafkin, 1988).

Television programming has become the target of Congress, religious groups, and educators who blame it for the increase in violence in the country, the decrease in attention span of children, and the decline in basic civility among the citizens of the country (Table 11.1). Research on the effects of television on children have not definitively proved these accusations, and many researchers believe that television viewing must be examined in the context of family dynamics (Fabes, Wilson, and Christopher, 1989).

FAMILY VIEWING PATTERNS

The television habits of children are often blamed on a lack of parental supervision; however, it appears that children develop their viewing habits as a result of being with their parents (St. Peters, et al., 1991). Studies show that 67 percent of the time, when children aged three to seven are watching adult programs, an adult is with them. Preschool children who remain at home with their mothers watch more television than children whose mothers go out to work (Pinon, Huston, and Wright, 1989). School-age children watch about the same amount of television, whether their parents are present or not.

TABLE 11.1   Then and Now Programming

The 1970s	The 1990s
On "The Brady Bunch," Greg feared telling the folks he wrecked the car.	On "Mad About You," Paul's sister feared telling the folks she's a lesbian.
On "Happy Days," sharing some Cokes meant sipping cola through straws from the same glass.	On "Beverly Hills, 90210," sharing some coke means snorting an illegal substance through straws on the same mirror.
On "Little House on the Prairie," Laura and Nellie both eager to satisfy their hunger for sweets, fought over the last cookie.	On "Friends," Monica and Rachel, both eager to satisfy their hunger for sex with their boyfriends, fight over the last condom.
On "The Beverly Hillbillies," the pill was Mr. Drysdale's leave-nothing-to-chance secretary, Miss Hathaway.	On "Roseanne," the pill is older daughter Becky's leave-nothing-to-chance method of birth control.

Almost one-half of all families impose rules concerning the programs children can watch (Comstock, 1991). Michele St. Peters (1991) identified four types of parenting in regard to TV viewing. *Laissez-faire* parents neither encourage TV viewing nor regulate their children's choices. *Restrictive* parents do not encourage viewing. They highly regulate the programming when children do watch, preferring Walt Disney shows and other prosocial programs. *Promotive* parents encourage TV viewing and impose few regulations about what their children can watch. These parents themselves watch children's programs, as well as comedies, dramas, game shows and adventure shows. *Selective* parents highly regulate TV viewing and encourage specific types of programs.

There is a striking change in family viewing from twenty years ago concerning what is considered acceptable during the "family hour" of 8 to 9 P.M., when many parents and children watch situation comedies (See Figure 11.2). The family hour was defined and established in 1975, when the Federal Communications Commission encouraged the major networks to set aside the first hour of prime time for nonviolent, wholesome programming. A 1996 survey by the Media Research Center, a conservative political organization, counted 29 uses of the word "ass" and 13 references to "bitch" during family hour (Rudolph and Hammer, 1996). Pressure from the government has led to the development of a rating system for violence, sex, and strong language, as well as the V-chip device that allows parents to block objectionable programming.

Television, after all, is a commercial enterprise that gears its programming to the marketplace. Parents do have the ability to encourage their children to

Figure 11.2
The Family Hour: Children, Parents, and TV

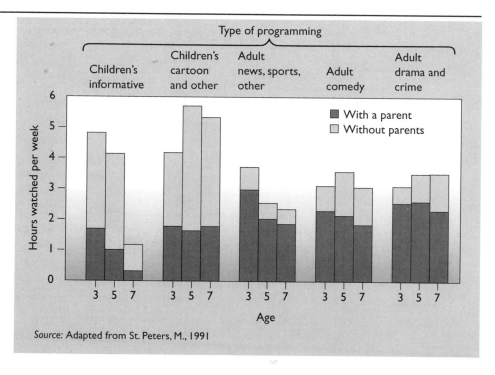

Source: Adapted from St. Peters, M., 1991

watch programs that are entertaining and educational, and to turn off the programming they find objectionable.

TELEVISION AND COGNITIVE DEVELOPMENT

One question that researchers ponder is whether or not educational television enhances academic skills. In the initial year of "Sesame Street," a group of 950 children were studied to assess the impact of the program on academic knowledge. The youngsters were placed in four groups, depending on how many times they watched the show during a six-month time frame. The results indicated that the more the children watched "Sesame Street," the more they learned (Ball and Bogatz, 1970). By comparison, children who watch cartoons are at a learning disadvantage by age seven (Huston and Wright, 1995) (Figure 11.3).

Mabel Rice and her colleagues (1990) found similar gains in their study, particularly in vocabulary development. In one project three- and five-year-olds were introduced to twenty new words during a fifteen-minute cartoon. All the children demonstrated an increased understanding of the words in as little

Figure 11.3
"Sesame Street" and Commercial Cartoons: A Learning Difference

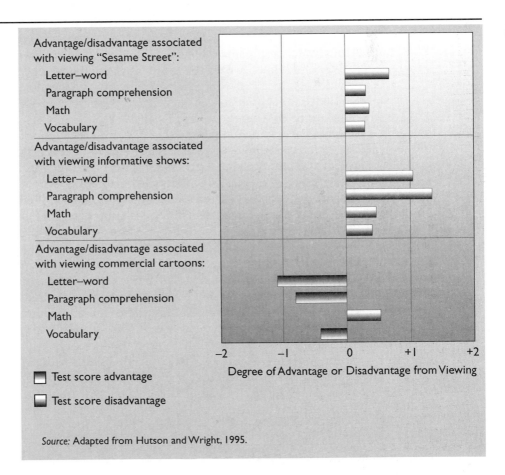

Advantage/disadvantage associated with viewing "Sesame Street":
Letter–word
Paragraph comprehension
Math
Vocabulary

Advantage/disadvantage associated with viewing informative shows:
Letter–word
Paragraph comprehension
Math
Vocabulary

Advantage/disadvantage associated with viewing commercial cartoons:
Letter–word
Paragraph comprehension
Math
Vocabulary

−2   −1   0   +1   +2

Degree of Advantage or Disadvantage from Viewing

□ Test score advantage

■ Test score disadvantage

Source: Adapted from Hutson and Wright, 1995.

as two exposures to the story, and they retained from two to five of the new words (Rice and Woodsmall, 1988).

Critics of these studies point to the fact that educational television may raise some academic skills, while doing little to close the academic gap between lower- and middle-class children (Sprigle, 1971, 1972). Jerome and Dorothy Singer (1981, 1983) believe that the more that children watched these programs, the lower their scores on tests of creativity. The Singers suggest that time spent viewing television takes away from reading, writing, and other activities that enhance creative thinking.

TELEVISION AND VIOLENCE

Prime-time shows include an average of five or six violent acts per hour, and cartoons include as many as 21 per hour (Gerbner, 1986). Many studies have shown that exposure to televised violence produces a small but significant increase in aggression, in specific children who come from homes where aggression and antisocial behavior are common (Heath, 1989). It appears that aggressive behavior and viewing television violence have a reciprocal relationship. In a three-year correlational study of approximately 1,000 youngsters, researchers found that children who were rated as most aggressive at the start of the study watched the most television violence. The children who viewed the most television violence over the three-year period developed the most aggressive behaviors. In other words, aggressive youngsters crave violent programs, and violent programs encourage aggressive youngsters to behave more aggressively (Huesmann, Lagerspetz, and Eron, 1984).

From a developmental perspective, the important question is whether exposure to television violence has any long-term effects on personality or behavior. One major problem with assessing this relationship is that many variables contribute to aggression. In any experiment, it would be impossible to control all the variables except the quantity of television viewing. In spite of this hurdle, several researchers have attempted to evaluate the long-term effects of watching violent television programs.

Monroe Lefkowitz and his colleagues (1972) conducted a ten-year longitudinal study to examine the effects of television on eight-year old boys. Those youths who watched the most violence on television were later rated as more aggressive than those whose television viewing was less frequent. When these same individuals were evaluated at the age of 30, it was found that those who had been rated highest in aggression and who watched the greatest amount of violent television had the most serious criminal records.

Brandon Centerwall (1992) has proposed that societal violence is an epidemic disease, linked to the advent of television. In a fascinating research project, Centerwall studied the homicide rates in Canada and among whites in the United States and South Africa since television was introduced to those societies. Murder rates began to rise sharply ten to fifteen years after television viewing became widespread, at about the time the first generation of TV viewers reached adulthood.

Jerome and Dorothy Singer (1983) propose that seeing violence on television may actually desensitize viewers, thereby neutralizing the impact of aggression. This is referred to somewhat misleadingly as the *no-effect model*.

The Singers hypothesize that watching too much television interferes with social development, creativity, and play opportunities. Children miss the chance to learn constructive problem-solving skills and techniques for interacting cooperatively with others (Singer and Singer, 1982).

PROSOCIAL BEHAVIOR AND TELEVISION: LEARNING TO DO GOOD DEEDS

Not all television programs contain violence. Some, like "Mr. Rogers' Neighborhood" or the reruns of "Lassie," attempt to teach or instill prosocial behavior, although older reruns expose children to outdated gender stereotypes. Lynette Friedrich and Althea Stein (1973) demonstrated that lower-class children who viewed "Mr. Rogers' Neighborhood" over a one-month period showed an increase in prosocial behaviors. Using "Sesame Street," Aimee Leiffer (1973) established that children who were exposed to scenes focusing on cooperative behavior later imitated that behavior, and she showed carry-over behavior to later situations. It has been demonstrated that youngsters can learn cooperative behaviors from seeing one episode of an old show such as "The Waltons," which highlighted themes of problem-solving and cooperation (Baran, et al., 1979). A study of children watching "Mr. Rogers' Neighborhood" showed that after viewing the program nursery-school children were more persistent, helpful, and cooperative (Huston, 1985). An analysis of almost 200 studies of the effects of prosocial television leads one to conclude that prosocial television has a more significant impact on children's behavior than does violent television (Hearold, 1986). It should be noted that modern prosocial shows, such as "Star Trek: The Next Generation," sometimes contain violent scenes.

CHILDREN AND COMMERCIALISM

Over the past 20 years, there has been an increase in the number of ads aimed specifically at children, despite the fact that, before the age of eight, children do not understand that commercials are intended to influence buying habits (Ward, Reale, and Levinson, 1972). Children in the United States have become a multi-billion-dollar market for clothing, toys, and other items.

Advertisers promote sugar-loaded foods and high-calorie snacks on children's programming, and children in turn request their parents to buy the products. So powerful are the consumer messages to children that the desire to purchase the items seen on television can lead to conflict between children and their parents.

TELEVISION GUIDELINES

Television provides education, relaxation, and entertainment for children; as such, it need not be looked at only negatively (Tangney, 1988). In the final analysis, the question is not whether it is best to turn off the television in a home, but how best to watch it. Dorothy and Jerome Singer (1987) proposed guidelines for parents to help their children get the maximum benefit from television.

- Start teaching good viewing habits at an early age.
- Help children plan what they watch.
- Encourage them to watch programs that feature their peers.
- Do not allow television to become a substitute for play or other activity.
- Discuss television programs, and give children opportunities to ask questions.
- Encourage time for reading. Children can follow up what they have seen on television by reading a book on the topic or character.
- Assist children in developing a well-rounded schedule of homework, play, athletics, and arts.
- Focus on positive examples of ethnic contributions to society.
- Mention how females show competence at work and in the home.

Chapter Review

- Middle childhood is a mirror into adult life as the intellectual and social competencies of infancy and early childhood stabilize during the childhood years of six to ten. In cultures throughout the world the middle childhood period marks the time when children are expected to begin functioning as useful members of their society.

- Erik Erikson refers to this period as one of industry versus inferiority. During this stage, children establish work habits that will carry them through life. They develop a view of themselves that will affect their future choices and relationships. At this stage also, children begin to venture away from the family and their parents, and peer-group activities become important.

- Middle childhood is about competence, the mastery of the environment, not just the exploration of it. It is a time of increased physical skills and the ability to engage in more organized group activities.

- Between the ages of six and twelve, children's faces take on a more mature look. The face becomes larger, the forehead flattens, the nose enlarges and the jaw widens. Physical growth is steady and moderate during middle childhood, except for a few spurt periods. Average height at six years of age is 3½ feet, and average weight is 45 pounds; boys are a little taller and heavier than girls.

- Middle childhood is generally a healthy period for children because the number of ear infections and illnesses common to early childhood decrease as physical immunities build. Accidents are the leading cause of middle-childhood injuries and death, primarily because as children become more coordinated they also engage in more dangerous pastimes.

- Children are less active today than they were 30 years ago, due to changes in the way we live. For this reason, one-fourth of school-age children are overweight and many, weighing at least 20 percent above their ideal weight, are considered obese. Obesity carries with it both physical and social problems.

- During the school-age years, children become more sophisticated in their thinking; they increasingly rely on logic and reasoning to understand the world. As they build up a pool of knowledge, they are no longer as bound by intuitions based only on what they see, smell, and hear. Rather their thoughts become more flexible and organized, to the point when they understand underlying operations used to solve problems.

- Jean Piaget divided middle childhood into two stages of intellectual development. The first, the preoperational period, spans from ages about four to seven, when a shift in thinking moves children forward in their understanding of the rationale behind solutions to problems. Stage two is called the concrete operational stage because at age seven children organize their thoughts based on the properties of what they see.

- Intelligence is the capacity for learning, reasoning and understanding. Parents often do not define intelligence the way Western psychologists do. In many non- Western cultures, intelligence is seen in the light of socially beneficial behaviors and motivations.

- Howard Gardner proposed the existence of multiple intelligences, at least seven forms. They are independent of each other, although they combine when it comes to certain kinds of thinking or skills.

- Robert Sternberg defines intelligence as "a kind of mental self-management—the mental management of one's life in a constructive, purposeful way." Intelligence involves the ability to shape, adapt to, and select one's environment.

- Moral behavior refers to obeying rules and regulations laid down by parents, a school system, the government, religious teachings, and others in the environment who influence children's thoughts, attitudes, and values. It is also about goodness and decency, the way one individual treats another, the degree to which a person can put himself or herself in another's place, respect for others, basic decency, and kindness.

- During the school-age years, children learn to think, study, and get along with others. Parental attitude very much affects the way children view school and learning. A parent who had an unsatisfying experience in school can project a negative attitude about

education, a view that can influence a child's expectations and performance. Parents who value education and support the school's objectives are more likely to raise children who view school positively.

- Children begin to perceive themselves as separate and distinct human beings while still in infancy. This awareness is self-concept, the basis of identity. A child's sense of self comes from his or her experience with and evaluation by parents and other significant people. Self-esteem is reflective of what a child thinks about his or her self. School-age children rate themselves on three self-esteem scales: cognitive competence, physical ability, and social worth. They combine the experiences from each of these settings into an overall sense of self-esteem.

- Four factors have been identified as significant to the development of a sense of self-worth. They include the degree to which parents show respect and acceptance of their children, the children's history of success, the praise and recognition they get for their efforts, the goals children have, the value placed on those goals, and children's ability to defend themselves when their self-esteem is attacked.

- An awareness of other people and an ability to imagine what they are thinking and feeling is part of social success, and it is in middle childhood that children build skills in perspective-taking. The children best at perspective-taking are better at problem solving in social situations. These children are the most popular among their peers because they are sensitive and cooperative in their relationships with other children.

- In middle childhood, parents begin to relinquish some of the control they have had over their children. Now, parent and children are engaged in coregulation, a transitional form of supervision in which parents exercise general oversight while permitting children to be in charge of moment-by-moment decision making.

- Psychologists view sibling behaviors in terms of *shared environment* and *nonshared environment.* Shared environments refer to those things in an environment that are the same for all the children in a family, such as the neighborhood and the family dog. Non-shared environments refer to things that are not the same for all the children, such as their friends and the individual way parents relate to each child in the family.

- There are five primary sources of sibling differences, all affecting the parent-child relationship. These are ordinal position or birth order, the age of the child when an event in the family occurs, gender of the child, the child's physical appearance, and idiosyncratic experiences.

- Television is a teaching tool that has become ingrained, and it is an incredibly influential part of the childhood experience. Parents must recognize that, as an educational medium, television affects children in a number of significant areas. Researchers have focused attention on specific areas of learning: cognitive functions, aggressive behavior, prosocial behavior, gender roles, and consumer attitudes.

Student Activities

1. Interview three different sets of siblings. Describe how they handle rivalry and conflict among themselves.

2. Develop a brief IQ test with the intention to guage the contextual intelligence of a child who has had little schooling but has managed to take care of herself in a dangerous and downtrodden neighborhood.

3. Develop an idea for a television show for school-age children that you think would be both interesting and prosocial.

Helping Hands

Action for Childen's Television
20 University Road
Cambridge, MA 02138
(617) 876-6620

An organization devoted to promoting quality television programming for children and to the elimination of commercials.

Council for Children's Television and Media
33290 W. 14 Mile Road, Suite 488
West Bloomfield, MI 48322
(313) 489-5499

An organization of parents, teachers, and citizens devoted to promoting quality programming and an improvement in children's viewing habits.

Association for Childhood Education
International (ACEI)
11561 Georgia Avenue, Suite 312
Wheaton, MD 20902
(301) 942-2443
www.udel.edu/bateman/acei

Organization promoting sound educational practices from infancy through adolescence. Publishes *Childhood Education*, a journal covering research, practice, and public policy issues.

National Association for the Education of Young Children (NAEYC)
1509 16th Street, NW
Washington, DC 20036
(202) 232-8777
(800) 424-2460
www.naeyc.org

Organization devoted to the needs of young children, with a focus on educational services. Publishes *Young Children*, a journal covering theory, research, and practice in child development and education.

CHAPTER

12

Parenting the Adolescent and Young Adult

Chapter Highlights

After reading Chapter 12, students should be able to:

- Understand the physical, emotional, and social changes in adolescence
- Understand the developmental stages in adolescence
- Understand the adolescent drive to achieve a sense of identity
- Recognize the changes that occur in the parent-child relationship during adolescence
- Recognize the behavior problems characteristic of adolescence

Chapter Contents

- Puberty: The Matured State
- What Should Parents Expect?
    Mid-life Parenting, Mid-life Issues
- The Physical Changes of Adolescence
    The Growth Spurt ▪ *Sexual Maturation* ▪ *Timing and Maturation*
- Cognitive Changes in Adolescence
    Adolescent Egocentrism ▪ *Creating an Identity* ▪ *James Marcia and Identity Status* ▪ *Identity and Culture*
- Patterns of Change Within Families
    Sources of Conflict Between Parents and Adolescents ▪ *Syles of Parenting and Adolescent Adjustment* ▪ *Family Structure and Adolescent Behavior* ▪ *The Influence of Peers* ▪ *The Adolescent as Consumer*

■ Educating the Adolescent
   Transition from Elementary to Middle School ■ *Attitudes Toward School*
■ The Problems of Adolescence
   Risk Taking and Sensation Seeking ■ *Substance Abuse* ■ *Risk Factors and Drug Use* ■ *Eating Disorders* ■ *Adolescent Depression* ■ *Parental Depression and Adolescent Distress* ■ *Suicide Among Adolescents*

Colin Powell rose through the ranks of the United States Army to become National Security Advisor to the president of the United States and then Chairman of the Joint Chiefs of Staff under George Bush. In his poignant autobiography, retired General Powell described himself as a teenager who could not figure out what he wanted to do with his life. Born in 1937 to parents of Jamaican background, he was raised in New York's South Bronx, which was at the time a multi-racial and multi-ethnic community. Colin, an average student in high school, won a letter in track but gave up the sport after a while. He made the church basketball team but quit after spending most of his time on the bench. He had previously joined the Boy Scouts but this didn't hold his interest for long. He tried piano and then flute lessons, but he showed no aptitude for either. "My inability to stick to anything became a source of concern to my parents, unspoken, but I knew it was there," General Powell later wrote.

At City College of New York, on the advice of family members, Colin began a major in engineering, despite his dislike of math and science. Soon after, he decided to switch to geology.

In 1954 Colin found himself attracted to the campus Reserve Officers Training Corps (ROTC), and he soon stood in line to receive the olive-drab pants and jacket that would mark him as a cadet. After becoming a member of the Pershing Rifles, an ROTC fraternity, Colin felt as though he had found himself. "For the first time in my life I was a member of a brotherhood," he writes. "We partied together. We cut classes together. We chased girls together . . . the discipline, the structure, the camaraderie, the sense of belonging were what I craved. I became a leader almost immediately (Powell, 1995).

What Colin Powell experienced in the years between high school and college is not unusual for youngsters in American society, who go through a transition that brings sharp physical, cognitive, and psychosocial changes. He was lucky enough to have parents who were loving and supportive, willing to guide their son while letting him experiment with life until he discovered a path that would lead him to a productive adulthood. This period of development, represented by a drive toward independence, peer-group loyalty, and intellectual growth is known as *adolescence*. Although generally we think of adolescence as the *teenage* years, from thirteen to eighteen, individual children and the children in some cultures begin adolescence as early as ten years old and emerge at age twenty two. Because the person who emerges from adolescence often barely resembles the child who entered it, parents can have a very difficult time, particularly if they are not fully aware of what is transpiring.

Adolescence is also referred to as *puberty*, which comes from the Latin term *puber* meaning "adult." *Pubescence,* the period preceding puberty, is the time during which changes occur. *Puberty* is the culmination of these changes, the final matured state. While physical changes during this time are universal, psychological and social reactions are contextual and cultural. In early adolescence, before age sixteen, the most obvious changes center on physical and psychological development, particularly the hormonal activities that direct biological change. In later adolescence, from age sixteen on, the focus is on peer relationships, sexuality, identity, and plans for the future.

PUBERTY: THE MATURED STATE

Around the world, in every country and culture, no matter how technologically advanced or primitive, every healthy child changes dramatically during this period. Some cultures celebrate the beginning of adulthood with social rituals that mark the event. It is through these rituals that individuals became full-fledged members of the adult community, and as such, they are expected to participate fully in adult society and behave according to culturally prescribed norms. There are cultures in which adolescent changes are viewed as shameful, embarrassing, socially troublesome, and cause for concern. American society is so culturally diverse that attitudes and actions in regard to adolescence vary significantly from one ethnic group to another. Because of this diversity and a lack of clear road signs or expectations, adolescents in the United States often face difficulty leaving childhood and moving toward adulthood while saddled with a confusing set of expectations set out by the family, school, and society at large.

Adolescence as we know it today did not exist until the 1930s in America, when the Great Depression sent teenagers away from farms and factories and into the high school setting, which previously had been reserved for youngsters taking subjects such as Latin and Greek and headed on to college. In 1900 only 6 percent of American seventeen-year-olds earned diplomas. By 1930 the figure had risen to 50 percent, after practical subjects such as home economics, stenography, and typing (for girls) and shop, mechanics, and woodworking (for boys) were added to the curriculum. According to Grace Palladino (1996) in *Teenagers, An American History*, once the teenage majority spent the better part of their days in high school, they began to look to one another and not to their parents for advice, information, and approval.

> Time and time again over the past sixty years, teenagers have proved that they cannot be separated from the "real"-world adult world or molded according to adult specifications: Ever since the architects of adolescent culture imagined a sheltered, adult-guided world of dependent teenage children, their high school descendants have yearned to breathe free. In the 1930s, they battled their parents over curfews, cigarettes, and swing music; half a century later, the issues were sex, drugs, and rock 'n' roll. But the basic conflict remains the same, regardless of the issue or the era: Who gets to decide

In the 1950s, James Dean and *Rebel Without a Cause* gave American society a vivid look at the anguished teen misunderstood by incompetent parents. Adolescence in the United States has never been the same.

how teenagers look, act, and experience life? And who decides what that experience means? Although adults often interpret this conflict as a simple attack on parental authority tempered by hormones and a biological need to stand apart, that is only part of the story. The evolution of modern teenage culture has as much to do with a changing economy, a national culture of consumption and individualism, and the age-graded, adolescent world of high school as it does with inexperience or hostility to adult rule. (Palladino, 1996)

WHAT SHOULD PARENTS EXPECT?

In the face of their children's biological, cognitive, and social changes, the parents of adolescents must understand what is happening to the young people they are raising. They must also be able to modify the parenting role they have long known.

As the young adolescent grows to adulthood, they seek to change the ways in which they are treated and the privileges they receive. In striving for identity and a sense of self, they make demands related to a desire for independence. Young male and female adolescents seek to be autonomous even while holding on to family ties. Parents find themselves living with children who look and think differently, and often—especially in the case of first-borns—parents feel fearful about giving up their authority too soon. Often both parents and adolescent children feel the need for change but they are not sure about the course this change should take. Families unable to make necessary adjustments often find themselves facing rebellious children. Nydia Garcia Preto (1988) has described why it is so difficult for parents to give up their decision-making role:

> ... from an adult perspective, the adolescent's decision in a rapidly expanding era of behavioral choices can leave much to be desired. The distinctions between choices that are merely unwise and self-defeating, and those that are self-destructive, even life-threatening, are often hard to determine. Uncertainty concerning when and how to act is common for parents of adolescents. (Preto, 1988)

Parents' ability to separate from adolescents is influenced by culture, because ethnic groups differ in their attitudes. For example, British Americans promote separation at an earlier age than do Italian, Hispanic or Jewish families, but they often provide inadequate support for this goal (McGill and Pearce, 1982). Portuguese families encourage an early transition to adulthood; however, they expect their adolescents to live at home until marriage, to get jobs, and to contribute to the financial support of the family (Moitoza, 1982). Jewish middle-class children generally go off to college after high school, leaving parents to support them while they live independently.

Adolescent autonomy is also influenced by the kind of community a family lives in. Urban adolescents can get where they want to go by public transportation. Their activities and friends can span the city, making them difficult for parents to keep tabs on. Suburban or rural adolescents must rely on parents for transportation to friends' homes or social events. This makes a driver's license of paramount importance to rural adolescents struggling for independence from parents.

MID-LIFE PARENTING, MID-LIFE ISSUES

At the point that a first child becomes an adolescent, parents are generally close to middle age. By the time their last child hits this stage, parents may be in their late forties or early fifties. Researchers have noted that parents' mid-life issues affects the parent-adolescent relationship as much as the changes that are occurring in the adolescent do (Galinsky, 1980). A teenager dressed in a short skirt might trigger an emotional overreaction from a mother who is lamenting that her own partying days are most likely over. A father's response to his child's laying around on a Saturday may reflect the father's mid-life dissatisfaction with a job he feels stuck in. In addition, many parents are experiencing other changes. Their own parents are aging and may need time and attention, their youthful aspirations and dreams must be reconsidered, financial concerns may become serious as tuition or parent-care costs loom, they may be experiencing the death of their loved ones; from many directions there may be uncertainty about the future.

This is also the time when parents are alone again, as increasingly their adolescent children separate from the family and spend more time outside the house and with friends. Betty Carter and Monica McGoldrick (1988) note that this is the time of personal exploration by many parents, a pursuit that can lead to a renegotiation of their marriage and sometimes even a decision to divorce.

THE PHYSICAL CHANGES OF ADOLESCENCE

Human beings are programmed for developmental change by their genes, and the program unfolds over time. As maturation occurs, factors such as health care, nutrition, physical labor, and body mass interact with genetic factors to trigger the pattern of changes that mark puberty. When the time is right *endocrine hormones*, powerful regulating chemicals, are excreted by the endocrine glands and carried through the body via the blood stream. Hormones cause the body to react in specific ways that affect anatomical and physiological development.

THE GROWTH SPURT

The earliest noticeable adolescent change occurring in both sexes is a *growth spurt*, a sudden, uneven, and unpredictable increase in a child's height. Because of its visibility, this is generally marked as the beginning of the pubescence sequence. Pituitary growth hormones and the thyroid hormones provoke the rapid skeletal changes that lead to the lengthening and increasing mass of the bones. The growth spurt occurs at about age ten and one-half for girls and lasts about two years. Boys begin the growth spurt at about age twelve and one-half and about two years later than girls; the spurt continues until approximately fourteen years old (Figure 12.1). It is not unusual for fourth-grade boys to be taller than girls in their class. But once the growth spurt begins, young women eclipse young men for the next couple of years.

Girls gain about three and one-half inches each year and boys closer to four inches (Faust, 1977). This growth spurt does not mean that full height is achieved. While the most growth occurs at the fastest rate at this time, there can be up to a 30 percent gain in later adolescence, up to age eighteen (Behrman and Vaughan 1988).

The growth process proceeds from the ends of the extremities and moves gradually inward to the center of the body. This means the hands and feet grow first, then the arms and legs, and finally the torso. This is why adolescents often appear lanky and awkward with long arms and legs, and big hands and feet before their centers catch up.

In girls, the pelvis widens; in boys, the shoulders broaden. During puberty, weight increases in a similar way to height. The rate of gain is greatest during the growth spurt but levels out toward the end of the two-year period. The round pudgy face of the child gives way to the longer, mature, adult-looking head. The face elongates as the lower jaw becomes longer. The eyes grow, the ears get bigger, the nose protrudes further, and the teeth in the jaw begin to

Figure 12.1
Adolescent
Growth Chart

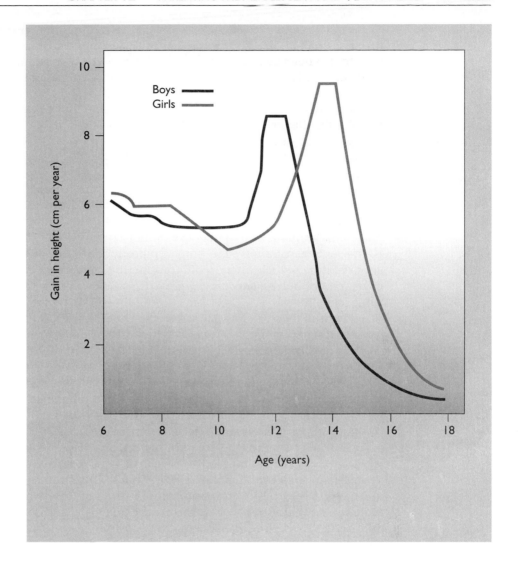

take on their adult appearance. During this period, many adolescents are unhappy about their physical appearance; they need assurances the changes taking place are normal and will pass within a relatively short time.

Initially, girls may be heavier and taller than boys, but as boys move beyond fourteen years old they overtake their female classmates in both height and weight. Between the ages of ten and fourteen, the typical adolescent girl gains about 38 pounds and grows about 9⅝ inches taller. During this same time, the typical adolescent boy gains about 42 pounds and grows about 10 inches. (Malina and Bouchard, 1991). During these gains, some adolescents require large quantities of food to fuel their growth and increased sleep to rest their actively expanding bodies.

While it is easy to see the external changes caused by puberty, less visible internal changes are also occurring. Both females and males increase their muscle mass during the growth spurt. Young women accumulate body fat at a faster rate and at a greater ratio to body weight than males; this accumulation is an important influence on the onset of a girl's first menstrual period (Frisch, 1985). Body fat provides shape around the legs and hips in ways that will eventually form the female figure. Cultural images of a female "ideal" cause some young women deep distress, to the point that some develop eating disorders.

SEXUAL MATURATION

Of all the changes taking place in the adolescent body, none cause as much parental and societal concern as the adolescent's newly found ability to reproduce. This ability is due to the development of *primary sex characteristics;* that is, the sex organs involved in human reproduction. Although not directly involved in the sexual function of reproduction, puberty is also marked by the development of *secondary sex characteristics:* the clear, physical signs that mark adult sexuality.

The primary sexual characteristics are those physical changes related directly to the reproductive system and genitals. In males there is an increase in penis length, enlargement of the testes/scrotal sac, and secretion of the androgens from the testes. In girls, the ovaries begin producing estrogens, the uterus grows, the lining of the vagina thickens. In girls the first signs of fertility is the *menarche*, (pronounced men-ark-ee), the first menstrual period. In boys *spermarche* (pronounced sperm-ark-ee), the first ejaculation of seminal fluid containing sperm, marks reproductive possibility. Actually the first occurrence of menarche or spermarche does not necessarily ensure reproduction possibility, as it takes some time—up to a year or two—before ovulation is regular enough and sperm production strong enough for reproduction to occur. This in no way means that a pregnancy cannot occur at this early stage of puberty, as national childbirth figures for teens show. A pregnancy is simply less likely during the time before an adolescent's body is fully developed sexually. When a pregnancy does occur at this early stage of sexual maturation, the growth and nutritional demands of the mother's body often conflict with those of the fetus, resulting in a low-birth-weight infant.

In actuality, the first occurrence of ejaculation of seminal fluid is *least* likely to happen during sexual intercourse. Rather, it occurs as a result of masturbation or "wet dreams." Males tend to be unprepared for this adolescent benchmark and they generally have little understanding of the changes going on in their bodies. Nevertheless, young men report strong positive feelings about this change (Gaddis and Brooks-Gunn, 1985).

For young adolescent women, the first menstrual period is the marker of womanhood. The physical symptoms associated with menstruation include cramps, water retention, pimples, and body aches. About half of all adolescent girls report having enough discomfort to curtail some of their physical activities (Widholm 1985). Researchers found no sense of debilitation or restriction on female lives, but rather a sense of mild upset and excitement around this event. More often than not, young women saw this event as the threshold into maturity and adulthood. While this experience might be scary to some, the actual negative side was minimal. Girls who matured early or were not educated about these bodily changes had more negative feelings, mixed emotions, as well as some confusion about what to do and what was happening to them. Even among well-educated women, knowledge and preparation was often incorrect, incomplete, and negative. (Koff, et al., 1990) In terms of expectations, those who had not yet experienced menarche were more likely to view it in a negative way than those who were postmenarcheal (Brooks-Gunn and Ruble 1982). Young women who learned about menarche from males (fathers, male friends) rated the experience with greater negativity than those who learned about it from books, magazines, educators, or girlfriends. A study of the menarcheal experience in 23 countries found that 32 percent of the female subjects received no maternal assistance, and if they had, it was mainly in terms of hygienic concern (Logan, 1980).

Sexuality is a process of development that begins in middle childhood in the form of attraction for one child to another. The hormonal changes that trigger this behavior begin as early as age six.

The outward signs of puberty are more obvious than the internal ones leading to reproduction. The body shape of boys and girls change drastically during this time and secondary sexual characteristics develop. Boys grow tall, female hips widen in preparation for future childbearing, hair appears in the pubic area and under the armpits, voices change, and boys grow facial hair. Young men often equate facial and body hair with virility. However, these characteristics, like other secondary sex traits, are controlled genetically and have little to do with "manliness."

Timing and Maturation

The young adolescent's reaction to puberty's onset occurs within a context of family, school, peers, and society. If maturation occurs earlier or later in comparison to peers, there is likely to be a variety of psychological reactions in terms of feelings, thoughts, attitudes, behavior, as well as interactions with family, teachers, and the same-sex and opposite-sex peers. In the classic studies of early maturers, boys were viewed in a more positive light by themselves and their peers. They had a greater sense of confidence and self-esteem than did late-maturing boys (Jones 1965). Furthermore, the early maturers were viewed as leaders, easier to get along with, and more able to handle themselves. In social contexts where sports and dating are a sign of prestige and status, the early-maturing boys were at an advantage over their late-maturing counterparts. Additionally, the early maturers had more successful peer relations than did the late maturers.

Data collected after the classic studies showed that early maturation in boys is not necessarily all positive. In a study of pubertal timing and its association with educational achievement for boys in middle and beginning high school, the early developers had the lowest school achievement in comparison to later and on-time maturers (who had the best achievement orientation). Of all groups, late-maturing girls had the highest achievement (Dubas, et al., 1991). In later measurements, the effects all but disappeared by twelfth grade, and the early maturers continued to show lower orientation toward achievement than both on-time and late maturers. Other studies show that the early-maturing boys also worried more about whether others like them and tended to be more rule bound and rigid in their adherence to rules. Data for later life show that while most of the differences disappear, the early maturers develop personalities that were often more serious, less playful, less flexible, and more inhibited in the long run. Early-maturing young men are treated like adults too soon and with full adult expectations. These young men did not have the same opportunity that the on-time and later-maturing adolescents had to slowly integrate the stressors that result from development during this period. Later maturers tended to have more feelings of insecurity and inadequacy, worried a great deal about rejection, had more conflicts within their own families, were more self-conscious, and had a poorer self-concept.

But all is not entirely negative for the late maturers. They may develop more flexible and adoptive roles due to their "longer" adolescence and having to learn to deal with their situations. If we look at data for early and later maturers some years later in life, we find that the late-maturing boys had a better sense of identity by the time they had reached their thirties. Therefore, this data suggest that while there are some positive effects of early maturation, there may also be a mildly negative effect on personality development during the adult years. While there are difficulties through adolescence for the later-maturing boys, they may develop personalities that allow them to navigate adult life demands in a more optimal way than the earlier-maturing boys.

Early-maturing young women appear to face more difficulties than their early-maturing male counterparts. These young women feel less attractive, often have a poor self-concept, and report lower self-esteem than on-time and later-maturing girls. Additionally they may face pressures to date early and to have sex. Often early-maturing young women have difficulty with body image and feel self-conscious (Nottleman, Eitha, and Welsh, 1986).

With regard to family interactions, the timing of puberty had greater importance to perceptions of the parents than to the adolescent. Parents generally report better relationships with early-maturing sons and late-maturing daughters as well as less conflict between those family members. Late-maturing sons and early maturing-daughters were a source of greater stress and anxiety. Generally, families reported most stress with early-maturing daughters. They will often experience more parental conflict that derives from parents' fears and attempts to restrict their young-developed daughters in their peer choices, autonomy, and dating (Savin-Williams, 1986).

Dealing with the budding sexuality of adolescent children is an important task for all family members. Parents who are comfortable with their own sexuality are better able to accept the growing sexuality of their children. In homes where the subject of sex is dealt with openly and honestly, realistic standards can be set. Denial or punishment of sexual impulses leaves adolescents with a sense of alienation, which often results in the desire to experiment and learn about sex on their own.

COGNITIVE CHANGES IN ADOLESCENCE

With adolescence comes a significant change in young people's understanding and perceptions of the world, as they enter an intellectual stage Jean Piaget calls *formal operations*. The formal operations stage begins at adolescence and continues throughout life. The teenager in formal operations has the capacity to problem solve by developing hypotheses and testing them out in his or her mind. Ideas can be silly, creative, or as outlandish as the mind can produce. The individual in this stage can think futuristically. He or she can plan ahead, avoid unpleasant situations, and imagine what life would be like under a variety of circumstances. This stage is a time of thinking about and understanding abstract concepts such as the meaning of religion, the purpose of war, morality, love, and freedom. The higher-order thinking that is characteristic of formal operations is a necessity for understanding traditional college subjects such as economics, art appreciation, and developmental psychology.

Formal operational thinking enables adolescents to look beyond their own families and imagine others, often in an ideal rather than a real way, a change that can precipitate conflict. Very young children perceive their parents as omniscient and omnipotent. As they mature into adolescents, they sometimes perceive the same parents as ignorant and unaware (Smollar and Youniss, 1989).

ADOLESCENT EGOCENTRISM

As children enter the transition from middle childhood to adolescence, they develop a way of thinking termed *adolescent egocetrism*. Given abstract thinking, they gain the ability to fantasize about the world and themselves as they wish them to be. A typical thirteen-year-old can be expected to comprehend and visualize what it is like to have to have a job, be a parent, or fight for social change.

Many parents have problems understanding three characteristics of adolescent egocentrism described by David Elkind (1978, 1984). The *imaginary audience* is a function of adolescent self-centeredness; teenagers are so preoccupied with their own looks and behavior that they believe everyone around them is equally interested. *Pseudostupidity* refers to indecisiveness and lack of prioritizing. Adolescents who are naturally bright have difficulty choosing from the many options they have.

Most frightening is the adolescent *personal fable*, a perception that they are so special as to be invincible and not subject to natural laws like everyone else. This perception explains why an adolescent is likely to say "Nothing is going to happen to me" when her mother refuses to allow her to go to a concert in a dangerous part of the city. Teenagers may experiment with drugs, thinking they can stop whenever they choose to; have unprotected sex because they believe they cannot get a disease or become pregnant; or drive above posted speeds and assume that they will not get a ticket. They sometimes weave around themselves personal stories or tales of heroism, greatness, or fortune to avoid feelings of insecurity or failure.

Adolescence is also a time when young people often view morality, the difference between right and wrong, differently than their parents. Lawrence Kohlberg (1986) believed that moral reasoning unfolded in stages. In early adolescence, children often adopt the moral standards of their parents; but in late adolescence and early adulthood, some children recognize that these are not the only moral and ethical options in life. When adolescents derive a personal code of morality, there is often conflict with parents over ethical conduct and adherence to rules.

CREATING AN IDENTITY

There is a prevailing view that adolescence is a time of storm and stress in most families; but this is not necessarily true (Gecas and Seff, 1991). Undoubtedly this is a period of difficult change for children and their parents because in modern Western society there are no rituals or guidelines that separate childhood from adulthood. The closest thing American society has to a rite of passage for teenagers is the issuing of a driver's license. This leaves adolescents with the dilemma of trying to figure out who they are and what they're going to do with their lives.

From approximately age eleven to age eighteen, a stage Erikson calls *identity achievement* versus *role confusion,* adolescents are faced with creating a coherent and unified sense of self, separate from their parents. Now they are concerned with "what they appear to be in the eyes of others as compared with what they feel they are, and with the questions of how to connect the roles and skills cultivated earlier with the occupational prototypes of the day." In essence, the "self" consists of experiences, values, beliefs, and ideology from the past, woven into the fabric of the present. This includes past successes, failures, triumphs, wounds and disappointments, as well as personal style and coping skills. Psychologists place strong emphasis on identity formation because adult intimate relationships, participating in family life, the choice of an occupation or career, and the development of beliefs and values is directly dependent on the adolescent's sense of self. Erikson believed that adolescents inevitably feel confused at this time and that this confusion accounts for some of the behaviors that most upset parents. He considers this time a *psychological moratorium*, a space between childhood security and adult autonomy, when adolescents can explore and test their options.

> In general it is primarily the inability to settle on an occupational identity which disturbs young people. To keep themselves together they temporarily overidentify, to the point of apparent complete loss of identity, with the heros of cliques and crowds. . . . They become remarkably clannish, intolerant, and cruel in their exclusion of others who are "different," in skin color or cultural background . . . and often in entirely petty aspects of dress and gesture arbitrarily selected as the signs of an in-grouper or out-grouper. It is important to understand . . . such intolerance as the necessary defense against a sense of identity confusion, which is unavoidable. . . . (Erikson, 1980).

Erikson stresses *fidelity* at this stage, the ability to sustain loyalties in spite of the contradictions of the adult value system. Even "love affairs" serve the important function of letting the adolescent get close to another person on whom to "project" him or herself. He or she can then test the "self" and make the necessary course corrections based on feedback from the other.

Role diffusion results when an adolescent doubts his or her sexual identity, is not accepted by peers, and is not able to reconcile the contradictions of society. Role diffusion carries with it a highly negative view of self in the present and for the future as well. The adolescent cannot pull together and integrate the necessary pieces of the self and as a result may feel alienated, angry, and confused. Erikson believed delinquency and psychiatric disorders come from the adolescent's inability to develop a defined sense of self.

Apathy, anger, anxiety, depression, and regression are signals that the adolescent is experiencing this life stage's process negatively. Behaviorally, the adolescent may look depressed, become a loner, may act out with sex, drugs,

Adolescents relieve the pressures of these transitional years by experimenting with roles, personal appearance, grooming, and clothing styles. Identity is often found in the social context of clubs, gangs, cliques, and other groups. This explains why each generation seeks to carve its own niche in terms of music, dance, language, gestures, and style.

or alcohol, or may skip school and drop out. Bullyish and belligerent behaviors are also signs of problems.

Some adolescents find that a negative identity is easier to live with than no identity at all. Membership in a gang serves as a defense against role diffusion. Immersing oneself in a group that provides an identity, albeit negative, and a set of ready-made values, morals, and behaviors can provide a kind of comfort to quiet the anxieties and tensions that come with adolescence. Erikson's theory helps us understand how and why adolescents allow themselves to become engulfed in totalitarian movements, gangs, or cults. Adolescence is a vulnerable stage of life and, if parents and society are not able to provide the stability necessary to forge a positive identity, the adolescent may be drawn to groups that offer a false sense of identity.

Kenneth Hardy of Syracuse University believes that black adolescents have fewer opportunities to define themselves because they are constantly grappling first with being black in a society that devalues them. He notes that black youngsters are less able to experiment or make mistakes than are their white counterparts. Just by being black puts an adolescent "into a slot that links him with drugs, guns, violence, crime, jail." This makes forging a positive identity—the developmental task of adolescence—particularly difficult (Hardy, 1996).

JAMES MARCIA AND IDENTITY STATUS

James Marcia (1966, 1980, 1987) has expanded Erikson's work to provide us with a richer understanding of the identity-development process in adolescence. Marcia defines identity as "an internal, self-constructed, dynamic organization of drives, abilities, beliefs, and individual history." It is a force that develops over time, one that shapes behaviors, emotions, coping abilities, social relationships, and occupational choice. It includes such aspects of development as moral reasoning, self-esteem, anxiety, and relationships. Marcia proposes that there are four states of identity, avenues that lead to resolving an identity crisis.

Identity diffusion refers to the state of adolescents who have not experienced an identity crisis because they have not yet explored any meaningful options in terms of personal beliefs or occupational possibilities. The identity-diffused adolescent may be aimless, taking up whatever comes along. These children often have poor self-esteem and poor self-image. Their unhappiness moves them from one set of peers to another, and their anxiety may lead them to the excitement and distraction caused by drugs, alcohol, and risky behavior (Waterman, 1992).

Identity foreclosure is the state when adolescents have made a commitment without experiencing a crisis. The commitment is not the result of thoughtful decision making but rather the passive acceptance of the desires and expectations of others, usually parents. Parents in identity-foreclosed families have a life plan for their children, a set vocational path. This does not mean children end up unhappy with their choices. Many enter adulthood feeling their lives are stable and safe because they have accepted parental goals.

Adolescents who are in the midst of a crisis, but unable to make a commitment to anything that can be defined are said to be in an *identity moratorium,* a state of exploring options and alternatives. Adolescents in this state will examine their thoughts, feelings, and perceptions, while bouncing ideas about the future off of family, friends, and teachers. This adolescent generally has a good sense of self and a flexibility that will enable the eventual resolution of the crisis.

Finally, there are those who feel *identity achievement*, meaning they have spent time exploring the variety of options and have made decisions about the future. These adolescents have been able to integrate the past self with the changes in the present into a coherence that will allow them to move into the future feeling socially competent and able to achieve their goals.

There are gender differences in regard to identity states. Sally Archer (1985) has found that girls in identity foreclosure and moratorium status are often conflicted in regard to family and career goals, while boys are less likely to be.

The resolution of the identity crisis is influenced by parental attitudes. Authoritative or democratic parents, ones who allow adolescents to think for themselves and be part of the family decision-making process, generally foster identity achievement. The adolescents in this group generally have a more positive attitude toward their parents. Adolescents whose identities are foreclosed often come from authoritarian homes where a high value is placed on conformity and obedience. These youngsters are not especially discontented with their status; there is a predictability and stability in many areas of their lives, although they may at some point feel anxiety. Young men in foreclosure status often have a lower sense of self-esteem and are more susceptible to the influence of others (Marcia, 1980). Permissive, neglectful parents who offer little advice or guidance often have children who remain in identity diffusion (Bernard, 1981; Enright, et al., 1980; Marcia, 1980). Detached, rejecting, neglecting, or "unengaged" parents often produced school dropouts. Adolescents in moratorium status feel the most anxiety as they struggle with trying to make decisions about their lives. These children are often ambivalently tied to their parents, sometimes loving and sometimes hating them, sometimes trying to find themselves but fearing parental disapproval and rejection if they choose the wrong course. Often college serves as the testing ground for adolescent decision making.

It should be noted that identity diffusion and foreclosure are more commonly found in early adolescence than in later adolescence. By high school, adolescents are often in achievement or moratorium status in regard to occupation choice, but in diffusion in their religious or political views.

IDENTITY AND CULTURE

Adolescents from minority American cultures, especially nonwhites, have particular problems in forging identities as they must develop an ethnic or racial identity as a part of their overall ego identity. Jean Phinney (1990) sees the development of ethnic identity in three stages. First comes *unexamined ethnic identity*, somewhat like Marcia's foreclosed status. Beliefs about one's culture come not from independent thoughts but rather from how the larger society

Flexible boundaries allow adolescents to be dependent when they need to be and independent when they are ready and able. In American society, getting a driver's license and borrowing the family car are rites of adolescent passage.

sees the culture. This can be a problem for Native American and African American adolescents who are frequently confronted with negative historical images of their cultures; however, if parents and others in their world present positive images, teens do not necessarily incorporate the negative views.

The second stage, *ethnic identity search*, is often triggered by an experience, such as a prejudicial remark, that makes an adolescent keenly aware of his or her ethnicity. Now the adolescent begins to make his or her own judgments about his or her group. This is a difficult time for many minority children who live in "two worlds." Black and Hispanic teens are often considered as "acting white" when they excel and achieve.

In the *resolution* stage, identity can be achieved in a number of ways. Some adolescents "give up" their own group and develop an identity more in keeping with their perception of white society. Others seem to develop two identities, which play out depending on whose company the adolescent is in. Still others incorporate the patterns and behaviors of their culture and remain separate from the culture at large (Phenney and Rosenthal, 1992).

PATTERNS OF CHANGE WITHIN FAMILIES

Adolescence is the time when parents must change from being primarily caregivers to being primarily counselors. This is the time when nonpower parental techniques of listening and problem solving are useful—as adolescent children slowly integrate themselves into adulthood. How successful that integration will be depends upon all the stages that came before. Did early childhood provide a sense of trust and a feeling of being loved and valued? Was the child able to initiate his or her own activities during middle childhood and move competently into the school environment? Parents who lament their children's problems during adolescence have to take a long view backward to see what earlier forces are contributing to making this transition difficult.

Many parents believe that adolescence is a time when less parental influence is needed, but this is not the case. More influence is needed, but of a different kind. A number of studies have shown that the greater the parental support for adolescents, the better these children do academically and socially. Support is often confused with control, but the two are quite different. Supporting children means listening to them without criticism, encouraging their positive aims, showing interest in their school and outside activities, sharing their companionship, knowing their friends, tolerating their style of dress and music, and displaying continued high regard and affection for them.

The transitions from child to adolescent to adult are so varied from family to family in today's world that it is difficult for parents to know what appropriate parenting is. Imagine the parent with two children, ages 18 and 22, both living at home. The 18-year-old has graduated from high school and has a job; she pays for her own clothes and has purchased a car with her own money, but she can't afford her own apartment. Her time on evenings and weekends is completely her own. The 22-year-old has graduated from college but is now enrolled in a rigorous graduate school program that allows him no time to work. His parents pay for his clothes and have provided him with a car. All his free time is spent studying. Which child is asked to help with household chores? How does a parent give both children the support they need? When do the parents, well into middle age, find time for themselves and their own needs? These kinds of modern issues make parenting more difficult than at any time in history.

As children move into adolescence, there is an increase in family tensions, disagreements, and conflict between parents and their children. Often adolescents distance themselves from the family as they strive for increased autonomy, and interactions with parents sometimes become chilly (Hill and Holmbeck, 1987; Paikoff and Brooks-Gunn, 1991; Steinberg, 1988).

A review of the literature of adolescence shows there is a broad behavioral range, from families in which discord is rare, to families in which there are occasional conflicts, on through to relationships in which conflict and discord are a dominant theme of daily living (Montemayor, 1986). The norm appears to be characterized by "temporary perturbations" rather than continual peace or constant conflict (Hill, 1985). In fact, the majority of adolescents and their families are healthy, and only a small percentage (upwards toward 20 percent) experienced significantly severe problems (Offer and Offer, 1975; Steinberg, 1988). In a study of 600 adolescents from ten countries—Australia, Bangladesh, Hungary, Israel, Italy, Japan, Taiwan, Turkey, the United States, and the former West Germany—it was found that the majority of teenagers had a positive attitude toward their parents and families (Offer, 1988). Only a small percentage felt otherwise, as illustrated by those who answered affirmatively to these questions:

- My parents are ashamed of me. (7 percent)
- I have been carrying a grudge against my parents for years. (9 percent).
- Often I feel that my mother is no good. (9 percent).
- My parents will be disappointed in me in the future. (11 percent)
- Very often I feel that my father is no good. (13 percent)

As adolescents age, their distance from the family increases, as both male and female children spend more time with their peers (Larson and Richards, 1991). In a study of children in grades five through nine, where electronic pagers were used to gauge companionship, location, and mood at random times, the older subjects reported spending more time with peers than with parents. Fourth graders were more likely to see both mothers and fathers as the most likely sources of support; however, as children progressed through school, they turned toward same-sex peers for support. From about tenth grade through college, romantic partners became important. Interestingly, although adolescents spend more time with peers and away from the family, mothers continue to be rated as a major source of support. Adolescents are more likely to seek advice from mothers than fathers, although it appears that girls seek advice on personal issues from their mothers. Boys do seek out advice from fathers but, when this relationship is rated negatively, boys are likely to seek their mother's advice. (Furman and Buhrmester, 1992; Greene and Grimsley, 1990). In a Scottish study, adolescents rated mother and same-sex friends as significant in their lives.

What do adolescents talk about with their friends and family? In one research project, adolescents reported that "discussions" with parents were generally one-sided, with parents more likely to explain their own views than to try and understand their adolescent children's perspectives (Hunter, 1985). The adolescents rated their conversations with peers as more mutual, allowing for both explaining and understanding. These peer conversations covered topics including the self, family life, school issues, personal philosophies, vocational questions, and peer and personal matters (Table 12.1). Note that on career or college issues, adolescents do not look to peers for advice.

SOURCES OF CONFLICT BETWEEN PARENTS AND ADOLESCENTS

Often the onset of puberty is a marker for the beginnings of parent-adolescent conflict (Table 12.2). Interestingly, pubertal status was associated with mother-son conflict but not father-son. For young adolescent women, when menarche occurred early, there was greater and longer-lasting conflict than when it

TABLE 12.1   Percentages of Teenagers Seeking Peer Advice

Issues	Girls	Boys
What to spend money on	2%	19%
Whom to date	47	41
Which clubs to join	60	54
Advice on personal problems	53	27
How to dress	53	47
Which courses to take	16	8
Which hobbies to take up	36	46
Choosing a future occupation	2	0
Which social events to attend	60	66
Whether to go to college	0	0
What books to read	40	38
How often to date	24	35
Participating in drinking parties	40	46
Choosing a future spouse	9	8
Whether to go steady	29	30
How intimate to be on a date	24	35
Information about sex	44	30

The Spirit of Parenting

The Color of Water

Helen didn't come home that night. Nor the next day. Nor the next. She was fifteen years old. Mommy called the police the second day. They came and took a report. They searched the neighborhood, but couldn't find her. Mommy called all Helen's friends. Still no Helen. The following week my sister Jack called Mommy from her apartment in Harlem. . . . "Ruth, she's with me," Jack said. "She doesn't want to see you, but don't worry. Let it blow over. Don't scare her off." But Mommy couldn't wait. She hung up the phone and summoned my brother Richie to the kitchen, gave him carfare and explicit instructions: Tell Helen all is forgiven. . . . Just come home. . . . He returned late that night with his hat pushed far back on his forehead. "She's not comin' home, Ma," he said.

Shortly after, Helen left Jack's altogether and disappeared.

Mommy was beside herself. She spent entire nights pacing up and down the floor. She called on preachers and friends from church, called on my stepfather, who made several rare, during-the-week appearances. More solutions were discussed. Prayers were said. Regrets taken. Apologies made. But there was no Helen. "She'll come back," Daddy said. "It'll work out."

Weeks passed, months, and Helen didn't return.

Finally Jack called. "I found her. She's living with some crazy woman . . . ."

Mommy got the address and went to the place herself. . . . "I'm here to see Helen," Mommy said.

Silence.

"Helen. I want you to come home. Whatever's wrong we'll fix. Just forget all of it and come on home."

"Please come home, Helen."

The door had a peephole in it. The peephole slid back. A large black eye peered out.

"Please come home, Helen. This is no place for you to be. Just come on home." The peephole closed.

From *The Color of Water: A Black Man's Tribute to His White Mother*
by James McBride

---

occurred at about the average age of onset (Hill, 1985). When adolescents were observed having pleasant and unpleasant conversations with their parents, researchers found that there were greater negative feelings expressed as adolescents physically matured. Compared to fathers and daughters, mothers and daughters were found to express more negative feelings in their conversations (Montemayor, 1986).

TABLE 12.2   Conflict Areas Between Parents and Adolescents

Poor school performance	Choice of friends
Misbehavior at school	Political views
Failure to do homework	Social activities
Disrespectful at home	General appearance
Putting off chores	Career plans
Untidy room	Sexual mores
Forgetting commitments	Religious values
Hair and dress style	

Parent-adolescent conflict can be grouped into two categories: superficial transactional quarrels and deeper psychological arguments about autonomy and independence. Parents generally assume they know what is "good" for their children until adolescence, when disagreements ensue over decisions, rules, family obligations, peers, habits, privacy, appearance, and so on. Family rules in these areas are generally established by the parents who may or may not permit input from their children. Family interaction tends to be unilateral, from parent to child, whereas peer interaction is more mutual (Holmbeck and Hill, 1991). In one study, which observed conversations between parents and adolescents, researchers noted that there tended to be a greater expression of negative feelings by parents as adolescents physically matured. Furthermore, greater negativity was generally expressed by mothers than fathers, and more in the mother-daughter dyad. As interpersonal issues become the focus of differences between parents and their adolescent children, disagreements can become quite heated. Interestingly, when conversations were pleasant, both were more positive with each other; but when conversations were unpleasant, parents and adolescents both were more negative toward each other (Montemayor, Eberly, and Flannery, 1993).

On measures of family communications, adolescents report consistently that parents dominate conversations and permit little room for an adolescent point of view (Noller and Callan, 1990).

Problems with parents are usually around separation and individuation. The typical pattern observed is that at the end of late childhood parents exert greater control and are closer, more supportive, and more nurturant than friends. As children move into early adolescence and are not yet autonomous, they use friends and peers as the intermediate step of gaining independence; they begin to lean more on them than on their parents. Researchers who studied adolescent behavior in shopping malls and amusement parks found expressive behaviors such as "touching, smiling, talking, gazing" decreased between mothers and their children as the children reached adolescence, and there was a corresponding increase in these same behaviors between peers (Montemayor and Flannery, 1989).

The studies interviewed or provided questionnaires to adolescents and their families regarding separation, individuation, autonomy, independence, and attachment. Both studies found that while the adolescent is undergoing changes and moving closer to peers, those adolescents who have higher-quality attachment to their parents through this time seem to fare much better through adolescence than those who had poorer quality attachment to parents. Overall, even as adolescents distance from their parents in gaining emotional autonomy, the quality of the attachment to the parents, not to the peers, predicted the quality of adjustment throughout adolescence. These adolescents reported being better able to handle problems and stressors, had higher reported self-esteem, and overall reported fewer negative feelings such as anxiety and depression (Papini and Roggman, 1992).

All in all, findings demonstrate that although adolescents continually report their dissatisfaction with the amount, speed, and types of changes that take place in their family, they still want the family to be a supportive and cohesive environment (Noller and Callan, 1986). The disagreeable fighting creates distance between parent and child, but it permits the child to stand on his own decisions, become more responsible, and gain control over her or his own life. This time may be referred to as *sturm und drang* (storm and stress), but it serves the psychological purpose of increasing distance in the family and providing a greater sense of autonomy for the adolescent.

In studying family conflict, one researcher raised the point that trying to understand the interaction between parents and adolescents in terms of conflict and harmony is "misdirected," rather, it is more important to view what goes on from other contexts (Montemayor, 1986). These contexts include the behavioral perspectives of communication and problem-solving skills, parenting techniques, and the positive and negative exchanges in the family.

Families that are unable to allow normal separation and growth may provoke undesirable behavioral symptoms in their children (Stierlin, 1979). While feelings of fear and guilt may prevent an adolescent from separating, the behavior the adolescent exhibits (drug-taking, delinquency, mental illness) may make parents feel so overwhelmed that they give up responsibility and call in the courts, social service agencies, or hospitals to take over the care of their adolescent child. Sometimes adolescents leave home themselves—to move in with friends, marry, or simply run away.

The expulsion of adolescents from the home can lead to a serious and even permanent family rift (Sager, et al., 1983). Nydia Garcia Preto warns of the consequence of this action.

> For the adolescent who is cast out or runs away, the casualty rate due to other-inflicted or self-inflicted violence (including drug overdose) is high. Vulnerability to exploitation is also high. Unemployment, under-employment, prostitution, and involvement with an abusive partner are more likely outcomes for the adolescent without family supports. The remaining members of the evicting or deserted family are likely to confront heightened guilt, mutual blame, self-reproach, bitterness, continued anger, depression, and unresolved feelings of loss. (Preto, 1988)

STYLES OF PARENTING AND ADOLESCENT ADJUSTMENT

There is a clear relationship between parenting style and adolescent adjustment. Diana Baumrind classified parenting into three categories: authoritarian, authoritative, and permissive (neglectful or overly indulgent) (Chapter 5). Numerous studies conclude that the authoritative style of parenting during adolescence is associated with the adolescent's better adjustment, higher self-esteem and self-confidence, better school performance, and lower deviance. The authoritative style benefited all adolescents, regardless of gender, socio-economic status, or racial or ethnic identity. Diana Baumrind (1991) found that authoritative parents were more successful in "protecting their adolescents from problem drug use and in generating competence." Are there specific parenting practices which have been found to be beneficial? Lawrence Steinberg and his associates found that "monitoring, encouragement of achievement, joint decision making" were related to higher academic achievement, greater self-reliance, and lower drug usage. (Brown, Mounts, Lamborn, and Steinberg, 1993).

FAMILY STRUCTURE AND ADOLESCENT BEHAVIOR

A number of studies that examine family structure indicate that problems and changes in family structure raise the risk of adolescent problems. Family structure may be viewed as a two-parent household, single-parent household, divorced household, remarried household with stepparents and siblings, or any combination and variation of these. Overall, the findings indicate that adolescents living in families with both biological parents (not separated or divorced) fared better than those in divorced, stepfamilies, or single parent households (Steinberg 1987). When another adult was present in a mother-only single-parent structure, there tended to be increased parenting and lesser amounts of misconduct than in mother-only circumstances (Dornbusch, 1985). While it is politically popular to link family breakups and adolescent problems, it is the changed economic situation that causes the stresses that lead to family problems. Generally mothers are left to parent alone with little emotional or financial support. The extra burden on a lone parent makes it harder to nurture, guide, and provide consistent discipline for adolescent children (Lempers, Clark-Lempers, 1990).

Due to the nature of divorce and remarriage, children undergo a variety of necessary adjustments to their living situations. They may have to adjust to living with a new stepfather, stepmother, step siblings, and combinations thereof. Relationships with biological parents need to be reworked, and the parent who is adjusting to a new living situation may not be as available to the child as before.

Adolescents left to fend for themselves for long periods of time are more likely to get into trouble. Parental or adult supervision is an important factor in family life and can mitigate the problems of stress and economic troubles (Forehand, Wierson, Thomas, and Armistead, 1991).

Psychologist Thomas Gordon (1991) believes that the most tragic consequence of parents misunderstanding adolescence is the number of teenagers who "divorce" their parents psychologically, withdrawing from the family relationship even while physically remaining at home. In *Discipline That Works* Gordon describes the family dynamics that can result from too many conflicts, severe punishment, and a lack of communication between parents and teenagers.

> Defeated in their efforts to gain freedom from the punitive control of their parents and weary of losing the never-ending conflicts and power struggles at home, these youngsters withdraw into sullen isolation and detachment, and cease all meaningful communication with their parents. Such youngsters arrange to stay away from home as much as possible, returning only to eat and sleep. Their parents know next to nothing about their activities, their beliefs, their values or feelings, because these kids make sure they divulge nothing about themselves to their parents. They've learned from daily experience that one way to avoid being controlled, deprived, and punished is to avoid being present in the relationship, or, if that's not possible, to avoid any open and honest communications.
>
> The more intrepid of these teenagers may eventually pack up and run away from home, preferring to risk the insecurities and dangers of the outside world rather than suffer the oppression of punitive and controlling parents. Studies of runaway children have shown that a very high percentage leave home in order to shake off the yoke of their parents' punitive power. In a related method of "escaping," many teenage girls get pregnant out of wedlock in order to use marriage as a way out of a tyrannical relationship with their parents.
>
> It has become clear recently that a surprising number of runaway teenagers don't run away from home at all—they are actually kicked out of their home by the parents! The most frequent reason given by the parents is that the youngsters were "incorrigible," "unmanageable," "rebellious," "uncontrollable." It so sad but true: some parents are willing to discard their children when they realize that they have lost the power to make them obey. Obedience becomes a higher value to these parents than their relationship with their offspring. (Gordon, 1991)

Gerald Patterson takes a combination of family systems approach and ecological approach to delinquency in children (Figure 12.2). He believes the excessive aggressiveness in children is due to parents' poor discipline techniques. The parents of children who exhibit antisocial behaviors are often lacking in family management skills, which have their roots in the parents' families of origin. In addition, societal factors such as employment and stress contribute to the way parents monitor and behave toward their children. Delinquency then is due to a variety of familial forces, many beyond the control of misbehaving children.

THE INFLUENCE OF PEERS

When teenage children get into trouble, it is not uncommon for parents to blame the influence of the adolescent peer group. What the research shows, however, is that problems already existing in the family trouble the adolescent so much that he or she seeks out the support of peers. Several studies compar-

Figure 12.2
Gerald Patterson's
Family Systems
Approach to
Delinquent
Behavior

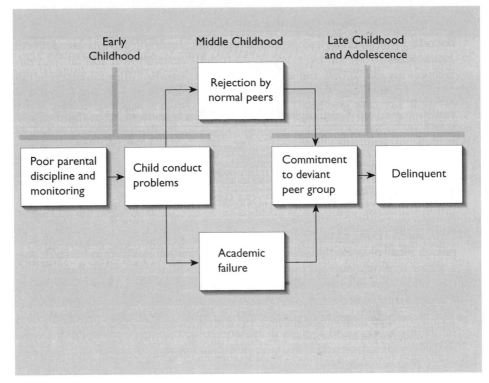

ing adolescent drug and alcohol abusers found that many of these children came from families where communication was impaired and parenting styles were authoritarian or permissive-neglectful. Often parents did not adequately monitor their children, there was a lack of discipline, and the teens themselves had inadequate social skills training (Brody and Forehand, 1993).

THE ADOLESCENT AS CONSUMER

The adolescent population of the United States began to grow in 1992 and reached almost 25 million. This is a growth rate twice that of the overall population (U.S. Census Bureau). By 2006, the number of adolescents will exceed 30 million. This growth has created an enormous consumer market of children—teenagers who do the family shopping, make dinner for themselves, and buy products with the money they earn from allowances or part-time employment. In 1992 teenagers bought 25 percent of all movie tickets in the United States and 27 percent of all videos, spending a total of $6.6 billion dollars. In 1994 they spent $1.5 billion on jeans and $3 billion on sneakers alone *(Fortune)*. The average adolescent allowance in 1994 was estimated at $15 a week, up from $11 two years earlier (Rand Youth Poll, 1994). One in nine high school students had their own credit cards. Clearly this is a cohort group like no other that has existed in American society; and this uniqueness explains why it is sometimes difficult for their parents to understand them.

The Informed Parent 12.1

Reducing Parent-Adolescent Conflict

Lawrence Steinberg has proposed a six-tiered collaborative problem-solving model designed to reduce parent-adolescent conflicts. It is best to try these strategies when children are fully available and willing to work on problems. Issues such as curfew, friendships, chores, social behaviors, dating rules, and the like can be handled this way if there are conflicts. Sometimes parents must make decisions their children disagree with, as in the case of health or safety, but otherwise most problems can be worked out more easily if adolescents participate in the decision-making process.

1. *Establish ground rules for conflict resolution.* First and foremost both parents and adolescents must be respectful when disagreeing. There should be no name-calling, criticizing each other's viewpoint, or putting each other down. This is considered "fair fighting."

2. *Try to understand each other.* Stay focused on the issues rather than personalities. Each party should state how they see the problem and what they see as a goal.

3. *Brainstorm ideas.* Generate as many solutions to a problem as you can. No idea should be rejected as dumb or crazy or too expensive. Allow a set period of time—5 to 10 minutes—to do this. Write all the ideas down.

4. *Try to agree on one or more solutions.* After discussing the options, select the one that seems best. A degree of give-and-take and some compromises will be in order here. Neither side should agree to something unacceptable.

5. *Write down the agreement.* This will ensure the agreement is accurately remembered. If one party forgets the agreement, it can be a reminder.

6. *Establish a time to review how things are going.* If the agreement is not working out or there are problems with it, the issues can be addressed.

Source: Adapted from *Adolescence* by John W. Santrock, Brown and Benchmark, 1993. Reprinted with permission of The McGraw-Hill Companies.

EDUCATING THE ADOLESCENT

High school provides adolescents with the academic information needed to function in the adult world. For those students planning to go to college, high school serves as a training ground for higher education. The variety of subjects offered in high school gives teenagers a glimpse at future career choices. School also provides a social milieu in which teenagers make and strengthen friendships.

TRANSITION FROM ELEMENTARY TO MIDDLE SCHOOL

The transition from the nurturant elementary school environment to the more independent middle school setting is often stressful. Instead of sitting in one or two classrooms the entire day, students in middle school move from class to

The Informed Parent 12.2

Negotiating Rules

David Elkind in *A Sympathetic Understanding of the Child: Birth to Sixteen*, offers three options for coming to agreeable terms with your adolescent:

- **Strike a bargain.** Offer a reward or delay an activity.
  "You can do the dishes after you return from the movies."
  "I'll drive you if you arrange for a ride home."
  "If you go to the store for me you can pick up a video to watch tonight."

- **Make an agreement.** This is best used with rules.
  "I'll loan you the car but you must be home by curfew."
  "You can go to the party but only if there's a parent in attendance."
  "If you complete all your homework you can talk on the phone."

- **Design a contract.** Write down the agreement. Each person should commit to the rules of the contract.

class, forcing interaction with larger groups of peers (Figure 12.3). During this time children are changing physically and cognitively. Family interactions change as young adolescents are expected to take on more responsibility and independence (Eccles, and Midgley, 1990). Compared to elementary school, the middle school offers the opportunity for more independence; there are more subjects from which to choose; and there is a greater chance for involvement in extracurricular activity.

The transition to high school can be difficult for teenagers because so much of the experience depends upon social interactions. A study of 3,781 students at a typical U.S. high school revealed that 70 percent of the students fit into one of six main "crowds" (Brown, et al., 1993) (Table 12.3).

ATTITUDES TOWARD SCHOOL

As a rule, children from middle and upper socioeconomic backgrounds put a high value on education, and have a positive attitude toward school. Students' attitudes are also influenced by the quality of the high school they attend. Theodore Sizer (1984) describes characteristics that are common to good high schools. In good high schools, everyone from the administrators to the parents and students believes in the importance of education. The teachers are dedicated professionals committed to giving the most to their students and to continually improving their skills. Students are not held back academically. There is flexibility for advanced students to take some of their courses at area colleges. Parent involvement is a high priority. Parents sit on school committees and attend functions such as parent open houses. Finally, teachers make students think critically rather than just memorize facts.

A good high school is one where a student feels welcome. The climate is positive and caring. Expectations are high. Rewards are bestowed for good work, and fair limits are set by the administration. Such schools tend to have better attendance rates, students who score higher on standardized tests, and fewer disciplinary problems (Rutter, 1983). Above all, good high schools are flexible, adjusting to the needs of their students.

THE PROBLEMS OF ADOLESCENCE

Adolescents are at risk for many serious problems. While approximately 80 percent of adolescents pass through this stage without major problems, the other 20 percent experience difficulties that may go untreated (Offer and Schoner-Reichl, 1992). Drug use has increased, especially in children age 15 and younger (Gans and Blyth, 1990). Mental illness is becoming a major disability among adolescents ages 10–18 (National Center for Education in Maternal and Child Health, 1990). Between 7 percent and 33 percent of adolescents are clinically depressed (Peterson, et al., 1993). The suicide rate among 10–14 years olds has almost tripled between 1968 and 1985 and doubled among 15–19 year-olds (Children's Safety Network, 1991). Homicide deaths among African American males, ages 15 to 19 have increased an astonishing 111 percent between 1985 and 1990. Sexually transmitted diseases, including HIV infection, have become epidemic among the nation's adolescents.

TABLE 12.3

Classification	Description
Popular	Socially competent; academically oriented; moderately involved in drugs and delinquency.
Jock	Focused on athletics; drug involvement limited to alcohol; interested in acceptable grades and good relationships with parents and teachers.
Brain	Strong focus on academic achievement; close relationships with teachers; avoidance of drugs and delinquency.
Normal	Largest group; the "average"; avoid deviant activities; no overriding focus on drugs or achievement.
Druggie	Strong focus on drugs; delinquency; inattentive to school and authority.
Outcast	"Loners" and "nerds"; low social competence; low self-image; low involvement in deviant behavior; average or above-average academic achievement.

A nine-year study of the Carnegie Council on Adolescent Development report concluded that the nation's 19 million young adolescents, ages 10 to 14, are being neglected to the point that half will have difficulty leading healthy, productive adulthoods. According to the researchers, parental involvement with children drops when children reach adolescence. While 75 percent of parents of 9-year-olds claim high or medium involvement in their children's lives, only 55 percent of parents of 14-year-olds say the same. The 27-member panel of the Carnegie Council suggest the following changes in order to deal with adolescent problems:

- Create schools that better suit adolescent developmental needs.
- Encourage family-oriented employer policies that would allow parents the time to re-engage with their children.
- Increase the educational and treatment options for troubled adolescents.
- Expand youth organizations so that adolescents can be reached and helped.
- Encourage a more responsible media, so that drug use, violence, and sexual activity are not glamorized.

RISK TAKING AND SENSATION SEEKING

Some adolescents appear prone to taking higher risks than others and consequently suffer the consequences of acts such as driving while intoxicated,

High school students often group themselves in cliques, representative of their interests and aptitudes.

driving above safe speeds, using drugs, participating in unprotected sex, and engaging in illegal actions such as vandalism and shoplifting. There are a number of hypotheses about why adolescents take more risks. David Elkind's work suggests the previously mentioned "personal fable," a form of egocentrism in which the adolescent feels protected from the impact of negative behaviors.

Jeffrey Arnett has approached "recklessness" in adolescents from the perspective of a predisposition to sensation seeking (Arnett, 1995). Arnett believes that some adolescents are attracted to the intensity of the sensations which certain experiences offer.

> It is interesting to note that the same individuals are likely to prefer hard rock and heavy metal music over other types of music. This does not mean that the music causes the adolescent to engage in reckless behaviors, but rather the need for higher intensity sensations is likely to be a possible common factor behind the attraction to both the music and experiences. In a related study, substance abusing adolescents were found to have a lower tolerance (more easily bored) in constant stimulation leisure activities than non-substance abusers. The authors hypothesize that when the activity fails to provide enough arousal, then boredom is the result, leading people to seek drugs as a way to raise arousal levels.

Arnett (1996) has delved deeply into the world of "metal heads," adolescents attracted to a musical subculture of American society characterized by a sense of alienation and estrangement from the overall culture, a deep loneliness arising from a lack of gratifying emotional connections to others, and cynicism about the ideals and possibilities for life that one's culture offers. Arnett believes that alienation is pervasive among American adolescents, including many who are not heavy metal fans. It is his position that American society values individualism above all social traits and American parents and schools tend to allow and encourage qualities that promote independence and creativity. Self-fulfillment and self-expression are held in higher value than self-restraint and self-denial. Heavy metal concerts are simply the extreme of what the American culture holds dear. The music is an active rejection of all social institutions and all forms of social restraint.

Arnett believes that American society has denied adolescent boys the rituals that show them how to *procreate, provide,* and *protect* as adult members of society. Because they are not guided properly by male elders, adolescent males are forced to construct their own view of what manhood is. Heavy metal concerts in some ways resemble ancient manhood rituals, serving the function of publically inducting boys into the role requirements that will be expected of them as adult men. But, as Arnett notes, heavy metal differs in that "it leads adolescent boys *against* adult ideals; it represents a declaration of rejection of the ways of the adults in the larger culture."

Richard Jessor (1992) viewed the factors leading to high-risk behaviors as part of a five-dimensional interrelationship that includes biology, the social environment, the perceived environment, personality, and actual behavior (Figure 12.3). When children engage in high-risk behaviors, parents often blame the schools, the availability of drugs, and peer influences (Jessor, 1993).

TABLE 12.4   Deaths Among Youths 15 to 24 Years of Age, United States, 1991

Leading Causes of Death	Number
1. Unintentional injuries (accidents)	15,278
2. Homicide (includes legal intervention)	8,159
3. Suicide	4,751
4. Cancer	1,814
5. Heart diseases	990
6. AIDS-related deaths	613
7. Congenital anomalies	449
8. Pneumonia and influenza	256
9. Cerebrovascular diseases	219
10. Chronic obstructive pulmonary diseases	209
Total, all causes	36,452

Source: National Center for Health Statistics (1994). *Health, United States,* 1993, p. 99. Hyattsville, MD: Public Health Service. Washington, DC: U.S. Government Printing Office.

Researchers like Jessor believe that the best defense against high-risk behavior in adolescence is the development of self-esteem, a sense of competence, a secure home environment, and a feeling of belonging to a stable family (Jessor, 1992).

SUBSTANCE ABUSE

Since 1975, annual surveys of teen drug use have been conducted across the country through research grants from the National Institute on Drug Abuse (NIDA). Most notable are the series of surveys titled "Monitoring the Future," also known as the National High School Senior Survey. The survey originally included only high school seniors but was expanded to a cross-sectional comparison by the inclusion of questionnaire data from 8th and 10th graders as well. This research is based on information from approximately 50,000 students attending 435 public and private secondary schools. The survey questions substance usage across time spans (within the last 30 days, past year, and lifetime) for a number of different drugs or substances (any illicit drug, marijuana, hashish, inhalants, hallucinogens, cocaine, crack, heroin, stimulant, sedatives including barbiturates and quaaludes), tranquilizers, alcohol, steroids, cigarettes, and smokeless tobacco.

Over a twenty-year period from 1975, drug usage increased through the late 1960s and into the 1970s, then decreased through the 1980s until about the early 1990s, when there appears to have been an overall increase in the usage of both licit and illicit drugs.

Beginning in 1997 there has been a modest drop in the use of drugs by adolescents (Figure 12.4). Marijuana use is slightly down, however, 1998

Figure 12.3   Adolescent High-Risk Behavior

Risk and Protective Factors

Biology/Genetics
- Risk factors
  Family history of alcoholism
- Protective factors
  High intelligence

Social Environment
- Risk factors
  Poverty
  Normative anomic
  Racial inequality
  Illegitimate opportunity
- Protective factors
  Quality schools
  Cohesive family
  Neighborhood resources
  Interested adults

Perceived Environment
- Risk factors
  Models for deviant behavior
  Parent-friend normative conflict
- Protective factors
  Models for conventional behavior
  High controls against deviant behavior

Personality
- Risk factors
  Low perceived life chances
  Low self-esteem
  Risk-taking propensity
- Protective factors
  Value on achievement
  Value on health
  Intolerance of deviance

Behavior
- Risk factors
  Problem drinking
  Poor school work
- Protective factors
  Church attendance
  Involvement in school and voluntary clubs

Risk Behaviors

Adolescence Risk Behavior/Lifestyles
- Problem behavior
  Illicit drug use
  Delinquency
  Drunk driving
- Health-related behavior
  Unhealthy eating
  Tobacco use
  Sedentariness
  Nonuse of safety belt
- School behavior
  Truancy
  Dropout
  Drug use at school

Risk Outcomes

Health/Life Compromising Outcomes
- Health
  Disease/illness
  Lowered fitness
- Social roles
  School failures
  Social isolation
  Legal trouble
  Early childbearing
- Personal development
  Inadequatae self-concept
  Depression/suicide
- Preparation for adulthood
  Limited work skills
  Unemployability
  Amotivation

TABLE 12.5   Trends of Drug Use Among 8TH, 10TH and 12TH graders, 1998

After a six-year increase beginning in 1992, there has been a slight decline in drug use among high school adolescents by 1998. Figures are percentages for those students who have tried a particular drug at some time in their lives.

Drug	8TH Grade	10TH Grade	12TH Grade	1997–1998 change for high school seniors
Marijuana/Hashish	22.2	39.6	49.1	−0.5
Inhalants	20.5	18.3	15.2	−0.9
Hallucinogens	4.9	9.8	14.1	−1.0
Cocaine	4.6	7.2	9.3	+0.6
Crack	3.2	3.9	4.4	+0.5
Heroin	2.3	2.3	2.0	−0.1
Stimulants	11.3	16.0	16.4	−0.1
Tranquilizers	4.6	7.8	8.5	+0.7
Alcohol	52.5	69.0	81.4	−0.3
Cigarettes	45.7	57.7	65.3	−0.1
Steroids	2.3	2.0	2.7	+0.3

Source: Monitoring the Future Study, University of Michigan, 1999.

figures show that nearly a quarter (22 percent) of all eighth-graders said they had tried marijuana, and about half (49 percent) of twelfth-graders said they had done so. While the use of alcohol is also slightly down, one-third (33 percent) of all high school seniors report being drunk at least once in the 30-day interval preceding the study.

After a long and steady increase in smoking among American teens, which began in the early 1990s, smoking rates among secondary school students have started to turn downward. The Michigan researchers note that adolescents in all three grade levels see smoking as dangerous. Nevertheless, over one-third of American students smoke by the time they leave high school.

While cigarette smoking and alcohol consumption are increasing, the survey found that hallucinogens, crack, inhalants, and heroin are being used by eighth graders. Because the survey does not account for the usage by students who drop out by twelfth grade, investigators believe that drug use rates are even higher than indicated.

RISK FACTORS AND DRUG USE

Many adolescents report that they have used drugs as a means to relax and handle stress (Johnston and O'Malley, 1986). Frequent users of drugs were found to be maladjusted, had personality problems, had a sense of alienation from others, showed poor impulse control, and manifested emotional distress (Shedler and Block, 1991). In an interesting study of adolescents self-rating their own physical attractiveness, females who rated themselves unattractive were more than four times as likely to use illicit drugs as those who saw themselves as average or attractive. And those who viewed themselves as unattractive and underweight as well, were six to ten times more likely to use illicit drugs. Self-ratings in males did not differentiate users from nonusers except for smokeless tobacco; those males who rated themselves as unattractive had a significantly higher usage rate (Page, 1993). A study of Latino adolescents found that alcohol and inhalant use were associated with depression and emotional distress (Felix-Ortiz, et al.). In a longitudinal assessment, children who manifested certain types of traits (fearlessness, difficulty controlling emotions, and unconventionality) were found to be more likely to use drugs than those who were not at risk (Brook, et al., 1995).

Family, peer, and socioeconomic status also play a role in adolescent drug usage. Collected data demonstrate that, when parents are actively involved with the adolescent and regularly monitor their children's activities, there is lowered delinquency and drug use (Dishion and Loeber, 1985). Diane Baumrind's work on parenting styles identified authoritative parenting as the only style (as compared with authoritarian and permissive styles) that was highly demanding and highly responsive with respect to "protecting their adolescents from problem drug use and in generating competence" (1991). Studies indicate that involved parents tend to provide solid communication with their adolescents, and keep an eye on their activities and peers; these factors relate directly to decreasing delinquent or problematic drug usage.

Are peers influential in drug use and abuse? While not a direct causal agent, it is true that social pressure from peers can be influential. For both males and females, peer pressure was associated with dating, sexual attitudes, and use of drugs and alcohol (Brown 1982). For drug abusers, it is not always the peer group that leads the adolescent into antisocial delinquent action, but rather it is the troubled adolescent who seeks out the deviant peers. Parents often overlook their own drug usage as an influence on their adolescent's behavior. Researchers in one study were able to predict which adolescents were problem drinkers simply by noting if a parent was an alcohol user when the adolescent was 12 to 13 years old (Peterson, et al., 1994).

EATING DISORDERS

A small percentage of adolescents experience life-threatening problems in the form of *eating disorders*: Over the past 20 years, *anorexia nervosa*, a form of self-starvation, and *bulimia*, a binge-purge syndrome, have emerged as serious psychological and health problems in adolescent women as well as in a small number of adolescent males. The emergence of these disorders is the result of a cultural ideal of slimness for women and a socialization process that insists on adherence to traditional feminine gender norms (Rodin, Silberstein, and Striegel-Moore, 1986). Many female athletes are encouraged to abnormal thinness by coaches, parents, and other participants in competitive sports activities (Taub and Blinde, 1992). It is also proposed that anorexia is the result of disturbed family interactions. The families of anorexics are often rigid and controlling, sometimes with an overprotective and hypochrondriacal concern for their children's health. An eating disorder is seen as a teenager's attempt to gain some control over life and body (Brone and Fisher, 1988).

The anorexic adolescent has a serious disturbance in body image; she sees herself as fat although she is generally not. An individual is considered seriously underweight for height on standardized weight charts if he or she is 85 percent or less of normal expectations. The anorexic will set goals to below 75 percent of normal body weight. When weight reaches this point there are noticeable and significant threats to health. Beyond the fear of weight gain, the adolescent will obsess about parts of her body (usually stomach, thighs, buttocks), which she mentally mismeasures and misperceives.

One of the diagnostic signs that weight loss has become too severe is amenorrhea. If the weight loss is so significant that the endocrine system is affected, the hormones that regulate monthly cycles diminish and menstruation ceases. Body organs and tissues begin to deteriorate. Other symptoms of anorexia include depression, irritability, sleep disturbances, and withdrawal

When world-class gymnast Christy Henrich tried out for the 1988 Olympics she weighed 52 pounds. By age 22 she was dead of anorexia nervosa.

from family and friends. Strangely, while these problems are occurring, the anorexic may become even more obsessed with food to the point of helping with food preparation and feeding others while starving herself.

In the United States, full-blown anorexia occurs in 1 percent of the population, and is considerably higher when the disturbance has not become the full-blown disorder (up to 3 percent). Statistically, there is a bimodal distribution (or two high-frequency peaks) in adolescence, occurring at ages fourteen and eighteen and the mean at age seventeen. This indicates that the onset may occur with life changes (such as going to college) or changes in family composition (loss by death or divorce).

Treatment for anorexia includes individual and family therapy, as well as medication for depression. If therapy is unsuccessful and weight loss reaches a critical level, then hospitalization is required because serious organ damage is the next stage. Death rate from anorexia is over 10 percent and occurs most commonly from electrolyte imbalance, starvation, and suicide.

Bulimia is a serious condition in which individuals binge (eat, often an inordinate amount of food) and then purge their systems by inducing vomiting or by using laxatives, diuretics, or vigorous exercise, the purpose of which is to prevent weight gain or to change body shape. Commonly, the binge-purge episodes are secret, and the adolescent may actually plan the episodes.

Bulimia may occur in conjunction with stressors such as family problems, school or social difficulties, perceptions of problems around weight, body shape dissatisfaction, and even by unpleasant mood states. The cycle begins with binge eating, which may work to alleviate feelings of loss of control, guilt, embarrassment, or depression. After purging (within two hours) often comes a sense of physical and emotional relief. If the purging behavior is vomiting, there may be many physical problems including serious dental problems caused by the stomach acid. As in anorexia nervosa, the bulimic adolescent is extremely concerned with weight and body image. Another study confirmed that these bulimic adolescents experience significantly greater feelings of depression and greater alcohol usage (Post and Crowther, 1985).

Beyond societal and cultural pressures, some young women face additional pressures to be thin. Dancers and athletes are frequently found to have bulimic symptoms. One study comparing adolescent dancers in the United States and China, found them to weigh approximately 14 percent below the ideal for their height and to have experienced delayed menarche (Hamilton, et al., 1988).

The bulimic profile is almost identical to that for anorexia nervosa: 90 percent are white adolescent females living in industrialized nations. Whereas full-blown anorexia nervosa affects about 1 percent of the population, bulimia nervosa occurs in up to 3 percent and is growing. Bulimia occurs in males, but only at a rate of about one-tenth the female rate. In males, bulimia usually develops in later adolescence or early adulthood, often after the individual has been on a diet or an intense stressor has occurred.

Psychotherapy, group therapy, family therapy, and medications are treatment option for bulimics. Even after successful therapy, however, there needs to be long-term support for work on coping skills, peer relations, family relations, and issues surrounding body image.

The Informed Parent 12.3

Anorexia Nervosa

Here are some of the symptoms that may point to anorexia in adolescents or adults.

Psychological Symptoms	Physical Symptoms
Preoccupation with thinness	Abdominal distress
Body image disturbance	Impaired mental function
Hyperactivity	Constipation
Moodiness	Metabolic changes
Depression	Electrolyte abnormalities
Feelings of insecurity	Hypothermia
Loneliness	Low blood pressure
Social isolation	Sexual dysfunction
Feelings of helplessness	Slow heartbeat

ADOLESCENT DEPRESSION

Depression is a disorder of affect or mood. While it is normal to occasionally feel down or blue, depression is a long-lasting, serious, clinical disorder requiring intervention or treatment. Depression is characterized by altered mood states, distorted thoughts, changes in the body's biology, and dysfunctional behaviors.

Depressed adolescents may feel sad or tired, become withdrawn, think hopelessly or negatively about their present and future, experience physical problems affecting appetite and sleep, have little interest in previously enjoyed activities, and have suicidal ideas. These symptoms can result from problems in the family, stress at school, excessively high personal expectations, relationship breakups, problems with the law, substance use and abuse, reactions to problems of others, problems due to the consequences of poor judgment (as in the case of an unwanted pregnancy or an accident while driving after drinking.)

Teenage depression is often masked by anxiety, eating disorders, substance abuse, or hyperactivity. As a result, parents may miss the traditional signs of depression. Whereas adults may directly report feelings of depression, adolescents often express it as boredom, irritability, or acting out. Parents should especially look for serious changes, such as loss of interest and withdrawal from things that were once important, or significant sleep or appetite differences.

PARENTAL DEPRESSION AND ADOLESCENT DISTRESS

Living with an ever-changing adolescent can put a strain on the healthiest of parents. When a parent—particularly a mother—is depressed, her adolescent children can have difficulty adjusting and may become depressed themselves.

Reed Larson and Maryse H. Richards (1994), who have studied the emotional lives of mothers, fathers, and adolescents, noted that depressed mothers feel less competent, are less energetic, and less actively engaged in parenting than women who are not depressed. They interact with less positive feelings, speak less, exchange few glances, and respond more slowly and less often. They are more self-focused and hypersensitve to negative events, expect more negative behavior from their children, and are more likely to view noncompliance as deliberate rebellion.

Larson and Richards pointed out that, since mothers in our culture are most responsible for child rearing, they are also most subject to the stress that raising children brings. Given the usual adolescent's inattentiveness, emotionality, and rebelliousness, it is not unreasonable to find that mothers often get depressed. The stress may be particularly harsh if the adolescent naturally has a difficult or unpleasant temperament. But which comes first, the depressed mother or the difficult child? Most likely, there is a reciprocal process at work: the mother's negative mood and the child's difficult behavior feed off each other (Larson and Richards, 1994).

Gerald Patterson's research showed that a mother's depression and a son's antisocial behavior develop together over time, beginning in early childhood and ending in adolescent deviance. The causes for each are interrelated. For the mother, they include lack of parental skills, financial difficulties, and depression; for the child they include a difficult temperament and lack of support from the father and other family members. These factors lead to tension between the mother and her child: frustration with the relationship, feelings of rejection on both sides, and aggressive and coercive behavior as a means for each getting his or her way. Having learned a dysfunctional way of relating, the adolescent son may carry this behavior over to school and peer relations (Patterson, 1986).

SUICIDE AMONG ADOLESCENTS

The National Center for Health Statistics (1991) reports that in 1988 a total of 2,059 adolescents (ranging from age 15 to age 19) and 243 children under age 15 committed suicide. In summary statistics that plotted the increase in suicide rates, numbers increased from 3.6 deaths per 100,000 children in 1960 to 11.3 deaths in 1988. These figures are probably underestimated. Religious taboos or concerns about insurance sometimes lead suicides to be reported as accidents.

Adolescents at risk for attempting suicide often have poor problem-solving skills and difficulties in social relationships, which make it harder for them to cope with and adapt to the changes of the age (Sadowski and Kelly, 1993; Jaycox, et al., 1994). Researchers have noted that there are *clusters of symptoms* that can serve as indicators for parents, who might then be able to intervene before their adolescent does himself harm. While the most outstanding indicator is depression, this symptom is accompanied by substance abuse, eating disorder, family conflict, failure in school, family history of suicide, feelings of loneliness, a diagnosed psychological problem, or abuse in the family. In stud-

The Informed Parent 12. 4

When to Seek Professional Help

If the adolescent is showing severe problem behaviors, such as depression, an eating disorder, drug addiction, repeated delinquent acts, or serious school-related problems, do not try to treat these problems alone. Seek professional support and advice.

If the adolescent has a problem but has not discussed it, he or she may want to talk to an objective professional. For example, an adolescent may be socially withdrawn and not have many friends. This could be due to extreme shyness, depression, stress at school, drug involvement, or other condition. A parent may not know what the adolescent's problem is or the reason for it. Professionals often can elicit information, on which they can make a specific diagnosis and provide recommendations for helping the adolescent.

If the adolescent is under stress and exhibits serious behavior changes (for example, becomes depressed or drinks a lot), due to a death or divorce in the family, he or she needs temporary assistance. Adolescents may not have the coping skills needs to get through difficult losses.

If parents have tried to solve the adolescent's problem but have not been successful, problems will likely continue to disrupt the child's life. Frequent truancy, chronic running away, or repeated, hostile opposition to authority are examples of problems that need professional treatment.

If parents realize they are part of the adolescent's problem, they may not be able to help with a solution. Constant, intense, bitter fighting that disrupts the everyday lives of the family members needs to be stopped. One individual is rarely the single cause of extensive family dissension. A therapist can objectively analyze the family's problems, help the family members to see why they are fighting so much, and find ways to reduce dissension.

Source: Adapted from Santrock, J. W. (1997) *Children 5E.* Brown and Benchmark Publishers, p484. Reprinted with permission of The McGraw-Hill Companies.

ies of Native American adolescents who attempt suicide, the clash of cultures and problems of identity are in a cluster that also includes drug use, depression, stress, lack of social support, school problems, and a pervasive sense of hopelessness (Howard-Pitney, et al., 1992).

Suicide is not an easy subject for parents or teachers to talk about with adolescents, and efforts to confront this issue directly are not likely to be successful. Other strategies have yielded more promising results. These include school programs that focus on issues or problems of substance abuse, competence building and problem solving, family relationships, and good mental health (Garland and Ziglar, 1993).

Parents, teachers, and friends of adolescents must be educated about the signs that indicate the possibility of suicide so that lines of communication must be opened up. These signs include:

- Previous suicide attempts
- Talking about death in a way that suggests the world would be better off with out them
- Alcohol and drug usage
- Reckless, risky, and dangerous behaviors; accidents
- Giving away possessions
- Changes in appetite, sleep habits, cleanliness, dress
- Change in enjoyment of normal activities
- Change in performance at school or work (including ability to concentrate)
- Withdrawing from activities, friends, and family
- Personality changes, including sadness, apathy, and anger
- Physical complaints, such as fatigue and tiredness
- Precipitating events, such as trouble with the law, a school course failure, or breakup of a friendship or romantic relationship
- Loss of a loved one or friend peer by death, especially suicide.

Parents of adolescents who display these signs, attempt suicide, or talk of suicide should seek professional help in the form of individual or family therapy.

Chapter Review

- Adolescence is a period of development represented by a drive toward independence, peer group loyalty, and intellectual growth. Although we generally think of adolescence as the teenage years, from ages thirteen to eighteen, depending upon individual children and the culture they grow up in, adolescence can begin as early as age ten and extend to age twenty two.

- Pubescence, the period preceding puberty, is the time during which changes occur. Puberty is the culmination of these changes, the final matured state. While physical changes during this time are universal, psychological and social reactions depend upon family and cultural contexts.

- In early adolescence, before age sixteen, the most obvious changes center on physical and psychological development, particularly the hormonal activities that direct biological change. In later adolescence, from age six-teen on, the focus is on peer relationships, sexuality, self-identity, and plans for the future.

- As young adolescents grow to adulthood, they seek changes in the way they are treated and the privileges they receive. In striving for identity and a sense of self, they make demands prompted by their desire for independence. Both male and female adolescents seek to be autonomous while holding on to family ties.

- As maturation occurs, factors such as health care, nutrition, physical labor, and body mass interact with genetic factors to trigger the pattern of changes that mark puberty. Hormones, secreted by the endocrine glands, are carried through the body via the blood stream, causing the body to react anatomically and physiologically.

- The earliest noticeable adolescent change, occurring in both sexes, is the growth spurt—a sudden, uneven, and unpredictable increase in height. Pituitary growth hormones and the thyroid hormones provoke rapid skeletal changes that lead to the lengthening and increasing bone mass. The growth spurt occurs at about age ten and one-half for girls and lasts about two years. Boys begin the growth spurt at about age twelve and one-half, two years later than girls, and continue until approximately fourteen years old.

- Puberty is marked by the development of primary sex characteristics, that is, the organs involved in human reproduction. Primary characteristics are those physical changes related directly to the sexual reproductive system and genitals. Puberty is also marked by the development of secondary sex characteristics, which are not directly involved in the sexual reproductive function, but are clear, physical signs that mark adult sexuality. These secondary sexual characteristics include facial hair in boys, body shape changes, change in voice, etc.

- Studies suggest early-maturing boys are viewed positively by themselves and their peers. They have a greater sense of confidence and self-esteem than do late-maturing boys. Early maturers are viewed as leaders, easier to get along with. Early-maturing young women face more difficulties than their male counterparts. These young women feel less attractive, often have a poor self-concept, and report lower self-esteem than on-time and later-maturing girls.

- The timing of puberty affects parents' perceptions. Parents generally report better relationships with early-maturing sons and late-maturing daughters, and they perceive there is less conflict between those family members. Late-maturing sons and early-maturing daughters were a greater source of stress and anxiety. Generally, families reported most stress about early-maturing daughters.

- With adolescence comes a significant change in understanding and perceptions of the world. Adolescents enter an intellectual stage called formal operations. The formal operations stage begins at adolescence and continues throughout life. Teenagers at this stage have the capacity to problem solve by developing hypotheses and testing them out in

their mind. They can plan ahead, avoid unpleasant situations, and imagine what life would be like under a variety of circumstances. They can think about and understand abstract concepts such as the meaning of religion, war, morality, love, and freedom.

- David Elkind describes three characteristics of adolescent egocentrism. The imaginary audience refers to teenagers' preoccupation with their own looks and behavior, to the point that they believe everyone around them is equally interested. The personal fable is a perception that they are so special as to be invincible and not subject to natural laws like everyone else. Pseudostupidity refers to the indecisiveness and lack of prioritizing shown by adolescents who are naturally bright but have difficulty choosing from the many options they have.

- From approximately age eleven to eighteen, adolescents are faced with creating a coherent and unified sense of self, separate from parents. The "self" consists of experiences, values, beliefs, and ideology from the past, woven into the fabric of the present. Role diffusion results when adolescents doubt their sexual identity, are not accepted by peers, and are not able to reconcile the contradictions of society. Role diffusion carries with it a highly negative view of self, in the present and for the future.

- James Marcia defines identity as "an internal, self-constructed, dynamic organization of drives, abilities, beliefs, and individual history." It is a force that develops over time, shaping behaviors, emotions, coping abilities, social relationships, and occupational choice. It includes aspects of development such as moral reasoning, self-esteem, anxiety, and relationships. Marcia proposes that there are four states of identity, avenues that lead to the resolution of an identity crisis. They include identity diffusion, identity foreclosure, identity moratorium, and identity achievement.

- Adolescents from minority American cultures, especially nonwhites, have particular problems in forging identities, as they must develop an ethnic or racial identity as a part of their overall ego identity. Jean Phinney sees the development of ethnic identity in three stages: unexamined ethnic identity, ethnic identity search, and resolution.

- Studies have shown a strong correlation between parental support for adolescents and the children's academic and social achievement. "Supporting" children means listening to them without criticism, encouraging their positive aims, showing interest in their school and outside activities, sharing their companionship, knowing their friends, tolerating their style of dress and music, and displaying continued high regard and affection for them.

- Parent-adolescent conflict can be grouped into two categories: surface transactional quarrels and deeper psychological conflicts resulting from a striving for autonomy and independence. Disagreements ensue over decisions, rules, family obligations, peers, habits, privacy, and appearance. Problems between parents and their children are usually around separation and individuation. As adolescents separate from the family, they turn toward peers for nurturance and support.

- Studies examining family structure indicate that problems and changes in family structure raise the risk of, and actually increase, adolescent problems. Family structure may include two-parent households, single-parent households, divorced households, remarried households with stepparents and siblings, or a combination and variation of these.

- Gerald Patterson believes that parents whose children exhibit antisocial behaviors are often lacking in family management skills, which have their roots in the parents' families of origin. In addition, societal factors, such as employment circumstances and stress, contribute to the way parents monitor their children and behave toward them.

- The transition from a nurturant elementary school environment to the more independent junior high school setting is often stressful. During this time, children are changing physically and cognitively. Family interactions change as adolescents are expected to take on more responsibility and independence.

- A good high school is one in which a student feels welcome. The climate is positive and caring, expectations are high, rewards are bestowed for good work; and fair limits are set by the administration.

- Adolescents are at risk for many serious problems. About 20 percent of teenagers experience serious difficulties, which may go untreated until too late. Problems include drug use, mental illness, suicide, homicide, eating disorders, and sexually transmitted diseases. Some adolescents appear prone to taking higher risks than others, doing things such as driving while intoxicated and engaging in such delinquent actions as vandalism and shoplifting.

- Many adolescents report that they have used drugs as a means to relax and handle stress. Frequent drug users tend to be maladjusted, have personality problems, feel alienation from others, show poor impulse control, and experience emotional distress.

- Teenage depression is often masked by other problems such as anxiety, eating disorders, substance abuse, or hyperactivity. Adolescents who are at risk for attempting suicide often have poor problem-solving skills and difficulties in social relationships.

- Strategies to prevent suicide include school programs that focus on problems of substance abuse, competence building, problem solving, family relationships, and healthy, mental states. Parents, teachers, and friends must be sensitive to specific signs that indicate the possibility of suicide; lines of communication must be opened up with the troubled adolescent.

Student Activities

1. Describe what adolescence was like for you. Were there times when you did not get along with your parents? What issues led to dissension?

2. Review the work of Erikson and Marcia, and determine where you were, in the search for identity, when you left or graduated high school. Were there areas of your life (sex-role

preference, religious beliefs, political beliefs, career choices) where you were in different states? Where do you think you are now?

Helping Hands

National Organization of Adolescent Pregnancy and Parenting
4421A East-West Highway
Bethesda, MD 20814
(301) 913-0378

An association that promotes community services that help with the problems of teenage pregnancy and childbearing.

National Committee on Youth Suicide Prevention
65 Essex Road
Chestnut Hill, MA 02167
(617) 738-0700

A volunteer network of professionals and parents working together to develop suicide prevention programs for schools and communities.

National Council on Crime and Delinquency
685 Market Street, No. 620
San Francisco, CA 94105
(415) 896-223

An organization of professionals working to develop programs to prevent and treat juvenile delinquency.

Job Corps
Employment Training Administration
200 Constitution Avenue, NW
Washington, DC 20210
(202) 535-0550
www.jobcorps.org

A federally sponsored training program offering disadvantaged people ages 16 to 21 education, vocational training and work experience.

Anorexia Nervosa and Related Eating Disorders
P.O. Box 5102
Eugene, OR 97405
(503) 344-1144

An association of anorexics and bulimics, their families and friends, and concerned professionals that provides information, support, medical referrals, and counseling.

Teens Teaching AIDS Prevention
3030 Walnut Street
Kansas City, MO 64108
(816) 561-8784

Provides teenagers with information on AIDS through peer counseling. Operates a toll-free hotline staffed by trained high school students and adult advisors at (800) 234-TEEN.

Do It Now Foundation
P.O. Box 27568
Tempe, AZ 85285
(602) 491-0393
www.doitnow.org

Works to provide information to adolescents and adults about alcohol, drugs, and related health issues. Assists organizations engaged in drug education.

CHAPTER

13

Launching Children

Chapter Highlights

After reading Chapter 13, students should be able to:

- Recognize the difficulty of launching children in today's world
- Understand how children leaving home affects family life
- Recognize the importance of helping children make career choices
- Understand the changing parent-child relationship as children become adults
- Understand the importance of grandparents in grandchildren's lives
- Recognize the myriad of forces working together to produce contented, productive adult children

Chapter Contents

- The Changing Family Life Cycle
  The Sandwich Generation ▪ *Letting Go in Stages*
- Getting Along Adult to Adult
  The Empty Nest ▪ *Boomerang Children* ▪ *Idealized Parental Expectations* ▪ *Helping Children Make Career Decisions* ▪ *Self-assessment in Career Choice* ▪ *Choosing for College* ▪ *Marriage While in College*
- Life After Launching
  Life Is Lived in Perpetuity
- Parenting into Old Age
  Grandparenting ▪ *Our Grandchildren's Favorite Thing*
- The Parenting Experience: A Summing Up

ne of the most famous love affairs in English literature occurred between the poets Robert Browning and Elizabeth Barrett. What makes their relationship so extraordinary is that the lovers, both well in their thirties, met in secrecy for a year before fleeing to Italy in 1846, where they married and had a son, Pen. The reason for their secrecy was that Elizabeth's father, Edward, forbade his children to ever leave him. He disowned and disinherited any of his sons and daughters who married. Although Elizabeth did manage to leave her father's home, she was unable to distance herself from him emotionally in order to live a contented, productive adult life. After her marriage, she kept her father's picture by her bedside and she sent him pleading letters, which he never opened. Overtaken by a mysterious illness, probably psychological in origin, Elizabeth retreated into invalidism and an addiction to morphine. She died at the age of 54, leaving her beloved Robert to raise their 12-year-old son alone.

Children reaching adulthood! Children leaving home! Whether they go off to marry, leave for college, or get a job and move into their own places, this can be a particularly difficult time for parents. It is especially difficult if adult children continue to rely on their parents for financial support or if, as occurs more and more frequently because of economic realities, the adult children continue to live at home. The parental role changes as children emerge from the transitional years of adolescence. A new relationship must be forged, based on equality and the mutual respect any two adults would show one other. Parents and their adult children may become part of a system that also includes in-laws and grandparents. Often the parents' marital relationship changes, too, when the children are launched into their adult lives.

THE CHANGING FAMILY LIFE CYCLE

Only a couple of generations ago, child rearing occupied parents for almost their entire adult lives. Today, because of low birthrates and the long life span of most adults, this same role takes only half that time, leaving parents with many years to contemplate and fulfill other goals. This change is especially difficult for women who have defined their role in light of family responsibilities.

Betty Carter and Monica McGoldrick (1988) point out that life today is built upon transitions. So many entrances and exits, departures and returns, losses and gains are experienced by the modern family that parents and children have difficulty negotiating all the changes. As children develop, parents "must shift to a less hierarchical form of relating." Many parents, however, encourage their adult children to continue dependence. Although some young adults do remain overly dependent, others rebel and break away in a move they believe is a strike for independence.

> The shift toward adult-to-adult status requires a mutually respectful and personal form of relating, in which young adults can appreciate parents as they are, needing neither to make them into what they are not nor to blame them for what they could not be. Neither do young adults need to comply with parental expectations and wishes at their own expense. (Carter and McGoldrick, 1988)

To get along with adult children, parents must change their attitude and forge a relationship based on equality and respect.

At the turn of the century, children reached puberty, took on adult work in farming or as artisans, and began thinking about marriage and parenthood. Today it is much more difficult to pinpoint the time of adulthood as our technological and service society makes it necessary for young adults to spend a lot of time training for employment, which will allow them to marry and raise a family. In a study of male development, Daniel Levinson (1978) pointed out that a young man today needs an incredible 15 years—from about age 17 to age 33—to emerge from adolescence and find his place in the adult world. Traditionally we consider people to be adults when they work full-time and support themselves financially. For some children, economic independence comes just after high school; for others it comes after undergraduate or graduate school.

The launching pattern in Western cultures is different from that found in Latin-American society. A study of launched children in six countries—Colombia, Costa Rica, the Dominican Republic, Mexico, Panama, and Peru—revealed that marriage is the major reason children leave home. About 80 percent of never-married children ages 15 to 29 continue to live at home (Goldscheider and DaVanzo, 1985). Economic security does not motivate Hispanic children to leave home; in fact, those who can help out financially are more likely to remain at home. Young Latin-American adult men live at home longer than young adult American men and women. Young adults in rural areas stay at home longer than those who live in cities. This may be caused by having children stay at home to work the land.

In some families, children stay at home with their parents until marriage. While at home they work and contribute financially to the household. In other families children are financially supported by their parents who expect them to continue their education before marrying and moving out.

Economics does play a part in who stays at home longest in Latin America. The average Latin American is educated to the eighth grade, and youths who continue on with their schooling generally come from higher socioeconomic backgrounds. Parents who have the nesessary financial resources keep their children home and support them while they continue their education (De Vos, 1989). Present trends in the six countries studied are for young people to leave rural areas for city life and for young adults to continue their schooling. This means that some Latin children will leave home earlier than in the past, while others will remain at home longer.

THE SANDWICH GENERATION

In 1800, a 37-year-old woman would expect both parents to be deceased. In 1980, the average 57-year-old woman had one parent still living. In 1996, one-half of all 60-year-old women had mothers still living (Watkins, Menken, and Bongaarts, 1987). These data mean that in middle age, women who are launching their children and providing them financial support and/or child-care assistance are also concerned with aging parents who need emotional, physical, and household-management assistance. For these reasons, mid-life mothers are sometimes called the *sandwich generation*.

LETTING GO IN STAGES

In reality, parents begin letting go of their children in early childhood, when little boys and girls strive for a level of autonomy that includes picking out their own clothing or choosing what they want for lunch. During adolescence, the separation intensifies. Indicators of successful separation by young adults include acquisition of skills necessary to embark on a job or career, independent living arrangements or plans in that direction, and the development of friendships and intimate relationships.

In some families, it is left to the young adult to make decisions about the future; the choice of a college, career, or mate is an individual one. In other families, parents place expectations upon children, and goals and aspirations are more a family affair than an individual one (McCullough and Rutenberg, 1988).

How parents respond to the separation from adult children depends on their success in transitioning during earlier stages. What is sometimes most difficult for parents is to recognize that the attitudes and values of adult children may be quite different from their own (Miller and Glass, 1989). In general, mothers are better able than fathers to take on a more peerlike adult relationship with their adult children (Fischer, 1986). This may be because fathers are usually more authoritarian than mothers, and it is harder for them to give up the superior father role for one in which the parties are more equal.

Parents who view their years with their children as successful tend to show support and interest as their children take up their own adult lives. One self-report study of 100 families asked the parents of adolescents how they thought they would feel when their children left home. About 33 percent expected a loss of a sense of family, 51 percent anticipated new opportunities, and 21 percent expected to feel relief at having raised their children to an adult stage (Anderson, 1977).

Jay Haley (1980) noted that some children become physically independent but are unable to separately emotionally from their families. Leaving home for the armed forces, an early marriage, an out-of-wedlock pregnancy, or drug or alcohol dependence are seen by Haley to be signs of *pseudolaunching,* as these actions mean that the family must still provide for financial and emotional support.

GETTING ALONG ADULT TO ADULT

In cultures where children are dependent on their parents longer, and because parents have increased life expectancy, it is likely that parents will need assistance from their children at some point. Consequently, it is especially important that the parent-child relationship be harmonious and satisfying rather than discordant and tension-filled. A number of studies reveal that the ultimate parent-child relationship evolves over time, beginning when the children are young (Brubaker, 1985, 1990). In a study of Italian American mothers and daughters, 46 percent of the mothers and 43 percent of the daughters cited their long-standing relationship as most revealing of their present one (Johnson, 1978). What was particularly important to these mothers and daughters was to be able to meet each other's expectations of their respective roles.

One aspect of past experience that impacts on the adult-child–adult-parent relationship is each party's perception of how well parents fulfilled their roles. Victoria Bedford (1992) found that parents' fairness toward their children was a key determinant of their future relationship. While it is difficult to achieve complete fairness because of maturational and temperamental differences between siblings, parents must strive to give each child what he or she needs by way of physical care, as well as the love, attention, approval, time, space, and possessions. As Bedford notes, "fairness implies consistency with principles, consistency between parents, and appropriateness to the needs of children." In fact, much of the conflict between adult siblings can be attributed to preferences parents are perceived to have shown throughout the family's life cycle. A favored sibling might be the target of a sister or brother's anger if it is too threatening to confront the parents about family unfairness (Ross and Milgram, 1982). Sometimes a less favored child strives to make up for feelings of deprivation by becoming oversolicitous to aged parents in order to now court their favor (Altschuler, Jacobs, and Shiode, 1985).

THE EMPTY NEST

When the last child leaves home, parents face a period of disequilibrium known as the *empty nest syndrome,* a sense of anxiety and dissatisfaction that accompanies this change in family life. At one time parents had many children and raised them until old age; but in the last two generations, fewer children are born in families and these children tend to leave while their parents are middle-aged. Parents face twenty or more years in which to create a "new" life, one in which the children are not the central characters. Sometimes parents have trouble accepting this reality and they hold on to their children longer than is healthy. A mother who has spent most of her adult life raising children may not know what to do with the time she now has on her hands.

It has been postulated that the empty nest brings with it a decrease in marital satisfaction; however, this is only true if both parents focused all their energies on their children, to the exclusion of their marital relationship. It has been found that, with the children grown and gone, marital satisfaction *increases* rather than decreases, as couples now have more time to be together and pursue mutual interests (Sherman, 1987). Sometimes one parent will exhibit emotional or physical symptoms in reaction to the last child leaving home. Family therapists often see such symptoms as an unconscious attempt to reconnect with a spouse who has been distant during the child rearing years (McCullough and Rutenberg, 1988).

Children today are taking longer to graduate from college and many are moving home to live with their parents again afterward. This necessitates new agreements between parents and adult children in regard to residence-sharing.

Boomerang Children

It is increasingly common in today's economic climate for the empty nest to be refilled, as children return home after college, after a divorce, or when a career doesn't earn them enough money to live on their own (Glick and Lin, 1986; Steinmetz and Stein, 1988). The 1990 census report indicated that 21 percent of 25-year-olds were living with their parents, a 15 percent increase since 1970. The refilled nest can be a trying time for both parents and their adult children. Researchers have found that 42 percent of middle-aged parents reported having conflicts with their resident adult children. The most common complaint of both parties is a loss of privacy. Adult children are unhappy about their cramped sex lives, the inability to play their music loudly, and their parents' attempts at limiting their independence (Clemens and Axelson, 1985). Parents complain the house is too noisy, meals are difficult to prepare because of conflicting schedules, they don't like staying up late worrying, they have too much responsibility, and their marital relationship is disturbed.

Parental relationships with renested children are more likely to go well if there is ample space for everyone's privacy, if parents do not resume the caregiver role, and if children do not resume a dependent-child position.

Idealized Parental Expectations

In middle-class America, parenting is considered an intense but time-limited investment in child rearing. There is an expectation that children will some day be successfully launched into their own lives and careers and that parents

The Informed Parent 13.1

Parental Expectations for Young Adults

Parents frequently have unrealistic expectations for their young adult children. The economic and social realities of today's world create situations that both parents and children can have difficulty adjusting to. Compare the idealized parental expectations and the reality of young adult life.

Idealized Parental Expectations

Education
College away from home

Postgraduate or professional

Entry-level position in career expected to provide sufficient income for independence and chance for advancement

Living Arrangements
Dorms, apartments, fraternity/sorority houses away from home

Independent household

Reality Patterns of Today's Young Adults

Education
Interrupted, postponed, or intermittent college

Interrupted, postponed, or intermittent post baccalaureate

Erratic job patterns, doubtful career path, no assured income level sufficient for independence

Living Arrangements
Commuting from home, occasional independence but basically reliant on parents for housing and/or money

Despite difficulties, a return home is acceptable

will then be able to plan for their own retirement and later years. Today many professional couples delay childbirth for career aspirations, with the result that adult children are being launched at a time when parents are less free to prepare for the future they desire. A study of parental expectations showed that parents have long had an idealized model concerning the launching of young adults from the family nest (Schnaiberg and Goldenberg, 1989). In reality, young adults today are caught between the expectations or desires of their parents and the realities of a workplace where economic independence is exceedingly difficult to achieve. With fewer lucrative career opportunities, if not college educated, plans for independent housing, as well as those for marriage and children, are postponed.

The Informed Parent 13.2

Parent Adult-Child Residence-Sharing Issues

Parents and the adult children who share their home must address and negotiate a number of issues.

1. How much money will the adult child be expected to contribute to the household? When is it to be paid?

2. What benefits will the child receive? For example, will the family's laundry soap or food in the refrigerator be at the young adult's disposal?

3. Who will have authority over utility usage? Who will decide, for instance, when the weather warrants turning on an air conditioner or where to set the thermostat?

4. What about telephone use? At what time is it "too late" for friends to call the house? At what point is a conversation "too long"? Should a second telephone line be installed for the young adult? Who will pay for the telephone charges?

5. What are the standards for cleanliness and orderliness? Who is responsible for cleaning what, and when? Who does the yard work? How will laundry be done or divided?

6. Who is responsible for cooking, and when? Who buys the food?

7. When are guests welcome in the house? How much notice must be given? What rooms will be available for guests? Will parties be allowed?

8. What are the rules about drinking and/or smoking in the house?

9. How will other household members be informed if one will be unexpectedly late or absent so that those at home do not worry unnecessarily?

10. What are the rules about using personal items of other members in the household?

11. If an adult child returns home with children, who is responsible for the children's care? Who may discipline the children? Are grandparents expected to babysit?

HELPING CHILDREN MAKE CAREER DECISIONS

Choosing a career is a process that takes many years, beginning with a *fantasy* stage at about age eleven, going through a *tentative* stage in adolescence, and ending with a *realistic* stage that can reach to age thirty six (Ginzberg, 1984). When they are young, and before they are in touch with their abilities and interests, children fantasize about being ballerinas, firefighters, rock stars, and basketball players. By the teen years they become somewhat more realistic. With parental help or that of teachers, adolescents can begin looking at their personal attitudes, likes and dislikes, and abilities as they relate to the world of work. In a study that questioned high school seniors about job characteristics they considered important, students rated "interest" highest and "high status" far down the list (Bachman, 1987) (Table 13.1). Gender differences are significant

TABLE 13.1   What High School Seniors Desire in a Job

Description	Percentage
Interesting to do	87%
Uses skills and abilities	72%
Good chance for advancement and promotion	67%
Predictable, secure future	64%
Chance to earn a lot of money	58%
Chance to make friends	53%
Worthwhile to society	41%
Chance to participate in decision making	33%
High status or prestige	32%

when adolescents are questioned about occupational values. Young women were more likely to value careers that allow them to help others, whereas men were more concerned with attaining money, social status, and security (Lueptow, 1992).

As they leave adolescence, children begin exploring their career options. They eventually select a career field and then a specific job. This does not mean that the choice is a stable one. Often there are feelings of ambivalence, and sometimes economic opportunity and social expectations influence the decisions young adults make (Ginzberg, 1984; Yost and Corbishley, 1987). Sons are particularly influenced by what their fathers do for a living (Barling, 1991). The sons of doctors, lawyers, and scientists, for example, are far more likely to choose these careers over other jobs. This occupation or employment influence comes through the father's behavior modeling and through the way the male parent communicates values and attitudes, indicating just how influential fathers are in helping sons define themselves.

A mother's employment influences a daughter's perceptions of appropriate roles for women. Daughters of working mothers are more likely to want to work when they become parents (Galambos, Peterson, and Lenetz, 1988). Both sons and daughters of working mothers expect women of their generation to work after they have children.

There are innumerable books and psychological inventories about career selection that parents can use in helping their children make choices based on their skills, interests, attitudes, and personalities, as well as opportunities in the marketplace (Table 13.2).

SELF-ASSESSMENT IN CAREER CHOICE

Many adults are unhappy about their job or career choice. In order to prevent dissatisfaction in their work, children should explore the kinds of jobs that suit their temperament and personalities, the kind of work environment they prefer, and the talents and skills they can use in their future careers.

TABLE 13.2 Helping Young Adults Look at Work Preferences

Work Tasks (What you like to do)	Examples
Routine, predictable work	Filing, assembly-line production, data coding
Physical work	Gardening, construction, making crafts
Work with machines and tools	Computer repair and installation
Work with numbers	Accounting, computer programming
Work with plants/animals	Medicine, research, therapy
Work with people	Sales, advocacy
Work with information	Teaching, editing
Clerical work	Filing, copying, sorting
Creative expression	Music, dance, cooking, drama
Working Conditions	
People relationships	Work with some people, a few, alone? Preferred authority structure
Movement and time	One location or more? Travel desires/ Work schedule
Performance conditions	Supervision expected/Degree of autonomy/ Degree of responsibility
Variety	Predictability of tasks/Schedule
Environment	Calm or bustling/Quiet or noisy/ Aesthetics/Size
Location	Indoors or outdoors/Geographical region
Benefits	
Salary/Benefit needs	Lifestyle desires/Expected dependents
Opportunities	Advancement/Connections/Skill development
Security and status	Is the position challenging? What are the chances of advancement? How important are security and status?
Worth of work	Does work enhance self, the community, others?
Personal rewards/Stimulation	Feel needed? challenged? appreciated?

Parents can help children identify interests and needs in regard to work by helping them explore four basic career elements.

■ **Motivation.** What needs, interests, values, and beliefs may affect what you like to do? What is important for you to retain in your work life? What motivates you to do your best work? What kind of work do you really want to do? What is it you really don't want to do? What do you want to put into work, and what do you want to get out of it?

- **Style.** How do you relate to the world? How do you like to work? What kind of work environment appeals to you? How do you communicate? How would you manage and lead others? What kinds of contributions can you to make to an organization? How do you relate to people? What kinds of bosses, colleagues, and subordinates do you work best around?

- **Skills.** What are you able to do? What are the things that you can do that you also really like to do? What skills can you take with you wherever you go? What skills do you most want to use in your work?

- **Internal Barriers and Developmental Needs.** What is it that blocks you from getting what you want out of your work life? What attitudes, opinion, beliefs, or behaviors keep you from experiencing success and satisfaction, or from performing as effectively as you need or want to? What is it you would like to be able to do better or differently, so as to make full use of your potential?

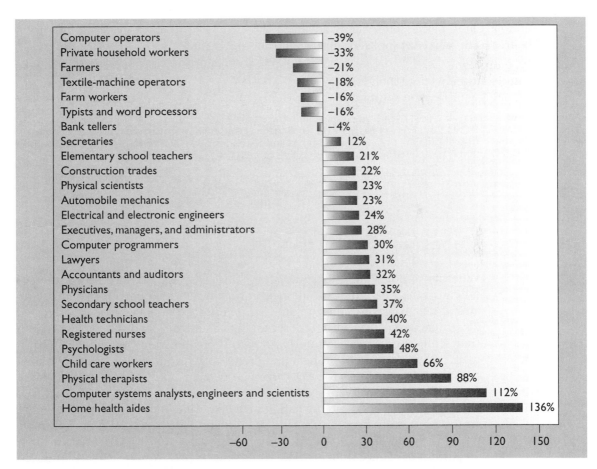

Figure 13.1   Projected Job Growth, 1992–2005
Source: U.S. Department of Labor, Bureau of Labor Statistics (1994): The American Workforce: 1992–2005. Bulletin 2452, April 1994, Washington, DC: U.S. Government Printing Office.

The Informed Parent 13.3

Career Inventories

The Myers-Briggs Type Indicator is one of many of career inventories that relate personal style to work activities. A career inventory can be helpful in identifying the direction a young adult should take. Here is an example of the kinds of questions asked.

1. When you start a big project that is due in a week, do you
   a. take time to list the separate things to be done and the order of doing them, or
   b. plunge in?

2. Are you
   a. easy to get to know, or
   b. hard to get to know?

3. Do you prefer to
   a. arrange dates, parties, etc., well in advance, or
   b. be free to do whatever looks like fun when the time comes?

4. Do you usually
   a. value sentiment more than logic, or
   b. value logic more than sentiment?

Source: Modified and reproduced by special permission of the Publisher, Consulting Psychologists Press, Inc., Palo Alto, CA 94303 from *Meyers-Briggs Type Indicator ®-Form G* by Katharine D. Briggs and Isabel Briggs Myers. Copyright 1977 by Peter Briggs Meyers and Katharine D. Myers. All rights reserved. Further reproduction is prohibited without the Publisher's written consent.

CHOOSING FOR COLLEGE

Whether or not high school graduates consider going to college depends very much on their parents' attitudes about higher education. Also, college graduates' career aspirations depend on their parents' experiences. College-educated daughters of mothers who work set higher career goals and achieve more than their college-educated counterparts whose mothers are homemakers (Hoffman, 1979). A study of professional men showed that 44 percent of the sons of doctors choose medicine as a career; 28 percent of the sons of lawyers favor the legal profession (Werts, 1968).

While thirty years ago the nation's colleges were filled with mostly affluent, white, eighteen to twenty-year-olds, the undergraduate population is now drastically changed. A three-year study by Ernest Boyer (1990) found that in 1960, 94 percent of college students were white and 63 percent were men. Within ten years, the number of minority students enrolled in college doubled. In the 1990s, enrollment of women increased so that women outnumbered men, and foreign students and "graying" students began to fill college classrooms.

The Informed Parent 13.4

The Ten Fastest-Growing Jobs for College Graduates: 1992–2005

Health and education careers appear to be among the most rapidly growing occupations that require college degrees. Parents can help children make realistic choices about future career opportunities by keeping up on the changes in the job market.

Job	Increase by 2005	Degree Recommended
Computer engineers and scientists	112%	Computer science Engineering
Systems analysts	110%	Computer science
Physical therapists	88%	Physical therapy
Special-ed teachers	74%	Special education
Operations research	61%	Engineering, math, physical sciences
Occupational therapists	60%	Occupational therapy
Preschool and kindergarten	54%	Early childhood education, teacher elementary education
Speech/language pathologists	48%	Speech and language pathology
Psychologists	48%	Psychology
Construction managers	47%	Construction management, civil engineering, business

More than one-half of all high school graduates enroll directly in college, and half of these students do not graduate within four years. Most youngsters who choose to attend college do so because they believe that a college education offers greater opportunity for job opportunities, career advancement, and financial security. However, the greatest impact on students will be development of their intellect, attitudes, and beliefs (Astin, 1977). The acceptance of gender equality, an enhanced self-concept, and a greater tolerance for divergent views are among the changes often seen in young adults after they spend some time in college classrooms.

Karen Coburn and Madge Treeger (1992) have written at length about the process of "letting go" as children head for college. They explain that parents often have mixed feelings about "losing" their adult children.

Parental ambivalence about sending a child off to college, particularly a first-born, is common. The sense that family life will never be the same again, a sense of loss, even jealousy—all are likely to be mixed with the anticipated satisfaction of launching one's offspring. For many parents in the midst of all the hustle and bustle of daily life, this is a period of reflection—of poignant memories about times past. For many there is a coming to terms with one's own limitations, while exploring that ever-expanding horizons of the next generation.

The Spirit of Parenting

Everyday Blessings

First child off at college freshman year, arrives home 1:30 A.M. for Thanksgiving, driven by a friend. When he had called earlier to say he would not make it home for dinner as we had hoped, we were all disappointed, and for a few moments there had been more than a slight current of annoyance in me. We leave the door unlocked, as arranged, having told him to wake us when he arrives. No need. We hear him come in. The energy is young, vital, spilling over even in his attempts to be quiet. He comes upstairs. We call to him, whispering, so as not to wake his sisters. He comes into our darkened room. We hug. My side of the bed is closer to him than Myla's. He lies down across my chest, backwards kind of, extends himself, and embraces us both with his arms, but even more with his being. He is happy to be home. He lies here, draped over my body sideways, as if it were the most natural thing in the world. Any trace of annoyance at the lateness of the hour and disappointment about him not making it by dinnertime evaporates instantly.

I feel happiness radiating from him. There is nothing overexuberant or manic here. His energy is joyful, content, calm, playful. It feels like old friends reunited, and beyond that, familial celebration. He is at home now, here in our darkened room. He belongs. The bond is palpable among the three of us. A feeling of joy fills my chest and is joined by a series of images of my life with him, captured in the fullness of this moment. This huge nineteen-year-old, lying across me, who I held in my arms as much as possible until he could and would wriggle out and run in the world, now with his scruffy beard and powerful muscles, is my son. I am his father. Myla is his mother. We know this wordlessly, bathing in our different happinesses that unite as we lie here.

After a while he leaves us to watch a movie. He has too much energy to sleep. We try to go back to sleep, but we can't. We toss for hours in a daze of sleepless exhaustion. It crosses my mind to go into his room to spend more time with him, but I don't. There is nothing to chase after here, not him, not even needed sleep. The depths of our contentedness finally hold sway, and we sleep some. I am gone to work in the morning long before he wakes up. My whole day is suffused with knowing that I will see him when I get home.

—Myla and Jon Kabat-Zinn
From *Everyday Blessings: The Inner Work of Mindful Parenting*

MARRIAGE WHILE IN COLLEGE

Until the late 1940s students who married while in college were often expelled. It became acceptable to be married after the Korean War when veterans, many of them husbands and fathers, returned to the classroom. Today about 15 percent of college students are married and living with their mates. Anthropologist Margaret Mead (1960) believed that early marriage inhibited intellectual and social growth so that job training became the goal of college instead of an experience leading to knowledge and self-development.

Intellectual life demands some kind of postponement of early domesticity . . . which has always been characteristic of . . . peasants and of the urban poor. . . . In European history it has been the young men of the elite class who have been permitted to postpone responsibility while they have a chance in some reasonably protected environment to think, and to make friends . . . and discuss things, and develop and change their minds and explore. This is the thing we're cutting out in this century.

Early student marriage is domesticating boys so early they don't have a chance for full intellectual development. They don't have a chance to give their entire time to experiment, to think, to sit up all night in bull sessions, to develop as individuals. . . . There is a tendency to substitute easy domesticity for a period of stretching one's intellectual and ethical muscles before one settles down. (Mead, 1960)

LIFE AFTER LAUNCHING

For parents who successfully launch their children, midlife can be the beginning of a long period of productivity and creativity. Erik Erikson refers to this time as *generativity versus stagnation*, a period built upon care and a concern with establishing and guiding the next generation. By itself, having children does not ensure a positive outcome at this point in life. Investing time and energy in rearing children in a way that benefits society is what's most important. In an interesting turnabout, Erikson proposes that adults *need* children because they need to take care of others. This does not necessarily mean their own children exclusively. There are many children in the world whose lives are devoid of the guidance and care they need to develop properly. Generativity is about working with others, youngsters or adults, to make the world a better place. Erikson believes that an adult who ignores the needs of others in order to concentrate on his or her own needs and interests becomes his or her own "infants and pets." *Stagnation* is a lack of psychological growth, leading to self-indulgence and ultimately a boring and unproductive midlife.

LIFE IS LIVED IN PERPETUITY

At no time is the "payoff" of parenting more evident than in the stage of life Erikson calls *integrity versus despair:* the final stage of development. Beyond age 60 to 70 people begin to reflect upon the lives they've lived. It is "the acceptance of one's one and only life cycle as something that had to be and that, by necessity, permitted no substitutions." If life is seen as an exercise in failed opportunities and missed experiences with one's children, a parent may reach the last stage of life with bitterness and despair. But a fine sense of integrity comes when a person feels he or she has lived up to life's responsibilities and has accepted the triumphs and disappointments that have come with living. It is a time for looking back with general satisfaction and few regrets. What can be more joyous than being proud of one's own children at this stage and sharing a positive relationship with them? What in life can bring more joy than seeing grandchildren being raised in loving, positive ways, much like their parents were?

The reward for the hard work of parenting is the joy of looking back on the wonderful experiences that are a part of raising children, and looking ahead to the love and friendship that comes when a close relationship exists between parents and their grown children.

PARENTING INTO OLD AGE

Eighty percent of elderly people have living children, some of them also in their late adult years (Aizenberg and Trea, 1985; Cicirelli, 1983). Over three-fourths of the elderly see an adult child at least weekly; more than four-fifths live within an hour of an adult child (Hagestad, 1987). The relationship between elderly parents and adult children, when positive, is based upon emotional support they give each other, the sharing of information and advice, and often the sharing of financial resources (Hamon and Blieszner, 1990). Sometimes, however, adult children are unable to assist their aging parents (Schmidt, 1980). The reasons include:

- Caretaker fatigue
- Competing demands, such as parent versus spouse
- Inability to face parents' decline; depression, anger, and denial of realities of parents' aging
- Expectations that the other parent would die first
- Rivalry about which sibling is most helpful
- Resentment of time expended and effort needed to care for the parent

When care is needed, female adult children provide more assistance and companionship to elderly parents than do male adult children. On issues that concern finances and the making of important decisions, male adult children participate as much as female adult children (Finley, 1989).

There is often a special closeness between adult children and elderly parents. In one study, adult children reported feeling close to both elderly parents, with 87 percent feeling close to fathers and 91 percent feeling close to mothers

(Fischer, 1986). When problems do arise, they are a result of the elderly parents' attempts to control and intrude into the lives of their adult children (Brubaker and Brubaker, 1981). Sometimes elderly parents are unhappy or embarrassed by their dependency on their offspring. While parents rely on the help of their adult children, many adult children also continue to rely on their parents. A study of 146 adult children (average age 32) living with their parents showed that 63 percent had never left home at all. About 75 percent had never married, 17 percent were divorced, and 8 percent were currently arried (Suitor and Pollemer, 1987). Of these stay-at-homes, 55 percent were daughters.

GRANDPARENTING

When president George Bush left the White House in 1964, he was asked what he planned to do in his retirement. He answered that he was "going into the grandparenting business."

The grandparent business differs considerably among families and grandparents; however, when there is a strong emotional attachment between grandparents and grandchildren, both parties benefit from the relationship. Grandparents take on a number of roles in the family. They act as a stable anchor for family members, as babysitters or assistants in emergency situations, as conflict mediators, and as keepers of the family traditions (Bengston, 1985). Sociologists Andrew Cherlin and Frank Furstenberg (1986) studied 510 grandparent relationships and found that about 12 percent of grandparents saw a

Relationships between grandparents and grandchildren are mutually beneficial.

grandchild daily (often they lived together), 25 percent saw a grandchild once a week or more, and about 20 percent saw their grandchildren less often than every two or three months. Of those interviewed, 82 percent had given grandchildren money during the previous year, and 14 percent had interceded in problems between a grandchild and his or her parents (Table 13.3).

Race and social class affect grandparenting interaction. In low-income and minority families, parents and children often rely on grandparents as well as other kin for essential help in raising grandchildren, particularly when an unmarried daughter has a child. For this reason Cherlin and Furstenberg found that 87 percent of black grandparents felt free to discipline a grandchild, compared to 43 percent of white grandparents (Cherlin and Furstenberg, 1986).

Cherlin and Furstenberg assigned grandparents to one of three basic styles:

Companionate: This relationship is marked by companionship, play, and affection. Companionate grandparents often live near their grandchildren, making it easier to interact with them. About 55 percent of the grandparents studied fit this category.

Involved: About 16 percent of grandparents are involved in grandparenting activities to the point of enforcing rules and disciplining the grandchildren. Grandmothers specifically come to the rescue when an unmarried adolescent grandchild gives birth. They often take over child-care duties when the new parent returns to the workforce.

Remote: Because of geographical distance, about 29 percent of grandparents are not an intimate part of their grandchildren's lives, although some are still closely linked emotionally. Some grandparents are distant from their grandchildren because of tensions between themselves and their children.

Other studies of grandparents identify a "fun-seeker" grandparent, one who likes to play with the grandchildren and take them on outings (Neugarten and Weinstein, 1994) (Table 13.3). Grandparents also serve as "family watch-

TABLE 13.3 Grandparents and Grandchildren: Shared Activities	
Activity	**Percentage of Grandparents**
Joke or kid with child	91%
Give child money	82%
Watch TV with child	79%
Talk to child about their own growing up	77%
Give child advice	68%
Discuss child's problems	48%
Go to church or synagogue with child	43%
Discipline child	39%
Take a day trip with child	38%
Teach child a skill or game	24%
Help settle a disagreement between child and his or her parents	14%

Source: Cherlin and Furstenberg, 1986.

dogs," as gender-role socializers, and as arbitrators of behavior (Thomas and Datan, 1983; Bengston and Robertson, 1985).

Today's grandparents have fewer grandchildren than in previous generations. Their longer life expectancy and increased quality of their lives allows them more time and energy for their grandchildren. The typical role of grandparent is somewhat ambiguous in our society, with a number of factors influencing the grandparent-grandchild relationship.

- Geographical proximity to grandchild
- Age of grandparent
- Health of grandparent
- Gender of grandparent
- Developmental level of grandchild

Most grandparents and adult grandchildren believe their relationship is important (Hartshone and Manaster, 1982). The most satisfied grandparents are those who have regular but not overwhelming contact with their grandchildren. Grandmothers enjoy their role more than grandfathers (Bergston, 1985; Thomas, 1986, 1989). Of all ethnic groups, African Americans, Asian Americans, Italian Americans, and Hispanic Americans are the most involved in grandparenting (Bengston, 1985; Taylor, 1988).

The degree to which grandfathers interact with their grandchildren is primarily due to proximity. Studies have shown that when grandfather and grandchildren live within ten minutes of each other, the relationship is closer. Other situations that encourage closeness include: the grandchild is a boy, the grandchild is younger than age 15, the grandfather's health is good. One study suggested that African American grandfathers got along better with their grandchildren and felt closer to them than white grandfathers (Kivett, 1991). In general, the grandfather role was seen as more important to African American men who had more kin living in their households. African American grandfathers looked at their grandchildren as the bridge to the future, whereas white grandfathers were more likely to see their grandchildren as a link to the past. Studies of Hispanic American grandparents show a high level of companionate relationships. These grandparents offer more help to their grandchildren and report greater satisfaction with the grandparenting role than do Anglo-Saxon Americans (Bengtson, 1985).

In an age of divorce and extended families, remarriage has made the role of grandparenting somewhat awkward and confusing. Stepgrandparents are often not sure of their place in their stepgrandchildren's lives. Even more problematic are instances when a divorce and remarriage occur and the parents of the noncustodial parent lose contact with grandchildren, who have become part of their custodial parent's new extended family. Research has shown that it is in the best interests of children to have contact with all their grandparents after a divorce (Bray and Berger, 1990). Generally one set of grandparents, most often on the maternal side, are closest to the children (Matthews and Sprey, 1985). Many children today are close to stepgrandparents and have contact with them past the high school years (Trygstad and Sanders, 1989). Problems can arise

The Informed Parent 13.5

Grandparenting Styles

Five distinct styles of grandparenting have been identified. Age is an important influencer in the interaction between grandparents and grandchildren. The older the grandparents, the less involved they will be.

Formal: These grandparents are interested in their grandchildren, but they rarely involve themselves in caretaking.

Fun-seeker: These grandparents have an informal and playful relationship with their grandchildren. They enjoy doing things with them.

Surrogate parent: These grandparents, usually grandmothers, share or are responsible for caregiving their grandchildren.

Reservoir of family values: These grandparents, usually grandfathers who are somewhat powerful and authoritarian, provide skills and resources.

Distant figure: These grandparents have little contact with their grandchildren, except perhaps on birthdays and holidays.

Source: Neugarten and Weinstein, 1964.

when lonely grandparents rely on their grandchildren to give them the attention and affection they are missing. Studies by Lucy Fischer have looked at grandparenting as it affects daughters, in comparison to daughters-in-law. While the birth of a child often decreases conflict with a woman's own mother, it often increases tension with a mother-in-law (Fischer, 1983). This tension comes when two grandmothers give parenting advice; but that offered by a woman's mother is often solicited, and that offered by a mother-in-law is seen as intrusive.

A number of research projects have suggested that family histories and intergenerational relationships strongly impact the grandparent-grandchild relationship. Children who are close to their parents are significantly closer to each of their grandparents, as compared with children who are not so close to their parents (Rossi and Rossi, 1990). A study of three generations of farm families reported a closeness between grandchildren and grandparents and frequent contact, when compared to nonfarm rural families. This difference is partly due to the proximity that comes with shared work on a family farm. Even in this setting, it is the grandparents' supportiveness toward the child's parents that enhances the quality of the grandparent-grandchild relationship (King and Elder, Jr., 1995). After studying more than 1,000 grandparent-grandchild relationships, Les Whitbeck (1993) found that the mediator role of parents greatly influenced these relationships. An absence of emotional closeness between the grandparents and their children lingered into the children's adulthoods,

The Informed Parent 13.6

Grandparenting: Pleasures and Problems

Grandparents play an important role in the lives of their children's children. Here are some of the benefits and problems of this relationship.

Benefits

- Grandparents can help children feel loved and secure.
- Grandparents can help children to know, trust, and understand other people.
- Grandparents can help children bridge the gap between the past and the present.
- Grandparents can provide children with experiences and supervision that parents do not have money or time to provide.
- Grandparents can give children a sense of values and a philosophy of life based on many years of living.
- Grandparents can give children a wholesome attitude toward old age.

Problems

- Grandparents are often puzzled about the roles they're expected to play in the lives of their grandchildren.
- Grandparents may have different ideas about raising children than their children do.
- Grandparents may offer unsolicited advice to parents and grandchildren.
- Parents may become jealous of the affection that children show their grandparents.
- Grandparents may become too possessive of their grandchildren.

making a warm adult-adult relationship less likely. This kind of relationship history not only affects interactions between grandparents and their adult children throughout their lives, but it also has an effect across generations.

Grandparents must remember that their grandchildren have parents who are, when possible, ultimately responsible for the care of the grandchildren. When problems arise between parents and grandparents over issues pertaining to grandchildren, all adults need to resolve differences in a way that enables grandchildren to have loving relationships with both.

Over 40 percent of elderly Americans are also great-grandparents, a role that brings a sense of family renewal, a marker of longevity and a new interest in life (Doka and Mertz, 1988).

OUR GRANDCHILDREN'S FAVORITE THING

The grandparent-grandchild relationship—when built on love, care, and guidance—enhances the life of all involved. Educator Eda LeShan (1993) believes that—while elderly people need their freedom, quiet, and rest—they suffer when they have little or no contact with young people. She also believes grandparents serve as important role models for children if they stay engaged with the community and people in it. LeShan emphasizes the importance of having a loving relationship with one's own children so that grandparents can become their grandchildren's "favorite thing."

> Helping our own children is often the best way to help the grandchildren. Giving parents a weekend away from the kids, helping to ease a depression over a lost job, comforting them when a child is seriously ill, supporting them when they make a mistake . . . it helps parents to feel better if we remind them of our own failures with them! And how they turned out just fine despite our imperfections . . . the more we comfort our own grown adult children, the more they can comfort our grandchildren. (LeShan, 1993)

THE PARENTING EXPERIENCE: A SUMMING UP

There is no question that parenting is among the most challenging, difficult, joyous, disappointing, and fulfilling experiences in life. But parent-child relationships have changed so much over the last 50 years that it is barely recognizable to people who raised their children before this time. Poet-writer Robert Bly (1996) pointed out that although mothers and fathers still teach values such as empathy, discipline, helpfulness, honesty, and community responsibility, they are often overwhelmed by forces in the society—music, videos, films, consumerism—that greatly influence their children. In Bly's view, many parents have abdicated their roles as mothers or fathers, to the point of leaving their children behind as they venture out in search of the lives they think they want. He believes that, when children see their parents behaving irresponsibly,

It is in the interest of all adults in the world to see that children are given the care, respect, love, and encouragement that will enable them to grow into healthy, contented, productive adults.

they do not want to move into adulthood. Bly questions the society's commitment to raising children, given the crumbling schools, the failure to protect children from guns, the cutting of funds for Head Start and breakfasts for poor children, the elimination of music and art programs in schools, the increase in numbers of children living in poverty, and the poor prenatal care provided to pregnant women. Bly implores Americans to resist retirement, leaving the nation's children behind. "The adult in our time," he writes, "is asked to reach his or her hand across the line and pull the youth into adulthood."

> If the adults do not turn and walk up to this line and help pull the adolescents over, the adolescents will stay exactly where they are for another twenty or thirty years. . . . If we take an interest in younger ones by helping them find a mentor, by bringing them along to conferences or other adult activities, by giving attention to young ones not in our family at all, then our own feeling of being adult will be augmented, and adulthood might again appear to be a desirable state for many young ones.

Today's parents are confronted with serious social problems—family breakups, societal violence, substance abuse, political upheaval, economic greed, and a lack of spiritualism—that make it difficult to raise contented, productive children.

Because children are the promise of the future, it is incumbant on parents—with the help of friends, neighbors, grandparents, teachers, the clergy, police officers, politicians, businesspeople, basically all members of the community—to see that they get the care, support, and educational opportunities they need to make them contented, productive adults.

Parenting is for posterity, so that the kind of parents we become influences not only our children but our grandchildren, great-grandchildren, and all the future generations within our families. The ability of parents around the world to raise caring, decent, productive, and resourceful children is unquestionably the best hope for the future of humankind.

Chapter Review

- As children reach adulthood and leave home to marry, go to college, get a job, or move into their own home, parents can have a particularly difficult time. As children emerge from the transitional years of adolescence, parental roles change. New relationships must be formed, based on equality and the mutual respect any two adults are expected to show each other.

- It is difficult to pinpoint adulthood today because our present technological and service society makes it necessary for youngsters to spend a lot of time training for employment

that will allow them to marry and raise a family. A young man today may take up to fifteen years—from about age 17 to age 33—to emerge from adolescence and find his place in the adult world.

- In some families, it is left to the young adult to make decisions about the future. The choice of a college or career or mate is an individual one. In other families, expectations are placed upon children and their goals and aspirations are more a family affair than an individual one.

- In general, mothers are better able to conduct a peerlike adult relationship with their adult children than are fathers. This may be because fathers are usually more authoritarian than mothers, making it harder for fathers to turn the superior role into one that is more equal.

- Jay Haley believes that in some families children become physically independent but are unable to separate emotionally. Leaving home to join the armed forces, an early marriage, an out-of-wedlock pregnancy, drug or alcohol dependence are seen as signs of pseudolaunching, as the difficulties provoked by these actions means the family must still provide financial and emotional support.

- Much of the conflict experienced between adult siblings can be attributed to parental preferences throughout the family life cycle. Parental fairness in regard to children is a key determinant of their future parent-child relationship. While it is difficult to achieve complete fairness because of maturational and temperamental differences between siblings, parents must strive to give each of their children what they need in terms of both physical care and the love, attention, approval, time, space, and possessions.

- Marital satisfaction often increases as couples now have more time to be together and pursue mutual interests. Sometimes a married parent will exhibit emotional or physical symptoms in reaction to the last child leaving home.

- It has become increasingly common in today's economic climate for children to return home after college, following a divorce, or when a career doesn't earn them enough money to live on. The most common complaint of parents and young adults is a loss of privacy. Conflict revolves around restricted sexual activity, noise, and independence.

- Choosing a career is a process that takes many years, beginning at a fantasy stage at about age eleven, going through a tentative stage in adolescence, and ending with a realistic stage that can reach to age thiry-six.

- Whether or not children leaving high school consider going to college depends consider-

ably on parental attitudes about higher education. More than one-half of all high school graduates enroll directly in college, and half of these people do not graduate within the usual four years. Most youngsters who choose to go to college do so because they believe higher education offers greater opportunity for financial security, career advancement, and job opportunities.

- Parents who successfully launch their children during midlife often begin a period of of productivity and creativity. Erik Erikson refers to this stage as a time of generativity versus stagnation, built upon care and a concern with establishing and guiding the next generation.

- The relationship between elderly parents and their adult children, when positive, is based upon emotional support they give each other, sharing of information and advice, and also sharing of financial resources. When care is needed, female adult children provide more assistance and companionship to elderly parents than do male adult children.

- Grandparents take on a number of roles in the family, including being an anchor of stability to family members, as babysitters or assistants in emergency situations, as conflict mediators, and as keepers of family traditions. Race and social class determine grandparenting interaction. In low-income and minority families, parents and children often rely on grandparents and other kin for essential help in raising grandchildren, particularly when an unmarried daughter has a child.

- Five distinct styles of grandparenting have been identified: formal, fun-seeker, surrogate parent, reservoir of family values, and distant figure. A close grandparent-grandchild relationship—when built on love, care and guidance—greatly enhances the life of all those involved.

- Parenting is among the most challenging, difficult, joyous, disappointing, and fulfilling experiences in life—one that has changed significantly since the 1950s. Parents today are confronted with serious social problems:

family breakups, societal violence, substance abuse, economic greed, and a lack of spiritualism. To raise contented, productive children, parents need the help of family, friends, neighbors, grandparents, teachers, the clergy, police officers, businesspeople—all members of the community.

Student Activities

1. What styles of grandparenting did all of your grandparents favor? What special things did you do with your grandparents that you didn't do with your parents?

2. Imagine you are the parent of three children, the last of whom is leaving for college within weeks. What would you like to do with the rest of your life as an "empty nester"? What dreams do you have that are outside the context of raising children?

3. Considering the state of the world, what advice would you give to new parents today about raising children?

Helping Hands

American Association of Retired Persons (AARP)
1909 K Street., NW
Washington, DC 20049
(202) 872-4700
www.aarp.org/

Organization devoted to providing information about late adulthood and old age.

Bibliography

Abbott, D. A., and Brody, G. H. (1985). The relation of child age, gender, and number of children to the marital adjustment of wives. *Journal of Marriage and the Family, 47,* 77–84.

Abbott, S. (1992). Holding on and pushing away: Comparative perspectives on Eastern Kentucky child-rearing practice. *Ethos, 20,* 33–65.

Aber, J. L., and Slade, A. (1987). *Attachment theory and research: A framework for clinical interventions.* Paper presented at the Regional Scientific Meeting of the Childhood and Adolescence Division of the American Psychological Association, New York.

Abramovitch, R., Freedman, J. L., and Pliner, P. (1991). Children and money: Getting an allowance, credit versus cash, and knowledge of pricing. *Journal of Economic Psychology, 12,* 27–45.

Adamson, L. B., and Bakeman, R. (1991). The development of shared attention during infancy. In R. Vasta (Ed.), *Annals of Child Development,* (Vol. 8), London: Kingsley.

Adler A. (1927). *The Practice and theory of individual psychology.* New York: Harcourt Brace.

Ahrons, C. R. (1994). *The good divorce: Keeping your family together when your marriage comes apart.* New York: Harper Perennial.

Ainsworth, M. D. (1973). The development of infant-mother attachment. In B. M. Caldwell and H. N. Ricciuti (Eds.), *Review of child development research* (Vol. 3). Chicago: University of Chicago Press.

——— (1979). Infant-mother attachment. *American Psychologist, 34,* 932–937.

——— (1985). Patterns of infant-mother attachments: Antecedents and effects on development. *Bulletin of the New York Academy of Medicine, 61,* 771–791.

Aizenberg, R., and T'rea S. J. (1985). The family in later life. In I. F. Birren and K. W. Schaie (Eds.), *Handbook of the psychology of aging* (2nd ed., pp. 169–190) New York: Van Nostrand Reinhold.

Alan Guttmacher Institute, 1994. *Sex and America's teenagers.* New York:

Alessandi, S. M., and Lewis, M. (1993). Parental evaluation and its relation to shame and pride in young children. *Sex Roles, 29*(5–6), 335–343.

Altemeier, W. A., O'Conner, S. M., Sherrod, K. B., and Vietze, P. M. (1984). Prospective study of antecedents for nonorganic failure to thrive. *Journal of Pediatrics, 106,* 360–365.

Altschuler, J., Jacobs, S., and Shiode, D. (1985). Psychodynamic time-limited groups for adult children of aging parents. *American Journal of Orthopsychiatry 53,* 397–403.

Amato, P. R., and Keith, B. (1991). Parental divorce and the well-being of children: A meta-analysis. *Psychological Bulletin, 110,* 26–46.

Anderson, C. A., et al. (1977, October). A computer analysis of marital coping styles in families of children of normal and atypical development. Unpublished paper, presented at the American Academy of Child Psychiatry Annual Meeting, Houston, Texas.

Anderson, C. W., Nagle, R. I., Roberts, W. A., and Smith, J. W. (1981). Attachment to substitute caregivers as a function of center quality and caregiver involvement. *Child Development, 52,* 53–61.

Anderson, E. S. (1984). The acquisition of sociolinguistic knowledge: Some evidence from children's verbal role-play. *Western Journal of Speech Communication, 48,* 125–144.

Anderson, J. Z., and White, G. D. (1896). An empirical investigation of interaction and relationship patterns in functional and dysfunctional nuclear families and stepfamilies. *Family Process, 25*, 407–422.

Apgar, V. (1953). A proposal for a new method of evaluation in the newborn infant. *Current Research in Anesthesia and Analgesia, 32*, 260.

Archer, S. L. (1985). Identity and the choice of social roles. In A. S. Waterman (Ed.), *Identity in adolescence: Process and contents (New directions for child development, No. 30)*. San Francisco: Jossey-Bass.

Ariès, P. (1962). *Centuries of childhood: A social history of family life*. New York: Random House.

Arnett, J. J. (1995a). Broad and narrow socialization: The family in the context of a multidimensional theory. *Journal of Marriage and the Family, 57*, 617–628.

——— (1995b). Adolescents' uses of media for self-ocialization. *Journal of Youth and Adolescence, 24*, 519–533.

——— (1996). *Metal heads*. Boulder, CO: Westview Press.

Asher, S. R., and Wheeler, V. A. (1985). Children's loneliness: A comparison of rejected and neglected peer status. *Journal of Consulting Psychology, 53*, 500–505.

Asmussen, L., and Larson, R. (1991). The quality of family time among young adolescents in single-parent and married-parent families. *Journal of Marriage and the Family, 53*, 1021–1030.

Astin, A. W. (1977). *Four critical years*. San Francisco: Jossey-Bass.

Azrin, N., and Fox, R. M. (1976). *Toilet training in less than a day*. New York: Pocket Books.

Bachman, J. G. (1987). An eye on the future. *Psychology Today, 23*, 292–297.

Ball, S., and Bogatz, G. (1970). *The first year of "Sesame Street": An evaluation*. Princeton, NJ: Educational Testing Service.

Baltes, P. B., Reese, H. W., and Lipsitt, L. P. (1980). Life-span developmental psychology. *Annual Review of Psychology, 31*, 65–110.

Bandura, A. (1977). *Social learning theory*. Englewood Cliffs, NJ: Prentice-Hall.

——— (1986). *Social foundations of thought and action*. Englewood Cliffs, NJ: Prentice-Hall.

Bank, L., Forgatch, M., Patterson, G., and Fetrow, R. (1993). Parenting practices of single mothers: Mediators of negative contextual factors. *Journal of Marriage and the Family, 55*(2), 371–384.

Baran, S. J. (1979). Television programs about retarded children and parental attitudes toward their own retarded children. *Mental Retardation, 17*(4), 193–194.

Barling, J. (1991). Father's employment; A neglected influence on children. In J. V. Lerner and N. L. Galanos (Eds.), *Employed mothers and their children* (pp. 181–209). New York: Garland.

Barrett, M. D. (1986). Early semantic representations and early word usage, In S. A. Kuczaj and M. D. Barrett (Eds.), *The development of word meaning*. New York: Springer-Verlag.

Bates, E., O'Connell, B., and Shore, C. (1987). Language and communication in infancy. In J. D. Osofsky (Ed.), *Handbook of infant development* (2nd ed.). New York: Wiley.

Bateson, C. M. (1984). *With a daughter's eye: A memoir of Margaret Mead and Gregory Bateson*. New York: Morrow.

Bauer, D. (1976). An exploratory study of developmental changes in children's fears. *Journal of Child Psychology and Psychiatry, 17*, 69–74.

Baumrind, D. (1967). Child-care practices anteceding three patterns of preschool behavior. *Genetic Psychology Monographs, 75*, 43–88.

——— (1971). Current patterns of parental authority. *Developmental Psychology Monographs, 4* (No. 1. Pt. 2).

——— (1988). Parenting styles and adolescent development. In J. Brooks, J. Belsky, and M. Rovine (Eds.), Nonmaternal care in the first year of life and security of infant-parent attachment. *Child Development, 59*, 157–167.

——— (1989). Rearing competent children. In W. Damon (Ed.), *New directions for child development: Adolescent health and human behavior*. San Francisco: Jossey-Bass.

——— (1991a). The influence of parenting style on adolescent competence and substance use. *Journal of Early Adolescence, 11*, 56–95.

——— (1991b). Parenting styles and adolescent development. In J. Brooks-Gunn, R. Lerner, and A. C. Peterson (Eds), The encyclopedia of adolescence. New York: Garland.

Beautrais, A. L., Fergusson, D. M., and Shannon, F. T. (1982). Life events and childhood morbidity, *Pediatrics, 70*(6), 935–940.

Beavers, J., and Gordon, I. (1983). *Learning from families*. Dallas: Independent School District.

——— Hampson, R. B., Hulgus, Y., and Beavers, W. R. (1986). Coping in families with a retarded child. *Family Process, 25*, 365–378.

Beavers, W. R. (1977). *Psychotherapy and growth: Family systems perspective*. New York: Brunner/Mazel.

Beckman, P. (1991) Comparison of mothers' and fathers' perceptions of the effect of young children with and without disabilities. *American Journal of Mental Retardation, 95*(5), 585–595.

Bedford, V. H. (1989). Understanding the value of siblings in old age: a proposed model. *American Behavioral Scientist, 33*, 33–44.

Bee, H. (1995). *The developing child* (7th ed.). New York: Harper and Row.

Behrman, R. E., and Vaughn, V.C. (1987). *Nelson textbook of pediatrics* (13th ed.). Philadelphia: Saunders.

Bell, R. Q. (1971). Stimulus control of parent or caretaker behavior by offspring. *Developmental Psychology, 4*, 63–72.

Belsky, J. (1980). Child maltreatment; An ecological integration. *American Psychologist, 35*, 320–335.

—— (1986). Determinants of parenting: a process model. *Child Development, 55*, 83–96.

—— and Braungart, J. M. (1991). Are secure-avoidant infants with excessive day-care experiences less stressed by and more independent in the Strange Situation? *Child Development, 62*, 567–571.

—— and Isabella, R. A. (1988). Maternal, infant, and social-contextual determinants of attachment security. In J. Belsky and T. Nezworski (Eds.), *Clinical implications of attachment*. Hillsdale, NJ: Erlbaum.

—— and Kelly, J. (1994). *The transition to parenthood: How a first child changes a marriage*. New York: Delacorte Press.

—— Rovine, M. J., and Taylor, D. G. (1984). The Pennsylvania Infant and Family Development Project, III: The origins of individual differences in infant-mother attachment: Maternal and infant contributions. *Child Development, 55*, 718–728.

—— and Rovine, M. J. (Eds.), (1988). Nonmaternal care in the first year of life and security of infant-parent attachment. *Child Development, 59*, 157–167.

—— Steinberg, L., and Draper, P. (1991). Childhood experience, interpersonal development, and reproductive strategy: An evolutionary theory of socialization. *Child Development, 62*, 647–670.

—— Youngblade, L., Rovine, M., and Rolling, B. (1991). Patterns of marital change and parent-child interaction. *Journal of Marriage and the Family, 53*, 487–498.

Bem, S. L. (1989). Genital knowledge and gender constancy in preschool children. *Child Development, 60*, 649–662.

Bengtson, V. L. (1985). Diversity and symbolism in grandparent roles. In V. L. Bengston and J. F. Robertson (Eds.), *Grandparenthood*. Beverly Hills, CA: Sage, 16.

Bentovim, A., and Kinston, W. (1978). Brief focal family therapy where the child is the referred patient. *Clinical Jouranl of Child psychology, Psychiatry and Allied Disciplines, 19*, 1–12.

Bepko, C. (1985). *A blueprint for treating the alcoholic family*. New York: Free Press.

—— and Krestan, J. (1985). *The responsibility trap: A blueprint for treating the alcoholic family*. New York: Free Press.

Berg, W. K., and Berg, K. M. (1979). Psychophysiological development in infancy: State, sensory function, and attention. In J. D. Osofsky (Ed.), *Handbook of infant development* (pp. 283–343), New York: Wiley-International.

Berk, L. (1993). *Infants, children and adolescents*. Boston: Allyn and Bacon.

—— (1996). *Infants, children, and adolescents* (2nd ed.). Boston: Allyn and Bacon.

Berko Gleason, J. (1989). Studying language development. In J. Berko-Gleason (Ed.), *The development of language* (pp. 1–34). Columbus, OH: Merrill.

Bernard, H. S. (1981). Identity formation in late adolescence: A review of some empirical findings. *Adolescence, 16*, 349–358.

Berns, R. M. (1997). *Child, family, school, community*. Ft. Worth, TX: Harcourt Brace.

Bernstein, A. C., and Cowan, P. A. (1975).Children's concepts of how people get babies, *Child Development, 46*, 77–91.

Bertalanffy, L. von (1952). *General systems theory: Foundation, development, applications*. New York: George Braziller.

—— (1968). *General systems theory*. New York: George Braziller.

Bettelheim, B. L. (1985). Punishment versus discipline. *Atlantic Monthly*, 51–57.

Bettner, B. L., and Lew, A. (1990). *Raising kids who care*. Newton Center, MA: Connexions Press.

Billingsley, A. (1992). *Climbing Jacob's ladder: The enduring legacy of African-American families*. New York: Simon & Schuster.

Black, C. V. (1993). *History of Jamaica*. Kingston, Jamaica: Carlong Publisher Caribbean Ltd.

Blakeslee, S. (April 17, 1997) Stimulating the infant brain *The New York Times*.

Bleichfeld, B., and Moely, B. (1984). Psychophysiological response to an infant cry: Comparison of groups of women in different phases of the maternal cycle. *Developmental Psychology, 20*, 1082–1091.

Block, J. H. (1983). Differential premises arising from different socialization of the sexes: Some conjectures. *Child Development, 54*, 1335–1354.

Blumberg, M. L.(1974, January). Psychopathology of the abusing parent. *American Journal of Psychotherapy, 28,* 21–29.

Bly, R. (1986).*The sibling society.* Boston: Addison Wesley.

Bombeck, E. (1991). Family: *Ties that bind and gag.* New York: Fawcett Books.

Bowen, M. (1966). The use of family theory in clinical practice. *Comprehensive Psychiatry, 7,* 345–374.

——— (1976). Theory in the practice of psychotherapy. In P. J. Guerin (Ed.), *Family therapy: Theory and practice.* New York: Gardner Press.

Bowlby, J. (1980). *Attachment and loss*: Vol. 3. Loss. New York: Basic Books.

Bowman, P. J. (1993). The impact of economic marginality among African American husbands and fathers. In H. P. McAdoo, et al. (Eds.), *Family ethnicity; strength in diversity* (pp. 120–137). Newbury Park, CA: Sage.

Boyd-Franklin, N. (1989). *Black families in therapy; A multisystems approach.* New York: Guilford Press.

Boyer, D., and Fine, D. (1992). Sexual abuse as a factor in adolescent pregnancy and child maltreatment. *Family Planning Perspectives, 24,* 4–11.

Boyer, E. L. (1990). *Campus Life: In Search of Community*, Princeton, NJ: The Carnegie Foundation for the Advancement of Teaching.

Boysson-Bardies, B., Halle, P., Sagart, L., and Durand, C. (1989). A cross-linguistic investigation of vowel formats in babbling. *Journal of Child Language, 16,* 1–17.

Bozett, F.W. (1987). *Gay and lesbian parents.* New York: Praeger.

Braswell, L., and Bloomquist, M. L. (1991). *Cognitive-behavioral therapy with ADHD children: Child, family, and school interventions.* New York: Guilford Press.

Bray, J. H., and Berger, S. H. (1992). Stepfamilies. In M. E. Procidano, C. Fisher, et al. (Eds.), *Contemporary families: A handbook for school professionals* (pp. 57–80). New York: Teachers College Press.

Brazelton, T. B. (1962). A child-oriented approach to toilet training. *Pediatrics, 29,* 121–128.

——— (1969). *Infants and mothers: Differences in development.* New York: Delacorte.

——— (1973). *Neonatal behavioral assessment scale.* London: Heinemann Medical Books.

——— (1983). *Infants and mothers: Differences in development* (2nd ed.). New York: Delacorte.

Briggs Myers, I. (1987). *Introduction to type: A description of the theory and applications of the Myers-Briggs type indicator* (4th ed.). Consulting Psychologists Press.

Brody, G., and Forehand, R. (1993). Prospective associations among family form, family process, and adolescents' alcohol and drug use. *Behavior Research and Therapy, 31*(6), 587–593.

Brody, J. (1982). *Jane Brody's New York Times Guide to Personal Health.* New York: Avon.

Brody, S. and, Axelrad, S. (1978). *Mothers, fathers, and children.* New York: International University Press.

Brone, R. J., and Fisher, C. B. (1988). Determinants of adolescent obesity: A comparison with anorexia nervosa. *Adolescence, 23,* 155–169.

Bronfenbrenner, U. (1977). Toward an experimental ecology of human development. *American Psychologist, 32,* 513–531.

——— (1979). *The ecology of human development: Experiments by nature and design.* Cambridge, MA: Harvard University Press.

——— (1986). Ecology of the family as a context for human development: Research perspectives. *Developmental Psychology, 22,* 723–742.

——— (1989). Ecological systems theory. In R. Vasta (Ed.), *Annals of child development* (Vol. 6, pp. 187–251). Greenwich, CT: JAI Press.

Brook, J. S., Whiteman, M., Cohen, P., Shapiro, J., et al. (1995). Longitudinally predicting late adolescent and young adult drug use: Childhood and adolescent precursors. *Journal of the American Academy of Child and Adolescent Psychiatry, 34*(9), 1230–1238.

Brooks-Gunn, J., Cherlin, A. J., and Furstenberg, F. F. (1989, March). Divorce doesn't always hurt the kids. *Washington Post.*

——— and Furstenberg, F. (1986). The children of adolescent mothers: Physical, academic, and psychological outcomes. *Developmental Review, 6,* 224–251.

——— and Ruble, D. N. (1982). The development of menstrual-related beliefs and behaviors during early adolescence. *Child Development, 53,* 1567–1577.

Brown, B. B. (1982). The extent and effects of peer pressure among high school students: A retrospective analysis. *Journal of Youth and Adolescence, 11*(2), 121–133.

———, Mounts, N., Lamborn, S.D., and Steinberg, L. (1993). Parenting practices and peer group affiliation in adolescence. *Child Development, 64,* 467–482.

Brubaker, T. H. (1990). Families in later life: A burgeoning research area. *Journal of Marriage and the Family 52,* 959–981.

——— and Brubaker, E. (1981, May). Adult child and elderly parent household: Issues in stress for theory and practice. *Alternative Lifestyles,* 242–256.

Burns, A. L., Mitchell, G., and Obradovich, S. (1989). Of sex roles and strollers: Female and male attention to toddlers at the zoo. *Sex Roles, 20*(5–6), 309–315.

Burns, D. D. (1980). *Feeling good: The new mood therapy.* New York: William Morrow.

———— (1989). *The feeling good handbook: Using the new mood therapy in everyday life.* New York: William Morrow.

Burton, L. M. (1992). Black grandparents rearing children of drug-addicted parents: Stressors, outcomes, and the social service needs. *Gerontologist, 31,* 744–751.

Butler, R. (1989). Mastery versus ability appraisal: A developmental study of children's observations of peers' work. *Child Development, 60,* 1350–1361.

Campbell, M., and Moen, P. (1992). Job-family role strain among employed single mothers of preschoolers. *Family Relations, 41*(2), 205–211.

Camras, L. A., Ribordy, S., Hill, J., Martino, S., Sachs, V., Spaccarelli, S., and Stefani, I. (1980). Maternal facial behavior and the recognition and production of emotional expression by maltreated and non-maltreated children, *Developmental Psychology, 26,* 304–312.

Carey, S. (1978). The child as a word learner. In M. Halle, J. Bresman, and G. A. Miller (Eds.), *Linguistic theory and psychological reality.* Cambridge, MA: M.I.T. Press.

Carpenter, L. (1994). *Unplanned parenthood: The confessions of a seventy-something surrogate mother.* New York: Random House.

Carter, B., and McGoldrick, M. (Ed.) (1988). *The changing family life cycle: A framework for family therapy.* New York: Gardner Press.

Centers for Disease Control (1996). *Warning: The AIDS virus may be transmitted though breast milk.* Atlanta, GA: Author.

Centerwall, B. S. (1992). Television and violence: The scale of the problem and where to go from here. *Journal of the American Medical Association,* 267(22), 3059–3063.

Chao, P. (1983). *Chinese kinship.* London: Routledge & Kegan Paul International.

Chan, S. (1992). Families with Asian roots. In E. W. Lynch and M. J. Hanson (Eds.), *Developing cross-cultural competence* (pp. 181–257). Baltimore, MD: Paul H. Brookes Publishing Company.

Chapman, M., and Skinner, B. F. (1989). Children's agency beliefs, cognitive performance, and conceptions of effort and ability: Individual and developmental differences. *Child Development, 60,* 1229–1238.

Cherry, L., and Lewis, M. (1976). Mothers and two-year-olds: A study of sex differentiated aspects of verbal interaction. *Developmental Psychology, 12,* 278–282.

Cherlin A. J., and Furstenberg, F.F. (1986). The new American grandparent: *A place in the family, a life apart.* New York: Basic Books.

Chess, S., Thomas, A., and Birch, H. G. (1965). Your child is a person: *A psychological approach to parenthood without guilt.* New York: Viking.

Children's Defense Fund (1991). *The state of America's children, 1991.* Washington, DC:

Children's Safety Network, (1990). *A data book of child and adolescent injury.* Washington, DC: National Center for Education in Maternal and Child Health.

———— (1991). *A data book of child and adolescent injury.* Washington, DC: National Center for Education in Maternal and Child Health.

Christmon, K. (1990). Parental responsibility of African-American unwed adolescent fathers. *Adolescence, 25*(99), 645–653.

Cicirelli, V.G. (1983). Adult children and their elderly parents. In T. H. Brubaker (Ed.), *Family relationships in later life.* Beverly Hills, CA: Sage.

Clark, H. H., and Clark, E. V. (1977). *Psychology and Language.* New York: Harcourt Brace.

Clarke-Stewart, K. A. (1973). Interactions between mothers and their young children: Characteristics and consequences. *Monographs of the Society for Research in Child Development, 38,* 1–109.

———— (1984). Day care: A new context for research and development. In M. Perlmutter (Ed.), *The Minnesota Symposium on child psychology* (Vol. 17, pp.61–100). Hillsdale, NJ: Erlbaum.

———— (1987). The social ecology of early childhood. In N. Eisenberg (Ed.), *Contemporary topics in developmental psychology* (pp. 292–318). New York: Wiley-Interscience.

———— (1991). A home is not a school: The effects of child care on children's development. *Journal of Social Issues, 47*(2),105–123.

———— and Gruber, C. P. (1984). Day care forms and features. In R. C. Ainslie (Ed.), *The child and the day care setting* (pp. 35–62), New York: Praeger.

Clemens, A. W., and Axelson, L. J. (1985). The not-so-empty nest: Return of the fledgling adult. *Family Relations, 34,* 259–264.

Clingempeel, W. G., Ievoli, R., and Brand, E. (1985). Structural complexity and the quality of stepfather-stepchild relationships. *Family Process, 23,* 547–560.

Clinton, H. R. (1996). *It takes a village : And other lessons children teach us.* New York: Simon & Schuster.

Coburn, K. L., and Treeger, M.L. (1992). *Letting go: A parents' guide to today's college experience.* Bethesda, MD: Adler and Adler.

Coie, J. D., and Koeppl, G. K. (1990). Adapting intervention to the problems of aggressive and disruptive rejected children. In S. R. Asher and D. Coie (Eds.), *Peer rejection in childhood* (pp. 309–337). New York: Cambridge University Press.

—— and Kupersmidt, J. B. (1983). A behavioral analysis of emerging social status in boys' groups. *Child Development, 54,* 1400–1416.

Cole, M., and Cole, S R. (1996). *The developing child* (3rd ed.). New York: Freeman

Coleman, J. S. (1988). Social capital in the creation of human capital. *American Journal of Sociology, 94,* 95–120.

Coleman, M., and Ganong, L. (1991). Remarriage and stepfamily research in the 1980s; Increased interest in an old family form. In A. Booth (Ed.), *Contemporary families: Looking forward, looking back* (pp. 192–206). Minneapolis, MN: National Council on Family Relations.

Coles, R. (1997). *The moral intelligence of children.* New York: Random House.

Colletta, N. D. (1983). At risk for depression: A study of young mothers. *Journal of Genetic Psychology, 142,* 301–310.

Comstock, G., and Paik, H. (1991). *Television and the American child.* New York: Academic Press.

Condry, J., Condry, S., and Pogatshnik, L. W. (1978, August). *Sex differences: A study of the ear of the beholder.* Paper presented at the meeting of the American Psychological Association, Toronto.

Conger, R., Ge, X., Elder, G., Lorenz, F., and Simons, R. (1994). Economic stress, coercive family process and developmental problems of adolescence. *Child Development, 65*(2), 541–561.

Coopersmith, S. (1967). *The antecedents of self-esteem.* San Francisco: Freeman.

Cowan, C. P., and Cowan, P. A. (1987). Men's involvement in parenthood: Identifying the antecendents and understanding the barriers. In P. W. Berman, F. A. Pedersen, et al. (Eds.), *Men's transitions to parenthood: Longitudinal studies of early family experience* (pp. 145–174). Hillsdale, NJ: Erlbaum.

——, Cowan, P. A., Heming, G., and Miller, N. (1991). Becoming a family: Marriage, parenting, and child development. In P. A. Cowan and E. M. Hetherington (Eds.), *Family transitions.* Hillsdale, NJ: Erlbaum.

Cowan, P. A. (1978). *Piaget with feeling.* New York: Holt, Rinehart and Winston.

Cox, M. J., Owen, M. T., Lewis, J. M., and Henderson, V. K. (1989). Marriage, adult adjustment, and early parenting. *Child Development, 60,* 1015–1024.

Crockenberg, S. B. (1985). Professional support and care of infants by adolescent mothers in England and the United States. *Journal of Pediatric Psychology, 10,* 413–428.

Crouter, A., Perry-Jenkins, M., Huston, T., and McHale, S. (1987). Processes underlying father involvement in dual-earner and single-earner families. *Developmental Psychology, 23,* 431–441.

Cutright, P., and Smith, H. (1988). Intermediate determinants of racial differences in 1980 U.S. normal fertility rates. *Family Planning Perspectives, 20*(2), 119–123.

Dahl, A., Cowgill, K., and Asmundsson, R. (1987). Life in remarried families. *Social Work,* 32, 40–44.

Darabi, K. F., Graham, E. H., Namerow, P. B., Philliber, S. G., and Varga. P. (1984). The effect of maternal age on the well-being of children. *Journal of Marriage and the Family, 46,* 933–936.

Dargatz, J. (1994). *Gain peace of mind.* New York: Thomas Nelson Publishers.

Daro, D. (1988). *Confronting child abuse: Research for effective program design.* New York: Free Press.

Davidson, J. K., and Moore, N. B. (1992). *Marriage and family.* Dubuque, IA: W. C. Brown.

Dean, A. L., Malik, M. M., Richards, W., and Stringer, S. A. (1986). Effects of parental maltreatment on children's conception of interpersonal relationships. *Developmental Psychology, 22,* 617–626.

Delany, E., Delany, S., and Hearth, A. (1993). *Having our say: The Delany sisters' first 100 years.* Kodansha.

deLissovoy, V. (1973). Child care by adolescent parents. *Children Today,* pp. 22–25.

De Vos, S. (1989). Leaving the parental home: Patterns in six Latin American countries. *Journal of Marriage and the Family, 51,* 615–626.

Dietz, W. H., and Gortmaker, S. L. (1985). Do we fatten our children at the television set? Obesity and television viewing in children and adolescents. *Pediatrics, 75,* 807–812.

Dinkmeyer, D. (1979). A comprehensive and systematic approach to parent education. *Journal of Family Therapy, 7*(2), 46–50.

Dinkmeyer, D., Sr., and McKay, G. (1976). *Parents' handbook (A part of the complete STEP program).* Circle Pines, MN: American Guidance Service.

Dishion, T. J., and Loeber, R. (1985). Adolescent marijuana and alcohol use: The role of parents and peers revisited. *American Journal of Drug and Alcohol Abuse, 11,* 11–25.

Dodge, K. A., Bates, J. E., and Pettit, G. S. (1990). Mechanisms in the cycle of violence. *Science, 250,* 1678–1683.

Dodge, K. A., Pettit, G., and Bates, J. (1994). Socialization mediators of the relation between socioeconomic status and child conduct problems. *Child Development, 65*(2), 649–665.

Doka, K., and Mertz, M. (1988). The meaning and significance of great-grandparenthood. *Gerontologist, 28,* 192–197.

Donaldson-Pressman, S., and Pressman, R. M. (1994). *The narcissistic family.* New York: Lexington.

Dore, J. (1978). Variation in preschool children's conversational performances. In K. E. Nelson (Ed.), *Children's language* (Vol. 1.). New York: Gardner Press.

——— (1985). Holophrases revisited, dialogically. In M. Barett (Ed.), *Children's single-word speech.* London: Wiley.

Dornbusch. S. M., Carlsmith, J. M., Bushwall, S. J., Ritter, P. L., Leiderman, H., Hastorf, A. H., and Gross, R. T. (1985). Single parents, extended households, and the control of adolescents. *Child Development, 56,* 326–341.

Downey, D. B., and Powell, B. (1993). Do children in single-parent households fare better living with the same-sex parents? *Journal of Marriage and Family, 55,* 55–71.

Draper, P. (1975). !Kung Women: Contrasts in sexual egalitarianism in foraging and sedentary contexts. In R. Reiter (Ed.), *Toward an anthropology of women.* New York: Monthly Review Press.

Dreikurs, and Soltz, V. (1964). *Children: The challenge.* New York: Hawthorne.

Dubas, J. S., Graber, J. A., and Petersen, A. C. (1991). A longitudinal investigation of adolescents' changing perceptions of pubertal timing. *Developmental Psychology, 27,* 580–586.

Dumas, J. E., and Wahler, R.G. (1983.) Predictors of treatment outcome in parent training: Mothers' insularity and socioeconomic disadvantage. *Behavioral Assessment, 5,* 301–313.

Dunn, J., and Plomin, R. (1990). *Separate lives: Why siblings are so different.* New York: Basic Books.

Dunn, J., and Shatz, M. (1989). Becoming a conversationalist despite (or because of) having a sibling. *Child Development, 60,* 399–410.

Dweck, C. S., and Elliot, E. S. (1983). Achievement motivation. In P. H. Mussen (Serial Ed.) and E. M. Hetherington (Eds.), *Handbook of child psychology:* Vol. 4 *Socialization, personality, and social development* (pp. 643–692). New York: Wiley.

——— and Leggett, E. L. (1988). A social-cognitive approach to motivation and personality. *Psychological Review, 95,* 256–273.

Dwivedi, K. N. (1997). *Enhancing parenting skills.* New York: Wiley.

Eccles, J. S., and Midgley, C. (1990). Changes in academic motivation and self-perception during early adolescence. In R. Montemayor, G. R. Adams, and T. P. Gullotta (Eds.), *From childhood to adolescence: A transition period?* Newbury Park, CA: Sage.

Edelman, M.W. (1992). *The Measure of Our Success.* Boston: HarperCollins.

Egeland, B., and Jacobvitz, D. (1984). International generational continuity of parental abuse: Causes and consequences. Presented at the conference on Biosocial Perspectives in Abuse and Neglect. York, ME.

Egbuono, L., and Starfield, B.(1982). Child health and social status. *Pediatrics, 69*(5), 550–557.

Eibl-Eibesfeldt, I. (1967). Concepts of ethology and their significance in the study of human behavior. In H. Stevenson, E. Hess, and H. Rheingold (Eds.), *Early Behavior.* New York: Wiley.

Eisenberg, N., and Miller, P. A. (1987). The relationship of empathy to prosocial and related behaviors. *Psychological Bulletin, 101,* 91–119.

Elder, G. H., Jr. (1974). *Children of the great depression.* Chicago, IL: University of Chicago Press.

——— (1979). Family history and life course. In T. Hareven (Ed.), *Transitions: The family and life course in historical perspective.* New York: Academic Press.

———, Caspi, A., and Nguyen, T. (1986). Resourceful and vulnerable children: Family influences in hard times. In R. K. Silbereisen, K. Eysferth, and G. Rodinger (Eds.), *Development as action in context: Problem behavior and normal youth development* (pp. 167–186). New York: Springer-Verlag.

——— and Hareven, T. K. (1993). Rising above life disadvantage: From the Great Depression to war. In G. H. Elder Jr., J. Modell, and R. D. Parke (Eds.), *Children in time and place: Developmental and historical insights.* New York: Cambridge University Press.

———, Nguyen, T. V., and Caspi, A. (1985). Linking family hardship to children's lives. *Child Development, 56,* 347–359.

Elkin, F., and Handel, G. (1972). *The child and society: The process of socialization.* New York: Random House.

Elkind, D. (1978). Understanding the adolescent. *Adolescence, 13,* 127–134.

——— (1981). *The hurried child.* Reading, MA: Addison-Wesley.

—— (1984). *All grown up and no place to go*. Reading, MA: Addison-Wesley.

Endes, J., and Rockwell, R. (1980). *Food, nutrition, and the young child*. St. Louis: C. V. Mosby.

Engfer, A. (1984). *Early problems in mother-child interaction*. Lincoln, NE: University of Nebraska.

Enright, R. D., Enright, W. F., Manheim, L. A., and Harris, B. E. (1980). Distributive justice development and social class. *Developmental Psychology, 16*, 555–563.

Epstein, J. L. (1983a). *Effects on parents of teacher practices of parent involvement*. Baltimore, MD: Center for Social Organization of Schools, Johns Hopkins University (Report #346).

—— (1983b). Longitudinal effects of family-school-person interactions on student outcomes. *Research in Sociology of Education and Socialization, 4*, 101–127.

Epstein, L. H., and Wing, R. R. (1987). Behavioral treatment of childhood obesity. *Psychological Bulletin, 101*, 331–342.

Epstein, N. B., Bishop, D. S., and Baldwin, L. M. (1982). McMaster model of family functioning: A view of the normal family. In F. Walsh (Ed.), *Normal family processes: Implications for clinical practice* (pp. 115–141). New York: Guilford Press.

Erikson, E.H. (1963) *Childhood and Society* (2nd ed.). New York: Norton.

—— (1980). *Identity and the life cycle*. New York: Norton (original work published 1959).

Fadiman, A. (1997). *The spirit catches you and you fall down: A Hmong child, her American doctors, and the collision of two cultures*. New York; Farrar, Straus and Giroux.

Faber, A., and Mazlish, E. (1982). *How to talk so kids will listen and listen so kids will talk*. New York: Avon.

—— (1990). *Liberated parents, liberated children: Your guide to a happier family*. New York: Avon Books.

Fabes, R. A., Wilson, P., and Christopher, F. S. (1989). A time to reexamine the role of television in family life. *Family Relations, 38*, 337–341.

Fagot, B. I. (1978). Reinforcing contingencies for sex role behaviors; Effect of experience with children. *Child Development, 49*, 30–36.

—— (1985). Beyond the reinforcement principle: another step toward understanding sex-role development. *Developmental Psychology, 21*, 1097–1104.

—— and Leinbach, M. D, (1987). Socialization of sex roles within the family. In B. Carter, *Of sex roles and sex typing: Theory and research*. (Ed.), *Current Conceptions*. New York: Praeger.

Falk, P. (1989). Lesbian mothers: Psychological assumptions in family law. *American Psychologist, 44*, 941–947.

Felix-Ortiz, de la, G. M., Newcomb, M. D., and Meyers, H. F. (1995). A multidimensional measure of cultural identity for Latino and Latina adolescents. In A. M. Padilla (Ed.), *Hispanic Psychology* (pp. 26–42). Thousand Oaks, CA: Sage.

Ferholt, J. B. (1991). Psychodynamic parent psychotherapy: Treating the parent-child relationship. In M. L. Lewis, et al. (Eds.), *Child and adolescent psychiatry: A comprehensive textbook* (pp. 869–877). Baltimore, MD: Williams and Wilkins, Co.

Fernald, A. (1985). Four-month-old infants prefer to listen to motherese, *Infant Behavior and Development, 8*, 181–195.

—— and Mazzie, C. (1991). Prosody and focus in speech to infants and adults, *Developmental Psychology, 27*, 209–221.

Fine, M., and Fine, D. (1992). Recent changes in laws affecting stepfamilies: Suggestions for legal reform. *Family Relations, 41*(3), 334–340.

Finkelhor, D. (1984). *Child sexual abuse. New theory and research*. New York: Free Press.

Finley, J. J. (1989, February). Theories of family labor as applied to gender differences in caregiving for elderly parents. *Journal of Marriage and the Family, 51*, 79–86.

Fischer, J. L. (1982). Mother-child relationships of mothers living apart from their children. *Alternate Lifestyles, 5*(1), 42–53.

Fischer, L. R. (1983). Mothers and mothers-in-law. *Journal of Marriage and the Family, 45*(1), 187–192.

—— (1986). *Linked lives: Adult daughters and their mothers*. New York: Harper and Row.

Fischman, J. (October, 1986). The Children's Hour. *Psychology Today*.

Fishman, K. D. (1992) Problem Adoptions. *Atlantic Monthly, 270*(3), 37–69.

Fleming, P. J., Gilbert, R., Azaz, Y., Berry, P. J., Rudd, P. T., Stewart, A., and Hall, E. (1990). Interactions between bedding and sleep position in sudden infant death syndrome: A population-based control study. *British Medical Journal, 301*, 85–89.

Forehand, R., Wierson, M., Thomas, A. M., and Armistead, L. (1991). The role of family stressors and parent relationships on adolescent functioning. *Journal of the American Academy of Child and Adolescent Psychiatry, 30*, 316–322.

Forman, E., and McPhail, J. (1989). *What have we learned about the cognitive benefits of peer interaction? A Vygotskian critique*. Paper presented at the annual meeting of the American Educational Research Association, San Francisco.

Fortune, May 16, 1994.

Fraiberg, S. (1987). *Every child's birth right: In defense of mothering*. New York: Bantam Books.

Frankenburg, W. K., and Dodds, J. B. (1967). The Denver developmental screening test. *Journal of Pediatrics, 71*, 181–185.

Frazier, E. F. (1939). *The Negro family in the United States*. Chicago: University of Chicago Press.

Freedman, D. (1974). *Human infancy: An evolutionary perspective*, Hillsdale, NJ: Erlbaum.

French, D. C., and Waas, G. A. (1985). Behavior problems of peer-neglected and peer-rejected elementary age children: Parent and teacher perspectives. *Child Development, 56*, 246–252.

Friedrich, L. K., and Stein, A. H. (1973). Aggressive and prosocial television programs and the natural behavior of preschool children. *Monographs of the Society for Research in Child Development, 38*(4, Serial No. 151).

Frisch, R. E. (1983). Fatness, puberty, and fertility. In J. Brooks-Gunn and A. C. Petersen (Eds.), *Girls at puberty: Biological and psychosocial perspectives* (pp. 29–49). New York: Plenum.

Fulton, A. M., Murphy, K. R., and Anderson, S. L. (1991). Increasing adolescent mothers' knowledge of child development: An intervention program. *Adolescence, 26*, 73–81.

Furman, W., and Buhrmester, D. (1992). Age and sex differences in perception of networks of personal relationships. *Child Development, 63*, 103–115.

———, Jones, L., Buhrmester, D., and Adler, T. (1989). Children's parents', and observers' perceptions of sibling relationships. In P. G. Zukow (Ed.), *Sibling interaction across culture* (pp. 163–180). New York: Springer-Verlag.

Furrow, D., Nelson, K, and Benedict, H. (1979). Mothers' speech to children and syntactic development: Some simple relationships. *Journal of Child Language, 6*(3), 423–442.

Furstenberg, F. F., Jr., Brooks-Gunn, J., and Morgan, P. S. (1987). *Adolescent mothers in later life*. New York: Cambridge University Press.

Gaddis, A., and Brooks-Gunn, J. (1985). The male experience of pubertal change. *Journal of Youth and Adolescence, 14*, 61–72.

Galambos, N. L., Petersen, A. C., and Lenetz, K. (1988). Maternal employment and sex-typing in early adolescence: Contemporaneous and longitudinal relations. In A. D. Gottfried and A. W. Gottfried (Eds.), *Maternal employment and children's development: Longitudinal research*. New York: Plenum.

Galinski, H. J., and Kopp, C. B. (1993). Everyday rules for behavior: Mother's requests to young children. *Developmental Psychology, 29*(5), 573–584.

Galinsky, E. (1980). *Between generations: The six stages of parenthood*. New York: New York Times Books.

Gambino, R. (1974). *Blood of my blood: The dilemma of Italian-Americans*. Garden City, NY: Doubleday.

Gans, J. E., and Blyth, D. A. (1990). *America's adolescents: How healthy are they?* (AMA Profiles of Adolescent Health series). Chicago, Il: American Medical Association.

Garbarino. J. (1982). *Children and families in the social environment*. Hawthorne, NY: Aldine de Groyter.

——— (1983). What we know about child maltreatment. *Children and Youth Services Review, 5*, 3–6.

Garcia-Preto, N. (1982). Puerto Rican families. In M. McGoldrick, J. Pearce, and J. Giordano (Eds.), *Ethnicity and family therapy* (pp. 164–186). New York: Guilford Press.

——— (1988). Transformation of the family system in adolescence. In B.Carter and M. McGoldrick (Eds.), *The changing family life cycle*. New York: Gardner Press.

Garland, A. F., and Zigler, E. (1993). Adolescent suicide prevention: Current research and social policy implications. *American Psychologist, 48*, 169–182.

Garvey, C. (1977). *Play*. Cambridge, MA: Harvard University Press.

——— and Hogan, R. (1973). Social speech and social interaction: Egocentrism revisited. *Child Development, 44*, 562–568.

Gately, D. W., and Schwebel, A. I. (1991). The challenge model of children's adjustment to parental divorce: Explaining favorable outcomes in children. *Journal of Family Psychology, 5*, 60–81.

Gecas, V., and Seff, M. (1991). Families and adolescents: A review of the 1980s. In A. Booth (Ed.), *Contemporary families: Looking forward, looking back* (pp. 208–225). Minneapolis: National Council on Family Relations.

Geissinger, S. B. (1984). Adoptive parents' attitudes toward open birth records. *Family Relations: Journal of Applied Family and Child Studies, 33*(4), 579–585.

Gelles, R. J. (1989). Child abuse and violence in single-parent families: Parent absence and economic deprivation. *American Journal of Orthopsychiatry, 59*(4), 492–501.

——— and Cornell, C. P. (1990). *Intimate violence in families* (2nd ed.). Newbury Park, CA: Sage.

George, C., and Main, M. (1979). Social interactions of young abused children. *Child Development, 50*, 306–318.

Gerbner, G., Gross, L., Signorelli, N., and Morgan, M. (1986). *Television's mean world; Violence profile* No. 14–15. Philadelphia: Annenberg School of Communications, University of Pennsylvania.

Geronimus, A. T., and Korenman, S. (1990). The socioeconomic consequence of teen childbearing reconsidered. *Quarterly Journal of Economics, 107,* 1187–1214.

Gibbs, J. (1989). Black American adolescents. In J. Gibbs, et al. (Eds.)., *Children of color* (pp. 179–223). San Francisco: Jossey-Bass.

Gil, D. G. (1970). *Violence against children.* Cambridge, MA: Harvard University Press.

―――― (1987). Maltreatment as a function of the structure of social systems. In M. R. Brassard, R. Germain, and N. Hart (Eds.), *Psychological maltreatment of children and youth* (pp. 159–170), New York: Pergamon Press.

Gilligan, C. (1982). *In a different voice: Psychological theory and women's development.* Cambridge, MA: Harvard University Press.

Ginott, H. G. (1965). *Between parent and child.* New York: Macmillan.

―――― (1973). *Between parent and teenager.* New York: Macmillan.

Ginsburg, G. S., and Bronstein, P. (1993). Family factors related to children's intrinsic/extrinsic motivational orientation and academic performance. *Child Development, 64*(5), 1461–1474.

Ginzberg, E. (1984). Career development. In D. Brown and L. Brooks (Eds.), *Career choice and development. Applying contemporary theories to practice.* San Francisco, CA: Jossey-Bass.

Glenn, E.N. (1983). Split household, small producer, and dual wage earner: an analysis of Chinese-American family strategies. *Journal of Marriage and the Family 45,* 35–46.

Glick, P., and Lin, S. (1986). More young adults are living with their parents: Who are they? *Journal of Marriage and Family, 48,* 107–112.

Gnepp, J. (1989). Children's use of personal information to understand other people's feelings. In C. Saarni and P. L. Harris (Eds.), *Children's understanding of emotion.* Cambridge, England: Cambridge University Press.

Goelman, H. (1986). The language environments of family day care. In S. Kilmer (Ed.), *Advances in early education and day care Vol. 4* (pp. 153–179). Greenwich, CT: JAI Press.

Goldberg, S., and Lewis, M. (1969). Play behavior in the year-old infant: Early sex differences. *Child Development, 40*(1), 21–31.

Goldenberg, I., and Goldenberg, H. (1996) *Family therapy: An overview* (4th ed.). Pacific Grove, CA: Brooks/Cole.

―――― (1994). *Family therapy.* Monterey, CA: Brooks/Cole.

―――― (1996). *Family therapy.* Monterey, CA: Brooks/Cole.

Goldman, D. (1995). *Emotional Intelligence.* New York: Bantam Books.

Goldscheider, F. K., and DaVanzo, J. (1986). Semiautonomy and leaving home early in adulthood. *Social Forces, 65*(1), 187–201.

Golombok, S., Spencer, A., and Rutter, M. (1983) Children in lesbian and single-parent households: Psychosexual and psychiatric appraisal. *Journal of Child Psychology and Psychiatry, 24,* 551–574.

Gordon, T. (1970). *P.E.T. Parent effectiveness training: The tested new way to raise responsible children.* New York: Plume Books.

―――― (1975) P.E.T. *Parent Effectiveness Training,* New York: New American Library.

Gordon, T. (1989). *Discipline that works.* New York: DAL/Dutton.

Gortmaker, S. L., Dietz, W. H. Jr., Sobol, A. M., and Wehler, C. A. (1987). Increasing pediatric obesity in the United States. *American Journal of Diseases of Children, 141,* 535–540.

Graziano, A. M., DeGioganni, I. S., and Garcia, K. A. (1979). Behavioral treatment of children's fears: A review. *Psychological Bulletin, 86*(4), 804–830.

―――― and Namaste, K. A. (1990). Parental use of physical force in child discipline: A survey of 679 college students. *Journal of Interpersonal Violence, 5,* 449–463.

Green, A. H. (1978). Child abuse. In B. B. Wolman (Ed.), *Handbook of treatment of mental disorders in childhood and adolescence.* Englewood Cliffs, NJ: Prentice-Hall.

Green, R., Mandel, J., Hotvedt, M., and Smith, L. (1986). Lesbian mothers and their children: A comparison with solo-parent heterosexual mothers and their children. *Archives of Sexual Behavior, 7,* 175–181.

Greenberger, E., Goldberg, W. A., Hamill, S., O'Neil, R., and Payne, C. K. (1989). Contributions of a supportive work environment to parent's well-being and orientation to work. *American Journal of Community Psychology, 17,* 755–783.

Greene, A. L., and Grimsley, M. D. (1990). Age and gender differences in adolescents' preferences for parental advice: Mum's the word. *Journal of Adolescent Research, 5,* 396–413.

Greenfield, P. M. (1994). Independence and interdependence as developmental scripts: Implications for theory, research, and practice. In P. M. Greenfield, R. R. Cocking, et al. (Eds.), *Cross-cultural roots of minority child development* (pp. 1–37). Hillsdale, NJ: Erlbaum.

Greven, P. (1992). *Spare the child*. New York: Vintage.

Griswold, R. L. (1993). *Fatherhood in America*. Basic Books, Inc.

Griswold del Castillo, R. (1984). *La Familia*. Notre Dame, IN: University of Notre Dame Press.

Grotevant, H. D. (1979). Environmetal influences on vocational development in adolescents from adoptive and biological families. *Child Development, 50*, 854–860.

Guelzow, M., Bird, G., and Koball, E. (1991). An exploratory path analysis of the stress process for dual-career men and women. *Journal of Marriage and the Family, 53*(1), 151–164.

Guisinger, S., and Blatt, S. (February, 1994). *American Psychologist, 49*, Number 2., 104–111.

Gundersen, B. H., Melas, P. S., and Skar, J. E. (1981). Sexual behavior of preschool children: Teacher's observations. In L. Constantine and F. Martinson (Eds.), *Children and sex: New findings, new perspectives*. Boston, MA: Little, Brown.

Hagestad, G. O. (1987). Parent-child relations in later life: Trends and gaps in past life. In J. B. Lancaster, J. Altman, A. S. Rossi, and L. R. Sherron (Eds.), *Parenting across the lifespan*. New York: Aldine de Gruyter.

Hale-Benson, J. E. (1986). *Balck children: Their roots, culture, and learning styles* (rev. Ed.). Baltimore, MD: Johns Hopkins University Press.

Haley, J. (1963). *Strategies of psychotherapy*. New York: Grune and Stratton.

—— (1973). *Uncommon therapy: The psychiatric techniques of Milton H. Erickson, M.D.* New York: Norton.

—— (1976). *Problem-solving therapy*. San Francisco: Jossey-Bass.

—— (1980). *Leaving home: The therapy of disturbed young people*. New York: McGraw-Hill.

Hall, E. G., and Lee, A. M. (1984). Sex differences in motor performance of young children: Fact or fiction? *Sex Roles, 10*(3/4), 217–230.

Hallahan, D., and Kauffman, J. (1994). *Exceptional children: Introduction to special education* (2nd ed.) Englewood Cliffs, NJ: Prentice-Hall.

Hallowell, E., and Ratey, J. (1994). *Driven to distraction: Recognizing and coping with attention deficit disorder from childhood through adulthood*. New York: Simon & Schuster.

Hamilton, S. F., and Frenzel, L. M. (1988). The impact of volunteer experience on adolescent social development: Evidence of program effects. *Journal of Adolescent Research, 3*(1), 65–80.

Hamon, R. R., and Biesmer, R. (1990). Filial responsibility expectations among adult child-older parent pairs. *Journal of Gerontology: Psychological Sciences. 45*, 110–112.

Hardy, K. V. (1996). May/June. Breathing Room Family Therapy Networker.

Harper, L. V., and Sanders, K. M. (1979). Preschool children's use of space: Sex differences in outdoor play. In M. S. Smart and R. C. Smart (Eds.), *Preschool children: Development and relationships*. New York: Macmillan.

Harrison, A. O., Wilson, M. N., Pine, C. J., Chan, S. Q., and Buriel, R. (1990). Family ecologies of ethnic minority children. *Child Development, 61*, 347–362.

Harter, S. (1982). The perceived competence scale for children. *Child Development, 53*, 87–97.

—— (1983). Developmental perspectives on self-system. In E. M. Hetherington (Ed.), *Handbook of child psychology, Vol 4: Socialization, personality, and social development* (4th ed., pp. 275–385). New York: Wiley.

—— *Self-perception profile for children*. Denver, CO: Department of Psychology, University of Denver.

Hartmann, E. (1981). The strangest sleep disorder. *Psychology Today, 15*(4), 14–18.

Hartshore, T. S., and Manaster, G. L. (1982). The relationship with grandparents: contact, importance, role conception. *International Journal of Aging and Human Development, 15*, 233–245.

Hartup, W. W. (1983). Peer relations. In E. M. Hetherington (Ed.), *Handbook of child psychology, Vol. 4: Socialization, personality and social development*, New York: Wiley.

—— (1989). Social relationships and their developmental significance. *American Psychologist, 44*, 120–126.

Haskins, R. (1989). Beyond metaphor: The efficacy of early childhood education. *American Psychologist, 44*, 274–282.

Hawkins, A. J., and Belsky, J. (1989). The role of father involvement in personality change in men across the transition to parenthood. *Family Relations, 38*, 378–384.

Harwood, R. L., Miller, J. L., and Irizarry, N. L. (1995). *Culture and attachment: Perceptions of the child in context*. New York: Guilford Press.

Healy, J. M. (1987, 1994). *Your child's growing mind*. New York: Doubleday.

—— (1992). *How to have intelligent and creative conversations with your kids*. New York: Doubleday.

Hearold, S. (1986). A synthesis of 1043 effects of television on social behavior. In G. Comstock (Ed.), *Public communications and behavior* (Vol. 1, pp. 65–133). New York: Academic Press.

Heininger, M. A. (1984). *Century of Childhood*. Rochester, NY: Margaret Woodbury Strong Museum.

Hess, R. D., and Shipman, V. C. (1965). Early experience and socialization of cognitive modes in children. *Child Development, 36*, 869–886.

Hetherington, E. M. (1993). An overview of the Virginia Longitudinal Study of Divorce and Remarriage with a focus on early adolescence. *Journal of Family Psychology, 7*, 39–56.

——— and Camara, K. A. (1994). Families in transition: The process of dissolution and reconstruction. In R. D. Parke (Ed.), *A review of child development research*, Vol. 7 (pp. 398–439). Chicago: University of Chicago Press.

——— and Clingempeel, W. G. (1992). Coping with marital transitions: A family systems perspective. *Monographs of the Society for Research in Child Development, 57*(2–3, Serial No. 227).

——— Cox, M., and Cox, R. (1979). Play and social interaction in children following divorce. *Journal of Social Issues, 35*, 26–49.

——— Cox, M., and Cox, R. (1985). Long-term effects of divorce and remarriage on the adjustment of children. *Journal of the American Academy of Child Psychiatry, 24*(5), 518–530.

——— and Parke, R. D. (1993). *Child psychology: A contemporary viewpoint* (2nd ed). New York: McGraw-Hill.

Hinderliter, K. (1988, Jan–Feb.) Death of a dream. *Exceptional Parent, 1*, 48–49.

Hill, J. P. (1985). Family relations in adolescence: Myths, realities, and new directions. *Genetic, Social and General Psychology Monographs, 111*, 233–248.

Hill J. P., and Holmbeck, G.N. (1987). Familial adaptation to biological change during adolescence. In R. M. Lerner and T. T. Foch (Eds.), *Biological-psychosocial interactions in early adolescence: a life-span perspective* (pp. 207–223). Hillsdale, NJ: Lawrence Erlbaum Associates.

Hilton, I. (1967). Differences in the behavior of mothers toward first- and later-born children. *Journal of Personality and Social Psychology, 7*, 282–290.

Hinde, R. A., Titmus, G., Easton, D., and Tamplin, A. (1985). Incidence of "friendship"and behavior to strong associates versus nonassociates in preschoolers. *Child Development, 56*, 234–245.

Hines, P. M., and Boyd-Franklin, N. (1996). African American families. In M. McGoldrick, J. Giordano, and J. K. Pearce (Eds.), *Ethnicity and family therapy* (2nd ed., pp. 66–84.). New York: Guilford Press.

Ho, D. Y. F. (1981). Traditional patterns of socialization in Chinese society. *Acta Psychologica Taivtanica, 23*, 81–95.

——— (1987). Fatherhood in Chinese culture. In M. E. Lamb. (Ed.), *The Father's Role: Cross-cultural perspectives* (pp. 227–245). Hillsdale, NJ: Lawrence Erlbaum Associates.

Hochschild, A. (1989). *The second shift: Working parents and the revolution at home.* New York: Viking.

Hoeffer, B. (1981) Children's acquisition of sex-role behavior in lesbian-mother families. *American Journal of Orthopsychiatry, 5*, 536–544.

Hofferth, S. L., and Phillips, D. (1987). Child care in the United States, 1970–1995. *Journal of Marriage and the Family, 49*, 559–571.

Hoffman, L. W. (1979). Maternal employment. *American Psychologist, 34*, 859–865.

——— (1984). Work, family and the socialization of the child. In R. D. Parke (Ed.), *Review of child development research* (Vol. 7, pp. 223–282). Chicago, IL: Chicago University Press.

——— (1989). The effects of maternal employment on the two-parent family. *American Psychologist, 44*, 283–292.

Hoffman, L. W. (1991). The influence of the family environment on personality: Accounting for sibling differences. *Psychological Bulletin, 110*, 187–203.

Hoffman, M. L. (1975). Altruistic behavior and the parent-child relationship. *Journal of Personality and Social Psychology, 31*, 937–943.

——— (1977). Sex differences in empathy and related behaviors. *Psychological Bulletin, 84*, 712–722.

Hofstede, G. (1991). Adapted from S. York. *Roots and wings: Affirming culture in early childhood program.* St. Paul, MN: Redleaf Press.

Holden, G. W. (1983). Avoiding conflict: Mothers as tacticians in the supermarket. *Child Development, 54*, 233–240.

Holmbeck, G. N., and Hill, J. P. (1991). Conflictive engagement, positive affect, and menarche in families with seventh-grade girls. *Child Development, 62*, 1030–1048.

Holt, L. E. (1894). *Food, health and growth: A discussion of nutrition of children.* New York: Macmillan.

Hopson, D. P., and Hopson, D. S. (1990). *Different and wonderful: Raising black children in a race-conscious society.* New York: Prentice-Hall.

Howard, J. (1978). The influence of children's developmental dysfunctions on marital quality and family interaction. In R. M. Lerner and G. B. Spanier (Eds.), *Child influences on marital and family interaction: A life-span perspective* (pp. 275–298). New York: Academic Press.

Howes, C. (1987). Peer interaction of young children. *Monographs of the Society for Research in Child Development, 53*, (1, Serial No. 217).

——— (1988). Peer interaction of young children, *Monographs of the Society for Child Development, 53*(1), 94–104.

——— Unger, O. A., and Matheson, C. C. (1992). *The collaborative construction of pretend: Social pretend play functions*. Albany, NY: State University of New York Press.

Huesmann, L. R., Lagerspetz, K, and Eron, L. D. (1984). Intervening variables in the TV violence-aggression relation: Evidence from two countries. *Developmental Psychology, 20*, 1120–1134.

Huggins, S. (1989). A comparison study of self-esteem of adolescent children of divorced lesbian mothers and divorced heterosexual mothers. In F. Bozett (Ed.), *Homosexuality and the family* (pp. 123–135). New York: Harrington Park.

Hughes, F. P. (1991). *Children's play and development*. Boston: Allyn and Bacon.

Hunt, C. E., and Brouillette, R. T. (1987). Sudden infant death syndrome: 1987 perspective. *Journal of Pediatrics, 110*, 669–678.

Hunter, F. T. (1985). Individual adolescents' perceptions of interactions with friends and parents. *Journal of Early Adolescence, 5*(3), 295–305.

——— (1985). Adolescents' perception of discussions with parents and friends. *Developmental Psychology, 21*(3), 433–440.

Hunter. R. S., and Kilstrom, N. (1979). Breaking the cycle in abusive families. *American Journal of Psychiatry, 136*, 1320–1322.

Huston, A. C. (1983). Sex-typing. In E. M. Hetherington (Ed.), *Handbook of child psychology, Vol 4: Socialization, personality, and social development* (4th ed., pp. 387–467). New York: Wiley.

——— and Alvarez, M. M. (1990). The socialization context of gender role development in early adolescence. In R. Montemayor, G. R. Adams, and T. P. Gullotta (Eds.), *From childhood to adolescence: A transition period?* (pp. 156–179). Newbury Park, CA: Sage.

Innocenti, M., Huh, K., and Boyce, G. (1992). Families of children with disabilities: Normative data and other considerations on parenting stress. *Topics in Early Childhood Special Education, 12*(3), 403–427.

Isabell, B. J., and McKee, L. (1980). Society's cradle: An anthropological perspective on the socialization of cognition. In J. Sants (Ed.), *Development psychology and society*, (pp. 327–365) London: Macmillan.

Izard, C. E. (1982). *Measuring emotions in infants and children*. New York: Cambridge University Press.

Izraeli, D. (1989). Burning out in medicine: A comparison of husbands and wives in dual-career couples. In E. Goldsmith (Ed.), *Work and family: Theory, research, and applications* (pp. 329–346). Newbury Park, CA: Sage.

Jackson, D. (1965). Family rules: Marital grid pro quo. *Archives of General Psychiatry, 12*, 589–594.

Jacobs, B. S., and Moss, H. A. (1976). Birth order and sex of sibling as determinants of mother-infant interaction. *Child Development, 47*, 315–322.

Jacobsen, R. B., and Bigner, J. J. (1991). Black versus white single parents and the value of children. *Journal of Black Studies, 21*, 302–312.

Jaycox, L. H., Reivich, K. J., Gillham, J., and Seligman, M. E. P. (1994). Prevention of depressive symptoms in school children. *Behavior Research and Therapy, 32*(8), 801–816.

Jendrek, M.P. (1993). Grandparents who parent their grandchildren: Effects on lifestyle. *Journal of Marriage and the Family, 55*, 609–621.

Jersild, A. T. (1960). *Child psychology* (5th ed.). Englewood Cliffs, NJ: Prentice-Hall.

Jessor, R. (1992). Risk behavior in adolescence: A psychosocial framework for understanding and action. In D. E. Rogers and E. Ginzburg (Eds.), *Adolescents at risk: Medical and social perspectives* (pp. 19–34). Boulder, CO: Westview Press.

——— (1993). Successful adolescent development among youth in high-risk settings. *American Psychologist, 48*, 117–126.

Johnson, E. S. (1978). "Good" relationships between older mothers and their daughters: A causal model. *The Gerontologist, 18*, 301–306.

Johnson-Powell, G., and Yamamoto, J. (1997). *Transcultural Child Development*. New York: Wiley.

Johnston, L. D., O'Malley, P. M., and Bachman, J. G. (1986). Drug use among high school students, college students, and other young adults: National trends through 1985. Washington, DC: National Institute on Drug Abuse.

Jones, M. C. (1965). Psychological correlates of somatic development. *Child Development, 36*, 899–911.

Jones, B. M., and MacFarlane, K. (Eds.), (1980). *Sexual abuse of children: Selected readings*. Washington, DC: National Center of Child Abuse and Neglect.

Julian, T. W., McKenry, P. C., and McKelvey, M. W. (1994). Cultural variations in parenting: Perceptions of Caucasian, African-American, Hispanic, and Asian-American parents. *Family Relations, 43*, 30–37.

Kaffman, M., and Elizur, E. (1977). Infants who become enuretics: A longitudinal study of 161 kibbutz children. *Monographs of the Society for Research in Child Development*, Vol. 42(2), 61.

Kagan, J. (1984). *The nature of the child*. New York: Basic Books.

———, Arcus, D., Snideman, N., Feng, W. Y., Hendler, J., and Greene, S. (1994). Reactivity in infants: A cross-national comparison. *Developmental Psychology, 30*, 342–345.

Kagitcibasi, C. (1990). Family and socialization in cross-cultural perspective: A model of change. *Nebraska Symposium on Motivation 37*, 135–200.

Kahn, M., and Bank, S. (1981, June). The sibling bond. Quoted in V. Adams, The sibling bond: A lifelong love/hate dialectic. *Psychology Today*, 34.

Karen, B. (1994). *Becoming Attached*. New York: Warner Books.

——— (1990, February). Becoming attached. *Atlantic Monthly*, 265.

Kaufman, J., and Zigler, E. (1989). The intergenerational transmission of child abuse. In D. Cicchetti and V. Carlton (Eds.), *Child maltreatment* (pp. 129–152). New York: Cambridge University Press.

——— (1991). Determinants of abuse: Compensatory and risk factors. In D. Cicchetti and V. Carlson (Eds.), *Child maltreatment*. Cambridge: Cambridge University Press.

Katz, A. J. (1979) Lone fathers: Perspectives and implications for family policy. *Family Coordinator, 28*, 521–528.

Kawasaki, C., Nugent, J. K., Miyashita, H., Miyahara, H., et al. (1994). The cultural organization of infants' sleep. *Children's Environments, 11*(2), 135–141.

Kearns, D. (1987). *The Fitzgeralds and the Kennedys*, New York: St. Martin's Press.

Kelder, L. R., McNamara, J. R., Carlson, B., and Lynn, S. J. (1991). Perceptions of physical punishment: The relation to childhood and adolescent experiences. *Journal of Interpersonal Violence, 6*, 432–445.

Kellam, S. G., Ensminger, M. E., and Turner, R. J. (1977). Family structure and the mental health of children. *Archives of General Psychiatry, 34*, 1012–1022.

Keller, W. D., Hildebrandt, K. A., and Richards, M. (1981, April). *Effects of extended father-infant contact during the newborn period*. Paper presented at the biennial meeting of the Society for Research in Child Development, Boston.

Kempe, C. H., Silverman, F. N., Steele, B. B, Droegemueller, W., and Silver, H. K. (1962). The battered child syndrome. *Journal of the American Medical Association, 181*, 17–24.

Kempe, R., and Kempe, C. H. (1978). *Child abuse*. Cambridge, MA: Harvard University Press.

Keogh, J., and Sugden, D. (1985). *Movement skill development*. New York: Macmillan.

Kerig, P. K., Cowan, P. A., and Cowan, C. P. (1993). Marital quality and gender differences in parent-child interaction. *Developmental Psychology, 29*(6), 931–939.

Kerr, M. E., and Bowen, M. (1988). *Family evaluation; An approach based on Bowen theory*. New York: Norton.

Kibria, N. (1993). *Family tightrope, The changing lives of Vietnamese Americans*. Princeton, NJ: Princeton University Press.

King, V., and Elder, G. H. Jr. (1995). American children view their grandparents: Linked lives across three rural generations. *Journal of Marriage and the Family 57*, 165–178.

Kinston, W., Loader P., Miller, L. (1987). Quantifying the clinical assessment of family health. *Journal of Marital and Family Therapy, 13*, 49–67.

Kirkland, J., and Hill. A. (1979). Crying and baby bashing. *Cry Research Newsletter, 2*(1), 5–6.

Kirkpatrick, M. (1987). Clinical implications of lesbian mother studies. *Journal of Homosexuality. 13*, 201–211

———, Smith C., and Roy, R. (1981) Lesbian mothers and their children: A comparative survey. *American Journal of Orthopsychiatry, 5*, 1.

Kishwar, M. (1987). The continuing deficit of women in India and the impact of amniocentesis. In G. Corea (Ed.), *Man-made women* (pp. 30–37). Bloomington: Indiana University Press.

Kivett, V. R. (1991). Centrality of the grandfather role among older rural black and white men. *Journal of Gerontology, 46*(5), 250-258.

Klaus, M. H., and Kennell, J. H. (1976). *Maternal-infant bonding. The impact of early separation or loss on family development*. St. Louis: C. V. Mosby.

Koff, E., Rierdan, J., and Stubbs, M. L. (1990). Gender, body image, and self-concept in early adolescence. *Journal of Early Adolescence, 10*, 56–68.

Kohlberg, L. (1986). A current statement on some theoretical issues. In S. Modgil and C. Modgil (Eds.), *Lawrence Kohlberg*. Philadelphia: Farmer.

Kolata, G. (1986). Obese children: A growing problem. *Science, 232*, 20–21.

Korner, A. F. (1979). Conceptual issues in infancy research. In J. D. Osofsky (Ed.), *Handbook of infant development*. New York: Wiley.

Kozol, J. (1991). *Savage inequalities*. New York: Crown.

Kressel, K. (1985). *The process of divorce: How professionals and couples negotiate settlements*. New York: Basic Books.

Kurokawa, M. (1969). Acculturation and mental health of Mennonite children. *Child Development, 40*(3), 689–705.

Ladd, G. W., Price, J. M., and Hart, C. H. (1988). Predicting preschoolers' peer status from playground behaviors. *Child Development, 59*, 986–992.

LaDue, R. (1994). Coyote returns: twenty sweats does not an Indian expert make, Bringing ethics alive. *Feminist Ethics in Psychotherapy Practice, 15*(1), 93–111.

Lahey, B. B., Hammer, D., Crumrine, P. L., and Fore-hand, R. L. (1980). Birth order: Sex interactions in child behavior problems. *Developmental Psychology, 16*(6), 608–615.

Lamanna, M.A., and Reidmann, A. (1994). *Marriages and Families.* New York: Wadsworth.

Lamb, M. E. (1979). Paternal influences and the father's role, *American Psychologist, 34,* 938–943.

—— (1980) The development of parent-infant attachments in the first two years of life. In Federson (Ed.), *The father-infant relationship.* New York: Praeger.

—— (1981). The development of father-infant relationship. In M. E. Lamb (Ed.), *The role of the father in child development* (2nd ed.). New York: Wiley.

—— (Ed.) (1987). *The father's role: Cross-cultural perspectives.* Hillsdale, NJ: Lawrence Erlbaum Associates.

Langlois, J. H. (1992). The origins and functions of appearance-based stereotypes: Theoretical and applied implications. In R. Eder (Ed.), *Developmental perspectives in craniofacial problems.* New York: Verlag.

—— Ritter, J. M, Casey, R. J., and Swain, D. B. (1995). Infant attractiveness predicts maternal behaviors and attitudes. *Developmental Psychology, 31,* 464–472.

Lansdown, R., and Walker, M. (1991). *Your child's development from birth through adolescence.* New York: Knopf.

Larrick, N. (1975). *A parent's guide to child rearing.* New York: Bantam Books.

Larson, R., and Richards, M. H. (1991). Daily companionship in late childhood and early adolescence: Changing developmental contexts. *Child Development, 62,* 284–300.

Larzelere, R. E., Klein, M., Schumm, W. R., and Alibrando, S. A. (1989). Relations of spanking and other parenting characteristics to self-esteem and perceived fairness of parental discipline. *Psychological Reports, 64,* 1140–1142.

Lash, J. P. (1971). *Eleanor and Franklin.*

Lefkowitz, M. M., Eron, L. D., Walder, L. O., and Huesmann, L. R. (1972). Television violence and child aggression: A follow-up study. In G. A. Cornstock and E. A. Rubinstein (Eds.), *Television and social behavior* (Vol. 3, pp. 35–135). Washington, DC: U.S. Government Printing Office.

Leifer, A. D. (1973). *Television and the development of social behavior.* Paper presented at the meeting of the International Society for the Study of Behavioral Development, Ann Arbor.

Lempers, J. D., and Clark-Lempers, D. (1990). Family economic stress, maternal and paternal support and adolescent distress. *Journal of Adolescence, 13,* 217–230.

Len, M. W. (1987). Parental discipline and criminal deviance. *Marriage and the Family Review, 12,* 103–112.

Lerner, R., and Lerner, J. (1977). Effects of age, sex, and physical attractiveness on child-peer relations, academic performance, and elementary school adjustment. *Developmental Psychology, 13*(6), 585–590.

——, Peterson, A. C., and Brooks-Gunn, J. (Eds), (1991). *The encyclopedia of adolescence.* New York: Garland Press.

Le Shan, E. (1993). *Grandparenting in a changing world.* New York: New Market Press.

Leung, A. K. D., and Robson, W. L. M. (1991). Sibling Rivalry. *Clinical Practices, 30*(5), 314–317.

Levine, D. U., and Havighurst, R. J. (1992). *Society and education* (8th ed.). Boston: Allyn and Bacon.

Levinson, D. (1978). *Season's of a Man's Life.* New York: Knopf.

Levy-Schiff, R. (1995). Individual and contextual correlates of marital change across the transition to parenthood. *Developmental Psychology, 30*(4), 591–601.

Lewis, J. M., Beavers, W. R., Gossett, J. T., and Pillips, V. A. (1976). *No single thread: Psychological health in family systems.* New York: Bruner/Mazel.

Lieberman, A. F. (1977). Preschoolers' competence with a peer: Relations with attachment and peer experience, *Child Development, 48,* 1277–1287.

Liebert, R. M., and Sprafkin, J. (1988). The early window: *Effects of television on children and youth* (3rd ed.). New York: Pergamon Press.

Lin, C. Y., and Fu, V. R. A. (1990). A comparison of child-rearing practices among Chinese, immigrant Chinese, and Caucasian-American parents. *Child Development, 61,* 429–433.

Lin, K. S. (1986). *The value of children for college students: A comparison of four ethnic groups.* Unpublished master's thesis. Colorado State University, Fort Collins.

Lips, H. (1993). *Sex and gender:* An introduction (2nd ed.). Mountain View, CA: Mayfield.

Lipsitt, L. P. (1982). Infant learning. In T. M. Field, A. Huston, H. C. Quay, L. Troll, and G. E. Finley (Eds.), *Review of human development.* New York: Wiley.

Littenberg, R., Tulkin, S., and Kagan, J. (1971). Cognitive components of separation anxiety. *Developmental Psychology, 4*(3), 387–388.

Logan, D. D. (1980). The menarche experience in twenty-three foreign countries. *Adolescence, 58,* 247–256.

Lowe, M. (1975). Trends in the development of representational play in infants from one to three years: An observational study. *Child Psychology, 16,* 33–48.

Lown, J., McFadden, J., and Crossman, S. (1989). Family life education for remarriage focus on financial education. *Family Relations, 38*(1), 40–45.

Lowry, G. H. (1978). *Growth and development of children* (7th ed.). Chicago: Medical Year Book.

Lozoff, B. (1989). Nutrition and behavior. *American Psychologist, 44*, 231–236.

Lozoff, B., Wolf, A., and Davis, N. (1994). Cosleeping in urban families with young children in the United States. *Pediatrics, 74*, 171–182.

Lueptow, L. B. (1992). Change and stability in the sex typing of adolescent work orientations: 1976–1989. *Perceptual and Motor Skills, 75*, 1114.

Lum, K. and Char, W. F. (1985). Chinese adoption in Hawaii: Some examples. In W. Tseng and D. Y. H. Wu (Eds.), *Chinese culture and mental health* (pp. 215–226). Orlando, FL: Academic Press.

Lyons, N. P. (1983). Two perspectives: On self, relationships, and morality. *Harvard Educational Review, 53*, 125–145.

Lytton, H., and Romney, D. M. (1991). Parents' differential socialization of boys and girls: A meta-analysis. *Psychological Bulletin, 109*, 267–296.

Maccoby, E. E. (1984a). Middle childhood in the context of the family. In W. A. Collins (Ed.), *Development during middle childhood.* (pp. 184–239). Washington, DC: National Academic Press.

——— (1984b). Socialization and developmental change. *Child Development, 55*, 317–328.

——— (1990). Gender and relationships: A developmental account. *American Psychologist, 45*, 513–520.

——— and Martin, J. A. (1983). Socialization in the context of the family: Parent-child interaction. In E. M. Hetherington (Ed.), *Handbook of child psychology*, Vol. 4: Socialization, personality, and social development (4th ed., pp. 1–102). New York: Wiley.

MacFarlane, A. (1977). *The psychology of childbirth.* Cambridge, MA: Harvard University Press.

Mahler, M. S., Pine, F., and Bergman, A. (1975). *The psychological birth of the human infant.* New York: Basic Books.

Main, M., and Solomon, J. (1986). Discovery of a disorganized/disoriented attachment pattern. In T. Brazelton and M. W. Yogman (Eds.), *Affective development in infancy.* Norwood, NJ: Ablex.

Malina, R. M., and Bouchard, C. (1991). *Growth, maturation, and physical activity.* Champaign, IL: Human Kinetics Books.

Manchester, W. (1978). *American Caesar.* Boston, MA: Little, Brown.

Mangione, J., and Morreale, B.(1992). *La storia: five centuries of the Italian American experience.* New York: HarperCollins.

Maratsos, M. (1973). Nonegocentric communication abilities in preschool children. *Child Development, 44*, 697–700.

Marcenko, M., and Meyers, J. (1991). Mothers of children with developmental disabilities: Who shares the burden? *Family Relations, 40*(2), 186–190.

Marcia, J. (1966). Development and validation of ego identity status. *Journal of Personality and Social Psychology, 3*, 551–558.

——— (1980). Identity in adolescence. In J. Adelson (Ed.), *Handbook of adolescent psychology.* New York: Wiley.

——— (1987). The identity status approach to the study of ego identity development. In T. Honess and K. Yardley (Eds.), *Self and identity: Perspectives across the lifespan.* London: Routledge and Kegan Paul.

Marotz, L., Rush, J., and Cross, M. (1985). *Health, safety, and nutrition for the young child,* Albany, NY: Delmar.

Matheny, A. P. (1987). Psychological characteristics of childhood accidents. *Journal of Social Issues, 43*, 45–60.

Masur, E. F. (1982). Mother's responses to infant's object-related gestures: Influences on lexical development, *Journal of Child Language, 9*(1), 23–30.

Mathew, R. J., Wilson, W. H., Blazer, D. G., and George, L. K. (1993). Psychiatric disorders in adult children of alcoholics: Data from the epidemiological catchment area project. *American Journal of Psychiatry, 150*(5), 793–800.

Mathew, R. J., Wilson, W. H., Humphreys D., and Lowe, J. V. (1993). Depersonalization after marijuana smoking. *Biological Psychiatry, 33*(6), 431–441.

Matthews, S. H., and Sprey, J. (1985). Adolescents' relationships with grandparents: An empirical contribution to conceptual clarification. *Journal of Gerontology, 40*, 621–626.

McAdoo, J. L., and McAdoo, J. B. (1994). The African-American father's role within the family. In R. Majors and J. Gordon (Eds.), *The American black male: His present status and his future* (pp. 286–297). Chicago: Nelson-Hall.

McBride, J. (1996). *The color of water: A black man's tribute to his white mother.* New York: Riverhead Books.

McCullough, P.G., and Rutenberg, S.K. (1988). In B. Carter and M. McGoldrick (Eds.), *The Changing Family Life Cycle.* New York: Gardner Press.

McGill, D. and Pearce, J. K. (1982). British families. In M. McGoldrick, J. K. Pearce, and J. Giordano (Eds)., *Ethnicity and family therapy.* New York: Guilford Press.

McGhee, P. E. (1979). *Humor: Its origin and development.* San Francisco: W. H. Freeman.

—— (1984). Introduction: Recent developments in humor research. *Journal of Children in Contemporary Society, 20*(1–2), 1–12.

McGoldrick, M. (July–August, 1994). The ache for Home. *Family Therapy Networker.*

—— (1995). *You can go home.* New York: Norton.

—— (1996). Irish families. In M. McGoldrick, J. Giordano, and J. K. Pearce (Eds.), *Ethnicity and family therapy* (2nd ed., pp. 544–566.). New York: Guilford Press.

—— and Carter, A. (1980). Forming a remarried family. In F. A. Carter and M. McGoldrick (Eds.), *The changing family life cycle: A framework for family therapy* (p. 272). Boston, MA: Allyn and Bacon.

McKenna, J. J. (1996). Sudden infant death syndrome in cross-cultural perspective: Is infant-parent cosleeping protective? *Annual Review of Anthropology, 25*, 210–216.

McKinney, J. D., and Speece, D. L.(1986). Academic consequences and longitudinal stability of behavioral subtypes of learning disabled children. *Journal of Educational Psychology, 78*, 365–372.

McLanahan, S., and Booth, K. (1991). Mother-only families: Problems, perspectives, and politics. In A. Booth (Ed.), *Contemporary families: Looking forward, looking back* (pp. 405–428). Minneapolis, MN: National Council on Family Relations.

McLoughlin, J., Clark, F., Mauck, A., and Petrosko, J. (1987). A comparison of parent-child perceptions of student learning disabilities. *Journal of Learning Disabilities, 20*(6), 357–360.

McLoyd, V. C. (1989). Socialization and development in a changing economy: The effects of parental job and income loss on children. *American Psychologist, 44*, 293–302.

—— (1990). The impact of economic hardship on black families and children: Psychological distress, parenting, and socioemotional development. *Child Development, 61*, 311–346.

Mead, M. A. (1960, June 6). New look at early marriage. *U.S. News & World Report*, 80–86.

—— (1972). *Blackberry winter: My earlier years.* New York: Simon & Schuster.

—— and Heyman, K. (1965). *Family.* New York: Macmillan.

Menaghan, E. G., and Parcel, T. L. (1991). Parental employment and family life: Research in the 1980s. In A. Booth (Ed.), *Contemporary families: Looking forward, looking back* (pp. 361–380). Minneapolis, MN: National Council on Family Relations.

Menyuk, P. (1977). *Language and maturation.* Cambridge, MA: M.I.T. Press.

Meredith, H. V. (1976). Findings from Asia, Australia, Europe, and North America on secular change in mean height of children, youth, and young adults. *American Journal of Physical Anthropology, 44*, 315–326.

—— (1978). Research between 1960 and 1970 on the standing height of young children in different parts of the world. In H. W. Reese and L. P. Lipsitt (Eds.), *Advances in child development and behavior* (Vol. 12) (pp. 2–59). New York: Academic Press.

Merrill, E. J. (1982). Physical abuse of children: An agency study. In V. DeFrancis (Ed.), *Protecting the battered child.* Denver, CO: American Humane Association.

Meyer, D. R., and Garasky, S. (1993). Custodial fathers: Myths, realities, and child support. *Journal of Marriage and the Family, 55*, 73–79.

Miller, A. (1990). *For your own good : Hidden cruelty in child-rearing and the roots of violence* (Hildegarde and Hunter Hannum, trans.). New York: Noonday Press.

Miller, B. C., and Moore, K. A. (1990). Adolescent sexual behavior, pregnancy, and parenting: Research through the 1980s. *Journal of Marriage and the Family, 52*, 1025–1044.

Miller, D. S. (1981) The "sandwich"generation: Adult children of the aging. *Social Work*, 419–423.

Miller, N., and Maruyama, G. (1976). Ordinal position and peer popularity. *Journal of Personality and Social Psychology, 33*, 123–131.

Miller, R. B., and Glass, J. (1989). Parent-Child attitude similarity across the life course. *Journal of Marriage and the Family, 51*, 991–997.

Miller, S. A. (1988). Parents' beliefs about children's cognitive development. *Child Development, 59*, 259–285.

Mills, D. (1984). A model for stepfamily development. *Family Relations*, 33, 365–372.

Minkler, M., Roe, K. M., and Price, M. (1992). The physical and emotional health of grandmothers raising grandchildren in the crack cocaine epidemic. *Gerontologist, 32*, 752–761.

Minton, C., Kagan, J., and Levine, J. (1971). Maternal control and obedience in the two-year-old. *Child Development, 42*, 1873–1894.

Minuchin, P. (1974). *Families and family therapy.* Cambridge, MA: Harvard University Press.

—— and Shapiro, E. K. (1983). The school as a context for social development. In E. M. Hetherington (Ed.), *Handbook of child psychology, Vol. 4: Socialization, personality, and social development* (4th ed., pp. 197–274). New York: Wiley.

Mirandé, A. (1991). Ethnicity and fatherhood. In F. Bozett and S. Hanson (Eds.), *Fatherhood and families in cultural context* (pp. 53–82). New York: Springer.

Moefesson, H. C., and Greensher, J. (1978). Childhood accidents. In R. Hoekelman, S. Blatman, P. A. Brunell, S. B. Friedman, and H. H. Seidel (Eds.), *Principles of pediatrics*. New York: McGraw-Hill.

Moitoza, E. (1982). Portuguese families. In M. McGoldrick, J. K. Pearce, and J. Giordano (Eds.), *Ethnicity and family therapy* (1st ed., pp. 412–437). New York: Guilford.

Money magazine (July, 1994). Vol. 23, No. 7.

Montemayor, R. (1986). Family variation in parent-adolescent storm and stress. *Journal of Adolescent Research, 1*, 15–31.

———, Eberly, M., and Flannery, D. (1993). Effects of pubertal status and conversation topics on parent and adolescent affective expression. *Journal of Early Adolescence, 13*, 431–447.

Montemayor, R., and Flannery, D. J. (1991). Parent-adolescent relations in middle and late adolescence. In R. M. Lerner, A. C. Petersen, and J. Brooks-Gunn (Eds.), *Encyclopedia of Adolescence*. New York: Garland.

Montessori, M. (1936b/1966). *The secret of childhood*. (M. J. Costelloe, trans.). New York: Ballantine Books.

——— (1949/1967). *The absorbent mind*. (C. A. Claremont, trans.). New York: Holt, Rinehart and Winston.

Morelli, G., and Tronick, E. (1991). Efe multiple caretaking and attachment. In J. Gewirtz and W. Kurtines (Eds.), *Interactions with attachment* (pp. 41–51). Hillsdale, NJ: Elbaum.

Mortimer, J. T., Shanahan, M., and Ryu, S. (1994). The effects of adolescent employment on school-related orientation and behavior. In R. K. Silbereisen and E. Todt (Eds.), *Adolescence in context; The interplay of family, school, peers and work in adjustment*. New York: Springer-Verlag.

Moskowitz, B. A. (1978). The acquisition of language. *Scientific American, 239*, 92–108.

Moss, H. A. (1967). Sex, age, and state as determinants of mother-infant interaction. *Merrill Palmer Quarterly, 13*, 19–36.

Moynihan, D. (1965). *The Negro family: The case for national action*. Washington, DC: U.S. Government Printing Office.

Nathanson, C. A., and Kim, Y. J. (1989). Components of change in adolescent fertility—1971–1979. *Demography, 26*, 85–98.

National Center for Health Statistics. (1991, June). Family structure and children's health: United States, 1988. *Vital Health Statistics* (Series 10, No. 178). Washington, DC: U.S. Department of Health and Human Services.

——— (1994). Health, United States, 1993. P. 99. Washington, DC: U.S. Government Printing Office.

——— (1996). *Vital statistics of the United States: Mortality*. Washington, DC: U.S. Government Printing Office.

National Commission on Children. (1991). *Beyond rhetoric: A new American agenda for children and families*. Washington, DC: Author.

National Safety Council (1985–1988). *Accident facts*. Chicago: Author.

——— (1995). *Accident facts*. Chicago: Author.

Nelson, K. (1973). Structure and strategy in learning to talk. *Monographs of the Society for Research in Child Development, 38*(1–2 Serial No. 149).

Neugarten, B.L., and Weinstein, K. (1964) The changing American grandparent. *Journal of Marriage and the Family, 26*, 199–204.

Newberger, C.M., and Newberger, E. (1982). Prevention of child abuse: Theory, myth and practice. *Journal of Preventive Psychiatry, 1*, 443–451.

Nielsen Television Services (1996). *Nielsen report on television*. Northbrook, Il: Nielsen.

Nitz, V., and Lerner, J. V. (1991). Temperament during adolescence. In R. M. Lerner, A. C. Petersen, and J. Brooks-Gunn (Eds.), *Encyclopedia of Adolescence (Vol. 2)*. New York: Garland.

Noller, P., and Callan, V. (1986). Adolescent and parent perceptions of family cohesion and adaptability. *Journal of Adolescence, 9*(1), 97–106.

Noller, P., and Callan, V. (1990). Adolescents' perceptions of the nature of their communication with parents. *Journal of Adolescence, 19*(4), 349–362.

Nottlemann, E. D. (1987). Competence and self-esteem during transition from childhood to adolescence. *Developmental Psychology, 23*, 441–450.

——— and Welsh, C. J. (1986). The long and short of physical stature in early adolescence. *Journal of Early Adolescence, 6*, 15–27.

Nugent, J. K., Lester, B. M., and Brazelton, T. B. (1989). *The cultural context of infancy Vol. 1*. Norwood, NJ: Ablex.

Offer, D. (1988). *The teenage world: Adolescents' self-image in ten countries*. New York: Plenum.

——— and Offer, J. B. (1975*). From teenage to young manhood: A psychological study*. New York: Basic Books.

——— and Schonert-Reichl, K. A. (1992). Debunking the myths of adolescence: Findings from recent research. *Journal of the Academy of Child and Adolescent Psychiatry, 31*, 1003–1014.

O'Hara, M. W., Zekoski, E. M., Philipps. L. H., and Wright. E. J. (1990). Controlled prospective study of postpartum mood disorders: Comparison of childbearing and nonchildbearing women. *Journal of Abnormal Psychology, 99*(1), 3–15.

Okagaki, L., and Sternberg, R. J. (1993). Parental beliefs and children's school performance. *Child Development, 64,* 36–56.

Olson, S., and Banyard, V.(1993). Stop the world so I can get off a while: Sources of daily stress in the lives of low-income single mothers of young children. *Family Relations, 42*(1), 50–56.

Olsen, D. H., and DeFrain, J. (1989). *Journal of Marriage and the Family.* Based on The Stepping Ahead Program, by E. Visher. In M. Burt (Ed.), *Stepfamilies stepping ahead.* Lincoln, NE: Stepfamilies Press.

Osgood, C. E. (1957). A behavioristic analysis of perception and language as cognitive phenomena, In *Contemporary approaches to cognition* (pp. 75–118), Cambridge, MA: Harvard University Press.

Page, R. M. (1993). Perceived physical attractiveness and frequency of substance use among male and female adolescents. *Journal of Alcohol and Drug Education, 38*(2), 81–91.

Pagelow, M. D. (1980). Heterosexual and lesbian mothers. A comparison of problems, coping, and solutions. *Journal of Homosexuality, 5,* 198–204.

Paikoff, R. L., and Brooks-Gunn, J. (1991). Do parent-child relationships change during puberty? *Psychological Bulletin, 110,* 47–66.

Palladino G. (1996). *Teenagers, an American history.* New York: Basic Books.

Papernow, P. (1984). The stepfamily cycle: An experiential model of stepfamily development. *Family Relations, 33,* 355–363.

Papini, D. R., and Roggman, L. A. (1992). Adolescent perceived attachment to parents in relation to competence, depression, and anxiety: A longitudinal study. *Journal of Early Adolescence, 12,* 420–440.

Parcel, G. S., Simons-Morton, G. G., O'Hara, N. M., Baranowski, T., Kolbe, L. J., and Bee, D. E. (1987). School promotion of healthful diet and exercise behavior: an integration of organizational change and social learning theory interventions. *Journal of School Health, 57,* 150–156.

Parke, R. D., and Sawin, D. B. (1975). *Infant characteristics and behavior as initiators of maternal and paternal responsivity.* Paper presented at the biennial meeting of the Society for Research in Child Development, Denver.

——— and Slaby, R. G. (1983). The development of aggression. In E. M. Hetherington (Ed.), and P. H. Mussen (Series Ed.), *Handbook of child psychology, Vol 4: Socialization, personality, and social development* (pp. 547–641). New York: Wiley.

Parker, F., Piotrkowski, D., and Peay, L. (1987). Head start as a social support for mothers: The psychological benefits of involvement. *American Journal of Orthopsychiatry, 57,* 220–233.

Parker, J. G., and Asher, S. R. (1987). Peer relations and later social adjustment: Are low-accepted children at risk? *Psychological Bulletin, 102,* 357–389.

Parker, J. G., and Gottman, J. M. (1989). Social and emotional development in a relational context: Friendship interaction from early childhood to adolescence. In T. M. Berndt and G. W. Ladd (Eds.), *Peer relations in childhood.* New York: Wiley.

Parsons, J. E., Adler, T. E., and Kaczala, C. M. (1982). Socialization and achievement attitudes and beliefs: Parental influences. *Child Development, 53,* 310–321.

Parten, M. (1932). Social play among preschool children, *Journal of Abnormal and Social Psychology, 27,* 243–269.

Pasley, K., and Ihinger-Tallman, M. (1987). Remarriage and stepfamilies. In C. Chilman, E. Nunnally, and F. Cox (Eds.), *Variant family forms.* Newbury Park, CA: Sage.

Patterson, C. J. (1992). Children of lesbian and gay parents. *Child Development, 63,* 1025–1042.

Patterson, G. R. (1982). *Coercive family process.* Eugene, OR: Castilla Press.

Patterson, G. R. (1986). Performance models for antisocial boys. *American Psychologist, 41,* 432–444.

Peck, M. S. (1978). *The road less traveled.* New York: Simon & Schuster.

Pei, A. (1952). *The Story of English.* New York: Lippincott.

Peele, S. (1989). *Diseasing of America: Addiction treatment out of control.* Boston: Houghton Mifflin.

Pennington, B. F., and Smith, S. D. (1988).Genetic influences on learning disabilities: An update. *Journal of Consulting and Clinical Psychology, 56,* 817–823.

Peterson, D. R. (1984). Sudden infant death syndrome. In M. B. Bracken (Ed.), *Behavioral teratology.* New York: Plenum Press.

Peterson, P. L., Hawkins, J. D., Abbott, R. D., and Catalano, R. F. (1994). Disentangling the effects of parental drinking, family management, and parental alcohol norms on current drinking by black and white adolescents. *Journal of Research on Adolescence, 4*(2), 203–227.

Phillips, D. A., and Zimmerman, M. (1990). The developmental course of perceived competence and incompetence among competent children. In R. Sternberg and J. Kolligian (Eds.), *Competence considered* (pp. 41–66). New Haven, CT: Yale University Press.

Phinney, J. S. (1990). Ethnic identity in adolescents and adults: Review of research. *Psychological Bulletin, 108,* 499–514.

Phinney, J. S., and Rosenthal, D. A. (1992). Ethnic identity in adolescence: Process, content, and outcome. In G. R. Adams, T.P. Gullotta, and R. Montemayor (Eds.), *Adolescent identity formation*. Newbury, CA: Sage.

Piaget, J., and Inhelder, B. (1969). *The psychology of the child* (Helen Weaver, trans.) New York: Basic Books.

Pinon, M. R., Huston, A. C., and Wright, J. C. (1989). Family ecology and child characteristics that predict young children's educational television viewing. *Child Development, 60*, 846–856.

Pletch, (1994). Environmental tobacco smoke exposure among Hispanic women of reproductive age. *Public Health Nursing, 11*, 229–235.

Plomin, R., and Daniels , D. (1987). Why are children in the same family so different from each other? *Behavioral and Brain Sciences, 10*, 1–16.

Poffenberg, T. (1981). Child rearing and social structure in rural India: Toward a cross-cultural definition of child abuse and neglect. In J. E. Korbin (Ed.), *Child abuse and neglect: Cross-cultural perspectives*, Berkeley, CA: University of California Press.

Polansky, N. A., Chalmers, M. A., Buttenweiser, E. and Williams, D. P. (1981). *Damaged parents; An anatomy of child neglect*. Chicago, IL: University of Chicago Press.

——— Gaudin, J. M., Ammons, P. W., and Davis, K. B. (1985). The psychological ecology of the neglectful mother. *Child Abuse and Neglect, 9*, 265–275.

Popkin, M. (1987). *Active parenting*. San Francisco: HarperCollins.

Pomerleau, A., Bolduc, D., Malcuit, G., and Cossette, L. (1990). Pink or blue: Environmental gender stereotypes in the first two years of life. *Sex Roles, 22*, 359–367.

Post, G., and Crowther, J. H. (1985). Variables that discriminate bulemic from nonbulemic adolescent females. *Journal of Youth and Adolescence, 14*, 85–98.

Poteat, G. M., Snow, C. W., Ironsmith, M., and Bjorkman, S. (1992). Influence of day care experiences and demographic variables on social behavior in kindergarten. *American Journal of Orthopsychiatry, 62*(1), 137–141.

Poussaint, A. F., and Comer, M. P. (1992). *Raising black children: Questions and answers for parents and teachers*. New York: NAL/Dutton.

Powell, C. (1995). *My American Journey*. New York: Random House.

Pulver, R. (Ed.), (1992). *Living with 10- to 15-year-olds: A parent education curriculum* (2nd ed.). Chapel Hill, NC: Center for Early Adolescence, University of North Carolina at Chapel Hill.

Radke-Yarrow, M., and Zahn-Waxler, C. (1984). Roots, motives, and patterns in children's prosocial behav-

ior. In J. Reykowski, J. Karylowski, D. Bar-Tel, and E. Staub (Eds.), *The development and maintenance of prosocial behaviors: International perspectives on positive morality* (pp. 81–99). New York: Plenum.

Rahner, E. (1980). Perceived parental acceptance-rejection and children's reported personality and behavioral dispositions: An intercultural test. *Behavior Science Research, 1*, 81–88.

Rand Youth Poll (1994).

Reich, P. A. (1986). *Language development*, Englewood Cliffs, NJ: Prentice-Hall.

Rice, M. L., Huston, A. C., Truglio, R., and Wright, J. (1990). Words from "Sesame Street": Learning vocabulary while viewing. *Developmental Psychology, 26*, 421–428.

Rice, M. L., and Woodsmall, L. (1988). Lessons from television: Children's word learning when viewing. *Child Development, 59*, 420–429.

Richards, M. H., and Duckett, E. (1994). The relationship of maternal employment to early adolescent daily experiences with and without parents. *Child Development, 65*, 225–236.

Richardson, R., Barbour, N., and Bubenzer, D. (1991). Bittersweet connections: Informal social networks as sources of support and interference for adolescent mothers. *Family Relations, 40*(4), 430–434.

Rivera, F., Sweeney, P., and Henderson, B. (1986). Black teenage fathers: What happens when the child is born? *Pediatrics, 78*, 151–158.

Roberts, T. W. (1994). *A Systems Perspective of Parenting*. New York: Brooks/Cole.

Roche, A. F. (1979). Secular trends in stature, weight, maturation, and development. In A. F. Roche (Ed.), *Monographs of the Society for Research in Child Development, 44*(3–4, Serial No. 179).

Rodin, J., Silberstein, L., and Striegel-Moore, R. (1984). Women and weight: A normative discontent. *Nebraska Symposium on Motivation, 32*, 267–307.

Roe, A. (1952). A psychologist examines 64 eminent scientists. *Scientific American, 187* (5), 21–25.

Roffwarg, H. P., Muzio, J. N., and Dement, W. C. (1966). Ontogenic development of human sleep-dream cycle. *Science*, 152, 604–619.

Rohner, R. P. (1975). *They love me, they love me not: A worldwide study of the effects of parental acceptance and rejection*. New Haven: HRAF Press.

——— and Chaki-Sircar, M. (1988). *Women and children in a Bengali village*. Hanover, NH: University Press of New England.

——— Kean, K. J., and Cournoyer, D. E. (1991). Effects of punishment, perceived caretaker warmth, and cultural beliefs on the psychological adjustment of children in St. Kitts, West Indies. *Journal of Marriage and the Family, 53,* 681–693.

——— and Rohner, E. C. (1981). Parental acceptance-rejection and parental control: Cross-cultural codes. *Ethnology, 20,* 245–260.

Roosa, M. (1991). Adolescent pregnancy programs collection: An introduction. *Family Relations, 40*(4), 370–372.

Rosenthal, R., and Jacobson, L. (1968). *Pygmalion in the classroom.* New York: Holt, Rinehart, Winston.

Ross, H., and Milgram, J. I. (1982). Important variables in adult sibling relationships: A qualitative study. In Michael E. Lamb and Brian Sutton-Smith (Eds.), *Sibling Relationships: Their Nature and Significance Across the Lifespan.* Hillsdale, NJ: Lawrence Erlbaum.

Rossi, A. S., and Rossi, P. H. (1990). *Of human bonding; Parent-child relations across the life course.* New York: Gruyter.

Rothbart, M. K. (1971). Birth order and mother-child interaction in an achievement situation. *Journal of Personality and Social Psychology, 17,* 113–120.

Rotundo, E. A. (1985). American fatherhood: A historical perspective. *American Behavioral Scientist, 29,* 7–25.

Rovee-Collier, C. K., and Lipsitt, L. P. (1987). Learning, adaptation, and memory in the newborn. In P. Stratton (Ed.), *Psychobiology of the human newborn,* New York: Wiley.

Ruble, D. N., Fleming, A. C., Hackel, L. S., and Stangor, C. (1988). Changes in the marital relationship during the transition to motherhood: Effects of violated expectations concerning divisions of household labor. *Journal of Personality and Social Psychology, 55,* 78–87.

Rumbaut, R., and Portes, A. (1998, March 21). Among young immigrants, outlook rises. *New York Times,* Section A.

Russell, J. A. (1990). The preschooler's understanding of the causes and consequences of emotion, *Child Development, 61,* 1872–1881.

Rutter, M. (1983). School effects on pupil progress: Research findings and policy implications. *Child Development, 54,* 1–29.

Sack, W. H., Mason, R., and Higgins, J. E. (1985). The single-parent family and abusive child punishment. *American Journal of Orthopsychiatry, 55,* 252–259.

Sadker, M., and Sadker, D. (1985, March). Sexism in the schoolroom of the '80s. *Psychology Today,* 54–57.

Sadowski, C., and Kelley, M. L. (1993). Social problem solving in suicidal adolescents. *Journal of Consulting and Clinical Psychology, 61*(1), 121–127.

Sager, C., Brown, H. J. S., Crohn, H., Engel, T., Rodstein, E., and Walker, L. (1983). *Treating the remarried family.* New York: Brunner/Mazel.

Santrock, J. W. (1993). *Adolescence.* Madison, WI: Brown and Benchmark.

——— (1997) *Children.* Madison, WI: Brown and Benchmark.

Sater, G. M., and French, D. C. (1989). A comparison of the social competencies of learning disabled and low achieving elementary-aged children. *Journal of Special Education, 23,* 29–42.

Satir, V. M. (1988). *The new peoplemaking.* Mountain View, CA: Science and Behavior Books.

Savin-Williams, R., and Small, S. A. (1986). The timing of puberty and its relationship to adolescent and parent perceptions of family interactions. *Developmental Psychology, 22,* 342–348.

Scarr, S., and McCartney, K. (1983). How people make their own environments. A theory of genotype/environmental effects. *Child Development, 54,* 424–435.

Scarr, S., and Weinberg, R. A. (1983). The Minnesota adoption studies: Genetic differences and malleability. *Child Development, 54,* 260–267.

Schacter, S. (1963). Birth order, eminence, and higher education. *American Sociological Review, 28,* 757–786.

Schaefer, C. E., and Millman, H. L. (1981). *How to help children with common problems.* New York: Van Nostrand Reinhold.

Schieffelin, B. B., and Eisenberg, A. R. (1984). Cultural variation in children's conversations. In R. L. Schieffelin and J. Pickar (Eds.), *The acquisition of communicative competence.* Baltimore, MD: University Park Press.

Schmidt, C. R., and Paris, S. G. (1984). The development of verbal communication skills in children. In H. W. Reese (Ed.), *Advances in child development and behavior* (Vol. 18). New York: Academic Press.

Schmidt, M.G. (1980) Failing parents, aging children. *Journal of Gerontological Social Work, 3,* 259–268.

Schnaiberg, A., and Goldenberg, S. (1989). From empty nest to crowded nest: The dynamics of incompletely launched young adults. *Social Problems, 36,* 251–269.

Schor, E. L. (Ed.) (1995). *Caring for Your School-Age Child Ages 5 to 12.* New York: Bantam Books.

Schulenberg, J. (1985, 1987). *Gay parenting: A complete guide for gay men and lesbians with children.* New York: Anchor.

Scott, W. J. (1986). Attachment to Indian culture and the "difficult situation": A study of American Indian college students. *Youth and Society, 17*(4), 381–395.

Sears, W., and Sears, M., (1995). *The Discipline Book.* New York: Little, Brown.

Sebald, H. (1989, Winter). Adolescents' peer orientation: Changes in the support system during the past three decades. *Adolescence, 24,* 940–941.

Segal, R. (1995). *The black diaspora.* New York: Farrar, Straus & Giroux.

Seligman M., Reivich, K., Jaycox, L., Gillham, J. (1996). *The optimistic child.* New York: Harperperennial Library.

Selzer, J. A. (1991). Legal custody arrangements and children's economic welfare. *American Journal of Sociology, 96,* 895–929.

——— (1991). Relationships between fathers and children who live apart: The father's role after separation. *Journal of Marriage and the Family, 53,* 79–102.

Shaffer, H. R., and Emerson, P. E. (1964a). Patterns of response to physical contact in early human development. *Journal of Child Psychology and Psychiatry, 5,* 1–13.

——— (1964b). The development of social attachments in infancy. *Monographs of the Society for Research in Child Development, 29* (No. 94).

Shaffer, J. P. (1977). Likability as a function of age, sex, and personality description. *Bulletin of the Psychodynamic Society, 9*(6), 402–404.

Shannon, D. C., Kelly, D. H., Akselrod, S., and Kilborn, K. M. (1987). Increased respiratory frequency and variability in high-risk babies who die of sudden death syndrome. *Pediatric Research, 22,*158–162.

Shapiro, F. (1994). *Eye movement desensitization and reprocessing.* Pacific Grove, CA: EMDR Institute.

Shatz, M., and Gelman, R. (1973). The development of communication skills: Modification in the speech of young children as a function of the listener. *Monographs of the Society for Research in Child Development, 38*(5, Serial No. 152).

Shedler, J., and Block, J. (1990). Adolescent drug use and psychological health: A longitudinal inquiry. *American Psychologist, 45,* 612–630.

Sherman, E. (1987). *Meaning in mid-life transitions.* Albany, NY: State University of New York Press.

Siegel, I. E. (1987). Does hothousing rob children of their childhood? *Early Childhood Research Quarterly, 2,* 211–225.

——— (1988) Commentary: Cross-cultural studies of parental influence on children's achievement. *Human Development, 31,* 384–390.

Silberman, C. E. (1985). *A certain people.* Summit Books.

Silberman, M. (1995). *When your child is difficult.* Champaign, IL: Research Press.

Simons, R. L., Conger, R. D., and Whitbeck, L. B. (1988). A multistage social learning model of the influences of family and peers upon adolescent substance use. *Journal of Drug Issues, 18,* 293–316.

Simons, R. L., Whitbeck, L. B., Conger, R. D., and Chyi-In, W. (1991). Intergenerational transmission of harsh parenting. *Developmental Psychology, 27,* 159–171.

Singer, D. G., and Singer, J. (1987). Practical suggestions for controlling television. *Journal of Early Adolescence, 7,* 365–369.

Singer, J. L., and Singer, D. G. (1981). *Television, imagination, and aggression: A study of preschoolers.* Hillsdale, NJ: Erlbaum.

——— (1982). Psychologists look at television. *American Psychologist, 38,* 826–834.

——— (1983). Implications of childhood television viewing for cognition, imagination, and emotion. In J. Bryant and Dr. R. Anderson (Eds.), *Children's understanding of television: Research on attention and comprehension* (pp. 265–297). New York: Academic Press.

Singer, L. M., Brodzinsky, D. M., Ramsay, D., Steir, M., and Waters, E. (1985). Mother-infant attachment in adoptive families. *Child Development, 56,* 1543–1551.

Sirignano, S., and Lachman, M. E. (1985). Personality change during the transition to parenthood: The role of perceived infant temperament. *Developmental Psychology, 21,* 558–567.

Sizer, T. (1984). *Horace's compromise.* Boston: Houghton Mifflin.

Slavin, R. E. (1994). *Educational Psychology.* Boston: Allyn and Bacon.

Slobin, D. (1970). Universals of grammatical development in children, In G. Flores D'Arcais and W. Levelt (Eds.), *Advances in psycholoquistics* (pp. 174–184). New York: American Elsevier.

——— (1972). Children and language: They learn the same around the world, *Psychology Today,* 71–76.

Slote, W. H. (1972). Oedipal ties and the issue of separation-individuation in traditional Confucian societies. *Journal of the American Academy of Psychoanalysis, 20*(3), 435–453.

Smith, D. S., and Luckasson, T. (1993). *Introduction to special education* (3rd ed.) (pp. 227–233). Boston: Allyn and Bacon.

Smith, D. W. (1977). *Growth and its disorders.* Philadelphia: W. B. Saunders.

Smith, P. K. (1978). A longitudinal study of social participation in preschool children: Solitary and parallel play reexamined. *Developmental Psychology, 12,* 517–523.

Spencer, M. B., and Dornbusch, S. M. (1990). Challenges in studying minority children. In S. S. Feldman and G. L. Elliot (Eds.), *At the threshold—The developing adolescent* (pp. 123–146). Cambridge, MA: Harvard University Press.

Spitze, G. (1991). Women's employment and family relations. In A. Booth (Ed.), *Contemporary families: Looking forward, looking back* (pp. 381–404). Minneapolis, MN: National Council on Family Relations.

Spock, B. (1946). *The common sense book of baby and child care.* New York: Duell, Sloan and Pearce.

Spock, B., and Rothenberg, M. (1992). *Baby and child care* (6th ed.). New York: Pocket Books.

Springle, H. (1971). Can poverty children live on "Sesame Street"? *Young Children, 26,* 202–217.

—— (1972). Who wants to live on "Sesame Street"? *Young Children, 27,* 91–108.

Sroufe, L. A. (1979). Socioemotional development. In J. D. Osofsky (Ed.), *Handbook of infant development.* New York: Wiley.

—— (1983). Attachment and adaptation in preschool, In M. Perlmutter (Ed.), *Development and policy concerning children with special needs.* Minnesota Symposium on Child Development, *16.* Hillsdale, NJ: Erlbaum.

—— (1979). The coherence of individual development: Early care attachment, and subsequent developmental issues. *American Pschologist, 34,* 1615– 1627.

—— and Cooper, R. G. (1988). *Child development: Its nature and course.* New York: Knopf.

Staso, W. (1997, April 17). *New York Times.* Science Section.

Stattin, H., and Klackenberg-Larsson. K. (1991). The short- and long-term implications for parent-child relations of parents' prenatal preferences for their child's gender. *Developmental Psychology, 27,* 141–147.

Steele, B. F., and Pollock, C. B. (1968). A psychiatric study of parents who abuse infants and small children. In R. E. Helfer and C. H. Kempe (Eds.), *The battered child* (pp. 103–147). Chicago, IL: University of Chicago Press.

Steinberg, L. (1987). The impact of puberty on family relations: Effects of pubertal status and pubertal timing. *Developmental Psychology, 23,* 451–460.

—— (1988). Reciprocal relations between parent-child distance and pubertal maturation. *Developmental Psychology, 24,* 122–128.

—— and Levine, A. (1990) *You and your adolescent.* New York: Harper Collins.

Steinem, G. (1983). *Outrageous acts and everyday rebellions.* New York: Holt, Rinehart and Winston.

Steinglass, P., Bennett, L. A., Wolin, S. J., and Reiss, D. (1985). *The alcoholic family.* New York: Basic Books.

Steinmetz, S., and Stein, K. F. (1988). Traditional and emerging families: A typology based on structures and functions. *Family Science Review, 1,* 103–114.

Stern, D. N. (1974). The goal and structure of mother-infant play. *Journal of the American Academy of Child Psychiatry,* 13, 402–421.

—— (1985). *Interpersonal world of the infant: A view from psychoanalysis and developmental psychology.* New York: Basic Books.

—— (1990). *Interpersonal world of the infant.* New York: Basic Books.

Stierlin, H. (1972). *Separating parents and adolescents.* New York: Quadrangle.

—— (1979). *Separating parents and adolescents: A perspective on running away, schizophrenia, and waywardness.* New York: Quadrangle.

Stipek, D. J. and MacIver, D. (1989). Developmental change in children's assessment of intellectual competence. *Child Development, 60,* 531–538.

Stipp, H. H. (1988). Children as consumers. *American Demographics,* 10(2), 27–32.

St. Peters, M., Fitch, M., Huston, A. C., Wright, J. C., and Eakins, D. J. (1991). Television and families: What do young children watch with their parents? *Child Development, 62,* 1409–1423.

Stoneman, Z., Brody, G. H., and Burke, M. (1989). Marital quality, depression, and inconsistent parenting: Relationship with observed mother-child conflict. *American Journal of Orthopsychiatry, 59*(1), 105–117.

Stoneman, Z., Brody, G. H., and MacKinnon, C. (1984). Naturalistic observations of children's activities and roles while playing with their siblings and friends, *Child Development, 55,* 617–627.

Storr, A. (1988). *Solitude: A Return to the Self.* Ballantine Books.

Straus, M. A. (1991a). Discipline and violence: Physical punishment of children and violence and other crime in adulthood. *Social Problems, 38,* 133–154.

—— (1991b). New theory and old canards about family violence research. *Social Problems, 38,* 180–197.

—— (1994). *Beating The Devil Out of Them: Corporal Punishment In American Families.* Lexington, MA: Lexington Books.

———, Gelles, R. J., and Steinmetz, S. K. (1980). *Behind closed doors: Violence in the American family.* Grand City, NY: Doubleday/Anchor.

Strong B. and DeVault, C. (1992). *The marriage and family experience.* New York: West.

Stunkard, A. J., Foch, T. T., and Hrubec, Z. (1986). A twin study of human obesity. *Journal of the American Medical Association, 256,* 51–54.

Suitor, J. I. and Pillemer, K. (1988, November). Explaining intergenerational conflict when adult children and elderly parents live together. *Journal of Marriage and the Family, 50,* 1037–1047.

Sung, B. L. (1987) *The Adjustment Experience of Chinese Immigrant Children in New York City.* New York: Center for Migration Studies.

Sutton-Smith, B. and Rosenberg, B. G. (1970). *The sibling.* New York: Holt, Rinehart and Winston.

Swiss, D. and Walker, J. (1993). *Women and the work/family dilemma.* New York: Wiley.

Szasz, C. M. (1977). *Education and the American Indian: The road to self-determination since 1928* (2nd ed.) Albuquerque: University of New Mexico Press.

Tafoya, N. and Del Vecchio, A. (1996). Back to the future: An examination of the Native American holocaust experience. In M. McGoldrick, J. Giordano, and J. K. Pearce (Eds.), *Ethnicity and family therapy* (2nd ed.). (pp. 45–54). New York: Guilford Press.

Takahashi, K. (1990). Are the key assumptions of the "Strange Situation" procedure universal? A view from Japanese research. *Human Development, 33,* 23–30.

Tangney, J. P. (1988). Aspects of the family and children's television viewing content preferences. *Child Development, 59,* 1070-1079.

Tanner, J. M. (1970). Physical growth. In P. H. Mussen (Ed.), *Carmichael's manual of child psychology* (Vol. 1) (pp.77–156). New York: Wiley.

——— (1973). *Growing up, Scientific American, 229*(3), 35–43.

——— (1978). *Fetus into man: Physical growth from conception to maturity.* Cambridge, MA: Harvard University Press.

——— (1990). *Fetus into man* (2nd ed.). Cambridge, MA: Harvard University Press.

Taub, D. E. and Blinde, E. M. (1992). Eating disorders among adolescent female athletes: Influence of athletic participation and sport team membership. *Adolescence, 27*(108), 833–846.

Taylor, R. J. (1988). Aging and supportive relationships among Black Americans. In J. Jackson (Ed.), *The Black American elderly.* New York: Springer-Verlag.

Teyber, E. and Hoffman, C. D. (1987). Missing fathers. *Psychology Today, 21*(4), 36–39.

Thevenin, T. (1987). *The Family Bed.* Wayne, NJ: Avery Publishing Group

Thomas, A., and Chess, S. (1977). *Temperament and development.* New York: Brunner/Mazel.

Thomas, A., Chess, S., and Birch, H. G. (1968). *Temperament and Behavior Disorders in Children,* New York: New York University Press.

Thomas, A., Chess, S., Birch, H. G. (1970). The origin of personality, *Scientific American, 223,* 102–109.

Thomas, A., Chess, S., and Korn, S. J. (1982). The reality of difficult temperament. *Merrill-Palmer Quarterly, 28,* 1–20.

Thomas, J. L. (1986). Age and sex differences in perceptions of grandparenting. *Journal of Gerentology, 41,* 417–423,

Thomas, J. R. (1989). Gender perceptions of grandparenthood. *International Journal of Aging and Human Development, 29*(4), 269–282.

Thompson, R. A., Lamb, M., and Estes, D. (1982). Stability of infant-mother attachment and its relationship to changing life circumstances in an unselected middle-class sample. *Child Development, 53,* 144–148.

Thurer, S. L. (1994). *The myths of motherhood: How culture reinvents the good mother.* Boston: Houghton Mifflin.

Tizard, B., Philips, J., and Plewis, I. (1976). Play in preschool centres. *Journal of Child Psychology and Psychiatry, 17,* 1976, 265–274.

Toda, S., A. Fogel, and Kawai, M. (1990). Maternal speech to three-month-old infants in the United States and Japan. *Journal of Child Language, 17,* 279–294.

Tomasello, M., Conti-Ramsden, G., and Ewert, B. (1990). Young children's conversations with their mothers and fathers: Differences in breakdown and repair. *Journal of Child Language, 17,* 115–130.

Tomasello, M., Mannie, S., and Kruger, A. C. (1986). Linguistic environment of 1–2 year old twins. *Developmental Psychology, 22,* 169–176.

Toner, I. and Smith, R. A. (1977). Age and verbalization in delay maintenance behavior in children. *Journal of Experimental Child Psychology, 24,* 123–128.

Trivette, C., and Dunst, C. (1992). Characteristics and influences of role division and social support among mothers of preschool children with disabilities. *Topics in Early Childhood Special Education, 12*(3), 367–385.

Trute, B. (1990). Child and parent predictors of family adjustment in households containing young developmentally disabled children. *Family Relations, 39*(3), 292–297.

Trygstad, D., and Sanders, G. (1989). The significance of step-grandparents. *International Journal of Aging and Human Development, 29*(2), 119–134.

Unger, D. G., and Wandersman, L. P. (1985). The relations of family and partner support to the adjustment of adolescent mothers. *Child Development, 59,* 1056–1060.

United States Bureau of the Census (1991). *Statistical abstract of the United States, 1991.* (111th ed.). Washington, DC: United States Department of Commerce.

United States Bureau of the Census (1995). *Statistical abstract of the United States: 1995* (115th ed.) Washington, DC: Author.

United States Department of Health and Human Services (U.S. DHHS), (1996). *Vital Statistics of the United States.* Washington, DC: National Center for Health Statistics.

U.S. Department of Health, Education, and Welfare (1978). *No easy answers: The learning disabled child.*

Vaughan, V. C. III, McKay, J. R., and Nelson,W. E. (Eds.), (1975). *Nelson textbook of pediatrics,* Philadelphia: W. B. Saunders Company.

Velleman, R., and Orford, J. (1993). The adult adjustment of offspring of parents with drinking problems. *British Journal of Psychiatry, 162,* 503–516.

Vigil, J. D., and Yun, S. C. (1990). Vietnamese youth gangs in Southern California. In R. Huff (Ed.), *Gangs in California.* Beverly Hills, CA: Sage.

Volling, B., and Belsky, J. (1993). Parent, infant, and contextual characteristics related to maternal employment decisions in the first year of infancy. *Family Relations, 42,* 4–12.

Wade, J. (1994). African American fathers and sons: Social, historical, and psychological considerations. *Families in Society, 75,* 561–570.

Wagner, B. M., and Phillips, D. A. (1992). Beyond beliefs: Parent and child behaviors and children's perceived academic competence. *Child Development, 63,* 1380-1391.

Walberg, H. J. (1986). Synthesis of research on teaching. In M. C. Wittrock (Ed.), *Handbook of research on teaching* (3rd ed. pp. 214–229). New York: Macmillan.

Walker, E., Downey, G., and Bergman, A. (1989). The effects of parental psychopathology and maltreatment on child behavior: A test of the diathesis-stress model. *Child Development, 60,* 15–24.

Wallerstein, J., and Blakeslee, S. (1989). *Second chances: Men, women, and children a decade after divorce.* New York: Ticknor and Fields.

Ward, S., Reale, G., and Levinson, D. (1972). Children's perceptions, explanations, and judgments of television advertising: A further exploration. In E. A. Rubinstein, G. A. Comstock, and J. P. Murray (Eds.), *Television and social behavior* (Vol. 4, pp. 468–490). Washington, DC: U. S. Government Printing Office.

Wanska, S. K., and Bedrosian, J. L. (1985). Conversational structure and topic performance in mother-child interaction. *Journal of Speech and Hearing Research, 28,* 579–584.

Wasik, B. H., Ramey, C. T., Bryant, D. M., and Sparling, J. J. (1990). A longitudinal study of two early intervention strategies: Project CARE. *Child Development, 61,* 1682–1696.

Waters, E., Matas, L., and Sroufe, L. A. (1975). Infants' reactions to an approaching stranger: Description, validation, and functional significance of wariness. *Child Development, 46,* 348–356.

Watkins, S. C., Menken, J. A., and Bongaarts, J. (1987). Demographic foundations of family change. *American Sociological Review, 52,* 346–358.

Watson, J. B. (1928). *Psychological care of the infant and child.* New York: Norton.

Weber, M. (1930). *The Protestant ethic and the spirit of capitalism.* London: Allen.

Weinraub, M. (1977). The determinants of children's responses to separation. *Monographs of the Society for Research in Child Development, 42*(4), 1–78.

Weisfeld, C. C., Weisfeld, G. E., and Callaghan, J. W. (1982). Female inhibition in mixed-sex competition among young adolescents. *Ethology and Sociobiology, 3,* 29–42.

Werts, C. E. (1968). Paternal influence on career choice. *Journal of Counseling Psychology, 15,* 48–52.

Whaley, L. F., and Wong, D. L. (1988). *Essentials of pediatric nursing.* St. Louis, MO: C. V. Mosby.

Whitbeck, L. B., Hoyt, D. R., and Huck, S. M. (1993). Family relationship history: Contemporary parent-grandparent relationship quality and the grandparent-grandchild relationship. *Journal of Marriage and the Family, 55,* 1025–1035.

White, J., and Parham, T. (1990). *The psychology of blacks: An African-American perspective.* Englewood Cliffs, NJ: Prentice-Hall.

Whitebook, M., Howes, C., and Philips, D. (1989). *Who cares? Child care teachers and the quality of care in America.* Executive summary of the national child care staffing study. Oakland, CA: Child Care Employee Project.

Whiteside, M. (1989). *Remarried systems. From children in family contexts.* New York: Guilford Press.

Wiesenfeld, A. R., Malatesta, C. Z., and DeLoache, L. (1981). Differential parental response to familiar and unfamiliar infant distress signals. *Infant Behavior and Development, 4,* 281–295.

Wilbur, J., and Wilbur, M. (1988). The noncustodial parent: Dilemmas and interventions. *Journal of Counseling and Development, 66*(9), 435–437.

Wilke, C. F., and Ames, E. W. (1986). The relationship of infant crying to parental stress in transition to parenthood. *Journal of Marriage and the Family, 48,* 545–550.

Williams, M. (1986). *Imperfect love.* Louisiana State University Press.

Williams, R. M. (1960). Generic American values. In W. Goldschmidt (Ed.), *Exploring the ways of mankind.* New York: Holt, Rinehart.

Williamson, N. E. (1976). *Sons or daughters; A cross-cultural survey of parental preferences.* Beverly Hills, CA: Sage.

Willis, W. (1992). Families with African American roots. In E. W. Lynch and M. J. Hanson (Eds.), *Developing cross-cultural competence* (pp. 121–150). Baltimore, MD: Paul H. Brookes Publishing Company.

Wilson, M. (1989). Child development in the context of black extended family. *American Psychologist, 44,* 380–385.

Wilson, J., and Baker, B. L. (1987). Siblings of children with severe handicaps. *Mental Retardation, 27*(3), 167–173.

Windell J. (1991). *Discipline: A sourcebook of 50 failsafe techniques for parents.* New York: MacMillan.

Winnicott, D. (1964). *The child, the family and the outside world,* London: Penguin.

——— (1971). *Playing and reality,* New York: Basic Books.

Wolf, A., and Lozoff, B.(1989). Object attachment, thumb sucking, and the passage to sleep. *Journal of the American Academy of Child and Adolescent Psychiatry, 28,* 287–292.

Wolff, P. H. (1966). The causes, controls, and organization of behavior in the neonate. *Psychological Issues, 5*(1, Serial No. 17).

Wolff, P. H. (1969). The natural history of crying and other vocalizations in early infancy. In B. Foss (Ed.), *Determinants of infant behavior Vol. 4.* London: Methuen.

Wong, H. Z. (1985). Training for mental health service providers to Southeast Asian refugees: Model, strategies, curricula. In T. Owan (Ed.), *Southeast Asian mental health: Treatment, prevention, services, training, and research* (pp. 5–40). Washington, DC: U.S. Department of Health and Human Services.

Wright, L., Schaefer, A. B., and Solomon, G. (1979). *Encyclopedia of pediatric psychology.* Baltimore; University Park Press.

Wynne, L. C., Jones, J. E., and Al-Khayyal, M. (1982). Healthy family communication patterns: Observations in families "at risk" for psychopathology. In F. Walsh (Ed.), *Normal family processes: Implications for clinical practice* (pp. 142–164). New York: Guilford Press.

Yarrow, M. R. (1978, Oct, 31). *Altruism in children.* Paper presented at program, Advances in Child Development Research, New York Academy of Sciences, New York.

Yeates, K. O., and Selman, R. L. (1989). Social competence in the schools: Toward an integrative developmental model for intervention. *Developmental Review, 9,* 64–100.

Yellowbird, M., and Snipp, C. M. (1994). American Indian families. In R. L. Taylor (Ed.), *Minority families in the United States: A multi cultural perspective.* Englewood Cliffs, NJ: Prentice-Hall.

Yogman, M. J., Dixon S., Tronick, E., Als, H., and Brazelton, T. B. (March 1977). *The goals and structure of face-to-face interaction between infants and their fathers,* Paper presented at the biennial meeting of the Society for Research in Child Development, New Orleans.

Youniss, J. (1980). *Parents and peers in social development: A Sullivan-Piaget perspective.* Chicago, IL: University of Chicago Press.

Yost, E. B., and Corbishley, M. A. (1987). *Career counseling—A psychological approach.* San Francisco: Jossey-Bass.

Young, K. T. (1990). American conceptions of infant development from 1955 to 1984: What the experts are telling parents. *Child Development, 61,* 17–28.

Ysseldyke, J. and Algozzine, B. (1990). *Introduction to special education* (2nd ed.). Boston: Houghton Mifflin.

Zajonc, R. B. (1983). Validating the confluence model. *Psychological Bulletin, 93,* 457–480.

——— (1986). Family factors and intellectual test performance: A reply to Steelman. *Review of Educational Research, 56*(30), 365–371.

Zigler, E. F. (1987). Formal schooling for four-year-olds? No. *American Psychologist, 42,* 254–260.

—— and Gilman, E. (1993). Day care in America: What is needed? *Pediatrics, 91,* 175–178.

—— and Hall, N. W. (1989). Physical child abuse in America: Past, present, and future. In D. Cicchetti and V. Carlton (Eds.), *Child maltreatment* (pp. 38–75). New York: Cambridge University Press.

—— and Hunsinger, S. (1977, Fall). Supreme Court on spanking: Upholding discipline or abuse? *Society for Research in Child Development Newsletter.*

Zuninga, M. E. (1992). Families with Latino roots. In E. W. Lynch and M. J. Hanson (Eds.), *Developing cross-cultural competence* (pp. 151–179). Baltimore, MD: Paul H. Brookes Publishing Company.

Photo Credits

Page 4   Ken Heyman/Woodfin Camp & Associates
Page 4   Ken Heyman/Woodfin Camp & Associates
Page 4   Ken Heyman/Woodfin Camp & Associates
Page 5   Malinda Jo Muzi
Page 13   Malinda Jo Muzi
Page 20   Lapira/Sestini/Liaison Agency, Inc.
Page 33   King Features Syndicate
Page 37   Erich Lessing/Art Resource, N.Y.
Page 46   Cornell University Photography
Page 49   George Malave/Stock Boston
Page 55   Archive Photos
Page 55   Robert Clay/Monkmeyer Press
Page 57   Malinda Jo Muzi
Page 57   Malinda Jo Muzi
Page 63   Karen Gelula
Page 67   Sonia Ochroch
Page 68   Jeffrey Ochroch
Page 80   Arlene Collins/Monkmeyer Press
Page 85   Amy C. Etra/PhotoEdit
Page 88   Kathy McLaughlin/The Image Works
Page 88   Vanessa Vick/Photo Researchers, Inc.
Page 102   Mimi Forsyth/Monkmeyer Press
Page 109   David Strickler/Monkmeyer Press
Page 117   Judy Gelles/Stock Boston
Page 130   Judy Gelles/Stock Boston
Page 140   Seth Resnick/Stock Boston
Page 152   Susan Woog Wegner Photography/Photo Researchers, Inc.
Page 156   Alan Carey/The Image Works
Page 158   Aneal Vohra/Unicorn Stock Photos
Page 169   Suzanne Arms/The Image Works
Page 184   Jeffrey Ochroch
Page 190   Malinda Jo Muzi

Page 196   D&I MacDonald/Unicorn Stock Photos
Page 200   Michael Newman/PhotoEdit
Page 204   Tony Korody/Sygma
Page 206   Malinda Jo Muzi
Page 226   Malinda Jo Muzi
Page 239   Malinda Jo Muzi
Page 244   Malinda Jo Muzi
Page 248   King Features Syndicate
Page 249   Malinda Jo Muzi
Page 261   Malinda Jo Muzi
Page 262   Renee Lynn/Photo Researchers, Inc.
Page 263   Universal Press Syndicate
Page 279   Malinda Jo Muzi
Page 289   Penguin Books USA, Inc.
Page 303   Malinda Jo Muzi
Page 318   Malinda Jo Muzi
Page 319   Elizabeth Crews/Stock Boston
Page 326   Hugh Rogers/Monkmeyer Press
Page 330   Spencer Grant/Stock Boston
Page 332   Malinda Jo Muzi
Page 346   Malinda Jo Muzi
Page 362   Corbis
Page 367   Malinda Jo Muzi
Page 372   Malinda Jo Muzi
Page 374   Malinda Jo Muzi
Page 387   Mark Richards/PhotoEdit
Page 393   Reuters/Kansas City Star/Archive Photos
Page 404   Karen Preuss/The Image Works
Page 405   James Carroll/Stock Boston
Page 408   Mike Kagan/Monkmeyer Press
Page 418   David Young-Wolff/PhotoEdit
Page 419   David Young-Wolff/PhotoEdit
Page 424   Deborah Yale/Monkmeyer Press

Text Permissions

Page 12 Informed Parent 1.1 From *Parents In Contemporary America, 5th edition*, by E. E. LeMasters and J. DeFrain. © 1989. Reprinted with permission of Wadsworth Publishing, a division of Thomson Learning. Fax 800-730-2215.

Page 18 Table 1.1 *The Journal of Psychology*, 120: 116, 1986. Reprinted with permission of the Helen Dwight Reid Educational Foundation. Published by Heldref Publications, 1319 Eighteenth St., NW, Washington, DC 20036-1802. Copyright © 1986.

Page 22 Figure 1.2 From *The New York Times*, 4/15/98. Copyright © 1998 by The New York Times. Reprinted by permission.

Page 24 Table 1.3 From Parent Satisfactions: Implications for Strengthening Families by W. H. Meredith, N. Stinnett, and F. Cacioppo. In *Family Strength 6: Ehancement of Interaction*, edited by Williams, Lihgren, Rowe, Zandt, and Stinnett, 1985. Reprinted by permission of Dr. John DeFrain.

Page 26 Informed Parent 1.3 From *The Marriage and Family Experience, 5th edition*, by Brian Strong and Christine DeVault. ©1992. Reprinted with permission of Wadsworth Publishing, a division of International Thomson Publishing. Fax 800-730-2215.

Page 39 Spirit of Parenting Ch 1 From *The Prophet* by Kahlil Gibran. Copyright 1923 by Kahlil Gibran and renewed 1951 by Administrators CTA of Kahlil Gibran Estate and Mary G. Gibran. Reprinted by permission of Alfred A. Knopf, Inc.

Page 48 Figure 2.1 R. Vasta (Ed.), *Annals of Child Development* (Vol. 6). Greenwich, CT: JAI Press.

Page 50 Figure 2.2 From "After Socialization and Development in a Changing Economy: The Effects of Paternal Job and Income Loss on Children" by V. C. McLoyd, *American Psychologist* 44, 294. Copyright © 1989 by the American Psychological Association. Reprinted with permission of the American Psychological Association.

Page 52 Figure 2.3 From Baltes, P. B., Reese, H. W. and Lipsitt, L. P. (1980). Life–span developmental psychology. *Annual Review of Psychology* 31, 65–110. With permission, from the Annual Review of Psychology, Volume 31, © 1980, by Annual Reviews www.annualreviews.org.

Page 54 Figure 2.4 From *The New York Times*, September 18, 1998. Copyright © 1998 *The New York Times*. Reprinted by permission.

Page 71 Informed Parent 3.1 Reproduced by permission. *Roots and Wings: Affirming Culture in Early Childhood Programs*, Stacey York, © 1991. Redleaf Press. St. Paul, Minnesota.

Page 75 Figure 3.3 From *The New York Times*, March 21, 1998. Copyright © 1998 *The New York Times*. Reprinted by permission.

Page 95 Figure 4.1 From *Family Therapy: An Overview, 4th edition*, by I. Goldenberg and H. Goldenberg. © 1996. Reprinted with permission of Wadsworth Publishing, a division of Thomson Learning. Fax 800–730–2215.

Page 97 Figure 4.2 From *Family Evaluation: An Approach Based on Bowen Theory* by Michael E. Kerr and Murray Bowen. Copyright © 1988 by Michael E. Kerr and Murray Bowen. Reprinted by permission of W. W. Norton & Company, Inc.

Page 98–99 Figure 4.3 From Betty Carter & Monica McGoldrick, *The Changing Family Life Cycle: A Framework for Family Therapy, 2e*. Copyright © 1988 by Allyn & Bacon. Reprinted by permission.

Page 100 Figure 4.4 From *You Can Go Home Again: Reconnecting with Your Family* by Monica McGoldrick. Copyright © 1995 by Monica McGoldrick. Reprinted by permission of W. W. Norton & Company, Inc.

Page 104 Table 4.1 From Kinston, W., Loader, P., and Miller, L. (1987) Quantifying the clinical assessment of family health. *Journal of Marital and Family*

Therapy 13, pp. 43–67. In *Handbook of Family Therapy,* Vol. 11 (Edited by Gurman, A. S., and Kniskern, D. P., p. 298). Reprinted by permission of Taylor & Francis, Inc.

Page 105 Table 4.2   From Kinston, W., Loader, P., and Miller, L. (1987) Quantifying the clinical assessment of family health. *Journal of Marital and Family Therapy* 13, pp. 43–67. In *Handbook of Family Therapy,* Vol. 11 (Edited by Gurman, A. S. and Kniskern, D. P., p. 298). Reprinted by permission of Taylor & Francis, Inc.

Page 110 Informed Parent 4.1   Excerpt from *Child, Family, School, Community: Socialization and Support, Fourth Edition* by Roberta M. Berns, copyright © 1997 by Holt, Rinehart and Winston, reprinted by permission of the publisher.

Page 121 Figure 5.1   From *The New York Times,* February 11, 1996. Copyright © 1996 by The New York Times. Reprinted by permission.

Page 127 Figure 5.4   From *The New York Times,* May 1, 1998. Copyright © 1998 *The New York Times.* Reprinted by permission.

Page 131 Figure 5.5   From Whiteside, M. *Remarried Systems,* from *Children in Family Contexts* edited by L. Combrinck-Graham, Guilford Press, 1989, p. 138. Reprinted with permission.

Page 137 Table 5.4   From Betty Carter & Monica McGoldrick (Eds.), *The Changing Family Life Cycle: A Framework for Family Therapy, 3e.* Copyright © 1999 by Allyn & Bacon. Reprinted by permission.

Page 138 Informed Parent 5.1   From Olson, D. H. and DeFrain, J. *Marriage and the Family,* pp. 58–59. Based on "The Stepping Ahead Program" by E. Visher. In *Stepfamilies Stepping Ahead,* edited by M. Burt, 1989, Lincoln, NE: Stepfamilies Press, 1989. © 1989 by Stepfamily Association of America. Reprinted with permission.

Page 144 Figure 5.6   From *The New York Times,* August 19, 1997. Copyright © 1997 by The New York Times. Reprinted by permission.

Page 157 Informed Parent 6.2   From *The Marriage and Family Experience, 5th edition,* by Strong/ DeVault. © 1992. Reprinted with permission of Wadsworth Publishing, a division of Thomson Learning. Fax 800-730-2215.

Page 172 Table 6.5   From Joan Kaufman and Edward Zigler, in *Child Maltreatment,* D. Cicchetti and V. Carlson (Eds.), 1991, p. 139. Reprinted with the permission of Cambridge University Press.

Page 173 Table 6.6   Reprinted with the permission of The Free Press, a Division of Simon & Schuster, Inc., from *Confronting Child Abuse: Research for Effec-* *tive Program Design* by Deborah Daro. Copyright © 1988 by Deborah Daro.

Page 186 Figure 7.3   Figure from Belsky, J. (1984), The determinants of parenting: a process model. *Child Development* 55, 83–96. Reprinted with permission.

Page 210 Informed Parent 8.1   From *How to Talk So Kids Will Listen & Listen So Kids Will Talk* by Adele Faber and Elaine Mazlish. Copyright © 1980 by Adele Faber and Elaine Mazlish. By permission of Rawson Wade, Publishers Inc.

Page 212 Informed Parent 8.2   From *Between Parent and Teenager* by Haim G. Ginott, Macmillan, 1969. Reprinted with permission of author.

Page 216 Spirit of Parenting Ch 8   From *Blackberry Winter* by Margaret Mead. New York: William Morrow and Company, 1972. Reprinted by permission.

Page 232 Informed Parent 8.5   From *The Discipline Book* by W. Sears. Copyright © 1995 by William Sears and Martha Sears. By permission of Little, Brown and Company, Inc.

Page 241 Table 9.1   From *Cultural Perspectives on Child Development* by Wagner and Stevenson © 1982 by W. H. Freeman and Company. Used with permission.

Page 248 Informed Parent 9.1   From Berk, Laura E., *Infants, Children & Adolescents, 3/e.* Copyright © 1999 by Allyn & Bacon. Adapted by permission.

Page 254 Spirit of Parenting   "A Poem for Emily" in *Imperfect Love* by Miller Williams. Louisiana State University Press, 1986. Reprinted with permission.

Page 272 Informed Parent 9.5   From *Your Child's Growing Mind* by Jane M. Healy. Copyright © 1987, 1994 by Jane M. Healy. Used by permission of Doubleday, a division of Random House, Inc.

Page 294 Informed Parent 10.3   From *How to Have Intelligent and Creative Conversations* by Jane M. Healy. Copyright © 1992 by Jane M. Healy, Ph.D. Used by permission of Doubleday, a division of Random House, Inc.

Page 295 Spirit of Parenting Ch 10   From *Diary of a Baby* by Daniel N. Stern. Copyright © 1990 by Daniel N. Stern, M.D. Reprinted by permission of Basic Books, a member of Perseus Books, L.L.C.

Page 297 Informed Parent 10.4   From "Everyday Rules for Behavior: Mothers' Requests to Young Children" by Gralinski, Heidi, J., and Kopp, C. B. *Developmental Psychology* 29, 1993, p. 567. Copyright © 1993 by the American Psychological Association. Reprinted with permission of the American Psychological Association.

Page 333 Informed Parent 11.2   From "How Kids Learn" by Barbara Kantrowitz & Pat Wingert in *Newsweek*, 4/17/89. Copyright © 1989 Newsweek, Inc. All rights reserved. Reprinted by permission.

Page 336 Spirit of Parenting   From *The People, Yes* by Carl Sandburg. Copyright 1936 Harcourt, Brace and Company and renewed 1964 by Carl Sandburg, reprinted by permission of the publisher.

Page 339 Informed Parent 11.4   Adapted from Sternberg, R. J., and Williams, W. M. (1995) Parenting toward cognitive competence. In Bornstein, M. H. (Ed.) *Handbook of Parenting*, Vol. 4, *Applied and Practical Parenting*, pp. 259–275. Mahwah, NJ: Lawrence Erlbaum Associates. Reprinted by permission.

Page 341 Informed Parent 11.5   From *Your Child's Growing Mind* by Jane M. Healy. Copyright © 1987, 1994 by Jane M. Healy. Used by permission of Doubleday, a division of Random House, Inc.

Page 345 Informed Parent 11.6   From *Caring for Your School-Age Child (Age 5–12)* by Edward L. Schor, M.D. Copyright © 1995 by the American Academy of Pediatrics. Illustrations © 1995 by Jeanne Brunnick. Used by permission of Bantam Books, a division of Random House, Inc.

Page 351 Table 11.1   From Radovsky, V., *TV Guide*, July 13, 1996, p. 14.

Page 352 Figure 11.2   From "Development of Television Viewing Patterns in Early Childhood: A Longitudinal Investigation," by A. C. Huston, J. C. Wright, M. L. Rice, D. Kerkman, and M. St. Peters, 1990, *Developmental Psychology* 26, pp. 409–420. Copyright © 1990 by the American Psychological Association. Reprinted with permission of the American Psychological Association.

Page 353 Figure 11.3 From Huston, A. C. and Wright, J. C., May 1995. The effects of educational television viewing of lower income preschoolers on academic skills, school readiness and school adjustment 1 to 3 years later: Report to Children's Television Workshop. Published originally by the Center for Research on the Influences of Television on Children (CRITC)—University of Texas, Austin. Reprinted with permission by John C. Wright.

Page 365 Figure 12.1   From J. M. Tanner (1962), *Growth at Adolescence, 2d ed.* p.3. Reprinted by permission of Blackwell Science Ltd.

Page 377 Table 12.1   From Sebald, H. (1989 Winter) "Adolescents' peer orientation: Changes in the support system during the past three decades." *Adolescence*, pp. 940–941. Reprinted by permission of Libra Publishers.

Page 383 Figure 12.2   From "One Theory of Parents' Early Role in the Development of Delinquent Behavior" by R. Patterson, B. D. DeBaryshe, and E. Ramsey, 1989, *American Psychologist* 44, 329–335. Copyright © 1989 by the American Psychological Association. Reprinted with permission of the American Psychological Association.

Page 384 Informed Parent 12.1   Adapted from *Adolescence* by John W. Santrock, Brown and Benchmark, 1993. Reprinted with permission of The McGraw-Hill Companies.

Page 390 Figure 12.3   From "Risk Behavior in Adolescence: A Psychosocial Framework for Understanding and Action" (p. 27) by Richard Jessor, 1992. In *Adolescents at Risk: Medical and Social Perspectives*, edited by D. E. Rogers and E. Ginzberg. Reprinted with permission of Eli Ginzberg.

Page 397 Informed Parent 12.4   Adapted from Santrock, J.W. (1997) *Children 5E*. Brown and Benchmark Publishers, p. 484. Reprinted with permission of The McGraw-Hill Companies.

Page 409 Informed Parent 13.1   © 1989 by The Society for the Study of Social Problems. Reprinted from *Social Problems* Vol. 36, No.3, Issue June 1989, pp.251–269. Reprinted by permission.

Page 410 Informed Parent 13.2   From **FC—Marriages and Families, 5th edition*, by Mary Ann Lamanna and Agnes Biedmann. © 1994. Reprinted with permission of Wadsworth Publishing, a division of Thomson Learning.

Page 412 Table 13.2   From Yost, E. B., and Corbishley, M. A. *Career Counseling—A Psychological Approach*. Table 13.2, p. 412. Copyright © 1987 Jossey-Bass, Inc., Publishers. Reprinted by permission.

Page 414 Informed Parent 13.3   Modified and reproduced by special permission of the Publisher, Consulting Psychologists Press, Inc., Palo Alto, CA 94303 from *Myers-Briggs Type Indicator®—Form G* by Katharine D. Briggs and Isabel Briggs Myers. Copyright 1977 by Peter Briggs Myers and Katharine D. Myers. All rights reserved. Further reproduction is prohibited without the Publisher's written consent.

Index

AA. *See* Alcoholics Anonymous (AA)

AARP. *See* American Association of Retired Persons (AARP)

Abbott, S., 251

Aber, J.L., 257

Abortion, 18, 31, 45, 130

Abrahamse, 128

Abramovitch, R., 343

Acceptance, 10, 11, 184, 185, 217

Accidents, 282–284, 285, 323

Acculturation, 73–89

ACEI. *See* Association for Childhood Education International (ACEI)

ACLD. *See* Children with Learning Disabilities (ACLD)

Action for Children's Television, 358

Active Parenting, 201, 219

ADD. *See* Attention deficit disorder (ADD)

Addiction
  child abuse and, 170
  narcissistic parents and, 187
  See also Alcoholism; Drugs; Substance abuse

ADHD. *See* Attention deficit hyperactivity disorder (ADHD)

Adler, Alfred, 216, 219

Adler, T.E., 335

Adlerian model, 199, 200

Adolescent drug use, 370, 380, 383, 386, 388–392
  identity and, 373
  organization regarding, 401
  parenting style and, 381
  peers and, 392
  personal fables and, 370
  physical attractiveness and, 392
  suicide and, 397, 398
  trends in, 389–391

Adolescent peers, 368–369, 376–377, 382–383
  drug use and, 392
  parents vs., 380
  school and, 385

Adolescents/teenagers, 111–112, 359–401, 425
  career choices of, 410–411
  child abuse and, 170
  communication with, 212
  as consumers, 383
  death and, 165
  delinquency in. *See* Delinquency
  depression in, 227, 230
  discipline of, 225, 381, 382, 383
  dysfunctional families and, 106
  early- vs. late-maturing, 368–369
  eating disorders in, 392–395, 396, 401
  emerging from, 404, 406
  expulsion from home of, 380
  family violence and, 174
  friendships of, 307, 384
  historical setting and, 52, 53
  individualism and, 75
  interdependent stage for, 14, 15
  "metal head," 388
  organizations regarding, 401
  parental responsibilities to, 16
  parenting style and, 198
  as parents, 116. *See also* Teenage fathers; Teenage mothers
  personal fables of, 129, 370, 388
  physical changes of, 364–369
  problems of, 386–398
  professional help for, 397
  puberty and, 361–362, 366–369, 377–378, 404
  Puerto Rican, 78
  risk taking by, 387–389
  self-control and, 302

single parents of, 122
social class and, 60
stepparents and, 134
suicide by, 55, 386, 395, 396–398, 401

Adoption, 143–146
  gay, 116, 141, 142
  infants and, 255, 256
  informal, 78

Adult Attachment Interview, 259

Adult children, 172, 360, 402–427
  of alcoholics, 175, 178
  career decisions of, 410–414, 415
  grandparents and, 423
  marriage of, 416–417
  staying at home, 404, 405, 408, 410, 419

AFDC. *See* Aid to Families with Dependent Children (AFDC)

Affection, 17, 30, 184, 185, 186, 188
  adolescents and, 375
  babies and, 254–255
  grandparents and, 422
  as love, 11
  socialization and, 198

Affective involvement, 108

Affective responsiveness, 108

African Americans/blacks, 66, 79, 81, 82, 322
  accident rate for, 283
  as adolescents, 372, 375
  cosleeping by, 251
  education and, 340
  as fathers, 31, 34
  as grandparents, 60, 83, 139, 141, 420, 421
  homicide and, 386
  identity and, 375
  as mothers, 38, 82, 83–84, 128
  organizations regarding, 91
  social class and, 60

Africans, 69, 328
  AIDS among, 53–54
  slavery of, 34, 81–82
Age
  children's. See Children's age
  parental, 20, 23, 56, 189,
    418–419. See also Mothers,
    older/menopausal
Age cohorts, 51–53, 55, 349
  adolescents as, 383
Agreement, adolescents and, 384,
  385
Aid to Families with Dependent
  Children (AFDC), 125
AIDS, 85, 116, 139
  in Africa, 53–54
  breastfeeding and, 253
  organizations regarding, 180, 401
  on television, 54
  in United States, 54, 55
  See also HIV
Ainsworth, Mary, 6, 169, 247,
  256–258, 260
Aizenberg, R., 418
Al-Anon, 176, 178
Al-Khayyah, M., 103
Alateen, 178
Alcoholics Anonymous (AA), 176,
  178
Alcoholism, 140, 141, 174–178
  ADD and, 160
  adolescents and, 372, 373, 383,
    389–391, 392, 398, 401
  Latino adolescents and, 392
  Native Americans and, 86, 89
  organizations regarding, 176,
    178, 180, 401
  suicide and, 398
  See also Addiction; Substance
    abuse
Alessandri, S.M., 61
Algozzine, B., 161
Alimony, 124, 136
Allowance (children's), 343–344,
  383
Allport, Susan, 9
Altemeier, W.A., 168
Altschuler, J., 407
Alvarez, 77
Amazon culture, 2
Ambivalent attachment, 257
American Association of Retired
  Persons (AARP), 427
American culture. See United
  States/America
Ames, E.W., 248
Ames, Louise B., 270
Anderson, C.A., 133, 312
Anger, 9, 191–192, 196, 219
  adolescents and, 380
  communication and, 215

modeling and, 223
  punishment and, 227
  self-esteem and, 335
  temper tantrums and, 302
Anglo-American culture, 73–76,
  94, 97, 328. See also United
  States/America
Anglo-Saxon culture, 76
Anorexia nervosa, 392–395, 401
Anorexia Nervosa and Related Eat-
  ing Disorders, 401
Anxiety, 207, 219
  adolescents and, 380
  alcoholic parents and, 175
  empty nest syndrome and, 407
  punishment and, 227
  separation, 256, 257
  stranger, 256, 257
  in young children, 298
Apgar, Virginia, 240
Apgar Scale, 240, 242, 250
Appalachian Americans, 251
Appreciation, 218
Arapesh, 2
Archer, Sally, 373
Arguments, 221
Aries, Philip, 29
Aristotle, 199
Armistead, L., 381
Arnett, Jeffrey, 388
Artificial insemination, 20, 142
Asher, S.R., 342, 343
Asian Americans, 79–81, 283, 421
Asian Indians, 79
Asians, 78–81
Asis, M.M.B., 19
Asmundsson, R., 135
Asmussen, L., 122
Association on American Indian
  Affairs, 91
Association for Childhood Educa-
  tion International (ACEI), 276,
  358
Associative play, 305
Assumptions, 67–72
Astin, A.W., 415
Attachment, 5, 187
  adolescents and, 380
  adoption and, 145
  avoidant, 7–8, 257, 258, 260
  child abuse and, 169
  death and, 163
  disabled children and, 157
  dual-income parenting and, 119
  friendships and, 308
  in infants, 255–261
  interview to assess, 259
  as love, 11
  parenting styles and, 197
  play and, 304, 306
  sibling position and, 97

stepparents and, 134
  transitional objects in, 261–262
  types of, 257–258
Attachment disorder, 145
Attention, 425
  desire for, 217
  grandparents and, 422
  language development and, 293
  nurturance and, 260
  siblings and, 349, 350
  visual, 272
Attention deficit disorder (ADD),
  160–163, 165
  alcoholic parents and, 175
  child abuse and, 168
Attention deficit hyperactivity disorder (ADHD), 160, 168
Attention spans, 326
Attitudes, 5, 8, 14, 319
  of adult children, 406
  assumptions and, 66, 68
  children's gender and, 62
  college education and, 415
  multi-ethnicity and, 72
  newborns and parental, 238
  social class and, 60
  toward school/education, 334,
    385–386, 414
Authoritarian parents, 77, 196–198
  adolescents and, 373, 381, 383,
    392
  adult children and, 406
Authoritative parents, 197–198,
  335
  adolescents and, 373, 381, 392
Authority, 14, 15, 31
  fathers', 32
  hatred of, 30
Autism, 35, 96, 150
Autonomy, 61, 95, 106, 110, 197
  adolescents and, 362, 363, 371,
    376, 379, 380
  communication and, 210–211
  culture and, 328
  misinterpretation as, 257
  in stages, 406
Avoidant children, 7–8, 257, 258,
  260
Axelrad, S., 258
Axelson, L.J., 408
Azrin, Nathan, 300
Azuma, 328

"Baby boom," 33–34. 237
Babyproofing home, 274
Bachman, J.G., 410
Baites, P.B., 52
Baldwin, L.M., 108
Ball, S., 353
Bandura, Albert, 223, 229, 292
Bank, L., 125

Bank, Stephen, 348
Banking scandal, 55
Banyard, V., 125
Baptists, 83
Baran, S.J., 355
Barbour, N., 129
Barling, J., 411
Bates, E., 268
Bates, J., 60, 171
Bateson, Catherine, 203, 206
Bateson, Gregory, 203
Baumrind, Diane, 5, 10, 83, 185,
    196–198, 213, 335, 381, 392
Baurer, 298
Beautrais, A.L., 287
Beavers, Jeanette, 154–155, 158
Beavers, W.R., 106, 107
Beck, 60
Beckerman, 250
Beckman, P., 157
Bedford, Victoria, 407
Bedrosian, J.L., 292
Bedwetting, 94, 301
Behavior control, 109. *See also*
    Control
Behavior modification, 219–231
Behavior window, 215
Behavioral disorders, 107
Behavioral theory, 301
Behaviors, 5, 8
    adolescent, 372, 376, 380,
        381–383, 388–389
    context dependent, 233
    correcting, 209–211, 226–231
    culture and, 71, 73, 328
    feelings and, 208–209
    of healthy families, 110
    infant, 240–243
    limits on, 219
    maladaptive, 184
    mis-, 213–215, 217, 226
    modeling. *See* Modeling;
        Parental models
    moral, 331, 370, 372
    motivations for, 217
    newborns and parental, 238
    parent training programs and,
        199, 200
    prosocial, 355
    rules for, 297
    television and, 354, 355
Behrman, R.E., 364
Belief systems, 190–195
Beliefs, 3, 5, 8, 14, 199
    adolescents and, 371
    Asian, 79
    assumptions and, 66, 68–70
    behavior and, 219
    college education and, 415
    ethnicity and, 89
    intelligence and, 328

newborns and parental, 238
"personal fables" as, 129
religious. *See* Religion
rigid, 107
self-defeating, 218
siblings and, 349
Bell, Richard, 198
Belsky, Jay, 22–24, 62, 111, 119,
    171, 172, 186, 187, 260, 238,
    263
Bem, S.L., 303
Bengali, 184
Bengston, V.L., 419, 421
Bennett, 85
Bentovim, Arnon, 105
Bepko, Claudia, 175, 178
Berg, Henry, 166
Berg, K.M., 246
Berg, W.K., 246
Berger, S.H., 421
Bergman, A., 145, 170
Berk, Laura, 248, 269, 270, 285,
    312, 343
Berko-Gleason, 62
Bernard, H.S., 374
Berndt, Thomas J., 79
Berns, Roberta M., 61, 110
Bernstein, A.C., 302
Bettelheim, Bruno, 35, 38,
    226
Bettner, Betty Lou, 218, 220
Bible, 228
Biculturalism, 81
Biesmer, R., 418
Bigner, J.J., 82
Billingsley, A., 83
Biology, 8–9, 23
    adolescents', 388, 395
    women's, 35
    See also Development
"Biracial," 81
Birch, Herbert, 243–245
Birth cohorts, 51–53
Birth control/contraception, 18,
    19–20, 31, 45, 130
Birth defects, 61
Birth order, 3, 346–348
    effective parenting and, 189
    language development and, 293
Birth rates, 44, 109, 123, 124, 127,
    128
    Native American, 85
Bishop, D.S., 108
Black, C.V., 82
Black, Claudia, 175
Blakeslee, S., 267
Blame shifting, 232
"Blank slate," 11
Blanket (as transitional object),
    261
Blatt, Sidney J., 8

Bleichfeld, B., 247
Blended family, 5, 116, 131
    Native American, 86
    problems in, 132, 139
    See also Remarriage; Stepfamily;
        Stepparents
Blinde, E.M., 393
Block, J.H., 61, 392
Blumberg, M.L., 168
Bly, Robert, 424–425
Blyth, D.A., 386
Bodily-kinesthetic intelligence, 329
Bogatz, G., 353
Bongaarts, J., 405
Borke, 290
Boszormenyi-Nagy, 145
Bouchard, C., 365
Boundaries, 101, 106, 111,
    374–375
Bourne, 166
Bowen, Murray, 95–97, 98
Bowlby, John, 163, 255, 256, 260,
    299
Bowman, P.J., 83
Boyd-Franklin, N., 82, 83
Boyer, D., 128
Boyer, Ernest, 414
Boysson-Bardies, B., 268
Brainstorming, 220, 384
Brand, E., 133
Braungart, J.M., 260
Bray, J.H., 421
Brazelton, T. Berry, 6, 239, 240,
    241, 249, 300
Brazelton Scale, 240, 241
Brazilian Americans, 76
Breastfeeding, 252–254, 277
Breznitz, 293
British Americans, 363
Brody, S., 258
Brody, G.H., 259, 322, 383
Brodzinsky, Advid, 146
Broken-record technique, 221
Brone, R.J., 393
Bronfenbrenner, Urie, 46–48, 79,
    95, 171, 259
Bronstein, P., 49, 238
Brook, J.S., 392
Brooks-Gunn, J., 128, 129, 366,
    367, 376
Brouillette, R.T., 250
Brown, 292
Brown, B.B., 381, 385, 392
Brubaker, E., 419
Brubaker, T.H., 419
Bruner, Jerome, 291
Bryant, D.M., 311
Bubenzer, D., 129
Buck, 250
Buddhism, 78, 79
Buhrmester, D., 377

Bulimia, 392, 395, 401
Burke, M., 259
Burnell, G.M., 18, 19
Burns, A.L., 61
Burns, David, 191, 193
Burton, L.M., 141
Butcher, 227
Butler, Iris, 145, 146
Butler, R., 320

Cacioppo, B.E., 23
Callaghan, J.W., 323
Callan, V., 19, 380
Calvin, John, 29
Camara, K.A., 348
Cambodian Americans, 79
Cambodians, 328
Campbell, M., 125
Camras, L.A., 170
Canino, I., 78
Care, by parents, 9, 11
Caregivers, 16, 83
  African American, 83
  attachment and, 257
  Chinese, 79
  death and, 163
  grandparents as, 141
  infants and, 246
Caretaker fatigue, 418
Caribbean culture, 82
Carlson, B., 229
Carpenter, L., 116
Carson, 227
Carter, Betty, 98, 109–110, 111,
  112, 364, 403
Carter, E.A., 137
Casey, R.J., 348
Caspi, A. 53
Castillo, Griswold del, 77
Catholics, 44
  African American, 83
  Filipino American, 79
  Latino, 76–77
Caucasians/whites, 73–76
  accident rate for, 283
  Chinese vs., 81, 242
  child abuse by, 168
  grandparents and, 139
Causality/causation, 191, 193
CCRC. See Children's Creative
  Response to Conflict (CCRC)
Centerwall, Brandon, 354
CHADD. See Children and Adults
  with Attention Deficit Disor-
  ders (CHADD)
Chaio, 79
Chaki-Sircar, M., 184
Chapman, 319
Chapman, M., 335
Char, W.F., 79

Cherlin, Andrew, 7, 141, 419, 420
Cherry, L., 293
Chess, Stella, 5, 13, 243–245
Chiao, 79
Child abuse, 166
  adoption and, 145
  in Africa, 53
  alcohol and, 175
  children's temperament and, 245
  contemporary, 9
  corporal punishment as, 228,
    229
  gay parents and, 143
  historical, 29
  intergenerational, 167–168
  Native American, 89
  organization regarding, 181
  sexual, 35, 53, 143, 145, 167
  by teenage parents, 130
  See also Maltreatment
Child Abuse Hot Line, 228
Child care
  fathers and, 21, 34, 35, 39, 118,
    262, 263
  gender roles and, 102
  settings for, 309–310
  single mothers and, 125
  Spock and, 38
Child Care Information Exchange,
  315
Child custody, 120, 139, 142
Child labor, 31, 102
Child management, 105
Child neglect/abandonment, 29,
  31, 166, 170
  alcoholism and, 175
  organization regarding, 181
  peer relationships and, 342
  by teenage parents, 130
  See also Maltreatment; Neglectful
    parents
Child support, 124, 126, 136
Children, 3, 22–23
  adult. *See* Adult children
  allowance for, 343–345, 383
  animals and, 332
  "battered," 166
  bedtime for, 252
  books for, 271, 279, 296, 303,
    308
  commercialism and, 355
  communication with, 207–213
  cost of raising, 24–28, 57–59
  crying by, 298
  death and, 163–165
  decision to have, 18–22
  development of. *See*
    Development
  disabled, 145, 146, 150–163, 168
  disorganized-disoriented, 258

divorce and. *See* Divorce
effect of dual-income parenting
  on, 119. *See also* Two-career/
  dual-income family
ethnicity of. *See also* Culture(s);
  Ethnicity; Race
exceptional, 150–163
fears of, 298
friendships of, 307–308, 342–343
"good," 170, 331
grown-up, 112. *See also* Adult
  children
growth rate of, 322
growth spurt in, 364–365
health and safety of, 282–287,
  297, 315, 323
historical changes in regard to,
  28–40, 51, 53
humor of, 306–307
"hurried," 55–56
immigrant, 73. *See also*
  Immigrants
listening and talking to, 207–211
lying by, 326–327, 331
in Middle Ages, 29, 30
number of, 28, 44. *See also*
  Fertility
nurturance of. *See* Nurturance
nutrition for, 253
obesity among, 323–324
one child vs. more, 28
"parentified," 177, 232
physical fitness of, 323–324
preschool. *See* Preschool children
reading to, 271, 312, 331
roles for, 211. *See also* Gender
  roles
scapegoat, 168, 177
schools and, 29, 31. *See also*
  School-age children
self-controlled, 280, 296–303
self-worth in, 6. *See also*
  Self-esteem
sheltered, 54
sleep by, 296–303
socialization of. *See* Socialization
"special needs," 154. *See also* Disabled children
temperament in. *See* Temperament
as toddlers, 282, 290
undifferentiated, 96
urban vs. suburban, 48
See also Adolescents; Infants;
  Middle childhood
Children and Adults with Attention Deficit Disorders
  (CHADD), 162
Children with Learning Disabilities
  (ACLD), 162

Children's age, 56–57, 187, 349
  adoption and, 145
  children's gender and, 62
  chronological vs. developmental, 3
  discipline and, 224
  effective parenting and, 183, 189
  egocentrism and, 288–290, 291
  parental responsibility and, 15–16
  stepfamily problems and, 134
  See also Age cohorts; Birth order
Children's Creative Response to Conflict (CCRC), 235
Children's peers, 307–308, 342–343
  ecological context of, 47, 48
  physical punishment and, 229
Children's responsibility, 53, 188, 216–219
  death and, 165
  freedom and, 219
  inappropriate, 55–56
  parent training programs and, 6, 199, 200
Chinese, 16, 67, 79
  adolescent, 394
  adoption of, 144
  child maltreatment and, 168
  education and, 342
  infants and, 242
  one-child policy and, 8, 62
Chinese American, 73, 79, 80–81
Christians, children of, 112
Christmon, K., 84, 130
Christopher, F.S., 351
Chronosystem, 47–51
Cicchetti, Dante, 169
Cicirelli, V.G., 418
Civil rights movement, 80
Clark, E.V., 268
Clark, F., 162
Clark, H.H., 268
Clark-Lempers, D., 381
Clarke-Stewart, Alison, 6, 62, 310, 312
Clemens, A.W., 408
Clingempeel, W.G., 133, 187
Coalition, 104, 105, 106–107
Coburn, Karen, 415
Cochran, 84
Cognition, 309, 339–340
  in adolescents, 369–375
  attachment and, 256–257
  day care and, 312
  humor and, 306-307
  in middle childhood, 324–331
  play and, 306–307
  parental, 190–192
  television and, 353–354

Cognitive theory, 194, 199, 219
Cohabiting families, 116
Cohesiveness, 110
Coie, J.D., 342
Coleman, 227
Coleman, J.S., 121
Coleman, M., 135
Coles, Robert, 112, 331
Collective monlogues, 291
Collins, 156
Comas Díaz, 78
Comer, James P., 84
Comfort, 106
Commercialism, 355
Communal families, 116
Communication, 6, 102–103, 208, 210–211
  adolescents and, 377, 379, 380, 382, 383
  alcoholic parents and, 175
  children's gender and, 61
  in dysfunctional family, 106–107
  effective, 108
  in healthy family, 110
  infants and, 268–270
  Native Americans and, 87
  plain speaking in, 221–222
  self-awareness and, 190
  spanking as, 229
  See also Language
Community
  adolescents and, 363
  children and, 47, 48
  dysfunctional family and, 107
  grandparents and, 424
  Native American, 86
Community class, 50
Compadrazgo, 77
Compensatory lies, 327
Competence
  in adolescents, 381, 389
  in middle childhood, 332–344
  types of, 328–329
Computerization, 55
Comstock, G., 352
Concrete operational stage, 325–326
Condry, J., 61
Condry, S., 61
Confidence, 217, 243
Conflict, 106
  adolescents and, 369, 370, 376–385, 396
  adult children and, 407, 408
  family maps and, 100
  friendships and, 307, 342
  in healthy family, 110
  suicide and, 396

Conflict resolution, 6, 199
  adolescents and, 384
  on family health scale, 105
  family meetings for, 220
  friendships and, 308
  "no lose" method for, 213
  organization for, 235
Confrontation, 209, 213, 214
Confucianism, 52, 78, 81
Conger, R.D., 53, 170
Connectedness, 79, 96
Conroy, Pat, 103
Consequences, 217, 219, 223, 224
Conservation (of objects), 325
Consumerism, 315, 355, 383
Context dependent behavior, 233
Conti-Ramsden, G., 270
Contract, 385
Control, 106, 109, 185–186
  adolescents and, 375
  punishment and, 227
  supportive, 198
Control theory, 198
Cook, 18
Cooney, 78
Cooper, R.G., 258
Cooperative play, 305
Coopersmith, S., 335
Corbishley, M.A., 411
Coregulation, 343
Cornell, Claire, 172, 174
Corporal punishment, 228. See also Physical punishment; Spanking
Cortes, 73
Cosleeping, 251–252, 299
Council for Children's Television and Media, 358
Cowan, C.P., 61, 111, 238, 263
Cowan, P.A., 111, 238, 263, 302, 325
Cowgill, K., 135
Cox, M., 48, 133, 187
Cox, R., 133
Creativity, 32, 307, 330
  culture and, 328
  television and, 354, 355
Criminal behavior, 85, 205, 401
  by adolescents, 388
  child abuse/neglect and, 170
  organizations regarding, 401
  rejection and, 343
  spanking and, 230
  on television, 54
  See also Homicide
Crisis, healthy families and, 110
Crockenberg, S.B., 302
Cross, M., 292
Cross-cultural parenting, 5
Crouter, A., 50, 263

Crowley, 388
Crowther, J.H., 394
Cults, 372
Cultural norms, psychological factors vs., 8
Culture(s), 2, 3, 29–30, 65–91, 199
  adolescents and, 361, 363, 388, 397
  adult children and, 404–405, 407
  African, 69, 81–82, 328
  African American. See African Americans/blacks
  Amazon, 2
  American, 39, 51, 53. See also United States/America
  Anglo-American, 73–76, 94, 97, 328
  Appalachian, 251
  Arapesh, 203
  Asian, 78–81
  Asian American, 79–81, 283, 421
  Asian Indian, 79
  assumptions and, 67–89
  Bengali, 184
  Brazilian American, 76
  British American, 363
  Cambodian, 328
  Cambodian American, 79
  Caribbean, 82
  child maltreatment and, 170, 172, 173
  Chinese. See Chinese
  Chinese American, 73, 79, 80–81
  Cuban American, 76
  Dominican, 76
  eating disorders and, 394
  education and, 342
  effective parenting and, 189
  English, 73–75, 82, 344
  Eskimo, 330
  European immigrant, 73–76
  examples of different, 2, 9–10
  Filipino, 328
  Filipino American, 79
  German, 7–8, 17, 171, 329
  Greek, 62
  growth rate and, 322
  Guatemalan, 251
  Havascupai, 85
  Hispanic. See Hispanics; Latinos
  Hmong, 87
  Hopi, 89, 323
  identity and, 374–375
  immigrant. See Immigrants
  Indian (American). See Native Americans
  Indian (East), 57, 73, 168, 322
  Indian (Nayar), 2
  Indian (Wauja), 2
  infant language and, 268, 270

  intelligence and, 328
  Inuit, 329
  Italian, 69, 363
  Italian American, 407, 421
  Japanese. See Japanese
  Japanese American, 72, 73, 79
  Jewish. See Jews
  Kalawali, 68
  Kamukuaka, 2
  Korean American, 73, 79, 79
  language and, 268, 270, 290, 293
  Latin American, 404–405
  Latino, 76–78, 392. See also Hispanics
  Manus, 203
  Mayan, 251, 252
  Mexican, 328, 404
  Mexican American, 76, 77, 91, 328
  middle childhood and, 317, 318
  mothers and, 38–40
  Mundugumor, 203
  Mundurucu, 2
  Native American. See Native Americans
  Navaho, 85
  New Guinea, 2, 68, 203
  Nigerian, 4
  organizations regarding, 64, 91
  parenting style and, 198
  Portuguese, 363
  Puerto Rican, 76, 77–78
  reasons for having children in different, 20
  social class in, 57–61
  South Pacific, 62, 203
  South American, 2
  Spanish, 78, 82
  suicide and, 397
  Swedish, 62, 171
  Tchambuli, 203
  tradition in, 3–4, 6
  Vietnamese, 52–53, 328
  Vietnamese American, 79
  Wauja, 2
  Western, 299, 328, 329, 404
  See also Ethnicity; Nations/countries; Race; Religion
Custodial fathers, 125–126
Custodial grandparents, 139, 140
Cutright, P., 128

Dahl, A., 135
Daniels, Denise, 345
Darabi, K.F., 128
Dargatz, Jan, 313
Daro, D., 173
Datan, 421
DaVanzo, J., 404
Davidson, J. Kenneth, 189–190

Dawson, 139
Day care, 119, 125, 309–310
  child abuse and, 169
  constructive, 312
  infant attachment and, 260
  organization regarding, 315
Day-care grandparents, 139, 140, 141
De Lissovoy, V., 129
De Vos, S., 405
Dean, A.L., 170
Dean, James, 362
Death, 125, 163–165
  of children, 323
  homocide, 386
  of infants, 249–251
  among Native Americans, 85–86
Decision making, 343
  adolescents and, 373, 374
  collective, 216–217
  culture and, 328
  on family health scale, 105
Defensive lies, 327
Defrain, J., 5, 6, 12, 138
DeGioganni, I.S., 298
Del Vecchio, Ann, 86
Delaney, Bessie, 344
Delaney, Sadie, 344
Delinquency, 229, 230, 380, 382, 392
  identity and, 371
  organization regarding, 401
  rejection and, 343
Deloache, L., 247
Demandedness, 10–11
Demandingness, 196–198
DeMause, Lloyd, 29
Dement, W.C., 246
Democracy, 34, 32, 68, 197
Democratic parenting style, 216–217, 335
  adolescents and, 373
Denver Developmental Screen Test, 272
Departure stage, 14, 15
Dependence, 68. See also Independence
Depression, 96, 125, 187
  adolescents and, 380, 386, 394, 395–396
  alcoholic parents and, 175
  child abuse and, 170
  in children, 192–194
  death and, 163
  disabled children and, 157
  eating disorders and, 394, 395
  physical punishment and, 230
  post partum, 256
  punishment and, 227
  self-esteem and, 335

Despair, 417
DeVault, Christine, 27, 154, 157
Development, 10, 46–51, 187, 238
  alcoholism and, 175
  cognitive. *See* Cognition; Cognitive theory
  day care and, 312
  death and, 164, 165
  discipline and, 225
  early childhood, 280–282
  effective parenting and, 189
  emotional, 256, 257
  grandparents and grandchild's level of, 421
  idiosyncratic experiences and, 349
  infant, 264–274
  influence of time on, 52
  language. *See* Language
  middle childhood, 317–331
  models and, 223
  motor, 270–274, 282, 322–323
  observational learning and, 223
  parental expectations and, 347–348
  parenting constructs for, 185–186
  primary vs. secondary context for, 46
  responsibilities and, 219
  of self, 293–296, 371
  social, 308, 310, 312, 355
Developmental models, 2
Dietz, W.H., 323
Differentiation of self, 95–97
Dinkmeyer, Don, 217
Directive parents, 198
Disabled children, 150–163
  adoption of, 145, 146
  child abuse and, 168
  hearing, 153
Discipline, 34, 37, 186, 232
  adolescents and, 225, 381, 382, 383
  African American, 83
  grandparents and, 420
  importance of, 223–231
  of infants, 266
  self-, 213–215, 225
  See also Physical punishment; Spanking
Discrimination
  African Americans and, 82
  Chinese Americans and, 79
  Native Americans and, 85
Dishion, T.J., 392
Divorce, 5, 7, 54, 116, 131, 139
  adolescents and, 112, 364, 381
  among Asians, 79
  children's gender and, 62

development context and, 46
  gender roles and, 102
  grandparents and, 421
  play after, 306
  See also Remarriage; Stepfamily; Stepparents
Do It Now Foundation, 401
Dodds, J.B., 273
Dodge, K.A., 60, 171
Doka, K., 423
Dolls, 61, 261
Domestic abuse, 230. *See also* Child abuse; Violence
Donaldson-Pressman, S., 187
Dore, John, 291
Dornbusch, S.M., 61
Down's syndrome, 152
Downey, D.B., 121
Downey, G., 170
Draper, Patricia, 69
Dreams, 298
Dreikurs, Rudolf, 192, 199, 200, 216–217, 219
Drugs, 205
  ADD and, 160
  adolescents and. *See* Adolescent drug use
  grandparents and, 116, 139, 140, 141
  infants and, 256
  Native Americans and, 85, 86, 89
  organization regarding, 401
  parenting style and children's use of, 198
  SIDS and, 250
  on television, 54
  See also Addiction; Substance abuse
Dubas, J.S., 368
Dubroff, Jessica, 183, 186
Dunn, Judy, 270, 350
Dunst, C., 158
Dweck, C.S., 335
Dyscalculia, 159, 160
Dysfunctional family, 103–109
  alcoholic parents and, 175, 178
  stepfamily as, 133
Dysgraphia, 159, 160
Dyslexia, 159–160

Eating disorders, 392–395, 401
  suicide and, 396
Eberly, M., 379
Eccles, J.S., 385
Ecological model, 171, 172, 259, 382
Ecological systems theory, 47–51
Economics
  adolescents and, 381
  adult children and, 403, 404, 409

of childrearing, 24–28
  children's age and, 349
  day care and, 312
  gender roles and, 102
  single mothers and, 123–124
  unwed mothers and, 122
Economy, 69
  birth rate and, 45
  fathers and, 32
  inflation and, 55
  mothers and, 38
  parent-child relationship and, 53
  See also Socioeconomic class
Ecosystem, 233
Edelman, M.W., 2, 191
Education, 358
  adolescents and, 384–386
  African Americans and, 83
  Asians and, 79
  child abuse and, 168
  culture and, 328
  early childhood, 308–312
  homework and, 341–342
  Jews and, 67, 70
  middle childhood, 317–320
  Native Americans and, 87–88
  organization for childhood, 276, 358
  parental expectations and, 338
  self-esteem and, 334–342
  television and, 353–354
  unwed mothers and, 122
  See also School
Egbuono, L., 286
Egocentrism, 287–290, 291, 325
  adolescent, 370, 388
Eibl-Eibesfeldt, Irenaus, 304
Eisenberg, A.R., 293
Eisenberg, N., 342
Eitha, 369
Elder, G.H., Jr., 348, 349, 422
Elder, Glen, 53
Elizur, E., 301
Elkin, Frederick, 73
Elkind, David, 55, 56, 129, 332, 370, 385, 388
Elliott, E.S., 335
Emerson, Peggy, 245
Emotional cutoff, 97
Emotional development, 256, 257
Emotional disorders, child abuse and, 170
Emotional distress
  drug use and, 392
  economy and, 53
Emotional neglect, 167
Emotions/feelings, 9, 108, 109
  behavior and, 208–209
  childhood illness and, 287
  (continued)

Emotions/feelings *(continued)*
cognitions and, 190–192
communication and, 210
differentiation of self and, 95–97
in dysfunctional family, 107
expressing, 70, 103, 106, 110, 207–208, 209, 220
family maps and, 100
humanist approach and, 199, 200
in infants, 266
school-age children and, 165
See also Social/emotional problems
Employment. *See* Unemployment/employment
Empty nest syndrome, 407
Endes, J., 252
Enmeshment, family maps and, 100
Enrichment programs, 310–312
Enright, R.D., 374
Ensminger, M.E., 128
Environment, 45–51
modifying, 214, 220
adolescents and, 388, 389
ethnicity and, 69
genetics and, 246
of infants, 267
language development and, 293
middle childhood and, 325
shared/unshared, 345, 346, 349
siblings and, 345, 346, 349
temperament and, 243
Environmental adaptation, 329
Environmental movement, 55
Environmental selection, 329
Environmental shaping, 329
Environmental structure, 186, 187, 188
Epstein, J.L., 49
Epstein, L.H., 324
Epstein, N.B., 108
Erikson, Erik, 129, 318, 371, 372, 417
Eron, L.D., 354
Ethnicity, 199
adolescents and, 374–375
assumptions and, 67–89
child abuse and, 168
grandparents and, 421
growth rate and, 322
multi-, 72–73
statistics on, 72, 74, 79
See also Culture(s); Nations/countries; Race
Europeans, 73–76, 285
Evolutionary biology, 8
Ewert, B., 270
Exosystem, 49, 171, 172
"Explanatory style," 193, 194

Extended family, 68, 77, 111, 131
adolescents and, 111
death and, 163
grandparents and, 421
single parents and, 122, 125
See also Kinship
Eyer, Diane, 39–40

Faber, Adele, 199, 206–211, 301, 302, 350
Fabes, R.A., 351
Fabish, Adele, 6
Fadiman, Anne, 87
Fagot, B.I., 61, 348
Falk, P., 142
Families and Work Institute, 21, 22
Familism, 78
Family, 93–114
adaptation of, 106
adolescents and, 375–386, 392
adoptive. *See* Adoption
centrifugal vs. centripetal, 107
changes in American, 116–130
death in, 163–165
definition of, 70–71
dysfunctional. *See* Dysfunctional family
egalitarian, 35
extended. *See* Extended family; Kinship
fearing, 232
healthy, 110, 155
maltreatment in, 165–174
matriarchal, 34, 35
noncustodial, 133
nuclear, 116, 117
patriarchal, 35
rituals of. *See* Rituals
step-. *See* Stepfamily; Stepparents
as system, 94–103, 106
two-career/dual-income, 54, 55, 58, 81, 118–119, 262
two-parent, 61, 116–119, 124, 344, 381
types of, 116–117
violence in. *See* Child abuse; Spousal abuse; Violence
Family bed, 251–252, 298–299
Family constellation, 216
Family health scales, 104–105
Family life cycle, 109–112
adoption and, 145
adult children and, 403–406, 407, 417
Family maps, 98–100
Family meeting, 218, 220
Family of origin, 3, 96, 382
child maltreatment and, 170
teenage mothers and, 129–130
Family protection process, 97

Family roles, 108, 131, 211
alcoholism and, 175–178
Family size, child abuse and, 168
Family structure, 2, 3, 100–103, 106
adolescents and, 111, 381–382
genograms and, 98
Family systems theory, 95–103, 231, 233
Dreikurs and, 216
Patterson and, 382
Family transitions, 109–112. *See also* Transitions
Fantastic lies, 326–327
Fatherhood Project, 42
Fathers, 20–22, 39
absent, 55, 124
adolescents and, 376–377, 379
adult children and, 406, 411, 414
African American/black, 31, 34, 83, 84
androgynous, 262–263
Asian, 78
attachment and, 262–263
as breadwinners, 34, 35
child abuse by, 168
child care and, 21, 34, 35, 39, 118, 262, 263
Chinese, 79, 81
custodial, 125–126
daughters and, 31
of disabled children, 155, 157
historical changes in regard to, 31–35
infants and, 247, 249, 255–256, 270
microsystem and, 48
as new parents, 238
noncustodial, 126
self-esteem and, 335
out-of-wedlock, 34
teenage, 34
Faust, 364
Fear, 298, 380
Fearing family, 232
Felix-Ortiz de la, G.M., 392
Feminism, gender roles and, 102
Fergusson, D.M., 287
Ferholt, J.B., 237
Fernald, Anne, 269
Fertility, 45
Fetrow, R., 125
Fidelity, 371
Fine, D., 128, 137
Fine, M., 137
Finkelhor, D., 167, 168
Finley, J.J., 418
Fischer, J.L., 238
Fischer, Lucy, 111, 406, 422
Fisher, C.B., 393

Fishman, K.D., 146
Flannery, D., 379
Fleming, P.J., 250
Flexibility, 106
Fogel, 270
Forehand, R., 381, 383
Forgatch, M., 125
Formal operations stage, 369–370
Foxx, Richard, 300
Fraiberg, Selma, 258
"Frames of mind," 328
Frankenburg, W.K., 273
Frazier, E.F., 89
Freedman, Daniel G., 242, 343
Freedom, 219
French, D.C., 160, 343
Freud, Sigmund, 17, 32, 120, 347
    Adler and, 216
    intelligence of, 329
Freudian theory, 38, 299
Friedrich, Lynette, 355
Friendship Force, 64, 91
Frisch, R.E., 366
Frodi, Ann, 169
Fromm, Erich, 11
Fu, Victoria, 81
Furman, W., 344, 377
Furrow, D., 270
Furstenberg, Frank, 7, 141, 128, 129, 419, 420
Fusion, 95

Gaddis, A., 366
Galambos, N.L., 411
Galinsky, Ellen, 14, 363
Gallois, 19
Gambino, R., 70
Gambling, 187
Gangs, 372
    Chinese, 81
    Vietnamese, 52
Ganong, L., 135
Gans, J.E., 386
Garasky, S., 125
Garbarino, J., 171
Garcia, K.A., 298
Garcia-Apreto, N., 77
Gardner, Howard, 328–329
Garland, A.F., 396, 397
Garvey, Catherine, 291, 304
Gately, D.W., 120
Gay parents, 116, 141–143
Gecas, V., 370
Gee, R., 274
Geissinger, S.B., 146
Gelles, Richard, 122, 167, 172, 173, 174, 229
Gelman, R., 291

Gender, 2, 3, 55, 61–63
    in Africa, 69
    birth order and, 348
    career choices and, 410–411
    education and, 340, 415
    effective parenting and, 189
    grandparents and, 421
    identity states and, 373
    language development and, 293
Gender roles, 102
    friendships and, 308
    gender identity and, 303
    household chores and, 119
    individualism and, 70
    self-concept and, 280
    television and, 355
Gender/sexual identity, 303, 371. *See also* Sex-role identification
Generativity, 417
Genetic factors, 199, 243, 246
    in bedwetting, 301
    in growth, 322
    in intelligence, 329
Genevie, 21
Genogram, 98–100
George, C., 169
Gerbner, G., 354
German culture, 7–8, 17, 171, 329
Geroniumus, A.T., 129
Gerson, Randy, 98
Gesell, Arnold, 270–271
Gibran, Kahil, 39
Gil, D.G., 166, 170
Gilligan, Carol, 20
Ginott, Haim, 6, 199, 200, 205–209, 212, 301
Ginsburg, G.S., 49
Ginzberg, E., 410, 411
Glass, J., 406
Glenn, E.N., 81
Glick, P., 408
Global causes, 194, 195
Gnepp, J., 308
Godparents
    Latino, 77, 78
    Puerto Rican, 78
Goldberg, S., 62
Goldberg, W.A., 187
Goldenberg, H., 95
Goldenberg, I., 95
Goldenberg, S., 409
Goldman, 301, 302
Goldman, Daniel, 243, 266
Goldscheider, F.K., 404
Golombok, S., 142, 143
"Good enough," 185, 198
"Goodness of fit," 13, 243–246
Gordon, Thomas, 6, 199, 204, 212–214, 301, 382

Gortmaker, S.L., 323
Gossett, J.T., 106
Gottlieb, 51
Gottman, J.M., 308
Gould, 9
Government assistance, 124–125
Government/laws, 31, 32
    child abuse and, 171
    stepparents and, 139
Goyco, 250
Gralinski, J. Heidi, 297
Grandparents, 111, 116, 418, 419–424
    adolescents and, 112
    African American, 60, 83, 139, 141, 420, 421
    family systems theory and, 101
    great-, 423
    infants and, 255, 256
    as parents, 139–141
    Puerto Rican, 78
Grant, 237
Graziano, A.M., 229, 298
Greece, 62
Green, A.H., 142
Greenberger, E., 187
Greene, A.L., 377
Greenfield, Patricia, 70, 175
Greven, Philip, 230
Grimsley, M.D., 377
Griswold, Robert L., 31–35
Grossmann, Karin, 7–8
Grossmann, Klaus, 7–8
Grotevant, H.D., 349
Gruber, C.P., 310
Guatemala, 251
Guelzow, M., 119
Guilt, 298, 380, 394
    parental, 192
    punishment and, 227
Guisinger, Shan, 8
Gundersen, B.H., 302
Guns, 425
Guttman, 120

Hagestad, G.O., 418
Hale-Benson, J.E., 340
Haley, Jay, 106, 335
Hall, E.G., 323
Hall, Nancy, 167
Hallahan, D., 151, 153
Hallowell, Edward, 160
Hamilton, S.F., 394
Hamner, 18
Hamon, R.R., 418
Handel, Gerald, 73
Hanks, 21
Hanlon, 292
Hardy, Kenneth, 372

Hareven, T.K., 53
Harlow, Harry, 258
Harper, L.V., 306, 322
Harrison, A.O., 82
Hart, C.H., 308
Harter, S., 334, 335
Hartmann, E., 298
Hartshore, T.S., 421
Hartup, W.W., 306, 307, 308
Harwood, R.L., 78
Haskins, R., 312
Havasoupai, 85
Havighurst, R.J., 60
Haviland, 2
Hawkins, A.J., 263
Head Start, 310–312, 315, 425
Health, 189, 284–287, 323
    scale for family, 104–105
Health care, 284–287
    Hmong, 87
    pregnancy prevention as, 130
    social class and, 61
    teenage parents and, 129
Healthy Mothers, Healthy Babies,
    277
Healy, Jane M., 266, 272, 293, 294,
    342
Hearold, S., 355
Heath, 354
Heininger, M.A., 28
Hembrismo, 78
Hendee, 129
Henderson, 343
Henderson, B., 84
Henderson, V.K., 187
Hess, R.D., 67, 293
Hetherington, E. Mavis, 133, 134,
    135–136, 187, 306, 334, 348
Heyman, Ken, 4, 100
Higgins, J.E., 122
Hill, A., 248, 249
Hill, J.P., 376, 378, 379
Hilton, I., 347
Hinde, R.A., 308
Hinduism, 79
Hines, P., 82, 83
Hispanics, 77–78, 79, 128
    as adolescents, 363, 375
    as adult children, 404
    as grandparents, 139, 421
    identity and, 375
    See also Latinos
Hitting, 205, 228–231, 266
HIV, 386
Hmong, 87
Ho, D.Y.F., 79
Hochschild, Arlie, 39, 118, 119
Hoeffer, B., 142
Hofferth, S.L., 128
Hoffman, Lois W., 20, 60, 346,
    348, 349, 415

Hoffman, Martin, 207
Hofstede, G., 70
Hogan, R., 291
Holden, George, 187–189, 230
Holmbeck, G.N., 376, 379
Holmes, 124
Holt, Luther Emmett, 199
Homicide, 386
Homosexual family, 116
Hopi, 89, 323
Hopson, D.P., 82
Hopson, D.S., 82
Houseknecht, 23
Houser, 338
Howard, Jane, 93
Howard-Pitney, 397
Howes, Carollee, 260, 304, 306,
    308, 312
Huggins, S., 143
Hughes, F.P., 282
Huie, 306
Humanist approach, 199, 200
Hunsinger, S., 167
Hunt, C.E., 250
Hunter, F.T., 377
Hunter, R.S., 168
Huston, A.C., 61, 351, 353, 355

Identity, 303, 371–375
Ihinger-Tallman, M., 132
Ilg, Frances L., 270–272
Image-making stage, 14, 15
Images, 237
Imaginary audience, 370
Imitation, 229, 331
Imitative lies, 327
Immigrants, 73–76, 80–82, 328
In-law relationships, 111, 422
In vitro fertilization, 20
Inadequacy, displaying, 217
Independence, 61, 68, 110
    adolescents and, 111, 362, 363,
        379, 380, 385
    adult children and, 403, 404,
        408
    Chinese parents and, 81
    cosleeping and, 251
    disabled children and, 156
    individualism and, 70, 75
    misinterpretation as, 257, 258
    teenage mothers and, 129
India, 2, 73, 79, 168, 322
    abortion in, 62
    social class in, 57
Indians. *See* Native Americans
Indifferent parents, 197–198
Individualism, 32, 53
    adolescents and, 388
    Anglo American parenting and,
        73–76, 94, 97
    collectivism vs., 70–72

European immigrants and,
    73–76
gender roles and, 70
Protestant ethic and, 73–74
Individuality, 106, 107
Individuation, 379, 380
Inductive methods, 207
Indulgence, 197–198
Industry, 318–320
Infanticide, 168
Infants/babies, 5, 6, 9, 14,
    236–277
    alertness in, 246–247, 267
    bonding of parents and, 254–263
    breastfeeding of, 252–254
    child abuse and, 169
    Chinese, 79
    crying by, 61, 247–249, 254, 290
    in family bed, 251–252
    fathers and, 21
    male vs. female, 348
    marital satisfaciton and, 111
    motor development in, 270–274
    newborn. *See* Newborns
    organizations regarding,
        276–277
    parental death and, 163–164
    parental responsibilities to, 16
    physical punishment of, 230
    play by, 262, 272, 304
    reflexes in, 240, 250, 256
    sleeping by, 247–252
    of teenage mothers, 128
Ingraham v. Wright, 167
Inhelder, B., 289
Innocenti, M., 157
Instability, 55
Integrity, 417
Intelligence
    birth order and, 347
    defined, 327–328
    moral, 331
    triarchic theory of, 329–330
    types of, 328–330
    See also Cognition
Interdependent stage, 14, 15
Intergenerational influences,
    98–100, 111, 422
Internal working model, 260
Interpretative stage, 14, 15
Interrelational components, 94
Intrapersonal intelligence, 329
Inuit, 329
Involvement, 108, 187, 188. *See
    also* Uninvolved parenting
Isabell, B.J., 247, 260
Islam, 83, 112
Iso-Ahola, 388
Italian Americans, 407, 421
Italians, 69, 363
Izraeli, D., 118

Jackson, D., 101
Jackson, Joan K., 178
Jacobs, B.S., 293
Jacobs, S., 407
Jacobsen, R.B., 82
Jacobson, Lenore, 336
Japanese, 251, 270, 328
  education and, 342
  infant communication and, 270
  spanking and, 51
Japanese Americans, 72, 73, 79
Jaycox, L.H., 396
Jehovah's Witnesses, 83
Jendrek, Margaret Platt, 140–141
Jersild, A.T., 298
Jessor, Richard, 388–389, 390
Jews, 44, 66–67, 68
  as adolescents, 363
  children of, 112
  Italians compared with, 69–70
Job Corps, 401
Johnson, E.S., 407
Johnson-Powell, G., 74
Johnston, L.D., 391
Jones, B.M., 143
Jones, J.E., 103
Jones, M.C., 368
Joy, 106
Julian, T.W., 83

Kabat-Zinn, Jon, 15, 416
Kabat-Zinn, Myla, 416
Kaczala, C.M., 335
Kaffman, M., 301
Kagan, Jerome, 6–7, 160, 242, 257,
  348
Kagitcibasi, C., 79
Kahn, Michael, 348
Kalawali, 68
Kamukuaka, 2
Kaplan, 326
Karen, B., 9
Karen, Robert, 255
Kashiwagi, 328
Katz, A.J., 120
Kauffman, J., 151, 153
Kaufman, Joan, 168, 172
Kawai, M., 270
Kawasaki, C., 252
Keh, Arceli, 20
Kelder, L.R., 229
Kellam, S.G., 128
Keller, W.D., 256
Kelly, M.L., 396
Kempe, C. Henry, 166, 170
Kennell, John H., 255, 256
Keogh, J., 272
Kerig, P.K., 61
Kerr, M.E., 96
Kibria, Nazli, 53
Kilstrom, N., 168

Kim, 18
Kin selection, 9
Kinesthetic intelligence, 329
King, V., 422
Kinship
  African Americans and, 82–83
  Native Americans and, 86
  Puerto Ricans and, 78
Kinston, Warren, 104, 105
Kirkland, J., 248, 249
Kirkpatrick, M., 143
Kishwar, M., 61
Kivett, V.R., 421
Klackenberg-Larsson, 63
Klaus, Marshall H., 255, 256
Knapp, Caroline, 179
Knowledge, 3, 6, 11
  child maltreatment and, 170
  of children, 11
  fathers', 31
Koeppl, G.K., 342
Koff, E., 367
Kohlberg, Lawrence, 370
Kopp, Claire, 297
Korenman, S., 129
Korner, A.F., 245
Kozol, Jonathan, 333
Krasner, 145
Krestan, Jo Ann, 175, 178
Kruger, 293
Kupersmidt, 342
Kurokawa, M., 283

La Leche League International, 277
Lachman, M.E., 259
Ladd, G.W., 308
LaDue, R., 85
Lagerspetz, K., 354
Lahey, B.B., 347
Lamanna, Mary Ann, 146, 410
Lamb, Michael, 21, 35, 39, 169,
  262
Lamborn, S.D., 381
Lambourne, 319
Langlois, J.H., 348
Language, 340
  culture and, 268, 270, 290
  day care and, 119, 312
  and development of self,
    293–296
  of immigrant children, 73, 80–81
  infants and, 267, 268–270, 272
  learning disabled and, 159
  meaning and, 294, 296
  middle childhood, 325
  social class and, 60
  socialization and, 208
  symbols and, 287, 325
  young children and, 287,
    290–296
  See also Communication

Lansdown, R., 322
Larrick, Nancy, 271
Larson, R., 122, 376, 396
Larzelere, R.E., 229
Lash, J.P., 334
Latin America, 404–405
Latinos, 76–78
  drug use by adolescent, 392
  See also Hispanics
Laws. See Government/laws
Lawson, 21
"Learned helplessness," 227
Learning, 67
  from children, 56–57
  imitation, 229
  observational, 222–223
  of optimism, 192–195
  about parenting, 3–8, 9
  reinforcement and, 222
Learning disabled children,
  159–163
Learning theory, 219
Learning-view theory, 170
Lee, A.M., 323
Lefkowitz, Monroe, 354
Leggett, 335
Leiffer, Aimee, 355
Leinback, M.D., 61
LeMasters, E.E., 5, 6, 12
Lempers, 381
Len, M.W., 230
Lenetz, K., 411
Lerner, J., 245, 348
Lerner, R., 348
LeShan, Eda, 423–424
Lester, B.M., 241
Leung, 349
Levine, D.U., 60
Levine, J., 348
Levinson, Daniel, 355, 404
Levy-Shiff, R., 238
Lew, Amy, 218, 220
Lewis, M., 293
Lewis, J.M., 61, 62, 107, 187
Lieberman, A.F., 258, 306
Liebert, R.M., 351
Lin, Chin-Yau Cindy, 80, 81
Lin, K.S., 408
Linguistic intelligence, 328
Lindgren, 60
Lino, Mark, 59
Lips, H., 308
Lipsitt, Lewis, 250
Listening, 207–211
Littenberg, R., 257
Living-with grandparents, 139,
  140, 141
Loader, P., 104, 105
Locke, John, 11, 17
Loeber, R., 392
Logan, D.D., 367

Logical-mathematical intelligence, 328
Lorenz, Konrad, 9, 29
Love, 11, 12, 30, 188, 208, 424
  and acceptance, 184, 185
  day care and, 312
  discipline and, 225
  expressing, 184
  grandparents and, 423, 424
  modeling and, 223
  punishment vs., 217
  siblings and, 349, 350
  transitional objects of, 262
Lowe, Marianne, 216, 304
Lowen, 136
Lowry, G.H., 281, 320
Lozoff, B., 252
Luckasson, T., 159
Luepnitz, Deborah Anna, 31
Lueptow, L.B., 411
Lum, 79
Lynn, S.J., 229
Lyons, N.P., 142

MacFarlane, A., 255
MacFarlane, K., 143
Machismo, 78
MacIver, D., 334
MacKinnon, C., 322
Macrosystem, 50–51, 171, 172
Mahler, M.S., 145
Main, Mary, 145, 258, 259
Malatesta, C.Z., 247
Malgady, 73
Malik, M.M., 170
Malina, R.M., 365
Maltreatment, 165–174
  myths about, 167–168
  prevention of, 171–172
Manaster, G.L., 421
Mangione, Jerre, 69, 70
Mannie, S., 293
Manus, 203
Maratsos, Michael, 291
Marcenko, M., 157
Marcia, James, 372–374
Margolies, 21
Marianismo, 78
Marital class, 3
Marital relationship, 186–187, 259
  adolescents and, 364
  alcoholism and, 175
  after children become adults, 403, 407, 417–424
  infants and, 259, 260, 263
Marotz, L., 292
Marriage, 18, 22–23
  during college, 416–417
  impact of, 2
  inter-, 72, 75, 89
  satisfaction in, 111

Marshall, Thurgood, 190
Martin, J.A., 10, 197, 207
Maruyama, G., 347
Mason, R., 122
Matas, L., 257
Mathematical intelligence, 328
Matheny, 283
Mathew, R.J., 175
Matthews, S.H., 421
Mauck, 162
Mayan culture, 251, 252
Mazlish, Elaine, 6, 199, 206–211, 301, 302, 350
Mazzie, 269
McAdoo, J.B., 83
McAdoo, J.L., 83
McAnaarney, 129
McBride, James, 66–67, 68, 378
McCartney, Kathleen, 246
McCullough, 406, 407
McGhee, Paul, 306
McGill, D., 363
McGill University study, 108–109
McGoldrick, Monica, 75, 89, 93, 98, 100, 109–110, 111, 112, 137, 364, 403
McHale, S., 50
McKay, Gary, 217
Mckee, L., 247
McKenna, James, 250
McKie, 320
McKinney, J.D., 160
McLoughlin, J., 162
McLoyd, Vonnie, 50, 60
McMaster Model of Family Functioning, 108–109
McNamara, J.R., 229
Mead, Margaret, 4, 100, 203, 216, 299, 416–417
Media
  adolescents and, 387
  child abuse and, 172
  organizations regarding, 358
Media Research Center, 352
Medicaid, 125
Melas, P.S., 302
Menaghan, E.G., 119
Menken, 405
Mental illness, 116, 140, 141
  in adolescents, 380, 386
  child abuse and, 170
  in children, 151
  warding off, 192
Menyuk, 291
Meredith, Howard, 282, 322
Meredith, S., 274
Meredith, W.H., 23
Merrill, E.J., 170
Mertz, M., 423
Mesosystem, 48, 49

Mexican American Cultural Center, 91
Mexican Americans, 76, 77, 328
Mexicans, 328, 404
Meyer, D.R., 125
Meyers, J., 157
Microsystem, 47–48, 171, 172
  attachment and, 259–261
Middle childhood, 16, 317–358
  cognitive development in, 320–331
  physical changes in, 320–324
  self-control and, 302
  self-esteem in, 334–342
  See also School-age children
Middle class, 30, 58, 60, 61, 119, 251
  adolescents of, 385
  adult children of, 408
  African Americans and, 84
  birth order and, 347
  fathers of, 33, 34
  language development and, 293
  mothers of, 37–38
  parenting style of, 198
  television and, 354
Midgley, C., 385
Milgram, J.I., 407
Miller, Alice, 17, 205
Miller, B.C., 129
Miller, L., 104, 105
Miller, N., 347
Miller, R.B., 406
Miller, S.A., 238
Millman, H.L., 335
Mills, D., 133
Milne, Alan Alexander, 279
Minkler, M., 141
Minority adolescents, identity and, 374–375
Minority children, education and, 340
Minority college students, 414
Minority grandparents, 420
Minton, C., 348
Minuchin, Salvador, 101, 105–106, 333
Mirandé, A., 83
Mirroring, 188, 208, 232
Misbehavior, 213–215, 217, 226
"Mistaken goals," 217
Mitchell, G., 61
Modeling, 110, 188, 190, 222–223
  early childhood and, 280
  friendships and, 308
  gender roles and, 303
  grandparents and, 423
  language and, 292
  lying and, 327, 331
  of perfection, 232
  See also Parental models

Models/methods, 202–235
  behavior change (ABC model),
    194
  behavioral, 220
  development, 2
  family assessment, 155
  family systems, 231, 233. *See also*
    Family systems theory
  images of parenting, 14–15
  no-effect, 355
  parent training, 6–7, 199
  process, 186
  psychiatric, 170
  social, 170–171
Moely, B., 247
Moen, P., 125
Moitoza, E., 363
"Momism," 35
Montemayor, R., 376, 378, 379, 380
Montessori, Maria, 282, 290,
  298–299
Moore, K.A., 129
Moore, Nelwyn, 189, 190
Moral behavior, 331, 370, 372
Morelli, G., 251
Morgan, P.S., 129
Morreale, Ben, 69, 70
Mortimer, Jeyland T., 343, 344
Moskowitz, B.A., 269
Moss, H.A., 293, 348
Mother-in-law, 111, 422
Motherese, 269–270
Mothers, 20–22, 111
  adolescents and, 376–377, 378,
    379
  adult children and, 407, 411,
    414
  African American/black, 38, 82,
    83–84, 128
  breastfeeding by, 252–254
  child abuse by, 168, 169
  children's gender and, 62
  children's language and, 292. *See
    also* Motherese
  Chinese, 16, 79, 80
  depressed, 396. *See also*
    Depression
  of disabled children, 155
  "good," 35, 37, 38
  grandparents and, 422
  historical changes in regard to,
    35–40
  household chores and, 237–238
  infants and, 237–238, 244–249,
    263
  Latino, 77
  microsystem and, 48
  mid-life, 405
  in Middle Ages, 36
  modern, 38–40
  as new parents, 238, 239

older/menopausal, 56, 112
  "second shift" of, 35, 39, 118
  stay-at-home, 38
  teenage. *See* Teenage mothers
  Victorian, 37–38
  widowed, 124–125
  working. *See* Working mothers
Mounts, N., 381
Movies/films, 171
Moynihan, Daniel, 34
Moynihan Report, 34, 35
Multi-ethnicity, 72–73
Musical intelligence, 328
"Multiracial," 81
Mundugumor, 203
Mundurucu, 2
Muzio, J.N., 246
Myer, Isabel Briggs, 414

NAEYC. *See* National Association
  for the Education of Young
  Children (NAFYC)
Namaste, K.A., 229
National Association for Family
  Day Care, 315
National Association for the Edu-
  cation of Young Children
  (NAEYC), 358
National Black Child Development
  Institute, 91
National Center for Clinical
  Infant Programs, 276
National Coalition Against
  Domestic Violence, 114
National Committee on Youth Sui-
  cide, 401
National Council on Crime and
  Delinquency, 401
National Head Start Association,
  315
National Information Center for
  Children and Youth with
  Handicaps, 156
National Organization of Adoles-
  cent Pregnancy and Parenting,
  401
National Sudden Infant Death Syn-
  drome Clearinghouse, 277
National Sudden Infant Death Syn-
  drome Foundation (NSIDSF),
  277
Nations/countries
  adolescents in different, 376
  Africa, 53–54
  America, 54
  birth rate in, 45
  European, 285
  health care in different, 285
  Netherlands, 130
  See also Culture(s); Ethnicity;
    Race

Native Americans, 62, 85–89, 323
  as adolescents, 375
  identity and, 375
  organization regarding, 91
  suicide by adolescent, 397
Naturalist intelligence, 329
Navaho, 85
Nayar culture, 2
Neglectful parents, 35, 387
  effective vs., 184, 185
  See also Child neglect;
    Permissiveness
Negotiation, with adolescents, 385
Nelson, Katherine, 292
Netherlands, 130
Neugarten, B.L., 420
Neumann, Sigmund, 51
New Guinea, 2, 68, 203
New York Longitudinial Study
  (NYLS), 243–245
Newberger, C.M., 166, 171
Newberger, E., 166, 171
Newborns, 238–240, 246–247,
  263–274
  attachment in, 255, 256
  bonding of, 255
  nutrition for, 252
  SIDS in, 249–251, 277
Nguyen, T., 53
Niche-picking, 246
Nigeria, 4
Night terrors, 298
Nightmares, 298
Nitz, V., 245
No-effect model, 355
Noller, P., 380
Norfleet, M.A., 18
Nottelmann, E.D., 334, 369
NSIDSF. *See* National Sudden
  Infant Death Syndrome
  Foundation (NSIDSF)
Nuclear family, 116, 117
  death in, 163
Nugent, J.K., 240
Nursery schools, 310
Nurturance, 5, 10–11
  adoption and, 146
  alcoholism and, 175
  day care and, 260, 312
  discipline and, 225
  family health scale and, 105
  fathers and, 21, 31, 32, 35
  girl children and, 336, 344
  in middle childhood, 319
Nurturing stage, 14, 15
NYLS. *See* New York Longitudinial
  Study (NYLS)

O'Hara, M.W., 238
O'Malley, P.M., 391
Obradovich, S., 61

Observational learning, 222–223
Offer, D., 376, 386
Offer, J.B., 376
Okagaki, Lynn, 328
Olson, D.H., 125
On-looker play, 305, 306
Ontogenetic level, 171, 172
Operant conditioning, 220
Optimism, 192–195
Orford, J., 175
Osgood, C.E., 268
Owen, M.T., 187

Page, R.M., 392
Pagelow, M.D., 142
Pai, 8
Paikoff, R.L., 376
Palladino, Grace, 361–362
Panterese, 269–270
Papernow, 133
Papini, D.R., 380
Parallel play, 305, 306
Parcel, G.S., 324
Parcel, T.L., 119
Parent, decision to, 18–22
Parent-child mix, 3
Parent-child relationship, 199
    as adult to adult, 406–413
    bidirectionality of, 5, 11–13,
        241–242
    changes in, 13–16
    chronosystem and, 49
    complexity of, 233
    divorce and. See Divorce
    on family health scale, 104
    family violence and, 172. See also
        Violence
    historical change in, 424–425
    historical events and, 53
    historical setting of, 29
    infant bonding and, 254–263
    love in, 11
    Native American, 86
    parent training and, 6
    parenting style and, 198. See also
        Parenting styles
    physical appearance and, 348
    social class and, 60
    social context of, 186, 216
    Spock and, 237
    in stepfamilies, 133, 135, 138
    temperament and, 5, 11–13
    work overload and, 119
Parent training/education, 5, 6, 15,
    199
    family systems approach to, 231
    fathers and, 21
    orientations for, 6
Parental control, 185–186. See also
    Control

Parental expectations, 14, 55, 119,
    196–198
    for adolescents, 362–364
    adult children and, 403, 406,
        407, 408–409, 414
    Asian, 78
    birth order and, 347–348
    for boys vs. girls, 336, 338
    about children's gender, 61, 62
    as demandedness, 10
    development and, 347–348
    effective parenting and, 189
    internalizing of, 207
    modeling and, 223
    romantic marital relationship
        and, 23
    play and, 323
    self-esteem and, 334–335
    social class and, 60–61
Parental models, 34, 170, 222–223
    child abuse and, 169
    language and, 292
    See also Modeling
Parental perceptions, 327–328,
    334
Parental responsibility, 40, 111,
    216–219
    children's age and, 11, 15–16
Parental support, 185–186
Parental thinking, distorted, 193
"Parentified" children, 177, 232
Parenting
    of adolescents. See entries begin-
        ning Adolescent
    of adult children. See Adult
        children
    active, 201, 219
    art of, 199
    aspects of, 8–10
    "bad," 9
    of boys vs. girls, 61–62. See also
        Gender
    co-, 77
    context of, 2–3, 43–64, 233
    culture and. See Culture(s);
        Nations/countries
    defining, 8–16
    effective, 183–201
    of elderly parents, 405, 427
    ethnicity and. See Ethnicity;
        Multi-ethnicity; Race
    examples of variation in, 2
    experience of, 1–42, 100,
        424–425
    experts/advice on, 16–17, 199,
        203, 205
    family maps and, 100
    goals of, 5, 185, 189, 206
    "good," 9, 170, 183, 185
    "good-enough," 185, 198

historical changes in regard to,
    28–40, 51
humane, 4, 6, 204–216
of infants. See Infants/babies
influences on, 2–3
learning about, 3–8, 9. See also
    Parent training/education
mid-life, 363–364
models of. See Models/methods
multiple, 86
myths of, 12
into old age, 418–419
organizations regarding, 41–42,
    148, 180–181, 201, 276–277,
    401, 427
patterns of, 184–190
of preschool children. See
    Preschool children
professional help for, 232
Puritan, 28–29
race and, 81–85. See also Discrim-
    ination; Ethnicity; Racism
research on, 6–8, 199
satisfaction in, 23
of school-age children. See Mid-
    dle childhood; School-age chil-
    dren
special, 139–146
special issues of, 149–181
study of, 4, 5–8, 199
support groups for, 6, 129. See
    also Social support
synchronicity of, 243–246
in transition. See Transitions
of young child, 278–315
See also Children; Parent-child
    relationship
Parenting Effectiveness Training
    (PET), 199, 201, 204, 211–213
Parenting skills. See Knowledge;
    Skills
Parenting styles, 5, 10–11, 34,
    195–198
    adolescents and, 373, 381, 383,
        392
    African American, 83
    children's gender and, 62
    Chinese, 79
    family maps and, 98
    Latino, 77
    responsibility and, 216
    self-esteem and, 335
Parents
    autonomous-secure, 259
    depressed, 395–396. See also
        Depression
    dismissing, 259
    disorganized, 259
    elderly, 405, 418–419, 427
    gay, 116, 141–143

grandparents as, 139–141
homosexual, 116
narcissistic, 187
new, 238
perfectionist, 192
preoccupied, 259
same-sex, 120
single. *See* Single fathers; Single mothers; Single parents
teenage, 116. *See also* Teenage fathers; Teenage mothers
undirected, 198
unengaged, 198
violence against, 174
Parents Anonymous, 171
Parents Without Partners, 148
Parham, T., 83
Paris, S.G., 291
Parke, R.D., 169, 334, 346, 348
Parker, J.G., 308, 343
Parker, F., 311
Parsons, J.E., 335
Parten, Mildred, 305, 306
Pasley, K., 132
Passive aggressiveness, 227
Patterson, Charlotte J., 143
Patterson, Gerald, 125, 342, 382, 396
Pearce, J.K., 363
Peay, L., 311
Peck, M. Scott, 56
Peele, S., 175
Peer counseling, 129
Peers. *See* Adolescent peers; Children's peers
Pennington, B.F., 160
Pennsylvania Project, 260
Permanence, 193–195
Permissiveness, 77, 197–198, 205
adolescents and, 374, 381, 383, 392
Perry Preschool, 311
Personal fable, 129, 370, 388
Personal history, 3
Personality, 2, 3, 186
child abuse and, 170, 171
adolescents and, 389, 398
bedwetting and, 301
discipline and, 224
drug use and, 391, 398
effective parenting and, 183, 189
infant attachment and adult, 260
of infants, 243–245, 263
puberty and, 369
television and, 354
Personalization, 193–194
Perspective-taking, 342
Pervasiveness, 193–194
Pessimism, 194–195

PET. *See* Parenting Effectiveness Training (PET)
Peters, 83
Peterson, A.C., 411
Peterson, P.L., 386, 392
Petrosko, J., 162
Pettit, G.S., 60, 171
Phillips, D.A., 334, 335
Phinney, Jean, 374–375
Phobias, 96, 175, 298
Physical disorders, 96
Physical fitness, 323–324
Physical maltreatment, 167
Physical punishment, 17, 229
child abuse and, 167, 171, 172
experiment in, 229
social class and, 61
See also Child abuse; Corporal punishment; Spanking
Piaget, Jean, 288–289, 291, 306, 369
Pill, C., 135
Pillemer, K., 419
Pine, F., 145
Pinon, M.R., 351
Piotrkowski, D., 311
Planned Parenthood Federation of America, 20, 41
Play
by boys vs. girls, 322–323
children's gender and, 61
creativity and, 307
disabled children and, 155
divorce and, 306
in early childhood, 280, 304–308, 332
friendships and, 308
gay parents and children's, 142
infants and, 272, 304
motor development and, 282, 322–323
safety and, 283, 284, 286
television and, 355
Pletsch, 77
Pliner, P., 343
Plomin, Robert, 345, 350
Poffenberger, T., 322
Pogatshynick, L.D., 61
Pogrebin, Letty Cottin, 116, 136
"Poisonous pedagogy," 205
Polansky, N.A., 170, 171
Politics, 30, 374
Pollock, Carl B., 168, 170
Pomerleau, 336
Popkin, Michael, 6, 199, 219
Portes, Alejandro, 73
Portuguese, 363
Post, G., 394
Post partum depression, 256

Post traumatic stress syndrome, 230
Poteat, G.M., 312
Poussaint, Alvin, F., 84
Poverty, 29–30, 425
abusive punishment and, 122
African Americans and, 60, 83
childhood illness and, 286
schools and, 333–334
single fathers and, 125
single mothers and, 122
Powell, B., 121
Powell, Colin, 360
Power, 106, 213
adolescents and, 382
attachment and, 257
non-, 214
punishment and, 226, 227
pursuit of, 217
scapegoat child and, 168
Power-assertive methods, 207
Poznansky, 298
Praise, 17, 211, 220, 225
moral behavior and, 331
Prejudice, modeling and, 223
Preoperational stage, 325
Preschool children, 309–313
attention span of, 326
criticism of, 195
death and, 164
development of, 281–282
enrichment programs for, 310–312
friendships of, 307, 308
language of, 290–293
parental responsibilities to, 16
play by, 306. *See also* Play
spanking of, 229, 230
television and, 351
as toddlers, 282
Pressman, R.M., 187
Preto, Nydia Garcia, 363, 380
Price, G.M., 308
Price, M., 141
Problem ownership, 214, 215
Problem solving, 6, 103, 105–109, 108
adolescents and, 380, 396
communication and, 215
cognitive development and, 325, 326
culture and, 328
effective parenting and, 189
on family health scale, 105
family meetings for, 220
family systems theory and, 233
feelings and, 209
in healthy family, 110
mirroring and, 208
(continued)

Problem solving *(continued)*
  parent education programs and,
    199
  peer relationships and, 343
  perspective-taking and, 342
  self-esteem and, 335
  suicide and, 396
  television and, 355
Protestant ethic, 73–74
Protestant Reformation, 37
Protestants, 29, 76
  Korean American, 79
  See also Baptists; Christians, chil-
    dren of; Puritans
Pseudostupidity, 370
Psychiatric model, 170
Psychological disorders, 96
  in adolescents, 371
  alcoholic parents and, 175
  in children, 143, 150, 151
  enrichment programs and, 311
  gay parents and, 143
  siblings and, 349
  suicide and, 397
Psychological factors, 8, 9,
    186–187, 188
  day care and, 312
  genetic and, 199
  physical growth and, 282
  single mothers and, 125
Psychological immunization, 192
Psychological maltreatment, 167
Psychological moratorium, 371
Puerto Ricans, 76, 77–78
Punishment
  abusive, 122
  adolescents and, 382
  consequences vs., 217
  discipline vs., 225–228. *See also*
    Discipline
  misbehavior and, 217, 226
  moral behavior and, 331
  negative reinforcement vs., 220
  physical. *See* Physical punish-
    ment; Spanking
  reward and, 219–231
  severe, 227
  temperament and, 243
  time out for, 224, 225, 227
Puritans, 28–29

Race, 81–85
  grandparents and, 420
  mixed, 81
Racism, 34, 82
Radovsky, V., 351
Rahner, E., 319
Ramey, C.T., 311
Ratcliffe, 320
Ratey, John, 160
Reale, G., 355

Rebelsky, 21, 293
Recognition, 218, 335
  siblings and, 349
Reconstituted family, 131
Regionality, 3
Reich, P.A., 269
Reinforcement, 219, 220
  genetics and, 246
  language and, 292
  moral behavior and, 331
  toilet training and, 300
  vicarious, 223
Rejection, 8, 184, 185, 342–343
  adolescents and, 374
  siblings and, 349
Relationships, 106–107, 111
  coalition and, 105
  parent-child. *See* Parent-child
    relationship
  sibling, 104
Relative deprivation, 346
Religion, 3, 19, 30, 112
  adolescents and, 374
  African American, 83
  ancestor worship in, 52, 78
  birth rate and, 44, 45
  child abuse and, 168
  motherhood and, 36, 37
  See also Buddhism; Catholics;
    Christians, children of;
    Confucianism; Hinduism;
    Islam; Jehovah's Witnesses;
    Jews; Protestants; Puritans
Remarriage, 132
  grandparents and, 421
  roles after, 131, 137
  See also Blended family; Stepfam-
    ily; Stepparents
Respect, 78, 189, 297, 424
  adult children and, 403, 404
  for animals, 332
  for children, 11
  discipline and, 225
  family meetings and, 220
  healthy families and, 106, 110
  for individuality, 106, 205
  moral behavior and, 331
  self-esteem and, 335
Responsibility, 106, 216–219
  of adolescents, 385
  See also Children's repon-sibility;
    Parental responsibility
Responsiveness, 10–11, 196–198
  affective, 108
Revenge, 217. *See also* Vengeful
  behaviors/lies
Rewards, 219–231, 229
  bedwetting and, 301
  moral behavior and, 331
  temperament and, 243
  in toilet training, 300

Rice, Mabel, 353–354
Richards, Maryse H. 376, 396
Richards, W., 170
Richardson, R., 129
Riedmann, Agnes, 146, 410
Rituals, 88, 89
  adolescents and, 111, 361,
    370–371, 388
  Asian, 79
Rivera, F., 84
Roberts, Thomas W., 231, 233
Robertson, J.F., 421
Robinson, 34
Robson, W.L.M., 349
Roche, A.F., 322
Rockwell, R., 252
Rodin, J., 392
Rodning, 306
Roe, Annie, 347
Roe, K.M., 141
Roffwarg, H.P., 246
Roggman, L.A., 380
Rogler, 73, 78
Rohner, Ronald P., 185, 198, 229,
    230
Rohner, E.C., 198
Role conflict, 118
Role confusion/diffusion,
    370–371
Role models. *See* Modeling;
    Parental models
Rolling, B., 263
Roosa, M., 128
Rosenberg, Ben, 347
Rosenthal, Robert, 336, 375
Ross, H., 407
Rossi, A.S., 422
Rossi, P.H., 422
Rothbart, M.K., 347
Rothenberg, M., 21, 251
Rousseau, Jean Jacques, 16–17
Rovee-Collier, 250
Rovin, Michael, 119
Rovine, M.J., 23, 260, 263
Ruble, D.N., 111, 367
Rule-governed system, 101–102
Rules, 224–225, 297
  adolescents and, 368, 370,
    385
  middle childhood and, 332,
    333
Rumbaut, Ruben, 73
Rush, J., 292
Russell, D., 167
Rutenberg, S.K., 406, 407
Rutter, M., 386

Sachs, 146
Sack, W.H., 122
Sadker, Myra and David, 338,
    340

Sadowski, C., 396
Safety, 284–287, 297, 315
Sager, C., 134, 380
St.Peters, Michele, 351, 352
Saluter, 139
Same-sex parenting, 120
Sandburg, Carl, 336
Sanders, G., 421
Sanders, K.M., 322
Sandwich generation, 405
Santrock, John W., 384, 397
Sater, G.M., 160
Satir, Virginia, 107
Savin-Williams, 369
Sawin, 346, 348
Scarr, Sandra, 246
Schacter, S., 347
Schaefer, C.E., 284, 335
Schaffer, Rudolph, 245
Schieffelin, 293
Schizophrenia, 96, 107
Schmidt, C.R., 291
Schmidt, M.G., 418
Schnaiberg, A., 409
Schoner-Reichl, 386
School, 332–334, 425
    adolescents and, 387
    adult children and, 404, 405,
        414–417
    boys vs. girls at, 338, 340
    physical punishment in,
        167
    traditional vs. open classroom
        in, 333
    See also Education
School-age children, 316–358
    attention span of, 326
    child abuse and, 170
    chronosystem and, 47–49
    death and, 164–165
    nutrition of, 324
    parental responsibilities to, 16
    success for, 337
    as teenage parents, 130
    television and, 351
    See also Middle childhood
School dropouts, 372, 374
Schreber, Daniel, 17
Schulenberg, J., 143
Schwebel, 120
Scott, W.J., 88
Sears, W., 232
Sears, M., 232
Sebald, H., 377
"Second shift," 35, 39, 118
Secure attachment, 257, 258, 260,
    306
    friendships and, 308
Seff, M., 370
Segal, R., 82
Self-awareness, 189–190

Self-concept, 280, 296
    college education and, 415
    self-esteem and, 334
    See also Development, of self
Self-control, 280, 296–303
    temper tantrums and, 301, 302
Self-defeating beliefs, 218
Self-discipline, 213–215, 225
Self-esteem, 189, 209, 334–342
    in adolescents, 368, 369, 380,
        381, 389
    alcoholic parents and, 175
    attachment and, 258
    communication and, 209, 211,
        213
    depression and, 192
    discipline and, 225
    fears and, 298
    gay parents and children's, 143
    identity and, 373, 374
    maltreatment and, 167
    obesity and, 324
    parenting style and, 198
    physical punishment and, 229
    self-discipline and, 213
    "special education" and, 160
    temper tantrums and, 301
Self-expression, 106. See also Emo-
    tions, expression of
Seligman, Martin, 192–194, 199,
    227
Selman, R.L., 308
Selzer, J.A., 126
Sensitivity, 106, 187, 188, 308, 342
Separation anxiety, 256, 257
Serpell, 328
Sex education, 20
Sex-role identification, 32. See also
    Gender/sexual identity
Sexism, 40
Sexual abuse, 35, 53, 143, 145, 167
Sexual maltreatment, 167. See also
    Child abuse, sexual
Sexuality, 85
    adolescents and, 366–368, 370,
        371, 373, 388
    family bed and, 299
    parenting style and children's,
        198
    punishment and, 227
    on television, 54
    young children and, 302–303
Sexually transmitted diseases, 386
Shannon, D.C., 250, 287
Shapiro, Ester, 163–165, 333
Shatz, M., 270, 291
Shedler, J., 392
Sherman, E., 293, 407
Shiode, D., 407
Shipman, V.C., 293
SI. See Survivors Insurance (SI)

"Sibling bond," 348
Sibling rivalry, 216, 349–350
Siblings, 344–350
    as adult children, 407
    attachment and, 97
    of disabled children, 155
    family health scale and, 104
    family violence and, 172, 173
    female vs. male, 348
    infants and, 255
    physical punishment and, 229
SIDS. See Sudden infant death syn-
    drome (SIDS)
Siegal, I.E., 338
Sigel, 78
Silberman, M., 189
Silberstein, L., 392
Silva, 319
Silverman, 164
Simons, R.L., 170, 229
Sinclair, 281
Singer, Dorothy, 351, 354–356
Singer, Jerome, 351, 354–356
Singer, L.M., 255
Single fathers, 120, 122, 125–126
    African American, 84
    childcare and, 262
Single mothers
    adolescents and, 381
    African American, 82
    myths about, 122
    Puerto Rican, 78
    stress and, 123–125
Single parents, 5, 116, 119–122
    adolescents and, 381
    allowances and, 344
    authoritative, 198
    organization for, 148
Sirignano, S., 259
Sizer, Theodore, 385
Skar, J.E., 302
Skills, 3, 6, 129, 186, 205
    "bag full of," 203
    fathers', 31
    spatial, 336
Skinner, B.F., 220, 222, 335
Skinner box, 226
Slaby, R.G., 169
Slade, A., 257
Slavin, Robert E., 159, 161
Sleeping
    co-, 251–252, 299
    by infants, 247–252
    by young children, 296–303
Slobin, Dan, 290
Slote, W.H., 52
Smith, 18, 19
Smith, D.S., 159
Smith, D.W., 282
Smith, M.L., 302, 306
Smith, S.D., 160

Smollar, 370
Snellman, 338
Snipp, C.M., _87
Sobol, A.M., 323
Social class, 30, 57–61, 199
    Chinese American, 81
    effective parenting and, 183, 189
    grandparents and, 420
Social development, 308, 310
    day care and, 312
    television and, 355
Social goals, children's gender
        and, 61
Social groups, 9
Social interaction, 187, 188, 270
Social learning theory, 187, 188,
        270, 292
    moral behavior and, 331
Social lies, 327
Social model, 170–171
Social network, 3
Social skills, 342
    adolescents and, 383
    play and, 304–308
Social speech, 291
Social support, 6, 168
    adolescents and, 397
    child abuse and, 171
    disabled children and, 157–158
    infants and, 260
    suicide and, 397
Social/emotional problems, 162
Socialization, 10–11, 45–51,
        94–104
    allowance and, 344
    day care and, 119
    eating disorders and, 392
    family health scale and, 105
    friendship and, 307, 308
    gender and, 96–97
    individualism and, 76
    infant, 243
    language and, 208
    Latino, 77
    parenting styles and, 196, 198
    play and, 304
    self-concept and, 280
    social class and, 61
Society for the Prevention of Cru-
        elty to Children, 166
Socioeconomic class, 3, 34, 57–61
    adolescents and, 385, 392
    adult children and, 405
    Anglo American parenting and,
        76
    child abuse and, 168
    day care and, 312
    motherhood and, 37–38
    SIDS and, 250
    working mothers and, 38
Sociopathy, 107

Soldier, 88
Solitary play, 305, 306
Solomon, G., 284
Solomon, J., 169
Soloway, 18, 19
Solution messages, 213
South America, 2
South Pacific, 62, 203
Spanish culture, 78, 82
Spanking, 30, 51, 196, 228–231,
        232
    frequency of, 229
Sparling, J.J., 311
Spatial intelliegence, 328
"Special education" classes, 160
Specific cause, 194, 195
Speece, D.L., 160
Spencer, M.B., 61
Spirituality, 112
    African American, 83
    Chinese, 80
    Native American, 89
Spitze, G., 118
Spock, Benjamin, 17, 21, 38, 237,
        251, 252, 254, 299
Spousal abuse, child abuse and, 171
Sprafkin, J., 351
Sprey, J., 421
Springle, H., 354
Sroufe, Alan, 5, 256–257, 258
Stability, 133, 389
Stagnation, 417
Starfield, B., 286
Stark, 268
Staso, William, 267
Steele, Brandt G., 168, 170
Stein, K.F., 408
Stein, Althea, 355
Steinberg, Lawrence, 381
Steinem, Gloria, 2
Steinglass, P., 175
Steinmetz, Suzanne, 173, 174, 229,
        408
STEP. *See* Systematic Training for
        Effective Parenting (STEP)
Step Family Foundation, 148
Stepfamily, 132, 148, 381
Stepfamily Association of America,
        148
Stepgrandparents, 421
Stepparents, 5, 7, 131–139
    infants and, 256
    organizations regarding, 148
Stereotypes, 107, 355
Stern, Daniel, 237, 290, 293, 296,
        304, 326
Sternberg, Robert, 328, 329,
        339–340, 376
Stierlin, Helm, 107, 380
Stinnet, N., 23
Stipek, D.J., 334

Stipp, H.H., 344
Stoneman, 259, 322
Stranger anxiety, 256, 257
Straus, Murray, 167, 173, 174, 228,
        229, 230
Stress, 6, 22–23, 55, 56
    adolescents and, 370, 380, 381,
        391, 394, 395
    avoidant children and, 8
    child abuse and, 170, 171, 173
    childhood illness and, 287
    children and, 146
    day care and, 312
    depression and, 395, 396
    disabled children and, 154, 157
    drug use and, 391
    eating disorders and, 394
    family socialization and, 96, 97
    grandparents and, 141
    healthy families and, 110
    infants and, 247–249, 252, 260,
        267
    physical punishment and, 230
    of poverty, 83, 122
    self-control and, 302
    single fathers and, 126
    single mothers and, 125
    unemployed fathers and, 50
    work overload and, 119, 125
Striegel-Moore, R., 392
Stringer, S.A., 170
Strong, Bryan, 27, 154, 157
Substance abuse
    by adolescents, 389–392, 395,
        396
    alcoholic parents and, 175
    child abuse and, 170
    organizations regarding, 401
    suicide and, 396
Sudden infant death syndrome
        (SIDS), 249–251, 277
Sugden, D., 272
Suicide, 96, 205
    adolescent/teenage, 55, 386, 395,
        396–398, 401
    Chinese, 80
    Native American, 85, 86
    organization regarding, 401
    physical punishment and, 230
Suitor, 419
Sung, Betty Lee, 81
"Supermom," 39–40
Supportive control, 198
Suppression, 227
Survivors Insurance (SI), 124–125
Suter, 60
Sutherland, 271
Sutton-Smith, Brian, 347
Sweden, 62, 171
Sweeney, P., 84
Swiss, D., 118

Symbols, 287, 325
Systematic Training for Effective
    Parenting (STEP), 199
Szasz, C.M., 86

Tafoya, Nadine, 86
Takahashi, 251
Tangney, J.P., 355
Tanner, James, 282, 320, 365
Taub, D.E., 393
Taylor, D.G., 260
Taylor, R.J., 421
Tchambuli, 203
Teaching, 187, 188, 223
Teddy bears, 252, 261
Teen pregnancy, 382, 401
Teenage fathers, 34, 84, 130
Teenage mothers, 19–20, 122–123,
    127–130
    grandparents and, 140
    income of, 58
Teenage parents, 116
Teenage runaways, 382
Teenagers. *See*
    Adolescents/teenagers
Teens Teaching AIDS Prevention,
    401
Telegraphic speech, 290
Television, 33, 54, 171, 350–356
    nutrition and, 324
    organizations regarding, 358
    play and, 287
Temper tantrums, 94, 301–302,
    308
Temperament, 3, 5, 11–13
    adolescent, 396
    attachment and, 259
    of babies, 241–243, 247, 263
    child abuse and, 171
    components of, 244
    impact on marriage of children's,
        23
    infant attachment and, 260–261
    types of, 242–243
Thevenin, Tine, 299
Thinking, distorted parental, 193
Thomas, 421
Thomas, Alexander, 13, 243–245,
    381
Thompson, R.A., 258
Thurer, Shari L., 36, 38–39
Tiede, 173
Tillitski, 126
Timberlawn-Beavers study, 106,
    107
Time out, 224, 225, 227
Tinbergen, Niko, 171
Tizard, B., 258
Tobacco use, 389, 390, 391
Toda, S., 270
Toddlers, 282, 290

Togetherness, 95, 96
Toilet training, 300–301
Tolerance, 110, 415
Tomasello, 270, 293
Toner, I., 302
Toys, 61, 261–262, 355
Tradition, 3–4, 6
Transactional process, 94, 106
Transitional object, 252, 261–262
Transitions, 109–148, 237–238
    adolescents and, 111, 363, 370,
        375–376, 384–385
    to day care/preschool, 313
    mid-life, 112
    SIDS and, 250
T'rea, S.J., 418
Treeger, Madge, 415
Triangles, 97, 100
Trivette, C., 158
Trust, 257
    alcoholism and, 715
    stepparents and, 133, 135, 138
Trute, B., 157
Trygstad, , 421
Two-career/dual-income family,
    54, 55, 58, 118–119
    child care by fathers in, 262
    Chinese, 81
Two-parent family, 116–119, 381
    children's allowance and, 344
    dual-career and dual-income,
        118–119
    economics and, 61, 124
Tucker, Nicholas, 29, 30
Tulkin, S., 257
Turner, R.J., 128

Undirective parents, 198
Unemployment/employment, 55,
    140, 187
    adolescents and, 380
    African Americans and, 84
    adult children and, 404
    male vs. female children and,
        348
    Native Americans and, 85, 86
    organization regarding, 401
    unwed mothers and, 122
    See also Working fathers; Work-
        ing mothers
Unengaged parents, 198
Unger, 130
Uninvolved parenting, 197
United States/America, 39, 51, 53
    adolescents in, 361–362, 388,
        394
    Anglo American parenting in,
        73–76, 328
    Appalachian, 76
    child sexual abuse in, 167
    depression in, 230

eating disorders in, 394
    ethnicity in, 72, 88. *See also* Eth-
        nicity; Multi-ethnicity
    growth rate in, 322
    immigrants in, 73
    individualism in, 70, 95. *See also*
        Individualism
    macroculture of, 76
    mothers in, 39–40
    punishment in, 228–229
    sheltered children in, 54
    social class in, 57–61
    teenage parents in, 130
United States Consumer Product
    Safety Commission, 315
Unoccupied play, 305
Unwed fathers, 130
Unwed mothers, 122–123, 124,
    127–128, 382

Values, 424
    adolescents and, 112, 371, 372
    of adult children, 406
    of American macroculture, 76
    Asian, 78
    assumptions and, 68–70
    of healthy families, 110
    multi-ethnicity and, 72
    self-esteem and, 335
    siblings and, 349
    Vietnamese, 53
Vaughn, V.C., 258, 364
Veevers, 25
Vega, 77
Velleman, R., 175
Vengeful behavior/lies, 327, 335.
    See also Revenge
Vietnamese, 52–53, 328
Vietnamese American, 79
Vigil, 52
Violence, 54, 172–174, 205, 114
    single-parent, 122
    television and, 354–355
Visitation, 139, 142
Voititz, Janet, 178
Von Bertalanffy, Ludwig, 94
Vygotsky, Lev, 296

Waas, G.A., 343
Wade, J., 84
Wagner, B.M., 335
Walberg, H.J., 333
Waley, 320
Walker, E., 170
Walker, J., 118
Walker, M., 322
Wallerstein, Judith, 7
Wandersman, 130
Wanska, S.K., 292
Ward, S., 355
Warmth, 184, 185, 188

Wasik, B.H., 311
Waterman, 373
Waters, E., 257, 308
Watkins, S.C., 405
Watson, John, 17, 254
Wauja, 2
Wax, Korey, 228
Weber, M., 73
Wegscheider, Sharon, 176
Wehler, C.A., 323
Weinraub, M., 257
Weinstein, K., 420
Weinitraub, 260
Weisfeld, C.C., 323
Weisfeld, G.E., 323
Welfare, 125
Wells, 18
Welsh, C.J., 369
Werts, C.E., 414
Wesley, John, 199
West, 18
Western culture, 299, 328, 329, 404
Wheeler, V.A., 342
Whitbeck, Les, 170, 422
White, 18
White, G.D., 133
White, J., 83
White race. *See* Caucasians/whites
Whitebook, M., 312
Whiteside, Mary F., 131, 132, 134
Widholdm, 366

Widows, 124–125
Wierson, M., 381
Wiesenfeld, 247
Wilbur, J., 126
Wilke, C.E., 248
Williams, Miller, 254
Williams, R.M., 76
Williams, Wendy M., 339–340
Williamson, N.E., 61
Willis, W., 82
Wilson, J., 284
Wilson, M., 82
Wilson, Mary Ellen, 166
Wilson, P., 351
Windell, James, 203, 223–225
Wing, R.R., 324
Winn, Marie, 54
Winnicott, Donald, 185, 261
Withdrawal of love, 185, 205, 207
Wolf, A., 252
Wolff, Peter, 246–247
Wong, 320
Wong, H.Z., 81
Woodsmall, 354
Work overload, 118–119
"Workfare," 125
Working fathers, 21, 22
Working mothers, 34, 38, 39–40, 111
  daughters of, 119
  in dual-career family, 118–119

infant attachment and, 260
  World War II and, 32, 33, 38
Working parents, 21
  chronosystem and, 49–50
Wright, J.C., 351, 353
Wright, L., 284
Wylie, Philip, 35, 38
Wynne, L.C., 103

Yamamoto, J., 74
Yarrow, M.R., 290
Yeates, K.O., 308
Yelling, 232, 266
Yellowbird, M., 87
Yogman, M.J., 262
York, Stacey, 71
Yost, E.B., 411
Youngblade, L., 263
Youniss, 308, 370
Ysseldyke, J., 161
Yun, 52

Zajonc, Robert, 347
Zaslow, 312
Zayas, L.J., 78
Zero Population Growth, 42
Zigler, Edward, 167, 168, 172, 311, 396, 397
Zimmerman, M., 334
Zuniga, M.E., 77